The Face of
London

'Mr Weller's knowledge of London was extensive and peculiar.'

Pickwick Papers

New, revised edition published 1970 by
© The Hamlyn Publishing Group Limited
London · New York · Sydney · Toronto
Hamlyn House, Feltham, Middlesex, England
The Hamlyn Publishing Group Limited 1969
SBN 6000 1276 X
Printed in Czechoslovakia

Contents

Illustrations

ILLUSTRATION ACKNOWLEDGMENTS: Aerofilms, Grahame Berney, Bildarchiv Foto Marburg, British Petroleum, J. Allan Cash, Central Press Photos, Keith Davis, Fairey Surveys, Financial Times, Fox Photos, Hamlyn Group Library, Michael Holford, A. F. Kersting, New Zealand High Commission, Picturepoint, The Rank Organisation, Shell, Vic Stacey, Daily Telegraph, The Times, E. R. Wethersett.

Editor's Preface

The face of London today changes much more rapidly than ever before. The most noticeable feature of the newer London is undoubtedly the ever-increasing number of multi-storey buildings, both commercial and residential, that are springing up in every direction.

In the City, the first of these now familiar 'skyscrapers' was Fountain House in Fenchurch Street, a modest 170 feet in height, of 14 storeys. This was opened in 1957, and duly recorded in an earlier edition of this work. Since then there have been so many more, so much alike that only those of exceptional height now attract attention. At the time of this revision, the latest and highest is Britannic House in Moor Lane, its 35 floors rising to 400 feet. The progress of the Barbican Redevelopment Scheme on the north side of the City lends colour to the theory that these gigantic slabs with their severe straight lines and rectangles look much better when grouped together in a cluster of their own kind than when mixed up with buildings of an architectural period such as Sir Christopher Wren's Cathedral and Chapter House.

Another notable aspect of the London scene is the continual intensification of traffic on the roads, though new roads and more Flyovers and Underpasses have done much to smooth the path of the motor vehicle. But for the pedestrian — and it is to the pedestrian that the following twenty-five walks are addressed — life is becoming rather less comfortable, for he is gradually being pushed underground into subways or up above on to *podia, pedways, walkways* and the like, to get him out of the way.

Most of these 'above or below' schemes for the protection of the pedestrian (who once had priority *on* the roads) involve the ascent and descent of varying numbers of steps, and it is pathetic to see elderly people struggling up 29 steps out of a subway at Hammersmith Broadway. As a further humiliation there are several places where foot-passengers, like animals in the Zoo, are penned in to the pavement by long lengths of metal railings, lest they should attempt to cross the road. These various protective devices have been well described as 'Safety with Indignity'.

The rapid outward spread of London into the surrounding Home Counties led to the setting up, in 1957, of a Royal Commission to consider the structure and working of local government in the Greater London area. This resulted in a most important development which, though without much noticeable effect upon the *face* of London, was drastic in the reorganisation of its administration.

Under the London Government Act of 1963, a new Greater London Area was formed, consisting of 32 new boroughs which, from 1 April 1965, replaced the Counties of London and Middlesex, plus county and municipal boroughs and small outlying districts (the City of London, having maintained its ancient constitution since medieval times, remained intact).

11

Of the two counties, London and Middlesex, the Administrative County of London was really an artificial rather than a geographical county and included a large part of Middlesex and smaller parts of Surrey and one or two adjacent counties; the whole area of 117 square miles being under the jurisdiction of the now defunct London County Council. As so frequently happens in the case of individuals, it was not until the LCC was dead and obituary notices appeared in the press that the general public realized the value of this very efficient body which had served them so well for nearly 80 years.

The County of Middlesex, on the other hand, was an ancient geographical county — and the natives had been known to call themselves, rightly or wrongly, *Middle Saxons*. As already noted, Middlesex suffered a great loss when a large part of the county went towards the formation of the County of London in 1888. The *coup de grâce,* however, was administered on All Fool's Day 1965, when the County of Middlesex was completely wiped off the map, to become part of the present Greater London. Most of the remains are buried in nine of the new London Boroughs, numbered 24 to 32. But it will need more than a stroke of the pen to efface a whole county; as John Betjeman said at Isleworth recently, *Don't bother about Greater London — this is Middlesex.*

E.R.W.

Introduction

The following work is an attempt to present, within the limits of a single volume, a bird's-eye view of the growth, progress, and development of the world's most wonderful city. When first published in 1932 its main features had been confined to the century immediately preceding, but much information dating farther back has now been included, which it is hoped will add to the historical interest of the book.

Later editions have enabled us to include with each successive edition the latest metropolitan improvements carried out during those intervening years. Vast indeed were the changes which took place in this great metropolis during the period between the first and second World Wars. On all sides private houses, small shops and famous hotels gave way to vast new blocks of offices, multiple shops, luxury flats, and the then all-conquering cinema. The outbreak of war in 1939 once again put an end for the time being to all further building activities, just as it had done in 1914-18. The courage and fortitude displayed by the citizens of bomb-scarred London throughout the six years of the second World War were such that history for the next thousand years may well place on record the words of Sir Winston Churchill: 'This was their finest hour'.

A work of this kind cannot claim to be original or to remain up-to-date for any length of time, having regard to the constant changes which are taking place daily, but no effort has been spared to incorporate such features as have not hitherto been chronicled in works on London.

In compiling a work dealing with the entire metropolis and its suburbs, the problem is to determine the most suitable method of portraying it in such a way as to render it useful and interesting. After careful consideration, we have come to the conclusion that a work of this sort can best be presented in the form of a series of walks and motor drives. The walks are described in the chapters covering the smaller areas in the heart of London, whereas the motor tours are intended to apply to those dealing with the more extensive areas of Greater London.

Owing to the vast amount of material contained in this work, it has not been found practicable to include a description of the interiors of our numerous churches, museums, and other public buildings, but since these figure in every history and guide-book of London, we feel that this would be superfluous.

Unfortunately a large number of these buildings have been either completely destroyed or severely damaged by enemy action, and some of the London churches now have only their bare walls and towers still standing.

Two hundred years ago London could properly be termed an oblong-shaped city with a much greater extent from east to west than from north to south. This was because previous to 1750, London Bridge was the only bridge which provided access to the south bank of the river. But owing to London's rapid growth on the south side of the Thames in more recent times, it now presents more the form of a square with bridges across the river at many points. Eighteenth-century London presented the anomaly of a city increasing greatly in size but almost stationary in population, despite a steady influx of people from the provinces. It extended already from Hyde Park on the west as far as Mile End and Limehouse on the east.

The estimated population in 1700 was 700,000, with no further increase down to 1750. This absence of progress was largely due to the heavy mortality from typhus and smallpox, which caused the deaths to exceed the births, and was further aggravated by the overcrowding of the poor in huge rookeries as squalid as any that had existed before the days of the Great Fire of 1666. Other contributory factors were primitive sanitation and the lack of any central authority to control the districts outside the City.

Medieval London with its frequent visitations of the plague is said to have had a lower death-rate than Georgian London with its constant ravages of infectious disease. The magnificent squares and spacious streets were offset by the rookeries of Westminster, St Giles, and Southwark. Yet even then London was deemed to be extremely well built, the houses being mostly of brick and the shops of much better appearance than those commonly seen in any other city in Europe. By 1700 it had already become the largest city in the world and was said to have been unexcelled in size by any other excepting ancient Rome. After the Great Fire of 1666, London had a splendid opportunity of laying out her streets and houses with due regard for domestic comfort, convenience, and beauty, but then, as now, private interests were allowed to stand in the way of London's future welfare. Thus the enlightened tradesmen of that age were more concerned with the contents of their warehouses and shops than with their approaches and appearance. The buildings were huddled and packed together like the bales and casks they contained, without any regard to fresh air and sunlight.

By 1801 the population of London had increased to 865,000, or taking that of the combined parishes within an eight-mile radius of St Paul's Cathedral, to 1,030,000. Even so, visitors arriving in London by road were impressed by the immense size of the outer villages and suburbs, a thing which largely escapes the notice of those arriving by railway.

Successive years of war, notably those of Napoleon and the recent World Wars, have been indirectly responsible for great developments in the metropolis. Vast resources have been brought into action by the financial situation then obtaining, and by the creation of paper currencies beyond all parallel, thus enabling individuals to spend much more money than they could otherwise have done. In addition, the emergency operations arising out of such wars have compelled the Governments of the day, as well as the various trading and commercial companies, to employ a larger number of people in London.

Thus between 1801 and 1831 the growth of London was remarkable, increasing from 865,000 to 1,474,000, or including the suburbs within the eight-mile radius, from 1,030,000 to 1,776,000, or nearly 75 per cent. in thirty years. That London could grow with such rapidity before the first railway or other rapid means of transit had been invented, was a phenomenon unparalleled even in the annals of ancient Rome. By the time the first railway entered the metropolis, London had actually doubled its population within the short period of thirty-five years, and had further increased by 1841 to 1,870,000, and including the outer districts, to 2,235,000.

A writer in the *Monthly Magazine* for February 1811 asserted that within the preceding forty years a thousand houses had been added each year to the metropolis, this increase being partly due to the number of retired people and civil servants quartered there. Between 1821 and 1831 London grew with such amazing rapidity that Paddington, Marylebone, and St Pancras doubled their populations within those few years; almost endless lines of new houses were then erected. To quote a remark made at that time, Kennington, Camberwell, Hackney, Bethnal Green, Stoke Newington, Highbury, Chelsea, Knightsbridge, and even Kensington, were making haste to join London. By 1939 places three times the distance of these inner districts from the City, such as Bromley, Downham, Eltham, Dagenham, Romford, Enfield, Barnet, Edgware, Southall, Hounslow, Kingston, and Croydon, were making haste to join, and even the distant towns of Watford, Uxbridge, and Caterham, over fifteen miles from the City, were rapidly becoming joined to the great province of houses by continuous lines of straggling suburban villas and large private residences.

The reign of George IV, justly termed the Augustan Age of London, did scarcely less for the metropolis than was boasted by the Emperor Augustus when he declared that he found Rome built of brick, and left it of marble. Richer and more varied architecture and park-like scenery replaced shabby houses and cowsheds, and fine new roads were constructed, inviting favourable comparison either with those of ancient Rome or the best which have been since constructed in or around this great metropolis. Certainly our grandfathers must be accorded their share of the credit for the great progress which has taken place since the dawn of the nineteenth century. The splendid wide streets of Bloomsbury, Belgravia, and St George's-in-the-Fields show that they greatly appreciated the blessings of fresh air and fine homes. The wide roads leading into the centre of London from both the north and south sides of the Thames, with their rows of well-built houses standing back in long front gardens, show that they knew how to build fine suburbs to suit the requirements of their own age.

By 1831 it was not only in architectural beauty and town-planning that London had improved, but its moral and intellectual progress had been commensurate with its embellishment. During the previous forty years the people themselves had altered as much in appearance as the place itself. Their dress, manners, and morals had improved, and already the use of machinery had made clothes cheap, resulting in an improved standard of behaviour and deportment. Coffee-houses had already done much to raise the character of the working classes; formerly artisans or single men had no better place than a public house to go to for their breakfast. Institutions and Savings Banks had already begun to confer great benefits upon the working classes.

The introduction of gas-lighting into the streets of London early in the nineteenth century greatly lessened the danger to its inhabitants of going out after dark. Mr Hughson, writing in 1817, asserts that owing to the vigilance and exertions of Mr Matthew Wood, then Lord Mayor of London, the City had been entirely cleared of common prostitutes and that the officers and their watchmen had been compelled to do their duty so thoroughly that according to the latest official report thieves then appeared afraid to enter the City.

Before the creation of the Metropolitan Police Force in 1829, the policing of the metropolis at night-time was chiefly entrusted to elderly men, mostly hired at a small weekly wage by the different parishes, and provided with a greatcoat, staff, and rattle. Each watchman had a regular beat which it was his duty to perambulate several times in the hour, and ludicrous though it may now seem, to proclaim aloud the time and the state of the weather. The entire force of watchmen, including the patrols and inspectors, did not exceed 4,000, whereas to-day the Metropolitan Police Force numbers more than 18,000.

Writing in 1833, Mr J. Britton, F.S.A., author of *The Original Picture of London,* says:

'We don't deny that there are various classes of sharpers and impostors in London, but as their places of rendezvous are generally gaming houses, brothels, and amongst the occasional crowds on public occasions, these may be fairly avoided by any stranger. He should also forbear to carry much money in his pocket and at places of public resort he should resist the apparently polite and kind attentions of unknown persons, guard against intoxication, the company of the frail sisterhood, retire to his home before twelve o'clock at night, and he will then be likely to avoid personal dangers and be freed from impositions.

When flats voluntarily place themselves in the way of sharps, the latter will readily transpose them into naturals. If fools obtrude themselves into the company of knaves, they have no right to complain of being cheated.'

The writer of these words added that he had lived in London for forty-seven years, had traversed the streets by day and night, frequented all its public places and thus mixed with various classes of society, and had never been robbed or suffered any personal injury.

The passing of the new Police Act produced the most beneficial effect upon the morals of the metropolis. The frightful scenes of bestial drunkenness no longer desecrated the Sabbath, and no longer rendered the public highways impassable to the well-conducted, nor were the slumbers of the tired citizens disturbed by the boisterous blackguardism of the drunken and dissolute. Stealing door-knockers and ringing bells ceased to be laughed at as fashionable frolics, and the fear of the treadmill proved the best cure for those outbursts of aristocratic wit.

Though London was generally admitted even then to be the finest city in the world, it was remarked by the leading authorities in 1831 that a review of the recent buildings erected between Buckingham Palace on the west and the Custom House on the east caused one to lament the many failures which they displayed. In some respects London was behind the other great cities of Europe, notably in the matter of hotel accommodation, which little more than a century ago was said to be inferior to all others with the exception of Constantinople.

London possessed a few high-class family hotels in the West End, but it was not until the fifties and sixties of the last century, when such hotels as the Westminster Palace, the Great Western, the Langham, and the leading railway hotels, were erected, that the supply became equal to the demand.

Five of London's great hotels which closed down during the Second World War were later converted into offices and business premises. These were the Carlton, the Langham, the Victoria, the Great Central and the Kensington Palace. All of them were very popular with both visitors and London residents. This greatly increased the shortage of hotel accommodation in London at a time when efforts were being made to develop the tourist trade, but a number of new hotels have been opened since the war, most of which are mentioned in their appropriate place.

Toll-gates persisted in London for long after they had been abolished in some other countries, and remained as an unmitigated nuisance to the free circulation of the traffic until 1868. The very objectionable window-tax also remained in force until well after 1850, despite the most strenuous efforts to get it repealed, and burials still took place in the crowded churchyards in the centre of London to the great detriment of the public health. Public executions at Newgate were not abolished until 1868.

In respect of its sanitation, London was probably superior, even a century ago, to most other great cities having regard to the backward state of affairs which prevailed everywhere. Even so, it was very defective from a present-day standpoint. Before the construction of the new main drainage system in 1859, the stench on the river between Westminster Bridge and Blackwall was abominable when hot weather set in. The gigantic improvement in the sanitation of London is reflected in the death-rate, which dropped from thirty-one in the thousand in 1831 to less than ten in the thousand in 1931.

Notwithstanding the success of the earlier railways laid down in the north of England, London was slow to adopt the new method of transit, and it was not until 1837 that the first line was opened between London and Deptford. Previous to that time some six hundred coaches and other conveyances brought fifty thousand toilers daily into the city from all parts of the metropolis. By 1845 the rage for railway speculation had become so great that there were more strangers in London than there had been at any time since the Coronation of Queen Victoria. Many of these were witnesses in attendance for the purpose of giving evidence before the special Parliamentary Committees, together with numerous solicitors and agents. However, many bogus railway companies were formed which never materialized as honest concerns and the general public declined to meet the calls due on allotment which could not successfully be enforced by law.

Omnibuses were first introduced into the streets of London by Shillibeer in 1829, and by 1853 their numbers had increased to three thousand, each carrying three hundred passengers daily. In 1856 various small omnibus companies were absorbed by the French General Omnibus Company of London, the management of which was afterwards taken over by an English Board of Directors. About 1849 the so-called knife-board type of omnibus came into general use on the streets of London. Stairs not yet having been evolved, passengers riding outside had to climb to the roof by a series of iron rungs on the right of the door. The knife-board was a central seat running the length of the roof and divided into two by a low vertical partition so that the outside passengers sat back to back with their feet against skirting-boards fixed to the edges of the roof. No selfrespecting woman was ever seen on the knife-board unless the vehicle was specially chartered for a picnic or outing, upon which occasions a ladder would be provided for their decent ascension, during which all males looked the other way. The floor inside the buses was usually covered with a thick layer of straw, dry and clean every morning, but in wet weather damp, dirty, and smelly for the rest of the day. The first omnibuses to be provided with stairs were those introduced by the Metropolitan Railway about 1864 between Portland Road Station and Piccadilly Circus in connexion with their trains.

In 1834 Mr J. A. Hansom of Birmingham invented the curious cab named after him, and in 1842 the Reynolds improved patent safety-cab was first put on the streets of London. It was designed to remedy the objection made to the driver sitting in front of the passenger so as to obstruct his view. The first double-decked motor omnibuses were placed on the streets of London in 1906, though the last of the horse-drawn omnibuses were not removed until 1916. During that period various private companies had placed altogether about seven hundred motorbuses on the streets of London. There were Vanguards, Victorys, Pioneers, Arrows, Union Jacks and Generals amongst others, but none of them had proved a financial success. Then in 1910 the London Underground Railways bought out all of the various London omnibus companies except that of Messrs Tillings and thus provided London with a unified and greatly improved transport service. The first taxi-cabs were introduced about the year 1907 and by 1910 nearly all hansom and four-wheeled cabs had vanished from the London streets.

Automatic traffic signals with alternating red and green lights, first adopted in New York, were installed in 1930 at Ludgate Circus and at the various crossroads in Oxford Street from St Giles's Circus to the Marble Arch. They are now in general use throughout the Kingdom. Roundabout traffic was first introduced in 1926 at Parliament Square and shortly afterwards at Hyde Park Corner, Aldwych, Trafalgar Square, Marble Arch and other great centres of traffic.

Despite the ever-increasing congestion of traffic existing in every great city at the present day, the problem seems to have been rather similar even in the forties and fifties of the last century, and we cannot do better than quote the following article from the *Illustrated London News* of 31 October 1846:

'Great as are the inconveniences which have arisen with the growth of London, we seem to have little of that courage which such difficulties should be grappled with; all our principal thoroughfares have become too small for the enormous stream of traffic hourly poured through them. We want new roads, long and wide, establishing perfect lines of communication between the extremities, yet the best we can do is to patch and mend bit by bit and, fearful of the cost of a real grand improvement, fritter away half a million in a back street. London, we repeat, is not now a city, it has outgrown the population and dimensions of a capital and has become a nation of itself, busier and more populous than many sovereign states that fill a considerable space on the map of Europe. What was the old city has become the mere centre of the mass surrounded for miles in every direction by thickly-populated districts. Their traffic passes through from point to point in every possible direction, railways pour in their hourly contributions from every corner of the kingdom, and from the centre outwards there is a never-ceasing export of men and merchandise, the material trade of nearly two millions of human beings, the intercourse and activity of an empire, and the commerce of half a world now run through streets and ways built nearly two centuries ago, and very badly even for the age that planned them, or rather built them without any plan at all. The result is that the streets of London are choked by their ordinary traffic, and the life blood of the huge giant is compelled to run through veins and arteries that have never expanded since the days and dimensions of its infancy.'

Those words were written over a hundred years ago, in reference to the forthcoming construction of the new Cannon Street, but for all practical purposes they might just as well have been written yesterday. Many wonderful improvements in the shape of new streets and the widening of the older ones have been carried out since that time, but thanks to our English method of doing things by halves, the advantages derived have been largely offset by the work which has remained undone. The noble Victoria Embankment and Northumberland Avenue have come into being and afford invaluable relief to the enormous traffic of the Strand and Fleet Street, which have themselves been greatly widened throughout almost their entire length from Ludgate Circus to Trafalgar Square. Victoria Street, Holborn Viaduct, and Shaftesbury Avenue also figure amongst the great London improvements of the nineteenth century.

Despite the exigencies of the second World War, three great metropolitan improvements were completed between 1939 and 1945. The first of these was the construction of the new West Cromwell Road bridge across the West London Railway in 1941. The second was the completion of the new Western Avenue from Hillingdon across the river Colne to join the main Oxford Road at Denham. This great arterial road now runs from Wood Lane, Shepherd's Bush to Denham and by-passes the busy suburbs of Acton, Ealing and Southall. The third monumental London improvement completed during war time was the new and noble Waterloo Bridge, partly opened to traffic in September 1942 and completed in

November 1944. The devastation created by enemy action in large sections of London's leading main thoroughfares enabled the London County Council, the City Corporation and the various metropolitan boroughs to carry out some much-needed street widenings. These include Leadenhall Street, Cannon Street, Aldersgate Street, the centre section of Cheapside, High Holborn, the narrow end of Tottenham Court Road and Piccadilly opposite St. James's Church.

Though the good work of ridding London of its worst slum areas, such as Clare Market, St. Giles's, Shoreditch, Bethnal Green, and Southwark, has progressed steadily during the past seventy years, the dangers from a sanitary and moral point of view arising from overcrowding seem to have excited no interest whatever before the dawn of the nineteenth century. This evil was very pronounced even as far back as the reign of Queen Elizabeth I when a proclamation to that effect was issued in 1580. But the anxiety felt was in no way due to sanitary considerations, but on account of the administration of justice and the provision of food at reasonable prices to meet the increase in population. Hence people were forbidden to erect any more houses within three miles of any of the gates of the City of London. Such legislation proving of no avail in preventing either the growth of the metropolis or the overcrowding in its centre, it was not until 1851 that Parliament first concerned itself with the quality and quantity of accommodation provided for the working classes in London. In that year Lord Ashley, later the Earl of Shaftesbury, called public attention to the disgraceful condition of the dwellings inhabited by the poorer classes in London and other great cities of the Kingdom. As the result of his efforts two Acts were passed, which were known as Lord Shaftesbury's Act and the Labouring Classes Act, which empowered the local authorities to deal with insanitary property. Later, in 1868 and 1885, further Acts were passed which gave much wider powers to the local authorities to deal with the overcrowding nuisance, including the right to condemn insanitary property or carry out improvements themselves in the event of the owner neglecting to keep them in a fit state of repair.

Happily the worst slum areas have now disappeared, but others still remain to be dealt with in back streets and neighbourhoods which largely escape the notice of the general public. In addition to the good work carried out by the London County Council and the various local authorities, much has been accomplished by private enterprise since the latter half of the nineteenth century, . notably by the Peabody Trust, the Guinness Trust, established in 1889, and by Sir Sydney Waterlow, who founded a limited company for the purpose of erecting blocks of workmen's dwellings.

Despite their monotonous streets and interminable rows of two-storied houses, such places as West Ham, Tottenham, and Earlsfield are a big improvement on the older working-class districts of Bethnal Green, Hoxton, and Walworth, but they in turn are now completely eclipsed by the garden suburbs of Dagenham, East Acton, Downham, Eltham, and Burnt Oak, erected by the London County Council between the first and second World Wars.

In order to draw off some of the surplus population of Central London satellite towns were built about thirty miles distant from the City and the West End. Stevenage in Herfordshire was chosen for North London, Harlow and Basildon in Essex for East London, Crawley in Sussex for South London, and Bracknell in Berkshire for West London. These new towns, each containing about fifty thousand inhabitants, are modelled more or less on the lines of Welwyn Garden City in Hertfordshire and Letchworth, the first garden city in Britain, founded in 1903 by the late Sir Ebenezer Howard. The industrial districts are separated from the residential quarters.

In the forty years between 1831 and 1871 Greater London more than doubled its population, and in the following forty years it nearly doubled again, rising to 7,256,000 by 1911. The numbers continued to rise steadily, but after 1921 (7,488,000) it was apparent that the increase was taking place in the Outer London area, and there was a decline in the population of the Administrative County (now the Inner London Area) and in the City of London.

This outward movement led to the formation in 1965 of the present Greater London Area of 620 square miles, with an estimated population of 8,000,000, of which the 766 acres (familiarly known as the 'Square Mile') of the City of London has a resident population of slightly less than 5,000.

If the reign of George IV was termed the Augustan Age of London, history has repeated itself a century later, for the improvements which were carried out in London during the reign of King George V, and more especially between the two World Wars, make even those of the reign of George IV appear trivial by comparison. George IV was responsible for the construction of Regent Street, but George V was privileged to witness its entire rebuilding. Accompanied by Queen Mary, he drove formally through the new street on 23 June 1927. Most of the new streets of London were constructed in the Victorian era, but the reign of George V witnessed the greatest amount of rebuilding all over the metropolis that had ever taken place within so short a period of time since the Great Fire of London.

The reign of King George V also saw the construction of new offices for the Port of London Authority in Trinity Square, as well as the King George's Dock and the new landing-stage at Tilbury erected at a cost of £700,000 and opened by Mr Ramsay MacDonald, then Prime Minister, on 16 May 1930. Statistics show that the traffic handled in the Port of London in 1929 was a record, and this at a time when the country was passing through a period of intense trade depression. The Port of London Authority celebrated its fiftieth birthday in 1959.

During September 1931 the leading public buildings and many of the principal commercial buildings were brilliantly illuminated for the first time by flood-lighting. The streets were thronged nightly by vast crowds of spectators and on several occasions became almost impassable so great was the public interest in this novel display. Such buildings as Buckingham Palace, the Houses of Parliament, Westminster Abbey and St Martin's Church presented a truly majestic appearance when viewed from the Mall and St James's Park. The cost entailed in floodlighting proved so moderate that many business houses adopted it as a permanent and attractive method of advertising. But in 1939 the second World War and its aftermath put an abrupt end to the lighting of all shop windows and illuminated sky signs and it was not until 2 April 1949, nearly ten years later, that lights again went up. On that Saturday night vast crowds of sightseers filled Picadilly Circus and the streets of the West End and children already ten years of age set eyes on the lights for the first time in their lives.

The threatened evils arising out of the rapid invasion of the countryside by this vast metropolis, which have caused misgivings since the time of the first Queen Elizabeth, have now lost most of their terrors. The difficulty is being solved partly by the ever-increasing areas which are being secured to the public as open spaces for all time, and partly by developing the newer suburbs on garden-city lines in place of the interminable rows of dreary streets which were thought good enough for our grandfathers. The parks and open spaces of Greater London already occupy some thirty thousand acres, or about 10 per cent of the entire Metropolitan area. Another unique feature of London is its numerous squares, which are said to occupy 1,200 acres and which were styled by von Raumer in 1835, 'the great and peculiar beauty of London'. An Act of Parliament now restrains the owners of the lands from building over any of the London squares and many of them have since been acquired as public open spaces.

Another unique attraction of London is the great variety of its component districts. Whereas the magnificence of other great capitals is mainly confined to particular quarters, the new grandeur of London is widely distributed and reveals itself in districts as far away from one another as the City proper, the West End, Kensington, Marylebone, and Westminster. This is largely due to the fact that London has been built up out of a conglomeration of places which were formerly separate towns and villages, but which have retained their ancient historical interest and the individuality and attributes of separate towns.

The suburbs of London can justly claim to be a hundred years ahead of those of the majority of the capital cities of the world in respect of their town-planning, roads, sanitary appointments, and other kindred blessings of modern civilization. To quote a recent article in the press, 'the new and nobler London has grown up silently and invisibly as an oak increases its girth and stature'. Tastes and opinions may differ on a question of this sort, but the impression of a particular city conveyed to the casual visitor is largely influenced by its clear atmosphere or sunshine. In that respect many other cities have a big advantage over London, but on the other hand, is there another piece of urban scenery in the world quite so beautiful as Westminster and its Government offices viewed from St James's Park on a fine spring day? If there is a finer city in the world, surely there never was a more interesting, varied, or wonderful one than London, the cradle of modern civilization. Dr Johnson, 190 years ago, said, 'When a man is tired of London, he is tired of life; for there is in London all that life can afford'. If that assertion was true in his day, it is doubly true at the present time.

Although the destruction of so many of our ancient churches, hospitals and other historical buildings by enemy action is a loss which every Londoner must deeply deplore, the disappearance on the other hand of large areas of mean streets totally unworthy of this city will ultimately prove a great blessing in disguise. The elimination of extensive squalid areas in Holborn, St Pancras, Bethnal Green, Stepney, Lambeth, Southwark, Bermondsey and other over-crowded quarters of Central London will pass unmourned by posterity. The blitz has created opportunities for beautifying great stretches of ugliness. Similarly the Great Fire of London in 1666 which swept away large areas of squalid and insanitary streets of that period conferred a great benefit on the inhabitants of London. Much of the property which has in fact been destroyed was destined to be pulled down even before the outbreak of war as part of the various schemes planned by the London County Council to rid London of its slums.

The same thing can truthfully be said of some of the older sections of the City of London, notably the Fore Street area and the quarter in the immediate vicinity of St Paul's Cathedral. Here most of the property which has been razed to the ground was very little less than a hundred years old and much of it would have been rebuilt within the next quarter of a century through the expiration of leases and the constant demand for more modern and up-to-date office accommodation. Thus it may well prove that the ravages of war, though inflicting grievous losses on the citizens of London, have their compensations in the extensive sites becoming available for the constructions of fine new streets and buildings.

The new London which will arise during the next thirty years, provided that we are spared the horrors of a third World War, should be a shining monument to the fortitude and enterprise of its inhabitants. It could be a city of fine wide streets and avenues with traffic roundabouts, of majestic vistas, beautiful parks, squares, and riverside drives and gardens, attractive suburbs with all the amenities of self-contained towns. The encirclement of London with an almost continuous Green Belt which will be preserved for all time is now practically completed. This grand scheme was sponsored in 1935 by the London County Council who offered grants amounting in three years to £2,000,000 towards its realization. The belt covers 28,500 acres of land and stretches from Egham to Rickmansworth in the west and thence eastwards towards Barnet and Epping Forest and southwards to the Thames near Rainham. The southern section includes a part of the North Downs, linking up with Box Hill and then bearing round to the west towards the Thames at Runnymede. Some four thousand acres in the north of Middlesex have been secured, and three thousand acres in Buckinghamshire. In Essex a stretch of farming country about six miles long and a mile deep, extending from Hainault Forest to Epping Forest, has also been mapped out for the Green Belt. This comprises over seven thousand acres, or a territory larger than Epping Forest, which covers over six thousand acres. Langley Park on the road from Gerrard's Cross to Slough acquired in 1944 is a beautiful stretch of woodland covering an area of a thousand acres similar to the famous Burnham Beeches. Although the Green Belt will be by no means always the same distance from the centre of London it will provide a permanent playground for the teeming millions of this great city.

Having regard to the enormous amount of detailed information contained herein, errors are liable to occur, even though the greatest possible care has been taken to avoid them. We shall always be glad to be informed by readers of any inaccuracies they may notice.

Needless to add, a work of this nature can only be compiled with the aid of numerous authorities and works of reference. To all these, and especially to the erudite and helpful staff of the London Public Libraries, we should express our grateful thanks.

First Walk

The Hub of the City; The Mansion House, The Royal Exchange, The Bank of England, and The Big Five Banks, The Stock Exchange, Broad Street and Threadneedle Street

"Those who walk see most."

The hub of the British metropolis, by which we mean the Royal Exchange, the Mansion House, the Bank of England, and the open space formed by the junction of the leading thoroughfares of the City of London, has been so completely transformed during the past hundred years, that we propose devoting the whole of our opening chapter to a general description and survey of what may aptly be termed the heart of the British Commonwealth.

Previous to 1835, six streets converged upon this great centre. These were Threadneedle Street, Cornhill, Lombard Street, Walbrook, Poultry, and Princes Street. Owing to the creation of King William Street and Queen Victoria Street since that time, their number has been increased to eight.

In 1831 the new London Bridge had just been opened with great ceremony by King William IV and Queen Adelaide, but as yet King William Street, designed to connect London Bridge with the Mansion House, had not been completed. To a stranger unfamiliar with the geography of London, a journey from the Bank of England to London Bridge may well have presented quite a tiresome ordeal, since he was compelled to proceed either by way of Lombard Street and along Gracechurch Street, or through Walbrook and along what was then only a very narrow precursor of the present-day Cannon Street. Only a native of London, possessing an intimate knowledge of its lanes and its courts, would have been able to shorten the journey by making short cuts through Abchurch or Clement's Lanes. Successive improvements carried out since that time have so enlarged and altered this 'Clapham Junction' of the City that it is now an open space of considerable size.

The visitor to the City is usually surprised to discover that such an important and impressive area has no official title; generally known as 'The Bank', there have been suggestions that a name associated with one of the three important buildings, such as Whittington, Gresham or Paterson, combined with Place, Square or Circus might be more suitable; though the area is irregular in shape, its claim to a geometrical description would be as good as that of, say, Piccadilly Circus, which has long since lost its circularity, and few of London's Squares are really *square*.

As for Queen Victoria Street, it was not until 1869, some thirty-eight years after the construction of the new London Bridge, that this thoroughfare was opened for traffic; prior to that time the whole of London's west-bound traffic passed through Cheapside. East-bound traffic passed mainly through Cornhill, as it still does at the present day, though of course the construction of King William Street relieved that thoroughfare of the traffic bound for London Bridge, which must necessarily have passed through Cornhill or Lombard Street in former times.

Moorgate Street had not yet come into being, and before the construction of that useful thoroughfare, which connected Moorfields with the Bank and was opened about 1840, traffic for Finsbury Square and City Road had to proceed by way of Coleman Street and London Wall.

The main streets of the City a century ago were mostly paved with granite blocks. Experimental wood paving had been laid down during the forties in certain sections of Cheapside, Newgate Street, and St Paul's Churchyard, but this had proved a failure, and it was not until many years later that wood paving became general in the streets of London. To-day wood paving is everywhere being replaced by tarred asphalt, though a length of Lombard Street was for a time experimentally laid with rubber.

Although traffic congestion in the centre of the City is certainly a very serious problem in our own day, it was no better, and lacking our present day organization and control, probably worse in 1831. That is, of course, if the most authentic accounts of the state of affairs then prevailing can be accepted at their face value.

Omnibuses had already started running from Paddington to the City in 1829, and by 1837 their number had increased to well over 200, serving various parts of the city. Some 600 coaches and other conveyances carried well over 50,000 workers daily to and from the City and from the outer residential districts of Marylebone, Paddington, Chelsea, Islington, Hampstead, Kennington, Clapham, Camberwell, Hackney, Mile End, and Stepney, all of which have long since become merged into London. The fares were 6d. for short distances, and 1s., 1s. 6d., 2s. for longer journeys to such places as Richmond and Ilford. Those whose incomes did not allow the daily sum of one or two shillings for conveyance to and from the City met this difficulty by walking in fine weather and riding only when it was wet, for, of course, until the last weeks of 1837, there were no railways.

One writer tells us that heavily laden wagons frequently broke down in the narrow streets and brought a long line of carriages to a standstill. Often a donkey-cart laden with firewood obstructed the traffic, followed by some elegant carriage, behind which would be a heavy dray loaded with beer-barrels, succeeded by an omnibus moving at snail's pace. This in turn would be followed by a cabman who had undertaken to convey his fare to his destination in a given number of minutes, dodging in and out amongst the narrow openings in the traffic in a way no one other than a London-born driver would have dared to risk.

Writing in 1829, Mr Thomas H. Shepherd describes London when viewed from the point where Cheapside terminates at the Mansion House and the Bank of England as being characteristic at once of metropolitan activity, commerce, and opulence, the gay and ever-moving throng of pedestrians and carriages giving indescribable life and animation to the scene. Designed by George Dance the Elder, and built on the site of the Stocks Market in 1739-53, the Mansion House was the first official residence of the Lord Mayors. Before that time, they kept their mayoralty in their own private houses or secured a suitable house elsewhere for their year of office: such a one was No. 73 Cheapside, the residence of Sir William Turner, who was Lord Mayor in 1668-9. Said to have been built by Sir Christopher Wren, it was long known as the 'Old Mansion House', and though now rebuilt as offices, the greater part of the remarkably fine old staircase still survives.

The Mansion House has undergone various alterations, notably the removal of the superstructure from the roof of the building and of the balustrade which formerly adorned the street front, but otherwise it appeared very much the same as it does at the present day. It was said to have cost £71,000. The superstructure, which was removed in 1842, consisted of two storeys designed to provide quarters for the servants, and was nicknamed 'The Mare's Nest'; it was regarded as a disfigurement that ought never to have been erected. It is strange how 'the whirligig of time brings in his revenges'; stand at the Royal Exchange and look at the Mansion House today: a 'Mare's Nest' is back again! – but this time it is the much less elegant superstructure of the colossal Bucklersbury House that rears its ugly head behind the Mayoral Residence and spoils the skyline.

The Mansion House itself is substantially built of Portland stone and is screened by a portico of six fluted Corinthian columns, but already it has become too small for present-day requirements and the City Corporation at one time seriously considered the advisability of pulling it down and erecting a larger building on another site, to make room for a traffic roundabout. However, the more recent development of London Wall on the north and Thames Street in the south is expected to result in considerable relief to traffic congestion at the Bank Intersection, as the traffic people call it.

In 1831 the second Royal Exchange, successor to that founded by Sir Thomas Gresham in 1566 and which perished in the Great Fire of London, was still in existence. In front of it stood two blocks of houses known as Bank Buildings. These occupied the open space in front of the present Royal Exchange, below which is now situated the Bank Station of the Central Underground Line.

A description of the first Royal Exchange founded by Sir Thomas Gresham and destroyed in the Great Fire of London in 1666 does not come within the province of this work, but the second building erected in 1669 much resembled the first, excepting that it was larger and more splendid. Designed by Edward Jarman, one of the City surveyors, its foundation-stone was laid by King Charles II on 23 October 1667, and the building, which was fronted with Portland stone, was completed and opened on 28 September 1669. The cost was £59,000, with another £7,000 for the enlarged site. It bore a stone tower erected in the

Italian style, which was greatly admired. The present Royal Exchange has a similar tower. In the year 1779 the Royal Exchange Assurance Corporation and Lloyd's made this building their headquarters, but later the second Royal Exchange was destroyed by fire.

This occurred on the night of Wednesday, 10 January 1838, when the fire started from the rooms of Lloyd's coffee-house. The conflagration was intense. Amidst the excitement of the crowd and the shouts of the firemen, coupled with the crash of the falling masonry, the chimes in the tower began to play their popular tune, 'There's nae luck aboot the hoose'.

The first stone of the third Royal Exchange was laid on 17 January 1842 by the Prince Consort, during the mayoralty of Alderman Sir John Pirie, and the building was opened with great ceremony on 28 October 1844, by Queen Victoria, accompanied by the Prince Consort.

Meanwhile the ground immediately in front of the new Royal Exchange had been cleared by the removal of the two blocks of buildings to the west of the site, in such a way as to provide an uninterrupted view from the junction of the streets in front of the Mansion House: an improvement which completely altered the appearance of the heart of the City. The sale of the first portion of the so-called Bank Buildings took place on 19 February 1844, and included the spacious banking premises of Messrs Ladbroke & Company, and three other houses. The second portion included the premises of the old Sun Fire Office, to-day located in Threadneedle Street, and one of the conditions attaching to the sale of both these blocks of buildings was that the buyers should remove the property within twenty-eight days so that the ground might be cleared by the end of March 1844.

In the space thus cleared was erected Chantrey's equestrian statue of the Duke of Wellington. It will be noticed that the Iron Duke has no stirrups – a peculiarity that is shared by the equestrian statue of George IV in Trafalgar Square, also by Chantrey. Before the calamity which resulted in the destruction of the second Royal Exchange it was the intention of the City Corporation to erect this statue in front of the recently-constructed building of the Liverpool and London and Globe Insurance Company at the junction of Lombard Street and Cornhill.

Of course, the Duke of Wellington himself was one of the principal guests at the opening ceremony of the new Royal Exchange, and upon his arrival the band stationed on the portico struck up 'See the Conquering Hero Comes', every head being uncovered and bowed low to do him reverence. The privilege of seeing one's own statue uncovered is an honour which falls to very few people, but notwithstanding this astonishing demonstration of national enthusiasm the Duke retained his composure, and ascending the portico calmly surveyed his own statue, and then quietly walked towards the door of the main entrance. Having no admission ticket, or considering it unnecessary to produce it, he merely glanced at the closed door, and then at the official. Thereupon the official, with profound obeisances, ushered His Grace into the building.

The present Royal Exchange has a length of 300 feet and a width of 175 feet at its eastern end, narrowing to 118 feet at the western end, and is considerably larger than its predecessor. It was built from the designs of Sir William Tite in the very short time of three years, at a cost of £150,000 and, most surprising of all, at a figure below the architect's estimate. Statues of Sir Thomas Gresham, Sir Richard Whittington and Sir Hugh Myddleton occupy niches on the outside walls and while lack of space precludes a detailed account of the interior of this and other buildings, it should be noted that, pending the erection of a more suitable building in the Barbican area, the exhibits of the Guildhall Museum are displayed in the Royal Exchange. There is a peal of bells, recast in 1921, which play English, Scottish, and Irish melodies at 9.0 and 12.0 o'clock in the morning, and at 3.0 and 6.0 in the afternoon. The eight Corinthian columns which adorn the main entrance to the building are 41 feet high and the tower fronting the north side is 177 feet. The steps of the Royal Exchange are one of the places from which a new sovereign is always proclaimed on his accession. Close to the statue of the Duke of Wellington stands the memorial, designed by Sir Aston Webb, R.A., to London troops who fell in the two World Wars, which takes the form of a pillar of Portland stone surmounted by a lion.

Since the removal of Lloyd's to their new quarters in Leadenhall Street in 1928, the rooms formerly occupied by them at the Royal Exchange have been taken over by the Royal Exchange Assurance Corporation as additional office accommodation. This Corporation has occupied the Royal Exchange for the whole period since its foundation in 1720, and in 1920 celebrated its bicentenary. To commemorate this event, the Corporation of London presented them with a fresco depicting the burning of the second Royal Exchange in 1838.

The space in front of the Royal Exchange also contains the entrance to the Bank station rebuilt a few years back, and second only in size to the more recently constructed station at Piccadilly Circus. Much damage was done to the Bank Station in September 1940, when a bomb fell here and destroyed the escalators. The original station opened in 1900 marked the terminus of the Central London Railway and was quite a modest affair by comparison with its successor. This line, which extended from the Bank to Shepherd's Bush, was virtually the pioneer of London tube railways and was popularly known as 'The Twopenny Tube' on account of the uniform fare of twopence for any distance. This facility prevailed for several years. The line was built between 1896 and 1900, and on account of the enormous volume of street traffic at this spot the temporary boards which covered the roadway during the construction of the Bank Station and the network of subways had to be renewed every day, an operation which was carried out in the early hours of the morning. The extension to Liverpool Street was opened in 1912; that beyond to Epping and Ongar in 1949.

At the junction of Lombard Street and Cornhill is the domed building of the Liverpool and London and Globe Insurance Company, and facing the south front of the Royal Exchange in Cornhill is the head office of Lloyds Bank, one of the 'big five', constructed between 1926 and 1930. It covers an extensive site and has imposing frontages both to Cornhill and Lombard Street. The building, which extends for the whole length of Change Alley, rises to an elevation of eight storeys above the level of the street, the two uppermost being zoned back a short distance to conform to the regulations governing the height of buildings permitted to be erected in London. It was designed by Sir J. Burnet & Partners and Messrs Campbell, Jones & Smithers, and occupies the site of the previous head offices of Lloyds Bank, together with a number of other buildings which were acquired for its extension, the frontage to Lombard Street being considerably wider than that to Cornhill.

One of the buildings thus acquired was Birch's restaurant on the south side of Cornhill, opposite the Royal Exchange. It was demolished in 1926, having till then the oldest shop front of its kind in London. In bygone days this establishment was much patronized by the Lord Mayors of London during their years of office. It was established as a confectioner's in the time of George I by a Mr Horton, after whom came Lucas Birch, whose son and successor Samuel Birch became Lord Mayor in 1840. His successors, although of a different family, have retained the name of Birch. The front of the old shop is preserved in the Victoria and Albert Museum, and the business has been transferred to Angel Court, Throgmorton Street.

As the result of the deep excavations made for the foundations of the new Lloyds Bank the roadway in Cornhill collapsed in August 1927 and had to be closed to traffic for some three months during repairs. A portion of the adjoining premises of the Commercial Union Assurance Company was involved in this catastrophe and necessitated the entire reconstruction of that building. The new structure which has since arisen is of the same elevation and scarcely less imposing than the neighbouring Lloyds Bank, and was completed in 1929 in the record time of eleven months. The collapse of the roadway in Cornhill was attributed to the loose character of the soil due to the fact that the Walbrook stream once flowed across this land on its passage to the Thames. At each side of the main doorway in the entrance hall of the Commercial Union building stands a figure clothed in the early 19th century uniform worn by the firemen of the Insurance Companies' private fire brigades. In addition to showcases of other interesting relics — some of which were unearthed during the excavations following the collapse of the roadway in 1927 — the walls are decorated with an exceptionally comprehensive and varied collection of nearly 200 Fire Marks, representing many different insurance companies of earlier days.

The space at the back of the Royal Exchange is now of considerable width, but previous to the destruction of the former Exchange it was very narrow and was originally known as Freeman's Alley and Sweeting Lane. Afterwards its name was changed to Freemans' Place, but to-day it is called Royal Exchange Buildings, after the building of that name, which faces the east side of the Royal Exchange. At either end of this space is a drinking fountain. That on the Cornhill side commemorates the Jubilee of the Metropolitan Drinking Fountain and Cattle Trough Association 1859-1909. But today, alas, it is quite dry. The fountain at the Threadneedle Street side, with an attractive 'Motherhood' group of three bronze figures signed Dalou and dated 1879, still has a trickle of water. Near the corner of Threadneedle Street, facing the east side of the Royal Exchange, is the statue of Mr George Peabody, an American philanthropist, occupying part of the site of the former parish church of St Benet Fink. During his lifetime Mr Peabody, who made a large fortune as a dry goods merchant in Baltimore and as a stockbroker in London, gave away for benevolent purposes a million and a half of money. From 1837 until his death he lived in London and is remembered today by the tenants of some forty Peabody Estates, most of them modernized, which house a population of nearly 18,000 people. He died in London in 1869 and, after a temporary interment at Westminster Abbey, his body was transferred to his native Danvers (now Peabody) Massachusetts, where he was buried beside his mother. Surely no foreigner ever deserved so well of Londoners as this great-hearted American who so loved London as to confer all this benefit upon her poorer people.

The church of St Benet Fink was destroyed in the Great Fire of 1666, rebuilt by Sir Christopher Wren, but demolished in 1844 on the erection of the present Royal Exchange. A semi-circular arrangement of coping stones remains to indicate the position of the West end of the church.

Until 1854 an unsightly block of buildings formed an obstruction in Thread-needle Street, nearly opposite Old Broad Street, and upon their removal the northern half of Threadneedle Street was opened up from the Royal Exchange to Bishopsgate as it appears at the present day. The owners of the property claimed about £36,000 compensation, little enough from a present-day stand-point, but they were awarded less than £29,000. During the excavations carried out in connexion with this improvement, Roman remains were found close to the site of St Benet Fink Church.

Crossing to the other side of Threadneedle Street we come to the Bank of England. This establishment was founded in 1694 by Mr William Paterson, a Scotsman, and grew out of a loan of £1,200,000 for the public service. The building was designed in 1734 by Mr George Sampson, and is typical of many other great British institutions inasmuch as it has grown from modest beginnings to world-wide importance. The east and west wings of the building were added by Sir Robert Taylor between 1765 and 1786, and necessitated the demolition of the church of St Christopher-le-Stocks, which, together with the churchyard, were purchased for the extension. The private residence and garden of the first governor, Sir John Houblon, occupied the site of the present bank. Between 1794 and 1823 various alterations were made to the building by Sir John Soane, and the former churchyard now marks approximately the centre of the new structure. The outer walls, which have been retained, are devoid of external windows in order to provide increased security, and at night the bank is guarded by a detachment of the Guards and by various watchmen. In 1861 the stone facing of the exterior walls showed rapid decay similar to that more recently exhibited by the Houses of Parliament. To stop this trouble a coating of a newly invented composition was applied to the surface of the frontage in Threadneedle Street.

The magnificent new structure designed by Sir Herbert Baker which has arisen within the confines of the original outer walls of Soane's building resembles a raised palace surrounded by a fortress, of which the central portion attains an elevation of about 100 feet. Begun about 1925, the reconstruction of the Bank of England, which was completed about 1938, was an undertaking which deserves to rank with the building of the new Houses of Parliament as the greatest event which has taken place in the rebuilding of London during the last hundred years. The fact that the Bank of England occupies an island site covering nearly three acres in the very heart of the metropolis has provided unlimited scope for the erection of such a splendid new building. The outer walls, besides furnishing a link with the past history of London, are eminently suited as a foreground to the new building. Notwithstanding the scale of Sir Herbert Baker's modification of Sir John Soane's structure, the increased accommodation it provided has already proved insufficient; a completely new building called New Change has been erected on part of the devastated area east of St Paul's Cathedral.

The east side of the Bank of England is bounded by Bartholomew Lane which connects Threadneedle Street with Lothbury and Throgmorton Street. At the Threadneedle Street Corner is the Sun Fire Office. The original building was erected as long ago as 1844, after the company had moved from their old premises in the Bank Buildings which stood in front of the old Royal Exchange. Built in the style of an Italian palace, it was at that period perhaps the finest office building in the City, but some sixty years ago considerable alterations were carried out and an extra storey added.

Midway along Bartholomew Lane is Capel Court, in which is the principal entrance to the Stock Exchange, inscribed over the doorway, 'Stock Exchange, 1801, altered and enlarged 1853'. At the end of the lane, Lothbury lies to the left and here is the Church of St Margaret, Lothbury, the parish church of the Bank of England. St Margaret also represents no less than seven other parishes of City churches that have been demolished or destroyed – but this number is exceeded by St Vedast, Foster Lane, which claims thirteen parishes in addition to its own. Also in Lothbury is the head office of the Westminster Bank, which rises to a height of seven storeys and has an extensive frontage to Angel Court.

To the right from Bartholomew Lane is Throgmorton Street, a narrow thoroughfare to Old Broad Street; it is practically given over to the Stock Exchange fraternity, who are continually popping in and out of 'the House', or standing in little clusters in the middle of the street discussing we know not what important business, so that vehicular traffic is not encouraged. It is here, by the way, that one may see a fair sprinkling of silk hats or 'toppers'. Although such headgear is not generally worn today, the tradition still persists in the Stock Exchange and top hats are by no means uncommon in the Throgmorton Street area; but, be it whispered, they are kept in the office wardrobe, put on in the morning and returned to the cupboard at the close of the day's business! Throgmorton Street derives its name from Sir Nicholas Throckmorton, Ambassador to France in the reign of Queen Elizabeth I.

The Stock Exchange had its first home in Jonathan's Coffee House in Change Alley – the attendants in the Stock Exchange today are still called 'waiters', an echo from those early days. The first stone of the present hall was laid on 18 May, 1801 and the building was opened in March, 1802. In 1853, additional space was acquired for a new building to the design of Thomas Allason, and there were further enlargements between 1885 and 1930. As one of the most important commercial buildings in the City, the Stock Exchange of today is not very impressive; it is of low elevation and faced with pink granite, which is dingy rather than distinguished, but plans have been prepared for a new building in the modern style to be erected on the present site. The 80-year old 'New House' at the Throgmorton-Old Broad Street apex has already been demolished and a 26-storey tower block, 320 feet high, is now being built in its place; when this is completed (in 1970), the older building of 1853 will be dealt with. Until a few years ago, it was strictly forbidden for any member of the public to enter the Stock Exchange, but a gallery has now been provided from which visitors may look down through a glass screen and witness the proceedings below. Admission is free and the gallery is open from 10.30 to 3, Monday to Friday.

The area enclosed by Moorgate, London Wall, Old Broad Street and Throgmorton Street consists principally of narrow streets and alleys leading to nowhere in particular, and it is here that the stockbrokers and jobbers have their offices. To roam at random through such byways as Angel Court, Drapers Gardens or Copthall Court affords all the delight of wandering through the narrow streets of some ancient University town, and the 'shortcuts' through Warneford Court, Pinners Hall, 19 Old Broad Street and many others are an essential part of the special knowledge acquired by a jobber's junior clerk who has to deliver stock or bonds to brokers on a busy Account Day.

Referring back to Throgmorton Street for a moment, mention must be made of the Drapers' Hall on the north side with its doorway flanked by massive caryatids. At the side of the hall is Throgmorton Avenue, entered through a pair of heavy iron gates surmounted by the coat of arms of the Worshipful Company, with their motto – 'Unto God only be Honour and Glory'. At the back of the hall one is surprised to find an unexpectedly large garden, with trees and a fountain though it is but a small remnant of the original garden, most of which was let for office building in the 1880's. This series of dingy old offices, known as Drapers Gardens, numbered 1 to 10 with large hemispherical brass number plates, stone staircases and dark basements, was demolished in 1964, and in their place there stands a modern office block of 30 storeys, and 335 feet high. Beyond this, Throgmorton Avenue continues to London Wall.

In Austin Friars, a left-right-left twisting byway from Old Broad Street, is the Dutch Church. The present building, the foundation stone of which was laid by Princess Irene of Holland, was opened in 1956, replacing a church that had 'all the magnificence of a cathedral', which was completely destroyed in 1940. The name Austin Friars recalls a 13th-century priory of begging friars dedicated to St Augustine, that originally stood here. Almost opposite Austin Friars is the

City of London Club in Old Broad Street. Built in 1832-4 by Philip Hardwick, it has a façade of a Palladian composition with a Doric order of seven attached pilasters. In a thoroughfare like Regent Street, it would not be particularly remarkable, but here, surrounded by twentieth-century office buildings, it provides a handsome contrast.

The present Gresham House, the greater part of which was rebuilt between 1920 and 1922, extends from Old Broad Street through to Bishopsgate, and stands on the site of the old Excise Office, built in 1763 and removed to Somerset House in 1848, The Excise Office was pulled down in March 1854 and during its demolition a Roman tessellated pavement was discovered about fifteen feet below the surface near Threadneedle Street. It was removed to the Crystal Palace, where it was destroyed when that building was burnt down in 1936. The Excise Office stood on the site of the college and ten almshouses founded by Sir Thomas Gresham in 1575 and consisted of a plain but handsome stone building fronting Old Broad Street, with another one of brick in the rear separated by a large courtyard. The adjoining Palmerston House, another large block of offices, also extends through to Bishopsgate and formerly contained the London office of the Cunard Steamship Company, now transferred to their new building in Leadenhall Street. The section fronting Bishopsgate was rebuilt in 1938-39 but the rebuilding of the section which faces Old Broad Street was delayed by the outbreak of war. Nevertheless this was completely destroyed, together with two adjoining buildings in Old Broad Street, by a bomb in August 1944. This section was rebuilt to provide premises for Barclays Bank, Dominion, Colonial & Overseas Branch.

The City of London Club, mentioned above, stands on the site of the Broad Street frontage of the old South Sea House, destroyed by fire in 1926. The main building of the South Sea House, however, was situated in Threadneedle Street, where it joins Bishopsgate. Charles Lamb, who was a clerk there, described it as 'a melancholy-looking, handsome, brick and stone edifice'.

The South Sea House was erected between 1720 and 1727 and was approached from a gateway leading into a court containing a piazza formed by Doric pillars. The South Sea Company itself was incorporated by Act of Parliament in 1710 to pay £10,000,000 due to the seamen employed in the wars of Queen Anne's reign, but after the scandals in speculation which took place in the so-called South Sea Bubble, the affairs of that Company were reduced to the narrow compass of recovering and distributing the Government dividends on their stocks. In 1853-54 the South Sea stock was converted and paid off by the Government, and this site, comprising half an acre of ground, was disposed of in 1854 for an enormous price. On this site today stands the British Linen Bank, a building of 1902, upon which the name 'South Sea House' is still maintained.

Turning into Threadneedle Street, a short distance farther west is an establishment of the Westminster Bank Ltd, scarcely less imposing than the head office of that bank in Lothbury. It was erected in 1925-26 and in 1930 was awarded the London Architecture medal of the Royal Institute of British Architects.

On the site of this building the Hall of Commerce formerly stood until about 1870. It was erected in 1842 by Mr Moxhay, a biscuit-maker, at a cost of £70,000. Opened with an inaugural banquet two years before the completion of the present Royal Exchange, it was designed to rival Lloyd's, the Baltic, Garraway's, and other similar institutions. It contained a reading-room and office accommodation for commission agents, where they could exhibit their samples. Mr Moxhay was also something of an amateur architect and it was thought that his Hall of Commerce was an expression of his disappointment when the selection committee rejected his own design for the new Royal Exchange.

Before the construction of the Hall of Commerce, a French Protestant church had occupied this site, and going back to much earlier times, it may amuse readers to learn that according to Mr David Hughson, LL.D., this centre of great opulence was once called Pig Street. That was because the animals belonging to the Hospital of St Anthony, which also stood on this site in more remote times, used to run about this street and be fed by passengers. This incident gave rise to the adage, 'Following like a Tantony pig'.

Concealed behind the premises of the Bank of New South Wales on the south side of Threadneedle Street is the Merchant Taylors' Hall, said to be the largest of any belonging to the City Companies. A few paces farther west will bring us back again to our starting-point, the Royal Exchange.

Second Walk

Cornhill, Leadenhall Street, St Mary Axe, Houndsditch, Liverpool Street, Bishopsgate, Gracechurch Street and Lombard Street

Cornhill at the present day consists mainly of tall modern office buildings. It derives its name from a corn market held here in olden times, and a century ago presented a long vista of gloomy dark-brick houses, typical of the period, never exceeding five storeys in height.

For this reason the Cornhill of that time appeared somewhat wider to the casual observer than does the Cornhill of the present day, and whereas St Michael's Church then towered well above all its neighbours and was a prominent landmark, to-day it is almost dwarfed by their modern successors.

On the south side, just beyond the Royal Exchange, and leading into Lombard Street, is Change Alley, now principally occupied by banks and insurance companies. Here stood until 1866 Garraway's coffee-house, a celebrated place for sandwiches, sherry, pale ale, and punch, which had enjoyed an existence covering 216 years. On the first floor was a sale room where business was transacted between 11.0 a.m. and 12.0 noon. Thomas Garraway was the first man who sold and retailed tea in the City of London and because of his care in obtaining the best tea, many noblemen, merchants, and gentlemen of position resorted daily to his house in Change Alley. Tea was then retailed at from 16s. to 50s. per pound. After an existence of nearly 120 years in its last quarters, Garraway's finally closed down on 11 August 1866. Its first building was burned down in the great fire in Cornhill of March 1748 which started in Change Alley and destroyed nearly a hundred houses, including the rival Jonathan's and Jerusalem coffee-houses, both of them in Change Alley. In 1930 Martins Bank set up a plaque at the rear of their Lombard Street premises marking the site of Garraway's Coffee House.

Jonathan's was next door to Garraway's and was the original rendezvous of the stockbrokers and jobbers who, ousted from the Royal Exchange by the merchants in 1698, came here before taking up their new quarters in Capel Court. It was closed down some years earlier than Garraway's. On the site of these two coffee-houses stands Martins Bank, which, like the adjoining head office of Lloyds Bank, has now been rebuilt, and, with its main frontage to Lombard Street, rises to a height of eight storeys. Certainly no more than fifty years ago the City fathers would have been shocked at the very suggestion that such tall buildings should be erected in these narrow streets, but the modification of restrictions regarding the height of buildings in the City — and the fifteen-storey skyscraper, Bucklersbury House — were yet to come!

Returning to Cornhill, at the south-east corner of the Royal Exchange is a pump which was placed in its present position on 6 December 1848. It bears an inscription to the effect that it was first erected in 1799 by the contributions of the Bank of England, the East India Company, and the neighbouring Fire Offices, together with the bankers and traders of the ward of Cornhill. The pump stands on the site of a well which served a House of Correction built there by Henry Wallis, Mayor of London, in 1282. The discovery of the well in 1799 led to the erection of the pump as recorded above. Opposite the pump, at Number 32 Cornhill, is the Cornhill Insurance Company. An interesting feature of this building is the pair of heavy teak doors with eight carved panels illustrating incidents in the history of Cornhill. One of the lower panels shows the author of *Vanity Fair* and the Brontë sisters (Charlotte and Anne) at the Cornhill office of their publishers, Smith Elder & Company. This would seem to be an anachronism, for (according to Mrs Gaskell) Charlotte's first meeting with Thackeray was in December, 1849 and poor little Anne had died at Scarborough in May of that year.

The principal turnings out of Cornhill are Finch Lane (derived from St Benet Fink) and Birchin Lane, a corruption of Birchover Lane, named after its first builder and owner. It was once inhabited by wealthy drapers and city merchants, but the modern buildings are occupied by banks and insurance offices. Next to Birchin Lane, in Ball Court (or 38½ Cornhill) is Simpson's Chop House, established in 1757 and still very popular. Penetrate a little further and 'The George and Vulture' (Thomas's Chop House) is reached; this has Dickensian associations, for it was here that Mr Pickwick stayed during the hearing of Bardell v Pickwick. The unwary wanderer, unless he is careful to remember the direction from which he entered this tangle of six back alleys, may emerge into a street quite remote from where he began, for after Ball Court he will encounter Castle Court and Bengal Court — either of which will take him to Birchin Lane, or George Yard which leads to Lombard Street, while Bell Inn Yard ends in Gracechurch Street and St Michael's Alley goes back to Cornhill! It is of interest to note that within this small triangle of Cornhill, Gracechurch Street and Lombard Street there are no less than three churches — and until 1933, when All Hallows was demolished, there were four.

No. 39 Cornhill, the Union Discount Company, stands on the site of the house where the poet Thomas Gray was born in 1716, and a commemorative bronze plaque quotes the first line of the *Elegy Written in a Country Churchyard*. Next we come to the church of St Michael Cornhill (with St Peter le Poer and St Benet Fink), where the poet was baptised; the font bears the date 1672 and among the church 'treasures' is Gray's own walking stick. The north, or Cornhill side of the church is quite hidden by office buildings, though a vaulted cloister dated 1868 leads from St Michael's Alley into the paved churchyard, from which the church is well lighted by four large stained-glass windows in the south wall. The tower, rebuilt in 1721 by Hawksmoor, rises to a height of 130 feet and is a copy of the Perpendicular chapel tower of Magdalen College, Oxford. Beyond the cloister in St Michael's Alley is the Jamaica Wine House; here stood the first London Coffee House, opened in 1652 at the sign of Pasqua Rosee's Head.

Another church rebuilt by Wren is that of St Peter upon Cornhill, situated at the corner of Gracechurch Street. Like St. Michael's, St Peter's Church is also surrounded by shops and office buildings so that the tower and cupola with its spire crowned by a large St Peter's Key can only be clearly seen from a few favourable viewpoints; one of the best is from the corner of Bishopsgate. The churchyard is raised some two or three feet above the normal ground level. As St Clement Danes in the Strand is the church of the Royal Air Force, so St Peter is now associated with the Royal Tank Regiment and inside the walls are decorated with highly coloured regimental badges and other warlike memorials. It is almost with a feeling of relief that one discovers high up on the south wall of the chancel the sad memorial to seven children — 'The whole offspring of James and Mary Woodmason' — who were burned to death when their home in Leadenhall Street caught fire on 18 January 1782, while their parents were attending a ball at St James's Palace.

Having reached the top of Cornhill, the easternmost of the City's two hills, we are faced by the two corners of Leadenhall Street; on the Bishopsgate side stands the domed clock tower of the London and Lancashire Insurance Company, whose 1925 building occupies the site of their original premises of sixty years earlier. At the Gracechurch Street corner the 'Leadenhall Buildings, 1883' still survive. In this area remains of a Roman Basilica were discovered in the early 1880s, furnishing evidence that a considerable group of Roman administrative buildings bestrode what is now Gracechurch Street on this eminence. Behind this corner is Leadenhall Market, formerly a poultry and game market, but today meat, fish and general provisions are also included. The market takes its name from a 14th century mansion belonging to Sir Hugh Neville that was roofed with lead, which seems to have been as unusual then as it would be today. The present buildings were erected from the designs of Sir Horace Jones in 1881, and the principal entrance to the market is in Gracechurch Street.

A short distance down Leadenhall Street on the right or south side is the entrance to Lloyd's, with the motto 'Fidentia'. This adjoins Royal Mail House which superseded East India Buildings that occupied this site until 1924. These buildings were erected in 1866 by Mr Tite, of the old East India House which, a City Corporation plaque reminds us, stood here from 1726 to 1861.

The former East India House in 1831 was quite the most imposing building in Leadenhall Street, and also extended nearly the length of Lime Street. The interior contained a grand concert hall, paintings illustrating India, marble statues, specimens of Indian architecture, a library of Indian literature, and a good museum of Oriental exhibits. The charter of the East India Company was given by Queen Elizabeth I on 31 December 1600. After the Indian Mutiny of 1857 the Government of India was transferred to the Crown and the East India Company was abolished by the India Act of 1858. Mr Weale, writing in 1851, remarks that for a company which governed a hundred million people, maintained armies, and made war with the greatest Asiatic powers, the East India House was but a humble and unpretentious edifice. It was erected in 1800, just two hundred years after the incorporation of the Company.

Amongst other remarkable curiosities contained in the museum was Tippu's organ, representing a tiger devouring a European. The music produced on turning the handle consisted of shrieks from the man, after every four of which came a growl from the beast. The East India House was pulled down in 1862, and the contents of its museums were transferred to the Victoria and Albert Museum.

It must never be forgotten, in referring to East India House, that that most delightful of essayists, Charles Lamb, was a patient, plodding clerk there for some thirty years. 'Thou dreary pile... in thee remain, and not in the obscure collection of some wandering bookseller, my "works". There let them rest, piled on thy massive shelves, more MSS in folio than ever Aquinas left, and full as useful!'

To return to Lloyd's—the insurance market, which should not be confused with Lloyds Bank or Lloyd's Register of Shipping.

Lloyd's began as a coffee house where business men, some of whom were prepared to insure against marine risks, foregathered and grew eventually to be an international centre for insurance of all classes.

The Leadenhall Street entrance, mentioned above, leads to the building of Sir Edwin Cooper's design which was opened by King George V in 1928. This has been somewhat overshadowed by the 'new building', extending from Lime Street to Billiter Street and southward to Fenchurch Avenue. The new building, whose architect was Mr Terence Heysham, was opened by Queen Elizabeth the Queen Mother, accompanied by Princess Margaret on 14 November 1957. The new Underwriting Room is 340 feet long by 120 feet wide and there sit Lloyd's underwriters transacting insurance business brought to them from all over the world. Above the Rostrum, from which the Caller announces the names of brokers wanted by colleagues, hangs the famous Lutine Bell which is rung to obtain silence when important announcements are to be made; one stroke for bad news and two strokes for good.

The Committee Room at Lloyd's is an adaptation of the Adam Great Room of Bowood House, Wiltshire, from which the original Adam ceiling, panelling, fireplace and other features have been taken out and re-erected. In the Nelson Room is a most interesting collection of Nelson relics, including the log-book of *H.M.S. Euryalus* recording the famous 'England expects' signal at the battle of Trafalgar. A bridge across Lime Street joins Lloyd's new building to their earlier premises, noticed above.

From the London and Lancashire Insurance building at the Bishopsgate corner of the north side of Leadenhall Street, tall office buildings survive as far as the Midland Bank (No. 140), beyond which, extending as far as St Mary Axe, everything has been demolished. The very large hole which resulted provided, for a time, an entirely new and unexpected aspect of the church of St Helen in Bishopsgate. On this extensive site a gigantic building is approaching completion which will include new head offices for the Peninsular and Oriental Group, the Commercial Union Assurance Company and others.

Lime Street, on the south side of Leadenhall Street, was until the close of the eighteenth century inhabited by wealthy city merchants. On the east side of this street, opposite Lloyd's, is a new building containing the City office of the Prudential Assurance Co. Ltd.

At the east corner of St Mary Axe (pronounced 'Simmery Axe') is the church of St Andrew Undershaft, erected in 1532. This is a church to which all lovers of London should make a pilgrimage, for it is the burial place of John Stow, whose *Survay of London,* published in 1598, is the first authority on the history of London.

The memorial, erected by his widow, is a life-size figure of the old historian seated at a table, writing, and the quill pen in his hand is renewed every year at a memorial service attended by the Lord Mayor and Sheriffs.

A century ago this thoroughfare was mainly inhabited by Jews, and until the dawn of the present century remained a shabby street. Its character was completely changed by the construction of the new Baltic Exchange in 1903 and by the various banks and steamship companies which have since invaded St Mary Axe and converted it into a first-class business thoroughfare. The Baltic Exchange covers the site of the former Jeffery's Square on the east side of St Mary Axe, traditionally where Dickens' Cheeryble Brothers lived. The foundation-stone was laid on 25 June 1901 by the Lord Mayor, the Rt. Hon. Frank Green, and the building was opened on 21 April 1903 by the Rt. Hon. Sir Marcus Samuel, Lord Mayor. The architects were T. H. Smith and W. Wimble.

East of Lime Street on the south side of Leadenhall Street are the Baltic House erected in 1903 and Albion House on the site of the New Zealand Chambers, both situated between Lime Street and Billiter Street. The New Zealand Chambers were designed by Mr Norman Shaw in 1874, and were an ambitious modern imitation of old architecture. Damaged beyond repair in the blitz of 1940, the New Zealand Chambers were demolished; but Baltic House, likewise greatly damaged, has been repaired and fitted with a new stone front. This has been set back about ten feet in order to conform with the plans of the City Corporation to widen Leadenhall Street between Lime Street and Aldgate. Between St Mary Axe and Creechurch Lane on the north side of Leadenhall Street, extensive rebuilding operations have been carried out, and the lofty new Cunard building has replaced a number of shabby old buildings which previously occupied the site. The new offices of the Cunard Steamship Company occupy an area of nearly half an acre, and were designed by Messrs Mewes & Davis.

At the east corner of Creechurch Lane is the church of St Katherine Cree (or Christ Church), erected in the year 1628. On the south wall is a curious triangular arrangement of brass rods, which proves to be a sundial, with the motto, *Non Sine Lumine*. This was put up in 1706, but as the opposite side of the narrow Leadenhall Street is now occupied by the seven-storey Furness Withy building, it is only at certain favourable times of a sunny day that the dial is able to function. Having survived the Great Fire of 1666 and suffered only minor war damage, the church was open for some time after the War, but further examination led to a thorough restoration in 1962. Under the provisions of the City of London (Guild Churches) Act of 1952, it was reopened as one of the fourteen Guild Churches and, relieved of parochial duties, is now the Guild Church of the Industrial Christian Fellowship.

A noteworthy feature of the restored church is the Laud Memorial Chapel of King Charles the Martyr, furnished by the Society of King Charles the Martyr. In the summer of 1965 the churchyard was reconditioned as the Fitch Garden, dedicated to 'all who work in the City', in memory of James Fitch who opened his cheesemonger's shop, east of the church, in 1784.

Between Billiter Street and Aldgate, immediately opposite the Church of St Katherine Cree, is a huge block of offices erected in 1919 by the City of London Real Property Company. It extends to Fenchurch Street and contains the headquarters of the Furness Withy Steamship Company. Here, in 1914, the City Corporation carried out an extensive widening of this portion of Leadenhall Street, but a few buildings still remain to be set back at the corner of Billiter Street in order to complete the widening of the street.

Entering Aldgate at the junction of Leadenhall Street and Fenchurch Street we immediately observe that the main thoroughfare between this corner and the Minories is far too narrow for its requirements. Being the only convenient approach from the City to the East End, it would seem that the City Corporation will some day deem it necessary to widen Aldgate to relieve the enormous volume of traffic passing through this bottleneck, extending from Leadenhall Street to the Minories. Some of its houses have been destroyed by bombing and others are now derelict. The first stage in the widening programme has commenced. One by one, in recent months the few remaining shops and offices that were still occupied have been vacated, and from No. 77 Leadenhall Street eastward, across Mitre Street and Duke's Place, to the corner of Houndsditch they have all been demolished. If one could shed a tear, it might perhaps be for No. 72 Leadenhall Street, an obscure and dirty old house with overhanging upper floors indicating late 17th century construction; but it has been derelict for so long that it would be unreasonable to wax sentimental about it now, especially as the remainder of the group, mostly dating from the 1880s, were also a very shabby lot.

At the point where Leadenhall Street and Fenchurch Street meet stands Aldgate Pump, a familiar landmark for hundreds of years. The old wall from which the pump formerly drew its water has long been filled in, but drinking water from the normal water supply is still available, via a dog's head in brass.

At the corner of Aldgate on the north side of Houndsditch is St Botolph's Church, Aldgate, built by George Dance in 1744, the third one erected on this site. During the Great Plague of 1665, this churchyard was utilized as a plague pit, and for many years afterwards the mark of this great pit could be seen on the surface, parallel with the passage by the west wall of the churchyard overlooking Houndsditch. It was 40 feet long, 16 feet wide, and in some parts 20 feet deep. Opposite Houndsditch at the corner of Aldgate and the Minories is the huge Portsoken House, erected in 1928, nine stories high, and faced with Portland stone.

Houndsditch derives its name from the old fosse which once encircled this quarter of the City and formed a useful depository for dogs. Affectionately nicknamed 'The Ditch' by its patrons, it is now the centre of the Jewish business quarter, and is also noteworthy for containing a church at both ends. Both churches are dedicated to that popular English saint, St Botolph, a Suffolk man who built an abbey near Aldeburgh. He was a sort of English St Christopher, who loved to help travellers on their way, for the three churches dedicated to St Botolph are at the City gates. Houndsditch specializes in what are known as 'Fancy Goods'; cheap and showy ornaments, low-priced imitations of more expensive and better quality articles of all descriptions; a popular source of supply for small shopkeepers, street traders and stall holders at fairs. For the retailer whose premises will not accommodate goods bought by the gross, in 'The Ditch' the small trader can order by the 'quarter-dozen'!

On the north side of Houndsditch, immediately opposite St Mary Axe, is the entrance to a court known as Phil's Buildings, which were pulled down in 1936. Here, many years ago, could be witnessed a daily scene, between four and five o'clock, of small traffic and bustle where hundreds of dealers of cast-off clothing used to assemble after their morning rounds, picking up whatever they could hope to sell for shillings or pence. The court was flanked by decently-built houses, one or two of which were occupied by persons in the trade. At the upper end was a lofty gateway near which was the entrance to a public house bearing the name and arms of a venerable Jewish patriarch of the City of London. The visitor to Phil's Court had to pay the sum of one penny for admission.

Only a short time back Houndsditch was the Cinderella quarter of the City, but of late years several fine buildings have been erected here. These include Audrey House and Greenly House on the south side and on both sides of the street, of the Houndsditch Warehouse Company: the Staple Hall, and the towering Stone House at the corner of Bishopsgate, erected on the site of the late Devonshire Hotel. A considerable widening has been carried out on the north side of the street. The fairy godmother has indeed been at work in stately Houndsditch. Small wonder therefore that a deputation of the most prominent business men in Houndsditch in 1927 petitioned the City Corporation to alter the name of this greatly-improving thoroughfare. The City Corporation, however, were wisely unwilling to accede to this request on the grounds that it would destroy the historical associations attaching to this thoroughfare. However, the petitioners were so far humoured as to be transferred from the E.1. postal district to the more dignified E.C.3.

Nearly all the houses which lined the south side of Houndsditch between

Bishopsgate and St Mary Axe have been destroyed by bombs and so also have most of the older buildings on both sides of the road at the other end of Hounds-ditch close to Aldgate. On a cleared site behind St Botolph's Church, extending to Stoney Lane is a new office block called St Botolph's House. The Houndsditch Warehouse is a large and handsome store which has been termed the 'Selfridge's of the Jewish quarter'. It was greatly enlarged in 1933 and also has extensive frontages to Stoney Lane and White Kennett Street. In another few years' time, Houndsditch looks like becoming a first-class thoroughfare. At the Bishopsgate end is the new Cotts House and next to it the fourteen-storey Kempson House built for the Wool Exchange and General Investment Co. Ltd.

Almost facing Houndsditch is the Church of St Botolph, Bishopsgate, rebuilt by James Gold in 1729. John Keats was baptized here in 1795. The churchyard has been made into a pleasant public garden and the former parish school, with its charming Coade figure of a boy and girl (one dated 1821), is now used as the hall of the Worshipful Company of Fanmakers. A long-disused Turkish Bath building near the churchyard, in the colourful style of architecture and decoration that was always associated with Turkish baths, has been brilliantly restored and is now open as the Gallipoli Turkish Restaurant.

A few paces north of St Botolph's Church on the west side of Bishopsgate will bring us to Liverpool Street Station, the city terminus of the former Great Eastern Railway, now merged into British Railways (Eastern Region).

Opened in November 1874, Liverpool Street Station occupies nearly ten acres of ground, standing on the site of the first Bethlehem Hospital — familiarly known as 'Bedlam' — which stood here from 1247 to 1676. The station was designed by Mr Edward Wilson, an engineer, the main-line departure platforms being approached from Liverpool Street and the arrival platforms from Bishopsgate. Near the booking office is a large mural war memorial flanked by bronze medallions of Captain Fryatt and Field-Marshal Sir Henry Wilson, who was assassinated shortly after unveiling the memorial to the Great Eastern men killed in the first World War.

The coming of the Great Eastern Railway into Liverpool Street in 1874 was one of the greatest boons conferred upon the travelling public of London during the nineteenth century. The old terminus, which was originally built by the Eastern Counties Railway, being situated close to Shoreditch High Street, necessitated a tiresome walk to the centre of the City. People residing in the eastern suburbs were thus put to great inconvenience and moreover Bishopsgate was not then the fine broad thoroughfare it is at the present day. It has been widened since that time between Liverpool Street and Shoreditch High Street, so that the great congestion of traffic which once prevailed in this thoroughfare has been enormously relieved.

Upon the opening of Liverpool Street Station, the Shoreditch terminus became the Goods Depot — until it was completely destroyed by fire on 5th December, 1964. It was the original intention that the new City station should not only stand boldly by Broad Street Station, which had been erected in 1865, but should advance further forward right up to the very boundary of London Wall, with impressive buildings surmounted by twin Gothic spires. But the City authorities would have none of it, and the tracks of the new station eventually had to be hidden below the level of the adjoining North London station. Liverpool Street, by the way, was named (in 1829) after Lord Liverpool, and has no direct connection with the Merseyside city.

With six lines running into eighteen platforms the much-abused 'bottleneck' is unavoidable and by no means peculiar to Liverpool Street among terminal stations. However, the electrification of the main line to Colchester and Clacton and most of the suburban lines, with the introduction of modernised signalling has done much to overcome the problem of congestion. Now that the steam locomotive has practically disappeared there is a noticeable absence of steam and smoke, and the familiar intermittent beat of the Westinghouse Brake has been replaced by the continuous roar of the Diesels.

Opposite Widegate Street, leading into Bishopsgate, stood until 1890 the picturesque Tudor house of Sir Paul Pindar, a wealthy merchant in the days of Queen Elizabeth I and James I, and for nine years Ambassador at Constantinople. It occupied a portion of the site now covered by the long range of shops in front of the east side of Liverpool Street Station and had a large garden in the rear. For something like a century before its demolition it had been used as a wine shop and tavern. The tall front of the house with its bay windows and unique carved panelling has been preserved and may be seen in the Victoria and Albert Museum.

Broad Street Station, the terminus of the North London Railway, immediately west of Liverpool Street Station, was opened in 1865, and was another far-reaching improvement. It enabled the City man wishing to travel to Kingsland, Islington, Camden Town, or Hampstead and Willesden, to save a journey of four miles and about twenty minutes in the time so occupied. Hitherto he had been obliged to make the long detour by way of Fenchurch Street and Bow, whereas now he was enabled to travel from the Broad Street terminus. This branch of the North London Railway was two miles long and had four stations, namely, Broad Street, Shoreditch, Haggerston and Dalston Junction, Kingsland. Here the lines form a fork, that on the west leading to Richmond and on the east to the docks, though the passenger service from Dalston to Poplar was withdrawn in 1944: today the line consists of $16\frac{1}{4}$ miles from Broad Street to Richmond, with 20 stations.

The North London Railway began life in 1846, with the high-sounding title of 'The East and West India Docks and Birmingham Junction Railway', an eight-mile run from Camden (Chalk Farm) to Poplar; the two-mile extension from Dalston to Broad Street came later. Although somewhat obscured by buildings that have subsequently occupied the forecourt, there is nothing insignificant about the architecture of Broad Street Station; it is spacious, with nine platforms well above the street-level, reached by thirty-two steps. A noticeable feature of many of the original stations on the line was generous size and sturdy design, and the surprising number and length of the platforms, which seemed to anticipate trains of exceptional length and capacity. The former Underground Railway station on the opposite side of Liverpool Street was opened in 1876, in which year the Metropolitan Railway extended their line from Moorgate to Aldgate. Since the construction of the new Underground booking Hall at Liverpool Street, with its escalators giving access to both the Central and Metropolitan lines, passengers were now able to get from the Eastern Region terminus and Broad Street Station to the Underground lines without the inconvenience of having to cross Liverpool Street. The old Bishopsgate Station has been merged into the underground Liverpool Street interchange station.

Old Broad Street, which commences opposite Broad Street Station, is lined at this end by several large blocks of office buildings, notably Broad Street House on the east side and until it was pulled down, Winchester House farther up on the west side. In the first Elizabeth's time Old Broad Street was one of the most fashionable streets in London, but New Broad Street, which runs at right angles to Old Broad Street between Liverpool Street and London Wall, was formerly called Petty France, and was built about 1737. The gloomy brown-brick houses which lined both sides of this street fifty years ago have now given way to modern blocks of offices, faced with stone. Some of them were damaged by enemy action.

We return to Bishopsgate through Wormwood Street. Until 1st January, 1911, this thoroughfare went under the two names of Bishopsgate Street Within and Bishopsgate Street Without, and the dividing line was of course the old City boundary, the reference being to the gate in the City Wall. These two titles have now been altered to plain Bishopsgate for the sake of greater convenience.

Going south we next come to St Helen's Place, a cul-de-sac on the east side of Bishopsgate, consisting some years ago of dreary-looking brown-brick houses, but now completely lined with new buildings. At the end of this street is a revolving platform erected for the convenience of motorists, who, by placing their cars on this contrivance, are saved the trouble of making the right-about turn when leaving this street. At the entrance to St Helen's Place from Bishopsgate is the stately building erected by the Hudson's Bay Company in 1925-27.

Next door, on the north side, is the tiny church of St Ethelburga, one of the smallest in London. It looks like a doll's house when compared with the tall office buildings on either side of it. This church, one of the few which survived the Great Fire of London in 1666, is a Gothic building which was erected about the year 1420. It originally had a stuccoed front with small shops which concealed the entrance to the church, but these were removed in 1933 in order to widen the pavement in Bishopsgate.

Some of the stained-glass windows in the church refer to Henry Hudson, the navigator who, with his crew, made communion here in 1607 before sailing on those voyages which led to the discovery of the river, strait and bay which bear his name.

A short distance farther south on the same side of Bishopsgate is Great St Helen's, giving access to the Church of St Helen and to St Mary Axe. The church escaped the Great Fire of London, and was restored in the nineteenth century, and the churchyard itself forms a pleasant retreat in the midst of the surrounding turmoil. By reason of its interesting monuments and brasses – the most important, perhaps, being that of Sir Thomas Gresham – St Helen's is sometimes called the 'Westminster Abbey of the City.' Among the many visitors to the church, practical appreciation was expressed by the members of the Mary Ward Settlement *Fascination of London* class recently. Under the direction of their tutor, Mr Hugh Mapleston, they spent several Saturday afternoons with pails of hot water, brushes and special detergents, scrubbing some of the monuments, including the earliest of them all, the splendid tomb of Sir John Crosby and his wife, Agnes, dated 1476. Next, in Crosby Square, a City Corporation plaque marks the site of the Hall of Crosby Place. Crosby Hall, a fine specimen of fifteenth century domestic architecture, was built by Sir John Crosby, Alderman of the City of London, in 1466. It later came into the possession of Richard, Duke of Gloucester (there is more than one reference to Crosby Place in Shakespeare's *Richard III*).

In 1868 the hall, which has a splendid hammerbeam roof, was converted into a restaurant, and in 1910 was dismantled and re-erected in Danvers Street, Chelsea, where it is now used by the British Federation of University Women.

Beyond Great St Helen's, opposite Threadneedle Street, is the Bank of Scotland. On the west side of Bishopsgate is Hambro's Bank, built in 1926 and faced with red brick with stone dressings, and a few doors farther north is the more recently completed building of Messrs Marcus Samuel & Company Limited. At the junction of Bishopsgate and Threadneedle Street is the head office of the National Provincial Bank. It was erected in 1865 on the site of an ancient inn called 'The Flower Pot'. In that year the National Provincial Bank extended its business to London, after having been for thirty-three years established in the provinces. The building is 53 feet high, of which 33 feet are accounted for by columns, and the roof is adorned by several groups of statuary. The Banking Hall with its glass domes and columns is most impressive, and a Preservation Order in respect of this building has recently been confirmed, as it is regarded as an excellent example of classic Victorian bank architecture. Beyond Threadneedle Street and across Cornhill, we come to Gracechurch Street, once known under the name of Gracious Street. A fountain known as the Cornhill Standard once stood at this important traffic junction. On the east side of this street is Grand Avenue, the principle entrance to Leadenhall Market, flanked by turrets surmounted by weather-vanes in the form of Golden (or at least, gilded) Pheasants. Here stood until 1865 the Spread Eagle Inn, one of the oldest in London, and approached from Gracechurch Street, through a galleried courtyard. Farther along is the foreign branch of Barclays Bank at the north corner of Fenchurch Street. The buildings lining the west side of Gracechurch Street include the English, Scottish and Australian Bank and the more recently constructed buildings of the Mercantile Bank and the Hong Kong and Shanghai Bank, completed in 1913. By St Peter's Alley and Corbet Court in Gracechurch Street is a new building for Guinness, Mahon & Co.

Turning next into Lombard Street on our right, at the north corner of Gracechurch Street is the head office of Barclays Bank, one of the so-called 'big five'. A large extension at the corner of George Yard was completed in 1932. In Gracechurch Street the building line has been set back a trifle; but the main frontage of this bank is in Lombard Street. This world-famous banking thoroughfare derives its name from the Lombards, merchants, money-lenders, and bankers who settled here in the twelfth century from the Italian republics of Genoa, Venice, and Florence. Because of their usurious practices they were ordered by Queen Elizabeth I to leave the country.

Behind Barclays Bank, occupying ground much sought after for business requirements, stood until 1938 the Church of All Hallows, Lombard Street. It was so completely hidden by the surrounding buildings that it was called the 'Church Invisible'. Many years ago Barclays Bank were said to have offered a large sum of money to the church authorities for this most valuable site, but their proposal was rejected. Finally, the walls of the church having become unsafe and in urgent need of repair, the building was condemned and pulled down in 1938. Work on an extension of Barclays Bank began on this site almost immediately and this is now completed. The beautiful stone tower of All Hallows Church has been re-erected as part of the modern church of All Hallows on the Great Chertsey Road at Twickenham. Many of the memorials have also been removed from the Lombard Street church to this new site.

On the opposite corner of Gracechurch Street and Lombard Street is the London Office of the Crédit Lyonnais, a building in the Italian style faced with Portland stone and erected in 1868 for the City Offices Company. In that year the approaches to Lombard Street from Fenchurch Street were considerably widened and the frontage of Lombard Street was set back seven feet. The requisite strip of land was purchased by the City Commissioners from the ground landlords, the Fishmongers' Company, for £2,000. The cost of the building was £70,000. In Plough Court, Lombard Street, Alexander Pope was born in 1688. By Clement's Lane is the new Clydesdale Bank, slightly convex in shape and decorated with half a dozen panels of quite puzzling modern design.

On the other corner of Clement's Lane, is the head office of the Royal Insurance Company, rebuilt and enlarged for the third time in 1910. The first building of this Company was erected in 1856-57 from the designs of Mr John Belcher and was located on the opposite corner to the existing building. This having soon proved too small, the directors secured the larger site on the south corner at the moderate cost of £45,000 and erected another building, also designed by Mr Belcher, which stood there until the present one was erected in 1910. On the same side of the street is Coutt's Bank on the site occupied by Lloyd's Coffee House between 1691 and 1785. Nearly opposite Clement's Lane at the corner of George Yard is the Church of St Edmund, King and Martyr, also restored by Wren, and occupying a more prominent site than did the neighbouring church of All Hallows.

An attractive feature that has disappeared from Nicholas Lane, which comes next on the south side of Lombard Street, was the pretty little churchyard of St Nicholas Acons, with its few tombstones; there is also a plaque recording that in the parsonage thereof, scientific Life Assurance began in 1762.

Until recent times, it was generally understood that these City churchyards were protected by Act of Parliament from being built on; but this obstacle seems to have been overcome, for approximately half of the west side of Nicholas Lane has been demolished for the rebuilding of the Lombard Street branch of the Westminster Bank, and we shall miss this diminutive relic of St Nicholas Acons.

The modern building at the south corner of Birchin Lane and Lombard Street occupied by Messrs Glyn Mills & Company Limited has replaced an earlier building which formerly belonged to the discounting house of Messrs Overend, Gurney & Company, which created a tremendous panic in the City on the afternoon of 10 May 1866 by closing its doors. This resulted in a rush on the leading banks, which were besieged by crowds of excited depositors. The present building, which is faced with red brick and stone, is of the same elevation as the adjoining Martins Bank and Lloyds Bank.

Before the construction of the new Martins and Lloyds Banks, already referred to in this chapter, a gloomy row of tall brown-brick buildings stood on these sites, fronting Lombard Street, south of Birchin Lane. The various banks had their trade sign in metal hanging above the street, which perhaps gave it an old-world appearance, but the houses themselves were more suggestive of the exterior of some prison or mausoleum. The buildings have been modernized, but Lombard Street is still noted for its attractive hanging signs.

The church of St Mary Woolnoth at the corner of Lombard Street and King William Street was designed by Nicholas Hawksmoor, a pupil of Sir Christopher Wren, in 1716. It was damaged in the fire raid of 29 December 1940. There is an underground railway station beneath this church, which caused a storm of protest in 1897. For this concession the Bishop of London obtained the sum of £250,000 from the City and South London Railway. So inextricably mixed are the church and the station that, ascending the stairs from the station to King William Street, one meets a church door surmounted by three winged cherubs and the exhortation 'Lift up your hearts'. As the church stands on such valuable ground, there have been many proposals to demolish it, but since it has become one of the Guild Churches, perhaps it now has a new lease of life. It has been described as one of the most striking and original, though not the most beautiful of the City churches. Though there are certainly more churches in the City than are required by its present day residents; a hundred and fifty years ago, when the City contained about ten times its present night population, the churches stood so dense that when viewed from a distance one could easily distinguish the City proper from all other parts of the metropolis. Before the Reformation the churches and monastic establishments occupied two-thirds of the entire area

1 The Mansion House, from the Bank, 1820.

2 The Stock Exchange, hidden away behind Throgmorton Street, as it appeared in 1830.

3 Threadneedle Street (showing the original Bank of England building), Cornhill, Lombard Street (behind the third Royal Exchange) and King William Street, 1837.

4ˉ The Merchant Taylors' Hall in 1830. The imposing entrance still stands, but much of the interior was damaged by fire in 1940.

5 The National Provincial Bank head office in Drapers' Gardens, E.C.2.

6 The Bank of England from Gresham Street.

7 Coade Stone figures of Charity Children on the old school buildings of St Botolph, Bishopsgate.

8 Elizabethan houses demolished in 1890 to make way for extensions to Liverpool Street Station.

9 The 15th century tower of All Hallows Staining in Mark Lane.

10 The Lord Mayor's Show passing under the half-built London Bridge in 1827. This bridge has now been sold to the United States.

11 The construction of King William Street. The Church of St Magnus the Martyr is now hidden behind Adelaide House.

12 Trinity House, Tower Hill, 1830.

13 The Custom House, from Thames Street, 1828.

14   Tower Bridge, from the east.

15   The City churches against the skyline in 1826; few of those still standing rise above the huge buildings.
now surrounding them.

16   A general view of the Tower of London and **Tower** Bridge.

17   One of the best examples of early Norman architecture in
Britain: the Chapel of St John in the White Tower.

within the City walls, so that adding the space occupied by the town residences of the bishops and clergy, all possessing large gardens and often assuming the dimensions of small palaces, it is difficult to imagine where the dwellings of the remainder of the inhabitants could have found even standing room.

Third Walk

King William Street, London Bridge, Eastcheap, Fenchurch Street, The Port of London Authority, The Minories, Great Tower Street, Lower Thames Street and the Monument

King William Street, connecting the Bank with London Bridge, was constructed between 1831 and 1835, and forms part of the main artery connecting South London with Islington through Moorgate and City Road. It could justly claim to rank next to Regent Street as the greatest London improvement carried out during the first half of the nineteenth century. The width and beauty of King William Street was considered very striking at that period, especially after emerging from the narrow streets and hilly lanes immediately adjoining. The making of the new street must have necessitated the demolition of a large number of houses which stood in its path across Abchurch, Nicholas, and Clement's Lanes. Yet compared with the construction of Regent Street or Kingsway, that of King William Street appears to have aroused very little public interest, since no details concerning this great event are to be found in any of the numerous histories of London which have appeared since that time.

Since 1914 practically the entire street has been rebuilt, and it is now lined with blocks of offices mostly six storeys high faced with stone as fine as any to be seen in the City. The old buildings, being only four storeys high, gave King William Street the appearance of a much wider thoroughfare than it actually is.

On the west side of King William Street are the buildings of the Scottish Provident Institution, the London Assurance Company, the Phoenix Assurance Company, the Comptoir National d'Escompte de Paris, and the larger Stafford House on the corner of Cannon Street. On the east side are the London Life Assurance Association, the Standard Bank, and the Australian Mutual Provident Society. On the wall of No. 27 Clements Lane, next to the Wren church of St Clement, Eastcheap, is a little-known marble tablet which records that Dositey Obradovich, an eminent Serbian man of letters, lived there in 1784.

At the junction of King William Street and Gracechurch Street overlooking the approach to London Bridge, is the imposing building of the Guardian Assurance Company, cometimes called the great white building, nine storeys high and crowned by a dome rising to 160 feet above the street level. A row of old buildings on the west side between Arthur Street and Cannon Street was destroyed in the blitz, and for several years the vacant space was used as an open-air cafe, but today a new eight-storey building accommodating the Moscow Narodny Bank, Westminster Bank and a number of shops occupies the site. A statue of King William IV which stood immediately in front of the Guardian Assurance building and was erected in December 1844 was removed to Greenwich Park in February 1935.

On the west side of London Bridge and fronting the river is the Fishmonger's Hall, built in 1831-33, and the third to be erected on this site. The first one perished in the Great Fire in 1666 and the second one was built in 1671. On the opposite site is the very much taller Adelaide House, erected between 1921 and 1924, which rises to a height of eight storeys above King William Street and ten storeys above the level of the river.

The new London Bridge, which is about 100 feet higher up the river than the old bridge, was erected under the supervision of Mr George and Sir John Rennie from the designs prepared by their illustrious father Mr John Rennie. After nearly a century of haggling the old London Bridge had been almost universally condemned as a nuisance to navigation and a reflection upon the architectural character of the City. Yet it was only removed in the teeth of strong opposition similar to that displayed in our own time towards the demolition of the old Waterloo Bridge. In 1823 an Act of Parliament was at last passed authorizing the construction of the new bridge together with the necessary approaches.

The first pile was driven on 15 March 1824, and the foundation-stone was laid on 15 June 1825. The new bridge was opened in great ceremony on 1 August 1831 by King William IV, accompanied by Queen Adelaide. They were entertained to a banquet by the Lord Mayor and members of the City Corporation in the pavilion erected on the bridge. With the object of enabling the watermen and a larger number of people to view the procession, His Majesty decided to make the journey by water, and between Somerset House and the stairs of London Bridge both sides of the Thames were lined with vessels, forming a passage about 150 feet wide. The total cost of the bridge, including the approaches, was £2,000,000, and the granite was obtained from Aberdeen, Haytor, and Peterhead.

A proposal to widen the bridge by building out brackets was defeated in 1854 and again in 1875 and it was not until 1906 that the bridge was widened from 52 feet to 65 feet. The width of the roadway was increased from 36 feet to 39 feet, and each of the sidewalks from 8 feet to 13 feet. The traffic over London Bridge is proverbial, and a still further widening is being considered, with the possibility of special facilities for pedestrians. A recent survey by the City Police showed that the number of vehicles crossing the bridge in an average 12-hour day was over 27,000. For pedestrians, the outstanding periods are, of course, the 'rush-hour's between 8.30 and 9.30 in the morning when over 17,500 crossed northward and from 5 to 6 in the evening when over 12,700 returned in the southerly direction. It was also found that, in both directions, two-thirds of the pedestrians favoured the footway on the eastern side of the bridge; this is probably explained by the fact that there are usually one or two large ships berthed in the Upper

Pool on that side, and the further possibility that the Tower Bridge might raise its bascules to let a big ship through – all of which adds interest to an otherwise rather tedious walk. The view from the other side of the bridge lacks shipping interest and is restricted by the Cannon Street railway bridge. The latest proposals to be put before the City Corporation, however, suggest the complete demolition, rather than widening, of London Bridge and its replacement by an entirely new bridge carrying six lanes of traffic at an estimated cost of £42 million. Already enquiries have been received from all over the world for souvenirs such as lamp standards or pieces of stone from the arches or parapets of the old bridge, but the Corporation preferred to sell the complete bridge, for re-erection elsewhere – and two widely-separated cities in Canada are reported to have favoured such a purchase as a tourist attraction. The matter has now been settled, however, and London Bridge is to go to the United States, where it will be rebuilt at Lake Havasu City in Arizona. £1,015,000 is the price to be paid and a ten per cent deposit of $246,000 has already been received by the City Corporation.

The dismantling of the 1005-ft. long bridge is now under way, each piece of granite is being numbered and will be stored at the Surrey Commercial Docks for shipment to Long Beach, California. The blocks will then be transported by road the 300 miles to Lake Havasu City. It is estimated that the entire process of dismantling, transporting and rebuilding old London Bridge will take about three years.

The contemplated demolition of London Bridge recalls Rennie's handsome Waterloo Bridge, which gave way under the strain of modern traffic and was pulled down in 1934-6. Much of it still lies in a stonemason's yard at Harmondsworth, Middlesex, awaiting sale; great heaps of massive blocks of stone – 60,000 tons of it – a most impressive sight.

The church of St Magnus the Martyr in Lower Thames Street, rebuilt by Wren between 1671 and 1687, formerly a prominent landmark viewed from London Bridge, is now practically obliterated by the obtrusive Adelaide House.

Returning to Eastcheap, up Fish Street Hill, an interesting building situated at the corner of Gracechurch Street was the National Provident Institution opened in 1862. At that period it was considered one of the finest buildings ever erected for this class of business, and was designed by Professor Kerr, who displayed great originality in the details of this edifice. Owing to expansion of business and the need for larger premises, the old building has been demolished and a new eight-storey structure to the designs of Mr W.A.S. Lloyd, F.R.I.B.A. has replaced it.

Eastcheap was so named to distinguish it from Westcheap, which was afterwards known as Cheapside. It contains several good office buildings, notably St Botolph's House on the south side of the street close to Botolph's Lane. On the north side, at the corner of Rood Lane, is the Church of St Margaret Pattens, another of those rebuilt by Sir Christopher Wren after the Great Fire. Leaving Eastcheap we proceed along Gracechurch Street. Some adjoining buildings on the east side were destroyed in the air raids of 1940. New offices for the English

Scottish and Australian Bank have been erected on this site. On the other side of the road, adjoining the Guardian Assurance Company's building, is a huge nine-storey edifice which was originally built for the Commercial Bank of London, one of the ill-fated Hatry Companies, and now occupied by the Bank of West Africa. On account of the wide expanse of roadway at this important traffic junction, these towering buildings present a majestic appearance when viewed from Eastcheap. Farther up Gracechurch Street, on the same side of the road, are the United Kingdom Provident Institution and Barclay's Bank (Dominion, Colonial and Overseas) branch.

At the south corner of Fenchurch Street, where until 1876 stood the church of St Benet, Gracechurch, is the new building of the Midland Bank, Overseas Branch. The chief exterior feature is the corner tower, which, with eleven floors, is fully glazed on the north side to show the staircase, each section of which is brilliantly illuminated after dark. Of course, the tower is also well furnished with lifts, but the staircase is something of a showpiece. On a marble wall by the main entrance is a sculptured figure of the god Hermes.

Turning next into Fenchurch Street, which is said to derive its name from Foin Church, near an ancient hay-market, a short distance up on the north side is a row of one-storey shops at the corner of Lime Street. Behind these shops stood the church of St Dionis Backchurch, demolished in 1878, the site of which is now covered by modern buildings. It is of interest to note that the font and pulpit of St Dionis Backchurch are now in the Church of St Dionis, Parson's Green. The peal of ten bells were transferred to All Hallows, Lombard Street and subsequently followed the tower of that church when it was re-erected at Twickenham.

A generation ago Fenchurch Street was still a gloomy thoroughfare with but few buildings out of the commonplace. But the hand of time has been busy here, and great improvements have been made. The centre section of the street, which forms almost a bottleneck, was partly widened between 1901 and 1903 by setting back the building line on the north side but the widening had not yet been completed at the Gracechurch Street end. Today Fenchurch Street is mostly modern buildings, the latest being the 24-storey structure on the south side between Philpot and Rood Lanes. On this side of Fenchurch Street between Rood Lane and Mincing Lane stands the London Commodity Exchange called Plantation House. (Architect, Mr Albert Moore, F.R.I.B.A.) The foundation-stone was laid by Sir Stephen Killick, Lord Mayor of London, on 27 March 1935. It also has entrances in Mincing Lane, Rood Lane and Eastcheap. On the north side of Fenchurch Street, near Cullum Street, is Fountain House, opened in May 1957, and the first 'skyscraper' office building to be erected in the City of London. It is a fourteen-storey structure covering an area of 27,000 square feet which before the war was occupied by twelve separate buildings. The general construction is of steel frame on mass concrete foundations. Steel was used instead of reinforced concrete in order to provide open floors with a minimum number of columns. Fountain House is 170 feet high and as it is higher than the escape ladders of the London Fire Brigade, an additional staircase and lift for firemen has been incorporated into the design. An unusual feature is the manner in which the building projects over the footpath in Fenchurch Street.

At the side of Fountain House is Fen Court, leading to the churchyard of St Gabriel, Fenchurch, which was destroyed in the Great Fire. The parish of St Gabriel was then united with St Margaret Pattens, Eastcheap until 1954, when the latter became a guild church and was relieved of parochial responsibilities. St Gabriel's parish was then added to those in the care of St Edmund the King, Lombard Street. In 1960 the churchyard was paved and planted by some of the owners and occupiers of the adjoining buildings. Three table-type tombs remain, but several trees and many plants and seats make this a pleasant lunch-time resort for the City worker.

At the west corner of Mincing Lane is a large new edifice containing a branch of the Westminster Bank. Mincing Lane, leading to Great Tower Street, is the centre of the tea and rubber trades, and is so named from some houses in it which belonged to the Minchuns or Nuns of St Helen's. On the east side is the new Clothworkers' Hall, recently rebuilt after having been completely destroyed in the air raid of 10 May 1941. The garden of the company is formed by the churchyard of All Hallows Staining, demolished in 1870 except for the tower which still survives.

Farther along on the same side of Mincing Lane stood the Commercial Sale Rooms erected in 1859-60 by Mr Lewis Glinton, upon land belonging to the Grocers' Company, specially as offices and sample rooms for merchants and Colonial firms. It contained two hundred offices and extended from Mincing Lane to an exit in Great Tower Street. Various other large blocks of offices in this thoroughfare extended through to Mark Lane on the east side and to Rood Lane on the west side, so that you could walk under cover through a series of long corridors from Mark Lane to Rood Lane, except that you had to cross the road in Mincing Lane. The merchants and their clerks located in these large buildings almost seemed to constitute a community of their own, similar to that of the stockbroking fraternity in Throgmorton Street and neighbourhood. A walk through this maze of corridors revealed to the astonished stranger various restaurants, tea-shops, tobacconists, and hairdressers' establishments, the existence of which must have been quite unknown to the outside world. But the Commercial Sale Rooms and practically the whole area between Rood Lane and the east side of Mark Lane, including nearly the whole of Mincing Lane and the north side of Great Tower Street, were wiped out in the air raids of 1940 and 1941. Today, however, the area between Mincing Lane and Mark Lane right down to Great Tower Street is fully covered by the great Plantation House with Dunster House, Colonial House and King's Beam House. The two former buildings have extensive public restaurants under the management of Mecca Ltd.

In Mark Lane, parallel with Mincing Lane, is the Corn Exchange, opened in 1747 and rebuilt in 1881 at a cost of about £40,000. It was badly damaged by bombs in 1942, and again rebuilt in 1947. Cereal House, next to the Corn Exchange, is a new block of offices completed in 1933.

Returning to Fenchurch Street, at the west corner of Mark Lane stood the London Tavern, famous for City banquets. It was originally called the King's Head and here Queen Elizabeth I, upon being delivered from the Tower of London on 10 May 1554, sat down to a hearty meal of pork and peas, after first offering up thanks at the adjacent church of All Hallows Staining. In honour of this event it was rechristened the Queen's Head, but upon being rebuilt in 1877 its name was again altered to the London Tavern.

On the opposite side of Fenchurch Street stood the Elephant Tavern, which was spared in the Great Fire of London, although everywhere else around was destroyed. For that reason it provided a valuable refuge for the homeless citizens of London. It was rebuilt in 1826 and when Fenchurch Street was widened in 1901 the front was set back a short distance to conform to the new building line. Both the London Tavern and the Elephant Tavern have likewise been destroyed in the great blitz. On this site, however, a new building, Victoria House, has risen and on the ground floor and basement Messrs Meux & Co. have resuscitated the old Elephant Tavern.

Next to the site of the Elephant Tavern was the former building of the Iron-mongers' Hall which was bombed during the first World War. It has since been modernized and taken over as offices by Messrs Cory & Son, a large firm of iron-makers, and the Ironmongers' Company have moved their headquarters to Aldersgate Street.

At the north corner of Fenchurch Street and Billiter Street is the National Provincial Bank and farther along, near the junction of Fenchurch Street and Leadenhall Street, is the Furness Withy House already noticed in our walk through Leadenhall Street.

Opposite the tower of All Hallows Staining in Mark Lane is the new Marine Engineers Memorial Building of thirteen storeys with two basements. The foundation stone was laid by the Duke of Edinburgh in 1955 and the building was opened by Earl Mountbatten in 1957.

London Street leads to Fenchurch Street Station, the terminus of the former London, Tilbury and Southend Railway, which was leased from the London and Blackwell Railway, a line opened in 1840. The present building dates from the mid-19th century and is a symmetrical design with round-headed windows, the whole front topped by a curved pediment. Whatever its architectural defects, they can be appreciated, as the foreground is free from the usual clutter of shops and sheds that obscure many of our railway stations. The platforms are approached by broad staircases with heavy iron balustrades.

The L.T. & S.R. was a popular railway with cheap fares and a reputation for punctuality. It owned a fleet of handsome tank locomotives, painted green with brass trimmings, but disfigured by uninspiring names such as 'Mile End', 'Black Horse Road', etc. In 1912 the line was taken over by the Midland Railway, after which its individuality disappeared. Electric traction has replaced steam, with the result that it is now possible to reach Southend in 47 minutes from

Fenchurch Street with four intermediate stops—compared with a previous 'best' of 59 minutes.

Beyond London Street is Lloyd's Avenue, a new thoroughfare connecting Fenchurch Street with Crutched Friars, opened by the Lord Mayor in 1899 and lined on both sides with handsome blocks of office buildings. It was constructed on land formerly occupied by the offices of the old London and India Joint Docks Company. On the south corner of Lloyd's Avenue and Fenchurch Street is the building of Lloyd's Shipping Register.

While Lloyd's Avenue is undoubtedly the most direct route from Fenchurch Street to Crutched Friars, a more interesting way would be via St Katherine's Row, which takes its name from the church of St Katherine Coleman that stood on the corner. The church was demolished as recently as 1925 and the church-yard made into a public garden. The narrow St Katherine's Row leads to a darkish, but sufficiently lighted *tunnel* (beneath Fenchurch Street Station) called French Ordinary Courg. En route, one encounters the most delicious aromas when passing the warehouses of merchants who trade in sweet-smelling essential oils and importers of otto of roses, musk and ambergris! Then from this fragrant twilight comes the sudden emergence into the deodorized daylight of Crutched Friars.

Crutched Friars, now consisting of warehouses, was once the residential quar-ter of the nobility, and in ancient times the Monastery of the Friars of the Holy Cross stood on this site. Many courts and alleys in this immediate neighbourhood were swept away between 1910 and 1912 to make room for the new headquarters of the Port of London Authority. This magnificent building, designed by Sir Edwin Cooper, stands on an island site enclosed by Trinity Square, Seething Lane, and the two newly-constructed thoroughfares called Pepys Street and Muscovy Street. Constructed between 1912 and 1922, it has a massive tower rising above a portico of Corinthian columns overlooking Trinity Square, and the offices are grouped round a lofty central apartment which has a domed roof of 110 feet in diameter. The frontage to Seething Lane is more extensive and is faced by a garden enclosed by iron railings. The building was opened by Mr Lloyd George in october 1922, this being the last public function carried out by him during his term of office as Prime Minister. The Act constituting the Port of London was passed in 1908, Mr Lloyd George himself being President of the Board of Trade at that time. The Authority consists of twenty-eight members. Lord Devonport was elected the first chairman, and on 31 March 1959 it celebrated its fiftieth birthday.

When the trade of the Port of London was languishing in the closing years of the nineteenth century, there was plenty of excuse for pessimism. Then when the newly-constituted Authority was faced with a long and costly list of re-constructions, improvements, and additions considered necessary if lost trade which had been diverted to Antwerp, Rotterdam, and Hamburg was to be restored to London, it might well have been dismayed. But instead of lying down to die, it faced its tremendous tasks courageously and confidently. Since then, acres of new docks and miles of new quays have been built, the bed of the river has been deepened from the Tower to the Nore, additional dry docks have been constructed, and costly new equipment and machinery have been installed.

On the south side of Trinity Square is a colonnaded memorial erected to the memory of the men of the Merchant Navy and fishing fleets who fell in the two World Wars. Affixed to each column are bronze plaques giving the names of the men and ships in which they served; altogether, some 36,000 names are recorded of men 'who have no grave but the sea'. Also in Trinity Square (which is oval rather than square) is Trinity House, the headquarters of the Trinity Brethren, a corporation controlling lighthouses and buoys round the British Coast, licensing pilots, and supervising navigation. This building was destroyed in the fire raid of 29 December 1940, but has now been rebuilt. The General Steam Navigation Company have left their offices in Great Tower Street and moved to a new building at Number 40 Lower Thames Street, next to Tower Pier. It has an attractive lawn and balcony overlooking the river. Part of their old premises have been acquired for a new headquarters of 'Toc H'.

The District Railway Tower Hill Station in Byward Street (known as 'Mark Lane' until 1946) has been closed, and on 5 February 1967 a new station was opened some 200 yards further east, at the corner of Cooper's Row. The new position provides additional platform space and reversing facilities for the trains. The engineering problems were considerable, for the widened lines run below the massive Merchant Navy and Fishing Fleets Memorial, which necessitated some under-pinning; moreover, this is an area where substantial remains of the old City Wall have to be considered. It is of interest to note that the new station stands on the site of the old 'Tower of London' station which was opened in 1882 and closed two years later. The ghostly platforms of the old station could always be spotted from the trains by the observant traveller, and one of these old platforms has, in fact, been adapted for use in the new station.

At the western corner of Pepys Street is the large new Walsingham House, which extends through to Crutched Friars. Adjoining is the more recent Mariner House of seven storeys. No. 1 Crutched Friars is 'Roman Wall House', so called on account of a very good fragment of the wall preserved in the besement. The collective result of the extensive building operation carried out in Lloyd's Avenue, Fenchurch Street, and round the Port of London Authority has been to transform this hitherto squalid section of the City into a first-class neighbourhood. In Hart Street and Seething Lane stands the church of St Olave, one of the eight to survive the Great Fire. It is frequently mentioned in the Diary of Samuel Pepys who, with his wife Elizabeth, is buried here. This church was severely damaged in the air raids of 1940, but it has been completely rebuilt and is again open.

From Crutched Friars and along Crosswall, we next come to the Minories, a wide and improving street connecting Aldgate with Tower Hill, at the eastern boundary of the City. A few good buildings have been erected here of late years, the most imposing of which is Portsoken House at the corner of Aldgate, already noted in our previous walk. Next to Portsoken House are Millbourn House and

Shipping Federation House, both recent office buildings, and on the other side of the Minories, St Clare House, a twelve-floor office block. About one-half of the buildings on the east side of the Minories have been destroyed in the blitz, but the newly-erected Ibex House escaped the damage. This is a gigantic block of offices completed in 1937. It is nine storeys high and also has a long frontage to Portsoken Street. At the corner of St Clare Street is 'The Three Lords', a tavern whose sign recalls the Lords Balmerino, Kilmarnock and Lovat who were beheaded on nearby Tower Hill for their part in the Jacobite Rebellion of 1745.

The Minories takes its name from an abbey of nuns of the order of St Clare, called the 'Sorores Minores', which stood here in the Middle Ages; it was founded in 1293 by Edmund, Earl of Lancaster. Upon its dissolution in 1539, the abbey church became the parish church of Holy Trinity, Minories, but though rebuilt in 1706, it was closed at the end of the nineteenth century and finally destroyed by bombs in 1941.

A remarkable discovery was made during excavations on the site of the old Abbey at the lower end of St Clare Street in December, 1964. Workmen digging the foundations of a new office building unearthed a leaden coffin with an inscription which very clearly showed that the coffin contained the remains of Anne Mowbray, Duchess of York. Anne, who died at Greenwich in November, 1481, was the child bride of Richard, Duke of York, one of the princes murdered in the Tower, to whom she was married in 1478 when just over five years of age. After careful examination by experts, the remains of the little Duchess were re-interred in the Henry VII Chapel, Westminster Abbey, on 31 May 1965. She now lies but a few feet away from the marble urn containing what are believed to be the remains of her husband and his brother, the boy king, Edward V.

In Jewry Street until recently stood a house (Number 7), built in 1650, which was decorated with a plaque stating that it 'survived the Great Fire of 1666 and the Blitz of 1940-45'. But it vanished and in its place now stands a new block of offices called 'Boundary House'.

The Royal Mint, situated on the east side of Tower Hill, was erected in 1815 and is the joint work of Mr Johnson and Sir Robert Smirke. It is an old-fashioned-looking Government edifice of three storeys with side wings, the centre block of which is decorated with a pediment and columns with wings.

A detailed description of the Tower of London, the oldest and most celebrated fortress in Great Britain, does not come within the scope of the present work. Suffice it to remark that it has done duty as a royal palace, as a place for assemblies and treaties, as a prison, and to-day, among other things, is the treasury of the ornaments and jewels of the Crown. Since 1856, the Crown Jewels have been displayed in the Wakefield Tower, but their increasing popularity has made it necessary to provide more suitable accommodation, and a new underground stronghold below the Waterloo Barracks in the Tower was opened recently. The most precious of the exhibits are kept in a lower vault, proof against every conceivable kind of felonious attempt; to reach this, the visitor has to descend 49 steps.

Tower Bridge, which is approached by the roadway on the east side of the Tower itself, was begun on 22 April 1886, constructed by the City Corporation at a cost of £1,500,000, and opened on 30 June 1894. The twin bascules, which have a span of 200 feet, are raised to allow the passage of large vessels, and a bell is rung when the bridge is about to be opened. The central span is 200 feet long and those on either side with chain suspensions 270 feet each. The bridge was designed by Sir Horace Jones and Sir J. Wolfe Barry. It is 880 feet long and the roadway is 49 feet wide. The main towers are 120 feet high from the river piers and the abutment towers are 44 feet high. The footbridge, 142 feet above high water, reached by stairs in the Gothic towers, is not now used as traffic is only held up very briefly when a ship passes through and pedestrians are not unduly delayed.

At the eastern entrance to Great Tower Street is the church of All Hallows Barking, which is so called on account of its possession in early times by the Abbey of Barking, Essex (founded c. 675). Samuel Pepys ascended the tower of this church to watch the Great Fire of 1666 and saw 'the saddest sight of desolation'; it is the church of Toc H and here also William Penn was baptized in 1644. Unhappily it was damaged in the air raid of 29 December 1940 and by fire three weeks later. Only the bare walls and the tower remained but the church has now been rebuilt.

For many years the church of All Hallows was concealed by the unsightly Myers Warehouse, an immense building popularly known as the 'Nightmare of Tower Hill'. This building which has been mercifully removed by bombs was erected in 1864, when property in this neighbourhood was only of small value. Probably much older than the Myers warehouse mentioned above, was Barber's Bonded Warehouse in Cooper's Row, north of Tower Hill, which was demolished recently to make room for the new Midland House. It was well known to those interested in such matters that within the old warehouse building was concealed the most complete fragment of the city wall that still survives. Its preservation was not due to any special regard for Roman antiquities on the part of the builder, but the wall is such a sturdy structure that it was easier — and cheaper — to make use of it as it stood rather than laboriously demolish it with pick and shovel; so the vaults and floors were added to the ready-made City Wall. A hundred and twenty feet long, its height is thirty-five feet, much of which was added during medieval strengthening and rebuilding. By a happy collaboration of the architects and contractors with the Ministry of Public Building and Works, the space behind the new Midland House was laid out as a piazza to which the public have open access to view the Wall, which is visible right down to its Roman plinth. This may be regarded as part of the development of the Tower Hill area as a 'precinct', to which the new buildings on the site of the old 'Tiger' tavern, an underground car park to receive the numerous tourist coaches that crowd the area during the summer months, and the re-siting of Tower Hill Station will contribute.

The relief road (complementary to the Route 11 by-pass north of the Bank intersection) which begins at the Blackfriars Underpass and continues with the development of Upper Thames Street, will also link up with the Tower Improvement Scheme.

Among the improvements carried out in this immediate neighbourhood during the latter part of the nineteenth century were the widening of Great Tower Street from St Margaret Pattens Church to Mark Lane, and the construction of Byward Street, which gives access to Trinity Square from the corner of Mark Lane without passing through the narrow eastern end of Great Tower Street. As a result of the widening of the western portion of Great Tower Street, the whole of the north side became lined with modern buildings, and the greater part of those on the south side had also been rebuilt in recent years. Thus Great Tower Street was practically a new thoroughfare. Both sides of the street suffered severe bomb damage and while there has been much new building on the north side there are still some blank spaces on the south. The City of London Real Property Company have now erected a huge nine-storeyed building with frontages to Great Tower Street, Mincing Lane, and Mark Lane, called King's Beam House.

Nearly opposite to Mincing Lane is St Dunstan's Hill, giving access to the church of St Dunstan in the East. The tower of this fine edifice was the work of Sir Christopher Wren, but the church itself was built by Mr David Laing, architect of the Custom House, in 1817. This church was also destroyed in the raid of 29 December 1940, but fortunately the tower with its elegant spire, poised on four curved ribs, still remains.

Passing down St Dunstan's Hill into Lower Thames Street, we next come to the Custom House, situated nearly opposite, and having an imposing stone frontage to the river. It was erected 1814-17 from designs by Mr David Laing, but was afterwards altered by Sir Robert Smirke, because the foundations were found to be defective, and the central parts had to be taken down. No less than five earlier custom houses erected on this site were destroyed by fire, the third being that which perished in the Great Fire of 1666. That built afterwards by Sir Christopher Wren was destroyed by fire in 1718, and was followed by another built by Ripley which met with a similar calamity in 1814. The east wing of the Custom House was destroyed in the war, but has recently been rebuilt in yellow brick and stone to match the style of the west wing.

Just west of the Custom House is Billingsgate fish-market, the oldest in London, dating from about the ninth century, and said to derive its name from Belin, a king of the Britons. The City Corporation erected a market here in 1830, but this was replaced by the existing building erected in 1877 by Mr Horace Jones. It is constructed of Portland stone with yellow-brick dressings between the upper windows. The riverside frontage is decorated with dolphins, which are not fish.

Opposite Billingsgate fish-market was the Coal Exchange, designed by Mr J. B. Bunning and opened in 1849 by the Prince Consort, Queen Victoria having been prevented by illness from attending the ceremony. It stood at the corner of Lower Thames Street and St Mary-at-Hill. The predominant feature was a circular tower 109 feet high. Inside was a rotunda with ornamental cast-iron galleries surmounted by a glass dome. The floor of the rotunda was composed of inlaid woods of many varieties and colours patterned in the form of a mariners' compass, and the elaborate decoration of the panels and pillars of the interior was of a kind which, though not appreciated today, was a valuable example of Victorian art. Threatened with demolition, reprieved, and threatened again, all endeavours to save the Coal Exchange were of no avail and it was demolished in 1962 to make way for the widening of Lower Thames Street. During the excavations of 1847, a Roman hypocaust was discovered; this has received a protective covering pending its re-opening to the public when the site is developed.

Many old buildings in both Upper Thames Street and Lower Thames Street have been destroyed or damaged in the earlier raids of 1940-41.

Pudding Lane, leading from Lower Thames Street to Eastcheap, marks the spot where the dreadful Great Fire of 1666 began, and in Fish Street Hill running parallel to Pudding Lane is the Monument, a fluted Doric column 202 feet high built in 1671-77 to commemorate that disastrous event. In 1842 the gallery at the top of the Monument was railed in to prevent people from committing suicide from that spot. Fish Street Hill was formerly the main thoroughfare leading to old London Bridge, and on the west corner at Upper Thames Street stood the church of St Margaret, destroyed in the Great Fire. After the closing of old London Bridge, the river approach, having become superfluous, was built over and is now covered by Fresh Wharf and the towering Adelaide House. The construction of Monument Street led to the demolition of the houses on the west side of Fish Street Hill, which had previously obstructed the view of the Monument.

The raised approach to the new London Bridge from King William Street necessitated the construction of the two new streets, namely, Monument Street giving access to Lower Thames Street from the east side, and Arthur Street immediately opposite, leading to Upper Thames Street from the west side of King William Street. Both of these streets run crescent-wise into Upper and Lower Thames Streets and contain some excellent buildings. At the south-west end of the curve of Arthur Street where it joins Upper Thames Street is Minster House, a new seven-storey block of offices. The construction of King William Street also necessitated the demolition of St. Michael's Church in Crooked Lane on the south side of Cannon Street. In 1935 a new subway was opened at the junction of King William Street and Cannon Street providing access to the Monument Station. From Cannon Street a walk through King William Street brings us back again to our starting-point at the Mansion House.

Fourth Walk

*Queen Victoria Street, Blackfriars Bridge,
New Bridge Street, Farringdon Street, Ludgate
Hill, Old Bailey, Southwark Bridge,
and Queen Street, etc.*

Queen Victoria Street was constructed by the late Metropolitan Board of Works as a continuation of the Victoria Embankment, with the object of providing London with a new main artery from the Mansion House to Charing Cross. It was the greatest improvement carried out in the City of London during the nineteenth century. Not only did it provide invaluable relief to the enormous traffic of Cheapside, but it completely altered the appearance of the City centre.

According to Mr J. Britton, F.S.A., author of *The Original Picture of London*, published in 1833, it seems that at the time the City Corporation had a scheme for the construction of a new street to connect the Mansion House with South-wark Bridge, but this never materialized.

The total length of Queen Victoria Street is not far short of a mile, the same as that of the Strand. It was opened to the public in sections, as its construction advanced and the different portions became available for use. The first portion, from the Mansion House to Cannon Street was opened on 18 October 1869, a second portion 200 yards long from Blackfriars Bridge to St Andrew's Hill in January 1871, a third instalment of 220 yards between St Andrew's Hill and St Bennet's Hill in May 1871, and the final section between St Bennet's Hill and what was then called New Earl Street, on 4 November 1871.

New Earl Street was the former name given to that portion of Queen Victoria Street situated between Trinity Lane and Cannon Street. It is considerably older than the remainder of Queen Victoria Street, and here the roadway, being only fifty feet wide compared with seventy feet in the other parts of the street, consti-tuted a tiresome bottleneck and also interfered with the architectural appearance of Queen Victoria Street. In 1871 it was hoped that this defect would soon be remedied. But instead of taking the necessary steps to purchase this offending block of buildings sixty years ago, when it could doubtless have been obtained upon reasonable terms, the Metropolitan Board of Works and the City Corpora-tion allowed the 'ship to be spoiled for a ha'p'orth of tar', and nothing further was done in the matter. In 1934 the City Corporation entered into negotiations with the property-owners concerned with a view to the early removal of this bottleneck, and in July 1936 the western portion of the protruding buildings, known as Baldwin House, was pulled down in preparation for this improvement. This 'Queen Victoria Street widening' is now proceeding and the block of buildings known as Mansion House Station Chambers – which also included the principal entrance to the District Railway Station – has been demolished.

The completed Queen Victoria Street was opened with a public ceremony by the Metropolitan Board of Works on Saturday, 4 November 1871. This took place at 3.30 p.m., when there was a procession of the officers and members of the Metropolitan Board of Works and of the City Corporation, headed by Colonel Hogg, Chairman of the Board, and the Lord Mayor of London walking arm-in-arm, the Sheriffs of London and Middlesex, and various London members of Parliament.

Work on the construction of Queen Victoria Street was commenced in 1867, and in February 1868 the Metropolitan Board of Works purchased the old leasehold offices of the Eagle Insurance Company at the corner of the Poultry and the now defunct Charlotte Row for £64,000. This property was required in order to effect a junction of Queen Victoria Street with the Poultry, and during the demolitions carried out here in January 1869 the remains of a Roman pavement were discovered close to Walbrook in the path of the new street. The tessellated pavement was seventeen feet below the surface, and although 1,400 years old was found to be in perfect condition.

In order to enable the general public to inspect the pavement, the work of excavation was suspended for one week, after which the Metropolitan Board of Works handed it over to the City Corporation for presentation to the Guildhall Museum. The pavement ran parallel with the course of the old Walbrook River, and there were traces of a building of importance on the west bank (which was probably the Mithraic temple discovered in 1954). During three days of the week after this discovery, no less than thirty-three thousand people were admitted by the authorities to inspect these interesting remains.

One of the sites cleared for the new street was the triangular slice of ground opposite the west side of the Mansion House, now occupied by the building of the National Safe Deposit Company, erected in 1873. But in 1869 the Metropolitan Board of Works were surprised to receive a deputation of City merchants and bankers asking them to preserve this piece of ground as an open space. The Board referred them to the City Corporation as being the proper party to approach on that subject, as the deputation could scarcely expect the Board to find £200,000, the value at that time placed upon this piece of land. Nevertheless it remained vacant until November 1871, when it was let by the Metropolitan Board of Works for £5,500 a year, or equal to £1 a square foot.

In October 1869 the directors of the Metropolitan District Railway wanted to secure this site for the Mansion House terminus of their new line from South Kensington, instead of the existing site in Cannon Street. In 1870 the Select Committee of the House of Commons gave its decision in favour of this scheme, but the City Corporation opposed it. They contended that it would interfere with the completion of the Inner Circle line. The Metropolitan Railway Company, who had previously obtained permission to extend their line to Mark Lane via Cannon Street, abandoned this scheme, and it was not until 1884 that they actually completed the Inner Circle.

An earlier scheme to connect the proposed new station at the Mansion House directly with the Metropolitan Railway station in Moorgate, by a short line running under Princes Street, was also defeated. The result was that the so-called Mansion House Station was placed in Cannon Street, and people who wanted to travel to and from the Bank in those days preferred an omnibus to the inconvenience of having to walk up Queen Victoria Street to the Mansion Hiuse Station. From a present-day standpoint the completion of the Inner Circle Railway, together with the later construction of the tube railways, has perhaps proved more beneficial to the requirements of the city.

Other valuable property which had to be cleared away for the construction of Queen Victoria Street included nearly one half of the houses in Bucklersbury and several more in Sise Lane a short distance farther west near Queen Street. Bucklersbury, which leads from Cheapside to Walbrook, derives its name from the house of the Bokelers, an ancient City family, and abuts close to St Stephen's Church, reconstructed by Sir Christopher Wren after the Great Fire of 1666. A curious feature was the narrow old-world bookshop of Messrs F. & E. Stoneham Limited, which had been located here since 1884. It stood like a dwarf in front of the lofty tower of this church and was originally the residence of the clerk of the parish. This house was completely destroyed in the raid of 29 December 1940 and St Stephen's Church was also badly damaged. Opposite the north end of Sise Lane (a corruption of St Osyth) is the churchyard of St Benet Sherehog, in Pancras Lane. A stone on the wall tells us that 'Before the Dreadfull Fire Anno 1666 Stood the Parish Church of St Benet Sherehog'. Twenty yards further along is the little churchyard of St Pancras. There is a possibility that it may become a public garden.

On the south side of Queen Victoria Street, between Bucklersbury and Sise Lane, stood until 1941 the Mansion House Chambers, one of the largest blocks of shops and offices in London, erected in 1872, and containing about five hundred rooms. It extended through to Budge Row at the rear and together with the adjoining buildings in Bucklersbury, Budge Row and the whole of Walbrook was destroyed in the air raids of 1940-41. This is the area now covered by Bucklersbury House. On a large site on the east side of Walbrook next to St Stephen's Church and extending to St Swithin's Lane, now stands a new ten-storeyed block of offices. This is St Swithin's House. There are eight storeys above the street level and two below. The site includes that of the Salters' Hall in St Swithin's Lane, which has been pulled down. During the excavation of this site, many interesting Roman relics were discovered by the workmen and by archaeologists from the Guildhall Museum who worked on Sundays for thirteen weeks. These included a number of wooden posts over a wooden raft upon which three houses are said to have been built, a second-century Roman well lined with wood, pottery, necklaces, and Roman boots and sandals. It is supposed that in Roman times this was marshland across which flowed the Walbrook River. On the west side Walbrook has been widened.

Crossing to the west bank of the Walbrook (as one might say) we see the colossal Bucklersbury House, completed in 1958, which marked the first stage in the development of one of the most important sites in the heart of the City. With frontages to Bucklersbury, Queen Victoria Street, Cannon Street and the whole of the western side of Walbrook, where it reaches a height of 165 ft, Bucklersbury House is fifteen storeys high with two basements and has a gross floor area of over 450,000 square feet.

The second stage in the development of this site is 'Temple Court', the head office of the Legal & General Assurance Society, the owners of Bucklersbury House and of this site. This has frontages to Queen Victoria Street, Cannon Street and Queen Street. A large foundation plaque depicting the Society's crest, Temple Bar, was laid by the Lord Mayor, Alderman Sir Edmund Stockdale, on 2 June 1960. In the development of this large site parts of Budge Row, Sise Lane, Tower Royal and Watling Street have been 'incorporated'; which means that those parts of Watling Street and Sise Lane south of Queen Victoria Street have gone – poor little Sise Lane, at no time very extensive, is reduced to some fifteen yards, while Budge Row and Tower Royal, though surviving in name, are 'improved out of all recognition'.

While the contractors were working on the foundations of Bucklersbury House, the Roman and Medieval London Excavation Council, under the direction of Professor W. F. Grimes, were making archaeological excavations on the site: in September 1954, the remains of a Roman Temple of Mithras and many pieces of sculpture were found some 18 feet below the present level of Walbrook. So great was the interest shown by the general public – as in 1869 – that a wooden stairway was erected down the steep slope and steel barriers were put up around the site to enable people – who queued in thousands – to obtain a closer view of the discoveries. The sculptures were presented by the owners of the site to the Guildhall Museum, together with a small silver ritual canister which was found buried in the north wall of the temple. Replicas of the sculptures are on view in the main Walbrook entrance to Bucklersbury House. The remains of the Mithraic Temple have been re-erected on a terrace in front of Temple Court, facing Queen Victoria Street, only a short distance from their original position, though their orientation, which was east-west, is now north-south.

Until 1875 St Antholin's Church stood on the corner of Budge Row near Sise Lane, in which year it was demolished and its parish amalgamated with St Mary Aldermary. It was rebuilt by Sir Christopher Wren in 1682, and bore a lofty spire, which showed up to advantage from Queen Victoria Street. When the church was pulled down, the spire was preserved and re-erected in the garden of a large house in Sydenham, where it still stands. On the north side of Queen Victoria Street is Wren's Gothic church of St Mary Aldermary with its principal entrance in Bow Lane.

By October 1873 Queen Victoria Street was so far completed that it was in a condition to be handed over to the care of the City Corporation. By that time only one-twelfth of the surplus land was unlet, and that was between St Bennet's Hill and Blackfriars Bridge. The total cost of the construction of the new street was £624,000.

West of Cannon Street the buildings which before the second World War lined Queen Victoria Street were with a few exceptions greatly inferior to those extending eastwards to the Mansion House, and were totally unworthy of what one might have expected to find in Queen Victoria Street no farther than four hundred yards from the Bank of England.

London is universally recognized as the Fur Trade capital of the world, and Garlick Hill with its adjoining little streets and courts behind the Mansion House Station down to Upper Thames Street is the ancient centre of the fur trade. Here the dealers have their premises, and a glance through their windows will disclose a display of Musquash, Silver Fox, Persian Lamb and other delights dear to the feminine heart, while for good measure, a man in a long white coat (for undressed furs are greasy) may brush past you with a string of fifty or so Mink skins slung over his shoulder.

At the corner of Great Trinity Lane is Beaver House, the headquarters of the Hudson's Bay Company, founded in 1670. Fitted with windows specially constructed to give a correct 'north light' for fur grading, and having special warehouse accommodation for upwards of two million pelts, Beaver Hall is one of the centres where fur sales are held. Entering from the street one meets a distinct *odour:* once inside, it is not so noticeable, but it is still there. Nearly all the buildings on the south side between Trinity Lane and St Bennet's Hill as far as opposite Godliman Street have vanished in the blitz, as well as those which faced them on the north side. Here the church of St Andrew-by-the-Wardrobe is again open, having been rebuilt in 1960, after being gutted in the great fires of 1940. The headquarters of the Salvation Army went up in flames during the early hours of the morning in the great raid on the City which occurred on 10 May 1941. Nothing was left of this building which employed several hundred workers except the bare façade, which was shortly afterwards taken down. A new International Headquarters building on the same site (which the 'Army' has occupied since 1881) was opened by Queen Elizabeth the Queen Mother on 13 November 1963. In 1965, the Salvation Army celebrated the centenary of its foundation by William Booth on 2 July 1865. Her Majesty the Queen visited the Royal Albert Hall during the Centenary Celebrations, and the Post Office issued an attractive set of colourful stamps to mark the occasion. Farther along on the same side of the street is the Auction Mart which has escaped destruction.

On the north side are also the Bible House of the British and Foreign Bible Society, the Heralds' College, and Faraday House, the Overseas Telephone Service of the G.P.O. The College of Heralds, which escaped destruction in the air raid of 10 May 1941, was originally the town house of the Earls of Derby and was remodelled in brick, probably by Sir Christopher Wren. Faraday House is nine storeys high, a height which would have shocked the City fathers of two generations ago. A large extension was completed in 1939 which covers the former site of the stores of Messrs Spiers & Pond the caterers. It also has a frontage to Godliman Street which has been considerably widened on the west side. On a part of this site in Godliman Street stands a gloomy-looking structure which resembles a prison or small fortress. This was specially built during the war to provide bombproof protection for the Communications Department. It is immensely strong and about thirty feet deep with walls of reinforced concrete. In Knightrider Street, to the north of Queen Victoria Street, stood until 1867 the Doctors Commons or College of Doctors of Law, which originally contained the Will Office. Here the doctors once lived together in the collegiate manner, and used to dine together every Court day. It was demolished to make room for Queen Victoria Street, which passes directly through the site of the quadrangular garden of the college. The dislodged Courts were eventually transferred to the new Law Courts in the Strand.

On the north side, close to Blackfriars Bridge, is *The Times* newspaper office, a much extended new building of seven storeys facing Queen Victoria Street that has replaced the former offices in Printing House Square, which lay further back. Several other old buildings and obscure little alleys have been removed, including a quaint little 'printer's pub' called 'The Lamb and Lark' and dated 1882. Printing House Square, however, is still the address where *The Times,* according to the imprint on the last page, is 'printed and published in the Parish of St Andrew-by-the-Wardrobe with St Ann Blackfriars in the City of London'. Almost opposite is Blackfriars Station, opened about 1891, once an important station and now a terminus for suburban trains of the Southern Region with a District Line underground station at a lower level. Deeply incised in the stone facings of the frontage is an alphabetical list of dozens of places to which one could travel from this former 'St Paul's Station' of the old London Chatham and Dover Railway; places such as Broadstairs, Berlin, Faversham, Frankfurt, Sheerness and St Petersburg, while warnings to 'check your tickets and change', in both English and French, are still to be seen at the booking office windows. Blackfriars gets its name from the monastery of the Dominicans or Black Friars, established by Hubert de Burgh, Earl of Kent, in 1221.

The first Blackfriars Bridge was erected between 1760 and 1769 and the foundation-stone like that of its successors was laid by the Lord Mayor of London on 31 October 1760. This bridge was opened on 19 November 1769. It was 995 feet long with a roadway 28 feet wide and footpaths each 7 feet wide. It was designed by Robert Mylne and erected at a cost of £153,000. The foundations having proved defective, it was pulled down in 1863.

The present Blackfriars Bridge was built at a cost of £350,000. The foundation-stone was laid by the Lord Mayor of London on 20 July 1865, and the opening ceremony was performed by Queen Victoria on 6 November 1869. Originally 80 feet broad, it was widened between 1907 and 1909 to 110 feet, in order to provide additional space for the London County Council tramways, which were then extended from South London across Blackfriars Bridge and along the

Victoria Embankment. Today it is probably the widest bridge crossing any river in Great Britain. Although it is generally assumed that the busiest traffic centre in the City is the Bank Intersection where seven busy roads meet and 40,000 vehicles pass every day, the simple four-road crossing at the north end of Blackfriars Bridge scores, somewhat surprisingly, with a daily total of 60,000. The new Underpass at Blackfriars, which was opened by the Minister of Transport on 26 July 1967, will ensure a smoother flow of traffic at this busy junction.

The construction of the first Blackfriars Bridge led to the formation of New Bridge Street, a broad thoroughfare leading from the Thames to Ludgate Circus. It occupies the site of a portion of the old Fleet ditch, which after the Great Fire of London was converted into the so-called Bridewell Dock, and extended from Fleet Street to the Thames. It was arched over in 1765 to make room for New Bridge Street. According to Knight's *London,* prior to 1756 the approaches to the Thames on both sides of the Fleet ditch were occupied by a body of miserable ruins at the back of Fleet Street on the one side and Ludgate on the other. Many of the narrow courts and alleys in this neighbourhood became the abodes of thieves and murderers, who upon occasion disposed of the bodies of their victims by dropping them into the Fleet ditch under cover of darkness.

Before the construction of the Victoria Embankment the northern approach to Blackfriars Bridge, which is now a wide sweep of open roadway, was through Chatham Place, so named after William Pitt, Earl of Chatham. This property was required by the Metropolitan Board of Works for the construction of Queen Victoria Street, and in November 1869 they purchased it from the Bridewell Hospital for £23,460.

When the first Blackfriars Bridge was built what is now Blackfriars Road went under the name of Albion Place and contained only a few buildings, so that the approach to the bridge from the Surrey side of the river was not a very costly undertaking. It was originally intended to name Blackfriars Bridge after William Pitt.

At the western corner of New Bridge Street and the Victoria Embankment is Unilever House, rebuilt in 1930-31, on the site of the former De Keyser's Royal Hotel which was opened on 5 September 1874 by Sir Polydore de Keyser, who came to London as a waiter from Belgium and became Lord Mayor of London. It was very popular with foreigners, and at one time every guest had to be introduced personally or by letter before he could secure accommodation. The hotel, containing four hundred rooms, was taken over during the first World War, in 1916, by the Royal Flying Corps, and was later acquired by Messrs Lever Brothers as their London offices. A peculiarity of Unilever House is the absence of any windows on the ground floor. Its architect was Mr J. Lomax Simpson.

Midway between the Victoria Embankment and Fleet Street, on the same side of the road, stood the Bridewell, originally a royal palace named after a well in the parish of St Bride's. It was at the Palace of Bridewell that Henry VIII, having met Anne Boleyn, began to have doubts about the legality of his marriage

68

with his deceased brother's widow, Katherine of Aragon. It was given by Edward VI as the first workhouse or house of correction for vagabonds and idlers, and was long regarded more as a hospital than a prison, and merely attracted more loafers to the capital. It was finally demolished in June 1863. A carved head of Edward VI is on the front of the present building, which is today used as offices.

On the opposite side of New Bridge Street stood Ludgate Hill Station, the former terminus of the London, Chatham and Dover Railway, opened on 1 June 1865. Having been found superfluous because of its proximity to Blackfriars and Holborn Viaduct Stations, it was finally closed to passenger traffic by the Southern Railway in 1929.

Ludgate Circus was formed between 1864 and 1875. When the railway bridge was constructed across Ludgate Hill the City Corporation purchased some ground belonging to the former London, Chatham and Dover Railway Company for the purpose of constructing a circus at this busy traffic centre. This enabled the Corporation to construct the eastern side of the circus at a cost of £5,000, and to add seventeen feet to the width of the roadway. The Metropolitan Board of Works agreed to contribute half of the money required for this improvement. Later an opportunity to form the north-west corner of the circus occurred when St Bride Street was constructed in 1868, and finally the work was completed in 1875 by the rebuilding and widening of the south-west corner of New Bridge Street and Fleet Street. Ludgate Circus will eventually be enlarged to facilitate the introduction of a roundabout traffic system, and this development may not now be long delayed. Anticipating that this improvement would involve the disappearance of the old King Lud tavern, a new King Lud has been established at the Seacoal Lane side of Hillgate House on Ludgate Hill; but as the Ludgate Circus development has not yet materialized, the old pub in the Circus has been smartly redecorated, so we now have the anomaly of two adjacent taverns with the same name.

Farringdon Street, leading north from Ludgate Circus, was the widest street in the City, and owed this distinction to the fact that it followed the line of the now invisible Fleet River, long since converted into a sewer. It was named after William Farringdon, a goldsmith and sheriff in 1281. On the west side until 1874 stood the Farringdon Market, built in 1829 at a cost of £80,000. It occupied one and a half acres of ground on a slope close to Stonecutter Street, and its situation was deemed most desirable from the standpoint of its drainage facilities, but it was otherwise quite inadequate for its requirements, and was removed to Smithfield in 1874. The Farringdon Market replaced the earlier Fleet Market, which stood on the adjacent site. With the exception of Gordon House, none of the buildings formerly lining the west side of Farringdon Street possessed any architectural merits. Farringdon Avenue has disappeared, for the original entrance opposite Turnagain Lane is completely obliterated by a new fifteen-storey building, erected on the Stonecutter Street-Farringdon Avenue site. This is the G.P.O. Telecommunications Centre, which has its own museum of exhibits which tell the story of telecommunications from 1837 — when telegraph first came into use — to the present day.

On the east side of Farringdon Street is the Congregational Memorial Hall, opened in 1874 to commemorate the bicentenary of the refusal of the Act of Uniformity. Some two thousand ministers were ejected from the Church in 1662. It has a frontage to Farringdon Street of eighty-four feet, and abuts upon the arches of the railway. Up to the plinth the front is faced with granite, and the remainder with limestone from the quarries of Devonshire. It stands on a part of the site of the old Fleet Prison, a four-storey building for debtors which occupied an extensive area. The principal building consisted of four storeys called galleries, nearly sixty yards in extent, in front of which was a large court for exercise. The railway now passes over a part of the site of the Fleet Prison.

The Fleet Prison was destroyed in the Great Fire on 4 September 1666, when the prisoners were temporarily removed to Caron House, South Lambeth. After 1641 the Fleet had become a prison for debtors only, and in 1780 it was again destroyed by fire during the Riots, when prisoners were liberated by the mob. It was rebuilt again immediately afterwards. In front of Farringdon Street was an arched opening commonly known as 'The Gate' from its crossed iron doors, above which was inscribed, 'Pray remember the poor prisoners having no allowance'. A small box was placed at the window-sill to receive the donations of sympathetic passers-by in the street, whilst the prisoners called out after them in a piteous tone. If a prisoner did not wish to go into the common-room with others, for which of course he paid nothing, he could be accommodated in the lowest story of the building upon payment of 1s. 3d., or upstairs in some better apartments for the same rent, but sharing them with a fellow prisoner. The fellow prisoner could be got rid of upon payment of 4s. 6d. per week or more, according to the fullness of the prison. In 1842 the Fleet Prison was abolished by Act of Parliament, and afterwards sold to the Corporation of London for £25,000. In March 1846 it was pulled down after an existence of nearly eight centuries. At a meeting of the Court of Common Council in 1854, it was proposed to construct a new street from the Old Bailey to Farringdon Street on the site of the late Fleet Prison, but this scheme failed to mature.

Seacoal Lane, on the same side of Farringdon Street, leading up to the Old Bailey, was so named from the fact that barges on the Fleet River at one time landed coal here. A noteworthy building on this side of the street is Fleetway House, the new headquarters of the Amalgamated Press Limited, erected in 1925. Next but one to Fleetway House is an eight-storey building for Fleetway Publications Ltd, erected by the Amalgamated Press and opened by their Chairman the Hon. Michael Berry in 1958. The ground presumably belongs to the Armourers and Brasiers Company, for the building bears their coat of arms with two mottoes, 'Make all sure' and 'We are one'.

Returning to Ludgate Circus, we see crossing Ludgate Hill an unsightly railway bridge. In May 1863 a petition against this disfigurement of Ludgate Hill, bearing more than a thousand signatures, was presented to the City Corporation.

The great difficulty encountered by any alternative plan to obviate the necessity of constructing this railway bridge across Ludgate Hill, was the short distance from the bank of the Thames to the junction with the Metropolitan Railway at Farringdon Street. This would have necessitated a very steep gradient, and in order to carry the line under Ludgate Hill it would have had to make a slight detour to reduce the ascent. Moreover, the cost would have been prohibitive, and the scheme would have involved the destruction of the Apothecaries' Hall and *The Times* Printing Office, as well as threatening the foundations of St Martin's Church in Ludgate Hill, and the Central Criminal Court in Old Bailey. Much disappointment has been expressed by the Press and the general public that the removal of the railway bridge which spans Ludgate Hill has not been included in the plans for the rebuilding of the City. But the same objection which was raised in 1863 against any alternative scheme still holds at the present day because of the prohibitive cost.

Just above Old Bailey is the site of the ancient gate of the City known as Lud Gate, which was demolished in 1760. A century ago Ludgate Hill was only forty-seven feet wide, whereas it is now sixty feet. It then went under the two names of Ludgate Street from St Paul's Churchyard as far as St Martin's Church, and Ludgate Hill from thence to New Bridge Street, but the name of Ludgate Street was altered to Ludgate Hill by the Metropolitan Board of Works in 1865.

The widening of Ludgate Hill was a long and tedious affair, and from start to finish covered twenty-nine years. During the years 1863 to 1891, the rateable value of property in Ludgate Hill more than doubled, and this great delay resulted in new interests being created, thus producing additional claims for compensation. The tenants who were called upon to vacate certain premises for the widening of Ludgate Hill and received handsome compensation, had secured other premises on the south side of the street, which ought previously to have been acquired by the City Corporation for this improvement, and thus obtained further compensation. But to-day it is no longer so easy to make money out of the City Corporation and the Greater London Council by that method, for notices are now served upon the occupiers securing such premises intended for demolition, barring any further claims.

Thus the width of Ludgate Hill was increased from forty-seven feet to sixty feet by setting back the entire building line, and before the blitz in 1940 the south side was lined with a handsome range of buildings extending from St Paul's Churchyard to New Bridge Street. Just beyond the railway bridge on this side of Ludgate Hill stood the famous linoleum establishment of Messrs Treloar & Sons, and immediately opposite La Belle Sauvage Yard, a cul-de-sac in which was located the well-known publishing house of Messrs Cassell & Company Limited. From time immemorial La Belle Sauvage had been a famous hostelry, having been very popular in the old coaching days. As recently as 1851 it was taken over by a new proprietor, who renamed it the International Hotel and remodelled it to meet the demand for improved hotel accommodation at the time of the Great Exhibition in Hyde Park. It was pulled down in 1873, when the inn yard was rebuilt and very much altered. Originally it consisted of two yards, the inn occupying the inner one, and the outer court leading through an archway into Ludgate Hill. The western section of Ludgate Hill from Old Bailey and Ludgate Court to Ludgate Circus was completely destroyed in the air raids of 1940 and all the buildings on both sides of the road were completely destroyed. So also were La Belle Sauvage Yard and the linoleum establishment of Messrs Treloar & Sons with shops on both sides of the road.

Higher up beyond Old Bailey, on the same side of the street, is the church of St Martin's, Ludgate, with a tall spire constructed by Sir Christopher Wren in 1684, which many people consider out of place there, since it obstructs the view of St Paul's from Ludgate Circus. Others think that it harmonizes admirably with the view of the cathedral, and by contrast adds to the majesty of the dome, which was evidently Sir Christopher Wren's intention. Today, the suggestion that the graceful spire of St Martin, Ludgate *obstructs* the view of St Paul's Cathedral is particularly droll now that the offending Juxon House has been completed. From Stationers' Hall Court up to the west corner Ave Maria Lane is Colonial Mutual House, a 7-storey building opened in 1962. When it was projected there were various rigid restrictions as to height, direction etc. imposed to prevent any diminution of the Cathedral vista. To this end, one may notice that while, from Stationers' Hall Court Colonial Mutual House continues the line of the adjoining buildings in Ludgate Hill, as it continues up the hill the front *curves away* to widen the view in a most praiseworthy manner. But despite this excellent example, in March 1964, there were murmurs and mutterings among the citizens when they saw steel girders rising on the opposite corner of Ave Maria Lane for a building that would clearly project some twenty feet or more beyond the unimpeachable corner of Colonial Mutual House. There were numerous complaints in the papers and protest meetings in front of St Paul's. But the 8-storey Juxon House, 90 feet high, is there. As if in mitigation of the offence, it was announced that there would be Viewing Galleries available to allow members of the public to enjoy the City scenery. Though Juxon House appeared to be still unoccupied, the promised galleries were opened in May 1968 — one on the first floor and another on the seventh. As the Ludgate Hill of the future is intended to be a purely 'processional' route, it would seem that the first floor was chosen with the Lord Mayor's Show and State Visits in mind (the public might peep between the television cameras). The panorama from the seventh floor, however, is rather disappointing, as it is not high enough. Now that the City has so many tower blocks ranging from fifteen to thirty floors in height, a modest seventh floor is too near the ground. In Old Bailey is the Central Criminal Court, built 1900-7 and now being extended. Designed by Mr E. W. Mountford at a cost of £250,000, it is crowned by a copper dome 195 feet high, as pleasing to the eye, on a smaller scale, as that of St Paul's Cathedral. This building was also badly damaged in the air raids of 1940 and a part of its façade in Newgate Street was destroyed. Old Newgate Prison, immortalized by Dick Turpin, Jack Sheppard, Claude Duval, and others famous in the annals of crime, was rebuilt in 1770-83 by George Dance, son of the architect of the Mansion House. It consisted of a rustic wall broken at intervals by grated windows and recesses partly filled with statues. The centre formed the house of the keeper. The first execution took place here, after the last one had occurred at Tyburn, on 7 November 1783, but after 1868, when public executions were abolished, they took place inside the walls of the prison, and were announced to the outside world by a black flag. After 1882 Newgate ceased to be used as a prison. The last man to be hanged in front of Newgate was Michael Barrett, the Fenian, on 26 May 1868.

On the occasion of a public execution crowds would flock to Newgate in the early hours of the morning to see the stage erected on which a real living actor was about to die. The neighbouring coffee-shops and gin-palaces were thrown open to those who desired to witness this horrible exhibition away from the crowds below, and people would then rush in and bargain for seats. Upon these occasions, one overheard cheery cries of 'Excellent situation, comfortable room, splendid view', as each rival establishment recommended its windows or the airy galleries on its roof. All night long the workmen would be engaged in erecting the gloomy scaffold, and the sounds of their hammers and saws would be drowned in the loud cheers and coarse jests uttered and responded to by a brutal mob. Temporary stands were also erected to accommodate the sightseers, and these structures were sometimes of such a temporary character that there were more deaths among the spectators than upon the scaffold. On 27 February 1807, thirty persons were crushed to death in the crowd which collected to witness the execution of Holloway and Haggerty at Newgate.

Returning to Ludgate Hill, Stationers' Hall Court, of course, leads to the hall of the Stationers' Company, at the back of which is the courtyard with a magnificent plane tree; then off Ave Maria Lane is Amen Corner, the approach to the charming Amen Court whose Wren houses, which still desplay link extinguishers, provide a secluded retreat for some of the Canons of the cathedral. The garden boundary on the west side is a considerable length of the City Wall, though its authenticity is doubted by some authorities.

Ave Maria Lane then becomes Warwick Lane, the east side being entirely new buildings – part of the Paternoster Development; the west side has its share of modernity, and the sole survivors of pre-war architecture are the red-brick Amen Court of 1880 and the hall of the Cutlers' Company, with its frieze of figures engaged in the various processes of the cutlers' craft.

In connection with the Warwick Lane development which will make an extension of the Central Criminal Court to provide twelve additional courts, little Warwick Square on the west side of the lane, has been bulldozed out of existence. There have been compensations, however; remembering that the Oxford University Press used to cherish a small fragment of the Roman Wall in the basement of their Warwick Square premises, it is some consolation, perhaps, to learn that the recent excavations uncovered a considerable length – about 130 feet – of the wall, part of which, it is hoped, may be preserved.

Other interesting discoveries included a massive outer wall of Newgate Prison and some evidence of a 15th century building which was possibly the inn or mansion of the Earls of Warwick. Augustus J. C. Hare in his *Walks in London* (1878) illustrates a curious relief in stone commemorating the 'King-maker'; bearing the date 1668, it depicted an armed knight with sword and shield and (in 1878) was 'on the wall of the last house (left) where Warwick Lane enters Newgate Street'—which would probably be on the site of the Warwick mansion.

North of St Paul's Cathedral, the triangular area bounded by Newgate Street, Warwick Lane and St Paul's Churchyard is the subject of what is known as the Paternoster Development, and is now approaching completion. The whole area is raised on a 'podium'—the modern device to provide space for a car park underneath, which in this case accommodates about 400 cars—and the podium is approached by various groups of steps from 10 to 24 in number, and two gentle slopes. The Panyer Alley end is a shopping 'precinct' called Cathedral Place, with provision for some 25-30 shops and two new taverns, 'The Sir Christopher Wren' and 'The Master Gunner'. The Warwick Lane side retains the name of Paternoster Square which formerly stood on that site. Distributed over the whole area are new office blocks, variously named Grindal, Walden, Courtenay, Laud and Sudbury House—the latter with an 18-storey tower.

Between these and St Paul's Churchyard, the base of the triangle, is the new Paternoster Row, truncated, though widened. It is now a cul-de-sac terminating at the Paternoster Car Parks, which are approached from Warwick Lane. Among all this towering grey concrete Sir Christopher Wren's redbrick Chapter House of 1714 survives in dignified insignificance.

Panyer Alley, nentioned above, was in the Middle Ages London's bread market, and on the wall of a house in the alley was a stone with a relief of a boy seated on a panyer, or bread basket, inscribed:

> 'When ye have sought the City round
> Yet still this is the highest ground
>   August the 27 1688.'

During several rebuildings over the years the Panyer Boy was taken down and replaced again, and throughout the Second World War was in the safe custody of the Vintners Company. He has now been set up again by the Panyer Steps near St Paul's Underground Station.

Before the raids of 1940, St Paul's Churchyard, east of the Chapter House, included a number of shops, of which Nicholson's the drapers was for many years a welcome oasis for the increasing feminine population in the man-made City desert. All these buildings have been demolished and made way for new ones, among which the replacement of shops has not been overlooked.

St Paul's Cathedral, the old metropolitan church, was destroyed in the Great Fire of 1666, after which the ground on which it stood began to be cleared for a new foundation on 1 May 1674. The first stone of the new cathedral was laid on 21 June 1675, and divine service was performed for the first time on

2 December 1697. But the last stone was not laid until 1710, thirty-five years after the first. The new cathedral, which cost £750,000, was paid for by a tax on every sea-borne chaldron of coal. It has been the scene of numerous thanksgiving services, notably that for the recovery of King Edward VII, when Prince of Wales, from a serious illness in 1872, and from another in October 1902, which delayed his coronation. A similar thanksgiving service took place in July 1929 for the recovery of King George V after his long and severe illness in 1928-29. Memorable among more recent events was the funeral service of the late Sir Winston Churchill on Saturday, 30 January 1965.

In 1925 the foundations of St Paul's Cathedral were discovered to be in danger, and the pillars supporting the dome instead of being built of solid stone were found to have been originally filled with rubble, thus producing further risk of instability. Thereupon public subscriptions were invited in order to provide funds for their restoration. Something like £200,000 was subscribed, and the work put in hand immediately. The eastern portion of the cathedral was partitioned off and closed to the general public to enable the work of restoration to proceed without interruption. The columns supporting the building have been strengthened by the process of pumping liquid cement into them to mix with and solidify the existing loose rubble. The work was completed by 1930, and the opening ceremony was performed by King George V and Queen Mary on 25 June 1930. When on 29 December 1940 a determined effort was made by German planes to fire the City of London by dropping showers of incendiary bombs, St Paul's Cathedral, though at one time ringed with fires, escaped destruction. Two days after the raid it was disclosed that the continuation of the attack with high-explosive bombs was checked only by the sudden development of bad weather over Northern France. Otherwise the damage might have been much heavier than it actually was and St Paul's Cathedral might indeed have been completely destroyed.

In August 1873 the City Corporation, desiring to widen St Paul's Churchyard, agreed to pay the Dean and Chapter of St Paul's Cathedral £20,000 for a portion of the land on the south side in order to remove the railings farther back and to widen the roadway. This improvement was then carried out and the roadway widened to nearly fifty feet. On the south side of the Cathedral eight feet of additional space were thus secured for the traffic. These alterations were completed in January 1874, and the old iron railings, which had originally cost £11,200, were sold by auction for no more than £349.

In October 1878 a new peal of twelve bells was presented to St Paul's Cathedral by the City Corporation, the leading City Companies, and Lady Burdett-Coutts, at a cost of £2,500. The new bells were hung in the upper story of the north-west tower. Another new bell, known as Great Paul, weighing seventeen tons, was placed in the south-west tower in 1882. In front of the Cathedral facing Ludgate Hill is a statue of Queen Anne.

St Paul's School, removed to Hammersmith Road in 1884, occupied the east side of St Paul's Churchyard. Founded in 1509 by Dr John Colet, Dean of

St Paul's, it was rebuilt in 1822 and considerably enlarged. It was a very handsome building fronted with stone, and consisted of a centre and wings ornamented with a Corinthian colonnade from the designs of Mr C. Smith. The south side of St Paul's Churchyard is fronted by a range of late nineteenth century buildings, occupied mainly by large wholesale drapery establishments, but some of the older warehouses have been destroyed. At the north corner of Watling Street and Old Change stood the church of St Augustine, built by Sir Christopher Wren in 1682. This also has been destroyed except the tower which still survives and, equipped with an elegant new spire of glass fibre, has been incorporated in the new Cathedral Choir School, replacing the old building in Carter Lane. The latest plans of the City Corporation for the rebuilding of the blitzed areas of the City of London include the widening and re-siting of Cannon Street, removing the road on the east side of St Paul's Churchyard so as to create a permanent open space to the east and south-east of the Cathedral. This will include an open space between Watling Street and Cannon Street and will extend from St Paul's to Friday Street. The area to which the plans of the City Corporation refer covers just over eight acres and is bounded by Cheapside on the north, Cannon Street on the south, Bread Street on the east, and St Paul's Churchyard on the west. It has also been proposed to construct a precinct or enclosed garden round St Paul's Cathedral and to close the eastern section of Ludgate Hill. Under that scheme the main-road traffic would be diverted on the south side into a greatly-widened Carter Lane opening into St Paul's Churchyard. The ultimate plan for the St Paul's Churchyard area is still far from settled. The principal building is the Bank of England extension which lies between Cheapside on the north and Watling Street on the south, bounded on the east by Bread Street and the west by an attractive curve called 'New Change'. South of the Bank building, between Watling Street and Cannon Street are the new yellow brick Wiggins Teape offices, 'Gateway House'. A most interesting feature of these two buildings is that they bestride Friday Street and though a right of way (for foot passengers only) has been preserved through both buildings, all that is left of old Friday Street is some eighty yards south of Cannon Street.

West of Gateway House, between New Change and the remains of Old Change, a public garden has been made and is well patronized by the lunch-time population of the district. On the low wall at the west end of the garden is an inscription, 'Old Change – a city street dating from 1293'.

Directing our steps along Cannon Street, we now propose to furnish our readers with a brief description of this important main City thoroughfare. While the original Cannon Street is one of the oldest streets in London, it came no further west than Walbrook. The extension to St Paul's Churchyard was not opened until 1854 and for several years was known as Cannon Street *West*. So, before that date, if you wanted to go from St Paul's to London Bridge, you either had to go round by Cheapside or through the very narrow Watling Street and its continuation Budge Row, leading into what was then only a short and narrow edition of Cannon Street, extending from Budge Row to King William Street.

It is interesting to learn from past records that the construction of Cannon Street was vigorously opposed by City men, who contended that it would fail to provide any adequate relief to the great congestion of traffic prevailing even in those days. The original Cannon Street was once named Candlewick Street from the candle-makers who lived here in olden times, and made candles for the Catholic Church.

Between King William Street and the point where Budge Row joined old Cannon Street, the alterations required to form the new thoroughfare were confined to the widening of Cannon Street itself by pulling down the houses on the southern side and rebuilding them on a greatly improved scale as regards their size and accommodation. This end of Cannon Street, being straight, now presents a very creditable appearance when compared to the standard of the fifties of the last century, with sufficient variety to avoid any appearance of monotony. But between 1930 and 1940 most of the former buildings which lined the south side of this section of Cannon Street were pulled down and replaced by modern blocks of offices. Thus between the last building on this side is Candlewick Houses a nine-storeyed block of shops and offices erected about 1931. On the two corner, of Laurence Pountney Hill are Provincial House and Eagle House, new blocks of shops and offices of uniform design and elevation, erected between 1935 and 1937. On the north side of Cannon Street near St Swithin's Lane is a tall building of nine storeys called Granite House which was erected in 1936. Farther west on the corner of Queen Street is a handsome building erected by the London Chamber of Commerce which was formally opened by the late Duke of Kent in 1935.

But new Cannon Street, strictly speaking, only begins westward from Budge Row, and here a start was made by the City Corporation on 25 October 1848 by the demolition of the houses on the south side next to Dowgate Hill and Walbrook. In February 1849 workmen commenced pulling down the buildings standing between Budge Row and the churchyard of St John-the-Baptist upon Walbrook, and in May 1849 the immense mass of houses bounded by Cloak Lane, Little St Thomas the Apostle, and Queen Street was removed, as well as another large cluster between Dowgate Hill and Watling Street. The old burial-ground of St John the Baptist was covered for the time being with the vast piles of rubbish, but was afterwards used to form a portion of the new street. Very little information concerning the church of St John the Baptist is available in any histories of London, and it would appear to have been a church of minor importance. There was another bite at the churchyard in 1884 when the District Railway was extended, and in the fragment that survives in Cloak Lane a stone memorial about 12 feet high tells us that the human remains displaced by the District Railway were 'carefully collected and re-interred in a vault below this monument.' The trains and platforms can be seen through the railings at the east side of the ground. Three gravestones still remain, and on the wall is an inscription of 1671 recording the destruction of the church in the Great Fire, and two plates marking the boundaries of Walbrook and Cordwainer Wards.

So St John the Baptist-upon-Walbrook is not completely forgotten.

Masses of buildings formerly occupied the space between Budge Row and St Paul's Churchyard, and here lanes and narrow streets crossed each other in every direction. The clearance of this crowded area was at that time regarded as one the greatest metropolitan improvements since the Great Fire of London. The new warehouses erected on the south side of the new Cannon Street appeared as stately to that generation of Londoners as any which have been erected in the City in our own time, and moreover they formed a good foreground to the vista of St Paul's Cathedral from this spot.

Between Queen Street and St Paul's Churchyard the most western section of Cannon Street was carved out of the former Basing Lane, so that the north side consisted mainly of old buildings, some of which were still standing until 1940 when they were destroyed in the blitz. The new buildings which replace them have been set back so that this section of Cannon Street is much wider than formerly.

In April 1852 the workmen employed upon the construction of the new Cannon Street discovered a Roman tessellated pavement a short distance east of Basing Lane at a depth of nearly thirteen feet below the surface. Here they also found piles which supported the walls of Roman masonry in the black soil, which were interspersed with horns, bones, teeth, and tusks of boars, oxen, goats, and other animals, as well as fragments of tiles, urns, and pottery of various descriptions. Cannon Street West was formally opened at one o'clock on 22 May 1854 by the Chairman, Mr J. T. Hall, and various other members of the Improvements Committee of the City Corporation. The cost of the new street from St Paul's Cathedral to London Bridge was £800,000, and by 1856 the long line of wholesale warehouses extending from St Paul's Cathedral all along the south side as far as King William Street had been erected.

One of these great blocks situated between Old Change and Distaff Lane was originally occupied by the large German firm of Berens, Blumenberg & Company, dealers in foreign fancy goods of all kinds who came to England shortly after the conclusion of the Napoleonic Wars. Such buildings at that period were an entirely new feature of the metropolis, and formed a most welcome contrast to the dingy, dark and illventilated tenements which had done duty as warehouses down to that time. They introduced a new architectural splendour into the vicinity of St Paul's Cathedral more worthy of that masterpiece of Sir Christopher Wren than their shabby predecessors. This block, however, has now been replaced by 'Old Change House', a six-storey (with two basements) building for Messrs Spillers Ltd.

A widening of Cannon Street between Queen Victoria Street and St Paul's Churchyard will afford a great relief to the very tiresome congestion of traffic caused by slow-moving vehicles. All the buildings which lined both sides of Cannon Street from the Mansion House Station to St Paul's Churchyard were destroyed except the Fire Brigade Station and Albert Buildings on the opposite corner. The latter is a gem of Victorian office architecture, with heavily ornamented windows that seem determined to keep out the daylight; viewed with the modern Temple Court and Bucklersbury House in the background, the contract is complete. Of the buildings which stood on the north side of the street, only one, namely the Cordwainers' Hall, had any claim to distinction, It was a handsome hall with a stone façade which had been rebuilt in 1910. It was destroyed by fire-bombs on the night of 20 December 1940. Between Distaff Lane – which has reappeared after being lost in the blitz – and Friday Street, on the south side of Cannon Street is Bracken House. This is an attractive – and 'reactionary' – new building for *The Financial Times,* finished in red and pink brick and stone. The architect was Sir Albert Richardson, Past President of the Royal Academy. Bracken House, opened at Easter 1959, consists of two seven-storey office blocks housing *The Financial Times,* with the printing works of The St Clements Press between them.

A special feature of the exterior is the Astronomical Clock, by Thwaites and Reed of Clerkenwell. It has three concentric dials which revolve at different speeds round a central point, the 'sunburst'. This clock shows the time, date, month, phase of the moon and the signs of the Zodiac. In fact, it appears to be a smaller version of the Great Clock at Hampton Court, made for King Henry VIII in 1540. On the reverse side is a conventional clock face, visible in the entrance hall of the building.

Referring to the modern trend in office building Sir Albert Richardson said: 'All that glass and concrete will be out of date in a hundred years. Bracken House will mellow in three or four years and will last three or four hundred. London is kind to brick. Modern buildings don't mellow; they get dirty'. Considerable new building is taking place in this blitzed area which extended from Queen Victoria Street across Cannon Street as far as Cheapside. Standing alone amongst the ruins were the tower and walls of the church of St Nicholas Cole Abbey in Distaff Lane. It was destroyed in the Great Fire of 1666 and was the first church to be rebuilt after the fire. It is now rebuilt for the second time. From this point can be seen the eight-pinnacled tower of St Mary Somerset in Upper Thames Street. The church was demolished in 1871, but the tower was allowed to remain.

In Dowgate Hill, at the side of Cannon Street Station, are three Company Halls – the Skinners (at No. 8½), Dyers, and Tallow Chandlers, while round the corner in College Street is the Innholders' Hall.

Upper Thames Street, which runs along the riverside parallel to Cannon Street from London Bridge to Blackfriars, has no glamour, but is full of interest. It was once said that in few streets of London have more Roman remains been found than in Thames Street; but that was some years before the bombing of the Second World War revealed – or at least facilitated the discovery of – other antiquities.

From King William Street, the first section of Upper Thames Street is not improved by the sight of two derelict and extremely untidy little churchyards. The first is that of All Hallows the Less; the City Corporation plaque recording the destruction of the church in the Great Fire is itself in two pieces – a result of the blitz. Next door, below the wall of Cannon Street Station, the churchyard of All Hallows the Great is entered by six little steps and a pair of iron gates; only one tombstone remains. This church, of 14th century origin, was rebuilt by Wren, but demolished in 1893 or 1894, according to which of two adjacent inscriptions is preferred. A belfry tower still stands in All Hallows Lane. From Suffolk Lane as far as Queen Street Place, a considerable widening has been made with a pleasant open space on the north side having seats that are much appreciated, for this is a terminal point for several bus routes. At the foot of College Hill is the church of St Michael Paternoster Royal, where the children's hero of legend and pantomime, Dick Whittington, is buried. Though now closed, memory seems to recall that this church has been open since the war, and among items of interest seen there was a glass case containing the mummified body of a cat! Restoration work on St Michael's is now proceeding.

Queen Street Place is the approach to Southwark Bridge, which was rebuilt, and opened by King George V, in 1921. The original Southwark Bridge, designed by Sir John Rennie, was erected by a public company at a cost of £800,000 and opened in 1819. In 1866 it was purchased by the City Corporation for £219,000, but had been made free of tolls in 1864. This bridge was of cast-iron and first known as 'The Iron Bridge' — by which name it is mentioned in Dickens's *Little Dorrit*.

West of Southwark Bridge is the Vintners' Hall, with bronze and brass gates decorated with swans; a reference to the privilege (which they share with the Dyers' Company) of owning a number of the swans that grace the waters of the Thames. The remainder of these handsome birds are the property of the Queen. On a side wall in Vintners' Place is perched a little Charity School boy, in Coade stone, dated 1840 and recalling an early school in the Vintry Ward.

Opposite the Vintners' Hall is St James, Garlickhithe, a church that was badly damaged but has been beatifully restored. A well-known curiosity in the vestry cupboard is the corpse of a man in a singular state of preservation. Parish boundary and property marks displaying the cockle-shell associated with St James may be seen on several buildings in the neighbourhood.

Wharves, overhead cranes and warehouses — some of them quite aromatic — are the principal features of Upper Thomas Street, but next along the riverside is Queenhithe Dock, one of the two popular harbours of the medieval Port of London; the dues from ships unloading there were said to be the Queen of England's 'pin-money'. In the old churchyard of St Michael, Queenhithe, on Huggin Hill is a mulberry tree which still produces an abundance of fruit in the season.

Passing Coffee House Alley, Stew Lane and High Timber Street, which are a few of the colourful names to be seen along here, one comes to the handsome eight-pinnacled tower of St Mary Somerset which stands at the foot of Lambeth Hill; the church was demolished in 1871, but the tower was suffered to remain. It was between Lambeth Hill and Huggin Hill that excavations in August, 1964 disclosed the remains of a large structure that was almost certainly a Roman public bath-house. A hypocaust system was identified, and broken blue tiles and pottery were found. About the same time, a mechanical digger, employed by contractors working on the site, struck a 112 lb. post-Roman unexploded phosphorus bomb.

Bennet's Hill winds round the red-brick church of St Benet, Paul's Wharf now known as the Welsh Church. Being near the College of Arms, several heralds or other officers of the College are buried here, including one Somerset Herald 'who died in the dreadful calamity which happened at the Theatre in the Haymarket on 3rd February, 1794, when twenty persons lost their lives and a great number were dreadfully bruised owing to a great crowd pressing to see His Majesty'.

Castle Baynard Wharf, the centre of the paper-making trade, recalls the occasion when the Duke of Buckingham offered the crown to the usurping Richard, Duke of Gloucester at the grim Baynard's Castle, which guarded the western approach to the City. Then to Puddle Dock and the Mermaid Theatre, opened in 1959. At this point, the new underpass, coming under Blackfriars Bridge from the Victoria Embankment, joins Upper Thames Street, which has here been dealt with rather more fully than its appearance would seem to merit because the proposed widening of the street to enable traffic to by-pass the centre of the City may effect a considerable change in its character.

It is now necessary to resume our consideration of Cannon Street and the station, which extends from Dowgate Hill nearly to Bush Lane. Opened by the old South Eastern Railway in 1866, it covers an area of over 152,000 square feet and is 855 feet long from the northern end of the railway bridge to the public highway, with a width of 187 feet inside the walls at platform level. The engineers were John Hawkshaw and J. W. Barry, and the famous arched roof, before the war, contained two acres of glass.

The post-war reconstruction of Cannon Street Station, at a cost of £$1\frac{1}{4}$ million, was part of the Modernization Plan for British Railways, and enables this important City terminus to deal with an increased number of longer trains and relieve the congestion that occurred on the North Kent suburban lines during rush hours. The most intricate stage of the work involved the under-pinning of the main building known as Southern House (originally designed and built as an hotel by E. M. Barry) to provide a modern Ticket Hall and Concourse area on the ground floor. Today, Cannon Street is almost entirely monopolized by the electrified suburban services, some 417 trains per day conveying 68,000 passengers, the majority of whom travel during the rush hour periods.

Opposite Cannon Street Station was St Swithin's Church, rebuilt by Sir Christopher Wren, which contained in its south front the celebrated London Stone which was placed there in 1798. Its origin is unknown but it is popularly supposed to have been a Roman milliarium. It is known to have been referred to as the London Stone as long ago as the time of the Saxon King Ethelstane. The church was badly damaged by bombs in the war and has now been demolished. The London Stone was removed to the Guildhall Museum at the Royal

Exchange and has now been replaced in the new office building for the Bank of China, which has been erected on the site. The present stone shows signs of having been shaped but bears no inscription or other means of identification — it is presumably only part of the original stone which John Stow, the Elizabethan topographer (in his *Survay of London,* 1598) describes as standing on the other side of the road 'near unto the channel... fixed in the ground very deep, fastened with bars of iron and otherwise so strongly set that if carts do run against it through negligence the wheels be broken and the stone itself unshaken'.

The little graveyard of St Seithun London Stone, with one tombstone remaining, is a public garden, entered from Oxford Court. The Hall of the Salters' Company — their fifth — next to the church, was completely destroyed and will be rebuilt on a site between Fore Street and London Wall in the new Barbican area.

New Court in St Swithin's Lane, the dignified headquarters of Rothschilds, the merchant bankers, although it escaped war damage, was demolished in 1962 and a modern building of six floors and two basements erected in its place. In the entrance hall is an impressive Brussels tapestry of Moses striking the rock, and in addition to busts of Nathan and Lionel Rothschild, there is a large canvas of the Rothschild family. A continuation of our walk through St Swithin's Lane will bring us back to our starting-point at the Mansion House.

Fifth Walk

Cheapside and its Tributaries, Guildhall, St Martin's-le-Grand, Newgate Street, Holborn Viaduct, Holborn, Chancery Lane, Temple Bar and Fleet Street

The Poultry, which is the eastern extension of Cheapside between the Mansion House and Bucklersbury, still bears the name of the commodity once displayed there for sale, and the same thing applies to Milk Street, Ironmonger Lane, Wood Street, Honey Lane, and Bread Street, all of them leading out of Cheapside. Bread Street was the birthplace of Milton in 1608. Cheapside, which was once an open market from end to end, derives its name from the Anglo-Saxon word 'ceapian', to sell or bargain.

Old Jewry, leading into Gresham Street, and dividing Cheapside from the Poultry, was so named from the Jews who once dwelt there and who were first brought from Rouen by William the Conqueror to live there. On the left-hand side are the headquarters of the City Police. We might also add that various attempts made during the last century to absorb that body into the Metropolitan Police proved unsuccessful, and that they continue to enjoy the undisturbed privilege of selecting their own 'thief takers'.

A century ago Cheapside had become one of the finest shopping streets in London, and one writer, describing it in 1851, says that although far inferior to many which had lately been built in the West End, it must strike a stranger with amazement. He further adds that half a dozen houses produced yearly double the income of numbers of foreign nobles, and that many an old lady and gentleman had retired to the quiet suburbs on the rents derived from a single house standing in this costly thoroughfare, for most of which two or three hundred pounds a year rent was paid. When these figures are compared with those obtaining at the present day in Cheapside they can hardly fail to cause mirth.

On the north side of Cheapside a new nine-storey block of offices with shops below extends from Old Jewry to Ironmonger Lane. Embodied in this is the new Mercers' Hall and Chapel, replacing the building that was destroyed in the air raids of 1940. The pre-war building was built in 1884 to replace an earlier Hall, the facade of which was preserved and removed to the town hall of Swanage, Dorsetshire, in 1882. At the east corner of King Street, leading to the Guildhall, is the building of the Atlas Assurance Company, a handsome edifice in the Italian style erected in 1835 from designs by Thomas Hopper.

The Guildhall, second only to the Tower in historical interest amongst City buildings, was begun about 1411, and was partly destroyed in the Great Fire of London. The Library was founded in 1423, and is maintained by the City Corporation as a free library. The walls of the Guildhall were restored in 1909, but its handsome roof, dating from 1865, was destroyed in the blitz of 1940. The original oak roof was entirely destroyed in the Great Fire of 1666 and the main front much damaged. The existing front was erected by Mr George Dance in 1789. Repairs to bomb damage recently completed include a new roof.

For more than 150 years it had been a reproach to the City that its fine hall had remained disfigured by its ugly flat roof, and its removal had long been urged by the Court of Common Council as an offence to architectural taste. In 1864 it was decided to erect a new roof of open oak with a tapering metal spire in the centre, and this work was carried out by the Committee of the Corporation with Mr Kelday as its Chairman. The architect was Mr Horace Jones, and the cost of the work was £20,000. The first stone was laid with some ceremony on 22 June 1864, when the members of the Improvements Committee, including four of the Aldermen, assembled on the roof. The hall was sufficiently completed to be used for the Lord Mayor's banquet on 9 November 1865. The present Guildhall Library and Museum were completed in November 1872, and opened free to the public in March 1873, at a cost of £50,000, in addition to £40,000 for the site. The Museum, originally in the crypt of the Guildhall, was for many years accommodated in the Royal Exchange, but in April 1968 the collection was moved to 55 Basinghall Street, a new building upon a podium at the south side of London Wall. While this is but an interim arrangement pending the completion of the Museum of London premises in the Barbican, the large area of window space in their new home allows the exhibits to be displayed and seen to better advantage than ever before.

The church of St Lawrence Jewry, on the west corner of the Guildhall Yard, was rebuilt by Sir Christopher Wren in 1671, after the Great Fire, at a cost of £10,000; this also suffered severely in the fire-raid of 29 December 1940, but is now rebuilt and re-dedicated. Here the Lord Mayor and members of the Corporation attend service on Michaelmas Day before electing a new Lord Mayor. In April 1853 burials were ordered in Council to be discontinued in this churchyard, the primary motive for the reform having been the fears of the Aldermen for the health of this district. On the east side of Old Jewry now stands a fine building erected in 1932 for the Commonwealth Bank of Australia. It is adorned by a row of stone columns extending from the third to the fifth storey. Fredericks Place, a quiet little cul-de-sac off the west side has several well-kept 18th century houses, and on the wall of No. 4a are boundary marks of the Cheap and Coleman Street wards, and the perishes of St Martin Pomary and St Olave Jewry — the tower of the latter still stands in Ironmonger Lane.

King Street has been largely rebuilt of late years, and contains some fine office buildings, and the same thing must be said of Queen Street directly opposite where the 1955 Bank of London and South America is faced by the later Aldermary House, of which Queen Elizabeth the Queen Mother laid the foundation stone in May, 1961. Cheapside has changed a great deal in recent years. and very little now remains of those which lined this street even fifty years ago. Dingy-looking, brown-brick houses have been replaced by tall and handsome new buildings, which give Cheapside the appearance of a new street.

Close to Bow Church stood until 1929 the premises of Sir John Bennett & Son, with its famous clock, long ago exiled to the U.S.A., which used to attract crowds to watch the hours being struck by the picturesque figures. On this and the adjoining site new buildings have been erected. Something like one-half of the buildings in Cheapside vanished in the blitz, notably those on the south side as well as in Bread Street and Friday Street. On the north side some of those opposite Bow Church shared the same fate. Farther west a handsome block of offices which stood between Gutter Lane and Foster Lane was destroyed by fire-bombs on 29 December 1940 when the water supply in the City failed and the fires spread. At the back of it stood the Saddlers' Hall, of which nothing was left but the broken marble pillars of its entrance at No. 141 Cheapside. A new building, 'Cheapside House' has been erected on this site and the new Saddlers Hall has been set back a little, with its principal entrance in Gutter Lane' instead of Cheapside as formerly. On the Gutter Lane front is the motto of the Saddlers, 'Hold fast, sit sure'. Further down this lane is a new building appropriately named 'Abacus House', for it is occupied by Chartered Accountants.

Bow Church or, properly speaking, the church of St-Mary-le-Bow, rebuilt by Sir Christopher Wren after the Great Fire, is greatly admired because of its tall steeple, 235 feet high, which some consider the finest Renaissance campanile in the world. This church was damaged in the air raid in September 1940 and burnt out in another raid in 1941, but it has now been rebuilt, its handsome steeple repaired and the famous Bow bells re-hung. Bow church embraces eight other church-less parishes, and a notice board at the entrance lists the names of no less than thirteen church wardens. In the churchyard is the bronze statue of Captain John Smith 'sometime Governor of Virginia,' presented by the Jamestown Foundation of Virginia and unveiled by Queen Elizabeth the Queen Mother in October, 1960.

In Milk Street on the opposite side of the road formerly stood the City of London School, established in 1835, and founded on an income of £900 a year bequeathed by John Carpenter, town clerk of London in the reign of Henry V. This establishment was opened in 1837, and removed to its present site on the Victoria Embankment in 1883.

A few paces farther west on the same side is Wood Street, with its familiar landmark, the flourishing plane-tree at the corner of Cheapside, marking the site of the churchyard of St-Peter-in-Chepe, destroyed in the Great Fire. It was this tree that inspired Wordsworth's simple little poem, *The Reverie of Poor Susan*. Three two-storey Cheapside shops which survived the blitz back onto this little churchyard. A tablet on the wall records that they were 'Erected at ye sole costs and charges of the Parish of St Peter's Cheape Ao Dni. 1687'. On the opposite corner of Wood Street is Cheapside's newest building, the nine-storey Mitre House.

Friday Street on the south side of Cheapside, leading into Cannon Street, was partly widened in 1931 by the City Corporation by setting back the buildings on the west corner of Cheapside, and more recently, about 1930, the houses at the east corner, said to have been the oldest in Cheapside, were pulled down. The whole street, however, was completely blotted out in the blitz and the greater part, from Cheapside to Cannon Street, has been 'incorporated' in new buildings, as previously mentioned.

Foster Lane, on the north side, running parallel to St-Martin's-le-Grand, contains the elegant hall of the Goldsmiths' Company, built by Philip Hardwick, R. A., and opened with a splendid banquet on 15 July 1835. Here also is the church of St Vedast, rebuilt by Sir Christopher Wren, with a tower built in 1695-98. Like many other City churches, it was seriously damaged in the raid of 29 December 1940, leaving little more than the walls and tower standing. After a complete restoration by Mr S. E. Dykes Bower, F.R.I.B.A., however, the church was re-hallowed by the Bishop of London in April, 1962. St Vedast *alias* Foster, to give its correct title, incorporates no less than thirteen other parishes of neighbouring churches — eleven which have been demolished, and two that have been relieved of parochial responsibilities. Notable features of the interior include the Renatus Harris organ of 1753 from St Bartholomew-by-the-Exchange, the 17th century pulpit formerly in All Hallows, Bread Street and the alabaster font, once in the church of St Anne and St Agnes, Gresham Street, The font in which Robert Herrick was baptized here in 1591 no longer exists. At the top of Cheapside stood until 1935 a statue of Sir Robert Peel, erected in 1851, which has been removed to the churchyard of St Botolph, Aldersgate, popularly known as 'Postmens' Park'.

There has been considerably building activity in the devastated Cheapside area, some of which has already been recorded. An important contribution is the eight-storey Sun Life Assurance Society building with a frontage of 250 feet extending from Milk Street to Lawrence Lane. This is of the familiar reinforced concrete construction with Portland Stone facings. During excavations, a Roman bath was discovered; it was measured and photographed and then covered up again. The ground floor has smart shops on either side of the entrance and there are three basements, the first of which provides garage accommodation. This building displays a nice new sundial.

At the junction of Cheapside and St Paul's Churchyard, an extensive widening of the roadway was carried out in 1900 by the City Corporation, thus affording much relief to the great congestion of traffic which hitherto prevailed at this busy centre. Here a new subway provides access to the Underground Station of St Paul's on the Central Line Railway. For many years the City Corporation had intended constructing a new St Paul's Bridge across the Thames, together with a new street, forming an approach, which was to have been continued north of Cannon Street by a widening of the east side of St Paul's Churchyard and

St-Martin's-le-Grand. Much of the property needed for this improvement had already been acquired by the Corporation, but the first World War intervened and further progress was delayed. Ultimately the scheme for the construction of St Paul's Bridge was abandoned, partly because of the hostility displayed towards the threatened great increase of traffic through the City, and partly because of the grave fears entertained for the safety of the foundations of St Paul's Cathedral resulting from the vibration to be expected from the heavy volume of traffic passing along the east side of the building. It was also considered that the north- and south-bound traffic of London would be more suitably accommodated by the construction of a new bridge at Charing Cross.

In 1926 a considerable widening of St-Martin's-le-Grand was carried out as a result of the demolition of the old General Post Office on the east side of that street. Erected in 1925-29 on the site of the church of St-Martin's-le-Grand, the old General Post Office was pulled down in 1912-13. It was a large two-storey building adorned with an Ionic portico, designed by Sir R. Smirke, R.A. Towards the end of the nineteenth century an extra storey was added to this building. For some twelve years, partly owing to the first World War, this site remained vacant, until the present handsome range of buildings was erected between 1925 and 1927. These contain a branch of the Westminster Bank, the Empire House, the new premises of Messrs Courtauld, and Union House. The latter building, which lost its three top storeys in the blitz, was repaired in 1950.

Today the business of the General Post Office is transacted in no less than eight buildings where one sufficed a century ago. The mail-coach service was inaugurated by Mr. J. Palmer of Bath, and the first coach ran between London and Bath in 1784. Coaches were provided with a well-armed guard, and travelled at the rate of nine miles an hour including stoppages.

The west block of the General Post Office at the corner of Newgate Street was erected in 1870-73 at a cost of £450,000, of which the site alone cost £300,000. This building was badly damaged in the air raids of 1940 and its three upper storeys have been taken down but the ground floor and the first and second floors are still in use. The north-west block at the corner of Angel Street was opened in 1894. On this site stood the Bull and Mouth Hotel, a coaching inn rebuilt in 1830 and renamed the Queen's Hotel. The latest addition to the General Post Office opened in 1910 is known as the King Edward Building, and occupies a part of the site of the old Bluecoat School. In front of the building is a statue, by Onslow Ford, of Rowland Hill, who introduced the Penny Post — 'one of the greatest blessings of civilisation'. Opened in 1927, a narrow gauge (2 feet) underground railway was constructed from the General Post Office to Paddington on the west and to Whitechapel on the east. The trains are electrically driven and automatically controlled, and this railway is said to relieve street traffic to the extent of 1,300 van-miles every day.

Newgate Street derives its name from the City gate which originally stood at the west end of this street. Most of it was destroyed in the raid of 29 December 1940, as were the various lanes on the south side of the street. Only a few buildings now remain, and these are mostly situated at the western end. Already before the second World War, a start had been made on the widening of Newgate Street by the City Corporation. The buildings on the north side which had concealed the view of Christ Church and its garden had been pulled down and the roadway slightly widened at this point.

Until 1902 the entrance to Christ's Hospital was situated on the north side of Newgate Street. This school was erected on the site of the Greyfriars' Monastery, and was founded by Edward VI on 26 June 1553, ten days before his death, as a hospital for poor fatherless children and foundlings. Later it was generally known as the Bluecoat School, from the dress worn by the boys. The first stone of the late building was laid by the Duke of York on 28 April 1825, and the hall publicly opened on 29 May 1829. The architect was Mr John Shaw, who designed the church of St-Dunstan's-in-the-West. In 1902 the school was removed to its present quarters near Horsham, Sussex. An opportunity of cutting a new street across the grounds of Christ's Hospital after the removal of the Bluecoat School was unfortunately lost. Christ Church Greyfriars, a fine edifice with a lofty square tower, stood on the site of an earlier Franciscan church which escaped the Great Fire but was rebuilt by Wren in 1704. It was completely ruined in 1941, but the tower has been repaired and the twelve ornamental urns which were removed from the steeple in 1828 have now been restored.

Paternoster Row, situated between Newgate Street and St Paul's Churchyard, was in olden times a fashionable centre for shopping, and was frequently rendered almost impassable by the congestion of carriages. Here Samuel Pepys used to go shopping with his wife. In more recent years Paternoster Row was almost entirely inhabited by publishers and booksellers. When the Row was consumed by fire in the raid of 29 December 1940, millions of books were burnt. It is now merely a narrow pathway, overgrown with weeds. The London headquarters of several large publishing houses, including Messrs Longmans Green, Hutchinson, Nelson and Hodder and Stoughton were obliterated as well as the curious little Locomotive Publishing Company office, tucked away at No. 3 Amen Corner, hard by the gates of Amen Court. Several large and well-known book-shops have also disappeared in the general destruction of Paternoster Row. In this terrific fire-raid among many famous buildings destroyed or damaged were the Guildhall and eight Wren churches, namely, St Bride Fleet Street, St Lawrence Jewry, St Stephen Coleman Street, Christ Church Greyfriars, St Vedast Foster, St Mary Aldermanbury, St Andrew-by-the-Wardrobe, and St Mary-le-Bow. A number of City Hall, including those of the Girdlers', Coopers' and Saddlers' Companies, Barbers' Hall and that of the Society of Apothecaries were also destroyed or badly damaged. Many offices, houses, and shops as well as three hospitals shared the same fate. On the following day the Royal Engineers and Pioneers were sent to dynamite a number of wrecked buildings which were stil, burning. Among the streets which suffered most severely were Cheapsidel Newgate Street, St Paul's Churchyard, Paternoster Row, Aldersgate Street, London Wall, Tower Hill, and the Minories. Despite the ferocity of this raid the A.R.P. and fire-fighting services worked heroically and succeeded in getting all the fires under control.

Between Ivy Lane and Warwick Lane on the north side of Paternoster Row stood Newgate Market until 1867, occupying the site of what is now called Paternoster Square, and forming a quadrangle between Newgate Street and Paternoster Row. It contained a market-house, and a clock and a bell turret in the centre, and was principally devoted to the sale of carcasses and butchers' meat. For many years Newgate Market was one of the greatest nuisances in the City, as not only were some six hundred sheep and fifty bullocks slaughtered there every day, but this took place in cellars underneath the shops where the joints were retailed to the public. The access to these cellars in the houses over-looking the market was by steps, over which a board was placed for the animal to slide down. But more often it was seized by the butcher and pitched headlong down into the cellar, where, unable to rise owing to broken limbs suffered in the fall, it awaited its turn to be slaughtered.

At the end of Giltspur Street opposite the Old Bailey is the large open space with a small garden in the centre now called West Smithfield, surrounded principally by the offices of several of the large meat companies and bounded on the north side by the new Smithfield Meat Market in Long Lane. It covers an area of over six acres, and until 1868 contained the old Smithfield Market, at that time the largest cattle-market in the world. It was long considered an even greater nuisance by the citizen of London than Newgate Market. It had an annual turnover of seven million pounds sterling, and its confined space often gave rise to scenes of dreadful cruelty. There was accommodation for 2,750 head of cattle, and standing room for 1,250 more, and 1,500 pens for sheep, each of which would hold sixteen, thus affording accommodation for over twenty-four thousand sheep. There were many slaughter-houses in the im-mediate vicinity, and great disappointment was felt by City people at the refusal for a long time of the Corporation of London to do away with this market, and in September 1848 they had even enlarged the market by purchasing a valuable block of houses on the north-east side of the Barbican for that purpose.

The market for living animals was eventually removed to Copenhagen Fields, North London, in 1855, and the new market erected on that site was begun in 1875. The last market for live animals to be held at old Smithfield was on 11 June 1855. The new Central London Meat Market was begun in 1862, and completed in 1868. It is a handsome building in the Renaissance style, fronted with red brick, and flanked by four corner towers, covering an area of three and a half acres, 630 feet long and 246 feet wide. It was designed by Mr Horace Jones and built at a cost of £200,000. The extension of the west side, which houses the Metropolitan Poultry Market, was opened in January 1875. The buildings were damaged in the air raids of 1940 and again in March 1945 when a bomb hit the fish, fruit and vegetable market at the corner of Farringdon Street and Charterhouse Street during morning shopping. Over a hundred people were killed and 123 injured by the falling masonry and girders and debris.

Connecting West Smithfield with King Edward Street, and branching also into Aldersgate Street, is Little Britain, a thoroughfare which commemorates the mansion of John Duke of Bretagne in the days of Edward II, and which in the time of the Stuarts was the great centre for booksellers. Here is the half-timbered Tudor front of the gateway leading to the church of St Bartholomew the Great — the oldest parish church in the City. Of special interest on account of the large amount of early Norman work which remains, the present building represents the choir of the old church of the Priory founded in 1123 by Rahere, the pious jester and courtier of Henry I. The well-preserved tomb of the founder is on the north side of the presbytery and the font in which the painter William Hogarth was baptized stands in the south transept. A custom of forgotten origin is still maintained on Good Friday morning, when a number of widows of the parish pick up sixpences and hot cross buns from a tombstone in the churchyard. In Bartholomew Close, which leads out of Little Britain, Milton was secreted at the time of the Restoration waiting for his pardon to be signed under the Act of Oblivion. Bartholomew Close was the birthplace of Hogarth. A memorial obelisk to Robert Waithman, Lord Mayor 1823-4, 'The friend of liberty in evil times,' which originally stood in Ludgate Circus, has been re-erected in Bartholomew Close. Here also on the night of 31 July 1944 a flying bomb hit the roof of Butchers' Hall and destroyed the two upper floors. A new Butchers' Hall, with heads of sheep and oxen over the windows, was opened in May 1960. The Company's motto is 'Thou hast put all things in subjection under his feet: all sheep and oxen'.

Between Giltspur Street and Little Britain is the famous St Bartholomew's Hospital, founded by Rahere in 1123 and refounded by Henry VIII after the dissolution of the monasteries. The buildings are approached by a gateway from Smithfield, and enclose a large square. A part of the site of the old Christ's Hospital is now occupied by an extension of St Bartholomew's Hospital, opened in 1907. St Bartholomew the Less, within the hospital grounds, is the parish church of the hospital, which is a parish in itself.

King Edward Street, leading into Newgate Street, and now containing the western block of the General Post Office, was once called Stinking Lane, owing to the filth which used to accumulate here from the neighbouring Newgate and Smithfield Markets.

The church of St Sepulchre at the eastern end of Holborn Viaduct, which has a very handsome Perpendicular tower, was damaged but not destroyed in the Great Fire of London. It is dedicated in honour of the Holy Sepulchre of Jerusalem, and was restored in 1875. There is a Musicians Memorial Chapel dedicated to St Cecilia, with memorial windows to John Ireland, Dame Nellie Melba and Sir Henry Wood. Roger Ascham, tutor to Queen Elizabeth I, is buried in the fifteenth century chapel of St Stephen, and Captain John Smith, sometime Governor of Virginia and Admiral of New England, who died in 1631, lies in the south aisle of the church. Another American association is that Roger Williams, founder of Rhode Island, was born in the parish and baptized in St Sepulchre's font.

On the wall of St Sepulchre, at the corner of Giltspur Street, stands the first public drinking fountain in London, the gift of Samuel Gurney in 1859. Like most of the older fountains today, it is quite dry. The 'pure cold drinking water' which it formerly supplied is now on tap in every home. When the Metropolitan Drinking Fountain and Cattle Trough Association was formed in 1859, the only drinking water available to the poorer people came from contaminated wells and pumps, to which were attributed the outbreaks of cholera in the mid-nineteenth century; one is reminded of the now-demolished St Luke's Church in Nutford Place, Edgware Road, which was dedicated in 1845 'as a thank-offering for mercies vouchsafed to this district at a time of visitation by cholera'. Much later is the memorial window in St James Church, Sussex Gardens, to five schoolboys (one of whom was the vicar's son) who, in 1890 'died from drinking impure water while on a walk together in the neigh-bourhood'.

Despite initial difficulties, within two years the Association had some 85 fountains working in London; once started, the movement grew and fountains of iron, stone, granite and marble sprang up all over London, for in addition to the simple utilitarian design approved by the Association, many large and elaborate structures of a memorial or commemorative description, suitably inscribed (and the inscriptions should be noticed), were erected at the expense of private donors. A considerable number of these Victorian designs still survive, and since all but a very few have ceased to function as fountains, the need for the space they occupy or the possibility that they are an obstruction to traffic will ensure their eventual destruction in this forward-looking age that requires everything to be strictly functional and severely rectangular.

The Metropolitan Drinking Fountain and Cattle Trough Association, however, is still active in providing drinking fountains in parks, recreation grounds and such places where people — especially children — congregate, and though horse-troughs are no longer supplied, the modern design of fountain usually has a small trough for dogs and the insanitary metal cups of bygone days have been displaced by the upward 'bubble' jet of water.

The bust of Charles Lamb — 'Perhaps the most loved name in English Liter-ature' — that survived the destruction of Christ Church, Newgate, now occupies a place on the wall of the restored watch-house in Giltspur Street, and a little further along at the corner of Cock Lane is the gilded figure of the Fat Boy, marking one of the places where the Great Fire of 1666 stopped.

We now direct our steps towards Holborn Viaduct. This magnificent artery was constructed by the City Corporation between 1863 and 1869 to carry the roadway over the valley of the Holebourne part of the Fleet River. It is 1,400 feet long and 80 feet wide, including an iron bridge of 107 feet, which crosses Farringdon Street. With the object of levelling the ascent from Holborn Bridge to Newgate Street, a new thoroughfare had already been constructed in 1802, called Skinner Street, which was named after Alderman Skinner, mainly through whose efforts it had been built.

The demolition of the houses and streets required to make way for Holborn Viaduct was begun in May 1863, but the first stone of the Viaduct itself was laid on 3 June 1867 by Deputy T. H. Fry, Chairman of the Improvements Committee of the City Corporation. The central object of this great London improvement was a stately viaduct across the Holborn Valley between Hatton Garden and Newgate Street, with another street opening opposite Hatton Garden into the newly-formed Holborn Circus, giving direct access to Ludgate Circus. This led to the construction of St Andrew Street, which passes by the back of St Andrew's Church into Shoe Lane, the widening of the latter street as far as Stonecutter Street, and from here the construction of another new street fifty feet wide called St Bride Street, with easy gradients leading down to the north-west corner of Ludgate Circus. In order to give direct access to Smithfield Market, another new thoroughfare known as Charterhouse Street had to be constructed on the north side of Holborn Circus.

At first the problem which confronted the engineer appeared a simple one, but on consideration of details the task soon assumed a more difficult and complex character, particularly as regards the placing of the numerous sewers, gas and water mains on higher levels. The Viaduct, being of considerable height above the level of the Holborn Valley, enabled the engineer to subdivide his vaulted passages into storeys. Thus a space was reserved for the areas and vaulted cellars of the houses, and against these at the top is the subway containing the gas and water mains, and electric-light cables. Below the subway is a vaulted chamber constructed with damp-proof courses through its walls of considerable depth, at the bottom of which, resting on a concrete bed, is the sewer. The subways, which are 11 feet 6 inches high and 7 feet wide, are constructed of brickwork, except where they are carried under the Southern Railway, where they are of tubular form and constructed of iron. Including the new streets from Holborn Circus to the Charterhouse and Ludgate Circus, the cost of this wonderful improvement was £2,100,000.

The most ornamental feature of the Viaduct is the cast-iron bridge across Farringdon Street, on the top of which are pedestals containing bronze statues representing Commerce and Agriculture on the south side, and Science and Fine Arts on the north side. During the clearance for the new streets nothing of special interest was brought to light, but frequent discoveries were made of concealed passages for escape, and nooks for hiding plunder in the squalid houses of Field Lane and its unsavoury neighbourhood, the removal of which alone was a great blessing to this part of London. The construction of St Andrew Street necessitated the removal of between eleven thousand and twelve thousand bodies from the churchyard of St Andrew's, which were transferred to the City cemetery at Ilford. Amongst other buildings demolished for the Holborn Viaduct improvement was the Saracen's Head Inn at Snow Hill, much frequented by stage coaches in the pre-railway days. A later hotel, bearing the same name with appropriate decorations on the front to remind us of Mr Wackford Squeers and Nicholas Nickleby, was destroyed in the last war.

Holborn Viaduct was formally opened by Queen Victoria on 6 November 1869, the same day as the new Blackfriars Bridge. The weather on that day was fine, and the people of London were glad to see the Queen once more coming amongst them after a long absence, which they had felt to be undeserved on their part. It seems that they failed to make due allowance for the domestic and personal hindrances to her more frequent appearance in the metropolis. Her Majesty appeared to be in excellent health and spirits, but she was still in deep mourning for the Prince Consort, although he had been dead nearly eight years, and all of her servants still wore a mourning band of crepe on one arm.

At the approach to the Viaduct near St Sepulchre's Church, seats under cover were erected for the guests of the City Corporation, as well as a pavilion with seating accommodation for six hundred persons. The festivities included a banquet in the evening, given by the Lord Mayor and Lady Mayoress at the Mansion House, in honour of this great event. Some 250 guests were entertained, including the members of the Court of Common Council, the Sheriffs, and other leading officers of the Corporation.

To all lovers of the ancient City of London, as distinguished from the greater metropolis, this enterprise on the part of the old-fashioned Mother Corporation in undertaking such great schemes of public utility appeared especially gratifying. This day of festivities was therefore so mapped out as to include a visit to the newly-opened Metropolitan Meat Market in Smithfield. During the decade from 1861 to 1871 London had been advancing more substantially, if perhaps a trifle less rapidly, than Paris in the matter of its great street improvements, embracing Holborn Viaduct, Queen Victoria Street, and the Victoria Embankment amongst others. St Bride Street, which cost £45,000, was only completed and opened to the public in November 1871.

In 1863 an alternative scheme to the construction of Holborn Viaduct was planned by Mr Bunning, in which it was proposed to raise the general level of the various roadways, so that instead of two steep hills, there would have been four moderate inclines running north, south, east, and west. This scheme upon examination was found to be too costly, and therefore that of Mr Marrable for the Viaduct was adopted.

Field Lane, on the site of Farringdon Road, north of the Viaduct, was an infamous rookery inhabited by the criminal class, and consisted mainly of filthy shops which were the headquarters of petty larceny. There were old-clothes shops, rag-merchants, public-houses, and fried-fish shops, many of which were frequented by pickpockets and thieves who trafficked in dark back-parlours. Huge bunches of pocket-handkerchiefs purchased from pickpockets were displayed in the shops here.

Opening into Field Lane, until pulled down in 1844, was Chick Lane, which contained a notorious thieves' lodging-house known as the Red Lion Tavern, with passages for concealment. At the rear was the Fleet Ditch over which the wrongdoer used to escape by climbing through a window and crossing the Ditch by a plank into the opposite collection of courts and alleys. The plank could be quickly removed into the opposite house in order to delay the progress of the pursuing policeman.

Holborn Viaduct Station on the south side of the road was opened on 1 March 1874 as the new City terminus of the London, Chatham and Dover Railway, and this improvement necessitated the widening of the Blackfriars Railway Bridge. The large hotel which fronted the Viaduct was requisitioned for Government service during the first World War, and was afterwards converted into business premises.

As part of the British Railways Modernization Scheme, the station buildings have been completely rebuilt and above the station is the nine-floor Williams National House, replacing the old Holborn Viaduct Hotel. West of the station, except for Remington House and the new W.D. & H.O. Wills tobacco showrooms on the north side, the buildings on both sides of the road, as far as the actual Viaduct, are of uniform height and dullness until we reach the City Temple on the south side. The whole building, erected at a cost of £35,000, was opened in May 1874, and was capable of holding three thousand people. It contained a marble pulpit presented at a cost of three hundred guineas by the Corporation of London. The City Temple was destroyed on 16 April 1941 and completely rebuilt and re-dedicated on 30 October 1958. On the buildings at each end of the south side of the actual bridge, statues of Henry Fitzalwin and Sir Thomas Gresham survive. Sir William Walworth and Sir Hugh Myddleton occupied similar positions on the north side, but have been destroyed. West of the Viaduct is the church of St Andrew, Holborn, rebuilt by Wren in 1686, destroyed in 1941 and now rebuilt and open again. It is much below the present level of the roadway owing to the subsequent construction of Holborn Viaduct.

Holborn Viaduct and the neighbouring thoroughfares suffered enormous damage in the air raids of 1940. On the north side all but seven buildings located between the church of St Sepulchre and the bridge over Farringdon Street were destroyed. These included the premises of Messrs Negretti & Zambra, the famous firm of opticians and makers of scientific instruments which stood on the north-west corner. Mr Negretti, originally a glass-blower from Como, and his partner Mr Zambra, who displayed their scientific instruments at the Great Exhibition of 1851, afterwards conducted a small meteorological station on the roof of their premises in Holborn Circus and then became vested with the title of 'Clerk of the Weather'. Their building was hit by a bomb on 12 September 1940 and on 9 October of the same year the premises were destroyed by fire and completely demolished. On the south side the railway station and the former hotel building were badly damaged, but both have been rebuilt, as noted above. So much property disappeared in the blitz between St Andrew's Street, Shoe Lane, and Farringdon Street that you could see right across the devastated area from Holborn Circus to Ludgate Circus. In the opposite direction many buildings in Charterhouse Street and round about Snow Hill have shared the same fate. H. M. Stationery Office is now in possession of most of Atlantic House, a twelve-storeyed block of shops and offices in Holborn Viaduct. The foundations cost over £75,000 and the building over £750,000. Three of the storeys are below ground on the blitzed site extending to Charterhouse Street. The architect for this new building was Sir Thomas Bennett.

At the western entrance to the Viaduct is a bronze equestrian statue of the Prince Consort, unveiled by King Edward VII, when Prince of Wales, in 1873. It was presented to the City Corporation by a private gentleman, and was designed by Mr Bacon, the sculptor.

On the north side of Holborn Circus is Hatton Garden, the headquarters of the London diamond merchants, leading to Clerkenwell Road, and so named after Sir Christopher Hatton, Lord Chancellor to the first Elizabeth. It contains some excellent buildings, and several jewellers' shops, which give this street quite an opulent appearance, almost worthy of the West End. In this connection may be mentioned Number 40 Holborn Viaduct a large new building for the Anglo-American Corporation of South Africa which appears to be mostly occupied by diamond merchants.

Ely Place, running parallel to Hatton Garden, from the entrance to Charterhouse Street, marks the site of the old palace of the Bishops of Ely, and was once entered by a great gateway. It was built by Bishop Arundel in 1388. Saffron once grew in the garden of Ely House, and hence the name of Saffron Hill given to an adjoining thoroughfare. To please Queen Elizabeth I, Bishop Cox leased the gatehouse and garden to Sir Christopher Hatton, who expended large sums of money upon Ely Place. Sir Christopher Hatton borrowed the money from Queen Elizabeth for that purpose, and when the Queen wanted her money back he died of a broken heart. Bishop Cox was obliged to consent to the mortgaging of the house and grounds to Sir Christopher Hatton, until all the money expended upon Ely Place had been repaid, but when Queen Elizabeth found his successor, Dr Martin Heton, unwilling to honour this agreement, she summarily ordered him to comply, failing which she would unfrock him. In the bar of the attractive little 'Mitre' tavern in Ely Court (claiming the date of 1546), stands the trunk of an old cherry tree which is said to have marked the boundary between the Bishop's garden and the part leased to Sir Christopher Hatton.

It was at Ely House that 'old John of Gaunt; time-honour'd Lancaster' died in 1399; the garden was famous for its strawberries, and the familiar incident in Shakespeare's *Richard III* where the Duke of Gloucester sends there for strawberries is well attested.

There is a tradition that Ely Place is considered to be in Cambridgeshire and therefore outside the jurisdiction of the Metropolitan Police. It is true that the police do not patrol Ely Place because the Commissioners have their own watchmen, but this does not confer the privilege of sanctuary upon any malefactor found therein. Since the Act of 1963, Ely Place is more likely to be in the London Borough of Camden than in Cambridgeshire.

The only remaining relic of old Ely House is the chapel on the west side of Ely Place, dedicated to St Ethelreda.

We turn next into Holborn, which derives its name from the Holebourne section of the Fleet River. This is a very broad thoroughfare from Holborn Circus as far as Chancery Lane and has undergone a complete transformation during the past fifty years. Until July 1898 Furnival's Inn stood on the north side. The site is now covered by the huge edifice of the Prudential Assurance Company. It was named after Sir William Furnival, who once owned this land, and was an Inn of Chancery attached to Lincoln's Inn. Its original buildings were regarded as exceedingly stately, having a front by Inigo Jones, but these were mostly pulled down in the time of Charles I and entirely rebuilt in 1808, when it was let to Henry Peto on a building lease of a hundred years. His statue, erected in 1830, stood in the former courtyard. Within Furnival's Inn stood Wood's Hotel, a high-class old-established house for gentlemen and for families. Dickens began the *Pickwick Papers* whilst living at Furnival's Inn. A bust of Charles Dickens stands in the courtyard of the Prudential building. Bartlett's Buildings, which was formerly a cul-de-sac, has now been converted into a thoroughfare called New Fetter Lane; it joins the parent Fetter Lane at a point opposite Bream's Buildings.

On the south side of Holborn Circus, a branch of Lloyds Bank Limited occupies part of a new nine-storey building of red brick with stone facings called 'Thavies Inn House'.

The Old Bell Inn at No 123, which was rebuilt in 1898, contained one of the most picturesque courtyards in England, surrounded by tiers of balconied galleries hung with flowers in summer. The rebuilt Old Bell was sandwiched in between two large modern blocks of buildings forming the well-known establishment of Gamages, who have since acquired the Bell and have built a new Food Hall on the site. Their premises are now continuous, without any break. The western block at the corner of Leather Lane occupies the site of the old Ridler's Hotel, and on part of the site of the eastern block stood the Black Bull Hotel. The large — and heavy — figure of a black bull that was its sign stood until recently over the doorway of a firm of solicitors in King Street, Hammersmith: Messrs Bull & Bull. These offices having been demolished, the animal was temporarily stored, but has now been liberated, as detailed in our 24th Walk. Other changes have taken place on the south side of Holborn, and here the most important building was the large drapery emporium of Messrs Thomas Wallis & Company Limited, at the corner of Holborn Circus. This was destroyed in the air raid of April 1941 and nothing was saved. Firemen fought the flames throughout the night and all the next day after showers of incendiaries and high-explosive bombs had been dropped on this great department store. Some two months later Messrs Thomas Wallis & Company Limited opened new shops in the Mount Royal building in Oxford Street. The eighteen-floor *Daily Mirror* building now stands on this Holborn Circus site. It rises to a height of 169 feet above street level and is the biggest newspaper office in Britain, with the most modern printing plant in the world. The printing presses are situated in the Press Hall, forty-six feet below ground. A staff of about 3,000 work in this 'graceful skyscraper', as the proprietors describe it. Farther west were the stately offices of Messrs Buchanans the whisky manufacturers, whose building has also been destroyed and replaced by a new building for the Midland Bank Ltd.

Opposite Gray's Inn Road is Staple Inn, now the property of the Prudential Assurance Company, consisting of two irregular quadrangles, and containing a small garden in the south court with a fountain. It was originally a hostelry of the woolstaple, serving as a kind of custom house, where wool was weighed and dues collected upon it. In all the hundreds of years since London became a city of importance it has not been able to sweep its roaring tide over that little island of quiet; but unfortunately its Elizabethan hall was wrecked by a flying-bomb in August 1944, though it has now been restored, with its garden. It is associated with Dickens and figures in *Edwin Drood*. Here also Dr Johnson moved on 23 March 1759 from Gough Square and wrote *Rasselas*. On the wall of the entrance to Staple Inn is a notice board which reads: 'The Porter Has Orders To Prevent Old Clothes Men & Others From Calling Articles For Sale, Also Rude Children Playing & c. No Horses Allowed Within This Inn.' Close by stood Barnard's Inn, demolished early in the present century, except the hall, which was occupied by the Mercers' School until September 1959 when the scholars were dispersed and the school closed down.

Close to Gray's Inn Road is the Holborn Cenotaph, a striking bronze statue by Albert Toft, forming the War Memorial of the Royal Fusilier. At the junction of Gray's Inn Road and Holborn, stone pillars and dragons mark the City boundary. On the south west corner of Gray's Inn Road is a new eight-storey building, 'Bishop's House', largely occupied by the Prudential Assurance Company, with a new Woolworth store on the ground floor.

Just west of Staple Inn was an imposing nine-storey building containing a branch of the Westminster Bank. It was erected in 1901 for the Birkbeck Bank, which closed its doors in 1911 after a chequered career. Eventually, after all the assets had been realized, the shareholders received 16s. 9d. in the pound. This remarkable building of glazed yellow and blue terracotta was smothered with decorative columns, statues and groups of statuary including a varied selection of undraped females and bright little boys; at intervals along the outside walls were medallions of eminent Victorians and earlier celebrities. Inside, the domed banking hall was equally impressive, with portraits of famous people, wrought-iron balustrades to galleries reached by elaborate staircases. In spite of all these visual incentives to integrity and thrift, the Birkbeck Bank failed. The building was demolished in 1965. In front of the grimy old buildings which had previously occupied this site stood until 1867 a row of old houses called Middle Row, which abutted on Holborn Bars, thereby greatly reducing the width of the main street in much the same fashion as Holywell Street formerly reduced the width of the Strand and Bozier's Court that of Tottenham Court Road. For at least a couple of centuries Middle Row had been regarder as an obstruction, for already in 1657 it is mentioned by Howell in his *Perlustration of London* as a mighty hindrance to Holborn, which, if it were taken down, would be from Holborn Conduit to St Giles one of the fairest rising streets in the world.

Here, in a house called the Golden Anchor, Dr Johnson lodged in 1748. On Saturday, 31 August 1867, the demolition of Middle Row was commenced, and a long-needed metropolitan improvement thus effected in this neighbourhood. The new roadway was completed for traffic by December 1867.

Chancery Lane, once called New Street, and then Chancellor's Lane, still follows very much the lines of an old country lane. It will surprise the average Londoner of today to learn that both of its approaches, from Holborn on the north and Fleet Street on the south, were at one time even narrower than they are at present.

In November 1850 rebuilding took place at the corner of High Holborn and Chancery Lane, and the inhabitants, desiring to have this corner widened, raised a sum of £5,350 by public subscription for that purpose, a part of which was paid to Mr Steel, the owner, for surrendering a slice of ground fifty-one feet long by seven feet wide. This improvement was carried out by resolution at a meeting convened by the parish officers at the request of inhabitants and occupiers of premises within the united parishes of St Andrew Holborn and St George-the-Martyr. The offer made by Mr Steel, who was rebuilding his corner premises at that time, was considered most reasonable, as it was said that if this splendid opportunity had been allowed to pass by, the eventual cost of this improvement would have been £40,000. Some of the buildings on the east side of Chancery Lane forming part of New Stone Buildings were destroyed in the air raids of 1940 and have been replaced by the new Chancery Lane Safe Deposit building, 'Chancery House'.

On the east side of Chancery Lane is the Public Record Office, a fine Tudor building extending to Fetter Lane, which has been the repository of State papers from as far back as the year 1100 to the present day. The buildings are in the Tudor Gothic style, with tall, deeply-embrasured windows, and were designed by Sir James Pennethorne, and added to between 1891 and 1900 by Sir John Taylor, with the frontage to Chancery Lane, at a cost of £200,000. The new buildings have incorporated part of the Rolls Chapel, and covered the site of the court of the Master of the Rolls. The older section of the Record Office, which is in Fetter Lane, was constructed in 1866, prior to which time the records were stored in the Tower, the Chapter House, and the Rolls Chapel in Chancery Lane.

Fetter Lane, running parallel to Chancery Lane on the east side, is said to derive its name from fewters of beggars which once infested it. At Clifford's Inn on the west side now stands a tall block of flats erected in 1936 which at that time was considered quite a novelty for the City of London. Most of the buildings on the east side of Fetter Lane have been destroyed in the blitzes of 1940 and so much property has been demolished in this immediate vicinity that here an unobstructed view across the steeply-sloping ground to Farringdon Sreet could be obtained until recently, but new buildings such as Newspaper House, Extel House and others now impede the field of view across this once desolate waste.

On the west side of Chancery Lane is the building of the Law Society, formed in 1823 for the purpose of providing a hall for the daily resort of the Solicitor's branch of the legal profession, a library, reading-room, and fire-proof rooms for depositing deeds and papers. Both Scotland and Ireland had already established halls and libraries for their solicitors before the English legal profession followed suit. In 1825 a sum of £50,000 was raised for that purpose in shares of 25s., with power to increase the capital to £75,000, and in 1827 the Comittee erected the present building. A Royal Charter of Incorporation was granted on 22 December 1831, and the institution opened for the use of members on 4 July 1832. Owing to the disadvantages occasioned by the joint-stock character of the undertaking, a new charter was granted on 26 February 1845, merging the individual liabilities of the earlier members into the new corporation. A new wing was opened by King Edward VII in 1904.

On the west side of Chancery Lane, near Fleet Street, where now stands a branch of the Bank of England, another widening was carried out in 1855. Two houses, Nos. 130 and 131 at the south-west corner, now occupied by a jeweller's shop, had already been pulled down in March 1853. These contained projecting windows, overhanging stories, and gabled fronts, and were nearly 250 years old.

Turning next into Fleet Street, nearly opposite Chancery Lane at the entrance to the Inner Temple is a stationer's shop with a projecting upper story built in 1610. On the first floor is a chamber known as Prince Henry's Room, once the Council Chamber of the Duchy of Cornwall. The London County Council and the City Corporation jointly purchased this building in 1900, when it was about to be demolished, and restored the premises at a cost of £30,000. Next door is a branch of Barclays Bank, erected on the site previously occupied by Gosling's Bank, where Warren Hastings, Clive, and Pope, and many other notable people, kept their accounts. Gosling's Bank was absorbed by Barclays Bank over forty years ago. Affixed to the wall of No 18 Fleet Street is a plaque unveiled by the Lord Mayor, Sir James Miller, in 1965 to mark the Diamond Jubilee of the Automobile Association, which opened its first office here in 1905.

A few yards farther west is Child's Bank, now acquired by Glyn Mills & Company, which adjoins the site of the old Temple Bar, demolished in 1878. The rooms over the Temple Bar used also to be occupied by Child's Bank, whose premises were adjacent. Child's Bank held the current accounts of Oliver Cromwell, Nell Gwyn, King William III, and Queen Mary, and they were the tenants of the City Corporation for the rooms over the gateway, for which they paid the modest rental of £20 per annum. In 1874 it was discovered that the keystone of the arch was out of the perpendicular, and but for this misfortune which befell the Temple Bar, the archives which have revealed so many interesting documents would never in all probability have come to light. Child's Bank itself was demolished in 1879, and rebuilt a few feet farther back from the old line of frontage.

The Temple Bar, a gateway of Portland stone, designed in 1670 by Sir Christopher Wren, had long been regarded as an obstruction to traffic, and already in 1858 the Metropolitan Board of Works passed a resolution that a communication be sent to the City Corporation to that effect. However, it was not pulled down until twenty years later, after which the present much-criticized pillar surmounted by a dragon was erected in 1880 as a memorial of the Temple Bar. Wren's famous gateway was reerected in 1888 in Theobald's Park, Waltham Cross, by its owner, Sir Hedworth Meux. In 1875 it had been proposed to remove the old Temple Bar to Hyde Park or the Thames Embankment, but this and more recent schemes to bring the gateway back to London have failed to mature.

On the north side of Fleet Street, between Chancery and Fetter Lanes is the church of St Dunstan-in-the-West; the church, built by John Shaw between 1829 and 1833, is octagonal in shape. It contains an imposing tower, and replaced an earlier church which was famous for its clock on which two giants struck the hour. This clock was reinstated in 1936 and was a gift of the late Lord Rothermere. The church and some adjoining buildings were slightly damaged in an air raid during March 1944, but have been repaired.

Nearly opposite is the Cock Tavern, which originally stood at No. 201 on the north side of the street, and was demolished in 1886 after an existence of more than three hundred years. The ancient sign of the Cock was set up again on the opposite side of the street in the present building, which was refronted some thirty years ago with a Tudor façade and set back two or three feet to conform to the new frontage of Fleet Street.

The widening of Fleet Street, like that of Ludgate Hill, was a long-drawn-out undertaking extending over a period of twenty years between 1897 and 1916, during which time practically the entire building line on the south side was set back between Ludgate Circus and the Temple Bar. To-day Fleet Street has a uniform width of sixty feet, the same as that of Ludgate Hill, and provides accommodation for four lines of traffic.

A start was made on the work in 1897 by rebuilding the three houses between Ludgate Circus and Bride Lane, including the Punch Tavern at the rear. This was followed in 1901 by the widening of the section between Bride Lane and Salisbury Court. Amongst other buildings then demolished were the former offices of *Punch*, situated on the east corner of St Bride's Avenue, and now removed to Bouverie Street. At the back of Fleet Street on the west side of Bride Lane is the Old Bell Tavern, which unfortunately was not included in the rebuilding of Fleet Street. Because of this defect the strip of land separating the Old Bell Tavern from Fleet Street is so narrow that only inferior buildings of a low elevation have been erected on this site, which have completely disfigured this part of Fleet Street.

For many years after 1901 progress was very slow, and only a few isolated buildings were set back to the new line of frontage. After 1911, when the handsome new building of the Norwich Union Insurance Society was erected at the west end of Fleet Street, the pace was accelerated, and by the end of 1916 practically all of the houses had been set back to the new building line. A few buildings still remained to be brought into conformity with the amended line of frontage, such as that of the Cock Tavern which only affected the width of the pavement, but with the solitary exception of Mooney's Irish House, which still protrudes about three feet beyond the amended building line, the widening of Fleet Street has long since been completed. As a result of this great improvement a new vista of St Dunstan's Church, hitherto concealed, has been opened up from Ludgate Circus.

Fleet Street lacks that uniformity in the height of its buildings which would be more pleasing to the eye, but its latest buildings are of a more imposing character and elevation. Although Fleet Street is to-day the centre of the newspaper industry, it did not start here until the nineteenth century. The *Morning Advertiser* came here in 1825 to No. 127 after an existence of thirty years in the Strand, and the *Daily Telegraph* was published at Peterborough Court in 1855. The tall and stately new buildings which have been erected on the north side of Fleet Street for the *Daily Telegraph* and the *Daily Express,* with their upper floors zoned back from the pavement, make some of the neighbouring buildings look very shabby. The *Daily Telegraph* is a very ornate building erected in 1930 with a stone façade rising to 120 feet and a row of circular columns extending from the third to the sixth floor. Its architects were Messrs Elcock and Sutcliffe and Messrs Burnet and Partners. The *Daily Express,* erected in 1932, has a glass front with its corners rounded off to admit additional light. It was designed by Messrs Ellis and Clerk. One wonders what the City fathers of a generation back would have said to the proposal to erect such lofty structures in the narrow Fleet Street of those days. The building next door to the *Daily Telegraph* now occupied by the *Liverpool Post* was originally the home of the *Standard,* which ceased publication during the first World War. Other fine buildings which have been erected of late years include Bouverie House and the Hulton Press offices a short distance west of the *Daily Telegraph* offices, and, on the south side, the *Chronicle* House and the adjoining Barclays Bank at the west corner of Salisbury Court.

Fleet Street is equally famous for its numerous taverns, where solicitors and journalists congregate for luncheon. In the olden days these taverns and coffee-houses were the Londoner's rendezvous, and those who wished to find any particular gentleman commonly inquired not whether he lived in Fleet Street or Chancery Lane, but whether he frequented the Grecian or the Rainbow. Some of these taverns have disappeared of late years but the Rainbow, first a coffee-house, then a tavern, has recently re-opened as an espresso coffee bar. In addition to those which we have already noticed, there is Peele's at the corner of Fetter Lane. A few doors farther east stood until 1936 Anderton's Hotel, once well known to commercial travellers and noted for City dinners and smoking concerts. The new Hulton Press building now stands in its place. The Hulton building is now occupied by the National Trade Press group of companies. Other well-known taverns include the Clachan on the other side of Fleet Street in Mitre Court, the King and Keys, and the world-renowned Cheshire Cheese, which is not really in Fleet Street at all but in Wine Office Court.

Fleet Street itself escaped serious damage in the blitz, but Sergeants' Inn, which stood at the back of the building of the Norwich Union Insurance Society and was reached through an archway, was completely destroyed in the air raid of 10 May 1941. Its original houses dated back a couple of centuries, but these had been mostly rebuilt in 1837 and its hall was occupied by the Church of England Sunday School Institute. It had been an inn in name only since 1793 when the sergeants quarrelled with the landlords, at that time the Dean and Chapter of York Minster. Sergeants' Inn and the offices of the Norwich Union Insurance Society have now been rebuilt.

A peculiarity of Fleet Street is the long unbroken stretch of buildings extending from Shoe Lane to Fetter Lane, without any side streets, but containing a veritable warren of courts and alleys, guaranteed to confuse even a regular frequenter who might be looking for, say, Johnson's Court, Bolt Court, or Gough Square. The house of Dr Johnson in Gough Square was purchased some years ago by Mr Cecil Harmsworth, and handed over by this gentleman as a gift in trust for the nation. It can now be visited at an admission fee of two shillings. Bouverie Street and Whitefriars Street, leading out of Fleet Street on the south side, are mainly devoted to the newspaper industry, as well as Tudor Street, which houses the Institute of Journalists and the head offices of the *Daily Mail.*

A detailed account of the glories of the Temple, situated between Fleet Street and the Victoria Embankment, away from the turmoil of the City traffic, cannot be included for want of space within these pages. This very delightful locality, boasting great antiquity, contains Gothic halls, interesting old buildings, lawns, dull old quadrangles, trees, and flower gardens, and the secluded Fountain Court with its rockeries and flowers. It bears all the appearance of some ancient university town, and is one of those pleasant surprises which only London seems able to reveal to the casual visitor familiar with the leading capital cities of the world. The Temple Church dates back to the year 1185, and the choir was finished in 1240. Restorations were carried out between 1839 and 1842 at a cost of £70,000. It was partially destroyed in the air raids of 1940, but has now been completely rebuilt. Pump Court, a cloistered little square centuries old was partly demolished in the air raid of 10 May 1941, including its archway and about half of its houses. The Middle Temple Library was also completely destroyed but the beautiful Hall, with its double hammerbeam roof, one of the finest of its period, still survives. Charles Lamb was born in Crown Office Row and Dr Johnson had rooms in the Inner Temple Lane, now covered by the modern Johnson's Buildings. Most of the war damage in the Temple has now been elegantly restored. In various parts of the Temple precinct framed maps in two colours have been affixed to the walls, showing the location of different buildings in both the Middle and Inner Temple, with helpful notes of historical interest. The Temple Church (both Round and Choir) is again open.

In Salisbury Square just off Fleet Street are the headquarters of the Church

Missionary Society, and also Salisbury Square House. Until some forty years ago this latter building was the Salisbury Hotel, once the great rendezvous of country squires and others concerned in agriculture. In Salisbury Square stood until 1940 Warwick House, the premises of Messrs Ward Lock & Company, the well-known firm of publishers, first established here in 1877. It was rebuilt in 1911 and included a handsome entrance hall and a fine mahogany staircase. The top floor was struck by a bomb on 27 December 1940 and destroyed. This was followed two nights later by the big fire-raid which destroyed about half of the remaining portion of the building. Kildare House, a new building for Van Den Berghs Ltd, now stands on this ground.

St Bride's Church at the back of Fleet Street was rebuilt by Sir Christopher Wren in the Italian style in 1680, and completed in 1703 at a cost of £11,400. The steeple, which was originally 234 feet high, was struck by lightning in 1764, and so damaged that it was deemed advisable to reduce its elevation by eight feet. This church was also damaged in the fire-raid of 29 December 1940, but it has now been rebuilt and was re-dedicated on 19 December 1957 in the presence of H. M. The Queen and Prince Philip. In 1952, during excavations connected with the rebuilding, remains of several earlier churches that stood on the site were revealed, and in the crypt a museum has been established which is unique because all the exhibits are seen in the place where they were found. Bride Lane contains the St Bride's Institute, consisting of a free library, reading and lecture rooms, a gymnasium, swimming-bath, and class-rooms for technical instruction.

The large block of offices now called Ludgate House at the northwest corner of Fleet Street and Ludgate Circus was until 1926 the head offices of Messrs Thomas Cook & Son, the well-known firm of tourist agents, who have since removed to Berkeley Street in the West End.

On the east side of Bouverie Street is the handsome building of the *News of the World,* the central portion of which is crowned by a square stone tower. Whilst the rebuilding of these premises was in progress, a perfectly formed crypt was discovered several feet below the ground level, which is supposed to have formed part of the old Whitefriars Monastery, founded in 1241. Across the marble and mosaic floor of the entrance hall, the builders have inserted stone slabs to mark the position of one of the buttresses of the monastery and part of the wall of the north aisle of the nave. In Britton's Court, Whitefriars Street, at the back of the *News of the World* premises, is a cell of the Carmelite Monastery, which may be seen upon application. On the south side of Fleet Street, covering the site between Salisbury Court and Bride Lane with a long frontage extending to Salisbury Square, now stands the large new building of the Press Association and Reuter's Telegraph Company. It is faced with stone and is nine storeys high with the two top floors zoned back a short distance from the pavement. It was erected between 1936 and 1938, and was designed by Sir E. Lutyens, R. A. in conjunction with Messrs Wimperis, Simpson and Guthrie. A handsome block of buildings erected in 1903 had previously covered the Fleet Street site. In Bridewell Place on a bombed site at back of New Bridge Street a large new office building, eight storeys high, called St Bridget's House, covers a part of the ground upon which formerly stood the Bridewell Prison.

A part of the bombed sites facing the north side of Ludgate Hill, including that of Messrs Benson's the jewellers and La Belle Sauvage Yard, was converted into the so-called Ludgate Gardens. Early in 1949 Mr Angus Darling conceived the idea of turning this, the worst and most conspicuous eyesore in the City, into temporary gardens. They were run as a commercial enterprise and were laid out by Mr Ian Walker of Godstone. There were about thirty exhibitors and here the public could buy all kinds of garden utensils and sports goods. The Ludgate Gardens site has now been built over by the new Hillgate House.

The blitzed area between Cannon Street and Watling Street, extending from St Paul's Churchyard to Friday Street, has now been levelled and here gardens are being laid out by the City Corporation. Our return journey from here to the Mansion House is by Ludgate Hill and Cannon Street, which we have already dealt with in our previous chapter.

Sixth Walk

Princes Street, Moorgate, London Wall, Finsbury Circus, Finsbury Square, Bunhill Fields, Chiswell Street, Fore Street, Barbican, Aldersgate Street and Gresham Street

We now take the last of our walks from the Mansion House. We have taken in turn each road leading from the hub of London, and we now turn into the last of these, Princes Street. Here, facing the west side of the Bank of England, are the National Provincial Bank and the huge new head offices of the Midland Bank, two of the so-called 'big five'. That situated on the corner of Princes Street and the Poultry, facing the Mansion House, is the nine-storey building of the National Provincial Bank of England. On the site now covered by these two latter banks stood a four-storey row of houses and offices erected about a hundred and twenty years ago, and faced with stucco. Until 1928 those corresponding to the site of the present Midland Bank in Princes Street were still standing, but the other portion of these houses, extending to the corner of the Poultry, were pulled down at least fifty years earlier to make way for the hand-some building of the Union Bank of London, now merged into the National Provincial Bank.

A survey of the foundations of this building, carried out in 1928 as a precaution against the possibility of its collapse, resulted in a decision to pull it down and erect the present modern building on this site. It was feared that the extensive excavations taking place on the adjoining site and at the Bank of England might otherwise result in this fine building sharing the fate of the Commercial Union Assurance Company in Cornhill, which fell down in August 1927.

On that portion of the site of the former Union Bank of London which faced Mansion House Street (that very short Street between Princes Street and St Mildred's Court), stood previously a very popular tavern known as the European. It was one of a row of brown-brick Georgian houses, and so brisk was business during the entire day at this establishment that freshly-drawn glasses of ale and stout stood ready on the counters for immediate consumption. There was also a huge demand for food snacks and sausage rolls, and one went in at one door and out at the other to avoid the crush of people.

In 1928 the City Corporation availed themselves of the opportunity thus afforded of purchasing a few feet of ground from the National Provincial Bank of England, to round off the sharp corner of the Poultry and Princes Street, at a cost of £78,000, a startling indication of the value of land in the heart of the metropolis.

The stately head offices of the Midland Bank, designed by Sir Edwin Lutyens, were completed in sections as the various leases expired and the necessary sites became available for rebuilding. Commenced in 1926, the entire building was not actually completed until twelve years later in 1938. The building is nine storeys high, with the upper floors zoned back from the street, like Lloyds Bank, and other buildings of the same period in the City and elsewhere. On a suitable promontory at either end of the building is the figure of a child embracing — or struggling with — a goose. These, it is said, are intended to remind us of the market that gave its name to 'Poultry'. The greater portion of the frontage to the Poultry was occupied until 1925 by the handsome building of the Gresham Life Assurance Company. This building was not more than half a century old at time of its demolition, but as the Midland Bank was particularly anxious to obtain this valuable site, it not only paid handsome compensation, but erected a new building for the Gresham Life Assurance Company in Fleet Street. St Mildred's Church, Poultry, one of the many which were rebuilt by Wren after the Great Fire of London, had previously stood on the site of the building of the Gresham Life Assurance Company, and was demolished in 1872.

Adjoining the Midland Bank in Princes Street is a block of red-brick buildings faced with stone dressings, containing premises. This rather attractive group bears the date 1891 and carries the arms of the Grocers' Company and their motto, 'God Grant Grace'. At the rear is a semi-circular drive leading to Grocers' Hall, which was badly damaged by fire in 1965 and has now been repaired.

At the corner of Gresham Street stood an elegant building occupied before the war by the Royal Bank of Canada. It curved round from Princes Street into Gresham Street and Old Jewry and was originally built in 1901 for the Governors of the Bank of England and was crowned with two stone towers. It was badly damaged in the blitz and a nine-storeyed building has now replaced it. Until 1901 the roadway in Gresham Street was very narrow at these crossroads, but in that year an extensive widening was carried out by the City Corporation at this corner, and a block of dark and gloomy houses was removed.

At the junction of Princes Street and Gresham Street begins Moorgate. This very important thoroughfare, constructed between 1835 and 1840, is a quarter of a mile long and about fifty feet in width, and connects Moorfields with the Bank of England. The construction of Moorgate followed upon that of King William Street as a matter of course, in order that a new direct thoroughfare could be opened from north to south connecting London Bridge with Islington, without passing by the narrow and inconvenient Coleman Street. It involved the clearance of dense masses of houses across Bell Alley and Swan Alley, which at that time extended through to Coleman Street. Already in 1740 Mr Robert Dingley, who designed the City Road, had planned a new street from Moorfields to the Bank, but strong opposition prevented this improvement.

For such an important undertaking the construction of Moorgate Street, like that of King William Street, appears to have excited little or no interest, and the multitude of historians and writers of London books have nothing to tell us on this subject. Yet strange to relate, there existed little over a century ago slum property within a stone's throw of the Bank of England, relics of which continued to exist for some time after the construction of Moorgate Street. In September 1856 two houses in Little Swan Alley running out of Coleman Street collapsed, burying the inmates and killing four persons. The floors of these houses were dilapidated and overcrowded with several families living in each room.

After the first World War, Moorgate Street was renamed Moorgate, and a similar alteration was made in the case of Bishopsgate Street. One wonders why the City Corporation did not also include Aldersgate Street and Newgate Street in this list of abbreviated names, or can it be that Newgate is too suggestive of unpleasant happenings to be included?

Moorgate, which formerly consisted of four-storey buildings fronted with stucco, has been rebuilt to such an extent since the first World War that, like King William Street, it can now almost be described as a new thoroughfare. Some of the buildings on the west side were destroyed in one of the German air raids over London in 1917, and these have been rebuilt with their upper storeys zoned back from the street. Others on both sides of the street are of more recent construction, and are chiefly occupied by banks and insurance companies. Special mention should be made of the Hall of the Institute of Chartered Accountants which may easily be missed, for it lies behind the east side of Moorgate. Built at the end of the 19th century, it is profusely decorated with columns and figures, while above the first floor windows along the Great Swan Alley and Moorgate Place frontages runs a stone frieze in low relief of over a hundred figures representing Arts and Crafts, Education, Building, etc. On the west side at the corner of Gresham Street, are the offices of the Northern Assurance Company, rebuilt about 1904, and adjoining them is Basildon House, once the home of the ill-fated London and Paris Exchange, which became known as the Vampire of Basildon House. Farther along are the new offices of the Provident Mutual Life Assurance Association.

Coleman Street, running parallel to Moorgate on the west side, was so named after Coleman, the first builder of that street. Tokenhouse Yard, the head-quarters of the estate market, is situated on the east side of Moorgate, and leads into Lothbury. It derives its name from the manufacture of tokens, which were the copper coinage of England prior to the reign of James I.

St Stephen's Church on the west side which faced Kings' Arms Yard was destroyed in the fire-raid of 29 December 1940. It was built by Sir Christopher Wren in 1676, but there had been earlier churches on this site since 1171. The site is now occupied by the new Swiss Bank Corporation building.

Further along Coleman Street, on the west wide, stood the Wool Exchange, recently demolished to make way for a new building called Woolgate House. The old Wool Exchange was an interesting building of 1874, and doubtless very up to date in its day. Outside, the capitals of its marble columns and the top of each window carried appropriate decoration in the form of sheep's heads, and the pediment over the main entrance displayed a full-size lamb. Inside, beneath a glass dome, a central iron staircase of criss-cross design rose to iron galleries leading to offices on the upper floors: the occupants complained that the building was cold in winter and too hot in summer. On the ground floor a confusion of corridors with quaint little shops led to salerooms where the bidding was rapid and competitive, while located in the basement was an extensive Mooney's Irish House which was very popular for quick lunches.

The old Wool Exchange had a certain musty charm, and one regrets its disappearance merely as a relic of the past; the wool brokers have now moved to more suitable accommodiaton in Brushfield Street, Spitalfields, where they use one of the sale rooms of the London Fruit Exchange.

At the north end of Coleman Street is the hall of the Company of Armourers and Brasiers.

We direct our attention next to London Wall, named from the wall which originally denoted the northern boundary of the City. A few words regarding the earlier history of this locality may prove of interest to our readers. The land immediately to the north of London Wall was originally a marsh or fen, and it is from this circumstance that the district received the name of Finsbury or Fensbury. This marsh appears to have acted as an obstacle to the movement of London towards the north, and thus largely accounts for the constant development of the Metropolis towards the west on a scale out of all proportion to the rate of expansion towards the north.

Only 180 years ago, when the population of this great metropolis was approaching a million inhabitants, and its houses already extended in an unbroken line from Hyde Park in the west to Mile End and Limehouse in the east, the district immediately north of London Wall was still very suburban, and large stretches of open fields were still to be seen no farther than half a mile from the Bank of England. The boundaries of the Fen or Great Moor were the City Wall on the south and the high ground near Islington on the north, and in olden times the young men of the City used to play on the ice when the Great Fen or Moor which watered the walls of the City was frozen. But according to Stow, the Lord Mayor caused the walls of the City to be broken towards the moor, and built the postern called Moorgate for the convenience of the citizens, to enable them to walk that way upon the causeways towards Isledon (Islington). Rubbish brought from the City through the nearest gates and posterns by degrees raised the surface, at all events of those parts next the City. From then onwards until the reign of Charles II, Finsbury Fields, as they were then called, were reserved as a grand arena for the use of the London archers. In 1512 Roger Ardley, mayor, made an attempt to drain the Fen, and in 1527 another mayor continued the good work by conveying the water over the City moat into the channel of the Walbrook, and thence to the Thames, so that by degrees the Fen was drained and made into hard ground.

But this handicap from which the City suffered in former times was destined in our own day to prove of inestimable advantage to its more recent development, for had there been no marsh or natural barrier in the past to check the growth of the City in this particular direction, this quarter of the town would have probably been covered with narrow streets and lanes in harmony with those of the neighbouring locality of an earlier age, instead of the existing wide streets and squares constructed in the early part of the nineteenth century. This has resulted in the erection of a large number of tall and very handsome buildings, amidst surroundings of plenty of light and fresh air, on a scale which, would never have been permitted in narrow streets. Moorfields or Finsbury, once a barren region, was first built on after the Great Fire of London, when all the City was topsy-turvy, and the poor homeless inhabitants were scattered broadcast from here as far as Highgate, some under tents and some in miserable huts and hovels, many without rag, bed, or board. Before that time Moorfields had been the drying-ground of London's laundresses, where acres of old linen were displayed.

The Great Fire of London was one such as had not been known in Europe since the conflagration of ancient Rome in the days of Nero. Nothing remained but stones and rubbish, all exposed to the open air, so that you could see from one end of the City almost to the other, and the City of London for the time being was almost comparable to what it looked like after its partial destruction in the second World War. Some 373 acres were burnt within the walls, including eighty-seven parish churches and 13,200 houses, contained in about four hundred streets and courts. Roughly, the flames destroyed an oblong area with its greatest length a mile and a half, and a depth of half a mile. The total value of property destroyed by the Fire was estimated at £10,000,000. It started on Sunday, 2 September 1666, in Pudding Lane near the Monument, and ended on Wednesday, 5 September, at Pie Corner near Smithfield, as we have already noted.

Although not cast in the heroic mould, King Charles II and his brother the Duke of York rendered great personal service on the day of London's tragedy, which could not be too highly valued. The supreme peril to the capital brought out in both of them a display of courage which intensified the loyalty towards the sovereign. The King, who was insensible to peril, paraded the City on horseback all day long, praying the populace not to resort to vengeful measures, and did much to calm them after the Fire was over. He and the Duke of York stood ankle-deep in water for many hours together, while they handled buckets with as much diligence as the poorest man, thus creating a good moral effect on the people, and causing them to work steadily with such good fellow-labourers.

The rush of people after the Fire was chiefly into Moorfields and Finsbury Fields. London resembled a city which had been sacked by some conqueror and left burning, and the rough camp of refugees extended as far as Islington and Highgate on the north and to St Giles's Fields and Soho on the west. Fortunately the weather at the time was warm and fine, otherwise the distress would have been very much greater than it actually was.

After the Fire the damage was so quickly repaired that Burnet said that to 'the amazement of all Europe London was in four years rebuilt with so much beauty and magnificence, that he who saw it in both states before and after the Fire cannot reflect on in without wondering where the wealth could be found to bear so vast a loss as was made by the Fire, and so prodigious an expense as was laid out in the rebuilding of the City'. The inscription on the south side of the Monument reduces this period to *three* years, but the late W. G. Bell in *The Great Fire of London* regards both claims as far too optimistic.

Before the Great Fire the houses were mostly of wood, with their upper stories projecting in overhanging floors in such a way as to impede the free circulation of air in the narrow streets except when high winds prevailed. People in the garrets could almost shake hands across from window to window, and so low were the rooms that a tall man with his hat on could hardly stand upright. In the reign of James I the precincts of the Court were so filthy that the ladies attending it complained of bringing away lice with them.

But it is time to proceed on our walk. The south side of London Wall contains the new Carpenters' Hall, adjoining Throgmorton Avenue, the Talbot Tavern, and several good office buildings. The Carpenters' Hall was destroyed on the night of 10-11 May 1941. The new building, the entrance hall of which is lavishly decorated with wood panelling of various kinds, was opened on 23 July 1956 by the Lord Mayor, Sir Cuthbert Ackroyd, 'Citizen and Carpenter'. Until the dawn of the present century, the buildings lining the south side were greatly superior to those on the north side, and could properly be regarded as the boundary line between wealth and poverty. Some of these are quite modern, notably those in the vicinity of Throgmorton Avenue. This is a modern thoroughfare which was commenced in 1876 and leads from London Wall into Throgmorton Street. Its site was previously covered by Carpenters' Buildings and a section of the Carpenters'Hall. This was removed for the construction of the new avenue and rebuilt at the corner of London Wall. The neighbouring Copthall Avenue which runs parallel to Throgmorton Avenue was formed in 1890 and covers the site of Leathersellers' Buildings and Little Bell Alley. The original buildings on the north side of London Wall replaced the old Bethlehem Hospital pulled down in 1814 and removed to St George's Fields, Lambeth, in 1815. They were originally private houses which in course of time had been converted into shops with a raised pavement approached by steps.

In front of the old Bethlehem Hospital, overlooking Moorfields, was an open space divided by gravel paths into four quadrangles planted with elm-trees. It was so much frequented by fashionable citizens as to obtain the appellation of the City Mall. After the removal of Bethlehem Hospital the square garden was converted into a circular one and laid out as Finsbury Circus in 1819. A short street opening into London Wall was then constructed across the centre of the ground occupied by the Bethlehem Hospital. It was not until several years later that the whole of the land fronting Finsbury Circus was let for building purposes, but afterwards it became a good-class residential centre, as did Finsbury Square, which was then the fashionable medical quarter of London.

By the end of the nineteenth century the north side of London Wall had become occupied by traders of a humble kind, and when the City Corporation decided to develop this property, there was a great uproar and many heated debates took place at the Guildhall. It was contended by those who opposed the scheme that if carried out it would bring widespread ruin and deal a death-blow to the trade of the district. But instead of this happening, the Corporation obtained for the estate a ground-rent far exceeding even their most sanguine expectations. The City was ready to expand and absorb additional office accommodation, and far from bringing ruin the development of London Wall placed it on a level with Threadneedle Street and Broad Street. Huge new buildings were erected and occupied by some of the largest financial companies in the City, with frontages to both London Wall and Finsbury Circus, which have given to this district an architectural dignity second to that of no other.

The huge island block of buildings comprising Salisbury House and Electra House, erected between 1899 and 1901, is enclosed by London Wall, Moorgate, and the south-west corner of Finsbury Circus. The south-eastern corner, also forming an island site with frontages to London Wall and Blomfield Street, is covered by the equally imposing London Wall Buildings, erected in 1901 and 1902, thus completing the reconstruction of the whole of the south side of Finsbury Circus and the greater part of the north side of London Wall. East of Blomfield Street, in London Wall, is the church of All-Hallows-on-the-Wall, built by Dance in 1765, in place of an earlier one which escaped the Great Fire and was pulled down in 1764. This was badly damaged in the war, but has been repaired and now, relieved of parochial duties, is open as a Guild Church.

In 1901 the City Corporation availed themselves of the opportunity of widening London Wall, which was set back about ten feet on the north side. They also acquired the gardens of Finsbury Circus as an open space for the general public, a boon which has been very much appreciated by City workers. The western section of London Wall between Moorgate and Wood Street was completely destroyed in the fire-raid of 29 December 1940.

The large block of buildings on the north-east side of Finsbury Circus was constructed in 1920 by the City of London Real Property Company, and extended through into Eldon Street. On the north-west corner is Britannic House, erected in 1922-24, an elegant building extending through to Moorgate, and including the site above the Northern Line Railway station of the tube between Moorgate and Finsbury Park. It is the headquarters of British Petroleum and was designed by Sir Edwin Lutyens, R.A. Adjoining Britannic House is River Plate House, formerly the London offices of the Buenos Aires and Great Southern Railway, which also extends through into Eldon Street.

The headquarters of British Petroleum have moved from the Britannic House mentioned above to a new building in Moor Lane, on the other side of Moorgate. The name of Britannic House has also been transferred to this new colossus which, being 400 feet high with 35 floors above ground level is (at the moment) the tallest building in the City of London.

Next to River Plate House stood until 1936 the London Institution, erected in 1819 by Mr William Brooks, and containing a double tier of Doric columns. It was originally built to provide an extensive library and a reading-room where foreign and domestic periodicals could be obtained by subscribers, and for the diffusion of knowledge by means of lectures. The London Institution was the only surviving building of the original Finsbury Circus, and accommodated the School of Oriental Studies, affiliated to London University. It was pulled down in 1936 and a new block of offices nine storeys high has now been erected on this site.

Returning to Moorgate, of which the northern extremity, from Ropemaker Street to Chiswell Street and Finsbury Square, is known as Finsbury Pavement, beyond London Wall on the east side are the City of London College and Binsbury Pavement House. Opposite is Moorgate Hall, a block of shops and offices erected in 1914 which extends through to Moorfields, a short street but important on account of the Moorgate terminus of the old Metropolitan Railway, which was opened in 1865. It was very badly bombed, but the pillared and pedimented entrance still stands.

At the northern end of Moorgate is Finsbury Square, the west side of which before its destruction in the air raids of 1940 comprised a row of four-storey houses built in 1777, and formerly known as Moore Place, after Mr Moore, a manufacturer who lived in one of them. They have all been replaced by a large block of offices. The other three sides of the square were built in 1789, 1790, and 1791, and Mr George Augustus Toole, writing in the *New British Traveller,* published about 1790, stated that Finsbury Square when completed would form with Moore Place one of the noblest squares in or out of the metropolis. About the commencement of the nineteenth century Malcolm vaunts Finsbury Square as a modern concentration of City opulence quite equal to the West End of the town in the splendour of its houses and furniture. It was the last relic of the ancient Finsbury Fields to be covered with buildings, but during the present century nearly all of it has been rebuilt on a sumptuous scale. None of the original buildings which fronted Finsbury Square now remain.

One wonders what Mr Malcolm and Mr Toole would say to Royal London House, the stately edifice of the London Friendly Society, which now adorns the north side of the square, with its lofty tower, 220 feet high and surmounted by a life-sized figure of Mercury as a symbol of progress, forming a prominent landmark when viewed from Moorgate. Or the imposing building of the London and Manschester Assurance Company with frontages to both Finsbury Square and Moorgate and the City Gage House on the south side. Perhaps they might have commented unfavourably upon the remains of Moore Place, in the midst of the new surrounding splendour, but a modern nine-storey block of offices now adorns the west side of Finsbury Square. The east side contains the new offices of the Maypole Dairy Company and also Finsbury Square House and doubtless in a few years' time the entire square will have been rebuilt.

During the second World War a large air-raid shelter was constructed under

18   The Monument to the Great Fire, completed in 1676; in the distance is its modern rival in height, the Post Office Tower.

19   A contrast in office fenestration: Albert Buildings of 1870 and the new Temple Court in Queen Victoria Street.

20 The discovery of a Roman pavement in the Poultry during the construction of Queen Victoria Street in 1869.

21 In 1688 the Panyer Alley Boy marked the highest ground in the City. He is now near St Paul's.

22 The Central Criminal Court (The Old Bailey).

23 Blackfriars Underpass and the Bridgehead Improvement scheme, designed to relieve traffic congestion, were opened in 1967.

24 Ludgate Circus in 1895. Buildings to the right of and beyond the bridge were completely demolished in the Second World War.

25 New office buildings round St Paul's. No 1 is Juxon House which, it is alleged, obscures the western perspective of the cathedral. No 6 is St Vedast Foster, No 8 Bank of England, New Change, and No 9 the site where the new Cathedral Choir School stands. The remainder are commercial 'houses'.

27 St Bartholomew's Hospital, founded in 1123.

26. This statue of Captain John Smith, 'sometime Governor of Virginia and Admiral of New England,' stands near St Mary-le-Bow, Cheapside.

29 The central 'sunburst' of the Astronomical Clock on the *Financial Times* building is said to represent Sir Winston Churchill.

28 The *Daily Mirror* building, Holborn Circus.

30 'Within the parish of St Andrew by the Wardrobe with St Anne, Blackfriars.' *The Times* building in Queen Victoria Street.

31 The Guildhall in 1831.

32   King Edward VII and Queen Alexandra (as Prince and Princess of Wales) driving through Temple Bar in 1863.

33   Furnival's Inn, demolished in 1898; the site of the present head offices of the Prudential Assurance Company.

34 Cheapside in the 1890s. Opposite Bow Church is the famous plane tree, still growing at the corner of Wood Street.

35 Ely House, of which only the chapel still remains.

the gardens of Finsbury Square when its railings were also removed for the war effort. Having been cleared of its war-time debris, the square has now been laid out as a public garden with grass lawns; below ground is a car park for 400 vehicles.

At the back of the west side of Finsbury Square are the headquarters and drill-ground of the Honourable Artillery Company, the oldest military body in the Kingdom, formed in 1537 under the title of the Guild or Fraternity of St George. Before the blitz its grounds were concealed from the public view by houses which surrounded them on every side. Close by in City Road were the headquarters of the London Rifle Brigade, but they have now moved to Sun Street, Finsbury. At the junction of City Road and Tabernacle Street, near Finsbury Square, a handsome building has been erected by Messrs Singer, the well-known sewing-machine firm. Fore Street, leading from Moorgate to Jewin Street, near the church of St Giles, Cripplegate, formerly consisted of warehouses but practically the entire street was destroyed in the fire-raid of 29 December 1940 when unfortunately the water supply ran out. It was in Fore Street at 12.15 a.m. on 25 August 1940 that the first bomb fell on the City of London. A new office building, Roman House, stands on this spot.

On the west side of City Road, just beyond the Artillery Ground, is Bunhill Fields (a contraction of bone hill), once the chief burial-place of Nonconformists. Near the central walk is the recently restored tomb of John Bunyan, with a recumbent figure put there in 1862. It also contains an obelisk to Daniel Defoe. Bunhill Fields was used as a Dissenters' Burial Ground from 1665, and in 1549 it had served as a place of deposit for a thousand cartloads of human bodies brought here from the charnel-house of St Paul's. In 1741 it was enclosed with a brick wall at the sole charge of the City of London, and subsequently leased to several of the great Dissenting sects who objected to the burial-service in the Book of Common Prayer. It was closed for further burials in 1852, when more than 120,000 bodies had been interred therein, and in 1869 was 'planted and restored for public resort'.

Bunhill Fields has frequently been confused with the 'Great Plague Pit' mentioned by Daniel Defoe in his *Journal of the Plague Year,* but this, it is contended, lies further north. Recent improvements by the City Corporation have cleared a transverse section in the centre, which allows John Bunyan's tomb to be examined more closely. The obelisk over Defoe's grave may be seen, also the gravestone of William Blake – though this is not in its original position. Previously, the public were restricted to a narrow railed-in path straight through the ground, but a large space on the north side has now been cleared of undecipherable tombstones and laid out as a public garden.

On the west side of the burial-ground is Bunhill Row, which connects Old Street with Chiswell Street. Before its destruction in the air raids of 1940 it consisted principally of warehouses. The west side was until recently a mass of luxuriant bomb-site vegetation, but is now replaced by the new City College for Further Education. Opened in 1965, the college consists of a group of three buildings containing a four-storey teaching block and assembly and dining sections linked at first floor level by open bridges. On the lower ground floor are fully-equipped workshops. The remainder of the site is occupied by Northampton Hall—a hall of residence, with 500 study-bedrooms—for students of the Northampton College of Advanced Technology.

Further north is the Bunhill Row-Banner Street development of the Greater London Council, comprising a new tower block of 18 storeys, plus two others of lower elevation, which together provide accommodation for 184 families.

On the east side a range of new offices with a frontage of about 120 yards is occupied by various Government departments. These offices back on to the H. A. C. Drill Ground. A warehouse stood on the site of a house, No. 124, where Milton wrote part of *Paradise Lost,* and here also he died in 1674. Nearly the entire quarter of the City bounded by Coleman Street, Moorfields and the grounds of the Honourable Artillery Company on the east side and by Aldersgate Street and Goswell Road on the west side, by Gresham Street on the south and extending almost to Old Street on the north side, was destroyed in the blitz. Almost every building has been demolished. This vast area includes the western section of London Wall, Wood Street, Fore Street, Jewin Street, Jewin Crescent and nearly all the east side of Aldersgate Street. It also includes the Barbican, a part of Chiswell Street, the whole of Red Cross Street and Golden Lane and Bunhill Row. Nothing like this has been seen in London since the Great Fire of 1666. Standing proudly by itself in the midst of this devastated area was the tower of St Giles Cripplegate Church, which, except for some damage to its turret in August, 1940, survived, though the church itself suffered severely in the fires of 29 December 1940. Another prominent landmark amongst the ruins is the huge building of Whitbread's Brewery, which although damaged in the blitz has escaped destruction. It is three hundred years old and was visited by George III and Queen Charlotte.

It is within this area that the Barbican Redevelopment Scheme of the City Corporation and the Greater London Council is in progress.

The Barbican site, one of the largest war-damaged areas to be comprehensively developed, covers almost 62 acres between Moorgate and Aldersgate Street, east and west, and from the Guildhall to the City Boundary near Fann Street, south to north. About 22 acres are allotted to an office zone, with a 'sentinel' block of 35 storeys, six blocks of twenty storeys and a number of lower buildings. In addition to offices and warehouses, this zone will include shops, restaurants, livery hall, an Underground station and the new Museum of London which, it is understood will eventually combine the collections at Basinghall Street and Kensington Palace and, one hopes, the residue still at Lancaster House. The remaining 40 acres of this project are intended for the creation of a residential population of 120,000 that today is a mere 5,000. This housing zone will have three triangular towers, each of 44 storeys, five of eight storeys and various other buildings which together will provide 2,100 flats and maisonettes, a theatre, concert hall and an art gallery. New buildings are planned for the Guildhall

School of Music and the City of London School for Girls (the foundation stone of this was laid by the Lord Mayor in 1965). A modern feature of the Barbican Area will be the high level walkways — sometimes called pedways — to separate the pedestrians from the traffic. The whole scheme is expected to be completed by 1971.

The new building in Old Street, combining a 16-storey office tower with shops and council dwellings, and extending from Bath Street to City Road, stands on the site of St Luke's Hospital. The hospital (for mental patients) was established at Moorfields in 1751, but the building, which has just been demolished, was built by George Dance the Younger in 1784. Prior to its demolition it was the Bank of England printing works.

St Luke's Church on the same side of Old Street is a building of stone which is crowned by a tall obelisk of grey stone. For many years there was some uncertainty about the identity of the weather vane which surmounts the obelisk. On the assumption that it represented a parasitic insect, the church has always been known as 'Lousy St Lukes'. But when the vane was brought down for repairs a few years ago, the 'louse' was found to be a harmless dragon with a forked tongue and tail of flames. St Luke's Church has now been vacated, as the foundations were found to be sinking. It is hoped that the tower with its unique obelisk may be preserved.

A walk through Whitecross Street will bring us to Chiswell Street, close to which is Whitbread's Brewery. Whitecross Street is a popular street market, restricted during the week to the middle of the day. The continuation of Chiswell Street opposite goes under the name of Beech Street, and leads to the Barbican, so called from a watch-tower for the defence of London, the remains of which still existed until towards the end of the eighteenth century. Here also Milton resided between 1645 and 1647, and published his English and Latin poems. The streets in this locality are fairly wide and before the blitz were principally covered with warehouses, but reveal little of interest to the visitor.

Bridgewater Square to the north of the Barbican is a tiny open space with a small public garden in the centre. It commemorates the residence of the Earls of Bridgewater. The two elder sons of the third earl were burnt to death here with their tutor in 1687. Golden Lane runs northwards from the Barbican and Redcross Street southwards to Fore Street and St Giles Cripplegate Church. Fore Street was the birthplace of Daniel Defoe in 1661, and before their destruction in the blitz consisted principally of warehouses. In Golden Lane the Finsbury Borough Council completed in 1962 a seven-acre housing estate with accommodation for 1400 people. There are nine separate blocks, of which the tallest, Great Arthur House of 16 storeys, was the highest in Britain when built. The usual amenities are provided, including central heating and, as in the Barbican area, separation of man and machine ensures the safety of the pedestrian.

St Giles Cripplegate is the church dedicated to the Hermit of the Rhone, who was the especial saint of cripples and lepers. It escaped the Great Fire of 1666, but was very nearly involved in that which occured in Jewin Street in 1897.

John Milton was buried in St Giles in 1674. A fine bronze statue by Horace Mountford which stood in the churchyard was blown off its pedestal during the raids and is temporarily standing in the entrance hall of the nearby Cripplegate Institute. Until recently, as previously mentioned, the tower of St Giles stood proudly by itself among all the surrounding devastation, a landmark for miles around. Today, however, the scenery has changed so much that St Giles frequently disappears as one walks round — obscured by one or other of the new cloud-capped office towers. Considerable war damage repairs to the church have been effected; the upper part of the tower has been made good and the walls and roof renewed. £40,000 are still needed to complete the restoration, but the church is open again and is at present being shared by the clergy and congregation of the ill-fated St Lukes, Old Street. At the western end of London Wall is the disused churchyard of St Alphage, situated on the north side of the road, and here a section of the original London Wall is still revealed to the passer-by. This church was demolished in 1923, but part of the 14th century tower is preserved.

Jewin Street, which leads from Redcross Street into Aldersgate Street, was the scene of what was perhaps the greatest fire which had occurred in the City of London proper since 1666. This occurred in November 1897, causing damage to the extent of £1,000,000. The fire, which started about one o'clock in the afternoon, consumed most of the buildings in Jewin Street, Jewin Crescent, Hamsell Street, and Australian Avenue, and was not got under control until nearly midnight.

We pass next into Aldersgate Street. This thoroughfare is so named from the northern gate of the City, the name of which in turn is derived from the alder-trees which once grew around the gate. Aldersgate, which resembled Temple Bar, was removed in 1761, and two pillars erected here in 1874 marked the northern limit of the City, where Aldersgate becomes Goswell Road. The pillars have disappeared, but a City Corporation plaque records that a drinking fountain was erected here in 1878 in memory of Robert Besley, Lord Mayor 1869-70. It was removed in 1934. The first section of the new 'Route Eleven', an extension of London Wall as far as Aldersgate Street, was opened by Princess Marina, then Duchess of Kent on 7 July 1959. This, the first new main thoroughfare to be created in London since the opening of Kingsway in 1906, runs across the north side of the City where some 120 acres were laid waste by enemy action. The portion that is now open (provided with underground garages) enters Aldersgate almost opposite Little Britain. The ultimate intention is to provide a through road from Aldgate to Ludgate Circus. On this new section of London Wall, near Aldermanbury, a new Hall has been built for the Worshipful Company of Brewers ('In God is all our trust').

Fifty years ago Aldersgate Street was a shabby thoroughfare, but during our own century it has greatly increased in importance. Unfortunately, most of it was destroyed in the war, and the east side is being rebuilt as part of the Barbican scheme. On the west side is the church of St Botolph, Aldersgate, one of three of that dedication in the City. Built in 1790, and the third on that site, it is not very attractive externally, but the interior is elegant. In 1954 it became a Guild Church and devotes special attention to the problem of after-care of discharged prisoners.

The churchyard, with additional ground, is now a public garden, popularly known as 'Postman's Park', from its proximity to the General Post Office. At the far end is an open loggia with seats and a number of memorial plaques commemorating brave deeds of self-sacrifice in everyday life — a conception of the Victorian artist G. F. Watts. A statue of Sir Robert Peel, founder of the Metropolitan Police, originally erected in busy Cheapside, has found a refuge here.

By Aldersgate Street Station, Carthusian Street leads to Charterhouse Square. On the north side of the square, just outside the City boundary, is The Charterhouse, which takes its name from a Carthusian Priory founded here in 1371. After the suppression of the monasteries there were changes in ownership and modifications of the buildings until 1611, when it was purchased by Thomas Sutton, a wealthy merchant who by his will established a home of refuge for 80 old men and a school for (at first) 40 poor boys. Today, the number of distressed gentlemen, or 'brethren', in residence is reduced to 35 and Charterhouse School, which was removed to Godalming, Surrey, in 1872, is now one of the foremost public shools. W. M. Thackeray was among the many illustrious pupils of the school, which figures in *The Newcomes* as 'Greyfriars', where Colonel Newcome was both an ex-pupil and later a 'poor brother'.

During excavations preliminary to the repair and rebuilding following the severe bomb-damage suffered in May, 1941, the grave containing the lead coffin of the founder, Sir Walter Manny, who died in 1372, was revealed. This and other discoveries compensated in some small measure for the losses sustained by this secluded retreat in the heart of busy London.

Returning to Aldersgate Street, on the east side in Shaftesbury Place is the splendid new hall of the Ironmongers' Company, which escaped destruction in the blitz, and at the corner of Gresham Street close to St-Martin's-le-Grand stands an imposing block of buildings called Alder House and Falcon House, erected in 1923. Until 1845 Gresham Street was called Maiden Lane as far as Wood Street, Lad Lane farther east, and Cateaton Street from Aldermanbury to Lothbury. It has been considerably widened both at the western end as a result of the rebuilding of St-Martin's-le-Grand, and at the eastern end opposite Old Jewry and Lothbury. At the corner of Gresham Street and Noble Street is the pretty little church of St Anne and St Agnes, once affectionately known as 'St Anne in the Willows'. Though not severely damaged in the war, its fate was for some time uncertain but it has recently been completely restored and is now a Lutheran church for the use of Latvian and Esthonian expatriates. While the east side of Noble Street has several new office buildings, on the west side, near the church, one may still see very clearly remains of the corner turret and west wall of the Roman Fort, brought to light by the excavations conducted by Professor W. F. Grimes and the Roman and Medieval London Excavation Council. Following the line of the fort wall (which was built about a hundred years before the Roman/*town* wall), an interesting section of *both* walls together may be seen.

Wood Street, the principal thoroughfare leading out of Cheapside, is a narrow street which previous to the destruction of nearly all its buildings in the blitz was the centre of the leading wholesale dry-goods establishments. The church of St Alban was destroyed in the blitz except for its bare walls and Gothic style tower, rebuilt in 1685 by Sir Christopher Wren. The widening of the street due to rebuilding has left the surviving tower standing almost in the middle of the road. On the grounds that it was an obstruction, an attempt was made to obtain parliamentary sanction to demolish it, but the new Wood Street police station at the corner of Love Lane has been set back in a most praiseworthy manner that widens the road and allows traffic to pass on either side of the church tower. On the west corner of Wood Street and Gresham Street stood the Haberdashers' Hall, which was rebuilt in 1862-64 at a cost of £30,000. This also was completely destroyed in the air raids, but has now been rebuilt.

Going down Wood Street from Cheapside, a little alley on the right leads us into Mitre Court, a rectangular space surrounded by office buildings. In the middle of the Court is a glazed iron canopy topped by a great old square lamp. This century-old canopy covers the entrance to the cellars of Messrs Norton & Langridge, Wine Merchants. The cellars are beneath the flagstones of Mitre Court and are the original underground dungeons of the old Wood Street Compter. This was a Debtors' Prison, first established in 1555, burnt down in the Great Fire, but rebuilt in 1670 and finally closed in 1790. The original window-less cells can still be seen, together with chains, fetters and iron-studded doors.

Running parallel to Wood Street to the east is Aldermanbury, so called from the ancient court or burg of Aldermen, and in a quiet tree-shaded corner in this street stood the church of St Mary Aldermanbury, erected by Sir Christopher Wren in 1677 but destroyed in a fire-raid on 29 December 1940, except for the bare walls and the tower. It occupied the site of an earlier church which appears to have stood for over five hundred years, but which was destroyed in the Great Fire of 1666. The infamous Judge Jeffreys was buried in this church. In the churchyard, crowned by a bust of Shakespeare, is a marble memorial to John Heminge and Henry Condell, friends of and fellow-actors with Shakespeare, who edited the 'First Folio' in 1623. They lived many years in the parish and are both buried here. The tower and walls of St Mary Aldermanbury (some 700 tons) have now been dismantled and shipped to the United States, where they were re-erected to form the chapel of Westminster College in the University of Fulton, Missouri, as a memorial to the late Sir Winston Churchill. In Oat Lane, opposite Love Lane, is the little churchyard of St Mary Staining, destroyed in the Great Fire of 1666; now a quiet oasis with garden seats for the comfort of the weary walker. Adjoining is the new Pewterers' Hall, opened in 1961, behind which is the churchyard of St Olave, Silver Street. Set in the wall is a stone which, beneath a grim outline of a death's head and crossbones, records that the church was 'destroy'd by the Dreadfull Fire in the year 1666.'

Farther east, at the corner of Gresham Street and Basinghall Street, is the Gresham College founded under the will of Sir Thomas Gresham. It was rebuilt in 1913 at a cost of £34,000. Basinghall Street, the centre of the wool market, is named, together with Bassishaw Ward, after the Bassings who resided close by in the reign of King Edward III. Basinghall Street and the neighbouring Coleman Street suffered unusually little damage from the air raids and most of their buildings have escaped destruction. Between Coleman Street and Moorgate a considerable widening of Gresham Street has been carried out by the City Corporation and amongst other new buildings erected on this site is the Swiss Bank. Our route from here back to the Mansion House is the same as that already described, either by way of Princes Street or through Old Jewry and Cheapside.

Seventh Walk

From Temple Bar to the Law Courts, Strand, Aldwych, Kingsway, Lincoln's Inn, Great Queen Street, Drury Lane, and Catherine Street

We have completed our walks along the spokes radiating from the central hub of the City, and we shall now have to begin our walks from various points. That quarter of the metropolis which we first propose to explore, situated between Temple Bar and Wellington Street, has been so completely transformed during the past century that with the exception of the two surviving churches of St Clement Danes and St-Mary-le-Strand, not a trace remains to show the present-day Londoner what this quarter was like in the time of Dr Johnson.

At the beginning of the nineteenth century a big clearance had been made in the immediate vicinity of Temple Bar by the removal of Butchers' Row, a street of tenements at the back of St Clement Danes Church and the Strand, so named from the butchers' shambles located there. In its earlier history it had even been celebrated as the residence of ambassadors and other eminent persons. These slums were removed through the efforts of Alderman Pickett, and on account of their narrowness were nicknamed the Straits of St Clements. They were the bane of ancient London, and here the Plague once frowned destruction on the miserable inhabitants and reserved its force for the renewed attacks of each returning summer.

The site of Butchers' Row is now the east side of the Strand opposite St Clement Danes Church, but was originally called Pickett Street after the Alderman. The improvements carried out by Alderman Pickett between 1790 and 1815 included the removal of a block of buildings which occupied the site now forming the wide opening on the west side of the old Temple Bar. The north side consisted of shops with wide extended fronts, and the western side was bounded by the vestry room and almshouses of St Clement Danes parish. At that time the view of St Clement Danes Church was almost concealed but the churchyard is now surrounded by an oval railing. In connexion with this improvement the south side of this part of the Strand was rebuilt and considerably widened.

Until April 1846 a relic of old London stood in the Strand, adjoining the west side of the Temple Bar. When Alderman Pickett did away with Butchers' Row and other adjoining tenements, this venerable domicile, consisting of a fried-fish shop, was left as the sole representative of their decayed glories. It was without decoration, but was noticeable because it displayed the last of the open projecting stalls which were a feature of the better-class shops of three hundred years ago. The neighbouring Temple Bar was said to have been a full century younger, having been erected in 1672.

The Law Courts, situated on the north side of the Strand opposite the Temple, occupy a space of eight acres, in the clearance of which some thirty-three streets, courts, and alleys containing 343 dwelling-houses, chambers, and lodging-houses were demolished in 1866-68; also some warehouses, stables, and printing offices, making a total of four hundred buildings of all kinds. During the course of the work one of the houses scheduled for demolition in the Strand, occupied by Professor Holloway and his patent pills, fell down of its own accord. But as a wooden hoarding had already been erected nobody was injured, and the police, observing a crack in the wall, stopped the traffic until the danger was past.

The total resident population of the cleared area was stated to be 4,125, and this colony presented a picture of the misery of an overcrowded district filled with human beings huddled together in houses in the last stages of neglect and decay. One contributing cause of this deplorable overcrowding was the dispensing of charity in the shape of coals, tea, bread, sugar, and other general necessaries for the poor. No sooner were these charities distributed, usually at Christmas time, than there would follow an exodus of about one-half of the population, many of whom came from St Giles's and took a room here solely for the purposes of obtaining coals. Finally it was resolved to restrict the charity tickets to people who had resided for not less than twelve months in the parish.

The Law Courts, which have a frontage of 483 feet to the Strand and a depth of 470 feet from north to south, were built between 1874 and 1882 in the Decorated Gothic style by G. E. Street, R. A., who never lived to see the completion of this his greatest work. It was finished by his son, A. E. Street, assisted by Sir Arthur Blomfield. Previous to the construction of the present buildings, the Law Courts were divided between Lincoln's Inn and Westminster.

The actual buildings cover a site of five and a half acres and the architecture is mainly Gothic. The principal feature is the magnificent Central Hall, which in dimensions is about equal to the nave of a first-class English cathedral. In height and width it comes between those of York and Lincoln, being 82 feet high by 48 wide and 231 feet long. Also prominent in the design are the clock-tower, 160 feet high, and the screen of arches fronting the Strand, but this otherwise noble pile of buildings is spoiled by the absence of the western extension and tower to balance that of the eastern side. It is obvious that the architect intended this to be built, and space was reserved to meet that future requirement. Instead of the Law Courts being entirely completed, the ground on the west side was laid out as a public garden on the understanding that should it be required at some future date for the completion of the Law Courts, it was to be surrendered for that purpose. In 1911 a considerable portion of this ground was appropriated for the construction of four additional courts, and what still remains of this open space is now used as a parking-ground for motor-cars and is so small and inconsequential that it might just as well be surrendered also for all the loss which would be felt by the very limited number of people who are able to use it, so restricted is the accommodation for cars. This would enable the Law Courts to be completed by the construction of the western wing and the missing tower.

The main building, which encloses two quadrangles, was begun in 1874 and was opened by Queen Victoria in great state in 1882. It is bounded on the east by Bell Yard, on the west by Clement's Inn, and on the north by Carey Street. The four additional courts were added by Sir H. Tanner, and strong-rooms and storage space in the basement that were used as air-raid shelters during the last war have recently been rebuilt to furnish a further six more or less permanent courts, so that there are now twenty-nine courts in all and 1,100 rooms. The main frontage of the building is of stone, but the part fronting the quadrangle and Bell Yard is a mixture of red brick and stone. At first the space acquired was deemed insufficient, and notice was given by the Commissioners of their intention to take 267,800 square feet of additional ground on the site of Clement's Inn, Dane's Inn, Chancery Lane, and New Square, Lincoln's Inn, and Portugal Street, all to the north of Carey Street, but this extra ground was never purchased. During the air raids of 1940 the quadrangles of the Law Courts were damaged but the main frontage in the Strand escaped destruction.

Meanwhile, an entirely different site, on the newly-constructed Thames Embankment, had been proposed in 1869 by Sir Charles Trevelyan for the new Law Courts. This scheme involved the appropriation of the ground between the Temple and Somerset House, so that all the principal Inns of Court should be located near the new Palace of Justice. The space already cleared on the north side of the Strand was to have been covered with quadrangles of buildings devoted to offices for solicitors, which it was contended would have been an enormous convenience to them. At that time the site between the Strand and the Embankment was occupied by inferior houses, including those formerly existing in Essex Street, Arundel Street, and Norfolk Street, with their adjacent squalid courts and alleys, long since rebuilt.

No finer site could well have been selected in all London for the new Law Courts, and the fact that the greater part of the land required belonged to the Duke of Norfolk would have facilitated its purchase. The transfer of the Society of Lincoln's Inn to Somerset House was regarded as quite feasible, and King's College was to have been removed to Lincoln's Inn. This scheme, however agreeable to the Inns of Court near the river, might not have appealed to the Benchers of Gray's Inn, 'up in the country', north of Holborn.

Finally, the Chancellor of the Exchequer, whilst admitting the superiority of the Embankment site from a purely architectural point of view, considered nevertheless that its adoption would have created an intolerable congestion of traffic in Fleet Street and the Strand, then much narrower than at present, by vehicles crossing from Holborn to the Law Courts, and that on the whole he regarded the Carey Street site as the more suitable of the two. As a result of the delay in arriving at a decision regarding the choice between these two rival sites for the new Law Courts, the ground which had been cleared for that purpose in the Strand remained derelict from 1868 until 1874.

Until 18 April 1853, when it was closed as a burial-ground under the Nuisance Removal Act, the churchyard of St Clement Danes and others in the centre of London were still being used almost daily for burials. During the epidemic of cholera in 1849, strong complaints had been raised against this practice. At St Clement Danes was a vault called the Rectors' vault, the descent to which was in the aisle of the church near the communion table, and when open, the stench from the decomposition of animal matter was so powerful that lighted candles passed through the opening into the vault were instantly extinguished. The men employed at various times dared not descend into the vault until two or three days after it had been opened, during which period the windows of the church were kept open to admit fresh air and neutralize the effect of the gases emitted.

The graveyards in the centre of London were so overcrowded with coffins in the 'forties of the last century that frequently space could be found only by forcing them into very tight enclosures, to the great indignation of the families concerned. Some of the bodies had to be removed in 1902 when a portion of the west side of the churchyard was required for the widening of the Strand by the London County Council. The churchyard of St-Mary-le-Strand was abolished in August 1872 for the widening of the roadway in the Strand and the footpath constructed alongside the church.

On the east side of St Clement Danes Church, which was erected in 1682 by Edward Pierce, is a statue of Dr Johnson, who regularly attended service here, and on the west side is the memorial to Mr Gladstone, designed by Hamo Thornycroft, R.A. Unhappily this church was completely burned out by an oil-bomb in the air raid of 10 May 1941 and only the tower and bare walls remained. Its rector, the Rev. W. Pennington Bickford, died in June 1941 of a broken heart. The church has been completely rebuilt and is lavishly decorated with R.A.F. insignia of various kinds since it is now the guild church of the Royal Air Force. At intervals during the day the 'Bells of St Clement's' play 'Oranges and Lemons' — though some authorities claim that it was St Clement Eastcheap in the City that was referred to in the old nursery rhyme.

Essex Street, leading to the water-gate of Essex House (part of the gate survives) and thence by stairs down to the Embankment and the Thames, derives its name from Robert Devereux, Earl of Essex, and favourite of Queen Elizabeth. High up on the wall of an alley leading from Essex Street to the Strand is a bust that probably represents his son, who led the Parliamentary forces at Edgehill, inscribed: 'This is Devereux Courte 1676'. Some good modern buildings have recently been erected on the east side of this street. The Outer Temple was so called to distinguish it from the Middle and Inner Temple and was never connected with the two Inns of Court, but at one time belonged to the Earls of Essex, mentioned above. Today, the name is carried by a block of offices, Nos. 222-225,

Strand. Situated between the two is the Middle Temple. Some of the buildings at the corner of Essex Street, overlooking the churchyard of St Clement Danes, are disfigured by unsightly advertisement hoardings which have been erected in front of the upper stories. Between Milford Lane and Arundel Street, also overlooking the churchyard, is a quite new building occupied by the Midland Bank and Standard Telephones and Cables.

On the slightly curved site between Essex Street and Milford Lane is the handsome new Huddersfield Building Society block, in the sixteenth century Italian classical style—a style dictated by the desire to harmonise with St Clement's Church opposite. 'This building', said the architect, Mr W. Braxton Sinclair, 'is a challenge to the match-box style of the present day'. During the great air-raid of 10 May 1941 offices on both sides of the Essex Steps archway were hit by a high-explosive bomb which likewise destroyed the corner of the old arch. These offices were reputed to be nearly as old as the street itself, which was built about 1680 on the site of the grounds of Essex House, the mansion of Robert Devereux. Before the construction of the Victoria Embankment the river came up to the foot of the steps.

The large building at the west corner of the Strand and Arundel Street, now occupied by Kelly's Directories, was erected in 1856 by Messrs W. H. Smith & Sons, the largest firm of booksellers and newsagents in the world, who now own some 1,500 shops and railway bookstalls. It stands on the site of the old Arundel House, famous in the annals of art and science, and is built in the Italian style. Eight houses previously stood on this piece of ground, four of which were in the Strand and four in Arundel Street, and this site is also interesting because on the occasion of the funeral of the Duke of Wellington a temporary building was erected here to accommodate two thousand persons.

The whole of the old buildings on the east side of Arundel Street, from the Strand down to the Embankment, have been removed and replaced by new ones. Between Arundel Street and Milford Lane a new, though short, street, called Maltravers Street, has appeared. The curiously named Tweezer's Alley, off Milford Lane, is still there. Norfolk Street at present seems to be undisturbed, but from Surrey Street to King's College there is an ominous emptiness among the shops and offices. The College, already occupying a number of buildings in Surrey Street, has plans for new construction to cover this area right down to the Embankment. We are also likely to lose the picturesque old Watch House of the parish of St Clement Danes in Strand Lane. Although Strand Lane will be effaced, it seems possible that the so-called 'Roman' Bath may be preserved, notwithstanding authoritative opinion that it is more likely to be 17th century than Roman.

The construction of Kingsway and Aldwych, together with the widening of the Strand from the Law Courts to Wellington Street, was carried out between 1900 and 1905, and with the possible exception of that of Queen Victoria Street and the Thames Embankment, is the greatest London improvement which has been carried out since the construction of Regent Street in 1820. Previously the

Strand, one of the most important thoroughfares in Europe, had possessed no direct communication with Holborn, and Kingsway has provided a connexion between north and south London at that part of the west central district which needed it the most. It has also solved the problem of connecting north and south London by means of a through omnibus system. The total length of Kingsway is 1,800 feet, and that of Aldwych 1,500 feet, with a uniform width of 100 feet in both thoroughfares.

The new street from Holborn to the Strand was planned in 1898, but the question of the formation of such a thoroughfare had actually been under consideration for more than sixty years. More pressing needs for other new arteries caused the former Metropolitan Board of Works to refrain from asking Parliament to sanction such a costly undertaking, but one of the first acts of the newly-created London County Council in 1889 was to refer the matter to its Improvements Committee for a general report on the matter. The formation of the new street was equally desirable because it cut through a large amount of slum property only fit to be demolished.

One scheme for the construction of a new street from the Strand to Holborn was planned about 1874 at the time of the construction of the new Law Courts, in which it was proposed to connect the Strand with the eastern side of Lincoln's Inn Fields by a new street running parallel to Chancery Lane, and from the north-east corner of Lincoln's Inn Fields by a short street leading into High Holborn near Great Turnstile. Another scheme planned in 1883 was for the construction of a street sixty feet wide commencing at Little Turnstile, High Holborn, thence through Gate Street to the western side of Lincoln's Inn Fields, and then curving southward entering the Strand near St Clement Danes Church. The scheme finally adopted for the construction of Aldwych and Kingsway was devised in 1892 by Mr Frederic Harrison, Chairman of the Improvements Committee of the London County Council. The central idea of this scheme was to provide direct access to Holborn both from Wellington Street on the west and Fleet Street and the Thames Embankment on the east, by means of the Aldwych Crescent leading into the southern end of Kingsway. In 1930 one-way traffic was introduced at the eastern end of the Strand and round the Aldwych Crescent, the eastbound traffic proceeding along Aldwych and the westbound traffic along the Strand.

The long delay which occurred in carrying out this much-needed improvement nevertheless proved a great blessing in disguise, because instead of s treet only sixty feet wide, involving the demolition of only a portion of the insanitary property between the Strand and Holborn, London has been provided with the magnificent Kingsway and Aldwych, both one hundred feet wide. Thus London has also benefited through the disappearance of Clare Market and the whole of the slums formerly centred round Drury Lane and Sardinia Street.

The tremendous changes which have taken place in this part of London since 1901 can scarcely fail to command admiration. Gone are the narrow and dark Holywell Street and Wych Street, the squalid Clare Market, and the innumerable gin-palaces of Drury Lane and its adjacent streets. As a piece of urban scenery, the Aldwych crescent, lined on both sides with stone-fronted buildings one hundred feet high, is unsurpassed in beauty when seen from either St Clement Danes Church or Wellington Street, and nothing of the same kind is to be seen in Paris, Berlin, or New York. With the exception of the twin Strand and Aldwych theatres on either side of the Waldorf Hotel, which in no way spoil the harmony of the crescent, all the buildings are more or less of the same elevation, and form a vista as impressive as that of the celebrated Regent Street Quadrant.

The demolition of Holywell Street, together with the houses facing the north side of the Strand between the churches of St Clement Danes and St-Mary-le-Strand, was commenced in August 1900. At first this end of the Strand was only widened to seventy feet, and a huge hoarding was erected here, which remained for over twelve months. In 1901 the long row of houses between St-Mary-le-Strand Church and Catherine Street was demolished, after which the whole of the eastern end of the Strand was set back to a uniform width of one hundred feet. The church of St-Mary-le-Strand, designed by Gibbs in 1717, was the first of the fifty new churches projected in the reign of Queen Anne.

Holywell Street, which ran parallel to the Strand, was also known as Bookseller's Row. It originally formed the continuation of Butchers' Row, and, like Middle Row in Holborn, was a great hindrance to traffic at the eastern end of the Strand between the two island churches. Wych Street, immediately north of Holywell Street, was practically the continuation of Drury Lane, and contained the old Globe Theatre erected in 1862 at the corner of Newcastle Street on the site of Lyon's Inn, which had once been an Inn of Chancery attached to the present inn of the Inner Temple. In the same street was the Olympic Theatre, built in 1805, which was destroyed by fire in 1849 and rebuilt shortly afterwards. Both of these playhouses were swallowed up in the great Strand-to-Holborn improvement. Newcastle Street, on the north side of the Strand, extended from St-Mary-le-Strand Church to the southern end of Drury Lane, and close by was the Coach and Horses Hotel, which also fronted the north side of the Strand.

Farther west, between Catherine Street and Wellington Street, stood the old Gaiety Theatre and Restaurant and the offices of the *Morning Post*. Parliament obliged the London County Council to reinstate these two concerns, and the later Gaiety Theatre was built at the Strand corner of the western end of the Aldwych curve in 1903, and a new building was erected for *The Morning Post* on the opposite corner in 1907, adjoining Wellington Street, approximately on the same site as the former building. The old Gaiety Theatre, built in 1864 for Mr Lionel Lawson, was originally called the Strand Music Hall. It was taken over in 1868 by Mr J. Hollingshead as a home of musical comedy and farce, and afterwards came into the possession of Mr George Edwardes. It had a side entrance in Catherine Street and stood on the ground now covered by the roadway of Aldwych. When this theatre was demolished in 1903, swarms of rats were disturbed; they invaded the Gaiety Restaurant next door, and much damage was done before they could be driven back into the sewers.

By this time the construction of both the new Gaiety Theatre and the restaurant was well advanced, and the following year the latter was removed to its new quarters. It was on a much grander scale than the old restaurant, but unfortunately it never enjoyed the same popularity and was therefore closed down altogether in 1908. This building afterwards became the headquarters of the Marconi Wireless Telegraph Company and was known as Marconi House; later it became the headquarters of the Ministry of Civil Aviation, and it is now the Marconi wing of English Electric House. From 11 May to 15 November 1922, it was '2LO', the first station of the British Broadcasting Company. A small portion of the ground floor was occupied by Short's, the well-known wine house, who have recently removed to the opposite side of the Strand.

Upon the occasion of the farewell performance at the old Gaiety Theatre in July 1903, there was keen competition among its patrons to secure admission, and the same eagerness was shown by these people to obtain admission to the opening performance of *The Orchid* at the new Gaiety Theatre on the 26th of the following October. Percy Greenbank—a name familiar to Gaiety patrons—was present on both occasions and in a letter to *The Daily Telegraph* in September 1960, said: 'I am the only survivor of that little band of authors and composers who provided the lyrics and music for all the Gaiety productions at that time and for many years after—Ivan Caryll, Lionel Monckton, Adrian Ross and myself.'

The handsome columns which adorned the exterior of the last Gaiety Theatre were not originally included in the design of Mr Norman Shaw, the architect, but the London County Council, wishing to make this corner building worthy of such a great London improvement, invited its proprietors to include these extra columns for the sake of effect, and agreed themselves to meet the extra expense which would be thus incurred. But when the formal claim for the cost of this work was presented to the London County Council, they regarded it as excessive and disputed the amount claimed. Litigation followed, as a result of which the Council had to pay the full sum claimed by the Gaiety Theatre Company.

By 1938 the interior appointments of the Gaiety Theatre had become out of date and to conform to the present-day regulations of the London County Council would have necessitated a heavy financial outlay before a renewal of the licence could be granted. The owners would not agree to carry out the necessary alterations and in 1938 the Gaiety Theatre was closed and its fixtures and fitting sold by auction. In 1946 the shell of the Gaiety Theatre, bombed during the war, was bought for £200,000 by Mr Lupino Lane who planned to modernize the building and reopen it as a centre of musical comedy. But after spending £35,000 on repairs, dryrot and worm-rot were encountered and restoration work was stopped altogether.

Heartbroken at his failure to restore the Gaiety Theatre, into which task he had put his life-savings, Mr Lupino Lane sold the building, which has now been demolished and a new eight-storey building for the English Electric Co. Ltd. has been erected on this site. The winning design of a competition held in 1955 was set aside and the £¼ million building opened in August 1960 is the modified design of an unsuccessful competitor. The main entrance is flanked by two 18-foot sculptures by Sir Charles Wheeler, President of the Royal Academy. They are of bronze covered with aluminium leaf, and represent 'Power' and 'Speed'. The familiar angel and trumpet figure – probably intended to symbolize 'Fame' – which used to surmount the Gaiety dome has, happily, been restored and now forms the centre-piece of a fountain in the courtyard of the new building.

The fine building at the junction of Wellington Street and Aldwych, erected for the *Morning Post,* was remodelled and as Inveresk House became the headquarters of Illustrated Newspapers Limited. It is now occupied by Lloyds Bank Limited.

Australia House, an imposing building in Doric style, occupies the island site at the eastern corner of the Strand and Aldwych and is one of the finest buildings erected in this new quarter of London. It was built by the Commonwealth to serve as offices for the various States and was opened by King George V in 1918, who had also laid the foundation-stone in 1913. The large site, comprising the central island now covered by Bush House and its two extensions, remained more or less derelict for nearly twenty years, and during the first World War temporary buildings were erected here for the American branch of the Young Men's Christian Association. The centre section of Bush House, designed by Mr Harvey Corbett, was erected between 1920 and 1923. The eastern extension was completed in 1930, but the western wing was not built until 1935. The erection of the south-western wing of Bush House in 1935 marked the conclusion of the great Strand-to-Holborn improvement started by the London County Council thirty years earlier. This section is now chiefly occupied by Government departments and the B.B.C. A portion of this island site, adjoining the western wing of Bush House, contains India House, opened by King George V on 8 July 1930, and comprising the London headquarters of the Indian Government.

Some time after the widening of this section of the Strand had been completed, a suggestion was made by Mr Hamo Thornycroft, R.A., and others, that the northern frontage of the Strand between the two churches should be amended in order to secure a good view of the Law Courts when approached from the Strand on the west. However, the London County Council were not convinced that by throwing open the vista of the Law Courts the architectural effect on the Strand would be greatly enhanced, and therefore they declined to incur the large additional expenditure which would have resulted from the sacrifice of the extra ground required for that purpose.

The handsome row of buildings which now lines the north side of the Strand from Wellington Street to the Law Courts is largely offset by the mean row of houses plastered over with advertisement hoardings on the opposite side of the street between Somerset House and Lancaster Place. That our finest thoroughfares should be thus disfigured is a burning shame and a thing which would not be tolerated in any well-ordered Continental city, where the owners of property can very properly be compelled to keep their buildings in a state of repair commensurate with the dignity of the neighbourhood in which they are situated. Indeed, some time ago the late Professor Reilly, F.R.I.B.A., remarked at a public dinner that the new buildings in the Strand made the old ones look as though they wanted a shave.

Returning once more to Aldwych, on the north side, between Catherine Street and Drury Lane, is the Waldorf Hotel, erected in 1906 and containing a row of Doric columns, and which, together with the twin Strand and Aldwych theatres on either side, forms an island site. The Strand Theatre, at the corner of Catherine Street, was formerly known as the Waldorf Theatre, and was opened in 1905. The Aldwych Theatre, at the Corner of Drury Lane, was originally built for Mr Seymour Hicks and was opened in 1906. The first Strand Theatre, erected about 1826 by Mr Rayner, a comedian, stood in the Strand itself on the site now covered by the Underground Railway Station at the corner of Surrey Street. Many successful musical plays were staged here, notably *The Chinese Honeymoon* in 1901, which enjoyed the longest run till then of any play in London.

The two fine blocks of buildings which form the entrance to Kingsway are designed in a uniform style, and are the work of Messrs Norman and Trehearne, architects. That on the east corner is devoted to the Television interest, while Crown House, on the west corner, is mainly devoted to shops and offices. In Houghton Street is the building of the London School of Economics, one of the youngest colleges of London University, opened by King George V in 1923.

The eastern section of Aldwych contains Columbia House, of Messrs Johnson & Phillips Limited, the electrical engineers, at the corner of Houghton Street, and next door, Aldwych House, a huge building erected in 1921, occupied by the Legal and General Assurance Society, with a row of Doric columns and of similar appearance to the Waldorf Hotel at the other end of the crescent. Other buildings on the north side of Aldwych are Astor House, the General Assurance Corporation Buildings, and Dane's Inn House, on the corner adjoining Clement's Inn.

Passing next into Kingsway, the first section to be completed was that between High Holborn and Great Queen Street. This portion of the new street practically followed the line of the former Little Queen Street which was swallowed up in this great improvement, and was in fact a setting-back of the east side of that street. The extension from Great Queen Street to Aldwych was a much greater undertaking and involved the clearance of acres of streets and buildings, some of them quite modern, such as those which fronted the south side of Great Queen Street. Amongst the obstacles which had to be removed was a great chimney-stack, and this was done by the simple method of blowing it up.

The subway for the London County Council's tramways running under Kingsway was of course constructed at the same time as the new street, but it originally terminated at the Aldwych station. It was extended some two years later, in 1907, to the Thames Embankment. It had been designed in the first place to accommodate only single-deck cars. The Council, wishing to remedy this defect, reconstructed the subway in 1929-31 at a cost of £300,000, to provide room for the double-deck cars in general use throughout the system. As one of the early stages in the ultimate replacement of tramways by omnibuses, which was completed in July 1952, this subway was closed when the last tram ran through it on 5 April 1952. Part of the subway has since been re-opened for general traffic between Waterloo Bridge on the Embankment and Bush House (one way only). The short branch line of the Underground Railway which connects Holborn with Aldwych station in the Strand was opened about 1905. During the second World War this line was closed and converted into an enormous air-raid shelter with accommodation for several thousand people. The line was restored and reopened to traffic in 1946, but is now in operation at rush-hours only, there being insufficient traffic to justify its continuous operation.

Kingsway and Aldwych were opened by King Edward VII and Queen Alexandra on Wednesday, 18 October 1905, assisted by the Chairman, Sir Edwin Cornwall, J.P., and members of the London County Council. The weather was fine, and the King and Queen drove from Aldwych to the end of the improvement through Kingsway and along Southampton Row. The opening ceremony was apparently fixed for a date which did not allow sufficient time to complete the work properly, with the result that Kingsway was closed again for a few days to vehicular traffic after the formal opening ceremony. The total length of the new thoroughfares, including Southampton Row and the side streets constructed, was 4,200 feet, or just over three-quarters of a mile. Aldwych owes its name to the fact that the district was in Saxon times the site of a Danish settlement, and Kingsway was so named in order to associate the new thoroughfare with the ruling monarch. The total cost of this great metropolitan improvement was close upon five million pounds.

Like Regent Street and Victoria Street, Kingsway failed to prove an immediate success, but today it is one of the most prosperous streets in London. For the first seven years after it was opened, its building sites were only let very slowly, but those in Drury Lane and the side streets were disposed of more rapidly. The first building to be erected between Great Queen Street and Aldwych was that of Messrs W. H. Smith & Son, the booksellers, in 1906, and for a long time this building stood in solitary glory. The headquarters of this firm are in Portugal Street.

The London Opera House, later the Stoll Theatre, on the east side, was erected by Mr Oscar Hammerstein of New York in 1910 at a cost of £200,000. This venture proved a failure, and it subsequently became a cinema in 1917, and then a theatre devoted to vaudeville and light comedy. The Stoll was demolished in 1958, and a new building with shops on the ground floor and seven floors of offices with three basements, has replaced it. Incorporated in the building is a new theatre, The Royalty — reviving the name of the old playhouse in Dean Street — which was opened by Dame Edith Evans on 23 June 1960. Curiously, its main entrance is down a side street (Portugal Street) while the Stage Door is in Kingsway. The auditorium is below street level. Within a year of opening live theatre was superseded by the cinema with performances of the film *Ben Hur*. The fine premises of Kodak Limited, on the west side, were also erected in 1910, and after 1912 the remaining Kingsway sites were disposed of more rapidly, so that by 1916 almost the entire street had become lined with stately buildings.

One of the finest of these is Sardinia House, the offices of the Public Trustee erected in 1914-15 at the north corner of Kingsway and Sardinia Street. The last building to be erected in Kingsway was the huge Africa House at the corner of Gate Street, completed in 1922, so that from start to finish it had taken seventeen years from 1905 for the new street to become completely lined with buildings. The latest addition to the Kingsway buildings is the seven-floor rectangular Space House at Nos 43-59, which is connected by a double-decker bridge to a 15-storey *circular* office building at the rear. One impressive feature of the latter seems to be the large number of windows, and although it is a rather dizzy business walking round a circular building counting the windows, the final estimate was 'about' 720.

From Great Queen Street to Aldwych, Kingsway is a noble thoroughfare, second only perhaps to Regent Street in the splendour of its buildings, which are of fairly uniform elevation, but the section from Great Queen Street to High Holborn has been badly disfigured by several small buildings of low elevation erected on shallow sites next door to huge structures like Africa House and Craven House.

The Roman Catholic Church of SS Anselm and Cecilia, at the corner of Kingsway and Twyford Court, opened in 1909, replaced the historic Sardinian Chapel which stood close to Lincoln's Inn Fields, but which was demolished for the Kingsway improvement. Holy Trinity Church, on the opposite side of the road, is the successor to a building erected in 1831, which was condemned as unsafe and demolished in 1912. This misfortune was variously attributed to the construction of the subway for the London County Council tramways on the one hand and that of the tube railway on the other. When a claim for compensation was made, each of the parties concerned blamed the other and disclaimed all liability for the damage, and that was all the satisfaction the Church authorities were able to obtain in the matter. It was originally proposed to add a tower to this church, but as no funds could be raised for that purpose, the tower remains a pious hope for the future. The church stands on the site of No 7 Little Queen Street, where Charles Lamb was living when his sister Mary, in a sudden fit of insanity, killed their mother with a table-knife.

Another large building on the west side of Kingsway is Kingsway Hall, containing the headquarters of the West London Mission. In August 1944 Aldwych and Kingsway were struck by a bomb which caused much damage to several large buildings in Aldwych and at the Strand end of Kingsway, as well as the roadway. Although these buildings, constructed of steel and faced with stone, stood up well to the bombing, every window was smashed and much internal damage resulted. Amongst the buildings struck by the blast were the

Air Ministry, Bush House, Crown House, Aldwych House and the Stoll Theatre. In the 1940 air raids buildings on the corner of Remnant Street next to the church of SS Anselm and Cecilia were destroyed.

Some of the magnificence of Kingsway extends to the western side of Lincoln's Inn Fields, where several of its new buildings, such as Sardinia House, and the adjoining Queen's House, have a second frontage. Lincoln's Inn Fields is twelve acres in extent and was purchased in the nineties by the London County Council as a public open space. It is the largest and best modern square in London, and boasts some magnificent plane-trees. It was laid out by Inigo Jones and was first railed off in 1735, but before that time it bore an evil reputation. Here Babington and other conspirators for Mary, Queen of Scots, were hanged and quartered for their sins, and in 1683 William Lord Russell was beheaded here for alleged high treason, after being led down the now defunct Little Queen Street to his execution. Lincoln's Inn Fields was likewise a noted resort for duellists.

On the south side of the square is the Royal College of Surgeons, erected in 1835, which was founded in 1740 and removed here from the Old Bailey, and also the offices of the Land Registry. Between them is the new Nuffield College of Surgical Science and west of the College of Surgeons is the new Imperial Cancer Research Centre. On the north side the principal object of interest is Sir John Soane's Museum, containing books, manuscript, and Egyptian and Oriental antiquities. Here also is the Institute of Auctioneers and Estate Agents. Lincoln's Inn itself, situated on the east side of the square, is one of the four great Inns of Court, and is approached by a picturesque gateway from Lincoln's Inn Fields. It contains a hall and library of red brick built in 1845, and a chapel erected from the designs of Inigo Jones in 1620. On the northern side is a quadrangle containing the so-called Stone buildings, begun in 1780 from the designs of Sir R. Taylor, but not actually completed until 1845. New Square lies immediately to the south, but does not form a part of Lincoln's Inn. Some of its old houses were damaged by a bomb in August 1944. The old gatehouse opening into Chancery Lane from Lincoln's Inn was built in 1518 by Sir Thomas Lovell and was restored in 1899. On the north-west corner of Lincoln's Inn Fields and Great Queen Street is Newcastle House, erected in 1685. From 1825 for nearly half a century it was occupied by the Society for the Promotion of Christian Knowledge.

In 1843 Sir Charles Barry designed new Law Courts which he proposed should be erected in Lincoln's Inn Fields, but this scheme was vetoed because of the opposition to the suggested appropriation of Lincoln's Inn Fields itself for that purpose. In Portsmouth Street, leading out of the south-west corner of Lincoln's Inn Fields, is a picturesque house which claims to be the 'Old Curiosity Shop' of Charles Dickens, but the validity of this claim is not generally conceded by competent authorities. Nevertheless, it is a popular establishment for the sale of Dickensian and other souvenirs and a regular stopping-place for coachloads of overseas visitors.

Crossing over to the opposite side of Kingsway, we next direct our attention to Great Queen Street, in which are now the headquarters of the Masonic Institutions of London. The new grandeur of Kingsway has spread in a westerly direction, so that today the whole of the south side of Great Queen Street has become lined with handsome modern buildings. At the Kingsway end are a few offices and shops, adjoining which are the Connaught Rooms, famous for public dinners and meetings.

The last remnant of squalor and poverty has now been removed from this side of Kingsway by the erection of the fine Masonic Temple, built at a cost of £1,000,000. It was opened on 19 July 1933 by the Duke of Connaught, who also laid the foundation-stone on 14 July 1927. It covers a huge triangular site, previously occupied by some of the worst slums in London. Now that the buildings in Drury Lane which back on to Wild Street have been cleared away, Great Queen Street has been brought into line with Long Acre, and the Masonic Temple thus enjoys an unobstructed view down Long Acre.

In connexion with this improvement the old Prince of Wales tavern was rebuilt in 1933 on a new site a few paces farther south, which brings it into alignment with Long Acre. Together with the Masonic Temple it presents a vista of almost Eastern splendour when seen from Long Acre. A sort of a square has been formed at the western end of Great Queen Street by this extensive road-widening opposite the Masonic Temple and Wild Street. A new building faced with stone has also been erected on the opposite corner of Great Queen Street.

On the north side of Great Queen Street was the Kingsway Theatre, formerly the Novelty owned by Penley, the comedian, and several modern buildings devoted to Masonic institutions and offices are sandwiched in between old Georgian houses. The Kingsway Theatre and the adjoining Georgian houses have been replaced by a new block of offices with a frontage of about sixty yards.

The large Winter Garden Theatre at the corner of Parker Street and Drury Lane, was recently demolished and the site is now used as a car park. Formerly a house of musical comedy and revue, it seemed to be misplaced, for it suffered long spells of emptiness. It was built in 1910 on the site of the Old Middlesex Music Hall. Extensive improvements and alterations to this theatre were carried out in 1919 by Messrs Grossmith and Laurillard at a cost of about £20,000. The Old Middlesex was itself rebuilt by a Mr Winder in the early 'fifties, and was regularly patronized by the butchers and other tradesmen of Clare Market. A good evening's entertainment could be enjoyed at the 'Old Mo', as the place was then familiarly termed, but upon occasion disappointed patrons in the gallery were said to have showered empty beer bottles on to the stage.

A few yards further north in Drury Lane once stood the Coal Yard, the birthplace of Nell Gwyn, and close by was the Cock and Magpie, alongside Drury Court, where in later years she had her lodgings.

A century ago Drury Lane contained numberless blind alleys, courts, and passages on either side, and gin was sold in public-houses which from their size and splendour might almost have been mistaken for the mansions of noblemen, and this in neighbourhoods where poverty and misery abounded. They stood mostly in conspicuous places such as the corners and crossings of the various streets, and here mothers would leave their children to play whilst they went into the gin-palaces to enjoy a farthings-worth of gin. They could be seen from afar, and could properly be termed the lighthouses which guided the thirsty soul on the road to ruin, for not only were they resplendent with plate glass and gilt cornices, but each house displayed signs informing you that it sold the only real brandy in London, or that it offered the famous cordial medicated gin strongly recommended by the faculty.

Externally these public houses were most magnificent, but inside they were extremely dismal and uncomfortable, and always crowded with people standing, staggering, or lying down groaning and raving under the influence of drink. The first and second floors of the narrow houses in this locality were occupied by small tradesmen and mechanics, some of them usurers preying upon poverty and coining gold from its vices and morbid cravings. But even here misery was less conspicuous than in St Giles's and Spitalfields. Saturday nights and Sunday after church hours were the times when Drury Lane appeared in all its characteristic 'glory'.

To the present generation, with its vastly improved standard of education and living, the conditions prevailing in those days must appear almost incredible. The sole place of relaxation for the poor man was the gin-palace, for churches and parks in those days held no attraction for the overcrowded and underfed artisans. Steamer, rail, or omnibus outings were too expensive, and of course there were no such attractions as tearooms or cinemas. There were penny theatres in those days where melodrama was played, and these contained a buffet with soda-water, lemonade, apples, and cakes. As a general rule the pit of the theatre would accommodate fifty persons, and there were galleries and wooden benches rising nearly to the ceiling. Strange to relate, the gentleman sat on one side and the ladies on the other, this separation of the sexes being prompted by a feeling of refinement. The gentlemen consisted principally of labourers and apprentices.

Most of the slums centred round Drury Lane were swept away in the construction of Aldwych and Kingsway, but some of the worst of them, situated between Wild Street and Drury Lane, had already been demolished many years previously, in order to make way for the large blocks of Peabody dwellings which now cover that ground. Others, situated at the northern end of Drury Lane, have not yet entirely disappeared in the tide of modern progress, but the whole of the southern end is now lined by respectable blocks of artisans' dwellings and business premises. Prominent amongst these is Bruce House, a large hostel containing nearly seven hundred cubicles, erected by the London County Council in 1906, at the southeast corner of Drury Lane and Kemble Street. This hostel has been popularly termed the 'Poor Man's Carlton', and here accommodation can be secured at prices within the reach of its patrons.

The famous Drury Lane Theatre, at the opposite corner of Russell Street, with its main frontage in Catherine Street, has been reconstructed several times on the existing site, the last occasion being in 1921, and before that in 1812. The portico was added some years later, but in 1921, when the interior of the theatre was razed to the ground and reconstructed on a very sumptuous scale, the outer walls and the colonnade in Catherine Street were preserved for reasons of sentiment. Today Drury Lane is internally one of the finest theatres in the world, but the old outer walls are so ugly that it would have been a greater ornament if a fine new façade had been erected in keeping with the internal magnificence and dignity of the new theatre. The Duchess Theatre on the opposite side of Catherine Street was opened in 1929, and the Fortune Theatre in Russell Street was completed in 1925.

It was in the upper end of Drury Lane near Long Acre that the Great Plague of London broke out towards the end of 1664. When two or three members of the same family died suddenly their timid neighbours took fright and moved into the City, whither they carried the infection. Said to have originated in the Levant, it had been raging for some months in Holland where in Amsterdam twenty thousand people had died, and a cargo vessel carried the infection to this country. In December 1664 a frost which lasted for three months suspended the plague's destructive progress, but no sooner had a thaw set in than it continued with increased violence. It reached its zenith in August and September 1665 when fifty thousand died, twelve thousand in one week. During that year the plague claimed a hundred thousand victims, grass grew in front of the Royal Exchange and in the main streets, churchyards were choked and large pits dug into which the dead and sometimes the living were thrown. Carts continually traversed the streets with the cry 'Bring out your dead', and stoppage of public business was complete. In the last week of September the plague began to abate, and by the following February had ceased altogether.

Eighth Walk

From Blackfriars Bridge along the Victoria Embankment, Northumberland Avenue, and the Strand to Wellington Street

We now start from Blackfriars Bridge, already described in our Fourth Walk, and proceed along the Victoria Embankment. This thoroughfare extending from Blackfriars to Westminster Bridge – perhaps the grandest riverside in Europe -- is one mile and a third in length and one hundred feet wide, and was formally opened on 13 July 1870 by the late King Edward VII, when Prince of Wales, accompanied by Princess Louise. The magnificent sweep from the Houses of Parliament to St Paul's is one of the finest views in London, and quite surpasses anything that can be seen beside the Seine, the Tiber, or any other river in Europe.

Londoners have never been sufficiently grateful to the late Metropolitan Board of Works for this wonderful improvement. The first idea of embanking the Thames originated with Sir Christopher Wren upon the occasion of the rebuilding of London after the Great Fire of 1666. Various previous attempts to secure the construction of the Thames Embankment had been prevented by strong opposition from vested interests. A Bill for that purpose was lodged in Parliament by Mr Cowper, First Commissioner of Works to the Metropolitan Board, and passed in 1862, after which plans for the Victoria and also for the Albert Embankment were prepared by Sir Joseph Bazalgette, engineer to the Board, to whom the Victoria Embankment is a monument of enduring fame. It is a piece of engineering second to none of the great achievements which marked the mid-Victorian period.

Work on the construction of the Victoria Embankment was commenced in February 1864 and on 20 July the first stone was laid by Sir John Thwaites, Chairman of the Metropolitan Board of Works, assisted by Sir Joseph Bazalgette. The river footway between Westminster Bridge and the Temple was opened to the public on 30 July 1868, but the completion of the roadway was delayed by the unfinished condition of the Metropolitan District Underground Railway between Westminster and Blackfriars, and this obstacle was not removed until the end of May 1870. The first passenger train passed under the Embankment to the temporary terminus at Blackfriars on 30 May 1870, and within six weeks from that time the roadway of the Embankment was completed and the northern footway had been paved. In 1862 it was proposed to construct a new street to connect the east side of Charing Cross Railway Bridge with Wellington Street, Strand, but this plan failed to mature.

The trees which adorn the Embankment are planted at intervals of forty feet. They have now reached maturity, but when they were first planted, in February 1872, strong complaints were made to the Metropolitan Board of Works that the public had cut and injured them, as a result of which a reward of £20 was offered for information leading to the conviction of any person thus damaging the trees.

The retaining wall is a work of extraordinary strength and is carried down to a depth of 32½ feet below high-water mark and 14 feet below the low-water mark. It is built throughout of brick faced with granite founded in concrete and Portland cement, and its uniformity is relieved at intervals by massive piers of granite with recesses partly occupied by stairs leading to the river. In 1940 during the second World War a massive stairway near Cleopatra's Needle which leads down to the water's edge was blown up as a defence measure in case the enemy attempted to land at this point. The process of narrowing the channel of the river led to the reclamation of some thirty-seven acres of waste ground, formerly comprising mud banks at low tide, of which nineteen are occupied by the roadway and the footpaths, and the rest partly converted into public gardens and partly given over to new buildings.

Some idea of the magnitude of the Victoria Embankment may be gathered from the following quantities of materials employed in its construction:

Granite	650,000	cub. ft.
Brickwork	80,000	”
Concrete	140,000	”
Timber for coffer-dam, etc. . . .	500,000	”
Caissons	2,500	”
Earth filling	1,000,000	cub. yds.
Excavation	144,000	”
York paving	125,000	superficial ft.
Broken granite	50,000	” yds.

The total cost of the work was £1,250,000, and for compensation relating to the purchase of the property £450,000.

For the opening ceremony a pavilion was erected near Charing Cross Railway Bridge, which had its main entrance in Whitehall Place, and a second stand was erected nearer Charing Cross, the two together accommodating fifteen thousand people. Naturally the bridges also provided excellent points of view and were crowded from an early hour, as were also the various river-boats. At ten o'clock the temporary barricades at Westminster and Blackfriars were removed and the Embankment thrown open to the public. Altogether 1,400 police were stationed at various points along the Royal Route from Marlborough House to the Victoria Embankment and the line of the Embankment itself was kept by the first battalions of the Grenadier and the Coldstream Guards. Visitors arriving in their carriages were admitted up to eleven o'clock and their Royal Highnesses arrived at twelve o'clock.

The Thames was not always the fine health-giving river it is today, for in 1859, only a few years before construction of the Victoria Embankment, it was still at times little better than an open sewer, and it was rapidly becoming worse and worse. After the compulsory abolition of cesspools in 1847, when the drainage of houses into the sewers had been made obligatory, upwards of thirty thousand cesspools were abolished in six years. But the evil was not thus removed, but only transferred, as all of the sewers which superseded these cesspools flowed directly into the Thames.

The construction of the new main drainage system in 1859 was preceded by ten years of rival schemes and debates between successive commissioners of sewers, followed by those of the newly-constituted Metropolitan Board of Works and various Parliamentary Commissions. In 1858 vigorous measures had to be taken to check the smells arising from the Thames, and the Government directed that 250 tons of lime should be discharged into the river near the outlets of the sewers at a cost of £1,500 a week, and the Metropolitan Board of Works also undertook deodorizing measures as a temporary expedient. In 1859, when Father Thames was in a particularly argumentative mood, Sir Joseph Bazalgette reported that, during the hot weather of that year, 4,281 tons of chalk lime, 478 tons of chloride of lime, and 50 tons of carbolic acid were used to keep the Thames quiet at a cost of no less than £17,733.

Owing to the fact that the sewers emptied themselves into the Thames at various levels, when the tide rose above the outlets of these sewers the entire draining of the district was stopped until the tide again receded, thus turning the riverside into a succession of cesspools. This state of affairs often created an unbearable stench in the neighbourhood of the Houses of Parliament, which upon occasion compelled the adjournment of the House of Commons for the day.

Fifty years earlier, the Thames was still a limpid stream on which it was a pleasure to go rowing and which was delightful for bathing. But, owing to sheer indifference on the part of both the Government and the people, it had become a foul sewer and a stream of death reeking with abominable smells and threatening an epidemic to London's three million inhabitants as the price of their ignorance and apathy.

The difficulty in remedying this great evil sooner lay in the fact that London at that time possessed no central government and it was not the City alone that was affected, but likewise the growing towns, boroughs, and villages which had sprung up around it, some of them being much larger than the City itself. The Government merely looked on and did nothing, so that year after year the evil went on increasing and was only checked by the fear of an epidemic, which frightened both the people and the Government.

Parliament itself could no longer sit in its own house without the fear of being poisoned, so that the transmission of the sewage to a place far down the river, where it could easily be carried out to sea by the force of the tides and the current, had become imperative. The result was that the Commissioners of Sewers were superseded by the Metropolitan Board of Works, and in 1859 work was begun on Sir Joseph Bazalgette's great drainage system of new sewers; the course of the Northern Outfall leads to Barking Creek, the Southern Outfall to Crossness on the Erith Marshes, and the main drainage works at both places deal with the final disposal.

Starting on our walk from Blackfriars Bridge, the first notable building is Unilever House, which has been rebuilt on a more magnificent scale than the former De Keyser's Royal Hotel, which we noticed in our Fourth Walk. Next door is the City of London School, which was moved here from Milk Street in 1883. It is a handsome stone-fronted building with a tall roof, worthy of the commanding situation which it occupies on the Embankment. In John Carpenter Street, immediately adjoining the City of London School, is the Guildhall School of Music, erected in 1886 by the Corporation of London in the Italian style at a cost of £22,000, to provide high-class musical instruction at moderate fees. Sion College, a clubhouse for clergymen, at the west corner of John Carpenter Street, was founded in 1630 and contains a library of 110,l000 volumes rich in theological works. The present building was erected in 1886, and is in the Gothic style of architecture. Beyond Sion House are New Carmelite House, the offices of the *Daily Mail*, Audit House, occupied by the Exchequer and Audit department, the building of the Post Office Contracts Department, and Hamilton House, the head office of the Employer's Liability Assurance Corporation, together forming a handsome range of buildings extending as far as the Temple Gardens. Some of this ground remained waste for many years after the opening of the Victoria Embankment.

New Carmelite House is a six-storeyed edifice with a stone front erected in 1936 on the site of the former offices of the Metropolitan Asylum Board. It forms an extension of their main offices in Carmelite Street.

The Temple Gardens once reached right down to the river but of course are now separated from it by the Embankment. In the gardens, standing some distance back from the river-front, is a large block of buildings fronted with Portland stone. It was erected in 1880 by the two Societies of the Inner and the Middle Temple and consists principally of barristers' chambers. As a piece of urban scenery the combined effect of these gardens and the buildings centred round them within the Temple is most pleasing and restful when seen from the Victoria Embankment. Nearly opposite the western boundary of the City is moored the training ship H.M.S. *President,* the headquarters of the London Division of the Royal Naval Reserve, and nearby are H. M. S. *Discovery* in which Captain Scott made his expedition to the South Pole, H.M.S. *Chrysanthemum,* and H.M.S. *Wellington,* the floating Hall of the Honourable Company of Master Mariners. A number of seats along the Victoria Embankment have bronze plaques affixed to them, which read: 'Presented by W. H. Smith Esq., M.P., 1873'. This was the 'Son' of W. H. Smith & Son, the booksellers—known as 'Pinafore Smith', for he was First Lord of the Admiralty in 1874 and immortalized by W. S. Gilbert in *H.M.S.Pinafore.*

The former offices of the London School Board, erected in 1874, which stood until 1928 near the Temple Underground Railway Station, were demolished about 1929 and on this extensive site now stands Electra House, a tall building erected in 1930 for Cable & Wireless Limited. A few paces farther west is the Norfolk estate, containing several handsome red-brick buildings dressed with stone, which overlook the Embankment Gardens. One of these, at the west corner of Arundel Street, was formerly the Arundel Hotel. Until January 1871 iron railings and a brick wall stood at the bottom of Norfolk Street, but these were removed in order to provide direct access between the Strand and the Temple Station of the Underground Railway.

After passing through the eastern section of the Embankment Gardens we come next to Somerset House, occupying the site of the Palace of the Protector Somerset, maternal uncle to Edward VI. The palace was begun in 1547, but Somerset never lived to see the completion, having been meanwhile executed in the Tower. After his death the palace became royal property and here lived the Queens of Charles I and II. Here also Inigo Jones, the famous architect, died in 1652. Towards the end of the eighteenth century it was decided to rebuild the palace and devote it to public uses, and in 1774 Sir William Chambers was appointed as the architect. The river frontage is eight hundred feet long with a noble façade in the Palladian style, and before the construction of the Victoria Embankment it was lapped by the waters of the Thames. Still affixed to the walls are heavy iron rings, formerly used for tying-up boats.

The eastern wing was added in 1824 and the western wing, with its handsome frontage to Wellington Street, in 1854—56. The building contains 3,600 windows and houses an entire army of civil servants, including those of the Inland Revenue Office, Wills Office, and those of the Registrar-General of Births, Marriages, and Deaths. The east wing of Somerset House is occupied by King's College, founded in 1828 and now affiliated to the London University, but King's College School for Boys was removed to Wimbledon Common over fifty years ago. As a preliminary to the first stage of the King's College Redevelopment programme, the demolition of buildings from Somerset House eastward to the Aldwych Underground Station is almost complete, and at the time of writing, only five shops, all empty, are still standing. Two buildings that had survived the Great Fire of 1666 were sacrificed some months ago.

The old Waterloo Bridge, once considered by Canova to be the finest in Europe, was designed by George Dodd and built by a private company, the engineer being John Rennie. The first stone was laid on 11 October 1811 and the bridge was opened on 18 June 1817, the anniversary of the battle of Waterloo. But for this historical event it was originally intended to call it the Strand Bridge. The Bill for its construction was strongly opposed during its progress through Parliament, opposition being particularly raised to its being built with stone, a thing which seems difficult to understand. The plans and estimate for a wooden bridge were laid before the Commissioners and favourably received, but when the architect was urged to name a sum for keeping it in repair during a certain number of years, he declined to make any proposals. Notwithstanding this the wooden project had many friends, and in the House of Lords the design for a stone bridge was carried only by a small majority. On this occasion the minority obtained the ironical and punning nickname of 'Wooden Peers'.

In May 1924, owing to the foundation of one of the main arches having become weakened, causing a sinking of a portion of the roadway, Waterloo Bridge had to be closed to vehicular traffic for several months until the necessary strengthening of the foundations had been carried out. A contract for the construction of a temporary bridge was immediately placed with Sir William Errol & Company Limited, of Glasgow, in case the old one should prove unfit for any further service, and this was completed within twelve months. In order to lessen the weight of the old bridge, the concrete roadway was taken up and wood substituted. At first it was intended that the old Waterloo Bridge should be replaced by a handsome new structure capable of taking six lines of vehicles, but, thanks to short-sighted opposition, the fate of Waterloo Bridge remained undecided for many years.

The intention was to spend upwards of £800,000 on the old bridge by building out brackets on both sides of the bridge and increasing its width from twenty-eight feet to no more than thirty-five feet. A Bill presented to Parliament in 1932 for the construction of a new Waterloo Bridge at a cost of £1,200,000, towards which the Government were asked to contribute two-thirds, was rejected by the House of Commons on ground of economy. In 1934 the Government again refused to make any contribution. Nevertheless the fates had been working against the retention of the old Waterloo Bridge in the earlier rejection of the Bill promoted in 1930 for the construction of a new Charing Cross Bridge, and after ten years of haggling wiser counsels were allowed to prevail. On 20 June 1934 a start was made on the demolition of the old bridge.

In 1934 Mr Herbert Morrison, then leader of the newly-elected Socialist party of the London County Council, formally removed the first stone of the old bridge. Though Parliament tried hard to save it from demolition, the legal ruling was that they had no power to prevent the London County Council from pulling down the bridge. To show their displeasure Parliament at first refused to contribute towards the cost of the new bridge, but in 1938 they relented and made a grant of £300,000. The new bridge, designed by Sir Giles Scott, is a handsome structure of five arches, one of which spans the Victoria Embankment. This is the first all-concrete bridge to be constructed across the Thames. Its intended completion, by 1940, was delayed by the outbreak of the second World War, and in September of that year it was damaged by bombing. The new bridge was partly opened to vehicular traffic in September 1942 but not finally completed until November 1944. The formal opening ceremony was performed by Mr Herbert Morrison on 10 December 1945. Spacious new stairs leading down to the Victoria Embankment have been constructed on both sides of Wellington Street. The temporary bridge, which after September 1942 had been reserved for pedestrian traffic, was pulled down in November 1943 after an existence of nineteen years. But when London workmen dismantled the temporary bridge, they little suspected that its great girders were to play an important part in winning the second World War. Neither did the London County Council employees who stored the girders. But the London County Council, the Ministry of Supply, and the War Office had conducted secret negotiations including plans for building mysterious additional sections. These were added for the purpose of bridging the Rhine, an operation already foreseen even at that time, several months before D-day. After the capture of Antwerp, the bridge, complete down to the last nut and bolt, was shipped across the Channel and then conveyed in special railway trucks. Thus it came about than when the Germans had destroyed the Rhine bridges and our only one across the river at Remagen had collapsed, there beside the wreckage lay this substitute bridge only waiting to be put together.

Engineers worked day and night under enemy fire to fling it across the Rhine, and the additional sections gave the bridge the exact length required to span the river. Within a week tanks, guns, lorries and troops were pouring over the resuscitated Waterloo Bridge spanning the Rhine, as Londoners had hurried across this same bridge for seventeen years to and from their offices on the Strand.

A century ago London, Blackfriars, and Westminster Bridges were the only ones open to the general public free of toll, the others being owned by private companies. Waterloo Bridge and the Charing Cross railway footbridge were freed of tolls in 1878 and, in accordance with an Act of Parliament passed in July 1877 for that purpose, five more bridges were freed to the public on 24 May 1879. These were Lambeth, Vauxhall, Chelsea, the Albert, and Battersea Bridges. Those of Wandsworth, Putney, and Hammersmith were freed a short time later. The Toll Houses at either end of the Albert Bridge still remain.

Proceeding beyond Waterloo Bridge, through the Embankment Gardens, which were opened in July 1872, we first pass the Institution of Electrical Engineers at the corner of Savoy Street, a red-brick building with stone dressings, and then the famous Savoy Hotel, opened in October 1889, covering nearly an acre of ground. It originally had terraced balconies on every floor; they overlooked the Embankment and were supported by granite columns and coloured pillars, but these were removed in 1912 when two additional storeys were added to the river frontage. It was the first great hotel in London to provide private bathrooms to each bedroom. In 1904 the Savoy Hotel was greatly enlarged and extended to the Strand.

Next door to the Savoy Hotel, also overlooking the Embankment, stood until 1930 the Hotel Cecil. Opened in January 1896, the Cecil was at that time considered the most magnificent hotel in Europe, and was named after Salisbury House, the residence of Robert Cecil, Earl of Salisbury and Lord High Treasurer to James I. It was erected by the Liberator Permanent Building and Investment Society in 1892, in connexion with which concern Jabez Balfour failed for £8,000,000 and was sentenced in 1895 to fourteen years' penal servitude. The Hotel Cecil closed its doors on 23 February 1930, and was demolished in the record time of sixteen weeks between September and December. A magnificent twelve-storey building crowned by a massive stone clock-tower has now been erected on this site by the Shell-Mex Company at a cost of over £1,000,000.

West of the Shell-Mex House stood until 1936 Adelphi Terrace, a handsome row of houses facing the Embankment Gardens, built by the brothers Adam in 1770. It had always been a favourite abode of actors, artists, and literary men. David Garrick died at No 5 in 1779 and No 7 housed the famous Savage Club. Also in Adelphi Terrace was the Dramatic Library of the British Drama League. The Terrace was pulled down to make way for the gigantic office building which has been erected on this site. The collection of buildings and streets, raised by the architects, John, Robert, James, and William Adam, on the site of Durham Yard at the south side of the Strand, are all named after the members of that distinguished family, and the term Adelphi also alludes to these talented brothers. The new Adelphi building covers the vast site bounded by the Embankment Gardens, Adam Street, John Street and Robert Street. It has thirteen floors rising to 130 feet above the Victoria Embankment and is about the same height as the Savoy Hotel, but not quite as high as the neighbouring Shell-Mex House. It has two basement floors below the Victoria Embankment level which are used as garages, and also a roof garden. The acrhitects were Messrs Colcutt and Hamp. On the east side of Adam Street is another new office building overlooking the Victoria Embankment which was erected in 1938. In John Street (now John Adam Street) is the Royal Society of Arts, established in 1754, and next door was the Little Theatre, originally a concert hall, now demolished. The old St Martin's Tavern at the Charing Cross end of John Adam Street, remembered for large slabs of cheese and jars of pickles on the bar counters, was demolished a few years ago and the new 'Gilbert and Sullivan' erected on the site. Like the 'Sherlock Holmes' of the same brewers, it is a 'speciality' pub and has an extensive display of photographs, model theatre sets, programmes and other *miscellanea* dear to the heart of the G. and S. enthusiast.

Cleopatra's Needle, which stands on the Embankment, was brought from Alexandria at a cost of £10,000, which was defrayed by Sir Erasmus Wilson, the eminent surgeon. This famous Egyptian obelisk, sixty-eight feet high and weighing 180 tons, was erected here in 1878, and originally stood in front of the great temple of Heliopolis. At its foot are two large sphinxes. Cleopatra's Needle was shipped from Alexandria by the *Cleopatra,* which was wrecked in a storm off the Spanish coast in October 1877. Here it was left until the following January, when it was towed from the Spanish port of Ferrol by the steam-tug *Anglia* in six days, and arrived safely in London on Monday, 21 January 1878. In the Embankment Gardens at the bottom of Buckingham Street is the Water Gate, said to have been built by Inigo Jones. This is the sole relic of York House, which was the residence of the Archbishop of York and afterwards of the Dukes of Buckingham. There also Francis Bacon was born on 22 January 1561. It is said that when the second Duke of Buckingham sold the property for building purposes, he stipulated that his name and title should be kept in memory by the streets built upon it. They were accordingly named *George, Villiers* and *Duke* Streets, *Of* Alley and *Buckingham* Street. George Court, Villiers Street, Of Alley (now York Place) and Buckingham Street still survive. Across the roadway is the Belgian monument commemorating the hospitality of the people of this country to Belgians during the first World War. Also facing the Embankment Gardens is a newly-erected monument to the memory of all the men and women of the Air Forces of every part of the Commonwealth and British Empire who gave their lives in the second World War, 1939-45.

Already a century ago the Thames was a great centre of local steamboat traffic and in 1831 steamers were running daily during the season from the City to Richmond and from St Katherine's Docks to the various seaside resorts. As early as 1815 Mr George Dodd purchased and fitted up a steam-vessel at Glasgow, brought it to London in 121 hours, and started running pleasure trips on the Thames. As time went on the number of steamboats running a regular service up and down the river multiplied enormously and this led to the most iniquitous competition between the rival companies, who carried passengers at fares which were incompatible with reasonable safety and efficiency for those electing to travel to and from the City by river. The steamboat companies on the Thames, owing to the absence of any control, did exactly as they liked in those days, although omnibus proprietors and owners of cabs were numbered and licensed. Thus what was punishable in the Strand was permitted on the river, though in practice the river was a hundred times more dangerous. In the absence of any proper landing-place the companies erected long lines of rickety piers made of dirty barges planked over, at any spot that suited their convenience. Sometimes two rival companies placed their piers side by side, so that the public were constantly deluded into taking wrong tickets for the boat which never came along. All along the river the piers were an eyesore, a public nuisance, and an obstruction.

Things reached a climax when on 27 August 1847 a steamboat called the *Cricket*, running between the City and the West End at a fare of only one halfpenny, was on the point of leaving the Adelphi pier for London Bridge. It had on board about 150 passengers, all quietly seated, when suddenly a loud report was heard, followed by a violent explosion. The vessel was immediately cleared, some of the passengers having actually been blown into the air, whilst others jumped over the sides and struggled in the mud that lined the shore. Only a few dumbfounded persons remained in the uninjured part of the boat, and about forty persons were seen at one time floating in the water, which fortunately happened to be at low tide, but some of them perished before assistance could be rendered. At the time of the accident the *Cricket* was aground near the shore and the explosion occurred during the attempt to get her off. One part of the boiler was hurled a hundred feet towards the Adelphi pier and another portion in the opposite direction towards Waterloo Bridge. Thirty people were in the cabin of the boat at the time of the accident, all of whom perished, and their bodies could not be recovered until the tide had receded.

Today, except for pleasure trips in the summer-time, the river is entirely out of favour as a means of transport with the average Londoner, who prefers the more rapid transit afforded by the motor-omnibuses and the Underground Railway. However, a half-hourly service of so-called water buses ran between Greenwich and Putney during 1950-51, but these no longer operate. At one time bathing in the Thames was a popular pastime, and in July 1875 a floating bath was opened on the Embankment near the Underground Railway station at Charing Cross. It was 135 feet long by 30 feet wide and contained good dressing-rooms and a saloon intended for use as a lounge.

The Victoria Embankment is now illuminated at night-time by a double row of arc-lamps suspended on wires extended across the roadway, and the effect is very impressive. A proposal as long ago as 1879 to light the Embankment by electricity was opposed by Sir Joseph Bazalgette, Engineer to the Metropolitan Board of Works, who maintained that this system of lighting still had defects which prevented its adoption as a serious competitor with gas lighting.

In 1906 the London County Council extended their tramway system across Westminster and Blackfriars Bridges along the Victoria Embankment, thus enabling the tramcars to follow a circular route instead of coming to a dead end as hitherto on the Surrey side of the river. Several attempts to bring about this improvement in previous years had proved unsuccesful, but in 1905 the necessary Bill was passed in the House of Commons by Mr Balfour's Government, though it was once again rejected in the House of Lords. With the advent of the Liberal Government in 1906 the Bill for extending the tramways passed both Houses without any further opposition and so rapidly was the work carried out that by December of that year they were already established along the Victoria Embankment. The tramways having now become obsolete, London Transport finally replaced them in 1952 with new omnibuses of the latest pattern.

Charing Cross Railway Bridge, which is an affront to the appearance of the Thames Embankment, was erected in 1860. It is the successor to the Hungerford Suspension Bridge designed by Mr I. K. Brunel and opened to the public on 1 May 1845. The latter is said to have cost £100,000 and has been removed to Clifton near Bristol. Permission to erect their Charing Cross Station on the north side of the river was granted to the former South Eastern Railway by Parliament at a time when a similar concession had been granted to the London, Brighton and South Coast Railway and the London, Chatham and Dover Railway to extend their lines to Victoria. The construction of the Victoria Embankment had not then been decided upon, or in all probability Charing Cross Station would never have been allowed to be constructed in its present position.

By universal consent Charing Cross Railway Bridge is now doomed and, whatever the present difficulties, its eventual removal will play a most important part in the reconstruction of London. In the words of one of our leading London newspapers, 'No visitor to the metropolis could fail to be distressed by the affront which Charing Cross or Hungerford Bridge offers to the view from Westminster Bridge and by the contrast between the stately buildings which line the north bank of the river and the wharves and sheds which happily have now been demolished and so disfigured the south bank as to suggest Lazarus in his rags and sores at the gate of the rich man's palace across the way.' But even wharves need not necessarily disfigure the river-front, and a notable exception is the one erected by the Oxo Company between Waterloo and Blackfriars Bridges, containing a tall, handsome clock-tower which looks well from the opposite side of the river.

In 1934 the London County Council decided to purchase the estate which lies between the County Hall, and the new Waterloo Bridge, at a cost of £1,500,000. Already by 1939 they had planned a south side embankment with gardens along the Thames but work on this project was suspended during the war.

The site which has now been cleared extends from the County Hall to Waterloo Road and from the Thames bank to York Road, covering an area of thirty-two acres. On this site was held the Festival of Britain which opened in May 1951. East of Charing Cross Railway Bridge, on the site of the former Lion Brewery, was erected the Royal Festival Hall at a cost of £2¼ millions. This is claimed to be the finest concert hall in Great Britain.

The Main Hall provides seating accommodation for 3,172 people and a large amount of additional accommodation, such as exhibition space and meeting rooms, is also provided. This has been placed around the main auditorium so that the Concert Hall becomes an inner core to the building, protected on all sides by its enclosing envelope, with the entrance foyer running under it. Simple and direct access to the auditorium is from side promenades. On the river front there is an upper and lower restaurant within the main foyer space.

The external shape of the building contains a large window area, mostly overlooking the river and affording exciting vistas of London's skyline unrivalled from any other vantage point. The whole of the structure is of reinforced concrete faced outside with Portland Stone. Inside as well as outside, special attention is given to the quality of the finish. An attractive feature is the ease with which sections of the building can be used simultaneously for different purposes.

The Hall was built in two stages, the first of which was completed by the time the Festival opened in 1951 and includes the Concert Hall, the restaurants, meeting rooms and additional accommodation.

London's famous Red Lion, erected in 1837 on the hundred-feet-high roof of the old Red Lion Brewery, has been carefully preserved and having stood for some years outside Waterloo Station, was in April, 1966 removed to a better position at the County Hall end of Westminster Bridge.

The famous Shot Tower, the second on this site, built in 1826, was retained. It is 140 feet high and the shot used to fall from a height of 120 feet.

Towering over the South Bank are the new offices for the Royal Dutch-Shell Group of oil companies. They have been designed by Sir Howard Robertson, A.R.A., and built between 1957 and 1962, they comprise two blocks, one on either side of Hungerford Bridge. The 'Upstream' building, consisting of ten storeys, is dominated by a twenty-six storey tower of 351 feet above street level. The 'Downstream' block has ten storeys with a three-storey annexe, fronting on to Belvedere Road. These outstanding buildings accommodate more than 5,000 employees.

With the building of the Shell offices the National Film Theatre had to move from its original home in the Festival of Britain Telecinema and the present National Film Theatre was built under Waterloo Bridge.

In recent years the Royal Festival Hall has been used in ways for which it was not originally designed. It now houses summer and winter ballet seasons which have necessitated the introduction of a demountable proscenium stage and its foyers have been used for exhibitions and social functions on a scale far greater than was originally envisaged.

The second stage in the development of the Royal Festival Hall has now been completed. The foyers and restaurant space have been considerably enlarged, the area of the bars doubled and the ballroom, which opens on to a sheltered terrace, enlarged to 100 feet by 81 feet. Backstage improvements include many new dressing rooms and storage accommodation. Four new lifts carry 30 persons each. The river front, containing new entrance foyers, has been extended. The Waterloo Bridge entrance is being retained for private functions.

Downstream, on the site originally intended for a National Theatre, for which Queen Elizabeth the Queen Mother laid the foundation stone, the second concert hall is now under construction. This will consist of two auditoria: The Queen Elizabeth Hall, seating approximately 1000 and The Purcell Room, with seats for about 360. Further back from the river will be an exhibition gallery (to be known as the Hayward Gallery, after Sir Isaac Hayward, the last Leader of the London County Council), on two levels with open-air sculpture courts cantilevered out from the main structure. The new buildings will be given dark finishes of Cornish granite and their sculptured outlines will contrast with the Shell offices and the Royal Festival Hall.

Upper level terraces will connect the three buildings and give access to Waterloo Bridge, Hungerford footbridge and Waterloo station free from vehicular traffic. Terraces at a still higher level (over the lower level of the exhibition gallery and the foyer of the small concert hall) will provide secondary access from Waterloo Bridge to the South Bank with spacious observation and seating areas. Two loop roads from Belvedere Road will carry motor traffic to the concert halls, gallery and the National Film Theatre and below the exhibition gallery will be a park for 170 cars. The riverside gardens are being reshaped into a continuous promenade through an avenue of trees from County Hall to Waterloo Bridge.

On the site now occupied by Charing Cross Station and Hotel formerly stood Hungerford Market, a large two-storey building opened in 1833 for the sale of meat, fish, fruit, and vegetables, which replaced an earlier market built in 1680 by Sir E. Hungerford. The hall possessed stalls for the sale of cheap prints, picture-frames, walking-sticks, shells, and sweetmeats, and a large exhibition hall and bazaar gallery were added to the building in 1851, beneath the upper portion of the structure. This was afterwards appropriated by Messrs Gatti & Morico for the sale of ices and coffee and fitted up as a small café with an orchestra, and when the building was pulled down in August 1862 for the construction of Charing Cross Station, this firm received £7,750 compensation. Hungerford Market was never a success. The quadrangle overlooked the Strand and was a convenient starting-place for the Paddington and Camden Town omnibuses.

Charing Cross Station was opened to the public on 11 January 1864, but the hotel not opened until 15 May 1865. Being one-of the first of the large modern hotels to be erected in London it was an immediate success and on the opening evening was already more than half occupied. The Eleanor Cross, seventy feet high, which stands in front of Charing Cross Station, was erected in 1865 by the Charing Cross Hotel Company; the design of this reproduction was carried out by Sir Edward M. Barry, A.R.A., who also designed the hotel.

In December 1905, whilst some twenty men were at work repairing the lofty semicircular roof of Charing Cross Station, a tie-rod snapped, thereby causing the entire structure to collapse. Fortunately no lives were lost, but some of the wreckage fell on to the roof of the adjoining Avenue Theatre, opened in March 1882 and now renamed the Playhouse, which was almost completely destroyed. The theatre had to be entirely rebuilt, and Mr Cyril Maude, the lessee, received £30,000 compensation from the South Eastern & Chatham Railway for the damage caused. The collapse of the roof of Charing Cross Station proved a blessing in disguise, as it led to the disappearance of a hideous eyesore from the Thames Embankment and the construction of a new flat roof in its place, more in harmony with the surrounding buildings. This also was damaged in the air raids and in 1944 the upper floors of the hotel were damaged by a flying-bomb. The Playhouse Theatre is now a B.B.C. studio.

Beyond Charing Cross Station, overlooking the Embankment Gardens, is Whitehall Court, another noble pile of buildings erected in 1887 by the Liberator Permanent Building and Investment Society and designed by Sir Alfred Water-house, R.A. It houses the National Liberal Club and various other London clubs.

We now leave the Victoria Embankment at Charing Cross and proceed up Northumberland Avenue. This exceedingly handsome thoroughfare, constructed across the grounds of Northumberland House at a total cost of £650,000, was opened to the public without ceremony on 18 March, 1876. Northumberland House, built in the reign of James I in 1605 for Henry Howard, Earl of North-ampton, was then known as Northampton House, It was purchased in 1874 from the Duke of Northumberland and his son Earl Percy for £525,000, under a special Act of Parliament for the purpose of constructing a new street to connect Charing Cross with the Victoria Embankment.

As early as 1865 it was proposed to purchase Northumberland House for the new street, and the Duke of Northumberland was served with a notice in December of that year by the Metropolitan Board of Works, but he was successful on that occasion in resisting compulsory purchase. There was much controversy at the time as to the necessity for destroying Northumberland House, and an alternative scheme was propounded by Sir James Pennethorne which would have avoided the necessity for so doing, by taking a slightly curved line opposite the King Charles statue to the Victoria Embankment, leaving the house intact by passing it on the west side, but shaving off a slice of the garden. It was urged that not only would Northumberland House have been spared under this plan, but that this alternative scheme would have concealed the ugly view of the Charing Cross Railway Bridge over the river. Northumberland House was the very last relic of all the noble mansions and palaces which in the seventeenth century adorned the river-front of the Strand.

Finally, at a meeting of the Metropolitan Board of Works held in July 1872, it was again decided to make an application for the purchase of Northumberland House with a view to obtaining the direct approach to the Victoria Embankment, which by that time had become imperative. It was said at the time that the ratepayers would be recouped by the purchase to the extent of £300,000 on the sale of the surplus land overlooking the new street.

A part of Northumberland House, including the ball-room, was destroyed by fire on the night of 19 August 1868. During its last days prior to demolition in July 1874, it was thronged with people who were furnished with tickets of admission by the Metropolitan Board of Works. Several adjoining houses in Charing Cross, at the entrance to the Strand, were also purchased for the construction of the new thoroughfare.

It was some years before the whole of the building sites in Northumberland Avenue were disposed of. The first building to be erected here was Grand Buildings at the corner of the Strand, which was opened in June 1880 by the Gordon Hotels Company. Originally called the Grand Hotel, it is built in the later Italian style, with a mansard roof, and was designed on the lines of the most modern French and American hotels of that period. Until the erection of other buildings in Northumberland Avenue it enjoyed a fine outlook over the Thames Embankment and the new Charing Cross Gardens. The hotel had three hundred rooms, and even in its earliest days was greatly frequented by non-residents for table d'hôte dinner. In 1928 the Grand Hotel was sold by the Gordon Hotels Company for conversion to offices, and an arcade was then constructed between the Strand and Northumberland Avenue containing shops on the ground floor. Commenting upon their decision to sell the Grand Hotel in 1928, Sir Francis Towle, Chairman of the Gordon Hotels Company, expressed the opinion that nowadays a great hotel resembled a battleship inasmuch as it tended to become obsolete after twenty years of existence and that visitors now preferred the newer hotels in the West End. Next to Grand Buildings was the Constitutional Club, a handsome building of six storeys in the Gothic style with a façade of terra-cotta. Built in 1884, it was designed by Sir Robert Edis. It was recently demolished and a new nine-storey building, occupied by the Standard Bank and other offices has replaced it. Just behind, in Northumberland Street is a tavern which until recently was known as the Northumberland Arms and its sign was the well-known Northumberland Lion, with his tail 'extended', as the heralds have it. It has now been re-named the Sherlock Holmes and contains an interesting collection of

'Holmesiana'; the dining-room on the first floor has been arranged to represent the celebrated sitting-room at Number 221b Baker Street.

The Hotel Metropole, opened in 1885, and the Hotel Victoria, opened in 1890, are both situated in Northumberland Avenue, and when first built by the Gordon Hotels Company were considered amongst the finest in the world. During the first World War practically the whole of Northumberland Avenue was requisitioned by the Government and the Ministry of Munitions, including the three great hotels, the Constitutional Club and, ironically enough, the offices of the Society for the Promotion of Christian Knowledge. In 1936 the Hotel Metropole was purchased by the Government for £300,000 in order to provide alternative accommodation for the various departments which had removed from Whitehall Gardens to make way for the construction of the magnificent new block of Government Offices recently erected on that site. The Metropole and the Victoria, now renamed Metropole Buildings and Northumberland House respectively, are still in use as Government offices. Facing the Metropole in Northumberland Avenue is the handsome building of the Royal Commonwealth Society erected in 1936. It was damaged in the air raids of 1940 but has now been repaired. The foundation-stone was laid on 3 June 1935 by the Duke of Windsor when Prince of Wales. In Craven Street and Villiers Street, both leading from the Victoria Embankment to the Strand, are several small hotels and restaurants which cater mostly for short-term visitors. The largest of these is the Adelphi Hotel and Restaurant in Villiers Street, which faces Charing Cross Station.

Passing next into the Strand, we miss Trafalgar Square, to which we shall come during another walk. Nearly all the old houses which had previously lined the north side of the Strand from Charing Cross to Wellington Street were pulled down between 1921 and 1831, and during the present century the majority of these have been rebuilt a second time. Duncannon Street was named after Lord Duncannon, who was Chief Commissioner in 1837, and William IV Street, running diagonally from the Strand to St Martin's Lane, and Agar Street were also constructed in the reign of William IV, when a considerable widening of this part of the Strand was carried out.

Between Duncannon Street and Agar Street is an interesting triangular block of buildings, the remains of the West Strand Improvements of 1830, but the identity of the architect is still the subject of discussion. With the Strand as the base of the triangle, the other sides are Adelaide Street and William IV Street; the western corner is adorned by a pair of imposing domed turrets and the other corners have one each, though one has lost its dome. The symmetry of the stucco frontage in the Strand is interrupted by the head office of Coutts & Company, bankers to the Royal Family. This building was completed in 1904, when they moved from No. 159 across the road where the bank had carried on its bussiness since 1739. The Banking Hall—or 'The Shop', as they call it—lies almost exactly on the site of the old Lowther Arcade, which ran diagonally from the Strand through to Adelaide Street. The Arcade, named after Viscount Lowther, Commissioner of Woods and Forests, was by the sixties a children's paradise, especially at Christmas, full of toy-shops – about thirty of them. A very popular song of the period – 'The Tin Gee-Gee' – which told the touching love-story of a toy soldier and a little doll in the Lowther Arcade, doubtless set the pattern for the Magnet and Churn type of song and later, the familiar 'bird' or 'animal' duet for the comedian and soubrette in subsequent musical comedies.

The Banking Hall at 440 Strand is full of interest for, in addition to a display of historical documents and objects drawn from the bank's archives, it will be noticed that the male staff wear frock coats of a style of long ago and, by an earlier tradition, are all clean-shaven. Charing Cross Hospital, at the corner of William IV Street, was founded in 1818, and the present building was erected in 1831 and greatly enlarged in 1904. The widening of the Strand, from Wellington Street westward, which for many years came to a halt opposite Agar Street, has now been completed. All the buildings on the south side from George Court to Viliers Street have been demolished. A new eight-storey building, 'Villiers House', with shops below and an arcade leading through to Buckingham Street (somewhat shortened) now occupies this stretch of the Strand. East of George Court is Halifax House, the London headquarters of the Halifax Building Society. This is a large building of nine storeys erected in 1933; next to it the New South Wales Government offices.

A start was made on the widening of the south side of the Strand in 1899 when the Hotel Cecil extended its frontage from the Embankment. It had previously possessed a small frontage to the Strand, but this entrance was almost concealed from view and, to make room for the imposing new building now fronting the Strand, something like a dozen houses were pulled down and the roadway set back to a width of eighty feet. In 1902 the Savoy Hotel decided to follow in the footsteps of its neighbour, and like the Hotel Cecil extended its building from the Embankment Gardens to the new line of frontage in the Strand. Amongst other buildings which were swallowed up in this improvement was the former world-famed chop-house of Messrs Simpson, which was then rebuilt and incorporated in the new building of the Savoy Hotel. Two new blocks of buildings were erected, one on each side of the new courtyard, both of elegant appearance, that on the east side forming part of the hotel and that on the west side being utilized for business premises and for many years as the head offices of the Metropolitan Water Board. The west side of the courtyard also includes the Savoy Theatre which was opened in October 1881. The top storeys of the Savoy Hotel fronting the Strand were damaged by bombing during the blitz, but have since been repaired.

For over ten years after the completion of the Savoy Hotel no further progress was made with the widening of the Strand, but in 1914 the old Tivoli Music Hall was pulled down. It was then to have been reconstructed but the outbreak of the first World War led to the abandonment of this scheme and the site remained vacant for the following two years. At first it was used as a recruiting station for Kitchener's Army, and after 1916 the famous Canadian Y.M.C.A. structure known as the Beaver Hut was erected on this site. It was removed to make way for the modern Tivoli Cinema, erected in 1922 on the new line of frontage. The comparatively new Tivoli Cinema, however, has now been demolished and in its place, between Durham House Street and Adam Street, stands a new Peter Robinson store. The range of new buildings between the Savoy Hotel and Wellington Street, forming a part of the estate of the Duchy of Lancaster, was also erected in 1924-25, but one building at the west corner of Savoy Street still remains to be set back to the amended line of frontage. This is Savoy House, at the corner of Savoy Street; it houses the Western Australia Government offices.

One of the buildings which have been swallowed up in this improvement is Terry's Theatre, which in later years was converted into a cinema. Close by were the former headquarters of the Art Union of London, a Palladian building erected in 1879, in which Sir Mallaby Deeley opened a tailor's shop after the first World War, for the purpose of defeating the flagrant profiteering in men's clothes which was taking place at that time. In Savoy Street is the Savoy Chapel Royal, restored at the expense of Queen Victoria in 1864 after a fire. It stands on part of the site of the ancient Palace of the Savoy presented by Henry III to his uncle, the Count of Savoy.

The demolition of the three remaining houses between Adam Street and the Hotel Cecil in 1927 completed the widening of the Strand from Wellington Street to nearly opposite Agar Street, and at the same time opened up a new vista of the Nelson Monument from the eastern end of the Strand.

Turning our attention once more to the north side of the Strand, at the corner of Agar Street is a five-storey building erected in 1908 for the British Medical Association and now occupied by the Rhodesian Government. It is built of grey granite and when newly erected created a great stir because of the alleged impropriety of the nude anatomical figures, designed by Epstein, which adorn its exterior, and which at that time were styled 'indecent' by one of our leading London newspapers. However, the Epstein figures are now so weather-beaten that they are almost unrecognizable. The British Medical Association has now removed to Bloomsbury. On the adjoining site, extending to Bedford Street, the Civil Service Stores in 1932 erected a new building with an entrance in the Strand.

At the east corner of Bedford Street is a large modern block of buildings known as Walter House named after Sir Edward Walter, K.C.B., who in 1859 formed the Corps of Commissionaires, whose headquarters are next door in Exchange Court. Sir Edward was the first Commandant of the Corps, and it is an interesting record of family succession that during a period of over a hundred years the Commandant has always been a Walter. Following the death of the Founder in 1904, the post of Commandant was held successively by a nephew, two great-nephews and, since 1960, a great-great-nephew of the founder, Lt. Col. R. F. Walter, who today commands the splendid Corps of Commissionaires of which Her Majesty the Queen is Chief Life Governor.

Adjoining the former offices of the New Zealand Government (now Barclay's Bank) is the Adelphi Theatre, originally built in 1806 by Mr John Scott, a colourmaker. Reconstructed in 1858, it became a celebrated house for melodrama and here the unfortunate Mr William Terriss was stabbed to death by a madman outside the theatre on 16 December 1897. The Adelphi Theatre was again reconstructed in 1910 and afterwards became a popular house for musical comedy under the management of Mr George Edwardes. In 1930 it was rebuilt for the third time, and the façade lined with black imitation marble. A few doors further east is the Vaudeville Theatre and next to it was Romano's, a popular restaurant in the days when the Strand was the centre of London's night-life. It is now a shoe shop, but remembrance of its gaudy past is preserved by the name 'Romano House'.

East of Southampton Street extensive rebuilding operations have been carried out on this side of the Strand in recent years, and what were once regarded as veritable skyscapers have replaced the four-storey stucco-fronted buildings erected here over a century ago, which were considered very fine in their day. Between Southampton Street and Exeter Street is Manfield House, and on the opposite corner of the Strand and Exeter Street extending to Burleigh Street is the huge Strand Palace Hotel, nine storeys high with nine hundred rooms.

The greater part of this site was formerly occupied by Exeter Hall, the head-quarters of the Y.M.C.A., now removed to Tottenham Court Road, but it had only a narrow frontage to the Strand, on both sides of which stood Haxell's Hotel, the two sections of which were connected with each other by a corridor running across the upper floor of Exeter Hall. Erected in 1831 by Mr Gandy Deering, Exeter Hall was at first used for meetings of all kinds, excepting political gatherings, which were not permitted there. Later it became the headquarters of the Young Men's Christian Association, and in February 1863 a monster anti-slavery meeting was held in this building. In 1907 Exeter Hall was pulled down and the greater part of the present Strand Palace Hotel was erected on the site, but the extension covering the site of Haxell's Hotel was not completed until 1930.

Another building which has been absorbed by the Strand Palace Hotel is that of the old *Globe* newspaper, founded in 1803, and which received its deathblow during the first World War. For an offence against the Defence of the Realm Act its offices and machine-room were raided in 1916 and closed down for several weeks. In 1921 it was absorbed by the *Pall Mall Gazette*, which was in turn absorbed in 1923 by the *Evening Standard*.

On the adjoining island site covered by the Lyceum Theatre and several shops fronting the Strand, it was proposed as long ago as 1858 to erect a huge hotel which was to have been called the International, and to have been designed on the lines of the Hôtel du Louvre in Paris, at an estimated cost of £100,000. For some unstated reason the whole scheme was abandoned, although London at that time was very badly off for first-class hotel accommodation, and the opening of the Hôtel du Louvre in Paris had excited great admiration and caused a demand for a similar establishment in London, a demand which was met by the erection of the much larger Strand Palace Hotel.

On this site previously stood the Exeter Exchange, overlooking the Strand, which was pulled down about 1820 for the Strand improvements. This was erected about 1680 as a rival to Gresham's Royal Exchange in the City, but for many years afterwards was a failure until this district became more populous. Before the construction of the Exeter Exchange this ground was occupied by Exeter House, the palace of Walter de Stapeldon (1261-1326), Bishop of Exeter and Lord High Treasurer.

The Lyceum Theatre was first built as an opera house in 1794, but was destroyed by fire and rebuilt in 1834 by Mr S. Beazley, an architect. From 1878 to 1904 it was managed by Sir Henry Irving and then became for a time a music-hall. Shortly before the first World War, the Lyceum Theatre was rebuilt, though the portico in Wellington Street was, like that of Drury Lane Theatre, preserved for reasons of sentiment. In 1920, owing to a quarrel between the brothers Walter and Harry Melville, lessees of this theatre, it remained closed for two and a half years. Each of the brothers was willing to buy out the other, but neither of them would alter his decision to retain control, until eventually they agreed in 1923 to settle their differences and reopen the Lyceum. It is now a dance hall.

Wellington Street was constructed in conjunction with Waterloo Bridge, in 1817, from the Thames as far as the Strand, and in 1924 its width was increased to eighty feet on the west side at the corner of the Strand where Wellington House now stands. In order to provide a spacious northern approach to Waterloo Bridge the London County Council in 1939 decided to purchase the entire block of buildings including the Lyceum Theatre, which forms a large island site, Inveresk House forming the adjoining island site in Aldwych, and Wellington House newly erected in 1925, and the buildings on the east corner of the Strand next to Somerset House. An island was to be constructed on the cleared sites around which one-way traffic would operate. The cost was estimated at £2,000,000 but the outbreak of war led to an idenfinite postponement of this ambitious scheme. However, a similar result has been achieved by arranging one-way traffic round the Aldwych island.

The northern portion of Wellington Street was not constructed until several years after the opening of Waterloo Bridge, and until July 1846 was known as Charles Street, Covent Garden. Before that time there was still no direct thoroughfare leading to Bow Street and Long Acre. The row of Georgian houses known as Lancaster Place, opposite the west front of Somerset House, was pulled down in 1930 and on this site an immense new building called Brettenham House was erected in 1932 by the Law Land Company. It extends to Savoy Street and has an elevation of ten storeys, with the two upper floors zoned back from the building line in Wellington Street. When viewed from the Victoria Embankment it forms a prominent landmark, and when seen from Blackfriars Bridge presents a high background which completely dwarfs the view of Somerset House. Here also the building line has been set back, and this has completed the widening of Wellington Street to eighty feet between the Strand and Waterloo Bridge.

On the south side of Waterloo Bridge a new roundabout has been constructed. This takes the form of a semicircular road, commencing at the approach to the bridge in Waterloo Road, then crossing York Road near the Royal Festival Hall and terminating in Waterloo Road opposite St John's Church. The new street is for the use of north-bound traffic whilst the south-bound traffic proceeds as before, direct along Waterloo Road. An attractive block of modern shops flanks the roundabout.

At the other end of York Road another roundabout has been constructed at the back of Westminster Bridge Road. This new street is in fact an extensive widening of Addington Street, which leads into Westminster Bridge Road near the railway bridge of the Southern Region railway. On the opposite side of Westminster Bridge Road another new street leads into Lambeth Palace Road and, passing at the back of St Thomas's Hospital terminates at the approach to Westminster Bridge. Thus the roundabout takes the form of the figure eight. The width of York Road has been increased to seventy feet.

Except for an interesting old bookshop, York Road before 1939 was a generally dull street of decaying houses and shops. Today, there are so many new office blocks that the General Lying In Hospital, built in 1828, is almost the only pre-war building left.

Ninth Walk

High Holborn, Bloomsbury, New Oxford Street, Tottenham Court Road, Euston Road, St Pancras, King's Cross, Pentonville, Clerkenwell and Theobald's Road

High Holborn, which will form the starting-point of this walk, extends from the City boundary at Gray's Inn Road westward to Shaftesbury Avenue, the section previously known as Broad Street having now become part of High Holborn. The name of High Holborn, as distinguished from Holborn proper, would appear almost superfluous, since most people are in the habit of referring to the entire thoroughfare as Holborn. In September 1874 it was actually proposed by the Metropolitan Board of Works that its title should be altered to Holborn simply, but vigorous opposition was offered by the inhabitants of High Holborn and a memorandum protesting against the proposed change was presented to the Board as the result of a meeting convened for that purpose. The more or less triangular space at the top of Shaftesbury Avenue, facing the Shaftesbury (previously Princes) Theatre, still has the former, now bears the Borough of Holborn's official name, 'Princes Circus'.

Gray's Inn Road, one of the principal tributary thoroughfares leading north from High Holborn, contains on the west side Gray's Inn, one of the four great Inns of Court, originally founded for the education and lodging of law students. It occupies an extensive area between Holborn and Theobald's Road and its buildings, which present a gloomy appearance when viewed from Gray's Inn Road, overlook pleasant gardens with fine plane-trees and lawns, laid out by Francis Bacon, who was admitted as a member in 1576 and held the office of Treasurer for nine years. The catalpa-trees in the centre are supposed to have been planted by him, and in the South Square is a statue of Francis Bacon by F. W. Pomeroy, A.R.A., marking the tercentenary of his election as Treasurer in 1608. In the air raid of 10 May 1941, the statue was toppled over and several houses on the north-east corner of Gray's Inn Square were destroyed, leaving a great gap. The interiors of the Hall, the Chapel, and the Library were also destroyed in the same raid, but all three have now been rebuilt. The gardens are now open to the public at certain hours during the summer months by kind permission of the Benchers of Gray's Inn.

Gray's Inn Road from Holborn to Theobald's Road was considerably widened in the 'eighties of last century and this improvement was evidenced by the long row of red-brick buildings lining its eastern side. Before that time it was called Gray's Inn Lane. At the east corner of Clerkenwell Road was Holborn Hall, originally the municipal offices of the Holborn Borough Council, and opened by the Lord Mayor of London on 18 January 1880. About 1908 the Holborn Borough Council removed to a new Town Hall erected in High Holborn close to the junction of New Oxford Street, which is now the Architects and Planning Department of the London Borough of Camden, into which Holborn has been absorbed. The only other building of much interest in Gray's Inn Road is the Royal Free Hospital, on the same side of the road, about half a mile distant from Holborn, and founded in 1828. Chancery Lane Station of the Underground Railway has its entrance from street level by Gray's Inn Road. This was opened in June 1934. When boring the tunnel, the contractors struck the old river Bourne which once flowed across Holborn to the Fleet River. On that account the escalators have been enclosed in an iron tank and the walls of the station lined with extra steel supports. The former station in High Holborn has now been converted into offices.

Returning to High Holborn, nearly opposite Chancery Lane on the north side stood, until 1940, the extensive First Avenue Hotel, formerly owned by the Gordon Hotels Company, and afterwards converted into offices under new proprietors. It was long a favourite rendezvous for lunch with solicitors and barristers. It was badly damaged in the air raids of September 1940 and has since been pulled down. On this site a nine-storeyed block of shops and offices called 'First Avenue House' has been erected and is principally occupied by the Ministry of Aviation and the War Office. Its architects are Messrs Gordon Jeeves. Of late years quite a number of fine buildings have been erected in High Holborn, principally on the north side, but the famous Inns of Court Hotel, which, before the first World War, stood on the south side, about midway between Chancery Lane and Kingsway, has been replaced by a large telephone exchange erected in 1920. Next to it is Princeton House, a nine-storey block of shops and offices which was erected in 1939 and faces Red Lion Street. Most of the older houses on the south side of High Holborn between Gate Street and Chancery Lane were destroyed in the air raids of 1940 and their sites are now occupied by new buildings.

Quite the largest building in this section of High Holborn is 'State House', a sixteen-storey block of offices on the corner of Red Lion Street. The abstract metal sculpture in the courtyard is by Barbara Hepworth.

Another important building in High Holborn is that of the Pearl Assurance Company, erected on the south side of the street and removed here in 1913 from Adelaide House, King William Street. It is adorned by a lofty clock-tower, and in 1930 a large new wing was added to this building on the east side in High Holborn. Farther west on the same side of the street was the Holborn Empire, formerly known as the Royal Theatre of Varieties, and opened in June 1867. It was severely damaged by a bomb in 1941, and has been completely demolished; it has been replaced by a seven-storey office block.

A few stages farther along is a building occupied by Messrs Crawford, the advertising specialists. It is a striking example of modernist architecture. The Holborn Restaurant, at the west corner of Kingsway, was originally the Holborn Casino, and in the 'seventies of last century was the largest and best-conducted dance hall in London. The first extension took place in 1874, the building was further enlarged in 1896, but quite recently the entire building was pulled down and a new office building for the Midland Bank and Burnley Building Society now stands on the site of the old Holborn Restaurant.

On the north side of High Holborn, a considerable widening of the roadway between Red Lion Street and Southampton Row was carried out in 1901 by the London County Council as part of the great Kingsway improvement and here a long row of modern buildings has been erected.

At Holborn Underground Station on the east corner of Kingsway and High Holborn, the Central and Piccadilly Line tubes were connected in 1934 by a subway and by escalators. This enabled passengers to travel under cover between these two lines, thus avoiding the former inconvenience of having to cross High Holborn to get from the former British Museum Station to the Holborn Station. The old British Museum Station was then abolished.

Southampton Row, formerly a very narrow street between High Holborn and Great Russell Street, is today, in consequence of the extensive widening carried out here by the London County Council, one of the finest thoroughfares in London. The portion between High Holborn and Theobald's Road was widened in 1904, but the section between Theobald's Road and Great Russell Street was not widened until 1915. The east side of Southampton Row contains the Baptist Church House and the Central School of Arts and Crafts, erected between 1906 and 1908, and at this point the underground tramway came to the surface. On the opposite side of the road are two picturesque blocks of buildings separated from one another by a wide passage known as Sicilian Avenue, containing shops and offices and leading into Hart Street, now renamed Bloomsbury Way.

On the large island site immediately north, enclosed by the west side of Southampton Row, Vernon Place, Bloomsbury Square, and Bloomsbury Place, is Victoria House, the Head Office of the Liverpool Victoria Friendly Society. This magnificent building, designed by Mr C. W. Long, is eight storeys high, with a tall, sloping roof and a central tower, and is far more suggestive of a large Government building than the office of a private business concern. It is splendidly proportioned and is a decided credit to the architectural features of the metropolis. The building has two spacious and well-equipped halls, known as Victoria Halls, which are in demand for dances, conferences, and other functions. The east side of the building facing Southampton Row contains a row of well-designed and attractive shops. The west side, facing Bloomsbury Square with its trees and lawns, provides a restful viewpoint for those working in this large office building. Sentinel House, a red-brick block of shops and offices which stood opposite Victoria House, was destroyed in the air raids of 1940, but has been replaced by a new building of the same name.

Forming part of the main thoroughfare connecting the Strand with the northern railway termini, Southampton Row is well known for its excellent shops and large hotels. The principal hotels are the Bonnington, the Imperial, and the imposing Hotel Russell on the east side, the last-named overlooking Russell Square, and the Bedford and some smaller hotels on the west side. At the back of the Bedford Hotel, which was recently rebuilt, a handsome pair of old wrought-iron gates lead to the gardens at the rear of Bedford Place. Southampton Row is a great centre of the tourist traffic and here the constant arrival and departure of motor-coaches laden with visitors or sightseers present a gay and animated scene. Close to Russell Square on the east side is Pitman's Business College, and farther south is Faraday House, a college for the study of electrical engineering.

Southampton Row comes to an end at Russell Square, laid out in 1805 and so called after the Russells, Earls and Dukes of Bedford, and one of the largest in London. On the east side of the Square formerly stood the twin hotels, the Russell and the Imperial. The former, of eight storeys and dated 1898, is of red brick and terracotta and is amply decorated with figures of four queens, Elizabeth, Mary II, Anne and Victoria, and many heraldic medallions; but this was quite overshadowed by the ornate Imperial, of 1911. Towers, turrets, spires, clock and sundial — everything — and so much more cheerful than the drab exterior of the Royal, on the other side of the road. It is with a feeling of regret that we have to record that this flamboyant spectacle was recently demolished. On the south side of Russell Square is a statue of Francis, fifth Duke of Bedford; the plinth is embellished with agricultural motifs. Russell Square, Southampton Row is continued under the name of Woburn Place. Here an extensive widening was carried out on the west side in 1922. On this site has been erected the Royal Hotel, opened in 1927, with an unusually long frontage extending from Russell Square almost to Tavistock Square, an excessively plain building in external appearance, more suggestive of a large factory than a hotel. On the other side of Woburn Place, formerly lined with Georgian houses long since converted into private hotels, now stands Russell Court. This is a bold block of bachelor flats, nine storeys high, erected in 1937. It is designed to provide small flats for university students and people unable to afford big rents. The originator of this scheme was Mr Gerald Glover, a London solicitor, and its architects were Messrs Val Myer and Watson Hart. On the neighbouring sites are two handsome new blocks of offices of uniform design, nine storeys high, erected in 1939, one of which faces Tavistock Square. Next to this is the new headquarters of the British Medical Association, a building of brick with stone dressings erected about 1928 and designed by Sir Edwin Lutyens, R.A., and Mr H. P. Adams. An extension now completed, was commenced in 1939 and its architect is Mr C. Wontner Smith. On the north side of Tavistock Square is a nine-storey block of flats called Tavistock Court. On the south side at the corner of Woburn Place the new Tavistock Hotel has been erected since the war. All the rooms of this modern hotel have private bathrooms.

Resuming our route from High Holborn, New Oxford Street was constructed at a cost of £290,000 and opened to vehicular traffic on 6 March 1847. It was designed to provide direct communication between High Holborn and Oxford Street, without passing by the tortuous route of St Giles's High Street — though, curiously, present day westbound traffic now has to proceed along this once 'tortuous toute'. New Oxford Street was driven through the heart of the so-called St Giles's rookery, which contained some of the worst squalor and slums in London. Of the compensation money, £114,000 was awarded to the Duke of Bedford for the freehold purchases of the land required for the new street, and in 1846 the whole of the houses facing St Giles's Church were demolished in connexion with this improvement. By 1849 all that remained of the infamous rookery was concentrated in ninety-five wretched houses in the former Church Lane and Carrier Street, wherein, incredible though it may appear, no fewer than 2,850 persons were crammed into a space of ground less than an acre and a quarter in area. In some of these noisome abodes, shelter could be obtained at threepence per head nightly. The most amazing fact was that amidst this great filth the inhabitants of St Giles's, who often slept fifty persons in one room, managed to survive, except perhaps in the hot weather, when these dens of misery and filth threw forth the most offensive smells, which were sometimes overpowering. In April 1843 a fever epidemic broke out in St Giles's and other metropolitan parishes, claiming more victims than were ever known during the worst periods of the cholera. It will also be remembered that the Great Plague of London, from which 100,000 people died in 1665, began in the St Giles's area.

In the squalid back rookeries of St Giles's picturesque scenes could sometimes be witnessed equal to those seen by tourists and artists who had travelled extensively in foreign cities. Here the place would be gay with costermongers' stalls containing fruit, vegetables, and flowers, bought in quantities from Covent Garden to be trimmed up and arranged for general sale.

In one of the streets was a large water tank, erected at a time when water in this densely-peopled district was almost as scarce and precious as in the desert, and this proved a great boon to the neighbourhood. In later years the sanitary authorities displayed greater vigilance in respect of the drainage, water supply, number of beds in apartments, and the cleanliness of rooms generally. In 1846 a model lodging house, eighty feet long and six storeys high, was erected in George Street by the Society for Improving the Conditions of the Labouring Classes.

The church of St Giles-in-the-Fields was so named to distinguish it from St Giles's Cripplegate. Constructed in 1733, it is the third church which has been erected on this site, and is built of Portland stone and has a spire 160 feet high, including the vane. After 1853, as the result of a petition to the Home Secretary, the churchyard was closed to further burials, as this practice had long since become dangerous to the health of this crowded neighbourhood. A prominent tomb in the churchyard is that of 'Unparallel'd Pendrell', who assisted Charles II to excape after the Battle of Worcester in 1651. He was rewarded with a pension in perpetuity which, it is believed, is still received by his descendents.

The buildings in New Oxford Street exhibited a great advance in taste at that period, and their elevation was well adapted to the width and requirements of the street. Its vacant building sites were soon disposed of, and it became an important shopping street. Looking at New Oxford Street and its side turnings at the present day, it is difficult to visualize what this neighbourhood looked like when it was covered by the St Giles's rookery. The construction of Shaftesbury Avenue in 1885 effected a further improvement in this locality, causing a number of houses to be swept away between Broad Street and Hart Street, Bloomsbury. Close to Shaftesbury Avenue, in Endell Street, stood Christchurch, St. Giles, a Gothic building which was erected in 1844, but pulled down in 1930.

Since 1928 the north side of New Oxford Street from Tottenham Court Road to Bloomsbury Street has been nearly all rebuilt, and is now lined by several stately structures. Prominent amongst these are the new premises of Messrs Burton, the popular tailoring establishment, at the corner of Tottenham Court Road, six storeys high, faced with stone, and erected at a cost of no less than £300,000. At the corner of Bainbridge Street is an entrance to the Dominion Cinema erected on the site of the old Meux Brewery within the record time of twelve months and opened in 1929. The main entrance is in Tottenham Court Road, adjoining the Horse Shoe Hotel. Other new buildings which have arisen in New Oxford Street are Imhof House at the east corner of Bainbridge Street, and that erected for the drapery store of Messrs Henry Glave & Son, which closed down in 1936. This building is being reconstituted.

The building on the south side of New Oxford Street formerly occupied by Messrs A. & F. Pears, the well-known firm of soap manufacturers, has now been renamed James House and is occupied by the Dick James Music Company and the Midland Bank. A fragment of the world-wide Pears' Soap advertising campaign still survives, however, in the form of two hinged brass plates in the pavement, each with the name of 'Pears' in raised letters; they cover sockets in which stood, it is said, large ornamental lamps which threw more light on the virtues of Pears' Soap. All the adjoining buildings on this side of the street as far as Earnshaw Street have been demolished. On this great site which extends back to Bucknall Street a huge new block of shops and offices, called Castlewood House, has been erected and is occupied by the Ministry of Aviation. Its architects are Messrs Lewis Solomon & Son. The popular Vienna Café which formerly stood at the junction of New Oxford Street and Hart Street was in later years converted into banking premises. It was pulled down in 1939 when all the buildings on the large triangular island site at the junction of Hart Street, now renamed Bloomsbury Way, New Oxford Street and Bury Place were pulled down for the erection of a huge block of shops and offices by Mr J. A. Phillips, the well-known London estate agent. Only the foundations had been completed before the outbreak of war. Building operations were suspended and in 1941 Mr Philips died. The basement was then requisitioned for a coal dump and partly for a large air-raid shelter, but a magnificent new building of nine storeys called

St George's Court has now been completed on this site, at a cost of £490,000. It is faced with stone up to the first floor and the upper part with yellow brick with stone dressings. It is at present occupied by the Ministry of Aviation. The architects are Messrs Lewis Solomon & Son. On another large triangular site at the junction of High Holborn and New Oxford Street nearly opposite St George's Court now stands Commonwealth House, a ten-storeyed block of shops and offices, completed in 1939. It was erected by the Pearl Assurance Company and is of a similar character to St George's Court. Its architect was Colonel Lafontaine. The increased height of the new buildings has in no way spoiled the appearance of New Oxford Street, although the old four-storey buildings are being mostly replaced by six-storey structures.

An explosion of gas-main pipes which occurred in December 1928 caused an upheaval in several important thoroughfares in this district, including New Oxford Street, Broad Street, High Street, St Giles's, and the eastern end of Shaftesbury Avenue, all of which were closed to traffic for many weeks, whilst the damage was being repaired. Many small shopkeepers were nearly ruined by this catastrophe, which led to numerous claims for compensation for loss of trade, and the Princes Theatre in Shaftesbury Avenue was compelled to close its doors for some weeks owing to the roadway having become impassable to traffic.

A considerable amount of demolition is taking place in New Oxford Street and Charing Cross Road to make way for road developments which will improve the traffic circulation in this area. New Oxford Street has now been made a one-way street and carries only traffic proceeding from St Giles Circus towards Holborn. Traffic from Holborn in the other direction passes down St Giles High Street to St Giles Circus or by way of Shaftesbury Avenue and Charing Cross Road.

At the New Oxford Street-St Giles High Street junction is the new 37-storey tower block 'Centre Point', a landmark for miles around that is only exceeded in height by the nearby Post Office Tower. The tower block, 371 feet above ground level, is constructed of polished capstone concrete, pre-cast in units, each of which is in the shape of an inverted 'Y'.

This shape not only takes care of the windforces and is therefore functional, but also enabled the building to be erected very rapidly by bolting together the reinforcements for the full height of the building. Pile foundations extend about 120 feet below ground level, slightly deeper than the Underground Railway.

The scheme includes a public house, restaurant and shops; there are also shops in the subways and a direct entrance to the Tower block from the Tottenham Court Road Underground Station.

At the St Giles's end of High Holborn is the High Holborn branch of Moorfields Eye Hospital, formerly the Westminster Opthalmic, which was removed here in 1930 from William IV Street, Strand. It is a towering red-brick structure which completely dwarfed every other building until the arrival of the 10-floor Berskhire House next door, at the corner of Endell Street.

On the north side of Bloomsbury Way is St George's Church, erected in 1731 by Nicholas Hawksmoor and adorned by a handsome portico, with a curious pyramidal spire topped by a statue of George I. Nearly opposite, next to St George's Court, is a tall new building of red brick erected by the Co-operative Permanent Building Society in 1928. Bloomsbury, the district to the north of High Holborn and New Oxford Street, derives its name from the Blemunds, afterwards known as the De Blemontes, and Bloomsbury Square on the north side of Bloomsbury Way dates from 1667. Bedford House, which once formed the north side of the square, was pulled down in 1800, and three years later Bedford Place and Montague Street were erected on its site and gardens.

The British Museum, in Great Russell Street, to the north of Bloomsbury Way, originated in 1753 with the purchase of the library and collection of Sir Hans Sloane, the necessary funds having been raised by a public lottery set on foot for that purpose. A larger building having become imperative, the present edifice in Great Russell Street was erected by the brothers Smirke on the site of Montague House between 1823 and 1847 at a cost of £1,000,000, The northern extension known as the King Edward VII galleries fronting Montague Place was erected between 1908 and 1914 at a cost of £200,000, the foundation-stone being laid by King Edward VII in 1908 and the opening ceremony being performed by King George V in 1914. Across the street the first block of buildings for the University of London together with the tower was completed in 1937. Another section fronting Malet Street has now been completed. The whole of this site, together with the adjoining Torrington Square, which has been pulled down, will be covered during the next few years by the new buildings of the University of London, but it is intended to preserve the garden of Torrington Square. When this is done the University, including University College Hospital, will stretch from the British Museum to Euston Road, and will form the most impressive university buildings in Europe. In May 1931 it was announced that the work had been entrusted to a single architect, Charles Holden, the architect of the St James's Park Underground Station.

Dr Holden, however, died in 1960 and a plan for the future development of the University Precinct has been prepared by Sir Leslie Martin and is now under consideration by the University and other interested bodies.

On 26 June 1933 King George V laid the foundation-stone of the new University Buildings. The tower is 210 feet high and has twelve main floors which are used for the storage of the library books. The base is constructed of granite and the upper portion is faced with Portland stone. The foundation-stone has been laid in the centre of the tower. The completed section comprises only one-third of the University buildings and includes the Senate House. The remaining sections will not be completed for some years. The main frontage is in Malet Street which has been extensively widened and converted into a noble thoroughfare. On the west side at the corner of Montague Place now stands the Institute of Hygiene and Tropical Medicine, which also has a frontage to Gower Street. Other notable buildings on the same side of this street include the Royal Academy of Dramatic Art and College Hall completed in 1933. Both were severely damaged in the air raids of 1940 and College Hall has been rebuilt.

In Gower Street is University College, chiefly founded by the exertions of Lord Brougham for the purpose of providing education in literature, science, and fine arts at moderate cost. The foundation-stone was laid on 30 April 1827 by the Duke of Sussex, and the building was opened on 1 October 1828, having been designed by W. Wilkins, R.A., the architect of the National Gallery. In 1869 it was incorporated by Royal Charter with additional powers and was divested of its original proprietary character. The site upon which University College stands was purchased for £30,000. The new stone building is the Institute of Anatomy, opened by King George V in 1923 University College Hospital, also in Gower Street, in connexion with University College, was founded in 1833 and rebuilt in the form of a diagonal cross by the late Sir J. Blundell Maple. Gower Street contains several large boarding-houses which cater specially for overseas students. University College now covers some 12 acres, has over 4,000 students and a teaching staff of over 900. Generous benefactions have helped in the establishment of residential halls close to the main college buildings. On the wall of the Engineering Department in Gower Street is a plaque which records that 'close to this place in the year 1808, Richard Trevithick, pioneer of High Pressure Steam, ran the first steam locomotive to draw passengers.'

Bloomsbury is also famous as a centre for large temperance hotels and boarding-houses, some of them containing upwards of two hundred rooms. Amongst the largest are the Ivanhoe and the Kenilworth, both of them in Bloomsbury Street, on the two corners of Great Russell Street, the County, the Ambassadors, and the Cora in Upper Woburn Place, in addition to those already noted in Southampton Row and Woburn Place. In Great Russell Street, Bedford Avenue, and Ridgmount Gardens are several fine blocks of flats. During the second World War the railings of all the Bloomsbury squares except those of Bedford Square were removed and the gardens thrown open to the public by the Duke of Bedford. These include Russell Square, Tavistock Square, Bloomsbury Square, Woburn Square, and Gordon Square. Because of its distinctive character Bedford Square has been left undisturbed. It was built between 1775 and 1780 at the back of the grounds of Bedford House. The appearance of Russell Square, still containing terraces of large Georgian houses, will be considerably altered in a few years' time by rebuilding on the north side and by the eastern façade of the new University buildings which will then line its western side. During the second World War a large underground air-raid shelter was constructed here. The Holborn Borough Council was justly proud of its newly-acquired public squares and the garden of Russell Square has been beautifully laid out after having been left in a derelict condition for several years. It now contains a tea-house and a children's playground, and concerts are given here during the summer months. Russell Square House on the north side of the Square at the corner of Woburn Place is a fine new eight-storeyed block of offices with a façade of red brick, completed in 1940.

We return to New Oxford Street once more and proceed along Tottenham

Court Road. This important main north-to-south thoroughfare commences at St Giles's Circus, as the junction of Oxford Street and Charing Cross Road is now called, and extends northwards for a good half-mile as far as Euston Road. Until 1900 a row of old houses known as Bozier's Court extended across what is now a wide approach to Tottenham Court Road, and like the old Middle Row in Holborn it constituted a great hindrance to the large volume of traffic at this busy corner. But even this improvement relieved the congestion of traffic in this part of London to only a very small extent. A one-way system has now been introduced and Tottenham Court Road now carries only northbound traffic. Southbound traffic from Hampstead and the north now makes its way via Gower Street and and Bloomsbury Street thus linking up these one-way streets with New Oxford Street and St Giles' Circus to form an island system of considerable size. This has greatly increased the speed of traffic circulation.

Tottenham Court Road was a favourite resort of Londoners in the early part of the seventeenth century, because it led to the old Manor House of Tottenham Court. It was then a country road with hawthorn hedges and good pastures and meadows on both sides, but occasionally rowdiness and disorders occurred in this locality. Here booths were erected and gaming and prize-fighting were indulged in, which culminated in riots and other offences calculated to create a breach of the peace.

Tottenham Court Road was mostly built between 1770 and 1800 and until the concluding years of the nineteenth century was a shabby street, but today it is the great centre of the London furnishing establishments and nearly the whole of the east side has been rebuilt during the past fifty years. At the corner of Great Russell Street is the building of the Central Young Men's Christian Association, which removed here from Exeter Hall in the Strand in 1908. It contains two large halls for meetings, restaurants, a gymnasium, swimming-bath, social rooms, and two hundred bedrooms for young men.

Farther up the street on the same side are the extensive furnishing emporiums of Messrs Heal & Son, and the world-famous establishment of Messrs Maple & Company Limited, which has been partly refronted of late years. Among these firms was the large and old-established store of James Shoolbred & Company which went out of business in 1935. Its extensive building which covered the site between Grafton Street and University Street was pulled down in 1936 and on this site now stands a large eight-storeyed block of shops and flats.

The west side of Tottenham Court Road from St Giles's Circus to Goodge Street is still lined by third-rate buildings mostly occupied by small shops, small cinemas, and night clubs. Many of them are also disfigured by slovenly advertisement hoardings erected above the groundfloor shops. An exception is the new 13-storey Metropolis House, between Percy Street and Windmill Street, to which Messrs Catesby have removed. Beyond Goodge Street, the buildings on this side of the road are of a better character and include some new office buildings with shops below, such as Bryan House, Matthew Hall House, and the former Grafton Hotel, now the University College Hospital nurses' home. On this side also stood the Whitfield's Tabernacle, an institutional church of the Congregational body, rebuilt in 1903 on the site of an earlier chapel erected in 1756 and damaged by fire on 23 February 1857. Unhappily it was destroyed by a bomb on Sunday, 25 March 1945. Of thirty-five people in the building seven were killed. Always known locally as Whitfield's, it is properly called The Whitefield Memorial Church. The Rev. Augustus Toplady, author of the hymn *Rock of Ages* was buried in the original church. The church has now been rebuilt.

Between Howland Street and Maple Street, off Tottenham Court Road, the Post Office Tower rises like a great lighthouse. The tallest building in Britain, the tower itself reaches 580 feet, on top of which is a trellis mast of 40 feet supporting a radar aerial to help short range weather forecasting.

The essential purpose of the tower is to provide more long distance telephone circuits and more television channels. Panoramic views of London from galleries near the top and a revolving restaurant are additional attractions for the visitor to London. The tower was opened to the public by the Postmaster-General on 19 May, 1966.

Turning next into Euston Road, and passing Gower Street, we come on the right-hand side to Unity House, the headquarters of the National Union of Railwaymen. Just beyond is Euston Square, which, together with Seymour Place, was partly erected in 1813 but not completed until 1831. Inasmuch as it actually forms a part of Euston Road it can hardly be considered a square at all, and moreover, the southern portion, which until 1926 was still an open garden, is now partly covered by the handsome building of the Society of Friends, the Weights and Measures office, and a business block, erected about 1928. Here an extensive widening has been carried out on the south side of Euston Road, giving it more the appearance of a boulevard. On this side the building of the Society of Friends has for its neighbour the Wellcome Museum of Surgery, an imposing building faced with Portland stone adorned with a row of Ionic columns above the ground floor, erected in 1931, by the late Mr Wellcome of the well-known firm of chemists, Messrs Burroughs Wellcome & Company Limited. On the other side of Euston Road are the equally imposing buildings of the Ministry of Pensions and other departments erected in 1931 and of the Cambridge University Press, called Bentley House, erected in 1937. With its many fine new buildings Euston Road is becoming one of the finest thoroughfares in London. On both sides of the road, some of its old houses, badly damaged in the air raids, have now been razed to the ground. A large site next to Unity House has been cleared of its old buildings and the new ten-storey Babcock & Wilcox Ltd building stands there. Unity House is now quite dwarfed between the Wellcome building and Babcock House.

Originally designed as the terminus of the parent London and Birmingham Railway, Euston was the first main line terminus in London and was brought fully into use on 17 September 1838. Writing in 1938, Mr Thomas Faulkner, a great authority on London topography, said that the London and Birmingham Railway was unquestionably the greatest public work ever executed in ancient or modern times, and that, when one considered the immense outlay of capital required, together with what were in those days regarded as the unprecedented engineering difficulties, it was evident that such a work could only have been undertaken in a country like Britain which abounded with capital and possessed engineering talent of the highest order.

The Act of Parliament for its construction was obtained in 1833 and the work was commenced in 1834 under the supervision of Mr Robert Stephenson. The entire line was built within four years at an average rate of one mile a fortnight and the first train conveying the directors to London accomplished the journey in four hours and thirty-five minutes for a distance of 112 miles. Yet London was slow to realize the advantages of railway travelling, since the Liverpool and Manchester Railway had already been opened eight years earlier, in 1830.

Plans for the new Euston Station, the principal London terminus of the London Midland Region of British Railways, have now been approved, and the former station and its adjoining hotel have been demolished. All that is left today seems to be just rails and platforms beneath some glassy shelters, which remind one of the pictures of old stations that were called 'train sheds' in the early days of railways.

The old Euston was certainly straggling and inconvenient in many respects, but being one of the oldest stations in the country, this was largely the result of piecemeal enlargement and improvisation. In 1838, the accommodation for trains consisted of two platforms, but from time to time there were various additions and extensions on either side of the Great Hall which explains the station's growth from the original two-acre site to its final area of eighteen acres with fifteen platforms.

The famous Doric Arch of Philip Hardwick was erected in 1836 when, standing in open ground in front of the old station courtyard, it appeared suitably impressive as 'The Gateway to the North'. The later enlargement of the station hotel closed the vista from Euston Road across the Square and the Doric portico became obscured and absurd. Within the station proper was the magnificent Great Hall, also by P. C. Hardwick, which was brought into use in 1849; it was the largest waiting room in the British Isles, measuring 126 feet in length, 61 feet wide and 64 feet high. The flat panelled ceiling was the largest of its kind in the world. The Doric Arch and the Great Hall have been smashed to pieces, but

'Praising what is lost
Makes the remembrance dear'.

The new station is the design of the London Midland Region's architect, Mr R. L. Moorcroft, under the direction of the Chief Civil Engineer, Mr W. F. Beatty. It will have for its central feature a large passenger concourse which has been designed to accommodate, without crowding or congestion, the maximum number of travellers that are likely to use the station at peak periods. This concourse will be kept entirely free from parcels traffic and luggage trolleys;

a decision that will be much appreciated, for we all remember the prompt and agile evasive action required when a motorized string of these luggage trolleys swung round the platforms as if the porters were 'playing at trains'. Escalators will connect with the London Transport station below, served by the present Northern and the new Victoria Lines. Every other facility required of a modern railway station will be provided and there will be fifteen platforms, as before— the only respect in which the new Euston will resemble its venerable predecessor.

On the opposite side of Euston Road, at the east corner of Woburn Place, is St Pancras Church, completed in 1822 at a cost of £76,000, and close to Seymour Street on the north side were the offices of the Hearts of Oak Benefit Society, opened by King Edward VII in 1906. This elegant building had become some-what outmoded and has been pulled down. The Society is replacing it on the same site with a modern office block, the principal part of which will be of moderate height, though there will also be a slender tower of some 15 floors. The well-known bronze statue of King Edward VII by H. Hampton, which formerly stood in the forecourt of the Euston Road premises, has been re-erected in the grounds of the Society's Convalescent Home at Broadstairs.

As another stage in the modernization of the north side of Euston Road a clearance has been made between Chalton Street and Ossulston Street where, in addition to a new Central Library for the Borough of Camden, an 11-storey office block is under construction. On the east side of Seymour Street facing Euston Station are the new Administrative offices of British Railways, Midland Region, completed in 1934. This is a nine-storeyed building faced with red brick and stone which is crowned by a massive-looking stone tower.

To-day the road from Paddington to Islington comprises the Marylebone, Euston, and Pentonville Roads, but until the middle of the last century it was called the New Road, and originated in an Act of Parliament in 1756 for the construction of an entirely new road beyond what was then the outer limits of London. It was vigorously opposed by the Duke of Bedford, who contended that the New Road would interfere with the privacy of Bedford House and his estate near Bloomsbury Square, but its advocates said that it would be a means of avoiding the driving of cattle through the streets to Smithfield Market and that in case of a threatened foreign invasion the New Road would enable His Majesty's Forces to march expeditiously into Essex and defend our coasts without passing through the cities of London and Westminster. A clause was inserted in the Act prohibiting the erection of houses within fifty feet of the road, the land in front of the houses to be reserved for gardens only, and vesting the authorities of those parishes through which it passed with power to pull down any erections in these front gardens and charge the expense to the offender's goods and chattels without proceeding in the usual way of indictment.

Unfortunately in many instances the law was evaded and in course of time shops of a very inferior character succeeded in coming forward to the frontage of the road, and what was designed by our grandfathers to become a magnificent boulevard has been largely spoiled, at least until the expiry of the existing leases.

Beyond Evershott Street, on the north side of Euston Road, is St Pancras Station and the stately Midland Hotel building, which is approached by a private roadway with an ascent of more than twenty feet. The roof of this station, said to be the largest of its kind in the world, is 700 feet long with a span of 240 feet unbroken by ties or braces and is 100 feet high. The Midland line from London as far as Bedford was opened on 13 July 1868, but pending the actual completion of St Pancras Station in 1870 the trains from the north ran for the time being into King's Cross Station. The hotel, which has a frontage to Euston Road of 575 feet, was opened on 5 May 1873, after having been five years in course of construction; at that time it was considered to be one of the finest in the world but for want of sufficient patronage it was closed down in 1935 and converted into offices of the railway company. It contains two lofty towers, both with ornamental turrets, that at the east end being 270 feet high and the west tower 250 feet high. The hotel was designed by Sir Gilbert Scott, had accommodation for six hundred guests and was erected at a cost of £500,000. The roof of St Pancras Station was badly damaged in the air raids of 1940, but Sir Gilbert Scott's beautiful building in Euston Road escaped unharmed.

To make way for St Pancras Station and the hotel, as well as the extensive goods depot to the north, comprising altogether some fifty acres, no less than three thousand houses in Somers Town and Agar Town were demolished, including Skinner Street, King's Road, and Brill Street, together with some of the worst slums in London extending more or less from Euston Road to Camden Square and the North London Railway. Somers Town was built after 1790 at the time of the French Revolution, but Agar Town, commenced about 1840 and happily wiped out altogether by the former Midland Railway, originated in a very disgraceful incident in the development of London.

The site of what was formerly known as Agar Town was meadow-land of comparatively small value at the time it came into the possession of Mr Agar about 1815. The Regent's Canal was then in course of construction and the Company wanted to carry it through this estate, but Mr Agar, who was a Queen's Counsellor at the Chancery Bar, successfully contested their right do do so. Until 1840 Mr Agar's grounds retained their park-like appearance and the approach to his private residence was through a neat lodge and gate in a road situated not far from York Road, King's Cross, then known as Maiden Lane.

In 1841 Mr Agar sublet the greater part of his estate on leases of twenty-one years. Tenements were run up in consequence by anyone disposed to take the land; many of them were hovels erected by journeymen bricklayers and carpenters on Sundays and in their spare time, and inhabited even before the ground flooring had been laid. Hence many of the first proprietors bitterly regretted the day they ever contemplated becoming owners of their dwellings in Agar Town or Ague Town as it was afterwards nicknamed, because of the absence of drainage or sewerage. The inmates contracted fevers which in some instances carried off an industrious father or mother, and sometimes several children in a family.

Of course the conditions of a new town springing up under such circumstances could not be concealed for long from the outside public, and in 1851 it attracted the attention of Charles Dickens, after it had been in existence about ten years. He wrote a graphic description of this neighbourhood in *Household Words* under the title of 'An English Connemara'. Rows of squalid and makeshift houses were erected opposite one another without any attempt to make the roadways, and when the rain came down, the ground, strewn with rubbish, was churned up into a thick paste. Every garden had its nuisance, the one containing a dungheap, the next a cinder-heap, and a third, belonging to the cottage of a coster, was a pile of periwinkle shells, rotten cabbages, and a donkey. The inhabitants themselves displayed a genuine Irish apathy, and as there were no sewers the stench on a rainy morning was overpowering.

When there was an outbreak of cholera an inspector of nuisances would appear on the scene, but directly the epidemic was over, his vigilance was again relaxed and things reverted to their former condition. In 1840 there was no Metropolitan Board of Works or London County Council to say no to Mr Agar, and one of these squalid streets even rejoiced in the very imposing name of Salisbury Crescent.

By the summer of 1868 the whole of Agar Town had disappeared, and thus London owes a debt of gratitude to the coming of the Midland Railway for a merciful riddance from this disgraceful rookery. But for this fortunate occurrence a later generation of Londoners would have been put to enormous expense in removing this blot upon the metropolis.

Some years after the construction of the New Road in 1756-57 the adjoining building sites were partly disposed of and eventually Somers Town was planned and so named after Earl Somers, Lord High Chancellor in 1695, who received this estate as a gift from Queen Anne after it had reverted to the Crown in 1539. Mr Jacob Leroux became the principal landowner under Lord Somers and built himself a handsome residence. Later the so-called Polygon and Clarendon Squares were built. The Polygon comprised a block of rather pleasant houses which at first overlooked open fields but was afterwards surrounded by the dingy Clarendon Square. The Polygon has been replaced by several blocks of artisan dwellings, which now occupy the centre of that square.

Between the two World Wars many slums in Somers Town were cleared away by the London County Council. Others have been removed by bombs in the vicinity of Stibbington and Drummond Streets. Here the so-called St Mary's Flats have been erected, and Queen Mary paid a surprise visit to them in February 1930 and also inspected a new model public-house called the Anchor Inn. About 1935 the London County Council redeveloped the area between Chalton Street and Ossulston Street and erected a large number of new blocks of workers' flats with spacious courtyards between these two streets. Those which face Ossulston Street are flanked by grass plots and have been planned in such a fashion as to avoid the typical monotony of long rows of artisan dwellings of the older type.

The influx of French emigrants contributed to the prosperity of Somers Town by their renting houses which had previously stood unoccupied, and this in turn created a demand for ground leases offered by the Duke of Bedford and the trustees of the late Foundling Hospital, who owned the greater part of the land on the south side of New Road. In due course this resulted in the erection of Guilford Street, Brunswick and Russell Squares, Tavistock Place, Woburn Place, and many other streets and squares. Euston Square and Seymour Place were erected about 1813. In Judd Street a huge new telephone exchange at the corner of Bidborough Street has been completed and many new blocks of flats have been erected since 1945 in Cromer Street and Argyle Street by the St Pancras Borough Council. In St George's Gardens, a disused burial ground near Brunswick Square, is the grave of Anna, sixth daughter of Richard Cromwell, the Protector (Oliver's son); she died in 1727. The Foundling Hospital, erected between 1739 and 1747, which has been pulled down, stood all alone at the dawn of the nineteenth century in Lamb's Conduit Fields. It was founded by Thomas Coram, a native of Lyme Regis, born in 1668, the son of a merchant captain. It occupied, together with its grounds, nearly ten acres, and was opened for the reception of five hundred boys and girls in 1743. A proposal in 1926 to remove Covent Garden Market to this site met with such a storm of opposition that it had to be abandoned. The vacant site was secured at great expense, and, thanks to generous contributions from Lord Rothermere, the London County Council, the local Borough Councils, and other bodies, has been laid out as a children's playground. It was formally opened in 1936. If the adjoining Brunswick and Mecklenburgh Squares could be purchased and added to the ground, it would assume the dimensions of a small park. These two squares were laid out in 1794 but most of the houses on the east side of Mecklenburgh Square have been destroyed in the blitz. On the north side of Brunswick Square is the new building of the School of Pharmacy, University of London. This is a handsome edifice of red brick with stone dressing. The west side of this square — and extending as far as Marchmont Street — has recently been demolished. Further north is little Regent Square, which was fortunate in the possession of two large churches, and unfortunate in losing both of them. St Peter, of which the massive six-columned Ionic portico and circular tower were an impressive ruin, recently demolished, overlooked the square from the east side. The Scottish Presbyterian Church on the south side was a copy of the west front of York Minster, by Sir William Tite, architect of the Royal Exchange. This was also severely war-damaged and, despite protests that the twin towers might have been saved, was demolished, and a new, though smaller, church in plain red brick and stone, stands in its place. In the neighbouring Guilford Street, noted for its many private hotels, is a large new building which is the Nurses Home of the Great Ormond Street Children's Hospital. Queen Square, just off Guilford Street, was built in the reign of Queen Anne after whom it is named. The statue in the Square, however, is generally considered to represent Queen Charlotte. Its north side was specially left open so that its inhabitants might enjoy an unobstructed view of Hampstead and Highgate. It has been largely rebuilt of late years and here are located the London Homoeopathic Hospital and the National Hospital for Diseases of the

Nervous System. On the west side are the offices of the Conjoint Examining Board and on the south side is the Italian Hospital. The Square is now a public open space. At the south west corner is the church of St George the Martyr, sometimes called 'The Sweeps' Church' because one of its charities provided free Christmas dinners for 100 apprentices to chimney sweeps in the Cities of London and Westminster.

In Lamb's Conduit (locally 'Lamb's Conduct') Street is an old stone 'Lamb's Conduit the Property of the City of London this pump is erected for the Benefit of the Publick.' This stone has been placed in the wall of a new building erected where the pump originally stood.

Between St Pancras Church and King's Cross Station, Euston Road has been partly widened of late years and some of the old houses have been pulled down. On a part of this ground, previously occupied by the Euston Market, now stands Clifton House, a seven-storeyed block of shops and offices. On the other corner of Judd Street is the handsome new St Pancras Town Hall completed in 1937, now the Town Hall of the new Borough of Camden, which faces St Pancras Station. Erected at a cost of £250,000, this is a building of four storeys faced with Portland stone with two porticos and a row of stone columns in the centre between the first and third storeys. Farther along on the same side of the road is the Century Cinema, formerly the Regent Theatre and originally the Euston Music Hall.

King's Cross Station, which was opened for traffic on 14 October 1852, replaced the temporary terminus of the former Great Northern Railway in Maiden Lane, now renamed York Way. To make way for the new station the old Smallpox Hospital, now removed to Highgate Hill, had to be pulled down, together with a number of houses on the west side of Maiden Lane which was then considerably widened. The station and goods yards occupy forty-five acres of ground. King's Cross Station is approached from Euston Road by a carriage drive and has two main arches, each of 71 feet span, separated by a clock-tower 112 feet high, the clock of which, by Dent, was originally an exhibit in the Great Exhibition of 1851. At the side of the station is the Great Northern Hotel, built in 1854.

The neighbourhood was formerly known as Battlebridge and underwent a great transformation many years ago. Before 1820 it had been a filthy and dangerous neighbourhood, and here the dustcarts of London used to be emptied. Afterwards all the mean hovels were removed and decent houses erected in their place. Battlebridge was renamed King's Cross after George IV and is supposed to have been the spot where King Alfred fought the Danes. About 1825, a building was erected at the junction of Maiden Lane, Gray's Inn Road, and Pentonville Road, which was crowned with a statue of George IV and christened King's Cross. At first this building was utilized as a place for exhibitions, then as a police station, and finally as a beer house until it was pulled down in February 1845. In 1907 when the North London tramways were electrified a new bridge was constructed over the Metropolitan Railway in order to bring Gray's Inn

Road into line with Caledonian Road. Here on the corner of Euston Road now stands the Gaumont Cinema. Viewed from this corner today, the outlook has changed suprisingly little in recent years; it is dull and shabby, and the same old buildings seem to be still there.

East of King's Cross is Pentonville which was mostly built between 1780 and 1820 and derives its name from Captain Henry Penton, M.P., the chief proprietor of the estate, who lived to see the hillsides all built over before his death, which occurred in Italy in 1812. The first houses of Pentonville were built in 1773 and were called Penton Place. It was then a beautiful hillside, from which you could see St Paul's Cathedral, the City of London, and the Surrey hills. Pentonville Prison is not in Pentonville at all, but in Barnsbury, and it is not clear how it came to be associated with this immediate locality, although Barnsbury never had any desire to be associated with that institution. Pentonville Road, which is to be considerably widened on the north side, will form part of the direct road across London which is to connect the Southend arterial road with the Western Avenue at Wood Lane. A few buildings have already been set back to the new line of frontage. One of these is a ten-storeyed building erected by Messrs Lilley & Skinner, the firm of footwear manufacturers. Half way up the hill — it is always called Pentonville *Hill* by the locals — is the little churchyard of St James, where Joe Grimaldi, the famous clown of the old Sadler's Wells Theatre is buried. According to the tombstone he died on 31 May 1837, aged 58. Most of the slums at the back of Pentonville Road have fortunately been removed by bombs. This applies especially to Collier Street, Cumming Street, Rodney Street, and Donegal Street, but Chapel Market, the busy shopping street, has escaped almost undamaged. On a part of this cleared ground, the so-called Busaco Street estate has been developed by the Finsbury Borough Council. Eight-storied blocks of flats have been erected in Cummings Street with open quadrangles at the back lined with four-storeyed blocks extending to Calshot Street. This has introduced a ray of light into this dreadful quarter of North London.

At the top of Pentonville Road is a lofty hill crest containing a reservoir surrounded by Claremont Square, the east side of which leads into Myddelton Square, adorned by the handsome Gothic church of St Mark in the centre. Most of the houses on the north side of the Square were destroyed in the raid of 11 January 1941 and were rebuilt — beautifully in keeping with the remainder of the Square — by the New River Company in 1947-8. Between Myddelton Square and Rosebery Avenue is the New River Head, containing the reservoir of the former New River Water Company, now merged into the Metropolitan Water Board. Pioneer amongst the old water companies of London, the New River originated in a contract made by Sir Hugh Myddelton in 1609 with the Corporation of London for making a river to supply the City with water from the springs of Chadwell and Amwell near Ware in Hertfordshire. This he succeeded in carrying out, but nearly ruined himself in the undertaking, and for a time the works were stopped at Enfield for want of capital. Myddelton then applied to the Corporation for assistance, which was refused, whereupon he appealed to James I, who agreed to provide half the cost in exchange for half the profits. The New River, thirty-eight miles in length, was thus completed and opened in 1613, and Myddelton was then made a baronet. Since 1946 the New River terminates at Stoke Newington Waterworks in Green Lanes and is now only 24 miles long.

The Metropolitan Water Board was constituted in 1902 in succession to the eight metropolitan water companies, of which the New River Company had been one. In Rosebery Avenue, adjoining the New River Head, are the extensive new offices of the Metropolitan Water Board, opened on 27 May 1920 at a cost of £300,000.

In October 1842 a number of labourers were employed in cleaning out the immense reservoir in Claremont Square, where the sediment had been allowed to accumulate for eleven years, and in some places it contained eleven feet of mud. In 1852 an Act was passed requiring all reservoirs within five miles of St Paul's to be roofed in or otherwise covered, and all water used for domestic purposes to be filtered.

Near the junction of Rosebery Avenue and St John Street is Sadler's Wells Theatre, which takes its name from a chalybeate spring discovered by a Mr Sadler in 1683 in the garden of a house which he had just opened as a 'Musick House'. Affectionately enshrined by Pinero in *Trelawney of the Wells,* the old theatre in its time offered almost every conceivable form of entertainment, though its most illustrious period was from 1846 to 1862 when Samuel Phelps produced more than thirty of Shakespeare's plays.

Finally closed in 1916, it lay derelict until the late Miss Lilian Baylis of the Old Vic campaigned for its rebuilding, after which it was re-opened in 1931 and flourished as 'the home of opera in English'.

Mr Sadler's spring has been preserved and is still in the theatre; actually there are two springs — one has been sealed off, but on the other a pump is continually working to keep the water down.

We retrace our steps down Rosebery Avenue, an important thoroughfare connecting Holborn with Islington, constructed in 1892. The northern end contains the Town Hall of the former Borough of Finsbury (now part of Islington), adjoining Myddelton Street, and was carved out of several previously existing streets, but the southern end is entirely modern and is built on a viaduct of fourteen arches spanning the valley of the old Fleet River. In the Skinner Street district a large development scheme is under way, which, covering an area of nearly half a square mile, will provide 450 new homes, a two-storey car park and a new library. The old Skinner Street Library, by the way, was the first in London to introduce the now familiar 'open access' system by which borrowers are able to 'browse' among the books.

King's Cross Road, running from north to south, which we shall next pass, is a modern name bestowed upon the former Bagnigge Wells Road in 1863, and its continuation, then named Coppice Row and Victoria Street, was altered to Farringdon Road. Bagnigge Wells in the parish of Holborn stood in the valley between Gray's Inn Road and Clerkenwell and was once a noted place of public entertainment. Two springs were discovered here in the reign of George III, and Bagnigge House, which up to then had been a small tavern, was enlarged by its enterprising landlord. A new, elegant, long room was built and an organ erected for the amusement of visitors. There was also a good tea-room and the grounds contained beautiful walks, and in the centre was a small round fish-pond containing a fountain representing Cupid astride a swan which spouted water through its beak to a considerable height. Close to the pond was the small stream of the Fleet River which traversed these grounds.

Set in the wall of No. 61 King's Cross Road is an old stone inscribed: 'This is Bagnigge House neare the Pindar A Wakefield 1680'. 'The Pindar of Wakefield' is a tavern in Gray's Inn Road, formerly much frequented by the waggoners of the Great North Road and commemorates a burly Yorkshireman who once thrashed Robin Hood himself. Just across the road is Gwynne Place – so named because Bagnigge House was once, it is said, a summer residence of Mistress Nelly. From here, Granville Square is reached by the ascent of 26 stone steps which, under the name of *Riceyman Steps,* were immortalized by Arnold Bennett in his depressing novel of that title.

Victoria Street, now forming a part of Farringdon Road, was commenced in 1845. It was 1,450 feet in length and extended from West St., Holborn, to the back of the Sessions House, Clerkenwell. To make way for this improvement a number of houses which stood in its path on Holborn Hill east of Field Lane had to be demolished, as well as Chick Lane and other filthy habitations devoted to offensive trades. The complete street was opened in 1856 from Holborn Bridge, including the extension to Bagnigge Wells Road, for which purpose many other houses were demolished in Great Saffron Hill and Coppice Row. The remaining portion of the Fleet Ditch, extending from Peter Street to Castle Street, which had been open for centuries, was arched over and converted into a sewer. Various minor thoroughfares, such as Vine Street, Castle Street, and Peter Street, were swallowed up in this improvement and their site is now covered by Farringdon Station.

In 1865 the extension of the London, Chatham and Dover Railway from Black-friars to Farringdon Road formed a connecting link between the great railways of the north and south, and at that time it was confidently predicted that the mile of the Metropolitan Railway from King's Cross to Farringdon Road would by 1870 become the great central artery for the internal traffic of the entire metropolis. It was calculated that since the Metropolitan Railway was already carrying 100,000 passengers a day, it would be almost impossible to forecast the amount of traffic likely to pass through Farringdon Street in 1870, and it would then become a second Clapham Junction.

But this forecast never came true, and that route was so little used by the travelling public that since the first World War the trains hitherto running from Blackfriars to Farringdon Road over the Southern Railway track have been abolished, and to-day only goods traffic passes over this connecting link between north and south.

On the site of the old Cold Bath Fields House of Correction in Farringdon Road, at the junction of Rosebery Avenue, now stand the modern buildings of the General Post Office, completed in 1900 and sarcastically renamed Mount Pleasant, where parcels are sorted and dispatched. Cold Bath Fields derives its name from a well of cold water formerly situated in fields built over by the house of correction in 1794. The latter was dismantled in 1887 to make way for the new post office buildings. It was constructed by a Mr Howard as an experiment in severe principles of discipline to correct and reform convicted felons and hardened criminals.

At the junction of Farringdon Road with Clerkenwell Road is the former Sessions House, now removed to South London, erected in 1781 from the designs of Mr Rogers. It has a stone front with columns and pilasters of the Ionic order and stands on Clerkenwell Green, which was formerly a small green, but is now a paved square on the hill slope. This building has now been converted into offices. Close by is the church of St James, built in 1788-92 on the site of an earlier church which formed the choir of a Benedictine nunnery founded in 1100 by Jordan Briset, and from which Clerkenwell derived its name. Clerkenwell is the especial abode of London clockmakers, working jewellers, and makers of meteorological and mathematical instruments, and work entrusted to West End jewellers is usually sent here to be executed.

In a hollow to the north of the church close to St John Street formerly stood the Clerkenwell House of Detention, which was the scene of the Fenian explosion of 13 December 1876, an outrage committed with the object of rescuing the prisoners Burke and Casey, in which a part of the wall was blown down with a barrel of gunpowder placed outside the prison. This building, which was first erected in 1775, was rebuilt in 1847 and finally pulled down in 1890, and its site is now occupied by a London County Council school. Up to the early 1920's, a blind matchseller used to stand in Holborn, near Gray's Inn; he had lost his sight when a boy, as a result of this Fenian explosion.

Clerkenwell Road, like Farringdon Road, is a modern thoroughfare designed to provide a direct route from New Oxford Street to Shoreditch and north-east London via Theobald's Road and Old Street. It starts at Old Street, runs along the northern side of the Charterhouse Grounds, past St John Street to Farringdon Road, after which it crosses a bridge over the Metropolitan Railway and leads thence to Gray's Inn Road opposite Theobald's Road. Clerkenwell Road was opened in April 1878 by Sir J. M. Hogg, Chairman of the Metropolitan Board of Works, and the gross cost of this improvement amounted to £1,600,000. It was cut through some of the worst slums in London, with which Clerkenwell a century ago appears to have been richly endowed, and it swallowed up a small thoroughfare running out of Gray's Inn Road, called Liquorpond Street.

From Clerkenwell Green Jerusalem Passage brings us to St John's Square. On the north side of the square is St John's Church, rebuilt on the site of the

36 The old General Post office in St Martin's-le-Grand shortly before its demolition in 1912.

37 The church of St Dunstan in the West, Fleet Street, in 1830.

38 The tower of Wren's church of St Alban's Wood Street.

39 The Wool Exchange, Coleman Street, built in 1874 and now demolished.

40 Some of the fifty tiled plaques, recording gallant deeds by civilians, erected in Postman's Park.

41 A view of the Barbican area, looking east along London Wall.

42 Left: The Church of St Mary, Aldermanbury, designed by Wren, as it was in 1820, and (43) its remains being dismantled for re-erection at Fulton, Missouri.

44 The tallest building in the City of London, Britannic House, is the 400-foot high headquarters building of the B itish Petroleum Group.

46 'The Old Curiosity Shop' in Portsmouth Street.

45 In Strand Lane is the Watch-House of the parish of St Clement Danes. The entrance to the 'Roman Bath' is through the railings.

47 Completed in 1882, the Royal Courts of Justice in the Strand were designed by G.E. Street.

48 Somerset House in 1820.

49 The *Cricket* disaster, 1847. Her boiler burst as she was about to leave the Adelphi pier.

50 Northumberland House, the entrance to the Strand and the Charles I statue, about 1800.

51 The Liverpool Victoria Friendly Society, (Victoria House) Southampton Row.

52 The Shell Centre, on the South Bank.

53 The Royal Festival Hall.

54 'Pocahontas, La Belle Sauvage,' reclines before the entrance to the Red Lion Square premises of Cassells, the publishers.

priory church of St John of Jerusalem, founded in 1140. A three-brick-wide semi-circle in the Square marks the outline of part of the circular nave of the old church, and the Norman Crypt still survives below. On the south side of the Square – which was cut in two by the Clerkenwell Road – stands the old gate-house of the priory, rebuilt by Prior Docwra in 1504. In the rooms over the gateway, then occupied by the publisher, Edward Cave, Dr Johnson wrote his contributions for the *Gentleman's Magazine;* the rooms are now used by the St John Ambulance Association. In July 1845 St John's Gate was pronounced a dangerous structure under a new building Act, and notice was given that unless it was put into substantial repair it would be pulled down. A public subscription was then invited to provide for its restoration, but for some time the amount forthcoming was quite inadequate to meet the cost. Though much of the surrounding property has been destroyed in the blitz, the gateway itself has escaped damage.

Theobald's Road which leads from Gray's Inn Road to Bloomsbury Way was so named because it led to Theobalds in Hertfordshire, the favourite hunting resort of King James I. Nearly all the north side of Theobald's Road was destroyed in the early raids of 1940. The devastated area included Old Gloucester Street, Boswell Street, New North Street and Harpur Street and extended north to Dombey Street. Fronting Theobald's Road on both sides of Harpur Street two massive blocks of Government offices were erected soon after the war. Both are nine storeys high and of uniform design and are fronted with red brick with stone dressings. Adastral House, the west block, extends to New North Street, and Lacon House, the east block, to Lamb's Conduit Street. 'Lacon', it appears, is a contraction for 'Lamb's Conduit'. The new buildings house three thousand Civil servants who have moved from requisitioned houses and flats in other parts of London. Adastral House, formerly Ariel House, is occupied by the Air Force department of the Ministry of Defence, which in November 1949 moved here from Adastral House in the Strand. Lacon House is occupied by the Ministry of Public Building and Works. The architect of these buildings is Mr Arthur S. Ash.

More recent office buildings along this stretch of Theobalds Road (sometimes pronounced *Tibbalds*) include Sentinal House, Rochdale House and Mercury House. A new Police Station with a 14-storey tower replaced the old one that stood at the corner of Gray's Inn Road in September, 1965, and facing the gardens of Gray's Inn, a new Public Library was opened by Queen Elizabeth the Queen Mother in November, 1960.

Bedford Row, between Holborn and Theobald's Road, is a wide thoroughfare built in the early part of the eighteenth century which is mainly tenanted by solicitors. John Street, which is continued by Doughty Street, leads to Mecklenburgh Square. This wide street of eighteenth-century Georgian houses reminds one very much of Pulteney Street, Bath. Here Charles Dickens lived in the earlier days of his prosperity. His house, No. 48, is now a Dickens Museum under the auspices of The Dickens Fellowship.

Facing each other across Mecklenburgh Square are London House and William Goodenough House, which together form a residential centre for post-graduate students from all parts of the Commonwealth and the U.S.A. The former, designed by Sir Herbert Baker, was opened by the late Queen Mary, in 1937.

Red Lion Square at the back of Theobald's Road, built in 1698, is now a public garden. On the north side, at the entrance to the offices of Cassell and Company, the publishers, is a reclining nude figure of 'Pocahontas, La Belle Sauvage', by David McFall, an emblem that recalls their former premises in Belle Sauvage Yard, Ludgate Hill. Number 17, on the south side, where Dante Gabriel Rosetti, William Morris and Sir Edward Burne-Jones lived, still stands.

Tenth Walk

Charing Cross, Trafalgar Square, Haymarket, Leicester Square, Covent Garden, Long Acre, St Martin's Lane, Soho, and Shaftesbury Avenue

Charing Cross, bounded on the east by the Strand, on the west by Cockspur Street, and extending a few paces south into Whitehall, is one of the great traffic centres of the metropolis. In the time of Edward I it was merely a route hamlet, and here was erected the last of the twelve crosses set up to mark the resting-places of the body of his beloved queen Eleanor on the journey to Westminster Abbey, where she was buried. The bronze statue of King Charles I which faces Whitehall was erected in its present situation at the expense of the Crown in 1776 after the Restoration. On 30 January each year, the anniversary of the King's execution, the Society of King Charles the Martyr hold a memorial service at the statue; in 1965, however, the *venue* of the ceremony was changed, owing to the funeral of Sir Winston Churchill.

Trafalgar Square is so intimately associated with the everyday life of the metropolis that it seems difficult to realize that this fine open space, designed between 1829 and 1841 as a kind of War Memorial to the Nelson victories, is little more than a century old, and is some ten years younger than Piccadilly Circus. It was laid out on the site of the King's Mews, erected in 1732 and once the royal stables, together with a slum area which surrounded St Martin's Church, known as the Bermuda and Caribbee Islands, and Porridge Island, famous for its cook-shops. Nearer Charing Cross several mean buildings were also swept away for the further enlargement of the square. It seems that there had previously been an open space of sorts on this spot, but of very much smaller dimensions. The fountains in the centre were designed in 1845 by Sir Charles Barry and the statues adorning three corners of the square are those of Sir Henry Havelock, Sir Charles James Napier, and George IV. In 1926 flag paving stones were laid down in Trafalgar Square, according to the scheme originally planned by Sir Charles Barry. After the first World War the fountains were improved and fitted with lighting and their first illumination brought dense crowds to the Square. Two long ornamental flower beds were added at the back of the Square; by the northern wall are set two bronze busts labelled simply 'Beatty' and 'Jellicoe', commemorating these two great admirals of the 1914-18 war. The four lamps at each corner of the Square are frequently, but quite erroneously, supposed

179

to have come from Nelson's flagship H.M.S. *Victory*, while flying above are the pigeons whose tameness is a perpetual source of wonder to the children.

The Nelson Column in the centre was erected between 1840 and 1843, and was designed by Mr William Railton. It is 186 feet high, sixteen feet lower than the Monument, and is surmounted by a statue of Nelson seventeen feet high by Mr E. H. Baily, R.A., which was placed in position on 3 November 1843, after a somewhat tardy recognition of Britain's great naval hero. The square pedestal is thirty-six feet in height and contains representations of Nelson's four great battles, and the four gigantic lions at the base were designed by Sir Edwin Landseer. For many years these lions, although constantly promised, were not forthcoming, and they were only set up in 1868. This furnished the newspapers with a standing jest which took the form of a suggestion that the old lion which then crowned the top of Northumberland House had refused to acknowledge them as brethren. On the east side of the square are the offices of the South African Government erected on the site of Morley's Hotel, acquired in 1921. On this island site, which includes Golden Cross House, the present magnificent building was completed in 1933. It is six storeys high, faced with Portland stone, and adorned in the centre by a row of four cylindrical columns. Its architects were Sir Herbert Baker and Mr A. T. Scott. On the west side are the Canadian Government offices, remodelled out of the former premises of the Union Club refaced with stone. The adjoining Royal College of Physicians building, with its great portico and columns at the corner of Pall Mall East has been taken over by Canada House. The College has moved to Regent's Park.

The National Gallery, fronting the north side of the square, had its origin in the purchase in 1824 by Lord Liverpool's Government of the Angerstein Collection of thirty-eight pictures. The building was erected between 1832 and 1838 and has a length of 460 feet, but the exterior is spoiled by its low elevation together with its insignificant dome and pepper pots, whatever its claim to interior architectural merit and appointments. Its Ionic portico was built with the columns removed from the old Carlton House in Pall Mall. Originally both the national collection and the Royal Academy were housed here, but in 1869 the Academy was removed to Burlington House. The building was extended in 1866-67 on land at the back of the north side of Trafalgar Square. The west side of the building was formerly joined to the buildings in Pall Mall, but in 1903 two of these houses were pulled down so as to isolate the National Gallery.

The church of St Martin in the Fields, overlooking the north-east corner of Trafalgar Square, replaced an earlier edifice and is noteworthy on account of its handsome portico and lofty spire. It was begun in 1721 and completed in 1726, when George I gave 100 guineas to the workmen in addition to £29,000 which he contributed towards the cost of the building and to the organ. The entire cost was nearly £70,000, of which sum over £30,000 was granted by Parliament, the rest being made up by voluntary subscriptions.

By virtue of its size and its prominent situation in the centre of the metropolis, Trafalgar Square soon became a popular centre for public meetings and demonstrations, some of which were occasionally held in defiance of the regulations prohibiting them. Perhaps the most memorable instance was that which occurred on Sunday, 13 November 1887, resulting in a set conflict in which the Metropolitan Police, supported by the Life Guards and the Grenadier Guards, succesfully defended Trafalgar Square against something like twenty thousand men and youths who had defied the legal prohibition to congregate there in processions with their bands and flags for the purpose of holding a public meeting.

Sir Charles Warren, the Chief Commissioner, had issued a police regulation, which been posted up in all parts of the metropolis, prohibiting any organized procession from approaching the square on the Sunday, and by one o'clock some 1,500 police had taken possession of the square. In addition there were three hundred Grenadier Guards behind the National Gallery until 4.0 p.m., when they were brought out with fixed bayonets to line the parapet adjoining the National Gallery. After 4.0 p.m. the 1st Life Guards were called out, and Sir Charles Warren kept the square clear by employing altogether four thousand constables in addition to the three hundred Grenadiers and the three hundred Life Guards, who remained on duty until past 6.0 p.m.

This imposing demonstration of force proving too much for the demonstrators, they hooted and cursed the soldiers, who, nothing daunted, dropped their rifles on the toes of all who ventured near them and struck them with their fists. Thus the square was soon cleared, and by 6.0 p.m. all further disturbance was at an end, though not before some 1,500 persons had been conducted to the neighbouring hospitals for treatment. It was then announced that whilst meetings would be prohibited in Trafalgar Square, they could be held without interference in Hyde Park, whereupon some forty thousand people, mostly idle spectators, availed themselves of this opportunity on the following Sunday.

Trafalgar Square seventy years ago was also an open-air dormitory for outcasts, who preferred to sleep in the open instead of seeking refuge in the casual wards. As a general rule between three and four hundred homeless of both sexes were disturbed here shortly after midnight by a police inspector who appeared with tickets for the Endell Street Casual Ward. The outcasts were then offered the tickets with the alternative of being charged under the Vagrancy Act if they persisted in remaining in the square.

Some accepted the tickets but some preferred to go to other quarters. The efforts of the Commissioners were to some extent thwarted by the benevolent attentions of those persons who brought food to the vagrants and thus attracted people who would otherwise have gone to the casual wards or common lodging houses. Only about one-third of these people had any regular calling or occupation, and the rest simply lived from day to day as best they could from childhood, and could hardly explain how they had managed to exist for so long. About 30 per cent of these people had come from the country in the hope of finding employment in London. Before the formation of Trafalgar Square, St. Martin's Lane extended down to the Strand, and opposite Northumberland House then stood the original Golden Cross Hotel. This was a busy and important coaching hotel which stood several yards to the west of its successor but was removed to make way for the laying out of Trafalgar Square.

The Admiralty Arch, which gives access to the Mall, is approached by a wide opening into Charing Cross at the south-west side of Trafalgar Square, which involved the demolition of five houses. Together with the Memorial in front of Buckingham Palace it forms part of the National Memorial to Queen Victoria and was designed by Sir Aston Webb. The rooms above form part of the premises of the Admiralty. It was erected in 1910, but the roadway into Charing Cross was only just completed in time for the Coronation Procession of King George V on 22 June 1911.

On the island formed by Trafalgar Square, Spring Gardens, and the Mall are the offices of the Canadian Pacific Railway Company, erected in 1907, the West End offices of the Sun Insurance Company, and Malaysia House, with a handsome pair of door-handles in the form of silver-bronze tigers. At the opposite corner of the Mall and Charing Cross is Drummond's Bank, and the Whitehall Theatre, erected in 1930 on the site of the former Ship Tavern. Immediately adjoining Martins Bank, two doors farther south, is another large extension of the Admiralty, the ground-floor portion of which is occupied by the banking premises of Messrs Glyn Mills & Company. It was completed in 1930, and replaced a shabby row of old houses with steps in front, which formerly contained H.M. Office of Works. The new building is six storeys high and faced with red brick. In Spring Gardens are the old offices of the Metropolitan Board of Works, erected in 1861 and enlarged in 1890 at a cost of £10,000 and until 1922 the headquarters of the London County Council. The building is now used partly as offices, but some of it is derelict as the result of bomb damage.

Cockspur Street, which is the continuation westwards of Charing Cross, originally consisted of small good-class shops, but since the dawn of the present century has been almost entirely rebuilt and has become the headquarters in the West End of most of the principal steamship companies. On the south side are the offices of the Royal Mail, and the P. & O. Companies, also those of the Compagnie Générale Transatlantique, the Canadian National Railways, and the imposing Norway House, nine storeys high, acquired by the Norwegian Government as a semi-official centre, and formally opened by King Haakon in 1911. On the opposite side of the street, at the junction with Pall Mall East, is Oceanic House, erected in 1903, formerly the offices of the White Star Line and associated companies and now occupied by Barclays Bank. On the site of Oceanic House there formerly stood a rather imposing Nash building called Waterloo House, which about sixty years ago, before the invasion of the neighbourhood by the various steamship and railway companies, was occupied by a large drapery emporium, Messrs Halling, Pearce & Stone, later merged into the business of Messrs Swan & Edgar, of Piccadilly Circus. The magnificent new building next door is that of the Sun Life Assurance Company of Canada. It was completed in 1929 and adjoins the Canadian Government Offices in Trafalgar Square.

Warwick House Street, a little cul-de-sac off Cockspur Street, leads to Carlton Mews, an interesting relic of Regency London. On the ground level of the Mews are the coach houses where the carriages of the Carlton House Terrace residents were kept—now, of course, garages. Of special interest, however, are the ramps by which the horses were led up to their stalls above the carriages they drew. These stables and coachmen's quarters were converted into comfortable homes which have now been vacated, for the Mews are due for demolition. On the walls may be seen the boundary marks where the parishes of St Martin-in-the-Fields and St James Westminster meet, while through the yard a dozen narrow steps lead up to Carlton House Terrace.

In Pall Mall East, next to the National Gallery, stood the celebrated furniture emporium of Hampton & Sons Ltd until the war, when it was demolished in the air raids of 1940. In Suffolk Street is the United University Club, also fronting Pall Mall East. Suffolk Street was formed in 1664 on the site of the town house of the Earls of Suffolk. At the top of this street, which ends in a cul-de-sac, stood until 1940 the old-established Garland's Hotel which has been destroyed in the blitz. Richard Cobden died in lodgings in Suffolk Street in 1865. On the eastern corner of the Haymarket and Pall Mall is Kinnaird House, containing a branch of Barclays Bank, and on the western corner was the Carlton Hotel; the two buildings together formed a very handsome approach to the Haymarket, along which we will next direct our travels. Down to the reign of William III, this fine, wide thoroughfare was the public highway in which carts loaded with hay and straw were allowed to stand for sale free of toll but in 1926 the street was paved, when a tax was levied on the carts according to their loads.

The Carlton Hotel, erected between 1897 and 1899 and pulled down in 1959, occupied the site of the old Her Majesty's Theatre, now rebuilt on the adjoining site at the corner of Charles Street. The first theatre erected on this site was opened as long ago as 1705, but this was destroyed by a fire in 1789, and was reconstructed in 1790. At that time it was the largest theatre in England, and together with the adjoining Opera Arcade was designed by M. Novosielski. The Royal Opera Arcade, to give it its full title, was reduced and rebuilt by John Nash and G. S. Repton in 1820. It is one of London's earliest arcades and the bow-fronted shops maintain their old-fashioned appearance.

On 13 December 1867 the old theatre was completely destroyed in less than an hour by a fire which broke out at eleven o'clock at night. It seems that the fire-alarm was rather slow in communicating with the headquarters of the brigade, then located in Watling Street, and it was said that the alarm was not given until twenty minutes past eleven, by which time the flames had attacked the roof. By midnight the scene had become one of fearful grandeur, when the roof collapsed amidst a shower of sparks and burning fragments which fell like so much hail in front of the clubs in Pall Mall. Several houses round the theatre were gutted, principally the shops in the adjoining Opera Arcade. The principal sufferer was Mr Graves, the well-known engraver and print-seller in Pall Mall, whose spacious galleries containing ancient and modern works of art collected during forty years were destroyed.

When the theatre was rebuilt the original façade was retained until 1895, when the entire theatre was pulled down, and re-erected on its present site at the corner of Charles Street. The new theatre, which is faced with Portland stone and crowned by a dome, is a great improvement on the old building. In earlier times boxes at Her Majesty's Theatre were let on lease, and in 1860 one of those facing the stage, measuring six feet seven inches by nine feet deep, with the right of admitting six persons nightly, was sold at the Auction Mart with an unexpired term of thirty-one years for £445.

The adjoining Carlton Hotel, opened in 1899, was fronted in the same style as Her Majesty's Theatre, and was also crowned by a lofty dome at the corner of the Haymarket and Pall Mall in such a way as to give these two buildings the appearance of being one. The vacant site of the Carlton Hotel was utilized on the occasion of the Diamond Jubilee of Queen Victoria in 1897 for the erection of a large stand to view the procession. The Palm Court of the Carlton Hotel was demolished by a bomb during the air raids of September 1940. The hotel was then closed down and requisitioned by the Government during the remaining years of the war. In 1948 the Carlton was purchased by the New Zealand Government, and, as previously mentioned, the celebrated hotel was demolished in 1959 and New Zealand House, with a 15-storey tower on a four-storey 'podium', now stands on the site.

On the opposite side of the Haymarket, facing Charles Street, which was re-named Charles II Street to avoid confusion with some twenty other streets of the same name, is the Theatre Royal, originally built from the designs of Nash and opened on 4 July 1821. It was completely rebuilt internally about 1907, but the original Corinthian portico of six columns has, like those of several other London theatres, been retained for reasons of sentiment. The well-known Pall Mall Restaurant which stood next door to the Haymarket Theatre was pulled down in 1930 and a commercial building has been erected on this site. As previously stated, a market of hay was formerly held in this street, but this was removed in 1830 to Cumberland Market near Regent's Park. Few streets in London have improved so much of late years as the Haymarket. Sixty years ago it was a second-rate street, and in the sixties of last century was frequently the scene of drunkenness and disorderly conduct at night time, when the public-houses were still permitted to remain open all night. The west side has been almost entirely rebuilt during the past fifty years and is now lined with stately structures, including the Carlton Cinema opened in 1927. A new street called St James's Market was opened from the Haymarket into Market Street in 1922 when the Capitol Cinema was built. Several large modern buildings also adorn the opposite side of the Haymarket, notably Dewar House at the corner of Orange Street, the premises of Messrs Burberry, and at the corner of Panton Street, Haymarket House, on the ground floor of which is The Design Centre. This street was so named after its landlord, Colonel Panton, who, having won money at a card table, refused to touch a card again. Panton Street contains the Comedy Theatre opposite to which stood Stone's Chop House which dated back to 1770 but was destroyed in the great air raid of 10 May 1941. Stone's has now been rebuilt in a very different, and doubtless much improved, style from the old house one remembers. Orange Street, so called after the Prince of Orange, contains a Nonconformist Chapel, next to which stood a house which was the last London residence of Sir Isaac Newton. A plaque on the wall of Orange Street tells us that it was originally 'James Street 1675'. Another, on a Wine Merchant's premises, reads: 'This building formerly known as the Royal Tennis Court, rebuilt A.D. 1887.'

We now pass Piccadilly Circus on our left, which is fully dealt with in our next chapter, and turn into Coventry Street. This thoroughfare was considerably widened on the south side in 1881, and several important buildings were erected, including the former Haymarket Stores, the Prince of Wales's Theatre, and the club premises at the corner of Whitcomb Street, now the Mapleton Hotel. The Prince of Wales's Theatre, famous for musical comedy and revue, was erected in 1885 and rebuilt in 1936. Whitcomb Street leading through to Pall Mall was originally called Hedge Lane and in the reign of Charles II was a real lane and passage to St Giles's Fields. In the reign of Queen Elizabeth I you could walk from here all the way to Hampstead without finding a dwelling-place. The extensive premises of the Haymarket Stores, which had frontages to both the Haymarket and Coventry Street, were pulled down in 1939 and on this site is a newly built block of shops and offices commenced before the second World War. The buildings on the north side include Scott's Restaurant facing the Haymarket, Lyons Corner House erected in 1908 at the corner of Rupert Street, and greatly enlarged in 1920-23, the Rialto Cinema, occupying the site of the old Globe Restaurant, demolished in 1911, and the recent Quality Inn at the corner of Wardour Street.

On the site of the extension of the Lyons Corner House formerly stood a street called Arundel Place, which ended in a cul-de-sac. The eastern corner was occupied by Messrs Lambert, the silversmiths, now removed to New Bond Street, and contained an interesting old Georgian shop-front. At the top of this cul-de-sac were two well-known foreign hotels called the Previtali and the Mathis, both noted for their excellent cuisine and very popular with Spanish and South American visitors to the metropolis. Interpreters on the staff of these two hotels placed themselves at the disposal of foreign visitors unable to speak English who required a guide to conduct them round the shops in the West End and assist them in their purchases.

Little more than a century ago there was no proper connecting street between Coventry Street and St Martin's Lane, and although one was already planned about 1825, it was not until 1845 that it was completed across Leicester Square. The first section of the new street, sixty feet wide, was then named New Coventry Street, and contained a block of buildings on the south side designed in 1845 by Mr Charles Mayhew. This was pulled down in 1926 to make way for the fine new premises of the Automobile Association, which also include a branch of the Midland Bank on the ground floor. The famous Leicester Lounge at the corner of Wardour Street and Coventry Street was closed in 1926, and the premises became a part of the former drapery establishment of Messrs Stagg & Russell. In 1949 this was purchased by Messrs Peter Robinson Limited, the well-known drapery emporium in Regent Street, as a branch store. Peter Robinson's having opened a new branch in the Strand, this large island site bounded by New Coventry Street, Wardour Street, Lisle Street and Leicester Street is now occupied by the new 'Swiss Centre', a multi-storey building accommodating, *inter alia*, the Swiss National Tourist Office, Swiss Federal Railways, Swissair and Swiss Watch Corporation.

On the opposite side of Leicester Square the extension of this new thoroughfare is fifty-four feet wide and is called Cranbourn Street, and here the original houses, none of which are still standing, were erected from the designs of Mr Herbert of Pimlico, and for that period were regarded as a meritorious specimen of street architecture. According to the *Illustrated London News,* the Improvement Commissioners in July 1845 originally intended to continue this line of thorough-fare via Long Acre, starting from the corner of Bow Street diagonally across Drury Lane, to Carey Street, and thence across Chancery Lane through the Rolls property midway between Holborn and Fleet Street to Farringdon Street, then passing under an arch to the wide part of the Old Bailey, but this admirable scheme stopped short.

Leicester Square prior to 1608 was commonly known as Leicester Fields, and was long a favourite resort of duellists. Leicester House, from which it derives its name, stood on the north-east corner of the square, and was built between 1632 and 1636 by Robert Sidney, Earl of Leicester. This mansion was purchased by George II when Prince of Wales after he had quarrelled with his father and been ordered to quit St James's. It seems that George II had a similar quarrel with his son Frederick, Prince of Wales, who took up his residence as his father had done before him at Leicester House, and added another mansion immediately west-ward called Savile House for his children. In 1777 a communication was built between the two houses for the convenience of the Royal Family. Here also Peter the Great was entertained in 1698.

In 1760 George III was proclaimed King in front of Savile House, and in 1806 Leicester House was pulled down, and Lisle Street built on the site of its gardens. Savile House, which occupied the site of the premises of Messrs Stagg & Russell. was destroyed by fire on Tuesday, 28 February 1865, as the result of an explosion, On that occasion King Edward VII, then Prince of Wales, accompanied by the Duke of Sutherland, was present attired in fireman's uniform.

In 1851 the ground on the square was leased for ten years to Mr Wyld, the geographer, for £3,000, who erected here a circular building ninety feet across, enclosing a globe sixty feet in diameter. Some three hundred men were employed on its construction for upwards of three weeks. On the removal of Wyld's Globe, in October 1862, after occupying the square for ten years, the enclosure became exposed in all its barren nakedness, and from that time to 1874 its condition was a disgrace to the metropolis. It became overgrown with weeds, and covered with rubbish such as tin pots, kettles, old clothes, cast-off shoes, dead cats and dogs, and was an eyesore to everyone forced to pass by it. Leicester Square also contained a gilt equestrian statue of George I, but this also was neglected and allowed to fall into decay, so that many pranks were played upon this ill-fated monument, and even *Punch* made fun of it. The statue had been relegated to a temporary retirement inside the Great Globe of Mr Wyld, and its re-appearance made it the target of practical jokers. It had even begun to fall to pieces and was kept up by a wooden prop.

The disgraceful state of Leicester Square attracted the attention of Parliament, and in November 1867 the Metropolitan Board of Works stepped in and obtained the right to take over Leicester Square on the ground that owing to wilful neglect it had become a kind of 'no man's land'. An action was tried in the Court of Queen's Bench on 13 November 1867, as to whether the Board of Works had the power to take charge of the enclosed garden. Unfortunately the decision went in favour of Mr Tulk the plaintiff, whose family were the owners of the garden, as well as the houses fronting three sides, and who had not only refused to reclaim the square himself, but had resisted every offer made by others who were willing to undertake the work.

In May 1872 Leicester Square was about to be sold by auction and it was supposed that it would be purchased for building purposes. The reserve price was fixed at £30,000 and the remains of the statue of George I were sold by auction and fetched £16. In 1873 a Mr Varques acquired nearly the whole of one side of Leicester Square as a site for a Continental Hotel, but was unable to proceed with its construction, because in the meantime Chancery suits had been instituted by the Committee for the Improvement of Leicester Square. Finally it was restored and beautified by Mr Albert Grant, M. P., at a cost of £28,000, and opened to the general public in July 1874. Out of this sum £13,000 was paid for the ground.

The principal ornament in the square is a white marble fountain surmounted by a statue of Shakespeare, supported at the corners by busts of four distinguished residents of the past, Hogarth, Hunter, Newton and Reynolds, and the trees planted in 1874 have now reached a state of maturity. The Alhambra Theatre which stood on the east side of Leicester Square was built in the Moorish or Arabesque style and was opened in 1852 as a place of popular instruction after the style of the Polytechnic, and was first called the 'Royal Panopticon of Science and Art'. But this speculation proved a failure, and the building was closed down for a time, and reopened as a theatre and a music hall under the name of the Alhambra. It remained in this capacity until December 1929, after which time it was utilized as a picture theatre until it was pulled down in November 1936. Like its famous rival, the Empire Theatre, before its demolition, the Alhambra had long been under sentence of death. Its site together with the adjoining Turkish baths was sold by Sir Oswald Stoll for £600,000 to Mr Oscar Deutsch, head of the Odeon Circuit, who died in 1945. A new Odeon Cinema was then erected on this site. The building is faced with black marble and is crowned in the centre by a lofty square tower. Its architects were Mr Andrew Mather and Mr Harry Weedon. It has a second entrance in Charing Cross Road together with a block of shops and offices nine storeys high. The Cavour Restaurant on the same side of the square, later rechristened the Café Anglais, enjoyed great fame and popularity under the management of the late M. Philippe, its former proprietor, who amassed a fortune.

The upper storeys of the Café Anglais together with the adjoining Leicester Corner House and several buildings in Bear Street were bombed in the great raid of 10 May 1941 and afterwards destroyed by fire. The Leicester Corner House was originally the Hotel de Provence, but in 1919 it was purchased by Messrs R. E. Jones & Sons, the firm of caterers. In the nineties and early nineteen-hundreds it had frequently been the abode of disorderly night-time patrons. Small restaurants of various kinds, which change with the changing tastes of their patrons still occupy this side of the Square, and the north-east corner now has a new super-public house called The Samuel Whitbread.

At the south-eastern corner stood Archbishop Tenison's Grammar School, moved from Green (now Irving) Street at the back of the National Gallery and erected here in 1872. The school has been demolished, and a modern office block will be erected on this site in the near future. Here previously stood the house in which Hogarth settled in 1733, and here after his death his widow lived until 1789. Hogarth's house afterwards became the Sablonnier Hotel which was kept by an Italian named Pagliano and was largely frequented by foreigners until it was pulled down in 1870.

All three of the other sides of Leicester Square having been practically rebuilt during the past thirty years, very little remains to indicate what it looked like when Mr Albert Grant laid it out as a public garden. The two handsome buildings situated on the corners of Leicester Place were both erected in 1898. That on the west corner, previously the Queen's Hotel, is now Queen's House, Queen's bar and a News Theatre. That on the east corner is Victory House, excepting the ground floor which contains a restaurant. This building was for many years the Hotel and Café de l'Europe, and after the first World War it became the Victory Hotel owned by Trust Houses Limited. This latter venture proved a failure and in 1922 the building was purchased for £60,000 by the N.S.P.C.C., who removed their offices here from another building on the opposite side of the square. They have again moved to Riding House Street, Langham Place.

Next door to the Queen's Hotel building is the new Empire Cinema, opened in November 1928, and standing on the site of the former Empire Theatre erected here in 1887. The final performance at this house took place on the evening of 21 January 1927, when the popular American musical comedy called *Lady Be Good* completed its successful run at the Empire. The Duke of Windsor, then Prince of Wales, was present on that occasion. This famous theatre which seated eight hundred people had very spacious accommodation and together with the

Alhambra and the London Pavilion was noted for its lounges or so-called promenades and saloon bars at the back of the stalls. The occasional boisterous celebrations indulged in by the young men about town incited the anger of the puritan elements who tried to get them banned. The promenades were a never-ending source of attraction to the *demi-monde* who frequented them, but during the first World War all three of these establishments did away with them altogether.

On the west side were the premises of Messrs Thurstons, the billiard table manufacturers, removed here from Newcastle Street, Strand, in 1901, owing to the construction of Kingsway and Aldwych. This building was severely damaged in the blitz and the whole of the west side of the Square is now taken up by 'Fanum House', the headquarters of the Automobile Association. One old house, formerly the residence of Sir Joshua Reynolds, which stood next door, became the famous auction rooms of Messrs Puttick & Simpson. Despite strong protests it was pulled down in 1936 to make way for a further extension of the building of the Automobile Association. On the south side of Leicester Square is the new Dental Hospital at the corner of St Martin's Street, erected about 1906, which replaced an earlier structure opened in 1874, and opposite is the new Leicester Square cinema, which in 1930 was erected on the site of the old premises of the N.S.P.C.C. Attached to this building is the Pastoria Hotel with its frontage to St Martin's Street. At the corner of Orange Street in the entrance hall of the Westminster Branch Library is a plaque recording that the house of Sir Isaac Newton, in which he lived from 1710 to 1727, stood here. It later became the home of Dr Charles Burney and his daughter Fanny, authoress of *Evelina*. Green Street, now renamed Irving Street, was opened in 1860. Next to the Empire Cinema on the corner of Leicester Street now stands a block of shops and offices nine storeys high erected in 1937. The short distance between Wardour Street and Leicester Street is now known as *New* Coventry Street.

Turning next into Cranbourn Street, on the north side, close to Leicester Square, is the Warner Cinema, erected in 1938 on the site of Daly's Theatre, for many years a centre of musical comedy under the management of the late Mr George Edwardes and remembered for such musical successes as *The Geisha* (1896), *A Country Girl* (1902) and *The Merry Widow* (1907) – all of which ran for over 700 performances. It was opened by Mr Augustin Daly of New York in 1893 as a London theatre for his American productions. Just beyond Daly's Theatre are the London Hippodrome and the adjoining Cranbourn Mansions, opened in 1900. The interior of The Hippodrome has been entirely rearranged and it is now a restaurant with dancing and a twice-nightly 'Floor Show'. On the opposite corner of Cranbourn Street and Charing Cross Road is Leicester Square Underground Station, which was rebuilt in lavish style in 1935. It has escalators and a large circular hall like that of Piccadilly Circus Station, but on a smaller scale.

At the junction of Cranbourn Street, Long Acre, and St Martin's Lane is Garrick Street, leading to King Street, Covent Garden, and opened on 20 February 1861. The construction of this new thoroughfare involved the removal of a number of wretched hovels in Angel Court and Rose Street. Its principal building is the Garrick Club, instituted in 1831 and removed here from King Street in July 1864. The club is built in the Italian style and contains an interesting collection of theatrical portraits which may be viewed at specified times on the personal introduction of a member. At the corner of King Street are the premises of Messrs Debenham & Storr, the auctioneers, erected in 1860.

King Street leads to Covent Garden Market, a corruption of Convent Garden, and originally a private square formed about 1631 at the expense of Francis, Earl of Bedford, from the design of Inigo Jones, though never actually completed or even, perhaps, designed in full. Only on the north side does a length of the Piazza or Colonnade survive, whereas the west side is taken up by St Paul's Church, also built by Inigo Jones, and the south side has modern buildings which occupy the site of Bedford House pulled down in 1704. The market is devoted to the sale of fruit, flowers, and vegetables, and the buildings date from 1831, but have since been much extended and improved. In 1926 it was proposed to move Covent Garden Market to Bloomsbury, but this scheme was abandoned owing to widespread opposition. A later proposal to move the market to Nine Elms, Battersea, is thought to be more successful. At the corner of Tavistock Street and Southampton Street is Tower House, a fine building erected in 1936 by Messrs George Newnes Limited, the well-known firm of publishers. It is nine storeys high and faced with Portland stone.

The building on the north side of King Street, overlooking Covent Garden, was until 1929 the headquarters of the National Sporting Club. It was a fine old mansion of the Restoration period, which originally belonged to Sir Kenelm Digby, an eminent physician. Afterwards it became the town residence of various notable people, and early in the nineteenth century Mr W. C. Evans converted the dining-room of this mansion into an attractive concert hall with a stage and supper tables. So successful did this venture prove that Mr Evans was enabled to retire in 1844 with an ample fortune. It was afterwards taken over by Mr John Green, whose death occurred in the seventies. Several clubs then leased the premises after that time until 1892, when the building became the home of the National Sporting Club. In 1911 the theatre of the club was rebuilt and enlarged, and in 1919 the building was disposed of by the National Sporting Club to Messrs George Munro & Company Limited, a large firm of fruit brokers who rebuilt the premises internally but have preserved its historic façade in King Street.

Before the first World War Covent Garden possessed several good hotels, but most of these have been closed down and converted into business premises. Prominent amongst these was the Tavistock Hotel, forming the north-eastern building of the Piazza at the corner of James Street, which was much patronized by the theatrical profession. The former Covent Garden Hotel on the south side has become a branch of Lloyds Bank, and Hummums Hotel on the east side of Covent Garden is now Russell Chambers. Burleigh Street, leading to the

Strand, was first opened through from Exeter Street to Tavistock Street on the south side of Covent Garden in August 1859. In 1932 the Tavistock Hotel was pulled down and has been replaced by a new building faced with stone. The Piazza has been reconstructed and the original height of its buildings maintained. At the same time a new street was constructed at the back of the Royal Opera House between King Street and Floral Street which has been named Mart Street. The Tavistock Hotel has been rebuilt since the last war in Woburn Place.

Passing into Bow Street, we next observe the Royal Opera House on the west side, the third theatre which has been erected on this same spot. The second theatre was opened in 1809 and was converted into an Italian Opera House in 1847, but this was destroyed by fire on 5 March 1856. The present building, designed by E. M. Barry, was erected in the short space of six months during 1858. and will accommodate some two thousand people. Bow Street police court on the opposite side of the road has been the principal metropolitan station for upwards of a century. Endell Street, the continuation of Bow Street northwards, was opened in 1845 and leads to New Oxford Street.

We turn to the left into Long Acre. This busy thoroughfare is principally occupied by wholesale fruit houses, but it also contains the extensive new buildings of Odhams Press on the two corners of Endell Street, erected between 1935 and 1939, and several large firms of motor-car dealers. In the days before motor-cars, the principal carriage builders had their premises in Long Acre. It suffers from the drawback of being far too narrow for its requirements and is therefore scheduled as a one-way street. Most of the buildings on the north side of Long Acre are modern, having been gradually reconstructed since 1905. One of these is the large wholesale warehouse of Messrs Pouparts Limited which covers the site between Langley Street and Mercer Street. It was rebuilt in 1938. The new buildings of Odhams Press have long frontages to both sides of Endell Street and to make way for the west block much slum property was demolished between Long Acre and Shelton Street. At the corner of Endell Street is a large open-air swimming bath, the 'Oasis', which has been constructed by the Holborn Borough Council on the bombed site of the former covered baths. A large area in this district is the property of the Mercers' Company, and thus we find Mercer Street and The Mercers' Arms. All buildings on the company's land bear the familiar Mercers' crest, described as 'The Virgin with a celestial crown', though the boys of the Mercers' School usually referred to it as 'Queen Anne'. An old book on the City Companies suggests that this crest was originally the head of King Richard II who gave the Mercers their charter in 1393; the somewhat effeminate features of the poetic Richard being responsible for this accidental change of sex. In the Long Acre area alone it is possible to count at least forty of these 'marks'. The richest example, however, is possibly that on the gateway of the old Mercers' School in Fetter Lane.

At the southern end of Long Acre is St Martin's Lane, leading to Trafalgar Square and containing the New Theatre and the Duke of York's Theatre on the west side, and the immense London Coliseum on the east side, erected in 1905 at a cost of £150,000. At first the Coliseum proved a failure and in 1907 was closed down for about eighteen months, but in 1909 it was acquired by Sir Oswald Stoll, and has since that time enjoyed success as a theatre for variety, and, more recently, American musicals.

At the foot of St Martin's Lane is the Nurse Cavell Memorial, designed by Sir George Frampton, R.A., and unveiled by Queen Alexandra on 20 March 1920. Across the roadway behind the National Portrait Gallery is a statue of Sir Henry Irving, unveiled in 1910. This was formerly a favourite corner for various street performers, but the ground surrounding the statue has now been made into attractive flower beds. At the junction of St Martin's Lane and Charing Cross Road is a branch of the Westminster Bank, which adjoins the former Westminster City Hall. The foundation-stone of this building, which cost £24,000, was laid by King Edward VII, when Prince of Wales, on 18 March 1890, but since that time it has been considerably enlarged.

Charing Cross Road, connecting Trafalgar Square with St Giles's Circus, was completed in 1887, and contains the Garrick Theatre, opened in 1889, the new and excellent Westminster Lending Library, and Wyndham's Theatre, adjoining Cranbourn Street, erected in 1900. A great many shops in Charing Cross Road are occupied by second-hand booksellers, and prominent amongst these is the establishment of Messrs Foyle, which claims to be the largest bookshop in the world. On the east side is the Phoenix Theatre and a new block of shops and flats. In West Street, between Charing Cross Road and St Martin's Lane, are the St Martin's and the Ambassador's Theatres, erected between 1914 and 1916. On the site of Aldridge's Horse and Carriage Repository in Upper St Martin's Lane is the new fourteen-storey 'Thorn House', headquarters of Thorn Electrical Industries Ltd, with a tower block 180 feet in height.

At the back of Cambridge Circus, which forms the junction of Shaftesbury Avenue and Charing Cross Road, is the area known as the Seven Dials, an unsalubrious but rapidly-improving district built on what was once 'Cock and Pye Fields', from which radiate seven minor streets, namely, Great Earl Street, Little Earl Street, Great White Lion Street, Little White Lion Street, Great St Andrew's Street, Little St Andrew's Street, and Queen Street. It was so named because there was formerly a column in the centre, at the base of which was a dialstone, believed to have had seven sundials, one facing each of the streets. The column was in 1822 re-erected at Weybridge, Surrey, where it can still be seen, and the streets have been renamed to avoid the confusion between 'Great' and 'Little'. The dialstone also stands in the forecourt of Weybridge Public Library, but curiously, it has only *six* faces, not seven. By way of explanation it has been said that two of the seven streets opened into one angle. At the corner of White Lion Street, now Mercer Street, is the Cambridge Theatre, erected in 1930.

In Cambridge Circus, at the corner of Shaftesbury Avenue, is the Palace Theatre built for R. D'Oyly Carte by Mr T. E. Colcutt. It was opened as the Royal English Opera House on 31 January 1891, with a great flourish of trumpets, when Sir Arthur Sullivan's grand opera *Ivanhoe* was produced for the first time. Though the first-night audience was tremendously enthusiastic, the opera only achieved 160 performances, with the result that in July of the following year the opera house was sold to Sir Augustus Harris, and its name was changed to the Palace Theatre. Since that time it has enjoyed a high reputation as a variety theatre and a house of musical comedy. Next to the Palace Theatre is Wingate House, an eight-storey building which has the new Columbia Cinema on the ground floor.

Shaftesbury Avenue, connecting Piccadilly Circus with Hart Street, Blooms-bury, now renamed Bloomsbury Way, was opened in 1886, and, together with the construction of Cambridge Circus, Charing Cross Road, and the enlarge-ment of Piccadilly Circus, formed the last of the great metropolitan street improvements carried out by the former Metropolitan Board of Works. The story of Shaftesbury Avenue reveals a wasted opportunity of providing the West End of London with such a thoroughfare as might have been the pride and glory of her citizens at the present day. Viewed from that standpoint it was almost a pity that the construction of Shaftesbury Avenue was not delayed until after the creation of the London County Council in 1889, as in that case it would in all probability have taken the form of a noble avenue one hundred feet wide, after the pattern of Kingsway or Regent Street. Running diagonally from Piccadilly Circus to New Oxford Street, it might have opened up a fine new vista, resembling that of the superb Avenue de l'Opéra in Paris.

But instead of being planned on a generous scale, Shaftesbury Avenue merely took the form of a widening of the former King and Dudley Streets, two mean thoroughfares which were adapted to the width of the neighbouring streets. The only portion of Shaftesbury Avenue comprising an entirely new street is that between Piccadilly Circus and Rupert Street. The net result was that Shaftesbury Avenue was conceived on a most niggardly scale, the north side being lined for many years by the ragged buildings of King Street and Dudley Street, whilst buildings of a very second-rate character were erected all along the south side, the majority of which would look all the better for a cleaning with the steam-brush.

In course of time the greater part of the buildings on the north side were rebuilt, and several handsome theatres, notably the Apollo, and the twin Globe and Queen's Theatres, betwen Rupert Street and Wardour Street, were erected here. The Queen's Theatre was badly damaged in the air raid of 24 September 1940. It was rebuilt and re-opened on 8 July 1959 by John Gielgud in a Shakes-peare anthology called *Ages of Man*.

The building at the corner of Denman Street, next to the Café Monico, became during the second World War the American Red Cross Services Club and was then known as Rainbow Corner. It was vacated in 1947 and became one of the popular cafés of Messrs Fortes who own several others in London and in the South Coast towns. Both the Fortes café and the Café Monico have now been pulled down and the whole of this Shaftesbury Avenue – Denman Street – Sherwood Street triangle is to be redeveloped. A public outcry against the designs for the new building proposed for the site has given the surviving buildings a temporary reprieve. The future of the site is still uncertain although there have been various plans for the development of the whole of Piccadilly Circus.

East of Cambridge Circus all of the mean buildings on the north side of Shaftesbury Avenue, the legacy of Dudley Street, have now disappeared. In their place now stands the Saville Theatre erected in 1930, also a new eight-storeyed building erected in 1948 by the Metro-Goldwyn-Mayer film company and Century House, a nine-storeyed block of offices erected in 1938 at the junction of Shaftesbury Avenue and New Compton Street.

The south side of Shaftesbury Avenue included the world-famous Trocadero Restaurant, opened on 5 October 1896 and afterwards greatly enlarged. Recently closed, the 'Troc' reopened again under another name with quite a different kind of entertainment. Otherwise this side of the avenue is almost entirely occupied by milliners' and dressmakers' shops, which are so numerous that one wonders how all of them can possibly obtain a living in the same street. On this side of Shaftesbury Avenue formerly stood the Shaftesbury Theatre, which was damaged in the air raids of 1940. It was again hit in 1941 and then demolished. Opened in October 1888, it was a handsome building of red brick with stone dressings and a row of columns in the centre above the ground floor. Here two famous musical comedies had long runs, namely *The Belle of New York* in 1898 and *The Arcadians* in 1909. Here also *The Sorrows of Satan,* a play founded on Marie Corelli's famous novel, was produced in 1897. The adjoining London Fire Brigade Station was also partly destroyed. Charing Cross Road between Cambridge Circus and Oxford Street is a widening on the east side of the former Crown Street, but thence to Cranbourn Street and Trafalgar Square it is a new thoroughfare. Like all the new London streets built during the past sixty years, Shaftesbury Avenue and Charing Cross Road are provided with subways to accommodate the sewers and the gas and water pipes, thus obviating the necessity of constantly pulling up the roadway. On the west side of Charing Cross Road between Old Compton Street and Manette Street is the Inner London Education Authority's College for the Distributive Trades and the adjoining St Martin's School of Art erected in 1938.

Soho, the quarter enclosed by Wardour Street, Shaftesbury Avenue, Charing Cross Road and Oxford Street, is supposed by some people to have derived its name from the watchword of the Duke of Monmouth on the battlefield of Sedgemoor, and by others from So Hoe, the cry used to call off the harriers in the fields where the Lord Mayor and members of the City Corporation occasionally hunted the hare in the days when this district lay far beyond the outer limits of London.

Today Soho is essentially the Italian quarter of London, and is noted for its many excellent restaurants. Wardour Street, formerly known as Princes Street, is now the principal centre of the film trade, and several handsome buildings have been erected here of late years. Film producers, distributors and cinema furnishers all have their premises here. This street is in gradual process of widening at the present time and at the back of Shaftesbury Avenue a portion of the churchyard of St Anne's, Soho, was appropriated for that purpose. This handsome church, crowned by a tall spire, was erected in 1686, and dedicated to the mother of the Virgin as a compliment to Princess Anne. It was destroyed in the air raids of 1940 and only a portion of its walls and the tower now remain. The churchyard has now been laid out as a garden with lawns and seats. William Hazlitt was buried here and there is also an interesting memorial to Theodore, King of Corsica, who died in 1756. He was imprisoned for debt and surrendered his kingdom for the use of his creditors. He died in poverty and his burial was undertaken by an oilman in Compton Street who said he was willing *for once* to pay the funeral expenses of a king.

'Wigs by Clarkson' was in every theatre programme in pre-war days and No. 43 Wardour Street (now a restaurant) was the establishment of the celebrated and mysterious Willie Clarkson. Inscriptions on the doorway tell us that Sarah Bernhardt laid the foundation stone in 1904 and the coping stone was laid by Sir Henry Irving in 1905. In March 1966, one of the familiar blue memorial plaques was affixed to the building. Between Wardour Street and Dean Street is quaint little Meard Street, bearing the date 1732, with at least a dozen eighteenth century houses (some with shops) on its south side.

In Dean Street, leading out of Shaftesbury Avenue, was the Royalty Theatre, formerly the Soho Theatre and built in 1840 as a school for acting by Miss Fanny Kelly. Miss Kelly was an actress of such popularity and charm that her life was twice endangered by disappointed admirers who attempted to shoot her — once at Drury Lane and again at a Dublin Theatre. However, she lived to be 92. Her Royalty Theatre was rebuilt in 1861, but finally destroyed by bombs. The new block of offices built on the site is called 'Royalty House'. The 200 years old shop-front of the newsagent and tobacconist at Number 88 Dean Street is unique and worth a visit. In Old Compton Street, at the corner of Greek Street, is the Casino, formerly the Prince Edward Theatre, built of red and yellow brick with a mansard roof, after the style of some Italian palace, and opened in April 1930. Not having proved a success, it was transformed in 1936 into a large cabaret restaurant which claimed to be the most sumptuous in the world. It is at present devoted to Cinerama. The names of Dean Street and Compton Street commemorate Bishop Compton, Dean of the Chapel Royal.

Continuing our travels through either Greek Street or Frith Street, running parallel, we shall next come to Soho Square, laid out in the reign of Charles II and originally called Monmouth Square, from the Duke of Monmouth having resided in a house in this square. Here so much rebuilding has taken place of late years that Soho Square now bears a completely modern appearance. Among its newest buildings is No 20 Soho Square, formerly the offices of Messrs Crosse & Blackwell, at the corner of Sutton Row and that of the Twentieth-Century Fox film company at the south-west corner of the square. On this side is also the new Parkwood House, a tall block of offices with its upper storeys set back from the street. At Nos. 23-25 Soho Square is a building of similar design completed in 1938. Nos. 27 and 28, on the south side, are the new premises of Novello's, the music publishers, removed here from Wardour Street. On the east side is the Roman Catholic Church of St Patrick and at the north-western angle of the square is the French Protestant Church. On the south side, at the corner of Frith Street, is a large hospital for women. At the corner of Sutton Row and Charing Cross Road is the Astoria Cinema opened in 1927 on the site of the old jam and pickle factory of Messrs Crosse & Blackwell. This brings vivid recollections of the atmosphere at the junction of Tottenham Court Road, Oxford Street and Charing Cross Road (now St Giles' Circus) many years ago. From Meux's Horseshoe Brewery (now the Dominion Theatre) emerged thick clouds of malt-flavoured steam that would permeate the whole area — were it not for the sugary-sweet smell of boiling fruit, or a pungent odour of hot vinegar (according to whether it was jam or pickle making day) that issued from Crosse and Blackwell's factory (now the Astoria Cinema) nearby. In September 1874 the residents of Soho Square expressed a desire to throw open the central enclosure to the general public, and Mr Albert Grant, who had already laid out Leicester Square, offered to do the same thing for Soho Square, at an estimated cost £7,000. He also offered to endow it with an annual income of £150 for its maintenance, but this generous offer nevertheless failed to secure the square for the people. Today, however, Soho Square is a public garden.

The Westminster City Council have fortunately secured the Square for public use so that, with St Anne's Gardens, there are now two open spaces in this densely populated district. In the middle of the Square is a much weatherworn statue of Charles II, which originally formed the centre of a handsome fountain. Sometime in the seventies, however, the statue was removed to Grim's Dyke, Harrow Weald, a Norman Shaw mansion built in 1872, which W. S. Gilbert purchased in 1891. It remained there until 1938, when it was restored to Soho Square by Lady Gilbert. The statue is the work of Caius Gabriel Cibber (1681). Although so much of it has been rebuilt of late years, Soho and the quarter bounded on the west by Regent Street still lacks a co-ordinated plan of construction. This area consists mainly of a maze of courts, dark, narrow streets and cul-de-sacs of a very mean character, none of which affords proper communication with the neighbouring main streets. Only Berwick Street with its famous street-market gives a picturesque touch to a dark and squalid neighbourhood. A modern eighteen-storey tower building at the southern end of Berwick Street is part of the Westminster City Council Housing Scheme and provides 57 flats, 2 floors of office accommodation and 13 shops on the ground floor. Here a tavern, formerly the 'City of London', has been more appropriately re-named 'The King of Corsica'.

On a large island site in St Giles's High Street a massive block of offices, called St Giles Court and occupied by government departments, has been erected. It is nine storeys high and of a very similar character to that on the neighbouring site in New Oxford Street, which we have already noted in our ninth walk.

Eleventh Walk

Charing Cross to the Mall, Carlton House Terrace, Waterloo Place, Piccadilly Circus, Regent Street, Portland Place, and Regent's Park

Starting out on our travels from Charing Cross, and passing through the Admiralty Arch, already noticed in our previous chapter, we come first to the Mall, leading to Buckingham Palace. This fine road is 65 feet wide, paved with tarred asphalt, and flanked on both sides by an avenue, 25 feet wide, planted with double rows of plane-trees. The new Mall, which forms part of the memorial to the late Queen Victoria, was principally constructed in 1903 and 1904, but the eastern section from the Duke of York's Steps to Charing Cross was not opened to vehicular traffic until 1911. It necessitated the sacrifice of a slice of St James's Park, together with a portion of the lake near Buckingham Palace. Until 1904 a small kiosk stood in St James's Park on the site of the new Mall, where cows were kept and fresh milk provided for the general public, and for several generations this privilege had been enjoyed by the same family. During the lifetime of the tenants the Crown authorities allowed a new kiosk to be erected, conditionally upon all further claims to this privilege being surrendered after their decease.

The old Mall, which is still in existence and runs alongside the new Mall, has been converted into a riding track. It extended from Buckingham Palace to the Duke of York's Steps, after which it connected with the road leading by the east side of St James's Park to Birdcage Walk. Before the construction of the new Mall practically all of the east-bound traffic from Hyde Park Corner via Constitution Hill proceeded by way of Marlborough Gate and Pall Mall to Charing Cross.

The two handsome blocks of houses known as Carlton House Terrace, by John Nash, which adorn the north side of the Mall, were completed about 1831, and occupy the site of Carlton House and its grounds, the residence of George IV when Prince Regent. A new entrance into St James's Park from Pall Mall between the two terraces of houses was opened here by order of King William IV on the day of his coronation. It is approached by steps made of granite obtained from the Island of Herm, near Guernsey, forming a base for the Duke of York's Column, which was erected by public subscription to the memory of Frederick, Duke of York, second son of George III, at a cost of £25,000. The column itself is 124 feet high and is surmounted by a bronze statue fourteen feet high. Within, a spiral staircase of 168 steps leads to a gallery which at one time was open to the public during the summer months between 12.0 noon and 4.0 p.m., but this concession has long since been abolished. Strangers in London so frequently confused the Duke of York's with Nelson's column that a descriptive tablet was affixed to the former a few years ago. Nevertheless, the present writer quite recently encountered a visitor waiting on the Duke of York's steps to keep an appointment at Nelson's Column!

The building of Carlton House Terrace proved a most fortunate speculation. Lord Goderich paid £25,000 for one of the houses, and the Count de Salis gave £10,000 for a smaller one. The house adjoining the steps on the west side before the first World War was the German Embassy and Consulate, and at No. 13, and afterwards No. 11, Mr W. E. Gladstone resided for many years. Viewed from the north side, Carlton House Terrace commands little notice from the casual observer, but when seen from the Mall, its appearance when newly painted is very fine, and if it were faced with Portland stone, instead of stucco, which is so badly suited to our London atmosphere, it would undoubtedly become a permanent ornament to the West End of London.

In 1932 the house on the south-west corner of Carlton Gardens at the back of Carlton House Terrace was pulled down and on this site a lofty block of offices was then erected. This is a very fine building nine storeys high faced with Portland stone with its upper floors zoned back from the pavement. During the war, this was General de Gaulle's headquarters, and attached to the wall is his declaration, dated 18 June 1940:—

A Tous les Français! La France a perdu une bataille!
Mais La France n'a perdu la guerre!

This threat to the sanctity of Carlton House Terrace caused an outcry at that time amongst those people who recognized it only as the favourite place of residence for titled people and foreign ambassadors. A more recent shock for the exclusive Carlton Gardens is the ultra-modern 10-storey office building at No. 5-7 just opposite. Opened in 1965, Wool House, the new home of the International Wool Secretariat, provides the British textile trade and industry with a comprehensive technological and fashion and fabric advisory service.

In front of the Duke of York's Steps, facing Waterloo Place, is an equestrian bronze statue of King Edward VII, designed by Sir Bertram Mackennal, with Sir Edwin Lutyens as the architect. On the west side of the steps is a statue of Sir John Franklin, and on the east side one of Lord Clive and another of Captain Scott, the Antarctic explorer, which was the work of Lady Scott and was erected in 1912 by officers of the Fleet. In Carlton Gardens is a statue of Lord Curzon of Kedleston and at the western end of Carlton House Terrace, facing the Mall, is a recent statue of King George VI by W. McMillan (1954).

Carlton House, which stood on this site and originally crowned the southern end of Waterloo Place, belonged to the Earl of Burlington, and was presented in 1732 to the Countess Dowager, his mother, together with the attached estate. In the same year that lady sold it to Frederick, Prince of Wales, father of George III, who then made it his principal residence. In 1783 it underwent numerous additions and improvements and was created a separate establishment for the Prince Regent by Parliament. It was pulled down in 1828 to make way for the new opening from Pall Mall into St James's Park. The grounds, which overlooked St James's Park, were very beautiful and as retired as though they were right out in the country.

On the south-west corner of Waterloo Place and Pall Mall is the Athenaeum Club, founded in 1824, and erected here in 1829 from the design of Mr Decimus Burton. On the pavement outside the Athenaeum, is a mounting-block, or horse-block, 'erected by desire of the Duke of Wellington, 1830'. On the south-east corner is the United Services Club, erected in 1828 from the designs of Nash, and enlarged in 1911.

Let us now direct our steps up Waterloo Place. This large open space forms an oblong quadrangle leading into Regent Street, and its construction necessitated the removal of a number of old and shabby houses extending from St James's Market to the north side of Pall Mall opposite Carlton House. The market itself was also removed shortly afterwards to make way for the construction of Lower Regent Street. Here is the Crimean Monument and also statues of Florence Nightingale and Sidney Herbert, Secretary for War in the days of her devoted services to her country. Being close to so many of the leading West End clubs, the southern portion of Waterloo Place adjoining Carlton House Terrace is utilized as a car park. A proposal made by the Westminster City Council about twenty-five years ago that Lower Regent Street should be renamed Waterloo Place, so as to include under that title the entire street from Piccadilly Circus to Pall Mall, was rejected by the local ratepayers and shopkeepers. The suggested change would have been a great convenience, owing to the confusion caused to people who regard Regent Street proper as extending only from Oxford Circus to Piccadilly Circus.

The old buildings in Waterloo Place, erected about 1814, were faced with stucco, and on both the east and west sides consisted of a centre formed by an Ionic portico raised on a basement, which formed the entrance storey, and two flanks of Ionic pilasters corresponding with the columns. The corners of Charles II Street, forming the north side of Waterloo Place, originally came forward in advance of the building line of Regent Street, but they were rebuilt between 1908 and 1912 and set back to the same line of frontage as the rest of the street. The rebuilding of Waterloo Place was delayed by the first World War and was not entirely completed until 1925.

Banks and Insurance offices abound on both sides of Waterloo Place. On the site now occupied by the North British and Mercantile Insurance Company formerly stood the premises of William Watson & Company, a prominent firm of Indian Army bankers and forwarding agents who went bankrupt in 1904 to the extent of £600,000 as a result of which many Army officers lost all their savings.

Crossing Charles II Street we next enter Regent Street, constructed between 1816 and 1820, and now one of the finest metropolitan thoroughfares in the world. It was designed to connect Carlton House with Regent's Park, where the Prince Regent originally intended to build a house either there or on Primrose Hill. After passing the County Fire Office and Piccadilly Circus, it forms a curve known as the Quadrant, and then continues in a direct line to Oxford Circus and Langham Place, where it links up with Portland Place, leading to Park Crescent and Marylebone Road.

The Prince Regent having approved the plans and obtained the sanction of Parliament, this great improvement was designed by Nash, and commenced in 1814. The estimated cost was only £300,000, but actually it cost a great deal more, and its progress was retarded by the improverished state of the country's finances due to the Napoleonic Wars, in much the same way as the rebuilding of Regent Street in our own time was held up for several years by the first World War. Thus on 15 July 1816 orders were positively issued to stop the improvements north of Piccadilly Circus, and to proceed only with the section from Piccadilly Circus to Carlton House, and it was not until 1820 that the entire street was completed. King George IV was responsible for the construction of the old Regent Street, but King George V witnessed the completion of the new Regent Street, over a century later. To commemorate this important event in the history of London, His Majesty, accompanied by Queen Mary, drove through the reconstructed Regent Street on 23 June 1927. The route on this auspicious occasion was profusely decorated by the shopkeepers and tradesmen, and was thronged with thousands of spectators.

Resuming our travels once again, we first pass, on the east corner of Charles II Street and Regent Street, a recently constructed building for the United Kingdom Atomic Energy Authority. This site was formerly occupied by the Junior United Services Club. On the opposite side of Charles II Street is British Columbia House, the foundation-stone of which was laid by the Duke of Connaught on 16 July 1914.

On this corner site a century ago stood Warren's Hotel, then much patronized by the nobility and the higher clergy. In 1848 this hotel was reconstructed with a very ornate exterior, and later became the well-known Continental Hotel, which achieved notoriety as an abode of the *demi-monde* and fast-living people. In the summer of 1906 this hotel was raided by the police and closed down. Some months later it was reopened under new management as the Hotel Chatham, in which capacity it survived until 1914, when the premises were pulled down.

The adjoining block of buildings, known as Crown Chambers, until 1939 occupied by a large book store and a Lyons's tea-shop, was some fifty years ago the large drapery and fancy goods emporium of Messrs Howell & James. Crown Chambers was the only building in Regent Street which ever possessed a brick frontage, no other edifice having been faced with any other material than stucco or stone. The reason for allowing this exception to the general rule relating to the street frontages in Regent Street appears to be somewhat of a mystery. Crown Chambers, together with a house next door which was the last relic of Nash's Regent Street, was pulled down in July 1939. During the war this cleared site was utilized for an emergency water-supply tank of the National Fire Brigade. A handsome new seven-storey building has now been erected on this site. This is faced with Portland stone. Two doors farther up the street is Carlton House, built on the site of the old St Philip's Chapel, erected in 1821. The chapel was designed by Sir William Chambers in the Roman Doric style, and was pulled down in 1904. On the same side of the road, at the corner of Jermyn Street, is the imposing Plaza Cinema, opened in 1926, together with a row of shops. Next to the Plaza Cinema is York Building, the only remaining relic of the old Regent Street and formerly the Junior Army and Navy Stores. The balconied windows, with pediments and columns, make it most distinctive, though the interior has been modernized and is now the West End office of the Cunard-White-Star Line.

On the opposite side of the street, adjoining the Junior United Service Club, stood until 1937 Carlton Chambers, which was one of the three surviving blocks of buildings belonging to the old Regent Street, and had been suffered to remain indefinitely because there were no prospective offers for this building site. This is now covered by Rex House, a handsome building of seven storeys with the top floor zoned back from the treet and faced with Portland stone. It is at present occupied by British Railways Travel Centre, the Society of Friends of Jewish Refugees, and on the ground floor is the Paris Cinema now used by the B.B.C. sound services. Occupying almost the entire frontage between Carlton Street and Jermyn Street is the huge Dorland House, one of the largest office buildings in the West End, occupying the site of the former Raleigh Club and its courtyard which overlooked Regent Street. The ground floor accommodates various tourist offices etc. Commercial exhibitions are frequently held at Dorland House. The building on the eastern corner of Jermyn Street, now a restaurant, was originally tenanted by Messrs Elkington & Company Limited, the well-known firm of silversmiths.

After crossing Jermyn Street we next observe the two fine corner blocks of buildings forming the south side of Piccadilly Circus. That on the east side of the street, erected in 1923, contains a new entrance to the Criterion Restaurant, the sports shop of Messrs Lillywhites Limited, and Messrs Dunn's hat shop. That on the west side, completed in 1929, is occupied by a branch of The Midland Bank.

The Criterion Restaurant, a handsome building erected by Messrs Spiers & Pond in 1873 at a cost, including the internal equipments, of £80,000, was designed by Mr Thomas Verity. The principal frontage is in Piccadilly Circus and is decorated in the French Renaissance style. The Criterion stands on the site of the White Bear Inn, which was formerly one of the busiest coaching houses trading with the west and south-west of England. The Criterion Theatre, which adjoins the restaurant and also has an entrance in Jermyn Street, was opened in March 1874 and is entirely below ground, a thing no longer permitted under the present-day regulations appertaining to the construction of new theatres.

The new buildings which front Piccadilly Circus have been made square instead of curved like the old ones, so that to-day it is hardly correct to designate it a circus. Nevertheless, the name of Piccadilly Circus has become such a household word with everybody that any attempt to rechristen it Piccadilly Square would certainly be doomed to failure. Originally it was known as the first Regent Circus, and to use the expression of George IV 'prevented the sensation of crossing Piccadilly being perceived'. The second Regent Circus is now called Oxford Circus, and was designed on precisely the same lines as the original Piccadilly Circus, but Nash, in erecting this great future centre of London traffic, probably never had this intention or idea.

With the object of providing an approach to the newly-constructed Shaftesbury Avenue in 1886 Piccadilly Circus was greatly enlarged by the demolition of the buildings forming the north-east corner, together with Titchfield Street, which stood at the back of the Circus and extended from Glasshouse Street into Coventry Street. This involved the demolition of the old Pavilion Music Hall, which was rebuilt on its present site at the junction of Coventry Street and Shaftesbury Avenue within the short period of about six months. The west side of Piccadilly Circus, which has been set back a few feet, in conjunction with the widening of Piccadilly, contains the handsome new building of Messrs Swan & Edgar Limited, erected 1926-27. But perhaps the most distinctive building in the Circus is that of the County Fire Office on the north side, forming the entrance to the new Quadrant, and completed in 1927. The old County Fire Office, demolished in 1924, although of a much lower elevation, was also considered a great ornament in its day to the old Piccadilly Circus.

The principal feature of Piccadilly Circus, to which all visitors are irresistibly drawn, is the Shaftesbury fountain, with its popular statue of Eros. This was erected in 1893 as a memorial to that great Victorian philanthropist, Anthony Ashley Cooper, seventh Earl of Shaftesbury, who did so much for London's poor. The elegant statue, which is of aluminium, stands high on its pedestal above the fountain, and a generous supply of water gushes from the mouths of fishes, dolphins, etc., at numerous points in the circumference of the four basins of the fountain. The whole charming structure is based on a group of eight spacious octagonal steps, upon which (since there are no seats in Piccadilly Circus) visitors love to relax; save that on a windy day the water is liable to overflow and the steps become very wet.

Upwards of forty-five thousand vehicles pass through the Circus in the course of a day, and it is one of the busiest traffic centres in the West End; until recently the roundabout system was in operation here. The circular underground station below the centre of Piccadilly Circus, opened in 1928, is the largest and finest in London, and was an engineering feat of considerable magnitude. No less than thirty-eight million passengers use this station yearly. Its construction involved the removal of Gilbert's statue of Eros, erected in Piccadilly Circus in about 1890, to the Embankment Gardens, but after the new station had been completed Eros was restored to his original site in the centre of Piccadilly Circus. During the second World War the statue was again removed and the pedestal boarded up as a protection against the air raids. The booking offices of the station are surrounded by a number of shops and show-cases, the majority of which are occupied by Messrs Swan & Edgar Limited, whose main establishment has direct access to the station. Unfortunately the entrances from the neighbouring streets have been made far too narrow for their requirements and this greatly impedes the movement of pedestrians. The old station, between the Haymarket, Piccadilly Circus, and Jermyn Street, has now been converted into an arcade.

The first underground station, situated on the south side of the Circus adjoining the Haymarket, together with the Baker Street and Waterloo Tube, was opened in 1905, but the completion of the Hammersmith and Finsbury Park Tube in December 1906 was an improvement which had been badly needed for a number of years. Before that time Piccadilly Circus was served only by horse-drawn omnibuses of very limited capacity, and no more tiresome lack of travelling facilities then existed at any other great centre in the metropolis.

On the north-eastern side of Piccadilly Circus stood the well-known Café Monico, with a second entrance in Shaftesbury Avenue. This popular establishment, long famous for its cuisine and wines, was founded in 1879 by two young Swiss and at that time was considered one of the handsomest restaurants in England. A row of mean houses betwen Shaftesbury Avenue and Sherwood Street wantonly disfigures the north-eastern corner of Piccadilly Circus with atrocious advertisement hoardings of the cheapest kind. Though Piccadilly Circus was bombed in both world wars, neither the bombs of Kaiser Wilhelm nor those of Hitler have succeeded in removing these eyesores which profane this side of the Circus in striking contrast to the splendid new buildings on the opposite side. Some day it is hoped greatly to enlarge Piccadilly Circus by clearing the island site at the north-eastern corner bounded by Piccadilly Circus, Shaftesbury Avenue, Denman Street and Sherwood Street, and many of the buildings, including the Cafe Monico, have already been demolished. Unfortunately our municipal authorities are not vested with power to compel property-owners to maintain their street frontages in a condition suited to the dignity of the surrounding neighbourhood, as they are on the Continent. Thus our finest streets and open spaces, such as the Strand, Fleet Street, and Piccadilly Circus, are allowed to be disfigured by large numbers of common advertisement boards which are a shame and a reproach to the metropolis; this is a thing which would never be tolerated, for instance, in the Avenue de l'Opéra at Paris or in Unter den Linden in Berlin.

Advertisements need not necessarily disfigure our streets, since many are to be seen on our larger buildings which in no way offend the eye or spoil the architectural amenities of the street. English people protest strongly against the disfigurement of our countryside by unsightly hoardings, and yet strangely enough they never raise a voice in protesting against the spoiling of our most beautiful town streets where so many people spend the greater part of their existence.

Some reference has already been made to the need to enlarge the Circus, and the Piccadilly Circus Redevelopment is a problem that has exercised the minds of planners and traffic specialists for some time. It seems to have begun several years ago when permission was sought to erect a 13-storey skyscraper on the old Cafe Monico site. Refusal led to a full enquiry, which resulted in a Plan. But the conflicting interests of different ownerships in the Circus and other difficulties proved something of a stumbling block.

A new Plan—believed to be the third—has recently appeared and is now being considered. Following the modern trend of development schemes, this will aim at a forcible separation of vehicles and pedestrians, the results of which will of course be a good deal more trotting up and down stairs for the poor foot-passenger, who will be banished, either to a 'walkway' above ground or a 'precinct' underground. Eros will be moved once more and the Circus will be *a Square*.

From Piccadilly Circus, Regent Street begins with a lovely curve, called the Quadrant, and as it was mostly rebuilt between 1923 and 1927, a few words relating to its vanished predecessor, constructed by Nash about 1816, may here prove of interest. The old Quadrant was lined by a colonnade consisting of cast-iron columns 16 feet 2 inches in height, exclusive of the plinth. The balustraded roof was recommended as a general promenade for the residents of the houses, but this proved a failure because the idea conformed neither to English taste nor to our uncertain climate. Another objection was that the colonnade rendered the mezzanine floors dark and gloomy and likewise restricted the ventilation of the ground-floor rooms. Moreover, the value of the property was also depreciated by the great number of doubtful characters to whom the covered promenade of the Quadrant provided a never-ending attraction, to the intense annoyance of the shopkeepers.

At first it was proposed to remedy this evil by glazing the colonnade roof, and also by more strict police supervision, but even then serious objections remained, until eventually the town authorities decided upon the removal of the colonnade, and accordingly obtained an Act of Parliament for that purpose in 1848. The columns, numbering 270, together with the granite plinths, were then sold by auction. They realized the sum of £2,900, but as the total cost of this improvement came to £3,900, the balance of the funds required was obtained by a rate levied on the inhabitants. The whole colonnade was cleared away within twelve days.

The buildings of the Quadrant were five storeys high, and, being faced with stucco, the tenants were compelled by the Crown authorities to repaint them once a year, usually in March. This partiality shown by Nash for plaster-and-stucco-fronted buildings gave rise to the following rhyme:

> Augustus at Rome was for building renowned,
> And of marble he left what of brick he had found.
> But is not our Nash too a very great master,
> He finds us all brick and he leaves us all plaster.

It was then the fashion amongst those whose enmity towards the favourite architect of George IV arose out of jealousy, to ridicule the genius, energy, and talent of Nash, who gave London so many wonderful improvement.

In the original designs for the new Quadrant the same error of judgment was committed as in the case of the old Quadrant, namely, that of encumbering the new buildings with heavy stone columns, tending to give a dark and gloomy appearance to the street. Thus the erection of the Piccadilly Hotel in 1907, with its heavy-looking arches on the mezzanine floor, caused such an outcry amongst the shopkeepers of Regent Street that the Crown authorities wisely consented to a modification of the plan for the remainder of the new Quadrant. It was urged at the time that unless some lighter and more attractive design was adopted, the general public would no longer be attracted to this part of Regent Street. Except for the heavy columns of the Piccadilly Hotel, the new Quadrant is an exceedingly handsome piece of town-planning, and when seen against a clear sky looks majestic. Several new arcades leading into Glasshouse Street adorn the eastern side of the Quadrant, the largest of which is the so-called Quadrant Arcade, near the corner of Air Street.

The continuity of the old Quadrant was broken by the intervening Air Street, except that the buildings were joined by small bridges on a level with the first floor across that street, whereas the new Quadrant has been built over Air Street, and presents an unbroken frontage throughout its entire length. Midway along the west side of the Quadrant is Man in Moon Passage; of little significance now, but which, in the 'good old days' provided a convenient short cut to Vine Street Police Station. This was a well-trodden path on Boat Race Night, New Year's Eve and similar festive occasions when, under police escort, exuberant young men were 'run in'—a distinction which also carried with it membership of the 'Vine Street Club'. We still have exuberant young men, but the Police Station has moved to Savile Row and Vine Street, alas!, is re-named Piccadilly Place. On the opposite side of the street is the Café Royal. Further along were Oddenino's Imperial Restaurant and Stewart's Restaurant, but both have now disappeared. The famous Café Royal was opened by Mr Nicol in 1865 in Glasshouse Street and was afterwards extended to Regent Street. Mr Nicol died in 1907 and it is now under new proprietors. It was rebuilt in 1925. A few doors farther along are the ornate showrooms of the Ford Motor Company, perhaps the finest in London. The buildings at the northern end of the Quadrant are crowned with two small towers.

All the buildings on the east side of the Quadrant back on to Glasshouse Street, where they are also faced with Portland stone. This street, formerly consisting of small shops and houses of a humble character, has been changed out of all recognition by rebuilding and so also has Sherwood Street. Almost the whole of the opposite side of Glasshouse Street is occupied by the extensive Regent Palace Hotel, erected between 1913 and 1915, nine storeys high and containing upwards of one thousand rooms. The Hotel, which is under the management of Messrs J. Lyons, occupies an island site with extensive frontages to Sherwood Street, Brewer Street, and Glasshouse Street, previously covered by buildings of an inferior type. A new bridge across Sherwood Street, connecting the main building with a large annexe housing the staff, looks picturesque when viewed from Piccadilly Circus. In Sherwood Street opposite the Regent Palace Hotel is the Piccadilly Theatre, erected in 1927, and in Warwick Street is the Catholic Church of Our Lady of the Assumption and St Gregory.

The centre section of Regent Street, extending from Vigo Street to Oxford Circus, follows the line of the old Swallow Street, which it replaced, excepting a small section which is still left between the Quadrant and Piccadilly. According to London topographers of a century ago, Swalow Street was a dingy, dirty thoroughfare, long and irregular, and is said to have contained a livery stable which was a noted house of call for highwaymen. It seems to have formed a kind of boundary line between the splendour of Bond Street and Mayfair on the west, and the poverty-stricken neighbourhood which then existed on the east side round about Soho and Leicester Square. This can easily be traced at the present day by comparing such thoroughfares as Conduit Street, Maddox Street, and Hanover Street on the west side of Regent Street, with Brewer Street, Beak Street, and Foubert's Place on the east side. Moreover, little more than a century ago the Haymarket, Coventry Street, and Leicester Square were still poor and shabby, and even Pall Mall East had not yet been opened up into the newly-projected Trafalgar Square. Nevertheless, the east side of Regent Street contains the largest shops and has always been most favoured by the general public.

On the east corner of Vigo Street, which has been widened as far as Sackville Street, is the London branch of the Commercial Bank of Scotland. Doubtless it is intended that the widening of Vigo Street shall be continued eventually as far as Burlington Gardens. Glasshouse Street has also been widened at the south corner of Regent Street as a part of the rebuilding scheme.

The Quadrant curve ends at Vigo Street, and thence Regent Street is practically straight until it approaches Oxford Circus, and this section comprises a number of terraces of shops and offices, so designed as to give each one of them the appearance of forming part of one and the same building. This scheme, adopted by Nash in designing the old Regent Street, has been faithfully adhered to by those responsible for the creation of the new Regent Street, which is in actual fact a superimposed edition of Nash's Regent Street. The new buildings are principally the work of Sir Reginald Bloomfield, R.A. Those which have disappeared, having been only three or four storeys in elevation, imparted a semi-suburban appearance to this great metropolitan thoroughfare, whereas the new six-storey buildings, which are faced with Portland stone, have given to the first street in Europe a dignity which was hitherto somewhat lacking. In October 1944

Regent Street was struck by a powerful V-bomb. Although its buildings stood up well to the blast, scarcely a window or single pane of glass escaped damage from one end of the street to the other.

The French National Guard, during their visit to London in September 1848, when asked what was their impression of our City, replied that Regent Street was an admirable thoroughfare, but that its houses lacked height compared with the beautiful structures on the Paris boulevards.

Some of the terraces which line the new Regent Street are really beautiful, particularly the three which front the west side between Vigo Street and Conduit Street and the two on the opposite side extending from Glasshouse Street to Beak Street. That between Vigo Street and Heddon Street contains the rebuilt New Gallery Cinema. This has been renamed The New Gallery Centre; films are still shown, but they are of a religious or 'improving' nature as the building is now occupied by the Seventh Day Adventists and admission is free. It has been said that Regent Street was built by John Nash and rebuilt by everybody else. Whatever the architectural defects of today's buildings, they combine to make one of the most attractive shopping thoroughfares in the West End, though to describe the glitter and glamour of the Regent Street shops which, with certain exceptions, are mainly feminine in their appeal, would require a daintier pen than is at present available and more space than can be spared.

Two outstanding buildings, each of quite different character, are the Liberty shops on the east side, nearing Oxford Circus. Founded in 1875, Liberty & Company, whose earlier premises were 'East India House', specialised in the importation of delicate Oriental silks, and the later development of 'Liberty Art Shades' probably coincided with the 'greenery-yallery' Aesthetic Movement of the late seventies. In 1924, their Regent Street premises were rebuilt in the Renaissance style decreed by the planning authorities, with the addition of a screen of tall columns rising from the mezzanine floor, surmounted by a concave frieze with figures in bold relief, centred by Britannia with her shield and trident. She is supported on either side by a group of characters—some forty in all—apparently bringing valuable merchandise from all parts of the globe, for the means of transport include a ship, camel, elephant and even a chariot. Above the cornice, two or three individuals lean over and look down upon this busy scene—a pleasing touch.

Round the corner, in Great Marlborough Street, is the contrasting 'neo-Tudor' building, erected by Liberty's about the same time. Reminiscent of Chester or Shrewsbury, this sham show-piece is composed of very genuine materials, including actual timbers from such old 'wooden walls' as H.M.S. *Impregnable* and *Hindustani,* with plenty of carved oak and teak inside. In the centre of the Kingly Street bridge which connects the Regent Street premises with the Tudor building is a chiming clock with a mechanical St George that pursues a dragon when striking the quarters.

The adjoining block of buildings, also very ornamental, is occupied by Dickins & Jones, and extends from Great Malborough Street to Argyll Place. On the opposite side of the road, between Princes Street and Maddox Street, is the rebuilt Verrey's Restaurant and Regent House, which occupies the site of the old St George's Chapel demolished in 1895.

The four corner blocks which open on to Oxford Circus in Regent Street, also very ornate, have been designed in the same style of architecture, and are each six storeys high. That on the east side between Argyll Place and Oxford Street once contained the Regent Arcade which extended through to Argyll Street but has now been abolished. Opposite are the offices of the South African and Italian Air Lines, in premises formerly occupied for many years by the millinery establishment of Messrs Jay's, who, one seems to remember, specialised in mourning wear. The north-east corner of Regent Street and Oxford Circus contains the new premises of Messrs Peter Robinson Limited. This corner building was badly damaged in one of the early air raids in September 1940 when its stone façade was wrecked between the second and fourth floors, but all the damage has now been made good. The north-west corner of the Circus was for several years the premises of the London branch of the Paris Louvre store. It is now occupied by Swears & Wells, the furriers.

Like so many other great thoroughfares, Regent Street at first proved a failure, and this resulted in the fixing of very low ground rents in its earlier days, but with the expiration of the original Crown leases their value was raised from less than £50,000 to about £450,000. While some of the smaller shopkeepers have migrated to the side streets, and one or two large concerns have been driven out of business by the great increase in rents and taxes, the great majority of the larger establishment still remain in Regent Street. Its popularity seems greater than ever and on the rare occasions when they are vacated the shops are rapidly taken up by new tenants, despite the high rentals which are asked for them.

Amongst the popular establishments which flourished in Regent Street fifty years ago was that of Lewis & Allenby, the drapers and milliners, which was located in St George's House, in the terrace between New Burlington Street and Conduit Street. This building had its principal frontage in Conduit Street, where a new building was erected in 1865-66 from the designs of Mr James Murray, in the Italian style. This building, which is faced with stone, is still a leading feature of Conduit Street, but is now occupied by several smaller shops. In the section between Conduit Street and Maddox Street a stone in the pavement is incised with the initials of two churches, St George, Hanover Square and St James, Westminster; this marks the boundary between the two parishes and is to be seen outside Nos 211-213, opposite Liberty's.

Another well-known establishment in the 'fifties of last century in the same terrace was that of James Holmes & Company, a firm of shawl manufacturers, where you could buy a three-hundred-guinea shawl from Cashmere, or a costly embroidered scarf from China. On the site of the present establishment of Austin Reed & Company, at the corner of Vigo Street, was that of Johnson & Company, hatters to Queen Victoria, which displayed the most approved qualities and the latest fashions in hats.

Many people considered Regent Street to be a smarter thoroughfare in the days of horses and carriages than at the present time. Doubtless in these days of rapid transit from the suburbs, it is more democratic than it was in the days of our fathers. Today Regent Street and the leading shopping streets of the West End are no longer plunged into sudden gloom after the closing of the shops, as many of the leading firms have now adopted the practice of illuminating their windows after closing hours as a suitable method of advertising their wares.

In former times the shops remained open until a much later hour, and in the 'forties and the 'fifties of the last century constant efforts were made to obtain a reduction in the working hours. Already in 1843 Swan & Edgar, Redmayne, and Hitchcock & Williams closed their establishments at 7.0 p.m., but this practice was not generally recognized by the vast majority of drapers' shops for many years afterwards. On 9 October 1844, a very numerously-attended meeting was held by the Metropolitan Drapers' Association at Exeter Hall to protest against the practice of keeping shops open to a late hour.

Of the tributary thoroughfares leading out of Regent Street, the most imposing from a shopping point of view is Conduit Street on the west side, leading to Bond Street. It takes its name from Conduit Mead, an open field of twenty-seven acres until 1713. In this street Charles James Fox was born on 24 January 1749. It contains the former building of the Royal Institution of British Architects, now converted into shop premises, on the north side of the street, as well as a number of tailoring establishments and elegant shops. Conduit Street suffered heavily in the raids of September 1940 and so also did New Bond Street and Bruton Street. Several buildings on the south side of Conduit Street including those at the corner of New Bond Street and on the opposite corner of Bruton Street were destroyed and have been razed to the ground. Here the Westbury Hotel stands, designed on luxury lines, and on the corner of Bruton Street the Time Life building which includes a sculptured screen by Henry Moore.

New Burlington Street leads to Savile Row, mainly occupied by leading West End tailors. Several new buildings have been erected in Savile Row of late years, one of which, Fortress House, is now occupied by the Civil Service Commission. Surely this must be one of the ugliest buildings in London? — so different from the Commission's previous home in Burlington Gardens. Maddox Street and Grosvenor Street are occupied by several of the principal London estate agents, and also contain some excellent shops. In 1937 Savile Row was extended across Savile Place into Mill Street and Conduit Street. The passage known as Savile Place was a picturesque spot which many Londoners were sorry to lose. It contained a tiny umbrella shop owned by James Smith & Sons which was known as Mr Gladstone's umbrella shop, and also a famous print-shop which Oscar Wilde used to declare he visited every day. There was a quaint archway leading into Mill Street next to which stood Picard's cosy little café which was owned by Miss Mary Wills and specialized in cakes, teas and light luncheons. On this site, which faces Old Burlington Street, a new police station was completed in 1939 to replace that of Vine Street.

Hanover Street and Princes Street both lead into Hanover Square, constructed in 1718, and so named from the popularity of George I. It contains a bronze statue by Chantrey of William Pitt, erected in 1831, on the south side, and the fashionable church of St George, built from the designs of John James in 1724. Beneath the Corinthian portico stands a pair of large sporting dogs in bronze — a sufficiently incongruous church decoration to provoke enquiry. Believed to have been cast from models by Landseer, it appears that they originally stood outside the shop of a sporting outfitter in nearby Conduit Street. During the war the dogs took refuge in the church vaults and, their owner's premises having been completely destroyed, they have remained with the church ever since. An unknown sportsman abstracted one of them recently, but it was later recovered and they are now firmly cemented in position. Hanover Square now consists mostly of shops and modern blocks of flats, notably Hanover Court on the east side. On the south east corner is the new Vogue House, containing seven floors of offices, show-rooms and studios. By a gentlemen's agreement with the owners the garden is now open to the public during the daytime.

On the east side of Regent Street the most important thoroughfare is Great Marlborough Street, originally the abode of the well-to-do classes, but which has now developed into a leading business street. The south side, which was considerably widened in 1923 from Carnaby Street to Regent Street, contains Liberty's Tudor building already noticed, and the north side is faced by the new buildings of Dickins & Jones Limited. On the east corner of Argyll Street is the so-called Ideal House, a building of imitation black marble with gilded window-frames erected in 1930 and occupied by the National Radiator Company, and just beyond is the famous Marlborough Street Police Court, rebuilt about 1906. This street comes to an abrupt finish just beyond Wardour Street, but it is earnestly to be hoped that some day it will be driven through into Soho Square, and thus provide a much-needed relief thoroughfare for the enormous traffic of Oxford Street. In Argyll Street is the Palladium Theatre of Varieties, erected in 1910 on the site of the former Hengler's Circus. During the great blitz of 1940 a land-mine fell among the rafters of the London Palladium stage, but the building was saved from destruction through the gallantry of two young naval men who with only a torch for light extracted the fuse and detonator and thus saved the theatre. These were Sub-Lieutenant Graham Maurice Wright of Swansea and Able Seaman W. H. Bevan.

Opposite Great Marlborough Street Police Court and the stage door of the Palladium is Carnaby Street, which for many years was a drab thoroughfare with an electricity sub-station along one side and the rest of the street chiefly inhabited by working and repairing tailors and (being near Golden Square) woollen merchants. The only place of any interest was the old-world shop of Inderwick's, pipe makers and tobacco blenders, who are still there, having been established in 1797.

Today, 'Carnaby Street' is the synonym for Male Boutique which, being interpreted, means men's wear for the very up-to-date, dressy and 'with it'

young—or, at least, not too elderly—man. The transformation of dingy old
Carnaby Street to its present array of modernised shops devoted to colourful
couture is one of the surprises of recent years and claims a passing glance on our
way to Beak Street and thence to Golden Square, immortalized by Dickens
in *Nicholas Nickleby*. Formerly residential, it is now in a thickly-populated
district, and of late years the old houses have almost entirely given way to large
new warehouses and offices principally devoted to the woollen trade. After the
removal of its iron railings during the second World War, Golden Square was
thrown open to the general public. In the centre of the Square is a statue of
George II in Roman costume which came from Canons Park, Edgware, when
that palatial mansion of the Duke of Chandos was demolished in 1747. At the
corner of Lower John Street is a stone marked 'This is Johns Street, Ano Dom
1685'. Near Broad Street, now renamed Broadwick Street, in 1853 new workmen's dwellings were erected on the site of a rookery comprising a quadrangle
of wretched hovels in which cows and pigs shared the accommodation with
thieves and similar characters. No 28 where William Blake, poet and painter,
was born in 1757, was demolished in 1964. In Tension Court, formerly Chapel
Place, a short turning off Regent Street, is the little church of St Thomas. Built
in 1702, it was at first known as Archbishop Tension's Tabernacle; being concealed by tall buildings, it is not very well known.

Crossing Oxford Circus, the northern end of Regent Street is crowned by
All Souls' Church, at the corner of Langham Place, built by Nash in 1822-25,
to facilitate the change of direction between Upper Regent Street and Portland
Place. It has a circular portico of Corinthian columns, in which is a terminal
figure of John Nash—a recent addition. The upper part of its spire was damaged
in the great blitz, but has now been repaired. This church, at no time a very tall
building, is now completely dwarfed by the massive yellow brick rear of the new
extension to Broadcasting House. A glance at a map of London in 1815 shows
that this end of Regent Street has absorbed Bolsover Street and its continuation
known as Edward Street, which then led past the east side of the grounds of
Foley House into what is now Hallam Street. The name of Bolsover Street has
now been given to another thoroughfare which runs parallel to Great Portland
Street on the east side into Euston Road.

Farther along on the west side at the corner of Cavendish Place is the Polytechnic Institute, erected in 1838 as a centre for lectures and exhibitions, and
converted in 1882 into an institution for young men by the late Mr Quintin Hogg.
It was rebuilt in 1911 at a cost of £90,000, and was formally opened by King
George V. It contains numerous technical and science rooms and all the advantages of a club.

After leaving Regent Street we come next to Langham Place, connecting with
Portland Place. It covers a part of the site of Foley House, a large mansion which
was formerly the town residence of Lord Foley. The gardens occupied a considerable space of ground and extended to the north-east corner of Cavendish Square. The house itself was the same width as Portland Place, and

the garden in front of it was separated by a brick wall from that street.

Foley Street, on the right, which was renamed Langham Street in 1864, also occupies a part of the site of the grounds of Foley House, and its continuation, still called Foley Street, commemorates its name. Foley House was pulled down about 1820 for the construction of Langham Place, which was named after an adjoining mansion which belonged to Sir James Langham. Close to Foley House also stood the mansion of the Earl of Mansfield on part of the site now occupied by the former Langham Hotel. This sizeable building which fills the southern end of Portland Place was opened on 12 June 1865, after having been visited by King Edward VII, then Prince of Wales, before the formal opening. The foundation-stone was laid by the Earl of Shrewsbury on 17 July 1863, and the hotel, which is seven storeys high, and covers an acre of ground, contains upwards of six hundred rooms and apartments. There were three hundred bedrooms, an entrance hall fifty feet square, a dining-room one hundred feet long by forty feet wide, and a spacious winter garden. The building is supplied with water from an artesian well constructed on the premises, nearly three hundred feet deep. The architects of the hotel were Messrs Giles and Murray, who also designed the Buckingham Palace Hotel, now converted into business premises.

On the opening day the Langham Hotel was visited by two thousand people. It is now occupied by the B.B.C. St George's Hall in Langham Place was opened in June 1867, and the adjoining Queen's Hall, accommodating nearly three thousand people, in 1893. Both of these halls were destroyed by fire-bombs in the great raid of 10 May 1941. The Queen's Hall was intimately associated with the late Sir Henry Wood, who, with Robert Newman, began the famous series of Promenade Concerts in 1895. He wept when he saw the ruins of his beloved Queen's Hall, with its twisted girders that had supported its fine organ. Today the famous Henry Wood Promenade Concerts continue at the Royal Albert Hall. In the meantime, the Royal Festival Hall has been built on the South Bank, with accommodation for an audience of over 3,000, and thus caters for a proportion of London's concert-lovers. After Sir Henry's death in 1944 an appeal was made for funds to build a new Queen's Hall and succeeded in raising some £80,000, which, it seems, was insufficient for the purpose. Meanwhile, on the site of Queen's Hall and the adjoining St George's Hall (long the home of 'Maskelyne's Mysteries'), Henry Wood House has been built, the first seven floors of which are occupied by the B.B.C., and the remaining six upper floors (with a separate entrance) comprise the St George's Hotel, opened in 1963.

The disposal of the Henry Wood Memorial Fund was the subject of an appeal to the High Court, and in 1966 it was directed that the greater part of the fund should be applied to an alternative project for the advancement of music.

Portland Place was mostly built by the brothers Adam in 1774, and was so named after the Duke of Portland, the ground landlord of this estate. It is 125 feet wide and with the exception of Parliament Street, is the broadest street in London. In 1875 it was proposed to plant trees in Portland Place, but for some unknown reason this was never done, though doubtless they would even now improve the appearance of the street. It is wide enough to provide a dual carriageway with a car park down the centre. At the southern end of Portland Place at the corner of Langham Street is Broadcasting House, the towering building of the British Broadcasting Corporation, with a semicircular façade, erected in 1930-31. Its architect was Lieut-Col. G. Val Myer. A big extension involving the demolition of the adjoining houses at the corner of Portland Place and Duchess Street was commenced in 1939 and work was stopped during the war, but has now been completed.

Of late years several new blocks of flats and offices have been erected in Portland Place, which, on account of its great width, is admirably suited to that type of building but the older Adam buildings have been sacrificed to make way for them. A feature of Portland Place is the building of the Royal Institute of British Architects, who moved here from Conduit Street. It is situated on the east side at the corner of Weymouth Street and was opened by King George V and Queen Mary on 8 November 1934 in the centenary year of the Institute at a cost of £125,000. A special feature of this building is the great staircase hall with a balustrade of glass. The entrance is flanked by two columns surmounted by figures of a man and a woman. Its architect was Mr G. Grey Wornum. At Nos 76-78 is the new City and Guilds of London Institute, the foundation stone of which was laid by their President, Prince Philip, in 1958.

Portland Place, being a broad thoroughfare, is a most suitable setting for the statues which line the centre of the road. Among them is the Quintin Hogg group (which includes a boy with a football under his arm), Field Marshal Sir George White, Lord Lister and Queen Victoria's father, the Duke of Kent.

At the northern end of Portland Place is Park Crescent, a fine semicircle of large houses opening on to the south side of Marylebone Road and overlooking Park Square and Regent's Park. It was originally intended that a similar range of houses would be constructed within the park, immediately opposite, the whole of which was to have been named Regent's Circus. It would have been the largest circle of buildings in Europe. The eastern block of houses in Park Crescent was partly destroyed in the blitz and some of its houses were badly damaged. These have now been rebuilt with the same façades to preserve the original design and have been spared 'redevelopment'. Nos 1-6 in the Crescent have been remodelled as the International Students House, which is a club for up to 2,000 men and women, with a residence for 130 male students. Some interior Nash features, such as mantlepieces and pillars have been preserved. At the Marylebone Road corner is a bust of the late President Kennedy. Across the Marylebone Road, instead of another semi-circle to match Park Crescent and complete the intended Regent Circus, there is Park Square (East and West). On the east side, the wide steps and three double doors of the old Regent's Park Chapel remain; in 1910, the minister, the Rev. F. B. Meyer, attracted much attention by his vociferous protest against the Johnson v Jeffries heavyweight boxing contest. A little further along, in St Andrew's Place, is the new (and fifth) home of the Royal College of Physicians, formerly in Pall Mall East. This very modern building was opened in 1964 by Her Majesty the Queen, and the old portraits of earlier members look curiously uncomfortable in their new surroundings. Old street lamp-posts bearing the monogram of George IV are still to be seen in this area.

Regent's Park, comprising 412 acres, was originally known as Marylebone Park, and was laid out on the site of an ancient royal hunting ground by Nash for the Prince Regent, from whom it derives its modern name, about 1814. It had been resorted to in the time of Queen Elizabeth I and James I. Until 1811 it was leased by the Crown to the Duke of Portland, after which no time was lost in beginning its improvement, which followed upon the construction of Regent Street. The Outer Circle is two-and-three-quarter miles in circuit and encloses the Inner Circle and the Zoological Gardens, besides a number of large houses. These included Bedford College for Women and the Institute of Archaeology, but the latter has since moved to Gordon Square. The Regent's Canal, also designed by Nash, runs within the northern boundary, and on the west side of the park is a winding lake with several arms, covering twenty-two acres. On 15 January 1867, whilst skating was taking place, the ice collapsed. Some two hundred people were immersed in the lake, and forty persons were drowned. The depth of the lake was then reduced to four feet. The Broad Walk, a fine avenue lined with chestnut-trees, runs from south to north in the eastern part of the park. Within the Inner Circle, the former Botanic Gardens vacated about 1936 contain Queen Mary's Rose Garden, a lily-pond, lawns and the open-air theatre.

The Zoological Gardens, comprising thirty-four acres in the northern part of the park, are the largest and finest in the world, and are visited annually by about two milion people. The Zoological Society was founded in 1826, principally by Sir Humphry Davy and Sir Stamford Raffles, and was incorporated by Royal Charter in 1829. Amongst the modern additions to the gardens are the famous Mappin Terraces, beneath which is the Aquarium, erected in 1923-24 at a cost of £26,000. Band performances are given during the summer months and here visitors may dine or have refreshments in Continental style. The Gardens are intersected by the Outer Circle, and are known as the North Garden, the Middle Garden, and the South Garden.

The various private institutions occupying a considerable portion of Regent's Park give it a somewhat different character from that of the other great royal parks. At first it was never contemplated that it should be opened at all to the general public, but only to those privileged with tickets of admission issued by the Royal Household, and it was not until 1838 that Regent's Park was finally thrown open to the public. At the north-west corner of the park now stands Winfield House, the palatial modern mansion of Barbara Hutton, the Woolworth millionairess, of which the private grounds are exceeded in size only by those of Buckingham Palace. It is now the London residence of the United States Ambassador. On the east side near the Zoological Gardens is St Katherine's Hospital.

The park is almost surrounded by a number of fine terraces of handsome appearance and unique architectural character designed by Nash and intended to surround the palace which the Prince Regent intended to build in the Park — but never did. This was to be the grand climax and culmination of the Royal Road from Carlton House via Regent Street and Portland Place.

On the east side are Cambridge, Chester and Cumberland Terraces. High up on the wall of No 3 Chester Terrace is a bust of John Nash. Of this eastern group, Cumberland Terrace is the most decorative, with a pediment full of sculpture, clearly signed, 'J. G. Bubb'. The central figure of the group is, presumably, Britannia, but the prongs of her trident are missing.

The terraces are mostly about 140 years old, and the Crown Estates Commissioners, who are the owners, are progressing with a scheme of restoration and conversion to preserve these fascinating examples of Regency architecture and planning. Of the several groups, which together consist of no less than 374 houses, Cumberland Terrace was the first to be dealt with, and behind the Nash stucco facade of 1826 are now modern four-storey flats that are calculated to last at least another 100 years. The 42 houses in Chester Terrace have also been restored — as houses — and not converted like the neighbouring Cumberland Terrace.

On the west side of the park are Clarence, Kent and Hanover Terraces, and Sussex Place. Hanover Terrace (H. G. Wells lived at No 13) is very attractive, with three pediments and statuary. It also has a very favourable position, for it overlooks the park lake, as does Clarence Terrace, usually attributed to Decimus Burton and now in process of restoration. George R. Sims — 'Dagonet' of the old *Referee* — journalist and dramatist (with a hirsute head that was very familiar in advertisements for a hair restorer called 'Tatcho'), lived in Clarence Terrace and always dated his contributions from 'opposite the Ducks'.

Sussex Place, of 1822, which is unoccupied at the moment, is most striking, for the roof is topped with pairs of rather pointed domes at intervals — five pairs in all — which appear to be quite unorthodox. On the south side are Cornwall and York Terraces.

At the south-east corner of Regent's Park formerly stood the Colosseum, a vast circular edifice with a glazed cupola and a massive portico, designed by Decimus Burton, at that time the largest building of its kind in the country. It was used for exhibitions and panoramas, but after a time it went out of fashion as a place of public recreation and for many years remained closed. In October 1869 it was proposed to convert the Colosseum into an opera-house, but this scheme failed to meet with any support and in 1875 the building was pulled down and Cambridge Gate, a terrace of first-class houses, erected on its site.

Near Hanover Gate on the west side of the park is Abbey Lodge, a block of flats erected in 1930. This is a six-storey building of red brick with stone dressings which has its main entrance in Park Road. The north side of the park is now lined with modern blocks of flats extending from Hanover Gate to Avenue Road.

We will terminate this walk, covering the area of the great metropolitan improvements carried out by Nash under the direction of George IV, by a visit to Primrose Hill. This delightful eminence on the north side of Regent's Park is so named from the primroses which once grew here in plenty. It comprises an area of sixty acres and rises to a height of 219 feet, from the top of which a fine view of the metropolis can be obtained in clear weather. Primrose Hill was secured as an open space mainly through the efforts of Mr Hume, M. P., in 1853, together with an association of his friends who persuaded the Government to transfer this delightful space to the public. The ground was obtained from Eton College in exchange for a piece of Crown land near Windsor.

Primrose Hill was also known at one time as Greenberry Hill, and was supposed by many people to have obtained that title from the names of three persons named Robert Green, Henry Berry and Lawrence Hill, who were executed in 1682 for the murder of Sir Edmundbury Godfrey, a Justice of the Peace, whose body was found in a ditch near the site of the Regent's Canal on 17 October 1678. He was a rich timber merchant who lived at the river end of Northumberland Street in the Strand and was knighted for his services in bringing thieves and criminals to justice during the Great Plague of 1665. It was supposed that the three criminals had brought the body to Primrose Hill, after murdering him at Somerset House. It is, however, open to doubt whether the name of Greenberry Hill has any connexion at all with the three men executed for the murfer, other than a mere coincidence in the names of the men concerned in the crime.

Less than 200 years ago the verdant slope of Primrose Hill was a mile distant from the nearest houses and was almost as secluded as the Sussex Downs or the Chiltern Hills at the present day. Small wonder that the Prince Regent contemplated building himself a palace on Primrose Hill, and one can but admire his very good taste. Running under the hill is the tunnel of the former London & North Western Railway, now British Railways (Midland Region) 1,182 yards long, constructed in 1838, which at that time and for long afterwards was regarded as a great engineering feat. Until well into the nineteenth century Primrose Hill was also a rendezvous for duellists, and here Colonel Montgomery fought Captain Macnamara in 1803, resulting in the death of the former at Chalk Farm. Here also Lieutenant Bailey was mortally wounded on 17 January 1818 by a pistol-bullet from Mr O'Callaghan.

During the second World War the summit of Primrose Hill was occupied by an anti-aircraft battery. Here a camp was erected and enclosed with barbed wire. All this has now been entirely cleared away. A fine view is obtained from the top of Primrose Hill in the direction of Hampstead Heath, but on the south-east side it is marred by the railway yards and industrial buildings of Chalk Farm and Camden Town.

Twelfth Walk

Piccadilly Circus to Bond Street, Mayfair, Hyde Park Corner, Park Lane, Marble Arch and Brook Street

Piccadilly Circus, one of the great centres of London traffic, has actually no official existence, since Piccadilly from its earliest existence has always been reckoned as beginning at the top of the Haymarket and therefore includes most of what is commonly known as Piccadilly Circus. Nevertheless, there are two City of Westminster name plates, 'Piccadilly Circus' on the wall of Swan and Edgar's premises. Although it was the beginning of the Bath Road, the earlier standing of Piccadilly was not of much account, but later it completely eclipsed the importance of Jermyn Street, which has long since become a back street.

Piccadilly is supposed to have derived its name from the pickadills or ruffs worn in the early Stuart period. Originally extending as far as Sackville Street, and then to Albemarle Street, this thoroughfare was called Portugal Street after Catherine of Braganza, Queen of Charles II. Beyond this point ran the great Bath Road, or, according to early maps, 'the way to Reding'. The Queen was never a favourite of the people and in time the name of Piccadilly displaced her memory altogether. With its varying assortment of towering buildings, great hotels, and clubs, today Piccadilly can properly be regarded as the show thoroughfare of London, that is to say, it reflects the splendour of modern London even more than the new Regent Street.

Before the improvements effected by the London County Council before the war, the width of Piccadilly varied considerably. From the Circus to Swallow Street it was only fifty-two feet wide, increasing west of Sackville Street to eighty feet, then narrowing again from Bond Street to the Green Park and beyond to about seventy feet. With the reconstruction of the premises of Messrs Swan & Edgar, together with the erection of the Piccadilly Hotel, the building line has been set back to a width of eighty feet as far as Piccadilly Place. Until they were blitzed in 1940 three buildings remained to be demolished between Piccadilly Place and Sackville Street to give Piccadilly a uniform width of eighty feet from the Circus to the Green Park. That which projected between Piccadilly Place and Swallow Street caused a substantial narrowing of the roadway. It had an unexpired lease extending to 1968 and was at one time a branch of Lloyds Bank. After 1933 it was acquired by a multiple firm of tailors. The site is owned by the Government and in 1931 when the London County Council wanted it in order to complete the widening of Piccadilly they failed to come to terms about the price to be paid for the ground. Now that the projecting buildings have been removed by Hitler's bombs, the much-needed widening of this section of the famous thoroughfare is almost complete. The removal of these buildings has opened up a splendid new vista of Piccadilly looking westwards to Devonshire House.

The fine store building of Swan & Edgar Limited covers nearly the whole of the island site between Piccadilly Circus, the Quadrant, Air Street, and Piccadilly, and has replaced a number of single houses which formed the original premises of this well-known drapery firm. The western corner of the building, facing Piccadilly and Air Street, contains the West End branch of the Bank of Scotland.

Ont the adjoining site, extending from Air Street, westwards to Piccadilly Place, is the immense Piccadilly Hotel, erected between 1905 and 1908 and adorned by a classic colonnade on the first floor. The building is nine storeys high in addition to four others below the level of the street, extending to a depth of fifty feet. Unfortunately, the appearance of this noble building has been largely spoiled by the insignificant Denman House, a small building on the west corner of Air Street erected three years earlier, which has broken the uniformity of the Piccadilly frontage.

On the greater part of the site now covered by the Piccadilly Hotel formerly stood the St James's Hall and Restaurant, opened in April 1858 at a cost of £60,000. This building, which also extended to the Quadrant, contained a large hall and two smaller ones. The Piccadilly frontage was designed in the Alhambrian style of architecture by Mr Owen Jones. In 1875 handsome and spacious new dining-rooms were added to the building, thus placing it on an equality with the newly-erected Criterion Restaurant in Piccadilly Circus.

On the opposite side of Piccadilly stood until 1935 the Museum of Practical Geology, opened on 12 May 1851 by the Prince Consort and now moved to South Kensington. The main entrance was in Jermyn Street, and a peculiarity of this building was that it contained six windows overlooking the Piccadilly side without any entrance from that street. It was pulled down in 1935 and in its place has arisen the famous Simpson man's shop, devoted mainly to the sale of men's wearing apparel.

A few paces farther west on the same side of the street is St James's Church, erected by Sir Christopher Wren, in 1684. The principal entrance was in Jermyn Street, and whilst the interior of the church was much admired, the exterior has been denounced as rather ugly. The original tower collapsed as the result of faulty workmanship, and has long since been replaced by the existing one. On the east side of the churchyard, which also contains an open-air pulpit, stood the rectory, and until 1922 the west side was occupied by the St James's Vestry Hall. It was an ornate building in the Italian style, erected in 1861, but it has now been replaced by the new Midland Bank building which was designed by Sir Edwin Lutyens. R. A., in 1924 to harmonize with the rectory on the opposite side of the churchyard. St James's Church suffered considerable damage in a big air raid in October 1940. Its steeple was demolished and only the tower escaped injury. Meanwhile, until repairs were finished services were held in the blitzed church. A beautiful restoration of the interior by the late Sir Albert Richardson, P.R.A. has been completed and a garden of remembrance has been laid out in the churchyard. The bombs also destroyed the rectory, killing the verger who was in the house when the raid occurred. A new Rectory and Church Hall have just been built. The top floors of the Piccadilly Hotel were also badly damaged, as well as the former Lyon's Popular Café.

Adjoining the Midland Bank is the Royal Institute of Painters in Water Colours, and on the ground floor of the same block of buildings is the new Pigalle. Princes Hotel, which formed part of the same building and extended to Jermyn Street, has now been converted into offices, and a new arcade has been driven through from Piccadilly into Jermyn Street. Another feature of this side of Piccadilly is the Monseigneur News Theatre which is housed in the new buildings erected on the south-west corner of Piccadilly Circus. Beyond Princes Arcade is the famous bookshop of Messrs Hatchard, rebuilt in 1910, beyond which is the fine building of Messrs Fortnum & Mason Limited, the old-established firm of provision merchants. It has extensive frontages to Piccadilly, Duke Street, and Jermyn Street, and was rebuilt and greatly enlarged in 1927-28. A popular addition to their premises since 1964 is an attractive clock from which, at the striking of the hour, two figures, said to be Fortnum and Mason, emerge; they are accompanied by 18th century music played on seventeen bells – but the usual roar of the Piccadilly traffic is inclined to be rather discourteous to *The Lass with the Delicate Air.*

Opposite Princes Restaurant is Sackville Street, leading from Piccadilly to Vigo Street and built about 1679. It makes the dubions claim of being the longest street in London without any side turnings, and consists of private houses which have long since been utilized as business premises, largely occupied by leading West End tailors. While there are still several 18th century houses on the east side, the west side has been almost entirely rebuilt.

West of Swallow Street, Piccadilly is now adorned with two magnificent buildings on the east and west corners of Sackville Street, both of them in the Classic style and a hundred feet high. That on the east corner, erected in 1930, is entirely faced with Portland stone and contains a branch of Lloyds Bank. On the west corner is Nuffield House, erected in 1938, which has a longer frontage to Piccadilly and is faced with red brick with stone dressings. It covers the site of six Georgian houses and extends from Sackville Street to Albany Court Yard. This opens out to a small square cul-de-sac in which is The Albany, comprising a long double row of chambers extending from Piccadilly to Burlington Gardens, and named after the Duke of York, second son of George III, and a former owner of the central block. In 1804 the Albany was converted into chambers for bachelors, the gardens were built over, and the name of Albany was then given to the whole of this property. The house was originally built for

Lord Melbourne by Sir William Chambers, the architect of Somerset House, and the more distinguished tenants of Albany include Lord Byron, Canning, and Lord Lytton. Among those who understand these things, it is usually regarded as a solecism to refer to *the* Albany — though one of its bestknown fictional residents, A. J. Raffles, invariably did so. Once an exclusive bachelor sanctuary, it has in recent years been violated – if that is not too ungallant an expression – by the admission of ladies.

After passing Albany Court Yard we come to Burlington House, occupying most of the ground between the Albany and Old Bond Street. The original mansion was built for Richard Boyle, Earl of Burlington, who was greatly interested in architecture and did much to revive the classical forms. It passed from the Boyles to the Cavendish family and was afterwards purchased by the Government in 1853 for £140,000, who then allotted it for the use of academic and scientific institutions. In 1859 the permanent appropriation of this site was decided upon by the Government and the present buildings were then erected between 1868 and 1874 to provide accommodation for the administrative departments of the University of London (since removed to Bloomsbury), the Royal Academy, and a Museum of Patent Inventions. The architectural work was divided into three separate portions; first, the rebuilding of the old Burlington House for the Royal Academy, which was performed by their own treasurer and architect, Mr Sydney Smirke; secondly, the construction of a new mansion at the rear in Burlington Gardens for the University of London from the designs of Sir, James Pennethorne in 1868-70; and, thirdly, the new buildings by Messrs Banks and Barry, the architects, at the sides of the front court, and the Piccadilly front with its façade in the Italian style. Much controversy raged at the time as to whether the fine Piccadilly frontage of the old Burlington House should be preserved. Today, the centre portion of the building is the Royal Academy, with a statue of Sir Joshua Reynolds in the forecourt; the buildings at the sides of the courtyard are occupied by various learned societies, among which are the Society of Antiquaries and the Royal Astronomical Society. The mansion at the rear of Burlington Gardens, liberally embellished with statues, is occupied by the Civil Service Commission (though their administrative offices are now in Savile Row) and the British Academy for the promotion of historical, philological and philosophical studies.

Adjoining Pennethorne's building on the east is the picturesque entrance to the back of Albany. A quaint lodge and gateway lead to a longish courtyard having a covered way along the middle between a row of chambers on each side. Among the residents this is known as 'The Ropewalk', and the apartments of some of the distinguished occupants of the past are suitably marked.

On the north side of Burlington Gardens is the West End branch of the Royal Bank of Scotland, formerly that of the Bank of England, opened on 1 October 1855. It is a handsome building, originally Uxbridge House, the town mansion of the Marquis of Anglesey, built in 1792 by Vardy for the first Earl of Uxbridge, father of Field-Marshal the first Marquis of Anglesey. The mansion was built on the site of Queensberry House, London residence of the Duke of Queensberry, and was sold by the second Marquess of Anglesey to the Bank of England in 1855.

On the west side of Burlington House, extending from Piccadilly to Burlington Gardens, is Burlington Arcade, constructed in 1819 by Ware, a long covered passage lined with elegant shops, largely hosiers, bootmakers, and jewellers, and regarded as a fashionable parade. In 1930 the iron gates were removed from the entrance in Piccadilly, and the two corner shops fitted with modern window fronts. Burlington Arcade was badly damaged in the early air raids of 1940, when many of its shops were completely wrecked.

On the south side of Piccadilly, almost opposite, is the short but equally fashionable Piccadilly Arcade, erected in 1910, leading into Jermyn Street. Between the Piccadilly Arcade and St James's Street is a handsome row of modern buildings faced with Portland stone, including Egyptian House erected in 1905 on the site of the old Egyptian Hall, and that of the Norwich Union Insurance Company, at the corner of St James's Street, erected in 1908. The Egyptian Hall was erected by William Bullock in 1812 from the designs of Mr G. F. Robinson at a cost of £16,000, as a museum of natural history, and was built in the Egyptian style, with inclined pilasters and sides covered with hieroglyphics. Later the hall was used for popular entertainments and was famous for the 'magic and mystery' performances of Maskelyne and Cook.

A few paces west of Burlington Arcade will bring us to Old Bond Street, London's most fashionable shopping thoroughfare, built in 1686 by Sir Thomas Bond of Peckham, Comptroller to the Royal Household of the Queen Mother, Henrietta Maria. He was created a baronet by Charles II and bought part of the Claredon estate from the Duke of Albemarle. Bond Street was first brought into fashion by the celebrated Duchess of Devonshire, who, being offended with the inhabitants of Tavistock Street, Covent Garden, the fashionable street at that time, drew off people of rank, whom she led to Bond Street, because most of the inhabitants of the former district voted against Fox. New Bond Street, which begins at Clifford Street, was not built until about 1721, and here Lord Nelson lodged after the battle of Cape St Vincent in 1797 and the expedition against Teneriffe, when he lost an arm.

Present-day Bond Street reveals a well-assorted combination of both new and old structures, but on account of the buildings being kept in such good external condition the contrast between the old and the new is less apparent here than in any other great thoroughfare in the metropolis. Bond Street is regarded by many people who are authorities on the subject as the only street in London in which both sides possess an equal attraction to the shopping public, and it may aptly be termed the High Street of Mayfair. Between the two world wars many fine new buildings were erected in this street, amongst others that formerly occupied by Messrs Atkinson, the perfumers, at the south corner of Burlington Gardens, adorned by a tower and containing an attractive carillon of bells. On the opposite corner another block of buildings was erected for the National

Provincial Bank, and the former Bristol Hotel in Burlington Gardens has been remodelled and converted into shops and offices.

Lack of space prevents us from describing the attractions of Bond Street in detail and a recital of the old-established shops and famous names associated with Bond Street (Old and New) would develop into something like a catalogue, but Asprey's, the jewellers, founded in 1781 may be mentioned on account of their striking mid-Victorian shop front on the west side of the street, with its large areas of plate glass between tall and slender ornamental columns. Further north, on the same side is the Aeolian Hall, with a B. B. C. studio next door, on the site of the old Grosvenor Gallery. Fine art dealers are well represented and there are several galleries here. On the east side are the famous auction rooms of Messrs Sotheby's, the art auctioneers.

Another attraction of Bond Street is the Royal Arcade leading into Albemarle Street, containing about twenty shops and opened in 1880. In the 'seventies a scheme for the construction of an arcade from Bond Street to Regent Street was defeated by strong opposition, after an Act of Parliament had been applied for with a view to carrying out this scheme. A few years ago the Westminster City Council proposed to abolish the separate titles of Old and New Bond Street and to rename the entire thoroughfare Bond Street, but upon submitting the decision to a poll of the local ratepayers, a majority voted against the suggested change. In Grafton Street are the Medici Galleries and the famous antique book-shop of Messrs Bernard Quaritch, who moved here from Piccadilly early in the present century.

Among the large hotels near Bond Street is Brown's Hotel in Albemarle Street. The old-established Burlington Hotel in Cork Street which had frontages to both Cork Street and Burlington Street was pulled down in July 1935. On this site now stands an eight-storey building of red brick which was at first the St Regis Hotel. It is now a blocks of shops and offices and has been renamed Trinidad House. Opposite Grafton Street, Old Bond Street narrows into a tiresome bottleneck, which might aptly be christened the Straits of Bond Street, and which exercises a stranglehold on the heavy traffic of this thoroughfare. Sometimes a long line of omnibuses and motor-cars is held up by stationary vehicles in this immediate locality. Whilst many people will be aghast at the very suggestion that this small section of Bond Street should be widened at enormous expense, yet taking a long view of the pressing requirements of London's traffic, even this improvement might not be incommensurate with the cost which would be incurred. So great is the traffic congestion caused by stationary motor-cars during the day-time in this part of the West End that its streets seem like one gigantic garage. However, at the time of this revision, one-way traffic from north to south operates in Bond Street and the severe parking restrictions now in force have probably been effective.

Grafton Street leads out of Bond Street past Albermarle Street into Dover Street, both of these thoroughfares running parallel with Old Bond Street into Piccadilly. They originally consisted of high-class residences, of which some have given way to modern buildings, and others have been converted into high-class shops in no way inferior to those of Bond Street. Albermarle Street, which derives its name from Christopher Monk, second Duke of Albermarle, contains the Royal Instituion for the promotion of science established in 1799, and the publishing house of John Murray, fifth in the dynasty of the John Murray whose house was founded in Fleet Street in 1768. Here too, the National Book League have their premises. Dover Street derives its name from Henry Jermyn, Lord Dover. Here stood the famous Bath Club which was destroyed by fire in 1940. At the west corner of Albemarle Street and Piccadilly is an elegant new building faced with Portland stone, erected in 1927 by the Westminster Bank Limited.

Turning once again into Piccadilly, at the west corner of Old Bond Street are the offices of Qantas, Australia's Overseas Airline, where Stewart's Restaurant formerly stood and between Albemarle Street and Dover Street is Hatchett's Restaurant, known as the White Horse Cellar, from which place coaches used at one time to run to Brighton, Dorking, Windsor, and Tunbridge Wells. This establishment is the successor to an older White Horse Cellar which was situated close to Arlington Street on the opposite side of Piccadilly whence Londoners on summer evenings, before the days of railways, used to watch the mailcoaches drive down Piccadilly *en route* for the West of England.

On the west corner of Piccadilly and St James's Street is the building of the Royal Insurance Company, erected in 1908, adjoining which is a very ornate building at the east corner of Arlington Street erected by the Wolseley Motor Company in 1921, and now occupied by Barclays Bank. This building secured the gold medal of the Royal Institute of British Architects in 1922 for the finest erected in London during that year. On the west corner of Arlington Street and Piccadilly, extending to the Green Park, is the Ritz Hotel, opened in 1906. This is a massive colonnaded building eight storeys high of highly dignified appearance, partly constructed over the footpath in Piccadilly, in order to allow for the widening of the roadway, without the necessity of sacrificing the building-space above the ground floor. On that condition the strip of ground required by the London County Council for the widening of Piccadilly was purchased at a greatly-reduced figure from the owners of the property. In appearance the Ritz Hotel strongly suggests a corner of the famous colonnaded Rue de Rivoli in Paris transplanted into Piccadilly. Its architects were Messrs Mewes and Davis. It occupies the site of the earlier Walsingham House Hotel, a tall red-brick building originally constructed in 1887 as a block of residential flats, and the much older Bath Hotel which stood on the west corner of Arlington Street.

Facing the Ritz Hotel is the luxurious Berkeley Hotel, under the same ownership as the Savoy and Claridge's and built on the site of the old Gloucester Coffee House. This was a famous inn from which coaches used to run to the West of England. The new Devonshire House on the opposite corner of Berkeley Street and Piccadilly, nine storeys high, was erected in 1925-26. It extends to Stratton Street and Mayfair Place, forming an island site, and consists of shops and luxury flats.

The former Devonshire House occupied the site of Berkeley House erected by Sir John Berkeley in 1658, which was destroyed by fire in 1733. It was built by William Kent for the third Duke of Devonshire in 1755, but was a very unpretentious building with a low-pillared entrance hall. The back entrance facing the courtyard in Piccadilly was very ugly, but its grounds gave it an unusual air of exclusion. In 1897 the dark brick wall facing Piccadilly was adorned by magnificent wrought-iron gates brought from the house of the Duke of Devonshire at Chiswick. In 1918 Devonshire House and its grounds were sold to Messrs Holland & Hannen & Cubitts Limited, the builders, for £1,000,000, and the wrought-iron gates were then removed to their present situation at the entrance to the Green Park opposite Half Moon Street. They now face the tree-lined avenue formed in 1905 between Piccadilly and the Queen Victoria Memorial.

For a long time no satisfactory offers were obtained for the site of Devonshire House, and it was not until the autumn of 1924 that a start was made on the demolition of the old mansion. Berkeley Street was then widened from thirty to fifty-three feet and the two new streets constructed across the site of the former grounds. The first of these, known as Mayfair Place, runs at the back of the new Devonshire House building, and the second, which is a prolongation of Stratton Street, runs at right angles to the original Stratton Street, which had previously ended in a cul-de-sac.

The second new island site, which extends from Mayfair Place to the new extension of Stratton Street, contains the head offices of Messrs Thos. Cook & Son Limited, facing Berkeley Street and Mayfair Place, removed here from Ludgate Circus in 1926, and a block of offices occupied by Esso Limited. On the remaining portion of the grounds of the former Devonshire House, extending from Stratton Street to Lansdowne Passage, now stands the huge Mayfair Hotel, containing four hundred rooms, opened by the Gordon Hotels Company in May 1927. It has replaced the Grand Hotel in Trafalgar Square, belonging to the same company, which has now been converted into business premises.

On the west corner of Stratton Street, covering the site of the former town mansion of the Baroness Burdett-Coutts, demolished in 1925, stands Stratton House, a sumptuous block of shops and offices nine storeys high, and like Devonshire House fronted with Portland stone. Until 1925 Stratton Street, which was built in 1693, was a very secluded residential street, but it has now assumed the character of an important business thoroughfare which carries one-way traffic. In Devonshire House, overlooking Piccadilly, are the showrooms of Messrs Rootes and Messrs Henlys, two large firms of motor-car manufacturers and dealers, and in the adjoining Stratton House are a branch of the Midland Bank, the showrooms of the University Motors Limited, and the West End offices of British Electric Traction Co. Ltd. During the second World War Stratton House became the official headquarters of both the Polish and the Netherlands Governments.

Close to the Ritz Hotel is the new Green Park Underground Station, built to replace those of Dover Street and Down Street. It was opened in 1933, and has a second entrance from Devonshire House on the other side of Piccadilly.

The Green Park, a pear-shaped open space of fifty-six acres, was at one time larger, but its size was reduced by George III in 1767 to enlarge the gardens of Buckingham Palace. It was not always the beautifully-wooded park which it now is, for until well into the nineteenth century it presented a barren and unsightly appearance. At the north-west corner of the park was a large reservoir constructed in 1829 by the Chelsea Waterworks Company, capable of containing 1,500,000 gallons. It extended from opposite Stratton Street as far west as Half Moon Street, but was done away with about 1855. At the bottom of the hill in the centre of Piccadilly near Half Moon Street there was once a bridge over a stream. Here in the Green Park the Tyburn widened into a large pond from which it ran past the spot where Buckingham Palace now stands and fell into the Thames in three branches, the main stream emptying itself at Chelsea. About 1830 there was some talk of constructing terraces and of laying out the park in a highly-ornamental style with public walks, fountains, and statues, but perhaps the present-day London is glad that is has been left more or less in a natural state. In common with all other London parks and squares, the railings of the Green Park were removed in 1941 for the war effort and have now been replaced by a low holly hedge with wire netting in front.

The east side of the Green Park is lined by some of the most stately mansions in London. The first of these is Lancaster House, formerly the London Museum, at the corner of the Mall. Adjoining is the splendid Bridgwater House, built in the Italian style by Barry in 1850, and north of this is Spencer House, with a Doric colonnade. Both are now occupied by commercial firms, which is fortunate; otherwise they would, no doubt, have been demolished long ago. Right next door, the elegant Spencer House is o'ertopped by a modern block of expensive flats, nearly twice its height, built in 1960. This has been described as a masterpiece. That next to the Ritz Hotel is Wimborne House which in 1948 was sold by Lord Wimborne for conversion into offices. Next to it is Arlington House, a nine-storey block of flats with its two top storeys zoned back from the building line. Its main entrance is in Arlington Street. It was erected in 1936. Between Berkeley Street and Half Moon Street in 1846 the hill in Piccadilly was partly dug away and reduced and then repaved with granite blocks. These of course have long since been worn out and removed. West of Half Moon Street, Piccadilly rises gently towards Hyde Park Corner. Until 1825 the Rangers' Lodge stood in the park opposite Down Street.

Returning to the north side of Piccadilly, at the west corner of Bolton Street, is Reed House, a new building of eight storeys, which stands on the site of Bath House, formerly the home of Lady Ludlow, originally built for Lord Ashburton and occupying the site of the Pulteney Hotel, which became the resort of many royal personages during their visits to London, including the Emperor Alexander of Russia in 1814. He came out on the balcony to greet the public shortly after his arrival. In 1708 Bolton Street was the most westerly street in London.

On the east side of Clarges Street is the Kennel Club, while No. 85 Piccadilly, previously occupied by the Turf Club, is being developed for showrooms, flats, etc., and beyond Half Moon Street is the Naval and Military Club, formerly Cambridge House, standing well back from the street and popularly known as the In and Out. Just beyond is the American Club, and on a brass plate, just inside the doorway, is inscribed Abraham Lincoln's Gettysburg Declaration. Next door is the Public Schools' Club, formerly the Badminton, which closed down about twenty years ago. The adjoining tall building was erected about 1890 by the Junior Constitutional Club, which closed down in 1940. It occupies the site of two private mansions and is one of the finest buildings in Piccadilly. Formerly Esso Ltd. offices, it is now unoccupied. Next door to the Junior Constitutional Club was before the war the Hotel Splendide (formerly the Green Park Hotel), remodelled in 1927 out of the former Isthmian Club, on to which three extra storeys have been built to provide increased bedroom accommodation. During the last war it became King George's Club for Officers but it has now been converted into offices. The early air raids of 1940 played havoc with the buildings on the north side of Piccadilly, most of which were damaged. That on the east corner of Half Moon Street was completely demolished and so also was a section of the Piccadilly frontage of the Naval and Military Club.

After passing the St James's Club we next come to the huge Park Lane Hotel, opened in 1927, occupying the site of a row of old houses demolished in 1912, when this site was acquired by the proprietor of the Curzon Hotel for the erection of a new hotel. Negotiations were then entered into with the adjoining Savile Club for the purchase of their property, with a view to the construction of a larger hotel, which after a long delay failed to mature. Meanwhile, the first World War intervened and this resulted in the work being suspended for many years, during which attempts were made to dispose of the half-completed building. By 1915, when the building operations ceased, the steel structure of the new hotel had been completed, and something like £3,000 per annum was spent on keeping the skeleton structure (currently known as the birdcage) in a proper state of repair, until finally it was acquired by a new company in 1925, who completed the Park Lane Hotel. In 1930 the company acquired the premises of the adjoining Savile Club, which were then pulled down for the extension of the Park Lane Hotel, and the Savile Club has now removed to Brook Street.

Being of British nationality, Mr Harwath, the proprietor of the Curzon Hotel in Curzon Street, was interned in Germany and lost his eyesight. In 1919, he sold the Curzon Hotel and retired from business with the result that work on the completion of the Park Lane Hotel was further delayed. In 1926, Mr Harwath returned to business again and bought the old Fleming's and Greenslade's Hotels in Half Moon Street which he modernised and converted into the present Fleming's Hotel.

The Junior Athenaeum Club which stood on the east corner of Down Street was pulled down in 1935, and has been replaced by Athenaeum Court, a ten-storey block of flats, part of which is now a hotel. This is the same height as the adjoining Park Lane Hotel and has also a long frontage to Down Street. The previous building at first called Hope House was converted into a clubhouse shortly after the death of Mr. Hope in 1861 and from 1868 until December 1931 was occupied by the Junior Athenaeum Club. Between Down Street and Park Lane are the Cavendish (now taken over by the Cavalry Club), the Cavalry, and the Royal Air Force Clubs. On the east corner of Park Lane is a block of flats and chambers, the ground floor of which is occupied by the West End branch of Messrs Coutts's Bank. On the west corner is Gloucester House, a much larger building, which formerly consisted of extensive luxury flats, having a frontage of about 250 feet to Park Lane and fifty feet to Piccadilly. It is now used as offices. The ground floor contains large motor-car showrooms. On this site stood, until 1904, old Gloucester House, originally the residence of William Henry, Duke of Gloucester, and afterwards of the Duke of Cambridge, who died in 1904.

Until the opening of Hamilton Place in June 1871, this very narrow end of Park Lane was the only direct thoroughfare leading from the Marble Arch to Piccadilly. The painful congestion then prevailing in the small bottleneck of Park Lane was described in 1864 as one of the most absurd sights which a Londoner could show to his country cousin, either at Christmas, in May, or any other time of the year. Omnibuses, carriages and pairs, donkey-carts, sheep and cattle, and pedestrians all added to the prevailing welter and confusion, for of course no omnibuses or heavy traffic were allowed to go through Hyde Park. Nevertheless there was great opposition at the time to the opening of Hamilton Place into Piccadilly, and in 1869 an anonymous lady donor actually offered through her solicitors a sum of £50,000 to the Metropolitan Board of Works if they would repeal the Act to open up Hamilton Place. Needless to add, the offer was politely declined. Hamilton Place derives its name from James Hamilton, Ranger of Hyde Park in the time of Charles II. The recent Hyde Park Corner Improvement Scheme has provided further relief, for Park Lane now splits into *three* as it joins Piccadilly; the new road emerges close to the east side of Apsley House (The Wellington Museum) and assumes the name of Park Lane. The termination of the once aristocratic and exclusive thoroughfare is de-graded to *Old* Park Lane, while Hamilton Place remains between them.

In the stately mansions between Hamilton Place and Apsley House, erected in 1862, several members of the Rothschild family formerly resided. Number 145 was the residence of King George VI and Queen Elizabeth before their accession. It was completely destroyed in an air raid of 9 October 1940 by a bomb which fell on the back of the house. Nos 142, 143 and 144 Piccadilly still survive and are now the Arts Educational Schools, where the curriculum includes special vocational training in the arts of the Theatre – dance, drama, music and painting. Apsley House, at the corner of Piccadilly which faces Rotten Row and Hyde Park, was presented to the Duke of Wellington by a grateful people in 1820 as a reward for his services to the British nation. It was originally built in 1785 as a red-brick mansion for Lord Apsley, who in order to secure this site had to buy out the proprietor of an apple stall, an old soldier named Allen to whom

George II had given it as a reward for bravery at the battle of Dettingen. The principal front on Piccadilly consists of a centre with two wings having a portico of the Corinthian order. In 1823 the mansion was enlarged and the exterior refaced with Bath stone. Apsley House in now, under the auspices of the Victoria and Albert Museum, the Wellington Museum.

In 1902 a great improvement was carried out at Hyde Park Corner by setting back the railings of the Green Park from the Wellington Arch as far as Down Street, thereby increasing the width of the roadway opposite Park Lane to 170 feet, and providing substantial relief to the heavy congestion of traffic which formerly prevailed at this busy centre. This improvement was carried out in the early spring in order to complete the work in time for the coronation of the late King Edward VII, which was to have taken place in June, but was unavoidably postponed until the following August on account of the sudden illness of His Majesty. Since 1926 the roundabout system of traffic has been in operation at Hyde Park Corner, which to-day is one of the world's busiest traffic centres. In 1958 the London County Council obtained Parliamentary powers to deal at one and the same time with the great intersections of Hyde Park Corner, the heaviest concentration of traffic in London (120,000 vehicles in twelve hours) and Marble Arch, the fourth heaviest (81,000 vehicles in twelve hours). With Park Lane these intersections form a vital part of London's inner circle route and link that route with the main arteries to north, west and south.

Work has now been completed on a £6 million development scheme to provide a new road pattern. The scheme includes a four-lane underpass between Piccadilly and Knightsbridge, a roundabout for the circulation of other traffic at Hyde Park Corner and a subsidiary roundabout north of Apsley House. This is linked with a new roundabout system at Marble Arch by the development of the East Carriageway of Hyde Park to carry northbound traffic leaving Park Lane free for southbound traffic. Together they form a twin carriageway outside the Park with a wide central reservation. A number of intersections now permit traffic to join and leave each stream. To the east of Apsley House a new road links Park Lane with the remodelled Hyde Park Corner which leaves Apsley House freestanding. Northbound traffic not already in the park uses this road instead of going through the arches of the fine screen erected in 1828 from designs by Decimus Burton.

The planners' intention is to continue the effect of parkland between Green Park and Hyde Park by creating one large, restful, grassed island aroung the Wellington Arch. The war memorials of the Machine-Gun Corps and the Royal Regiment of Artillery and the equestrian statue of the Duke of Wellington, unveiled on 1 October 1846 have been retained on the new island. The processional route from Buckingham Palace to Marble Arch will cross this island passing through the Wellington Arch. Pedestrian subways now link the central island with surrounding points on the outer pavements and paths also connect the places where these subways enter and leave the island; the remainder have been grassed, with seats arranged by the various low retaining and boundary walls.

St George's Hospital, at the corner of Grosvenor Place, originated in 1773 with a party of dissentient governors of Westminster Hospital, who converted Lanesborough House into an infirmary. It then contained only sixty beds, but in 1829 it was rebuilt by Wilkins, the architect of the National Gallery, and enlarged in 1868 by the erection of a new wing in Grosvenor Crescent. The principal front of the hospital, facing the Green Park, is nearly two hundred feet in length. In 1913 Sir Mallaby Deeley proposed to acquire the site of St George's Hospital for the erection of a huge hotel. Great interest in the subject was aroused at the time, but the scheme failed to mature. Curiously enough, according to Mr J. Britton, it was proposed as long ago as 1819 to rebuild St George's Hospital on a site near Sloane Street. Undoubtedly the hospital occupies one of the most valuable sites in the metropolis, one which would be ideal for the erection of either a great hotel or a multi-storey block of luxury flats whenever the demand arises, though the 30-storey Hilton Hotel across the road may have realised the first of these suggestions. But after careful consideration it was decided to rebuild the hospital on its present site on a sumptuous scale at a cost of £1,000,000 as soon as conditions will permit.

We return to Park Lane by way of Hamilton Place. At the point where these two streets meet was an ornamental fountain known as the Poets' Fountain, from the marble statues of Chaucer, Shakespeare, and Milton on its circular pedestal. It was the work of Thomas Thornycroft and was erected in 1875, the cost being defrayed by a lady who died intestate and who wished that a fountain should be erected at this point. Becoming an obstruction to traffic, it was unceremoniously broken up in 1949, and the shattered remains of the three poets were to be seen lying in the road. A number of Park Lane houses between Hertford Street and Pitts Head Mews were destroyed in the blitz. On this extensive site now stands the London Hilton Hotel, opened in 1963. The building consists of a 4-storey base with a Y-shaped tower, whose three wings stretch 70 feet from the centre. As 'western Europe's largest luxury hotel', the Hilton, of course, is brimful of statistics; height, 328 feet, 30 storeys, plus four below ground, over 500 rooms— radio and television in every guest room—five restaurants, same number of bars, and a thirty-mile view from the Roof Restaurant. Total cost: about £8 million.

At one time the most fashionable part of London, much of the area covered in this chapter is popularly known as Mayfair, though this name is not officially recognized. It extends from Park Lane to Regent Street, from west to east, and from Piccadilly to Oxford Street, from south to north. It derives its name from a large open space between Berkeley Street and Park Lane where the notorious May Fair was held annually until it was suppressed at the end of the eighteenth century as a public scandal. Brick Street, at the southern end of Park Lane, leads to Shepherd Market, a group of buildings which formed the centre of the Fair. Until quite recently it remained a quiet old-world spot, but Carrington House, a large new block of flats, now covers a part of this site, and most of its older features have now disappeared, so that it is rapidly being merged into the adjoining fashionable quarter, of which it really forms a part. Nevertheless, with some buildings bearing the date of 1860 and its numerous cafes and antique shops, it is still a picturesque and unexpected little backwater that should not be missed.

In Hertford Street, leading from Park Lane to Down Street, resided Dr Jenner, the discoverer of vaccination against smallpox. He lived at Number 4 from 1804 onwards, but being unable to succeed as a doctor, returned to Gloucestershire. At the corner of Hertford Street and Park Lane was Londonderry House, the residence of the Marquess of Londonderry, built in 1850 from the designs of Mr B. Wyatt. Demolished in 1965, the site is now being 'developed'. Londonderry House, though nothing spectacular from the outside, had a magnificent interior, enriched by a notable collection of pictures and sculpture. Several of the houses in Park Lane between Hertford Street and Great Stanhope Street boast very ornamental façades. Number 18 next door to Londonderry House, now unoccupied, is built on a semicircular bay supported by stone columns and so also was Number 24 at the corner of Pitts Head Mews, a beautiful private residence which escaped destruction in the blitz, but not the attentions of the property developers who have pulled it down. That on the south corner of Great Stanhope Street, now renamed Stanhope Gate, was built in 1896 by the unhappy Barney Barnato, the South African financier, but was never occupied by him. Later it became the residence of Sir Philip Albert Sassoon who died in 1939. Recently modernised, it was formerly known as Park Lane House and was principally used for trade exhibitions and demonstrations. On the opposite corner of this street is Stanhope House, originally built for Mr Hudson, the soap magnate. It has a distinguished façade and is now occupied by Barclays Bank Ltd.

At the top of Stanhope Gate stood until 1934 Chesterfield House, erected in 1750 for Philip, fourth Earl of Chesterfield, and until about 1930 the residence of Princess Mary and the Earl of Harewood. It was then pulled down and a ten-storey block of balconied flats designed by Mr T. V. Burnett was erected on this site in 1935. Curzon Street takes its name from the third Viscount Howe, and in this street is Crewe House, erected about 1735 and formerly the residence of the Marquess, which stands back behind its wall and courtyard. It was purchased by Lord Crewe in 1899 for £90,000. During the first World War Crewe House became the Ministry of Propaganda, under the direction of the late Lord Northcliffe who died in 1922. It was purchased in 1937 by Messrs Tillings Limited for their new headquarters, who removed the unsightly brick wall which had previously concealed the house from view in Curzon Street. Stately mansions of this kind used to be much more common in this part of London than they are now, and Crewe House, with its trees and well-kept lawns, is a charming sight. At night it is floodlit—which, of course, is quite 'out of period'—but as the lighting is soft, it is quite attractive. On the north side of Curzon Street is Chesterfield Gardens, a fine range of large Victorian mansions with portico balconies, and on the south side near the approach to Shepherd Market is Sunderland House, a modern stone-fronted building erected on the site of a chapel long famous for hasty marriages. The Curzon Cinema at the corner of Hertford Street was erected in 1935. On the north side is the Third

Church of Christ Scientist, erected in 1910, and crowned by a tower facing Half Moon Street. Next door is the Washington Hotel which, during the second World War, became the Washington Club for American Officers. At the corner of Clarges Street opposite is a large block of flats erected in 1934 on the site of the former Curzon Hotel. On the ground floor is the fashionable Mirabelle Restaurant. Leconfield House, also in Curzon Street next to Chesterfield House, is a building of seven storeys erected in 1938 containing shops and flats. Number 21, 'Curzon House', now a residential club, is a well-preserved Georgian house, with fine railings and a pair of link-extinguishers. The western end of Curzon Street, which formerly terminated in a cul-de-sac, known as Seamore Place, was opened up into Park Lane in 1937 and so provided a useful relief thoroughfare to Piccadilly. When a cul-de-sac, it was approached from Pitts Head Mews by a curious little flight of stone steps, which still remains; it is now re-named Curzon Place. A new ten-storeyed block of shops and flats erected on the south corner of Curzon Street and Park Lane is now owned by the Alliance Building Society.

Returning once again to Park Lane, just inside the park opposite Stanhope Gate stood the Adrian Jones Cavalry Memorial, now re-sited in Hyde Park, near Rotten Row, and close to Tilney Street is Fitzherbert House, a block of flats which has been erected on the site of Mrs Fitzherbert's town house, demolished in 1927.

On the site of the late Dorchester House, at the corner of Park Lane and Deanery Street, which was pulled down in 1929, now stands the Dorchester Hotel which was erected for the Gordon Hotels Company Limited, at a cost of £1,750,000. It contains four hundred rooms and an open-air restaurant. The floors are lined with seaweed and the bedrooms with cork, in order to render the building absolutely soundproof. The architect was Mr W. Curtis Green. Dorchester House, erected by Vulliamy in the Italian style for the Holford family in 1851, was a magnificent mansion probably second to none in the metropolis, and was noted for its marble staircase, which is said to have cost £30,000. The exterior of the building was faced with Portland stone and stood back some distance from the roadway. The house was occupied by the Shah of Persia during his second visit to England, and it had also been the temporary residence of other foreign potentates. In later years it was occupied by Mr White-law Reid, the American Ambassador, but for some time before its demolition this mansion was for sale. Next to the Dorchester Hotel is a large ten-storey block of flats with its two top storeys zoned back from the street. It has a long frontage to South Street and covers the site of several private houses which had been unoccupied for several years before their demolition.

In 1935 the houses between Aldford Street and Mount Street overlooking Park Lane were pulled down, and on this site now stands Fountain House, a nine-storey block of flats, which has an underground garage. Aldford House, a handsome private mansion faced with stone, which stood on the adjoining site, was pulled down in 1931, and in its place now stands a nine-storey block of shops and flats. Park Lane now presents an unbroken vista of towering new buildings from Grosvenor House to the Hilton, giving it a typical American appearance. The central section of Mount Street derives its name from Oliver's Mount, an earthwork in the ring of fortifications constructed by Cromwell's army in 1643 to defend London from the Royalists.

The site of Grosvenor House, the former residence of the Duke of Westminster, extending from Mount Street to Upper Grosvenor Street, is now covered by the Grosvenor House Hotel, nine storeys high, erected between 1927 and 1928, which has been dubbed the 'Park Lane Cliffs'. It is built in the typical American style and resembles some of the apartment houses in the uptown district of New York. The two lower storeys are faced with stone, but the upper floor consist merely of straight brick walls, capped at the top with small towers, but otherwise utterly devoid of all external decoration, and more suggestive of some huge warehouse or penitentiary than a block of luxury flats in Park Lane. Its former aggressive appearance has matured with the passage of time.

The old Grosvenor House was demolished in 1927, and had its main entrance in Upper Grosvenor Street. It contained one of the finest collections of pictures in London. At the back, facing Park Lane, was a stone screen 110 feet long with columns in front and two carriage-ways with pediments sculptured with the Grosvenor arms. The house was erected in 1842 by Cundy, and the Corinthian colonnade, based on Trajan's Forum at Rome, was the most ornamental feature to be seen from Park Lane. It was sold by the Duke of Westminster to the late Lord Leverhulme, whoes executors in turn sold the site to the present owners.

In Mount Street, leading from Park Lane to Berkeley Square, the gloomy-looking houses of our great-grandfathers were replaced in the 'eighties of the last century by new buildings faced with red brick and terracotta, many of which are high-class flats and shops. Of special interest is Number 116, the poulterer's shop of John Baily & Son, established in 1720. Among the florid ornamentation of the flats may be seen a niche with a bust of Queen Victoria and another that is presumably the Prince of Wales (later King Edward VII). Some of the flats are dated in the late 'eighties. Here also several of the principal London estate agents have their offices. At the corner of Carlos Place is the Connaught Hotel, formerly the Coburg Hotel. More recently a similar transformation has been effected in Park Street, where the whole of the west side from Mount Street to Oxford Street is now lined by handsome new blocks of flats and private houses, in marked contrast to some of the old ones still remaining on the east side of the street. Many fine new houses have also been erected in Green Street and in Dunraven Street, formerly Norfolk Street. Here, on 6 May 1840, Lord William Russell was murdered in his bed by a Swiss valet named Courvoisier, who had been discovered by his master in the act of robbing him.

Near the west corner of Park Lane and Upper Brook Street is Dudley House, named after the eccentric Earl who lived and died here in 1833. The building has been adapted for commercial use, but behind the temporary partitions the original walls, ceilings and much of the decoration remain. On the opposite corner stood until 1933 Brook House, formerly the residence of Sir Ernest Cassel and until then occupied by Lord Louis Mountbatten. This famous Park Lane mansion was inherited by Lady Louis Mountbatten from her grandfather, Sir Ernest Cassel, and after having been purchased by Messrs Coutts & Company, the well-known firm of bankers, was pulled down in the autumn of 1933. For some time previously this palatial mansion had been unoccupied with boards hanging outside announcing that it was for sale. It had been the scene of brilliant social gatherings for forty years past and was built by Lord Tweedsmouth from whom it was purchased by Sir Ernest Cassel. The latter spent hundreds of thousands of pounds upon improvements and eight hundred tons of marble were imported from the Tuscan quarry of Sarravezza for the great hall, central staircase and galleries, extending to the glass dome in the roof. The sale of Sir Ernest Cassel's art collection in 1933 realized £26,000. On this large site a new block of flats was completed in 1934, but provision was also made in the plans for Lady Mountbatten to have a large flat or penthouse which occupied the greater portion of the two top floors. A smaller block of flats of the same design and elevation now stands on the opposite corner of Brook Street and Park Lane next to Sutherland House, which contains the Mayfair branch of Coutt's Bank. After passing Green Street we next come to the Marble Arch, which replaced an earlier brick gateway by Sir John Soane at what was then known as Cumberland Gate. Originally erected in front of Buckingham Palace by Nash at a cost of £75,000, it was removed to its present site in 1851 at a cost of £4,340, all the stones being numbered for that purpose. The Marble Arch was originally intended to bear a colossal bronze emblematic group of Victory in a four-horsed car, but the design was eventually changed to an equestrian statue of George IV, executed by Chantrey at a cost of 9.000 guineas. This was afterwards erected on a pedestal at the north-eastern angle of Trafalgar Square. The Marble Arch contains a large room in its attic which is utilized by the Metropolitan Police. Cumberland Gate was so called from William, Duke of Cumberland, the hero of Culloden.

In 1908 a wonderful improvement was carried out at the Marble Arch, when owing to the increasing congestion of traffic at the junction of Park Lane, Oxford Street, and Edgware Road the railings of Hyde Park facing the entrance opposite to Edgware Road were set back a distance of 180 feet. The corner was thus converted into a noble square, in such a fashion that the Marble Arch which formerly stood level with the park railings is now situated on an island in the roadway outside Hyde Park. Handsome iron gates have replaced the former railings. Some years later the building line at the corner of Park Lane was set back to bring it into alignment with the widened roadway in front of the Marble Arch and Hyde Park.

The traffic system at Marble Arch has been rearranged as part of the Hyde Park Corner to Marble Arch improvement scheme. Traffic for Edgware Road and the west now circulates around a large island and enters the Bayswater Road some distance west of the Edgware Road junction. A link road called Tyburn Way cutting the island in two carries traffic from the south into the Oxford Street stream. Although cut by this link road the whole is treated as one island. At the east end the processional route from Buckingham Palace passes across the island on the axis of Marble Arch. There are grass lawns, which when viewed from the processional route are terminated by a stone screen in front of which is a pool with fountains and sculpture. The two parts of the island are linked with each other and adjacent pavements by pedestrian subways. To avoid an excessively long subway from the north side of Bayswater Road to Hyde Park by way of the central island an area at the western end of the island is at a lower level with access to public conveniences so that pedestrians may come out into the open air, and if they wish, reach the upper level by steps. Seats on the island are arranged facing south. Near the Marble Arch, an underground Car Park to accommodate 1000 cars has been constructed.

Proceeding along Oxford Street, which is fully described in another chapter, we come first to Park Street and then to North Audley Steet, through which we next direct our steps to Grosvenor Square. North Audley Street, which has been considerably widened on the west side, contains some excellent shops, and so does South Audley Street, on the other side of Grosvenor Square. Like Mount Street it has been mostly rebuilt since the 'eighties of the last century. The former St Petersburg Hotel, situated on the east side of this street, was appropriated by the Government during the first World War and has been retained by them for permanent use as income-tax offices. North Audley Street is named after Mr Hugh Audley, a barrister of the Inner Temple, who bought land here for building purposes and amassed a fortune of nearly half a million sterling. In this street is St Mark's Church, erected by Mr John Deering in 1828 in the Ionic style, and in South Audley Street is the Grosvenor Chapel built in 1740. The former burial-ground at the back of this chapel is now a delightful public garden which affords a secluded retreat from the turmoil of the surrounding streets. It lies between South Street and Mount Street. In this chapel the Armed Forces of the United States held Divine Service during the second World War and here also is buried John Wilkes who died in 1797.

Grosvenor Square, six acres in extent, takes its name from Sir Richard Grosvenor, who died in 1732. It was built between 1720 and 1730, and has retained its popularity as a centre of wealth and fashion ever since that time. Both Lord Grenville and Lord North lived in this square when they were Prime Ministers. Number 29 was the scene of the so-called Cato Street conspiracy to assassinate the Cabinet Ministers of George IV while they were dining with Lord Harrowby, President of the Council. Happily they were warned in time and the conspirators were seized in an attic in Cato Street, Marylebone Road, only a few hours before the intended outrage. Arthur Thistlewood and four other ringleaders were lodged in the Tower and paid the supreme penalty of the law. Cato Street was afterwards renamed Horace Street, but its original name was recently restored and it is Cato Street again. Grosvenor Square is traversed from east to west by the two broad thoroughfares of Brook Street on the north side and Grosvenor Street on the south side. On the two corners of Carlos Place, opening into Grosvenor Square, are two handsome blocks of flats erected about 1928. Much of the square was rebuilt between the two World Wars. At the Duke Street corner is the new Europa Hotel, opened about two years ago, while on the east side is the Italian Embassy, and the large building, McDonald House, which extends round the corner into Grosvenor Street, is occupied by the Trade, Immigration and other departments of the Canadian Government. The Indonesian Embassy is at No 38 on the south side, and a yawning chasm separates it from Nos 43 and 44.

Grosvenor Square has not been deserted by society through its change of character; wealthy families who formerly resided in large private mansions now live in these new and more convenient flats. Their two top stories are built into dormer roofs. So extensive has been the rebuilding of the square that No 44, on the south side, the home of Lady Illingworth, was the last 18th century house in private occupation. An attempt to preserve it as an historic building led to much discussion when, in 1961, confirmation of a preservation order was refused. Now the houses from No 39 up to and including 44 with its link extinguishers and lampholders, have been demolished to make room for a £3½ million luxury hotel, The Britannia, which is scheduled for opening in 1969. This will be a 'sister' hotel to the Europa at the Duke Street corner of the other side of the square. During the second World War the entire square was requisitioned by the United States Expeditionary Force. In 1948 a memorial statue was erected in memory of the late Franklin Delano Roosevelt, President of the United States, on the east side of Grosvenor Square garden at a cost of £50,000, as a token of gratitude for his friendship to the British Nation during the second World War of 1939-45. Contributions to the fund were limited to five shillings each person, thus enabling two hundred thousand people to participate. The fund was reserved exclusively for British subscribers and the entire sum was contributed in less than twenty-four hours. The statue was unveiled on 12 April 1948 by Mrs Eleanor Roosevelt, that day being the third anniversary of the President's death. The Duke of Westminster has presented Grosvenor Square to the British Nation, and this has now been laid out as a beautiful public garden. For more than twenty years Grosvenor Square has been largely occupied by the United States Embassy and other U.S. offices, and the occupation was spread over all four sides of the Square. Many of these departments have now been transferred to the new American Embassy building which has just been completed at a cost of £1,720,000 and occupies the whole of the west side. Topped by a golden coloured American Eagle with a wing span of thirty-five feet, the new building has a private suite for the Ambassador, who has hitherto lived at the Regent's Park Embassy Residence. The architect is Mr Eero Saarinen and the British architects are Messrs Yorke Rosenberg and Mardall. The American influence in Grosvenor Square, however, is not so recent as may be imagined, for John Adams, the first American Ambassador to Britain, and later second President of the U.S.A., came to live at No 9, on the north-east corner of the square in 1785. From there his daughter Abigail was married. Long derelict, the house has been renovated and is now occupied by a department of the Japanese Embassy.

In Brook Street, which derives its name from the Tyburn brook, are some elegant shops and also the world-famous Claridge's Hotel, at the south corner of Davies Street. This hotel, formerly Mivart's, was opened in 1808 by M. Mivart, a Frenchman, at a time when sumptuous accommodation was very much lacking in the metropolis. It was bought some years later by Mr Claridge, and as Claridge's Hotel the one big square house was presently to become the abode of all the visiting Royalties to London. So well did M. Mivart prosper that he added four adjoining houses to the one originally leased before he sold his business to Mr and Mrs Claridge. This was in the middle of the last century. In 1895, after the death of Mr Claridge, the old premises were pulled down and the present magnificent hotel erected in their place. In 1930 it was greatly enlarged by a new wing erected on the site of three houses facing Brook Street. The late Marshal Foch stayed at Claridge's Hotel during his various visits to London. On the opposite corner of Brook Street is a fine new building erected by Lloyds Bank.

Davies Street, leading to Berkeley Square, until some twenty-five years ago was a ragged-looking street, but the whole of the east side is now lined by modern buildings. Next to Claridge's Hotel is a large new block of residential flats, and beyond Grosvenor Street is another called the Manor, with shops on the ground floor, erected on the site of the Davies Street swimming-baths, pulled down in 1912. This street also contains the headquarters of the Queen Victoria's Territorial Rifles. St Anselm's House on the corner of Weighhouse Street, a huge new block of offices, has now been completed and is occupied by the British Council.

Berkeley Square was built between 1730 and 1740 and takes its name from Berkeley House, the predecessor of Devonshire House already noticed during this walk. Noted for its plane-trees, of which it is possible to count at least thirty-three, it is now open to the public and is one of the most richly-wooded squares in London, and in summertime is most delightful. Lord Clive died at Number 45 and Horace Walpole at Number 11. Gunter's famous catering establishment which formerly stood on the east side was removed in 1937 to Curzon Street near Park Lane. This has now been closed and from an office in Bruton Street this old-established firm now deals with outside catering only. On the north-east corner is a handsome block of flats erected on the site of the former Thomas Hotel. Lansdowne House, on the south side of the square, was built by Robert Adam in 1784 for the Marquess of Bute when Minister to George III, and was sold by the Marquess, before its completion, to Lord Shelburne, afterwards Marquess of Landsdowne, for £22,000. In 1921 Landsdowne House was let on a short lease to Mr Gordon Selfridge, and was opened in 1934 as the Lansdowne House Club. The west wing has been rebuilt in order to provide additional accommodation including a swimming-bath. A ten-storied block of flats erected in 1934 now covers the site of the former grounds of Lansdowne House. This has frontages to both Berkeley Street and the south side of Berkeley Square and includes the showrooms of Messrs Stewart & Ardern Limited, the distributors of Morris motors for the metropolis. This building was struck by one of Hitler's flying-bombs in October 1944 which almost demolished its two top floors.

Lansdowne Passage, running between Berkeley Street and Curzon Street, and now closed, formerly divided the grounds of Devonshire House from those of Landsdowne House. Its entrance is still closed by a bar erected in the eighteenth century to prevent the escape of highwaymen by that way, after a mounted policeman had ridden full gallop up the steps in pursuit of the bandits who had robbed their victims in Piccadilly. It has now been closed and replaced by the new Lansdowne Row running parallel to it. On the east side of Berkeley Square now stands Berkeley Square House, one of the largest blocks of shops and offices in Europe. It was erected at a cost of £2,000,000 and stands on the site of twenty historic houses which fronted Berkeley Square and Bruton Street. The greater part of this site was sold by Lord Bearsted in 1930 to the Canadian Pacific Railway, who had originally planned to erect a great hotel, but had to abandon the scheme because of the world trade depression of 1931.

Begun in July 1937 and completed in September 1938 in the record time of fifteen months, Berkeley Square House is nine storeys high and divided into four wings by three open courts above the mezzanine floor and in such a way that every room has an open view. Between the second and third wings is the tower which is 140 feet high and contains three additional storeys built into it. The whole of the eight upper floors are at present occupied by the Ministry of Transport. The building is faced with Portland stone up to the first floor and the upper part with yellow brick. Its architects were Mr S. Gordon Jeeves and Mr Hector Hamilton. Like Grosvenor House, it is devoid of all exterior decoration. During the second World War it was damaged by enemy action, which also demolished the houses on the east corner of Berkeley Square and Davies Street. Another nine-storeyed block of shops and offices has also been erected on the opposite corner of Bruton Street which has a long frontage to Berkeley Square extending to Bruton Place. On the west side of the square stands another handsome block of flats, also nine storeys high and faced with Portland stone. On the adjoining site the large town house of the Earl of Rosebery stood until 1939 when it was pulled down. It was one of the few surviving mansions in Berkeley Square but was rarely inhabited by its owner. Here the Berger group of companies have erected a nine-storeyed block of offices. During the second World War a large underground shelter was constructed in Berkeley Square, but the garden, which lost its turf after the removal of the railings, has now been restored to its original beauty.

In 1935 a new thoroughfare called Fitzmaurice Place was constructed in front of Lansdowne House which is to connect it with Curzon Street, but owing to a difference of about eight feet in the level of the two thoroughfares has only just become available to through traffic from Curzon Street to Berkeley Square. In 1939 some twenty-nine old houses situated in the triangular site between

Curzon Street, Clarges Street and Clarges Mews were pulled down and Curzon Street House was then erected on this site. It covers an area of over an acre and is now the head offices of the Ministry of Education.

Hill Street and Charles Street on the west side of Berkeley Square remain almost unaffected by the spread of modern houses and large blocks of flats in other parts of Mayfair. Their brown-brick Georgian fronts still reflect the external gloom of the Mayfair of our grandfathers, splendid though they may be in their internal appointments. Hill Street indeed was described by Thackeray as the 'Great Gaunt Street'. One tall block of flats has been erected at the western end of Hill Street at the corner of John Street.

On the east side of Berkeley Street are several tall modern buildings, and most of the former private residences between Hay Hill and Piccadilly have been gradually converted into shops, with the result that Berkeley Street has now blossomed out into an important business thoroughfare.

Bruton Street, on the east side of Berkeley Square, leading to New Bond Street and named after Sir John Berkeley of Bruton, has undergone a similar transformation. This was previously one of the most exclusive corners of Mayfair and here many notable people have resided during the past two centuries. At one time Queen Elizabeth the Queen Mother lived at No 17 Bruton Street, and it was here that our present Queen was born in 1926. Here private houses one after another have been turned into high-class shops, which are largely occupied by ladies' tailors and dealers in antique wares. Arthur Tooth & Sons and the Lefevre Galleries have their fine art galleries here. It now differs but little from Conduit Street, of which it forms the continuation west of Bond Street.

Thirteenth Walk

Jermyn Street, St James's Street, Marlborough Gate, St James's Palace, Buckingham Palace, St James's Park, Constitution Hill and Pall Mall

The district commonly known as St James's is enclosed by Piccadilly, Lower Regent Street, Pall Mall, and the east side of the Green Park. It is essentially a quarter of London designed to meet the requirements of bachelors and members of West End clubs, and is notable for the comparative absence of women and of shops dealing in feminine requirements. The majority of London's principal clubs are situated in the St James's quarter, which also contains numerous colonies of bachelor flats and chambers, many first-class restaurants and men's shops.

Jermyn Street, which we have selected as our starting-point for this walk, derives its name from Henry Jermyn, Earl of St Albans, and was built about 1667. Many famous people are numbered amongst its earlier inhabitants. This street has been mostly rebuilt during our own century, and though it contains many fine buildings, these cannot be seen to advantage owing to the narrowness of the street, which scarcely exceeds thirty feet in width. To a large extent Jermyn Street is a backwater of Piccadilly, inasmuch as several large buildings have frontages to both streets. Figuring amongst these are the Criterion Theatre, the newly-erected buildings on the west side of Piccadilly Circus, the Simpson building, St James's Church, the Pigalle Restaurant and arcade, the extensive buildings of Messrs Fortnum & Mason Limited, and the Piccadilly Arcade.

On the site now covered by the Piccadilly Arcade previously stood the Brunswick Hotel, and here Louis Napoleon took up his residence in May 1846, under the assumed name of the Comte d'Arenberg, after his escape from captivity in the fortress of Ham. On the adjoining site is Bury Court, a handsome block of shops and offices which has replaced the former Cox's Hotel, demolished in 1924.

Turning to the south side of Jermyn Street, the Plaza Cinema has a frontage to this street, and various shabby houses at the corner of Wells Street have given way to modern buildings. A few doors farther west are the headquarters of the Royal Society for the Prevention of Cruelty to Animals, founded in 1824. The present building was erected in 1869. On the same side of the street is the former Jules Hotel, with a portion of its frontage zoned back and the remainder built forward to the line of the street, thus giving it a clumsy appearance. This is now used by the National Coal Board, but was previously known as Canberra House, so named because it was formerly occupied by the Commonwealth of Australia.

A few doors farther west is the new 250-bedroom Cavendish Hotel, opened in June 1966 on the site of the old Cavendish, made famous by that eccentric genius Rosa Lewis, the proprietrix who reigned there as the 'Duchess of Jermyn Street' for over half a century. When she died in 1952, at an uncertain but considerable age, a legendary personality was lost to London. The old hotel closed its doors in 1962, but it is remembered with nostalgia and affection by a great many people. In the new Cavendish a number of links with the old era have been preserved. One of the two bars has been named the Sub Rosa, the telegraphic address is 'Rosatel', and the old carriage lamps which shone on many distinguished visitors are again in position at the Jermyn Street entrance. Apart from these senti-mental links with the past, the 15-storey new Cavendish is a 1966 building of reinforced concrete construction, designed and equipped to provide a modern hotel service in complete contrast to its predecessor. Between Duke Street and Bury Street, at Number 76, stood until 1940 Hammam's Hotel and Turkish Baths, opened about 1860 as the London and Provincial Turkish Bath Company. The Unicorn Tavern is now on this site.

Hammam's occupied the site of the former St James's Hotel, and here Sir Walter Scott lodged for some time after his return from the Continent in 1832, setting out on 7 July for Abbotsford, where he died on 21 September of that year. On the east corner of Bury Street a new block of shops and offices occupies the site of the house in which lived the great Duke of Marlborough, when Colonel Churchill, between 1675 and 1681. On the corner of the building, in relief, are more-than-life-size figures showing Charles II presenting the title deeds of Jermyn Street to Henry Jermyn in 1665. The west end of Jermyn Street suffered badly from the October raids of 1940 when all the buildings on the south side between Duke Street and Bury Street were destroyed except one newly-erected building called Duke's Court, together with the rebuilt Unicorn Tavern on the south-west corner of Duke Street completed in 1935.

York Street, now renamed Duke of York Street, on the south side of Jermyn Street, leads to St James's Square, built in 1676. Formerly consisting of aristo-cratic private residences, this square now contains several large office buildings and one west-end club, whereas several years ago there were at least six. The Sports Club, which stood on the corner of Duke of York Street, was pulled down in 1939 and on this site now stands a new seven-storied block of offices which is at present occupied by the Ministry of Labour. The Sports Club has since amalgamated with the East India Club at No 16. In the south-east corner of the square stood until 1938 Norfolk House, a fine mansion built in 1748-52 by Matthew Brettingham, for the ninth duke, and here also George III was born in the older house at the back on 4 June 1738. This mansion was pulled down in

55 Sadler's Wells Theatre in 1830.

56 Russell Square and statue of the Duke of Bedford, 1930.

57   At St Giles Circus the 37-storey Centre Point tower looms above the cupola of the 1911 Y.M.C.A. headquarters in Tottenham Court Road.

58　The Post Office Tower and (left centre) the Gothic St Pancras Station.

59 Trafalgar Square with the National Gallery and, on the right, St Martin-in-the-Fields.

60 The Christmas Tree in Trafalgar Square, an annual gift from the people of Norway.

61 The circular stone Police Station at the south-east corner of Trafalgar Square.

62 Morley's Hotel and the Nelson Column in 1845. Landseer's lions did not appear until 1868.

63 An illegal demonstration by unemployed in 1887; Life Guards and police keep Trafalgar Square clear.

64 The Carlton Hotel, now demolished, and Her Majesty's Theatre, Haymarket.

65 The Haymarket Opera House, 1830. Her Majesty's Theatre is now on this site.

66 New Zealand House, offices of the N.Z. High Commission, on the site of the Carlton Hotel.

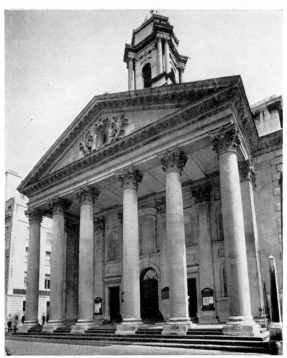

67 St George's, Hanover Square, invariably associated
with fashionable society weddings.

68 This handsome pair of sporting dogs took shelter at St George's during the war and have remained
there ever since.

69 The Quadrant, Regent Street, built to Nash's original design. The colonnade was removed in 1848.

70 Langham Place in 1828. All Souls' Church, designed by John Nash, is on the right.

1935 and on this site now stands a handsome seven-storeyed block of offices, which still maintains the name of Norfolk House. It is faced with red brick with stone dressings and is at present occupied by the British Aluminium Co. Ltd. During the war, General Eisenhower used Norfolk House as his headquarters and there in 1942 was planned 'Operation Torch' for the liberation of North Africa and in 1944 'Operation Overlord' for North West Europe.

At Number 14, on the west side of the Square, is the London Library. A sale at Christie's in June 1960 recalls the efforts of the Committee to deal with an unexpected crisis. For eighty years the Library, as a recognised cultural and educational institution, had been exempt from the payment of rates, but in 1956 the Inland Revenue decided that this exemption should cease and made an assessment upon the Library of £5,000. After an unsuccessful legal battle lasting three years the Committee found themselves faced with a debt of £20,000 for accumulated rates and for legal costs, plus a future payment of £5,000 a year in addition to their normal expenses. This financial problem was tackled by means of increased subscriptions, an appeal to members and well-wishers (which raised £16,000) and the sale referred to above, to which Her Majesty the Queen and Queen Elizabeth the Queen Mother graciously presented gifts.

Cleveland House, a large red-brick building of shops, flats, etc. erected in 1896, has recently been demolished for development. On the north side of the square is Chatham House, which has been the residence of three British Prime Ministers, namely William Pitt, the Earl of Derby, and Mr Gladstone. During the first World War a rather picturesque-looking hut resembling a country inn was erected in the centre of St James's Square, which was christened the Washington Inn, and was principally used by Americans and Overseas officers. It remained standing until 1921. King Street on the west and Charles II Street on the east of St James's Square were so named in honour of Charles II, whereas York Street on the north side and Duke Street leading from Piccadilly to King Street were named after the Duke of York.

Bury Street, running parallel to Duke Street on the west side, is said to derive its name from a half-pay officer named Berry. Ryder Street, leading at right angles into St James's Street, contains a colony of bachelor flats and shops called St James's Chambers, and on the opposite side of the street is the Eccentric Club, occupying the former premises of the Hotel Dieudonné.

We turn next into St James's Street. This broad and handsome thoroughfare, built in 1670, leads from Piccadilly to Pall Mall and is crowned at its southern end by the picturesque gateway of St James's Palace. It had been fashionable since its earliest days and was at first called Long Street. Being situated on rising ground, the Surrey hills can frequently be seen from the top of the street over St James's Palace in clear weather. On the east side, between Piccadilly and Jermyn Street, is White's Club, successor to White's Chocolate House, established in 1698, and built from a design by Wyatt. As a club it dates from 1736. Below Jermyn Street on the same side is Boodle's, the country gentleman's club, opened in 1762, with a distinctive façade, in the manner of the Adam brothers.

Next to Boodle's is a surprise development of modern buildings, the first of which is the addition to the club of a Ladies' Annexe and a residential block of seven floors. The principal building of this new group, however, is the 17-storey tower block for *The Economist* at the Ryder – Bury Street Corner, while at the angle of St James's Street and Ryder Street is a triangular building of four floors, of which the chief occupants are Martins Bank. All the buildings have a reinforced concrete structure of flat slabs between the outer columns and are intended 'to make a worthy and novel contribution to the civic architecture of London and the town landscape of St James's'.

With the exception of White's and Boodle's Clubs, virtually the whole of the east side of St James's Street is now lined with stately new buildings and elegant shops. Yet despite the changes which have taken place in St James's Street it still retains its original homely appearance. On the south east corner of Jermyn Street is Cording House, where the Italian Shipping Lines have their offices, but the finest buildings on this side of St James's Street are those situated between Ryder Street and King Street, which have been so designed as to appear like a single edifice. The older portion, called Bank Buildings, at the corner of King Street, erected in 1910, contains the principal West End branch of Lloyds Bank, but the newer section, known as St James's House, was not completed until 1927, and, previously used by the Royal Air Force, is now occupied entirely by the Dunlop Rubber Company. Before crossing the road, there are two famous 18th century shops at the lower end of the street which must not be overlooked: No 6 is Lock & Company, hatters, with interesting period hats in their window, and No 3, nearer Pall Mall, is Berry Bros & Rudd, wine merchants, well known for their huge scales on which many famous people have 'tried their weight'. At the side, a quaint oak-panelled passage leads to the charming little cul-de-sac Pickering Place which, according to tradition, was a secluded duelling-ground where Georgian 'bucks and blades' retired to settle their differences.

Directing our attention to the west side of St James's Street, the first note-worthy building is the Devonshire Club, two doors from Piccadilly, formerly Crockford's a famous London gaming-house built in 1827. It originated with William Crockford, a fishmonger, whose shop was situated next to the Temple Bar. The stakes were high, and Crockford is reputed to have made £1,200,000 out of his venture. He retired in 1840 and died on 24 May 1844. The building was designed for Mr Crockford by the brothers Wyatt, and in 1872 it was acquired by its present owners as a club for Liberals, but it is no longer essentially a political club. In 1872 it underwent a complete alteration and partial rebuilding. Another man called Smart, who started gaming-rooms at Number 34 on the opposite side of the street, now forming part of the site of the new Cording House, was not so fortunate. On 22 February 1843, Smart's gaming-rooms were raided by the police, when one of Smart's sons, who was in bed at the time, endeavoured to escape over the roof of the house and fell from the parapet into the street from the fourth storey. He was conveyed by cab to hospital, where he died.

Between Bennett Street and Park Place, two smaller clubs having moved elsewhere, the only building of any importance is Brooks's Club, erected from designs by Holland in 1778. Brooks's takes its name from its first proprietor, a wine merchant and money-lender under whom the club migrated from Pall Mall. South of Park Place were Arthur's Club and the Cocoa Tree Club. The premises of the former have been occupied by the Carlton Club since they were bombed out of Pall Mall in 1940. Queen's House (British Travel Association) stands on the site of the Cocoa Tree Club.

At the top of Park Place is Vernon House, the world headquarters of the Overseas League, adjoining which is the League's clubhouse. At the top of St James' Place, a cul-de-sac, is the entrance to Spencer House, mentioned in the previous 'walk'. Between Little St James's Street and Cleveland Row are the Constitutional Club, the former premises (No. 74) of the Bath, or Conservative Club, and the West End offices of the Alliance Assurance Company. The Conservative Club, opened on 18 February 1845, was erected from the designs of Basevi and Sydney Smirke on the site of a part of the former Thatched-House Tavern, and a house in which Gibbon the historian died on 16 January 1794. This club was established in 1840 to receive Conservatives, then too numerous to obtain admission to the Carlton Club. The Union Club is in the same premises as the old Thatched-House Club, which were erected in 1865, and occupied the main portion of the site of the once-celebrated Thatched-House Tavern, long famous for its public and club dinners. On the site of the offices now occupied by the Alliance Assurance Company originally stood English's St James Royal Hotel.

In King Street, on the opposite side of the road, was the St James's Theatre built in 1835 by Beazley for John Braham the singer and remodelled in 1879. The late Sir George Alexander, Sir Gerald du Maurier, and Sir Laurence Olivier, were amongst the well-known lessees of this theatre. Despite all protests and a vigorous campaign led by Lady Olivier (Miss Vivien Leigh), who went so far as to interrupt the proceedings of the House of Lords with an appeal from the Strangers Gallery, the theatre was pulled down in 1957. In its place now stands the new seven-storey St James's House of the Dunlop Rubber Co. Ltd. In addition to its name, the new building recalls the illustrious past by a series of four carved panels depicting people prominent in the history of this distinguished old theatre. The first (which, on account of its musical *motif* the present writer assumed to be John Braham the famous singer who founded the theatre) is Gilbert Miller, the impresario, flanked by a figure of music in the form of Pablo Casals, the famous 'cellist. The remaining three panels appropriately depict Sir George Alexander, Oscar Wilde and Sir Laurence and Lady Olivier. Immediately adjoining the St James's Theatre stood, until 1944, Willis Sale Rooms, formerly Almack's, a noted house for public dinners, balls and meetings, named after Mr Almack, one of the founders of Brooks's Club. It was opened in 1765, but was afterwards renamed Willis Rooms by its new proprietor in 1843. It contained a supper room with a spacious gallery and a ballroom 100 feet long by 40 feet wide, in which as many as 1,700 persons were present upon one occasion. The premises have long since been rebuilt. Willis Rooms were last occupied by Messrs Robinson & Foster Limited, auctioneers and valuers, who have removed to Queensberry Hall, South Kensington. The building was badly damaged in the air raids of 1940, and then completely demolished in another raid in March 1944. On this site a new block of offices, seven storeys high, has been erected. On the opposite side of King Street are Messrs Christie's sale rooms, celebrated for their picture and china sales. The sale rooms of Messrs Christie were also damaged in the raids, and the firm was temporarily at Spencer House, St James's Place, during the rebuilding.

Returning to St James's Street and turning to the left we come to St James's Palace, the official residence of the sovereigns of England from the reign of William III until the accession of Queen Victoria in 1837. Though no longer the residence of monarchs it still gives its name to the English Court, and Royal levees are still held in St James's Palace. For several years it was the residence of the Duke of Windsor when Prince of Wales.

Cleveland Row, opposite St James's Palace, leading into the Mall, derives its name from Barbara, Duchess of Cleveland, one of the mistresses of Charles II. Near here stood Berkshire House, which the Merry Monarch purchased and presented to this Duchess of Cleveland, whom John Evelyn described as 'another lady of pleasure and the curse of our nation'. He also refers to the house (later named Cleveland House) as 'a noble palace, too good for that infamous...'. It probably stood on or near the site of the present Lancaster House. Handsome modern buildings have been erected here opposite the Palace, but this thoroughfare is not available to through vehicular traffic except by special permission. Clarence House, close to St James's Palace, was the town residence of the Queen before her accession in 1952 and is now occupied by Queen Elizabeth, the Queen Mother. This house was built for the Duke of Clarence, afterwards William IV, and later was renovated for another Duke of Edinburgh, second son of Queen Victoria upon his marriage to the Princess Marie of Russia. Here Princess Anne was born on 15 August 1950. At the west corner of Cleveland Row and the Mall is Lancaster House, which used to house the exhibits of the London Museum. It was built in 1825 from designs by B. Wyatt for the Duke of York, son of George III, but he never lived to see its completion and in 1841 the Duke of Sutherland purchased the Crown lease for £72,000, the original cost of the building. The proceeds were used for the purchase of Victoria Park. On the death of the late Duke in 1913, this property came into the market and was purchased by the late Lord Leverhulme and presented to the nation. There seem to be two opinions about this. While most people have the impression that Lord Leverhulme presented Lancaster House to the nation expressly to contain the London Museum — and many of us visited it as such — a recent official leaflet states that it was presented to the nation for the *dual purpose* of housing the London museum *and* providing a centre for Government hospitality! (the italics are ours). A newspaper correspondent in 1961 rightly made public the 'dishonesty of successive Governments who alienated the house from the intentions of the donor'.

Meanwhile that part of the London collection which is still at Lancaster House is not accessible to the public, and the remainder is in a section of Kensington Palace.

A walk of about a hundred yards along the Mall will bring us to the Victoria Memorial, designed by Sir Thomas Brock, R.A., and unveiled by King George V on 16 May 1911. The height of the memorial is eighty-two feet in all, the statue of Queen Victoria being thirteen feet. The groups alongside represent Justice and Truth, and facing Buckingham Palace itself is a group symbolic of Motherhood. The whole is surmounted by a winged figure of Victory, this figure being poised on a sphere supported by the figures of Courage and Constancy. At the base is a marble basin with fountains. In front of the Memorial, forming the entrance to the Mall, is a semicircular colonnaded screen with arches and gateways which encloses the Queen's Garden. This great improvement involved the sacrifice of a small portion of the lake in St James's Park, and also a corner of the Green Park immediately opposite.

Buckingham Palace, the London residence of the Royal Family, facing the Mall and St James's Park, stands on the site of Buckingham House, built in 1703 by a Dutch architect for John Sheffield, Duke of Buckingham. It was acquired by George III in 1761 for £21,000 shortly after the birth of the Prince of Wales at St James's Palace. Their Majesties then moved, and all their succeeding children were born here. In 1775 the property was settled on Queen Charlotte in exchange for Somerset House, and thenceforth Buckingham House was called 'the Queen's House'. It was reconstructed between 1825 and 1836 in the Palladian style from the designs of Nash, but as William IV did not like the building, Buckingham Palace was not occupied until the accession of Queen Victoria. Later several alterations and improvements were effected, and new buildings added on the south side. The palace as constructed by Nash consisted of three sides of a square, the fourth side being enclosed by iron palisades. In front of the central entrance formerly stood the Marble Arch, now removed to Cumberland Gate, Hyde Park. The original east front of the palace was built in 1846 by Mr Edward Blore at a cost of £150,000. The south wing and the ballroom, measuring 111 feet by 60 feet, were added in 1856. Prince Charles was born at the Palace on 14 November 1948.

Architecturally the garden or west front of the palace with its balustraded terrace is regarded as the principal one. The pleasure grounds cover an area of forty acres, five of which are occupied by a lake, but the general public are not privileged to inspect this Royal residence or its delightful gardens. One surviving relic of olden times, totally inconsistent with the dignity of a Royal residence in the capital of the British Commonwealth, is the long hideous stable-wall fronting Grosvenor Place, with spikes on the top. Possibly this is a necessary evil, but at least an ornamental wall would be more in keeping with the splendour of Buckingham Palace and of the aristocratic Grosvenor Place. An ornamental wall of more recent construction fronts that part of the palace which faces Buckingham Palace Road.

In 1912 a new east front was built by Sir Aston Webb at a cost of £60,000 provided from the surplus funds subscribed by the public for the Victoria Memorial. It is of a straightforward Renaissance design and of Portland stone, with tall pilasters between all the windows, and gives the building a dignity which it previously lacked. A stone-balustraded balcony projects from the first floor, below which the stone-facing is rusticated. The work was carried out in the record time of less than three months, arrangements having been made that it should be put in hand between August and November during the period when their Majesties the late King George V and Queen Mary were out of town. All the blocks of stone for the new façade were numbered beforehand in order that the work might proceed as rapidly as possible. After the completion of the new front in the following November, His Majesty signified his great pleasure at the way in which the work had been carried out by inviting the men who had been engaged on this contract to a dinner at Buckingham Palace.

In its new mantle of splendour, Buckingham Palace bears a striking resemblance to the former palace in Brunswick, utilized as a public museum since the establishment in 1918 of the German Republic. But unlike the Brunswick Palace, it lacks the bronze statue on its roof, and let us hope that some day a bronze figure of a chariot and horses will be erected on the roof of Buckingham Palace to complete its appearance. Buckingham Palace is a never-ending source of attraction both to Londoners and visitors alike who flock here to witness the changing of the guard and other interesting events. A military band frequently performs of a morning in the courtyard, which attracts crowds of passing spectators.

The additions made to Buckingham Palace between 1846 and 1852 gave London a most welcome street improvement. On 26 July 1847 the tenants of the houses in Stafford Row opposite the private entrance to the palace, now forming a part of Buckingham Palace Road, received notice from the Commissioners of Woods and Forests to vacate their premises owing to the ground being required for the enlargement and improvement of Buckingham Palace. A few other houses were also removed in Great James Street, now renamed Buckingham Gate. This led to the construction of the fine range of buildings opposite the south front of the palace, including the offices of the Duchy of Cornwall and the Buckingham Palace Hotel. The former building was erected in 1855 on the corner of Buckingham Gate, the site having been purchased from the Land Revenues for £5,300. The architect was Mr Pennethorne and the cost of the building was £10,000. It was badly damaged in the early air raids of 1940 but has lately been repaired. Previously the offices of the Duchy of Cornwall had been located at Somerset House.

The Buckingham Palace Hotel, built in the Venetian style, was opened in April 1861 and was designed by Mr James Murray. From that time until the first World War it remained one of London's most aristocratic hotels, but after being released by the Government from war service it was acquired by Messrs

Nobels Limited, the manufacturers of explosives, a subsidiary company of Imperial Chemical Industries Limited. That company having removed its head offices in 1928 to Imperial Chemical House, Millbank, the former Buckingham Palace Hotel is now a block of offices.

In 1857 new iron gates were erected at the entrance to St James's Park, and the former Park Lodge, which stood at the west end of Birdcage Walk, adjoining the Wellington Barracks, was then removed. A new lodge was afterwards built at Buckingham Gate, and this improvement, including the new gates and approaches to the park, cost £2,450. In more recent times these gates have been replaced by handsome new gilded gates and railings, forming part of the improvements effected by the construction of the Victoria Memorial in 1904. Birdcage Walk, skirting the south side of St James's Park, derives its name from the aviary established there in the reign of James I, and contains the Wellington Barracks erected in 1834-59 for part of the household troops. On a Sunday morning in June 1944 the Guards' Chapel of the Wellington Barracks was hit by one of Hitler's flying-bombs during a parade service. The bomb exploded in the aisle among 180 worshippers, bringing down the roof, the upper walls, the massive Doric pillars and the portico. Many people were killed including Lieut-Col. Lord Edward Hay of the Grenadier Guards who was struck down while reading the lesson. The Bishop of Maidstone, Dr Leslie Owen, who was waiting in the sanctuary to preach, escaped unharmed. Of the original chapel only the apsidal sanctuary, brilliantly decorated in marble, mosaic and gold, survives. A new chapel (architect, Bruce George, A.R.I.B.A.) was completed in 1963. Built into the foundations are the remains of some two thousand memorials, damaged beyond repair when the former building was destroyed, and a Memorial Cloister containing Books of Remembrance for the seven regiments of the Brigade was opened by Her Majesty the Queen on 28th May 1956.

Running obliquely from Buckingham Palace to Hyde Park Corner is Constitution Hill, formerly a narrow thoroughfare, but widened in 1907 to ninety-five feet in connexion with the improvements in front of Buckingham Palace. For that purpose a strip of land about twenty-five feet wide, separating the roadway from the wall of the palace grounds, was taken, together with a small slice of the Green Park. Here no fewer than three attempts were made upon the life of Queen Victoria, the first by a lunatic named Oxford on 10 June 1840, the second by John Francis, another lunatic, on 31 May 1842, and the third by a man named Bean on Sunday, I July 1842.

John Francis, who made the second attempt on the Queen's life, was tried and condemned to death for attempted murder, and was sentenced to be conducted to the place of execution on a hurdle, there to be hanged by the neck until he was dead. The head was to be afterwards severed from the body, which was then to be divided up into four quarters, to be disposed of in such a manner as Her Majesty should deem fit. But instead of hanging the prisoner, Queen Victoria exercised her prerogative of mercy and commuted the death sentence to transportation for life to the former penal settlement in Tasmania.

The third attempt was made upon the life of the Queen whilst on her way from Buckingham Palace to the Chapel Royal. Upon that occasion the would-be assassin was seized by a spectator and the pistol taken from him, but owing to the stupidity of the police constables he was allowed to escape. Subsequently he was apprehended and lodged in Tothill Fields Prison, and eventually sentenced to eighteen month's imprisonment at the Millbank Penitentiary.

On Saturday, 30 June 1850, whilst riding in Constitution Hill, Sir Robert Peel was thrown from his horse after having made a call at Buckingham Palace. Whilst Sir Robert Peel was exchanging greetings with Miss Ellis, one of Lady Dover's daughters, his horse became restive, turned sharply, and threw Sir Robert over its head upon his face. Medical aid was obtained from St George's Hospital, but Peel died on the following day.

St James's Park, which next calls for notice, comprises an area of about ninety acres, which originally belonged to the Palace of St James's. It was first created and enclosed by Henry VIII, but was replanted and beautified by Charles II, and finally arranged by George IV in the years 1826-28 much as it appears at the present day. A Chinese bridge once spanned the so-called canal, which was erected for the occasion of the visit of the Allied Sovereigns to London in 1814, but it was destroyed a few years afterwards. The canal was then fashioned into a lake, consisting of a winding sheet of water. The original canal was formed by Charles II out of several previously-existing ponds, and he also built a decoy for ducks. The chain bridge which spanned the lake and afforded such delightful views of the Foreign Office and Whitehall Court was erected in 1857. The lake was then cleared out and raised, so that the greatest depth of water does not now exceed four feet. About twenty-five years ago it was suggested that the chain bridge should be replaced by a new stone structure, and after a hundred years' service the old suspension bridge has now been replaced by an elegant concrete bridge which was opened in October 1957.

During the first World War of 1914-18 the lake in St James's Park was drained, and an extensive collection of temporary buildings erected on this ground. For a considerable time the Passport Office was located here, and it was not until 1922, eight years after the outbreak of the war, that these huts were removed and the lake restored once again. Owing to the fact that the lake had been dry for so many years, some of the minor repairs to the basin proved inadequate, with the result that no sooner had the lake been refilled than the water slowly trickled out and left it almost empty again. The source of the trouble was located without much difficulty, and the water was prevented from escaping again.

Marlborough Gate, leading from the Mall and St James's Park into Pall Mall, was opened to the public in November 1856 by appropriating the private road hitherto used as the approach to St James's Palace. A portion of the wall of the palace was removed and rebuilt in a line with the new road, and on the opposite side a strip of ground was added to the garden of Marlborough House. In 1925 the wall of St James's Palace was again set back a short distance, so that a pavement could be provided on the west side of the roadway. Hitherto it had only contained a sidewalk on the east side, making it dangerous to pedestrians crossing the Mall at this corner.

Marlborough House, at the corner of Pall Mall, was built in 1710 for the first Duke of Marlborough from Wren's design. It became state property in 1817, when it was purchased for Princess Charlotte and her husband Prince Leopold. It was also the residence of Queen Adelaide after the death of William IV, and in 1850 this mansion was settled on the Prince of Wales, afterwards King Edward VII. Later, it became the home of Queen Alexandra during her widowhood, and then of Queen Mary. Today, it has the sub-title of Commonwealth Centre, and when it is not in use for conferences and the like, it is possibly open to the public.

Pall Mall is considered by many people to be the handsomest street in London. It derives its name from Paille Maille, a ball-game played by Charles II and his friends in St James's Park. On the corner site, adjoining Marlborough House, formerly occupied by the New Oxford and Cambridge Club, stands Hambro's Bank, a fine building of stone erected in 1931. On the adjacent site, formerly containing the Guards' Club, now removed to Brook Street, is another fine building erected by the Midland Bank in 1927. Farther along on the same side of the street is the Oxford and Cambridge Club, designed by Smirke in 1835-38, and at Numbers 81-82 are portions of Schomberg House, built about 1650 during the government of Cromwell. At that period Pall Mall was planted with elm trees to the number of 140, described as standing in 'a very decent manner' on both sides of the walk. In the reign of William III it was the residence of Frederic, Duke of Schomberg, killed at the Battle of the Boyne in 1690. Later it was occupied by William, Duke of Cumberland, the hero or the butcher of Culloden, as the case may have been and Thomas Gainsborough, the celebrated landscape and portrait painter (1727-1788) had his studio in Schomberg House. A part of the house was long since pulled down and the remainder is now occupied by the Commercial Union group of companies.

Next door to Schomberg House, adjoining the Royal Automobile Club, are the offices of the Car and General Insurance Corporation and of the R.A.C. Touring Department. The extensive Royal Automobile Club, erected between 1908 and 1910 at a cost of £250,000, occupies the site of the old War Office. It is built in the French Renaissance style, and is faced with Portland stone, with a row of stone columns above the ground floor. The Adam ceiling which adorned the old building has been retained in the smoke-room of the new club-house. Amongst the special features of the Royal Automobile Club, which boasts a membership of twenty thousand, are the handsome swimming-bath, the great gallery for concerts and teas, the gymnasium and rackets courts, the large restaurant, to which ladies are admitted, and the terrace overlooking the Mall. The building was slightly damaged in the early raids of 1940 and again in March 1944.

The old War Office was a very grimy-looking building, far more suggestive of a mausoleum than a leading Government office. The western portion was originally a house built for the Duke of Cumberland, brother of George III, and the eastern portion, next to the Carlton Club, formerly Buckingham House, was added to the building in 1855.

The Carlton Club, which adjoined the Royal Automobile Club, was erected in 1855, but was originally founded in Charles Street by the Duke of Wellington in 1831. The following year it removed to Lord Kensington's house in Carlton Gardens, and in 1836 Sir Robert Smirke built a new house of Grecian design to which in 1846 an addition was made by Mr Sydney Smirke. Eight years later the original club-house was pulled down, and a new wing and a centre were then added, the entire design presenting a façade of 130 feet.

The new building was a copy of Sansovino's Library of St Mark in Venice. Unfortunately it was faced with Caen stone, totally unsuited to the London atmosphere, resulting in its rapid decay, and eventually giving this fine building a most poverty-stricken appearance when viewed from Pall Mall. In 1923 the Carlton Club was refaced with Portland stone at a cost of £60,000, one-half of which was defrayed by Sir Mallaby Deeley. To celebrate the completion of the work the men who had been employed on the contract were entertained to a dinner by the members of the Carlton Club. The club-house was destroyed in the blitz except for its fine façade, but this has now been removed. The club is now at 69 St James's Street and on the Pall Mall site a new office building has been completed and is occupied by Lloyds Bank Europe. On the opposite corner of Pall Mall and Carlton Gardens is the Reform Club, an imitation of the Farnese Palace at Rome, founded in 1834, two years after the passing of the Reform Bill at 24 Great George Street, Westminster, the residence of Sir Matthew Wood, twice Lord Mayor of London. It was afterwards removed to a house standing on the site of the present building at Number 104 Pall Mall, but this was totally inadequate for the needs of the members. Within a few months it was decided to build a club-house, and there being an adjoining site previously occupied by three houses available for extension, this was purchased. The committee then resolved to erect a new building at a cost of not less than £19,000, but when the bill was finally settled it reached the sum of £80,000. The Reform Club was designed by Sir C. Barry, who also designed the adjoining Travellers' Club, which is a copy of the Palazzo Pandolfini at Florence. Adjoining the Travellers' Club is the Athenaeum, at the corner of Waterloo Place, already noticed in a previous walk.

Unlike the south side of Pall Mall, which is almost entirely occupied by large club-houses, the north side contains various handsome modern blocks of shops and offices. Nevertheless, there are two leading clubs located on this side of the street, namely, the Junior Carlton and the Army and Navy. The Junior Carlton, which faces the Royal Automobile Club, is an entirely new building which replaces the stately palace that was designed by David Brandon, and was opened in 1868 at a cost of £40,000. It has extensive frontage both to Pall Mall and the south side of St James's Square.

The Army and Navy Club, on the west corner of Pall Mall and St James's

Square, was founded in 1838 and the original club was built in 1848-51 on the model of Sansovino's Palazzo Cornaro on the Grand Canal at Venice. The present club is also a new building, of which the foundation stone was laid in October 1962. The Marlborough Club stood a few doors farther west on the site of Almack's Club, the great gaming-house of the eighteenth century and afterwards the Shakespeare Galleries. It was established in 1869, largely through the instrumentality of the Prince of Wales, afterwards King Edward VII, who was a member until the end of his life.

Westward to St James's Street and eastward to Waterloo Place, the north side of Pall Mall includes a handsome range of commercial buildings, a large proportion being Insurance offices.

Fourteenth Walk

Whitehall, The Government Buildings, Westminster Bridge, Houses of Parliament, Westminster Abbey, Dean's Yard, Westminster School, Millbank and Great Smith Street

Starting out on our travels from Trafalgar Square and proceeding down Whitehall we first pass the Whitehall Theatre on our right, occupying the site of the famous Ship Tavern, demolished in 1929. Adjoining Martins Bank is a red-brick edifice containing the banking premises of Messrs Glyn Mills & Company Limited, on the ground floor, and an extension of the Admiralty buildings on the five upper storeys.

Immediately adjoining these newly-erected buildings is the Old Admiralty, built in 1725, with a classic portico and a stone screen designed by Robert Adam in 1760. Next door is the Office of the Paymaster-General which which is now under reconstruction, and the Horse Guards, with a clock-tower and an archway dating from 1758 leading through to the parade ground in St James's Park. It stands on the site of an old tiltyard of the Palace of Westminster, where tourneys were held in former times. The stone front of these buildings overlooking the parade ground and St James's Park is very pleasing to the eye, but the frontage to Whitehall, consisting largely of yellow brick turned black, looks very dingy. Built by John Vardy, the design of the Horse Guards is generally attributed to William Kent. Many of the buildings which front the west side of Whitehall between the Old Admiralty and the Treasury are at present in a very dilapidated condition, partly caused by the blitz, but their restoration is gradually approaching completion.

At right angles to the Old Admiralty and the Horse Guards on the north side of the Parade Ground is the imposing quadrangular pile of the New Admiralty, which is connected with another block at the eastern end of the Mall containing the residences of the First Lord and the First Sea Lord, and the triple Archway with its wrought-iron and bronze gates designed by Sir Aston Webb, P.R.A. The New Admiralty was built in 1895 from the designs of Messrs Leeming & Leeming of Halifax in the Italian Palladian style, and is faced with red brick and stone. It contains three corner towers and a campanile which rises to a height of 170 feet. Its façade was damaged in the air raids of 1940 but only temporary repairs have been carried out in front of the New Admiralty, and unfortunately concealing the view of this fine building from the Mall is a frowning new structure which is officially named the Citadel. It was built 1940-41 to provide bomb-proof protection for the vital Admiralty operations, wireless and communication rooms. During the second World War the Admiralty became a huge nerve-centre into which poured signals from all over the world, all day and all night. In structure the Citadel resembles a ship upside down. The whole structure is immensely strong and its foundations are some thirty feet below the ground with heavily-reinforced concrete walls rising above them in several layers. It is not yet decided whether this building will remain as a permanency or be removed as a war-time disfigurement, but it will certainly remain for a long time to come as a feature of the London landscape.

The Parade Ground, the scene of the Trooping of the Colour, is the largest clear space in London, and contains statues of Field-Marshal Earl Kitchener, Viscount Wolseley, and Lord Roberts. On the western side is the Guards' Division Memorial, unveiled by H.R.H. the Duke of Connaught in memory of the fourteen thousand guardsmen killed in the first World War. Another memorial, designed by Sir Edwin Lutyens, R.A., stands at the corner of the New Admiralty to the officers of the Royal Naval Division who fell in the same War.

Returning to Whitehall, on the east side is Craig's Court, formerly the home of Cox's Bank. In the court is Harrington House, built in 1702, with a fine old Queen Anne front, until 1917 the residence of the Earls of Harrington and the last of the old private mansions of Whitehall. It is now the Whitehall Telephone Exchange. Farther along is Great Scotland Yard, so named because the Scottish Kings were housed here. It was once the official residence of the Royal architects and surveyors, notably Inigo Jones, Sir John Denham, Sir Christopher Wren, and Sir John Vanbrugh. Until 1891 it was the headquarters of the Metropolitan Police, but is now used by the Army Authorities as a recruiting centre.

Between Great Scotland Yard and Whitehall Place is the handsome building of the Ministry of Agriculture and Fisheries, completed in 1908. It is faced with Portland stone and harmonizes admirably with the adjoining War Office and with the Banqueting Hall on the opposite corner of Horse Guards Avenue. An extension of this building has now been carried out opposite the War Office in Whitehall Place. The Crown Estate Office occupies part of this building, facing Whitehall. The new War Office erected between 1899 and 1906 from the designs of William Young at a cost £1,000,000, is faced with Portland stone, with groups of Corinthian pillars, and contains four circular flanking towers, 156 feet high. The building occupies the whole of the island site between Whitehall Place, Horse Guards Avenue, and Whitehall Court, and contains about a thousand rooms and two and a half miles of corridors. Owing to the increase in size and the number of Government departments in recent years, the location and description of some offices change quite frequently; thus the building referred to above as the *new* War Office is now known as the *old* War Office.

Beyond Great Scotland Yard the roadway in Whitehall widens out considerably, increasing to 130 feet between Downing Street and Parliament Square. A very welcome improvement might some day be effected by setting back the building line on the east side of Whitehall between Great Scotland Yard and Trafalgar Square, bringing it more or less into alignment with the War Office and the Crown Estate Office. Some of the buildings are over a hundred years old and sandwiched between modern buildings erected in our own century, and the sacrifice of some twenty feet of ground could be largely offset by the erection of much taller buildings, similar to those of Northumberland Avenue. Since 1 January 1931 the name of Whitehall has been given to the entire thoroughfare from Trafalgar Square to Parliament Street. Before that time the northern section from Trafalgar Square to Great Scotland Yard was called Charing Cross. Here the roadway is only about half as wide as in Whitehall proper and there is often serious traffic congestion. Any long-term scheme for rebuilding Central London should include this suggested road-widening which would make Whitehall one of the grandest thoroughfares in the world. This is the High Street of the British Commonwealth and the wide sweep of roadway crowned by the National Gallery at the northern end with the Houses of Parliament at the southern end would be one of the finest vistas in London.

In the centre of Whitehall, opposite the War Office, is an equestrian statue of the Duke of Cambridge, a former Commander-in-Chief of the British Army. Lower down Whitehall, also in the centre of the road, opposite the Foreign Office, is the Cenotaph, a world-famous monument designed by Sir Edwin Lutyens, R.A., and erected in 1920 in place of a temporary memorial erected for the Peace Celebrations of July 1919. Between them is the equestrian statue of the bare-headed Earl Haig, which caused considerable comment when it was erected in 1937.

At the south corner of Horse Guards Avenue is the Banqueting Hall of the former Royal Palace of Whitehall built by Inigo Jones in 1622, and all that remains of the buildings destroyed by fire in 1698. This Palace, built by Cardinal Wolsey when Archbishop of York, was then called York Place and became the residence of the kings of England from Henry VIII to William III. It was said to have extended from the river to St James's Park and to have covered a site of twenty-four acres.

Macaulay tells us that, on the evening of 4 January 1698, a Dutch woman who was employed as a laundress at Whitehall, lighted a charcoal fire in her room and placed some linen round it. The linen caught fire and burned furiously. The tapestry, bedding, and wainscots were soon in a blaze. The unhappy woman who had done the mischief perished. Before midnight the King's apartments and those of the Queen, the Wardrobe, the Treasury, and office of the Privy Council had been destroyed.

The Banqueting Hall, celebrated for its painted ceiling by Rubens, was used as a Chapel Royal (though never consecrated) until 1890, when it became the museum of the Royal United Service Institution, founded in 1831, whose premises are next door. In 1964 the museum was removed, the interior re-decorated in its original colours and the Hall is again open to the public. It was from a window of the Banqueting House that King Charles I stepped on to the scaffold to be executed in January 1649.

At the back of the United Service Museum stood until 1938 Whitehall Gardens, and here at Number 2 Benjamin Disraeli resided from 1873 to 1875, and Number 4 was the town house of Sir Robert Peel, to which he was brought home to die after falling from his horse in Constitution Hill. Adjoining the United Service Institution is Gwydyr House which dates from 1772 and is now an office of the Ministry of Land and Natural Resources, though it is understood that this is not a permanent allocation.

Montagu House close by, which has lately been pulled down, was formerly the town mansion of the Duke of Buccleuch and afterwards the offices of the Ministry of Labour. Montagu House was completed in 1864, having been five years in course of erection. It was 144 feet long and 88 feet wide, and the elevated roofs above each wing rose to a height of 90 feet, giving the house a stately appearance. The garden formerly extended to the river, but when the Victoria Embankment was constructed, the Duke of Buccleuch received a large sum as compensation for the strip of ground required for this improvement. Overlooking the garden of Montagu House is Richmond Terrace, built on the site of Richmond House destroyed by fire in 1791.

This terrace of houses is now appropriated by various offices of H. M. Treasury, but its appearance is shabby and dilapidated. Facing the terrace, a magnificent pile of Government offices has now been erected at a cost of £5,000,000, and forms a continuous chain of Government buildings in Whitehall between Great Scotland Yard and Parliament Street. It is one of the largest in the world and covers the vast rectangular site bounded by Whitehall, Horse Guards Avenue, Richmond Terrace and the Victoria Embankment. It consists of a single block with three large internal courts and its two main facades face Whitehall and the Victoria Embankment. Each contains eight main storeys above the basement with a total elevation of eighty-seven feet but there is an additional upper storey set back ten feet and rising another six feet. The four internal blocks are eleven storeys high, and rise to 128 feet, and they tower, therefore, above all other adjacent buildings except the Victoria and Clock Towers of the Houses of Parliament.

The new building provides accommodation for 5,360 Civil Servants, an increase of 4,175 in the number previously occupying this site. The architect is Mr E. Vincent Harris who also designed the famous Circular Library Building in Manchester and who, by setting the new building further back behind Whitehall, prevents the Inigo Jones Banqueting Hall and Gwydyr House from appearing unduly dwarfed. The new buildings include an underground service yard reached by a sloping road from Horse Guards Avenue for delivery of supplies. Demolition of the houses in Whitehall Gardens was completed in 1939 and building operations were stopped during the war, but since then rapid progress has been made, and the Ministry of Defence is now in complete occupation. The principal entrances are in Horse Guards Avenue on the north, and at the southern end, the building faces Richmond Terrace. Reclining over the Horse Guards Avenue entrance are two colossal nude female figures said to represent Earth and Water. Known to the staff as 'The Windmill Girls', they weigh thirty tons each – and look every ounce of it. A companion pair, Air and Fire, are to be provided for the south doorway, but have not yet arrived.

On the eastern, or Embankment side of the new building may be seen 'Queen Mary's Steps'. In 1691 Sir Christopher Wren designed for Queen Mary II a terrace overlooking the Thames in front of the old river wall of Whitehall Palace, built by Henry VIII. A curving flight of steps was made at each end to give access from the Royal Apartments to the State Barge. In 1939, excavations for the new Government building revealed the river wall of the Tudor palace, the later terrace wall and the northern flight of steps. Thanks to careful repairs and restoration, these interesting relics can now be seen by the passer-by.

Henry VIII kept a huge wine cellar in his Palace of Whitehall which still exists and has been carefully preserved for incorporation into the new buildings. It is a fine example of a Tudor brick-vaulted roof 70 feet long, 30 feet wide and weighing 800 tons. But the cellar jutted out into the roadway and would have spoiled the line of the new building. In December 1946 it was decided to perform a miracle by moving the cellar more than forty feet to one side, lowering it twenty feet and then pushing it back to its original site, this time entirely below ground level. A huge excavation was first made and here a giant platform of girders was erected 60 feet long, 50 feet wide and 20 feet high. Then the cellar was embalmed in steel, brick and concrete to prevent damage. After that it was placed on mahogany cushions, carriage rails and two hundred special steel rollers. It was then shifted a quarter of an inch at a time until it had travelled 43 feet 5¾inches and rested completely on the platform. Then the original site was excavated to a depth of twenty feet and a concrete floor laid for the cellar to rest again on the ground. By May 1949, nearly two and a half years after the work began, the cellar was rolled back and restored to its original position. This gigantic operation cost the Government £100,000.

Crossing over to the other side of Whitehall, next to the Horse Guards is the Scottish Office and then the Treasury, an extensive edifice built of stone from the designs of Kent, consisting of three storeys. It was constructed at different periods, and considerable alterations were made in 1816, when the frontage to Whitehall was cased with brick, washed over in a dirty stone colour. The present façade was built by Sir Charles Barry in 1846-47 to replace the heavy front built by Sir John Soane. A grey antiquated building adjoining the Treasury in Whitehall was then pulled down to make way for an extension of that building. It differed entirely from the architecture of the adjoining buildings and contained a Gothic doorway enriched with carvings. In 1960 began a large-scale undertaking called 'The Downing Street and Treasury Reconstruction', by which the Treasury building in Whitehall and parts of Nos 10 and 11 Downing Street were rebuilt behind their original façades, while also preserving certain features of historic interest. During the course of this operation, it looked as if the Treasury building had been completely gutted, and in parts only the bare walls were left standing. Nevertheless the Whitehall exterior gives no indication of the recent conflict within.

Turning the corner into Downing Street, one is perhaps surprised to discover a rather pleasant open space called Treasury Green. From here the reconstruction work can be clearly seen and, in addition to the new work, a large expanse of Tudor wall has been uncovered, with doorways and windows plainly indicated. This is a relic of Whitehall Palace, formerly Wolsey's York Place —

> Sir,
> You must no more call it York Place; that's past;
> For since the Cardinal fell, that title's lost:
> 'Tis now the King's, and call'd Whitehall.'
> *(Henry VIII, Act IV, Sc. 1)*

Past the Green is No 10 Downing Street, the official residence of the British Prime Minister; a drab and humble-looking house to be sure, and among the cluster of sightseers that are always to be found standing on the opposite pavement and staring at the famous doorway, many must surely feel surprised and disappointed that, though surrounded by palatial government offices, the head of the government is confined to such an insignificant little house, so inconsistent with the dignity of his high office. But No 10 is not so simple as it looks. If the sightseer will retrace his steps to Treasury Green and, after noticing, on his left, the side of the house, walk through the tunnel-like Treasury Passage to the Horse Guards Parade, he will obtain a glimpse of *another* house which stands back-to-back with, and in fact has long been part of, No 10. Taking into account the several additions and extensions made from time to time since the original house was built (late 17th century), and not forgetting the garden hidden by a high wall, it is possible to realise that the Prime Minister's residence is something more than the familiar three bed- and two reception-roomed domestic dwelling that it might seem to be.

No. 11, next door, accommodates the Chancellor of the Exchequer, while at No 12, recently rebuilt, is the Government Chief Whip. Originally a cul-de-sac, there is now a gateway and steps down to St James's Park at the west end of Downing Street, which would provide a useful alternative exit if required by a harassed Prime Minister.

The Foreign Office, with the Home Office and Commonwealth Relations Office, are now housed in the fine quadrangle of buildings enclosed by Whitehall, Downing Street, St James's Park, and King Charles Street. These were erected between 1868 and 1873 at a cost of £500,000 from the designs of Sir Gilbert Scott, in the Italian style. The courtyard, which is entered from either Downing Street or King Charles Street, is very ornate, and surrounding the windows of the third floor are numerous statues. Work on the demolition of the houses in Duke Street, next to St James's Park, and in King Charles Street, was commenced in August 1861, and the last brick of the old Foreign Office in Downing Street was removed in January 1862. It seems, however, that the clearing of the site for the new buildings proceeded in a very leisurely fashion, as the actual work of construction was not commenced until 1868.

In June of that year it was planned to build a new War Office on the site of the present Treasury and Dover House, so as to adjoin the Horse Guards. Under that scheme the new Treasury was to have been constructed on the site of the buildings now containing the Ministry of Housing and Local Government. King Street was to have been swept away entirely to make room for this great improvement and Parliament Street widened to 130 feet. It was also suggested at the time that St Margaret's Church should be removed to the west of the Victoria Tower in order to open up an uninterrupted view of Westminster Abbey. At that time the total cost of the new buildings, together with the large amount of ground to be acquired, was estimated at £3,322,000, against which it was said that a sum of £525,000 could be offset for the value of previously existing premises no longer required, thus reducing the net cost to £2,797,000.

This scheme failed to mature, possibly on account of its magnitude, and it was not until 1898, exactly thirty years later, that the second and larger instalment of this grand improvement was commenced. The huge island site enclosed by Parliament Street, King Charles Street, St James's Park, and Great George Street, was then cleared of its many streets and houses, and in 1900 a start was made on the construction of the buildings now housing the ministry of Housing and Local Government. These were designed by J. M. Brydon in the Renaissance style. The portion fronting Parliament Street was completed by 1907, but the extension to St James's Park, which involved the disappearance of Delahay Street and the former premises of the Institute of Civil Engineers in Great George Street, now removed to the opposite side of the road, was not completed until 1915. These buildings are connected with the Foreign and Commonwealth Relations Offices by an overhead bridge which crosses King Charles Street.

King Street, which ran parallel to its modern sister, Parliament Street, between it and St James's Park, was the ancient highway between the regions of the Court of Whitehall and Westminster Abbey, and was completely swallowed up in this great improvement. It extended from the Cockpit Gate in Whitehall, on the site of the office of the Privy Council, to Great George Street, and in former times was the residence of many distinguished personages because of its proximity to the Court and the Parliament House. Through this street Charles I was carried in a sedan chair on his way to Westminster Hall on the first and last days of his trial, and singularly enough Oliver Cromwell was himself a resident in King Street at the time of the execution of his sovereign. The length of King Street was halved by the construction of the Foreign and Colonial Offices and the remainder was obliterated in 1898 by the later improvements. Parliament Street was created after the burning of Whitehall Palace in order to provide a wider street to Westminster Abbey.

The east side of Parliament Street from Richmond Terrace to Bridge Street consists mainly of shops and business premises, including a branch Post office. Nearly opposite King Charles Street is Derby Gate, leading to New Scotland Yard which consists of two dignified turreted buildings somewhat resembling a Scottish baronial castle, and was designed by R. Norman Shaw in 1890. The main building, which is on the north side of Derby Gate, has been the head-quarters of the Metropolitan Police since 1891, but that on the south side of the street was added about 1912. The main building occupies the site upon which it was originally intended to build a large National Opera House. It had already been designed by Mr Francis H. Fowler, and the foundation-stone of the new building, which was to have been one-third larger than Covent Garden Theatre, had been laid by the Duke of Edinburgh on 16 December 1875. It was expected that the building would be completed by 1877, but this unfortunate enterprise languished for want of capital, and after the foundations had been erected the work was stopped for many years, until finally the new headquarters of the Metropolitan Police were built on this site. The remains of the foundations of the Opera House are still to be seen in the cellars of New Scotland Yard. To meet the urgent demand for increased accommodation a large annexe to Scotland Yard was in 1938 erected on the site between Richmond Terrace and the Victoria Embankment. The new building is a handsome structure of eight storeys with a façade of Portland stone with its main frontage to the Victoria Embankment. In February, 1967, the headquarters of the Metropolitan Police were transferred to Victoria Street, as recorded in our Fifteenth Walk. It now has the new Government Offices for its neighbour. The stone-fronted building in the Italian style at the south corner of Derby Gate and Parliament Street was built in 1866 for the Whitehall Club, but at present it is occupied by the new Welsh Office (Y Swyddfa Cymreig).

At the corner of Bridge Street and the Victoria Embankment is St Stephen's Club, largely resorted to by Members of Parliament. It was opened in January 1875 at a cost of £120,000, and was designed to accommodate 1,500 members. The building, which is much larger than required by its present membership, has recently been sold to the Ministry of Works, who intend to develop the site. The club, which has since moved to Queen Anne's Gate, had a subway to the Houses of Parliament and a bell to warn members of division. On the embank-ment, at the corner of Westminster Bridge, is a statue of Queen Boadicea in her war chariot, designed by Thomas Thornycroft in 1902.

Westminster Bridge, one of the widest and handsomest bridges in Europe, consists of seven low segmental arches supported on granite piers. The central arch has a span of 120 feet, the others of 114 feet. It is 1,160 feet long in all and 85 feet wide, with footways each 15 feet wide. It was erected at a cost of £250,000, and opened on Saturday 24 May 1862, and replaced an older stone bridge erected between 1738 and 1750. The new bridge is slightly lower down the river than was the old one. Vast sums of money, amounting within forty years to £500,000, had been spent upon repairs to the old bridge, which was taken down in 1861, whereas the break-up price realized on its sale was only £7,465.

The architect of the old Westminster Bridge was a naturalized Swiss subject named Labelye, and to this is perhaps to be attributed one of its special features, namely a domed octagonal recess over every pier, intended as a shelter against rough weather and a resting-place for wayfarers. However, in those days before the establishment of Sir Robert Peel's police, these recesses also afforded shelter to robbers and other dangerous characters, and thus twelve watchmen were needed at night-time to protect passengers crossing the bridge. It was erected partly out of money raised by public lotteries between 1737 and 1749 and partly by grants made by Parliament, and cost £390,000. Labelye asserted that the quantity of stone used in its construction was nearly double that employed in the building of St Paul's Cathedral. The first stone of the old bridge was laid by the Earl of Pembroke in 1739, and the last in 1747, but the opening of the bridge was retarded until 1750, on account of the sinking of one of the piers. It consisted of fifteen stone semi-circular arches, and was 1,160 feet in length and 43 feet wide.

After the removal of the old Westminster Bridge more than one of the piers gave way, and to stop the subsidence the roadway was closed in August 1846. The balustrades and heavy stone alcoves were then removed, the stonework stripped to the cornice, and the roadway lowered, thus lightening it of thirty thousand tons of weight. Timber palings were then erected at the sides and the bridge was reopened. In November 1846 it was definitely decided to pull down the old bridge, but not without the usual strong opposition from cranks and sentimentalists. Thus on 4 January 1847 a meeting of protest was held at the Literary Institution when a counter-proposal for a new bridge at Charing Cross was approved by the meeting. Looking back on the long-drawn-out opposition to the construction of a fine new Waterloo Bridge coupled with a similar though far more justifiable demand for a new Charing Cross Bridge, the fate of which remained in the balance for some ten years, it is possible to draw a most interesting parallel.

To provide a new approach to the new Westminster Bridge four houses on the south side of Bridge Street had to be removed in 1860, as well as a block of buildings on the Surrey side, after which that half of the bridge which had then been completed was thrown open for vehicular traffic. Foot-passengers continued to use the old bridge whilst the remainder of the work was being carried out, and a footway was built over the central arches to enable them to be removed. In 1864 the remainder of the houses on the south side of Bridge Street, in front of the Victoria Tower, were removed, and the existing garden laid out on that site.

When composing his famous sonnet on the old Westminster Bridge at day-break, Wordsworth wrote, 'Earth has not anything to show more fair'. But if the shabby Westminster of his day, which presented no special features of interest other than Westminster Abbey when viewed from the Thames, could thus command his admiration, what would the great poet have said to the wonderful transformation which has taken place? What would he have said to the superb view of the Houses of Parliament as seen from the new Westminster Bridge, ncluding the Victoria Tower, and the majestic sweep of new buildings beyond, which now line Millbank as far as Lambeth Bridge, with the Victoria Tower Gardens as a foreground? What would he have thought of the view down the river of the Victoria Embankment with the majestic pile of new Government Offices, Whitehall Court, and the white cliffs of the new Adelphi, Shell-Mex House and the Savoy, terminating with Somerset House in the background?

But it is not only from the river that the incomparable beauty of Westminster reveals itself. Its wide and handsome streets, open spaces, public and private buildings, and its many Government offices, whether viewed from Parliament Square, Whitehall, or St James Park, constitute a piece of urban scenery unsurpassed for beauty and magnificence in the whole world. Westminster has clothed itself in the mantle of majesty, and Vienna alone amongst the great cities of Europe can show such an imposing array of public buildings within so confined an area.

Travelled Londoners return from the Continent dazzled by the splendour of the Champs Elysées or the Place de la Concorde in Paris, and they are enchanted with the buildings and churches or Rome of Florence. Yet nothing quite so beautiful is to be seen in the other great capital cities as Westminster, though here the average Londoner regards it with comparative indifference. Only the Englishman is so blind to the beauties of his own capital and country. In 1940 when Britain was in danger of being invaded, three temporary wooden bridges were built across the Thames in case the permanent bridges were destroyed by bombing. One of these spanned the river between Horse Guards Avenue and the County Hall. It was thrown open to the public in 1944 but very few people ever used it. The other two were higher up the river, one at Millbank, opposite the Tate Gallery and the other opposite Battersea Park. They were both pulled down in 1948 and one of them now spans the Kafue River in Rhodesia.

We turn next to the Houses of Parliament. The rebuilding of this noble pile, following upon the destruction of the old Royal Palace of Westminster by fire on 16 October 1834, was the most important architectural work undertaken in this country since the rebuilding of St Paul's Cathedral. Designed by Sir Charles Barry, R.A. at a cost of over £3,000,000 the new Houses of Parliament cover an area of eight acres and are probably the largest Gothic edifice in the world. After the fire in 1834 considerable delay occurred in the rebuilding of the Houses of Parliament, for although the designs of Sir Charles Barry were selected in 1836 it was not until 27 April 1840 that the foundation-stone of the new edifice was laid.

The stone employed for the exterior of the building was a magnesian limestone from Anston in Yorkshire, which was selected in 1839 with great care by scientific commissioners from all the building stones of England. Unfortunately it proved unable to withstand the corroding effect of the London atmosphere and necessitated external repairs to the stonework of the Houses of Parliament, which were carried out between 1929 and 1939 at a cost of £1,000,000. Various Members of Parliament and collectors of souvenirs have acquired pieces of the old stonework as mementos.

The buildings have four principal fronts, that facing the river being 940 feet long, and the Clock Tower, completed in 1857, with Big Ben for its bell, is 40 feet square and 320 feet high. The edifice contains eleven open quadrangular courts, five hundred apartments, and eighteen official residences, besides the Royal State Apartments, the House of Commons, the House of Lords, and the Central Hall, and from start to finish occupied nineteen years in its construction, which was completed in 1857. The Victoria Tower is 75 feet square and 340 feet high, and its entrance archway to the House of Lords is 65 feet high. The chief entrance for the public to the Houses of Parliament is through Palace Yard and Westminster Hall, and up the broad flight of steps at the farther end into St Stephen's Hall. The new House of Lords was completed by Easter 1847, but the House of Commons was not completed until some time afterwards.

At first the drainage of the new Houses of Parliament was defective, and in October 1848 it was discovered that a main line of sewer passed through the whole length of the building, discharging its contents into the Thames at Westminster Bridge. When this sewer was entered the stench was so great that it extinguished the lamps carried by some of the party. An opening was then discovered in the crown of the sewers large enough to permit the passage of a man, and as the sewer was above the level of the floor of the vaults no difficulty was experienced in stepping out into the underground apartments of the Houses of Parliament. The deposit in some places was almost knee-deep and could only be waded through with difficulty, and was, in fact, one continuous cesspool. Surprise was felt that whereas special attention had been given to the ventilation of the Houses of Parliament, no notice had been taken of the offensive drainage below the new buildings.

On 10 May 1941, the debating chamber of the House of Commons was bombed in one of London's worst air raids when the building, including the Members' Lobby, was completely destroyed by fire. It has now been rebuilt at an estimated cost of £1,000,000 and was opened by the late King on 26 October 1950. The architects were Sir Giles Gilbert Scott and Mr Adrian Scott. Big Ben was damaged but its mechanism remained intact. At the suggestion of the late Sir Winston Churchill, the archway from the Members' Lobby into the Chamber, 'which was smitten in the blast of the explosion, and has acquired an appearance of antiquity that might not have been archieved by the hand of Time in centuries', has been preserved and is known as the Churchill Arch.

Westminster Hall, which escaped the fire at Westminster Palace, was rebuilt by Richard II in 1397, and contains a wide span of roof built of English oak having no central supports. The roof was also pierced by bombs in the same big air raid.

Turning to Parliament Square, which was the birthplace in London of the roundabout system of traffic, first introduced here in 1926, the dominating features of this open space are the Houses of Parliament on the east side, and Westminster Abbey on the south side, in front of which is St Margaret's Church. Being attached to the House of Commons, the Speaker and Members of Parliament attend service at this church upon special occasions. It was erected in the reign of Edward I, but has undergone many restorations. The north side of Parliament Square is overlooked by the Government offices in Great George Street, and on the west side by the Middlesex Guildhall, rebuilt in 1931 from the designs of J. S. Gibson, with a square tower in the centre. A shabby block of offices which until about 1938 stood on the west side of the square at the corner of Great George Street has been pulled down. This site was purchased at great expense by the Middlesex County Council for the enlargement of Parliament Square. This is adorned by statues of Lord Palmerston. the Earl of Derby, Sir Robert Peel, George Canning, Lord Beaconsfield, Abraham Lincoln and, more recently, Field Marshal Smuts. Near Westminster Hall is a statue of Cromwell by Hamo Thornycroft. Facing the north side of Broad Sanctuary stood the building of the Westminster Hospital, founded in 1720. It was erected in 1832, and was enlarged in 1925 by the addition of an extra storey. The hospital was removed in 1939 to its splendid new headquarters in St John's Gardens, Mill-bank, and the old building in Broad Sanctuary has now been pulled down and the site is at present waiting attention.

Westminster Abbey, or the Collegiate Church of St Peter, to give the Abbey its official title, was originally a Benedictine monastery. Here our kings and queens have been crowned from William the Conqueror to Queen Elizabeth II, and here many of them are buried, some with and others without monuments. Like all our great churches, the Abbey has been the growth of centuries. A church already existed here in the days of Sebert, King of the East Saxons, having been built about 605, and a new one was erected by Edward the Confessor about 1065. This stood for about two centuries, until Henry III decided to rebuilt it on a more magnificent scale. It was largely completed about 1269, when the new church was consecrated, but the erection of the nave was spread over more than two centuries. The last great structural addition to the fabric of the church was in the early part of the eighteenth century, when the two western towers, 225 feet high, were added by Hawksmoor, after their lower parts had been restored by Wren. The 900th anniversary of Westminster Abbey, which was consecrated on 28 December 1065, was celebrated by a programme of events which began on 28 December 1965 and continued throughout the following twelve months. There were special services of various kinds, in many of which other churches took part, programmes of orchestral and choral music and an exhibition, called 'One People', in the Chapter House. The permanent exhibition of the Wax Effigies, second Coronation Chair etc., in the Norman Undercroft, was augmented and the layout much improved for the occasion.

The external stonework of the Abbey having largely perished and fallen into a state of decay restoration work became imperative, and in 1923 the Dean of Westminster issued an appeal to the public for funds to meet the cost. The appeal met with an immediate response and a sum of about £150,000 was raised by public subscription, after which the work of repair was immediately carried out. A further appeal, to restore the fabric of the Abbey and endow the Abbey choir School, was launched by Mr Winston Churchill in January 1953. The response was such that the target of a million pounds was achieved by Empire Day 1954.

Adjoining the great west door of the Abbey is the Jerusalem Chamber, now the Chapter Room, and immediately behind is the College Hall of Westminster School. In front of the west door is the new Abbey Bookshop for historical and religious books, and the Sanctuary, with a granite column to the boys of Westminster School who died in the Crimea and the Indian Mutiny. Originally the precincts of the Abbey were walled, and King Street included part of the square. There was then a rookery of mean streets adjoining the Sanctuary, which although its privileges had been abolished, was still regarded as a refuge. Pigs ran about the churchyard and carters loaded their vans here.

In course of time wonderful improvements were carried out in this immediate locality. The Gothic houses at the entrance to Dean's Yard were erected in 1854 under the provisions of the Westminster Improvements Act, as the result of the clearing away of several small and mean streets which before 1851 occupied the space to the west of Westminster Abbey. The Act required that the new houses should be built upon an improved scale in a style suitable to the dignity of the neighbourhood of Westminster Abbey, the cost being defrayed out of the compensation paid on behalf of the improvements carried out in Westminster. There are altogether eight houses, one of which forms the entrance and the gate-tower to Dean's Yard. The Gatehouse gives one the impression of the whole forming one public building, but the architect obviated this as far as possible by making the houses on the western side of the gateway slightly different from those on the east side.

After passing through Dean's Yard we next come to Westminster School, one of the great public schools of England, which was founded by the first Elizabeth in 1560 and attached to the Collegiate Church of St Peter at Westminster. The College Hall, dating from the time of Edward III, is now used as the dining-room of the school, and the tables are said to be made of timber from ships of the Spanish Armada. During the second World War the school was evacuated to Worcestershire. The College Hall was destroyed in the fire-raid of 10 May 1941 and the College Dormitory, designed by Sir Christopher Wren, was also gutted that same night. The Busby Library had already been destroyed in 1940.

In 1860 much complaint was levelled against the want of repair, comfort, and convenience at Westminster School, and a Committee of Investigation reported in favour of carrying out immediate improvements. At that time it was proposed to move the school to the country, but it was found that the sale of the old buildings would not realize so large a sum as had been anticipated by the Dean and Chapter. In June 1860 a great meeting was held in the Jerusalem Chamber of Westminster Abbey to consider this proposal, and amongst those present were the Archbishop of York, the Marquess of Landsdowne, the Marquess of Westminster, and the Dean of Westminster. A long discussion took place and the Archbishop of York was in favour of the removal of the school, but the Marquess of Westminster was against the proposal. The Marquess of Lansdowne, whilst favouring its removal, was dubious as to the wisdom of taking any step in the dark without further information. The Dean and Chapter of Westminster preferred to express no opinion on the subject.

A walk through Dean's Yard along Great College Street will bring us to Abingdon Street and its continuation south, known as Millbank. Abingdon Street before the second World War consisted of one long terrace of shabby Georgian houses partly facing the west front of the Houses of Parliament and partly overlooking the Victoria Tower Gardens, and was a magnificent specimen of real English ugliness. It was the only surviving relic of unsightly property in this immediate neighbourhood. Its appearance suggested the dustman sitting on the doorstep of the nobleman's mansion. It was largely inhabited by Members of Parliament on account of its convenient situation opposite the House. Most of the houses in Abingdon Street were damaged in the blitz and have since been pulled down and the space has been laid out with grassy lawns, now known as Abingdon Street Garden and provides a splendid setting for the ancient Jewel Tower; below is an Underground car park. The only house remaining is No 7, the fine Georgian house faced with Bath stone which stands on the corner of Old Palace Yard. In front of it now stands the statue erected to the memory of King George V, which was unveiled in 1948.

Opposite the Victoria Tower in Abingdon Street is the recently restored Jewel Tower. Built in 1365-6 to provide a treasury for the jewels and vessels of gold and silver belonging to Edward III, it is the only surviving building of the ancient private palace of the Kings of England. It is surrounded by an attractive fourteenth century moat, the existence of which was wholly unsuspected, for it had been filled in before 1700 and afterwards built over. The moat has been well stocked with rainbow trout; which caused a delighted cockney visitor to exclaim 'Blimey! rainbow trout in the middle of London—*you could win bets on that!*'

Millbank, formerly a poor street, is now lined by stately buildings extending from Great College Street to Lambeth Bridge, and overlooks the new Victoria Tower Gardens, which were laid out in 1912-13. Of late years poverty has been banished from this immediate locality, though as recently as 1930 slums could still be found in Marsham Street, a short distance away, and overcrowding was still said to prevail in the poorer districts of Westminster. Amongst the new buildings overlooking the Victoria Tower Gardens are Millbank House, Westminster House, containing the offices of the British-American Tobacco Company, Imperial Chemical House at the east corner of Horseferry Road, and Thames House on the south side of Horseferry Road, consisting of two blocks of buildings joined by an overhead bridge across Page Street.

Both Imperial Chemical House and Thames House were designed by Sir Frank Baines, F.R.I.B.A. These two great buildings were erected within the short period of three years, between 1929 and 1931. In January 1928 The Thames overflowed its banks between Vauxhall and Westminster, bursting the old embankment wall near the Tate Gallery and flooding the basement of the nearby houses. The present new embankment wall was completed in 1929. A Londoner who revisited his native city after an absence of ten years could scarcely fail to be astonished by the startling transformation which has taken place in the Millbank quarter of Westminster, once a large slum area and a reproach to the wealthy City of Westminster. Here the entire quarter centred round Millbank, Horseferry Road, Marsham Street and Page Street has been rebuilt. This is mainly due to the courage and foresight of Associated London Properties Limited, who purchased eight and a half acres of what was then slums and derelict property. On this site in place of workmen's cottages damaged by the Thames floods of 1928 have been erected magnificent residential and office buildings equal to any to be found elsewhere in London. Credit must also be given to the architects, Messrs Bennett & Son, who designed nearly all of these imposing buildings, as well as to Sir Robert McAlpine & Sons, the principal contractors for this large scheme of redevelopment on the Millbank Estate. In its general appearance the new Westminster is unlike any other quarter of London for it consists almost entirely of lofty buildings more suggestive of some modern quarter of Paris.

Horseferry Road has been widened from the south side to nearly double its former width and is already one of the finest streets in London. It takes its name from a ferry which in olden times forded the Thames opposite Lambeth Palace. On the south side is the new Westminster Hospital — erected at a cost of £700,000 — and comprising two ten-storeyed buildings overlooking both the east and west sides of St John's Gardens. These are faced with red brick with stone dressings and were designed by Messrs Adams, Holden, and Pearson, F.R.I.B.A. The foundation-stone was laid by the Duke of Windsor when Prince of Wales on 26 June 1935. To secure this splendid site the Westminster Hospital had to raise the sum of £100,000 — which they did within the short period of five months. It has for its neighbour Great Westminster House, a fine block of shops and offices seven storeys high erected in 1937. In Marsham Street, which has also been considerably widened, now stands Westminster Gardens, a ten-storeyed block of luxury flats erected in 1935, the modern equivalent of the stately homes of England. Facing it on the opposite side of Marsham Street is a similar building called Marsham Court. Cleland House, a handsome office building of ten storeys, stands on the corner of Page Street and John Islip Street. In this latter is Abell House completed in 1940 and at present occupied by the Ministry of Works. In Page Street, opposite the Westminster Hospital, is Neville House which also faces St John's Gardens and was erected in 1938. Within this building is incorporated the Paviors Arms Tavern, the elm panelling for which was obtained from the piles of the old Waterloo Bridge and had been under water for 120 years.

The western end of Page Street contains several large blocks of artisan dwellings erected by the Westminster City Council between 1930 and 1934. These are six storeys high and faced with yellow brick and concrete. Many of these flats have balconies which overlook wide courtyards used as children's playgrounds. Open spaces, hitherto considered impossible in the heart of London, have also been created around Westminster Gardens, Marsham Court, Neville House,

Cleland House and Great Westminster House. Practically all the vacant sites in the Millbank quarter of Westminster are covered with new buildings and all accommodation of both offices and residential flats was let as fast as it was completed. Being completely fire-resisting, direct hits by high-explosive bombs have done little more than damage those parts of the buildings with which they came in contact. Thus the total collapse of Thames House, Cleland House and Romney House which were heavily blitzed in April 1941 and in 1944 proved almost impossible. Romney House is a huge block of offices with its upper floors zoned back from the pavement which has long frontages to both Marsham Street and Tufton Street.

In Smith Square is Transport House, headquarters of the Transport and General Worker's Union, and also of the Labour Party. The Conservative Party Central Office is at No 32, and at No 36 in the same square are the headquarters of the Liberal Party.

> *And Party leaders you might meet*
> *In twos and threes in every street*
> *Maintaining, with no little heat,*
> *Their various opinions.*

Nearby are Lord North Street, Cowley Street and Barton Street—the latter bearing the date 1722—all containing a number of extremely well-preserved Georgian houses.

Smith Square is almost filled by the unusual Church of St John the Evangelist, the second of Queen Anne's 50 churches, burnt out in 1941, though the walls with a large tower at each corner, still remain. Built in 1728 to the design of Thomas Archer, it is believed that the four towers were added to counteract a tendency to sink into the marshy soil.

Ever since Charles Dickens (who could always produce an amusing description of *anything*) described it as a 'petrified monster, frightful and gigantic, on its back with its legs in the air', the church has been the object of superficial criticism; it is therefore encouraging to note that it is now being restored under the auspices of 'The Friends of St John's'.

Horseferry Road, where the former Gas, Light and Coke Company had its headquarters, forms the western approach to the new Lambeth Bridge, which was formally opened by King George V on 19 July 1932. The old suspension bridge, which was pulled down in 1929, was a very tawdry-looking structure opened on 10 November 1862 and erected by a private company at the very small cost of £40,000, including the purchase of the land. Reputed to have been the cheapest and the ugliest bridge ever built, it was designed by Mr Peter Barlow and was only wide enough to accommodate two lines of traffic. For many years prior to its demolition it had been closed to vehicles and was only available to pedestrians. One of the largest office buildings in Europe now occupies the four acre site in Horseferry Road, where the old Gas, Light & Coke Company formerly stood. This is a new group of Government offices, consisting of three 20-storey tower blocks 200 feet high, standing on a podium, with a basement and sub-basement. An ultra-modern speciality of the construction was that all the pre-cast concrete units were made *on the site* – a method known as 'industrialised building'.

The new Lambeth Bridge, crowned on the north side of the river by the Thames Houses and Imperial Chemical House on the two corners of Horseferry Road, and by Lambeth Bridge House and St Mary's Church on the south bank, now affords a fine view from the river almost rivalling that of Westminster Bridge in its beauty. The roadway is forty feet wide and the footpaths fifteen feet. When viewed from the centre of Lambeth Bridge the panorama looking down the Thames presents one of the finest urban riverside vistas in Europe. In the foreground are the Houses of Parliament, Westminster Abbey, the Victoria Tower Gardens and St Thomas's Hospital whilst in the background can be seen the County Hall, the new Adelphi and the Shell-Mex Building, the Savoy Hotel, Brettenham House and Bush House with the Central Hall of the Royal Courts of Justice closing the field of view as the river ends its dramatic northward progress through Westminster and turns at Waterloo Bridge to resume its easterly course.

Returning to Millbank, the Millbank Tower stands between Thorney Street and the Military Hospital. On part of this site stood the stables (later the garage) of the Speaker of the House of Commons. The gateway was decorated with the traditional horse's head and bore the date 1864 – though the gate was said to be that of the old Millbank Prison, mentioned below. On this site, with a frontage of 215 yards, has been erected a group of buildings, the outstanding feature of which is the 390-foot tower block for Vickers Ltd. This has 31 floors and a basement and, until the Post Office Tower appeared in Tottenham Court Road, was the highest building in the country. It has a system of automatic cruising lifts continuously in action and is fully air-conditioned and completely sealed off from outside, the temperature within varying on the different sides of the tower according to the direction of the sun. Additional buildings include a three-level car park with accommodation for 250 cars and an eleven-storey block of flats-specified by the Westminster City Council – to replace houses demolished. The architect of this undertaking is Mr Ronald Ward, F.R.I.B.A. and it was completed in 1963.

Continuing our walk along Millbank past the Queen Alexandra Military Hospital, we next come to the Tate Gallery, opened on 16 August 1897, and which owes its existence to the munificence of Sir Henry Tate, who not only presented the nation with a collection of pictures valued at £75,000, but contributed £80,000 towards the cost of erecting the gallery to house them. A new Turner wing was added to the building in 1910. The Tate Gallery occupies a part of the site of the old Millbank Prison erected in 1816 on ground bought from the Marquess of Salisbury. It resembled a fortress and was designed by Jeremy Bentham, and is said to have cost £500,000. The external walls formed an irregular octagon, which enclosed over sixteen acres of land, and the building contained accommodation for 1,120 prisoners. It was closed on 6 November 1890 and pulled down shortly after.

In June 1888 the Home Office invited the Metropolitan Board of Works to purchase the site of the Millbank Prison for the erection of artisans' dwellings, but the Board rejected the proposal on account of the expense. When the London County Council superseded the old Metropolitan Board of Works in 1889, the Home Secretary renewed his offer made in the previous year. After inspecting the site, which covered between twenty-two and twenty-three acres, the London County Council found that owing to the nature of the subsoil, which was probably a marsh when originally purchased by the Government in 1799, heavy expense would be incurred in building upon this land.

The prison itself had been built upon piles, and before the site could be laid out for building purposes it had to be raised several feet in order to give a proper fall to the drains. The Government's valuer assessed the site at £5,500 per acre, including the river frontage, but the Council made an offer for eight acres of the land at £3,000 per acre. This was rejected by the Home Secretary in April 1891, but another invitation was issued by the Treasury in November 1892 to negotiate for the purchase of this land, with the result that the Council finally agreed to pay £2,500 per acre for the back portion of the Millbank site. Several large blocks of dwellings were then erected, with accommodation for 3,700 persons. These proved very useful to the Council at a later date, when they had to provide alternative accommodation for 1,500 persons displaced by the Strand-to-Holborn improvements of 1900. At the present day many people of good position inhabit these blocks of dwellings because of their excellent situation in the heart of London.

The principal blocks are situated in Dundonald Street, now renamed John Islip Street, at the back of the Tate Gallery and have been named after celebrated artists. John Islip Street leads into Marsham Street, formerly a poor neighbourhood, typical of the Westminster of a century ago before it became the beautiful city of the present day. Before its redevelopment Marsham Street, despite its shabby appearance, still afforded a picturesque contrast to the new splendour of Millbank, only a few yards away, especially when it was enlivened by its busy costers' stalls. Marsham Street is continued at its northern end by Great Smith Street, which of late years has developed into a first-class thoroughfare. It contains the Westminster public baths, Church House, a Tudor building by Sir Reginald Blomfield, R.A., and one of the four public libraries owned by the City Council. It also contains the Sanctuary Buildings, a large eight-storeyed block of offices at the corner of Victoria Street, erected in 1920. On the east side is the new Church House which had just been rebuilt before the last war and was unfortunately badly damaged in the blitz. It is an immense building of eight storeys faced with red brick and also has frontages to Little Smith Street, Tufton Street, and Dean's Yard.

Fifteenth Walk

Parliament Square, Victoria Street, Broadway, Tothill Street, Westminster Cathedral, Victoria Station, South Belgravia, Buckingham Palace Road, Birdcage Walk

A century and a quarter ago the garden space known as Parliament Square was covered by a block of buildings which extended from Great George Street to St Margaret's Church, and one side of which formed a part of the now defunct King Street. Very little information is available regarding the exact period when this great improvement was carried out, but this site appears to have been cleared of its former buildings about the time when a start had been made upon the new Houses of Parliament. The removal of other buildings next to Westminster Abbey and also in Bridge Street enabled this open space to be considerably enlarged some years later.

Victoria Street, opening into Broad Sanctuary and Parliament Square, was commenced in 1845 and was seven years in course of construction, being opened to the public on 6 August 1851. Victoria Street owes its origin to the zeal of Sir Edwin Pearson and the Commissioners of the Westminster Improvements, as well as to the skill of the architect, Mr Henry Ashton. With the exception of Regent Street, none of the great metropolitan street improvements carried out in London up to that time could invite comparison with the future possibilities of Victoria Street, Westminster. When first opened it was one of the sights of London, if only by its contrast to the narrow streets and alleys through which it was driven, and the necessity for such a thoroughfare was obvious at a glance. It opened up a magnificent new vista of Westminster Abbey and the new Houses of Parliament.

The area of the district affected by the construction of Victoria Street was about four hundred acres, containing between three thousand and four thousand houses, and the first labour of the Commissioners after clearing away the houses was the construction of deep and efficient drainage for the surrounding houses. This was especially necessary on account of this district having been formed by deposits from the Thames and certain small rivulets which once formed Thorney Island. This low-lying district is often considerably below the level of the Thames at high water, so that the drainage of an extensive portion of this land was merely on the surface until after the construction of this new street. Victoria Street is over a thousand yards long and eighty feet wide, but the formation of six other streets and the lines of sewers, some two miles in length, necessitated the laying of about three miles of new drains. The principal of the new streets was James Street, now Buckingham Gate, connecting Victoria Street with Birdcage Walk and Buckingham Palace. This street had to be raised seven feet above its former level.

The Act of Parliament for the construction of Victoria Street was passed in 1845. Under this Act the Commissioners, the Government, and the parishes of St Margaret's and St John's undertook jointly to furnish money up to the sum of £150,000, but the entire work eventually cost £350,000, including the purchase of the frontages to Victoria Street.

The first houses to be pulled down were at the south corner of Tothill Street where Victoria Street actually commences. Several sinks of iniquity and vice, including the low houses in the Almonry, Orchard Street, Duck Lane, New Pye Street, and part of Old Pye Street as far as Strutton Ground, were then demolished. Thence the course of Victoria Street was by Woods's Brewery in Artillery Place, through Palmer's Village to the north-west side of the Westminster Bridewell or Tothill Fields Prison, terminating in Shaftesbury Terrace, now forming that part of Victoria Street opposite the Underground railway station.

One of the most celebrated houses to be pulled down was Caxton's house, then in the Almonry, on the site of the present Abbey House, formerly the Westminster Palace Hotel. Here the Abbot of Westminster permitted Caxton to set up his press about the year 1476 or 1477. Another relic which was removed was the Pest Houses or Five Chimneys abutting on the Vauxhall Bridge Road. These were used as homes for poor people affected by the pestilence, and were built in 1644, some twenty years before the Great Plague. Early in the eighteenth century they were converted into almshouses.

Considerable delay was experienced in carrying out the Victoria Street and adjacent improvements, and this became a source of grievance to the inhabitants, who complained of the injury to their trade. As a result of this annoyance they formed a society to protect their interests. In January 1849 the Commissioners obtained possession of the houses between Pye Street, Pear Street, and the Broadway and Artillery Row, near Strutton Ground, which were then evacuated and demolished immediately. Shortly afterwards St Margaret's Workhouse was also pulled down.

On 6 August 1851 Victoria Street was formally declared open by Sir Edwin Pearson, accompanied by Mr Foster Brown, the High Constable of Westminster, the Commissioners of the Westminster Improvements, Mr Hunt, surveyor to the Dean and Chapter of Westminster, and Sir James Pennethorne, surveyor to the Woods and Forests Office.

In July 1853 the Committee of the House of Lords sanctioned a Bill for the Westminster Improvements with the object of carrying out the further improvement of Victoria Street. A mass of houses adjoining the east end of Victoria

Street was then removed, and that portion of the street widened through to Broad Sanctuary. At the same time Francis Street was widened and opened into Victoria Street and Vauxhall Bridge Road, and the Westminster Chambers were then erected at the eastern end of Victoria Street on the south side. This was an extensive block of buildings between Great Smith Street and Orchard Street with a frontage of about 450 feet and containing about five hundred rooms. Here the India office had its temporary quarters until 1866, prior to the construction of the present buildings in Whitehall. The Westminster Chambers were bombed in the air raids of 1940 and the whole block has now been demolished and occupying this site of 327,000 sq. ft is the new ten-storey office block completed in 1964 to the design of Ronald Fielding, F.R.I.B.A., which has accommodation for 2,000 staff and is equipped with 22 lifts and ample garage space. It extends from Great Smith Street to Abbey Orchard Street and is at present the only new building on the south side of Victoria Street; the remainder, with the exception of the Army and Navy Stores and many of the smaller shops which have been modernised, date from the sixties of the last century and are now largely commercial offices above and shops below.

These were arranged as dwellings containing suites of apartments on each storey varying in accommodation from three to as many as twenty-two rooms, but averaging from eight to fifteen each, including domestic offices. They were built in the style of those in Paris and other Continental cities, and not unlike blocks of flats then already existing in Edinburgh and Glasgow. These buildings are six storeys high, and were so popular that they were occupied as fast as they were completed by families in very comfortable circumstances, including Members of Parliament. The domestic economy which they afforded in servants was quite a novelty of that now remote period, especially as these buildings were heated by hot water in place of coal fires.

The introduction of this class of dwelling into the metropolis was due to the enterprise of Mr Mackenzie, who was very successful in making them known to the public. They were designed by Mr Ashton.

About 1905 a great change came over this end of Victoria Street, and the whole of the west end of this thoroughfare is now lined with rows of high-class shops.

We now cross to the north side of Victoria Street, where, in 1860 the Westminster Palace Hotel was erected at the corner of Victoria Street and Tothill Street, with a view to providing hotel accommodation for Members of Parliament, as well as foreign and provincial visitors frequenting the law courts, which were then centred in Westminster. With a view to constructing a thoroughly up-to-date hotel, Messrs W. and A. Moseley, the architects, were commissioned to visit various foreign hotels. At that time London was stated to be inferior in hotel accommodation to every great capital city in Europe with the exception of Constantinople. The Westminster Palace Hotel, which contained four hundred rooms, was then the most luxurious in the metropolis, and the first really fine one to be constructed. During its erection, in May 1859, an upper stage of the scaffolding collapsed, killing five men and injuring eight others.

This hotel was acquired during the first World War by the National Liberal Club to replace their quarters in Whitehall Court, which had been requisitioned for Government service. After the war, when the National Liberal Club had vacated the Westminster Palace Hotel, that large building was renovated and converted into shops and offices, and has been renamed Abbey House.

Close to the Westminster Palace Hotel formerly stood the Oriental Turkish Baths, a fine building with a Corinthian portico, erected in 1862 by a number of Irish gentlemen who formed a limited company for the purpose of opening Turkish baths, then quite recently introduced into England. A portion of the building contained baths for ladies. The Oriental Baths have long since been demolished, and their site occupied by tall blocks of offices and flats.

On the north side of Tothill Street, opposite Abbey House, is the Wesleyan Central Hall, a monumental building designed by Lanchester and Rickards in the Renaissance style at a cost of £250,000, and used not only for religious services but for political and other conferences, as well as concerts and exhibitions. It possesses the third largest dome in London, being exceeded only by those of St Paul's Cathedral and the British Museum Reading Room. It has a diameter of 90 feet and the height to the lantern is 220 feet. On a portion of the ground floor is a branch of the Midland Bank. The ornamental towers of this building are still lacking because of the objection of the Westminster Hospital in former years to the diminution of its lights. Now that the Hospital has vacated its former building in Broad Sanctuary this difficulty no longer exists.

On the site of the Wesleyan Central Hall, and covering the whole of the north side of Tothill Street, previously stood the Westminster Aquarium and the adjoining Imperial Theatre, erected in 1875. The idea of establishing a grand aquarium in the metropolis was that of Mr W. W. Robertson, who commissioned Mr Bedborough, the architect, to prepare the plans. The first stone was laid by Mrs Bedborough, wife of the architect, in February 1875. The site, acquired at a cost of £80,000, covered an area of two and a half acres, and the contract for the building was undertaken by Messrs Lucas Brothers for the sum of £88,000. It was constructed of red Fareham brick, with Portland and Bath stone dressings elaborately carved. The length of the building was 600 feet, and the front hall at the east end was 85 feet wide and 140 feet in depth. The winter garden was 400 feet long and 66 feet wide and capable of accommodating 2,500 persons. The central avenue of the Aquarium was adorned by fine groups of sculpture, together with a fountain and a variety of exotic plants. The building was opened on 22 January 1876 by the Duke of Edinburgh, and it was claimed that in no other similar establishment in the world could so many different sights be seen.

Despite these attractions, the Aquarium only enjoyed an existence of a quarter of a century, having been demolished in 1902. It shared the fate of many other similar establishments, for it was far too large and unwieldy and much too expensive to be run as a paying concern, with the result that it degenerated into a state of decay and neglect. The Imperial Theatre, which adjoined the west end of the Aquarium, was leased during the concluding years of its existence to

Lily Langtry, and this brought it more into popularity with the London public than had hitherto been the case.

On the remaining portion of the Aquarium site now stands an immense block of buildings known as Caxton House, together with the adjoining Portland House, and these buildings are separated from the new Wesleyan Central Hall by a small thoroughfare called Matthew Parker Street. The entire north side of Tothill Street is now lined by modern structures. At the west end of Tothill Street is the Broadway, which leads back again into Victoria Street past the churchyard of the former Christ Church, Westminster, designed by Ambrose Poynter and erected in 1843. This stood on the site of an old chapel founded in the time of Charles I, which had previously been surrounded by poverty, sheds, hovels, and gin-palaces. The garden was once a burial-ground and amongst those interred here was Colonel Blood, who attempted to raid the Crown Jewels. The style of the church was Gothic and it was originally intended to crown its tower with a spire two hundred feet high. Like so many others this church was destroyed in the blitz and its remains have now been completely cleared away. On part of this site a new building for the General Post Office has been erected; it includes a new automatic telephone exchange, a branch Post Office and a Cable and Wireless Office.

Orchard Street, now Abbey Orchard Street, on the opposite side of Victoria Street, originally extended across the site of that thoroughfare into Broadway, the southern portion of which was then called Great Chapel Street. So many slums, courts, alleys, and nests of poverty and vice were swept away in 1845 for the construction of Victoria Street that it is difficult to convey a correct idea of the topography of this neighbourhood as it appeared before that time.

Orchard Street contained one of the residences of Oliver Cromwell, as well as some of the oldest houses in Westminster, and in former times Palmer's Village, which was situated close to the site of Christ Church and Buckingham Gate, was the seat of gentlemen's country houses. In James Street, which has been renamed Buckingham Gate, stood the almshouses of Lady Dacre, the Foundress of Emanuel Hospital, which she bequeathed to the City of Westminster, including the estate of Palmer's Village, which comprised an area of between two and three acres of ground. Though the almshouses have gone, Emanuel School still flourishes at Wandsworth Common, whither it was removed in 1883.

Palmer's Village, which now survives in Palmer Street, was named after the Reverend James Palmer, who here founded almshouses in 1654 for twelve poor persons and a school for twenty boys, known as the Black Coat School, under the parochial authorities. In 1881 the almshouses were re-erected in Rochester Row, an attractive creeper-covered red-brick group of buildings opposite St Stephen's Church. Another benefactor, Mr Nicholas Butler, founded two almshouses for 'Two of the Most Ancient Couples of Best Report' (1675). At the dawn of the nineteenth century, Palmer's Village boasted a village green, upon which the maypole was annually set up, and there was also an old wayside inn called the Prince of Orange. For a number of years before its demolition,

Palmer's Village was occupied as small tenements for working people, but in February 1851 twenty-seven of its houses were disposed of by auction by the Westminster Improvements Commissioners to make room for the construction of the west end of Victoria Street. The Roman Catholic authorities then made overtures for a large portion of this ground for the purpose of erecting a new cathedral, but their application was rejected.

The east side of Broadway overlooks the garden of Christ Church and is lined by large blocks of shops and offices, nine storeys high. That on the corner of Victoria Street contains a branch of Lloyds Bank. On the west side is St James's Park Station, above which is the new headquarters of London Transport, a twelve-storeyed building designed by Mr Charles Holden and completed in 1929. The upper floors are zoned back from the street, and the tower, which forms a prominent landmark when viewed from St James's Park, is in normal times flood-lit at night. The London Transport Board originated in the amalgamation in 1907 of the Metropolitan District Railway, parent line of the Underground group, and the tube railways. In that year Albert Stanley, who afterwards became Lord Ashfield, came to London from Detroit, U.S.A., as general manager of the London Underground Railways. Born at Derby on 8 November 1874, as a child he went with his parents to Detroit, U.S.A. There his first job was as messenger in the Detroit City Street Railway Company. At twenty he controlled the entire tramway system at a salary of £1,000 a year. In 1910 the Underground Group bought out all the separate omnibus companies except Messrs Tillings In that year the remaining horsebuses were taken off the London streets and replaced by motor-buses. In 1914, at the age of forty, Albert Stanley was knighted and during the first World War became President of the Board of Trade from 1916 to 1919. In 1920 he was raised to the peerage and returned to the Underground group, having become its chairman in 1919. Until about 1910 the management of London's buses centred around the General and Tilling groups and the earlier gaiety of the various colours gave way to a uniform red and grey, except for the 'British' route which ran from Pimlico to Hampstead, and whose fleet was a bright green and cream.

About 1920 a group of ex-service men, however, began a small fleet of modern buses in chocolate and cream — the motto 'Ubique' suggested they were old gunners — which were soon dubbed 'pirates' by the witty Cockney. London was soon lively with the Leyland 'City' buses in tan and cream, 'Pickup' in red and white, the blue 'Admirals' and silver 'Timpsons' to mention but a few. To meet this competition the older companies threw every bus on to the busiest routes and chaos soon resulted. On 1 July 1933, after protracted negotiations, the London Passenger Transport Board came into being, with Lord Ashfield as its first Chairman, and every vehicle bore the one uniform of 'General' red. The present organisation is known as the London Transport Executive which assumed control on 1 January 1948 and consists of a Chairman, vice-chairman and five members. London Transport serves an area of 2,000 square miles within a radius of approximately 25 miles of Charing Cross, including certain districts outside this area. To serve the needs of this area and to cater for over nine million passenger journeys a day, 8,300 buses and coaches, and nearly 4,200 railway vehicles are in use. The Executive has over 74,000 employees and its annual operating expenses amount to £93 millions.

Today London Transport is building the first underground tube railway across the centre of London for over 50 years. Called the Victoria Line, it will run for ten and a half miles from Victoria through the heart of the West End out to densely populated Tottenham and Walthamstow in the north-east suburbs. Of the 12 stations on the new route, 11 are existing important 'interchange' stations that will require extensive reconstruction. The line is estimated to cost £56 million to build and equip, including rolling stock. Begun in 1962, it is hoped to open the new railway in sections, starting at the end of 1968, and as a result, some alleviation of London's ever-growing traffic congestion is anticipated.

In Tothill Street is the newly-erected Broadway House, another lofty block of offices, and farther along at the corner of Queen Anne's Gate and Petty France is the huge brick pile known as Queen Anne's Mansions. This building, 180 feet high, was, when erected in 1884, the tallest in London, and was modelled on the American skyscraper. Twelve storeys high, it was erected before the passing of the London Building Act, which severely restricted the height of buildings; but that is now ancient history and today, the sky seems to be the limit. Queen Anne's Mansions are faced with yellow brick turned black with the dirt of ages, without any external decoration, and for real ugliness are unsurpassed by any other great building in all London. It was hit by a bomb in the earlier raids of 1940 when a small section of the side fronting Petty France was demolished from top to bottom as though it had been cut clean away with a knife. The rest of the building escaped damage.

In Caxton Street, formerly known as Little Chapel Street, is St Ermin's Mansions, approached by a courtyard. It is a seven-storeyed building containing flats and a restaurant on the ground floor, and is attached to the St Ermin's Hotel, much frequented by American visitors to London. After having been requisitioned during the first World War, it remained empty for several years until 1927, when it was converted into flats. Further along Caxton Street is the red-brick Caxton Hall, formerly the Westminster Town Hall, now used for political meetings, social functions, offices, and kindred uses, while on the south side is the charming little red-brick building (attributed to Sir Christopher Wren) with the figure of a schoolboy standing over the porch and an inscription below 'The Blew Coat School, built in the year 1709'. On the wall at the back, facing Brewers' Green, is a large painting of a similar boy, and, 'This School founded in 1688'. It is now National Trust property. At the corner of Victoria Street and Palmer Street, facing the west side of the garden of Christ Church, is Windsor House, another large block of shops and offices. It was formerly the Windsor Hotel, and has a very decorative entrance hall with marble pillars and statuary; the former ballroom, also rather ornate, is now occupied by Lloyds Bank. That

Westminster should thus have lost nearly all of its great hotels seems a pity, having regard to their convenient situation in this important quarter of the metropolis.

Across the way on the south side of Victoria Street, leading to Horseferry Road, is Strutton Ground, a street market that conveys a good idea of what the whole of this district was like not much more than a century ago. Artillery Mansions, a large block of service flats in Victoria Street, run on the lines of a private hotel, is very popular with Londoners, and is situated between Strutton Ground and Artillery Place.

Although now one of London's finest thoroughfares, Victoria Street, like Kingsway and Regent Street, was at first a failure. With its continuous rows of tall buildings, it is perhaps the most Continental-looking street in London, but some people consider that this spoils its appearance by making it appear narrow. For many years Victoria Street remained devoid of many buildings, but in 1868 large blocks were erected on the north side between Palace Street and Allington Street. These have now gone.

An increased impetus was given to building by the opening in 1860 of Victoria Station, making it one of the leading streets of the metropolis.

In 1861 Mr Train, an American citizen, was permitted to lay down one of his tramway lines along Victoria Street from Westminster Abbey to Pimlico. Such lines had been working successfully in the United States for years when Mr Train undertook to introduce them into England and on the Continent of Europe. He obtained leave to construct these routes experimentally. The track consisted of a step rail, which could only be crossed at right angles by ordinary vehicles at the expense of much jolting and diagonally only with great difficulty. A similar result was avoided at Birkenhead, where Mr Train inaugurated the first tramway service in England, by substituting flat grooved rails for the step ones. The doubledeck cars which ran every five minutes along Victoria Street held twenty-four people inside and the same number outside and were crowded every journey. But as the rails were raised above the ground, they proved an insufferable nuisance to the cross-traffic. Owners of carriages objected strenuously, with the result that Mr Train was ordered to remove his tramways by 4 October 1861, after a very brief term of existence. Naturally he was very angry at thus getting badly treated, to the great detriment of his banking account, and accordingly conceived an animus against England which nothing could assuage.

Another factor which contributed largely to the prosperity of Victoria Street was the coming of the Army and Navy Stores in 1872. They were originally intended for the use of the members of the united services and their families, but membership tickets are now no longer required and the stores are open to the general public. The shop-fronts of the Army and Navy Stores in Victoria Street were constructed in 1924, and, together with the wing at the corner of Francis Street, were designed by Sir Aston Webb, R.A.

On the island site bounded by Dacre Street, Victoria Street and Broadway, is the new office building, at first known as Ten Broadway, but which has been New

Scotland Yard since February 1967 when the headquarters of the Metropolitan Police moved in from their old Norman Shaw premises on the Victoria Embankment and, since there is no specific geographical location of that name, brought the world-famous address with them. The new building, of reinforced concrete clad with gray granite slabs, covers an area of 74,000 square feet and consists of three blocks: the 20-storey tower, which is 225 feet high, a lower block of nine storeys fronting Victoria Street and a 'link' block of seven storeys which joins the other two. So 'New Scotland Yard, Broadway S.W.1', where about 2,700 people are employed, will provide modern and efficient accommodation for the many important department snecessary for the administration of a Metropolitan Police District that covers $785\frac{1}{2}$ square miles.

Buckingham Gate, originally called James Street, on the north side of Victoria Street, leads to Birdcage Walk and Buckingham Palace. In this street is a huge block of flats on the west side called St James's Court, erected in 1897, which is approached through a spacious courtyard. On the opposite side are some Peabody dwellings which have been converted into flats and offices, and renamed Chandos House. Here also are the drill-halls of the Queen's Royal Rifles and the London Scottish Territorials, in the latter of which the inquiry into the loss of the Titanic in 1912 was held. Buckingham Gate also contains the Westminster Chapel of the Congregationalists, some old-fashioned houses on the west side near Birdcage Walk, and a large eight-storeyed block of flats erected in 1935. Petty France, leading to Tothill Street, was renamed York Street early in the last century, but some years ago its original title was restored to it by the London County Council.

At the junction of Buckingham Gate with Petty France is the showy Wellington House, built in 1908. In red and yellow terra cotta with Art Nouveau decoration, it has six little statuettes of Hood, George IV, Nelson, Wellington, Heathfield and Picton.

In Ashley Gardens, on the south side of Victoria Street, is the Westminster or Roman Catholic Cathedral. This vast and imposing structure was designed by J. F. Bentley in the Early Byzantine style, but his early death in 1902 deprived him of the satisfaction of seeing his work completed. The foundation-stone was laid by Cardinal Vaughan on 29 June 1895 and the building was finished in the early part of 1903. Apart from the cost of the site, nearly £250,000 was expended on this cathedral, which Mr Norman Shaw considered beyond all doubt the finest church which had been built for centuries. The great campanile is 273 feet high and another feature of the building is its dignified west front with its finely-balanced pillars and arches.

The balcony of the campanile has on two or three occasions been the objective of persons bent on committing suicide, and the year 1925 witnessed a ghastly tragedy, in which a woman threw herself and her three children to death from the balcony into the street below. As a result the Cathedral authorities withheld any further permission to the public to ascend the tower until new high railings had been erected round the balcony.

On the site of the Roman Catholic Cathedral previously stood Tothill Fields Prison, also called the Westminster Bridewell, a strong brick edifice, first erected in 1618, and then enlarged in 1655. It was rebuilt in 1836 at a cost of £146,000 and again enlarged in 1850 by the purchase of an expensive piece of ground known as Elliott's Lawn, and was eventually pulled down in 1884. To this prison the Westminster magistrates committed people provisionally for imputed crimes, and it was also used for debtors and vagrants. Here were witnessed all the evils arising from overcrowding, filth, deficiency of food, and damp, unventilated cells. It was characterized by a Committee of Inquiry appointed by the House of Commons in the early part of the last century as a disgrace to a Christian country. In 1818 no less than 2,650 persons were confined in this prison. This large site was earmarked as long ago as 1875 for the intended Roman Catholic Cathedral.

Ashley Gardens, close to Westminster Cathedral, which leads into Francis Street, contains large blocks of flats, with balconies, eight storeys high, faced with red brick. Others have been erected in Morpeth Terrace and Carlisle Place, also leading into Francis Street. At the western end of Ashley Place, adjoining Carlisle Place, was St Andrew's Church, a Gothic structure designed by Sir Gilbert Scott, and containing a lofty nave. It was destroyed by bombs and a new block of offices, Borax House, stands on the site.

On the north side of Victoria Street, at the corner of Allington Street, is the Victoria Palace of Varieties, erected on the site of the old Standard Music Hall, and one of only two music halls still open in London. Also in Allington Street was the main entrance to Messrs Watney's Stag Brewery, Pimlico. A company having been formed to develop this area, the ceremony of 'The Last Mash' took place on 23rd April 1959; so, after three hundred years, ended the brewing of beer on this site. The rebuilding of this ten-acre site gives a very clear indication of the size and shape of the new Victoria Street of the immediate future. Where the old brewery stood there are now six lofty office buildings, a block of flats, a multistorey garage and a new public house. The original intention of the developers was to use the Stag Site entirely for office buildings, but persuasion from local authorities led to the inclusion of the 16-storey block of luxury flats, Roebuck House, on the Palace Street side of the area, but its appearance is somewhat impaired by the adjacent filling station. In the middle is an open space called Stag Place, with an ornamental pool of very shallow water which has some artificial rocks resting on a concrete table well above the water line. Nearby is a symbolic stag—but this is no *Monarch of the Glen*—it is difficult to tell whether he is bowing to the audience or about to sit up and beg, though there are so many perforations in his anatomy that he is clearly incapable of either.

The extreme height of the surrounding buildings have a rather overpowering effect on Stag Place as an open space.

From Buckingham Palace Road, Princes Row has been extended as Bressenden Place, a new thoroughfare which curves round into Victoria Street. The several 'Houses' in the Stag area are named Eland, Roebuck, Glen (with shops on the ground floor), Watney, Portland – of 28 storeys – Carrier and Esso, which has a frontage to Victoria Street comprising a number of new shops. Next to Carrier House is the octagonal tavern, 'The Stag'.

East of the Stag area, the section between Palace Street and Buckingham Gate is dominated by the 250-foot tower of the Westminster City Council, which rises to 22 floors and adjoins the ten-storey Kingsgate House, with a range of new shops below which includes a large supermarket. That part of Victoria Street which extends from Vauxhall Bridge Road to Grosvenor Gardens was originally called Shaftesbury Terrace, and was already in existence long before the con-struction of that new thoroughfare. It is considerably wider than the rest of Victoria Street, but has been disfigured by the erection of all sorts and conditions of buildings without regard to their relation to the street. It includes a fine block of shops at the corner of Allington Street, the small but comfortable Cameo Cinema, the large Metropole Cinema and a tall new building erected in 1937 by Messrs T. M. Sutton Limited, the well-known firm of pawnbrokers.

Every architect and town-planner who wishes to see an illuminating example of how individual owners of property can make or mar a fine street should have a look at this terrace of buildings. On the opposite side of the street is the Victoria Underground Railway Station, adjoining which is Stewart's Restaurant and an arcade connecting Victoria Street with the station yard. Above the Underground station is a fine building called Victoria Station House. The Windsor Hotel on the corner of Wilton Road and Vauxhall Bridge Road has been rebuilt and set back a considerable distance.

Victoria Station, now one of the finest in London, was rebuilt and greatly enlarged in 1902-08 at a cost of £2,000,000, and covers an area of sixteen acres, comprising nine platforms, each more than a quarter of a mile long, and providing accommodation for eighteen trains. The platforms are divided into two portions, and, owing to the special track lay-out and signalling, trains using the rear portions can leave or arrive although the other section of the platform may be occupied. This applies only to the Brighton section of Victoria Station and does not take into account the neighbouring South-Eastern Station, which now forms a part of the Southern Region section of British Railways and has been joined to the Brighton Station by an opening giving direct access between the two stations. Thus, with platforms numbers one to eight on the South Eastern side, the combined station now has, in effect, seventeen platforms.

The old Victoria Station of the London, Brighton and South Coast Railway and the London, Chatham and Dover Railway was first opened to traffic on 1 October 1860. The buildings at that time were merely of a temporary character, with wooden frontages, more suggestive of those in some new town of mushroom growth in the wilds of Canada or Australia than one of the leading railway stations of London. Nevertheless they remained for nearly fifty years until the completion of the new station in 1908. The old station had a light but substantial roof about forty feet high, and piling had to be carried out to provide a foundation.

It was erected on the site of the huge basin at the head of the Grosvenor Canal, one of several constructed in various places on both sides of the Thames to enable barges to enter the heart of the metropolis before the days of the railway. Curiously enough Victoria Station was owned by neither the London, Brighton and South Coast Railway nor the London, Chatham and Dover Railway, but belonged to the Victoria Station and Pimlico Railway, who leased their line at a fixed rental to these two companies. Under the grouping system it became the property of the Southern Railway in 1923. Great opposition was offered to the Bill in Parliament for its construction by neighbouring property-owners, who feared the effects of smoke and noise, and the promoters were compelled to roof the railway in with iron and glass nearly all the way to the Thames at Grosvenor Road Bridge. The trains therefore appeared to be travelling through a glass tunnel for about half a mile before reaching the station. The original station cost £675,000 and covered eleven acres, but the superstructure was removed when the station was rebuilt.

To make room for the extension of Victoria Station a long row of buildings which formerly fronted the south side of Buckingham Palace Road were pulled down in 1902. The first part of the work to be put in hand was the construction of the new South Station, together with a new entrance from Buckingham Palace Road, and the erection of the long ornamental wall which now lines that thorough-fare. This was completed about 1905 and was followed by the reconstruction of the original North Station, after which the entrance to the station was set back some twenty-five feet, and the old wooden railings were replaced by new iron ones.

In 1907 the adjoining South-Eastern Station was refronted with a handsome new stone building in the Georgian style, which replaced the ugly wooden building that previously overlooked the Victoria Station courtyard. Like most other great London terminals, Victoria Station was bombed during the great air raids of 1940-41 and again in October 1944 but was never out of action. The roof of the Brighton station was badly damaged whilst that of the older South-Eastern Station was completely destroyed. During the September raids of 1940, a Dornier bomber which was shot down fell in the courtyard outside Victoria Station, its crew making a parachute descent which landed them at Kennington Oval. The Dornier remained on view to the general public for several days. The Grosvenor Hotel, which was opened in 1861, shortly after the completion of Victoria Station, is a handsome building 300 feet long and 100 feet high, with its main frontage to Buckingham Palace Road. The foundations of the hotel, which stands on a part of the site of the old Grosvenor Basin, were sunk through a series of quicksands, mudbanks, and old peat-bogs down to the solid mass of London clay. The main building is six storeys high, but when Victoria Station was rebuilt the handsome new annexe was built above the main entrance to the station.

The Grosvenor Railway Bridge between Battersea Park and Chelsea was the widest in the world at the time of building, and contained a station at which it was the custom to collect all tickets for Victoria. The construction of the new South Station necessitated the raising of the roadway in Buckingham Palace Road by several feet as well as the creation of a hill in the central portion of that thoroughfare in order to bring the new bridges over the station into line with Eccleston Street and Elizabeth Street.

On an extensive site between Wilton Road and Vauxhall Bridge Road, cleared in 1926, has been erected the Abford House, containing a large Chicken Inn Restaurant and the New Victoria Cinema, with a plain-looking stone front, containing scarcely any windows. A large and up-to-date Woolworth store has been built on the site of Parnell's Drapery Emporium. Here the building line on the east side of Wilton Road had been set back a considerable distance, including the Windsor Castle Hotel at the corner of Vauxhall Bridge Road. In October 1944, Parnell's building and the New Victoria Cinema, the Wilton Hotel and various other neighbouring buildings were badly damaged by a flying-bomb. Girders of shop fronts were twisted and every pane of glass smashed by the blast from the explosion. Farther along Wilton Road at the corner of Gillingham Street, another huge site was cleared of its old houses in 1930 and on this site now stands a large London Transport garage for their omnibuses and coaches. From the Woolworth store in Wilton Road to the Biograph Cinema, both of which also have a frontage to Vauxhall Bridge Road, recent development includes the ten-storey Chestergate House, and the two last-mentioned roads are now connected by a new thoroughfare called Neathouse Place; this revives an old Pimlico name, for this district was part of the ancient Manor of Neate or Neyte, and the old Neate Manor House was the residence of the Abbots of Westminster. The Biograph Cinema at Nos 47 and 48 Wilton Road is the oldest cinema in England, having opened (as 'The Bioscope') on 28 February 1905 and still flourishes with the showing of vintage films. •

The fine buildings in Grosvenor Gardens, close to Victoria Station, now mostly converted into offices, including Grosvenor Gardens House, formerly the Hotel Belgravia, were erected by the Duke of Westminster in 1868, as well as those immediately south of St George's Hospital in Grosvenor Place. They are built in the French style, mostly with stone façades and high steep roofs, and afford a pleasant and complete contrast to the ugly yellow-brick houses of the Georgian era and the Regency, in which style so many large houses in the West End were built. Those in the centre portion of Grosvenor Place between Wilton Street and Chester Street, their grimy black brick façades overlooking the hideous brick wall of Buckingham Palace, give this part of Grosvenor Place the appearance of a mausoleum. However, the new Associated Electrical Industries building, opened in 1958, has improved the appearance of this section. Hobart House, which now covers the site between Hobart Place and Wilton Street, is a large new block of offices erected in 1939. It is faced with red brick and has a long frontage to Grosvenor Place. It is at present occupied by the National Coal Board. Iron Trades House on the north corner of Chester Street is another new block of offices erected in 1938 and fronted with Portland stone. No 17, at the corner of Chapel Street, is the Irish Embassy.

In the triangular garden, opposite the entrance to Victoria Station, is the statue of Marshal Foch, unveiled in June 1930 by the Duke of Windsor when

Prince of Wales, and here the roundabout system of traffic has been introduced. Terminal House on the west side of Grosvenor Gardens, next to Buckingham Palace Road, is a fine block of offices erected in 1931. It is nine storeys high and faced with Portland stone. Next to it at the corner of Belgrave Street is Universal House, another distinctive block of offices erected in 1938. The former Hotel Belgravia, now Grosvenor Gardens House, was the headquarters of the American Expeditionary Force in 1918, and a panel by Sir Edwin Lutyens R.A. commemorating this event used to be in the entrance hall, but is now 'downstairs somewhere'. The hotel closed down in 1936 and is now offices.

Vauxhall Bridge Road, to which we will now return, is a rapidly-improving thoroughfare. It was built about 1816, at the time of the erection of the bridge, and provides direct communication between Hyde Park Corner and Grosvenor Place and the south of London. It divides old Westminster from the quarter of Pimlico or South Belgravia, a region of spacious squares and broad streets mostly lined with five-storeyed stucco-fronted houses laid out by Thomas Cubitt between 1830 and 1840.

About half-way along Vauxhall Bridge Road on the east side is Rochester Row, leading to Horseferry Road. A notable feature of this street is St Stephen's Church, founded by the Baroness Burdett-Coutts, who gave £30,000 for that purpose. The foundation-stone was laid on 20 July 1847 by the Bishop of London, and the building was opened on 24 June 1850. The church has a spire two hundred feet high. At the top of Rochester Row, adjoining Horseferry Road, is the Greycoat School, founded in 1698. In Greycoat Street is the new hall of the Royal Horticultural Society. Just south of Rochester Row is the old-fashioned Vincent Square, used as a playground by the boys of Westminster School. Bordering on the Square are three hospitals, the Grosvenor (for women), the Infants and the Gordon, while other buildings include the Technical Institute and the Old Hall of the Royal Horticultural Society.

At the southern end of Vauxhall Bridge Road stood Holy Trinity Church, designed by J. L. Pearson, R.A., in 1851 at a cost of £10,000, defrayed by an anonymous donor. The church was completely destroyed in the war and the parish has been joined with St James the Less in Moreton Street. The first Vauxhall Bridge was erected by a private company in 1811-16, but the existing bridge was built by the County Council at a cost of nearly £600,000 and opened in 1906. A peculiar feature are the iron screens on the parapets and the bronze statues on the piers of the arches. As originally designed the bridge was to have been entirely of granite, but only the piers and abutments are of that material, the superstructure being of steel. There are five spans and the bridge is eighty feet wide, of which fifty feet is allotted to the roadway and fifteen feet to each of the footpaths. At the south-west corner of Grosvenor Road, is a fine block of flats erected about 1930 by Messrs Hovis Limited, the flour manufacturers, whose own premises are immediately adjoining. This building is crowned by a stone clocktower at the corner of Vauxhall Bridge.

George IV proposed clearing the entire space between St James's Park,

Vauxhall Bridge Road, and the Thames, and laying it out with spacious streets crossing each other at right angles. The removal of the Court to Buckingham Palace in 1830 gave considerable impetus to the building of Pimlico, and by 1843 Mr Cubitt had completed the direct road from Belgrave Square through Eaton, Chester, Eccleston, Warwick, and St George's Squares to the river.

Prior to 1835 the whole of this quarter of Pimlico between Vauxhall Bridge Road and Buckingham Palace Road, now commonly known as South Belgravia, consisted of market gardens and waste land, with the exception of a few stray cottages here and there and a few blocks of houses near the river. On a considerable portion of the space between these two roads were osier beds, now covered by Eccleston Square and the adjacent streets. Warwick Square, between Belgrave Road and St George's Drive covers part of the old Neat House Gardens, occupied by market gardeners. It contains St Gabriel's Church, a large building of Early English architecture, with a spire 160 feet high, erected from the designs of Mr Thomas Cundy, who was also the architect of St Saviour's Church in St George's Square, nearer to the river. The Church of St Gabriel seems to have suffered from the frequent attentions of unwelcome visitors, for above the offertory box inside the church are two notices, one — 'To those who want to put something *in* — Thank you very much!' The other is addressed 'To those who want to take something *out*', and emphasises that, since the box is cleared every day, the most they are likely to get for their trouble is a few coppers, and as it costs about £10 to repair the box each time it is broken open, the Vicar has decided that it is cheaper to leave it unlocked — *so help yourself!* Opposite St Gabriel's, at 114 Cambridge Street, lived Aubrey Beardsley, whose illustrations in the early numbers of *The Yellow Book* were among the sensations of the 'nineties. Warwick Street, now renamed Warwick Way, running west at right angles to Vauxhall Bridge Road, was once called Willow Walk.

This quarter suffered severely from the earlier raids of 1940 because of its proximity to Victoria Station and the Southern Railway, notably Claverton Street, Lupus Street, Vauxhall Bridge Road, Wilton Road, Belgrave Road, Sutherland Terrace and Hugh Street, where many houses have disappeared. A newer feature of South Belgravia is the Eccleston Hotel at the corner of Eccleston Square and Gillingham Street. This was opened in 1930 by Sir James Monteith Erskine (Member of Parliament for St George's from 1921 to 1929) who purchased the old house, formerly the property of the Marquess of Bute, and enlarged and modernized it. Finding that the accommodation was insufficient to meet the demand, Sir James then purchased the adjoining property in Gillingham Street and built the present attractive new hotel and ballroom.

South Belgravia is a fine piece of town-planning, particularly such thoroughfares as Belgrave Road and St George's Drive, and if George IV was unable to realize his ambition by clearing the entire space from St James's Park to the Thames, at least the next best thing occurred when Mr Cubitt planned South Belgravia. Could our grandfathers, anticipating the tremendous growth of the metropolis, have commissioned Mr Cubitt to plan a series of great arterial roads radiating from the West End through the open fields to Kensington, Fulham, and Hammersmith, what a blessing it would have proved to Londoners of the present day.

On the site formerly occupied by the Royal Army Clothing Department in Grosvenor Road, covering seven and a half acres, now stands Dolphin Square, the largest self-contained block of flats in Europe. It extends from Grosvenor Road to Chichester Street and on its east and west sides is shut in by the houses backing on to St George's Square and Claverton Street. It contains 1,250 flats and its special features include a large square garden which is approached through wide archways from both Grosvenor Road and Chichester Street, a large restaurant and ballroom and a garage for hundreds of cars. Dolphin Square is ten storeys high and has a bold frontage of red brick with stone dressings to Grosvenor Road. The first section facing Grosvenor Road was opened by Lord Almulree on 23 November 1936, and the northern section facing Chichester Street was completed in 1937. Dolphin Square has its own street of shops, and residents can do all their shopping under cover. Opposite Dolphin Square, on the river side of Grosvenor Road are the pleasant Pimlico Gardens, in which stands the statute of William Huskisson, statesman. Born at Liverpool, which he represented in Parliament, Huskisson was killed by a locomotive at the ceremonial opening of the Liverpool and Manchester Railway on 15 September 1830. The procession of trains had left Liverpool, and at Parskside, the engines stopped for water. Contrary to instructions, the travellers left the carriages and stood upon the permanent way. Huskisson went to speak to the Duke of Wellington, and at that moment, several engines were seen approaching along the rails between which he was standing. Everybody else made for the carriages, but Huskisson, who was slightly lame, fell back on the rails in front of the locomotive *Dart,* which ran over his leg; he was carried to hospital, where he died the same evening – probably the first fatality of the Steel Highway.

In this immediate vicinity the Westminster City Council in 1947 began to clear a site of some thirty-three acres, bounded by Grosvenor Road, Westmoreland Terrace, Lupus Street and Claverton Street for the Council's principal post-war housing scheme. This estate, named Churchill Gardens, which is to provide 1,680 dwellings housing a population of over 5,000, has now been completed.

The blocks of dwellings range from three to eleven storeys in height and consist of different types of flat or maisonette having from one to five rooms each with built-in fittings of the most modern kind. Each house is named after some person eminent in literature, music, science etc., providing they have some associations with Westminster. Thus we have Shelley, Nash, Jane Austen, Wedgwood, Sullivan and so on. A much better arrangement than one finds in some parts of the metropolis where this form of immortality is frequently conferred upon otherwise obscure local politicians. A most interesting feature of Churchill Gardens is the Pimlico District Heating Undertaking, by means of which exhaust steam from two specially designed turbines at the Battersea Power Station, just across the river, is used to heat Council's water to a temperature of 200°F. This water is then pumped through a closed circuit of pipes under the River Thames to the 125 foot high accumulator (or storage tank) at the substation in Churchill Gardens; and thence to taps, towel-rails and radiators in the various buildings. The hot water, its temperature now reduced to about 130°F., then returns to the Battersea Power Station for re-heating and re-circulation.

The Westminster City Council have several other housing schemes in hand, among them the Abbots Manor Estate near Victoria Station, where eleven six-storey blocks of flats are under construction. Incorporated in this group is the site of the old 'Monster' public-house, once the starting-point of horse-drawn omnibuses, which was destroyed in an air-raid. At Hide Place, near Vincent Square, a 200 feet high block of twenty-two storeys consisting of 160 flats with wholly electric under-floor heating has been built. This is known as Hide Tower.

Buckingham Palace Road, which may be considered the dividing line between South Belgravia and the more fashionable quarter of Belgravia proper, was formerly a shabby thoroughfare, but is now lined with blocks of flats and business premises, as well as the St George's Baths on the north side, and the B.O.A.C. building, the long ornamental wall of the Southern Railway, and the Grosvenor Hotel, on the south side. North of Victoria Station Buckingham Palace Road becomes a first-class shopping street, and on the south side is adorned by a long row of handsome buildings faced with red brick and stone.

From Allington Street to Bressenden Place is the extensive drapery store of Messrs Frederick Gorringe Limited, one of London's most modern stores. Founded in 1858, this old-established business which, to quote an elderly customer, 'is as much an institution as Big Ben or Nelson in Trafalgar Square', was at one time threatened with demolition and 'development'. But in 1962 the old building was demolished, and by February 1964, a new multi-storey building had taken its place, with Gorringe's occupying the first three floors. Gorringe's are the holders of two Royal Warrants as Drapers to H.M. The Queen and to H.M. Queen Elizabeth, the Queen Mother. A turning opposite Gorringe's leads to the charming little Victoria Square. Beyond Bressenden Place is the Hotel Rubens, built in 1912 on the site of a row of small shops typical of the Georgian era, and the Imperial headquarters of the Boy Scouts' Association. In Palace Street is the Westminster Theatre, the first to be erected in the Victoria district. After a drastic rebuilding at a cost of £350,000, it was renamed The Westminster Theatre Arts Centre, for plays, films, concerts, exhibitions, lectures etc. Also in Palace Street is the Westminster City School. In the forecourt is a statue of the late Sir Sydney Waterlow, a former chairman of the Board of Governors. This statue is a copy of the one in Waterlow Park, Highgate, and is unusual in that Sir Sydney carries a trilby hat and umbrella. Lower Grosvenor Place, leading to Grosvenor Place, once owned to the very unpretentious name of Arabella Row.

After passing Buckingham Palace our return route to Parliament Square is by way of Birdcage Walk, which, like Constitution Hill, underwent an extensive widening in connexion with the improvements carried out thirty-odd years ago in front of Buckingham Palace. Birdcage Walk is fronted at its western end by the Wellington Barracks, but is also overlooked by Queen Anne's Mansions and a number of old-fashioned houses. Amongst the notable modern buildings erected in Birdcage Walk is that of the Institution of Mechanical Engineers, next to Storey's Gate. On the south side of Great George Street is the handsome stone-fronted building of the Institution of Civil Engineers. At the back of Birdcage Walk is Queen Anne's Gate, which leads from Queen Street to Dartmouth Street. This is a picturesque relic of Georgian London. Its houses were built early in the eighteenth century by William Paterson, founder of the Bank of England. These have fine doorcases and porches and grotesque masks. On the south side of the street is a statue of Queen Anne.

Sixteenth Walk

St Giles's Circus, Oxford Street and Tributary Thoroughfares, Marylebone, Edgware Road, Maida Vale, St John's Wood, etc.

Dominated by the 37-storey tower of the new Centre Point Building (described in our Ninth Walk), St Giles's Circus, forming the starting-point of this walk, is the title which is bestowed upon the important open space formed by the junction of Oxford Street, Tottenham Court Road, New Oxford Street, High Street, St Giles's, and Charing Cross Road.

Oxford Street, slightly over one mile in length, forms part of the great high-way through the metropolis extending from the Bank of England to Shepherd's Bush, and from St Giles's Circus to High Street, Notting Hill, with scarcely a curve. Although it is today one of the finest thoroughfares in London and the most popular shopping-street in the British Commonwealth, sixty years ago it was a rather shabby thoroughfare, consisting principally of third-rate houses, practically all of which have since given way to splendid modern buildings. The eastern end of Oxford Street, for the short distance between Tottenham Court Road and Rathbone Place, is far too narrow for the requirements of its traffic, but the exclusion of south-bound traffic from Tottenham Court Road and the introduction of High Street, St Giles as part of the one-way scheme has modified the congestion at this point.

On the north side of Oxford Street, four doors from Tottenham Court Road, is the Oxford Corner House erected by Messrs J. Lyons & Company Limited, between 1926 and 1928, on the site of the former New Oxford Theatre. Opened in the first place as the Oxford Music Hall, it was one of the first and most popular amongst the London variety houses, and was twice destroyed by fire. Previous to that time the site of the Oxford Music Hall had been occupied by the Boar and Castle Hostelry and Posting House, which dated back to the year 1620.

In 1839 experimental wood-paving was first laid down in Oxford Street near Tottenham Court Road by contract at 2s. 2d. per yard, but the public taste was not yet ripe for this change. Being completely worn out, it was removed again in 1844 and replaced by granite paving.

A few doors west of the Lyons Oxford Corner House was Frascati's Restaurant, originally opened as Krasnapolski's Dutch Restaurant about sixty years ago. It was closed recently and, having been entirely rebuilt, has now re-opened as the Language Tuition Centre.

Rathbone Place, the first turning on the north side of Oxford Street, is a narrow thoroughfare leading to Charlotte Street, by which it is continued to Fitzroy Square and Euston Road. It is named after Captain Rathbone, its builder, and on a building at the corner is a stone inscribed, 'Rathbones Place in Oxford Street 1778'. It is a centre for artists' materials and wholesale antique-houses, and also for dealers in musical instruments. Messrs Winsor & Newton, on the west side, have been in Rathbone Place for well over 100 years—though not at the present site. Nearly half of its buildings on the west side and a few on the east side have been destroyed in the air raids of 1940 and since pulled down. On the west side also a new Postal District Sorting Office, opened in 1963, extends for over a hundred yards.

Charlotte Street, named after the queen of George III, contains a number of foreign restaurants, catering for the foreign community which of recent years has overflowed into this neighbourhood from Soho on the other side of Oxford Street. At Number 76 Charlotte Street, Constable, the great painter, resided from 1822 until his death in 1837. On the east side is the Scala Theatre, and farther north the Swiss Club. The Church of St John the Evangelist, consecrated by the Bishop of London on 16 July 1846, stood next to Constable's house. It was damaged during the war and has been replaced by a new office building. An important new building, the Middlesex Hospital Medical School, is nearing completion on a site between Charlotte, Howland and Cleveland Streets and adjoins the Out Patients Annexe in Cleveland Street. The third and last phase of the building is the seven-floor students' hostel Astor College.

Fitzroy Square, lined by well-built terraces faced with stone, was designed by the brothers Adam. It was begun about 1790, but only the east and south sides had been completed before 1831. It was named after Charles, Duke of Grafton, son of Henry Fitzroy, lessee of the Manor of Tottenhall, formerly the property of the Dean and Chapter of St Paul's. Sir Henry Fitzroy was raised to the peerage in 1780 and then assumed the title of Lord Southampton. Today Fitzroy Square is no longer the artistic residential area it used to be. At No 29 on the west side is a plaque which records the residence there of George Bernard Shaw from 1887 to 1898, and adds, 'From the coffers of his genius he enriched the world'. On the south side is the London Foot Hospital. The north side contains the St Luke's Nursing Home for the Clergy, and on the east side is the British Drama League.

But for the narrowness of Rathbone Place, Charlotte Street and Fitzroy Square would provide a most useful relief thoroughfare for the heavy traffic of Tottenham Court Road, and, incidentally, could be made a one-way-traffic street from Euston Road to Oxford Street. If Rathbone Place were widened it could be brought directly into line with Charlotte Street at its northern end and with Soho Street on the south side of Oxford Street, thus providing a through route from Euston Road to Shaftesbury Avenue by way of Soho Square and Dean Street.

After passing Rathbone Place Oxford Street becomes a reasonably wide thoroughfare, sufficiently broad to accommodate a cab-rank in the centre of the roadway. Newman Street, the next turning on the north side, was built between 1750 and 1770, and was originally inhabited by artists, including Benjamin West, a president of the Royal Academy, and Banks and Bacon the sculptors. In March 1870 the Marylebone Vestry ordered the removal of a disused pump in Newman Street in consequence of its being frequently mistaken for a letter-box. Today Newman Street contains some good shops, but it is largely populated by textile and gown manufacturers.

Between Soho Street and Dean Street on the south side of Oxford Street are the former premises of Messrs Drages Limited, the popular firm of house furnishers, who started business in a small way about thirty-five years ago in High Holborn. This building, which is eight storeys high, is one of the finest on the south side of Oxford Street and is faced with imitation black marble. Next door was the Dean Hotel and Restaurant, formerly the Tudor Hotel, standing on the east corner of Dean Street. It was bombed in the air raids of 1940 and has been rebuilt and now matches up with the adjoining Polytechnic Tours building. Much rebuilding took place before the war on the north side of Oxford Street between Rathbone Place and Berners Street, and many shabby houses were replaced by handsome stone-fronted buildings. But few main leading London thoroughfares have been so heavily bombed as Oxford Street and many buildings, both new and old, have been destroyed or badly damaged in the great blitz and razed to the ground. East of Oxford Circus, on the north side of the street between Rathbone Place and Newman Street a new eight-storey building called Colgate-Palmolive House has been erected and on the south side new buildings can be seen at frequent intervals between Soho Street and Oxford Circus. Buszard's famous cake-shop, which had been a landmark for over a hundred years, was hit by a big bomb which, at two o'clock in the morning on 16 April 1941, smashed the shop-front and wrecked the handsome Palm Court which was a fashionable rendezvous for sumptuous teas. The building was demolished and a row of temporary one-storey shops stood here for some time, with a London County Council popular-price Ramillies Restaurant next door. They have all gone. A Littlewood store now occupies the site.

Berners Street, leading from Oxford Street to the Middlesex Hospital in Goodge Street, was so named after the family-title of its ground landlord. Built about 1750, like Newman Street, it was long celebrated as the home of artists, painters, and sculptors. Amongst its celebrated residents were Sir William Chambers, the architect, and Opie and Fuseli, the painters. Number 6 Berners Street was the Banking House of Marsh, Stracey, Fauntleroy & Graham, in which Fauntleroy committed forgeries involving the Bank of England in a loss of £360,000.

Today Berners Street is an excellent business thoroughfare and can boast some fine shops and hotels. At the east corner of Oxford Street is a branch of the Westminster Bank, and farther along, at the south corner of East Castle Street is the Berners Hotel, a lofty building with an imposing red-brick frontage to

Berners Street. On the opposite corner of East Castle Street stands York House, extending through to Newman Street. This was formerly the York Hotel, but is now converted into a hostel to provide accommodation for the nurses of the nearby Middlesex Hospital. On the opposite side of Berners Street is the principal frontage of the great drapery store of Messrs Bourne & Hollingsworth, extending from Oxford Street to East Castle Street. It was rebuilt in 1929 and also has extensive frontages to Oxford Street and Wells Street. This firm started business in a small way about fifty years ago, and migrated to Oxford Street from West-bourne Grove. Farther up, on the same side of Berners Street, are the premises of Messrs Sanderson & Sons, the well-known firm of wallpaper manufacturers.

The Middlesex Hospital, now at the top of Berners Street, was established in Windmill Street in 1745, and removed to its present site in 1755, when the first stone was laid by the Duke of Northumberland. About 1926 the foundations of the hospital were found to be defective, and this necessitated the immediate reconstruction of the building. The new Middlesex Hospital, erected between 1929 and 1935, is a handsome building of seven storeys, with a façade of red brick with stone dressings designed by Alner Hall and built round an open quadrangle. On the west side is the Bernard Baron Memorial Wing and on the east side is the Queen Alexandra Memorial Wing. In Wells Street stood until 1932 the Church of St Andrew, the foundation-stone of which was laid on 13 January 1846, and the building consecrated on 18 January 1847. The tower and spire were 155 feet high, and the building cost £7,000. The ground landlord, Archdeacon Berners, gave the freehold of the site, valued then at about £2,000. In 1932 the church was pulled down and a modern commercial building erected on this site called St Margaret's House.

The great dry-goods stores of Oxford Street commence at Berners Street, and together with the intervening shops now extend westwards to Park Lane, a distance of nearly a mile. After passing the buildings of Messrs Bourne & Hollingsworth, we come to that of the C. & A. Modes on the opposite corner of Oxford Street and Wells Street, and then the third London branch of Messrs Swears and Wells. Next comes the huge Waring & Gillow establishment extending along Oxford Street from Winsley Street to Great Titchfield Street and back to East Castle Street. It towers well above the neighbouring buildings, and was erected between 1901 and 1905, but owing to a dispute over the question of 'Ancient Lights' considerable delay was incurred in its completion. One small house which stood until 1933 on the corner of Great Titchfield Street and Oxford Street formerly belonged to Messrs Ridgway, the tea merchants. Later it was taken over by Messrs Waring & Gillow, who pulled it down in order to complete the rebuilding of this vast furniture emporium.

In Great Titchfield Street, opposite the premises of Messrs Waring & Gillow, formerly stood Oxford Market, so named after Lord Harley, Earl of Oxford, het original ground landlord. It was erected in 1721, but was rebuilt in 1815, when small dwelling-rooms were added to the shops below. In February 1876 the site of this market wad disposed of by public auction, and the property purchased for £27,500. In 1936, the buildings which stood on this site were pulled down and replaced by Kent House, a handsome block of shops and offices faced with stone.

Amongst the old buildings which stood in this part of Oxford Street was the former Princess's Theatre, which for years past had been used as a furniture warehouse. This building, together with the adjoining houses, was pulled down in 1931 to make way for a large Woolworth store. It was erected on the site of a building formerly known as the Queen's Bazaar, which extended back as far as Castle Street. It was destroyed by fire in 1829 and then rebuilt. For ten years, commencing from 1849, it became famous for the Shakespearian revivals of Mr Charles Kean; it was demolished in 1880 and rebuilt from the designs of Mr C. J. Phipps. Later it passed into the management of Mr Wilson Barrett and for some years became a home of melodrama, though it was never a great success. About forty years ago it was proposed to erect a large hotel on this site, but the scheme failed to mature.

On the other side of Oxford Street stood until 1938 the Pantheon, which was occupied by the firm of wine merchants, Messrs W. & A. Gilbey Limited. It was originally built in 1770-71 as a place of public amusement, including concerts, balls, and promenades, and was erected at a cost of £60,000 from the designs of James Wyatt and opened early in 1772. It was destroyed by fire in 1792, rebuilt on the same plan, and then pulled down in 1812. The Oxford Street front was preserved and the building was remodelled and converted into a bazaar, until acquired by Messrs W. & A. Gilbey about sixty years ago. The Pantheon was pulled down in 1938 and a new store erected on this site by Messrs Marks & Spencer Limited is again named, 'The Pantheon'.

After passing Great Titchfield Street we next come to Market Court, on the corner of which is a branch of the Midland Bank. Adjoining is the former eastern block of Messrs Peter Robinson's premises, erected in 1925-26, and extending to Great Portland Street. Now occupied by C. & A. Modes, a plaque on the wall of this building records that 'From June 1952, for fifteen years, it was the head-quarters of the B.B.C. Overseas Service. During the war direct broadcasts were made to America from the roof while air-raids were in progress'. The western block, which is the main building of Messrs Peter Robinson, is on the other corner, and covers the island site formed by Oxford Street, Regent Street, Castle Street, and the west side of Great Portland Street, and was erected in 1920-23. On the other side of the road is Oxford Circus Underground Station, above which a tall block of offices has been erected at the corner of Argyll Street.

Great Portland Street, leading to Marylebone Road, close to Park Crescent, was formerly a shabby street of no great importance, but during the past sixty years has gradually developed into one of the finest in the West End of London, and is now a leading centre of the dressmaking industry and also has a number of motor-car showrooms. Nearly half-way up, on the west side, was the former building of the Philharmonic Hall, erected in 1907 to replace the former St James's Hall in Piccadilly. In 1930 this building was enlarged by the addition of an extra storey and converted into a block of offices and shops. The Portland Hotel, which formerly stood on the adjoining site, was pulled down in 1935 and Western House, a new block of shops and offices, was then erected on this site. It lost its three top storeys in the blitz but has now been repaired. On the other side of the road stood until 1940 the well-known Pagani's Restaurant, which was completely destroyed in the air raids of September 1940. Various other buildings in both Great Portland Street and the neighbouring Great Titchfield Street have likewise been destroyed. Another architectural feature of this street was the Central Jewish Synagogue, opened in 1870. It was built in the Moorish style, and the cost was partly defrayed by the Rothschild family. This too was destroyed in the earlier air raids of 1940, but has now been rebuilt.

Sixty years ago the houses on each side at the northern end of Great Portland Street stood back from the roadway, with the ground-floor shops built over the original front gardens. These were mostly of an inferior character and have long since been replaced by new buildings extending from Clipstone Street to Marylebone Road. On the west side are the premises of Messrs S. Smith & Son, dealers in motor accessories, and Messrs Curry & Paxton, the opticians. On the east side is Portland Court, a large block of office buildings, faced with terracotta, erected in 1902. Farther up on the same side of the street are the National Institute for the Blind, and the National Orthopaedic Hospital for Children. Today Great Portland Street, with its fine rows of six-storeyed buildings, mostly faced with stone, reminds one of the leading thoroughfare in some large Continental city. The rental value of Great Portland Street is said to have increased 100 per cent since the first World War.

In New Cavendish Street and Weymouth Street, on the west side of Great Portland Street, and in Hallam Street, acres of new blocks of flats have been erected during the past twenty-five years. In Little Titchfield Street is the new extension building of the Polytechnic Institute for the use of women members.

Mortimer Street, running parallel to Oxford Street, contains the handsome building of Messrs Samson Clark & Company, the firm of advertisers, and a number of millinery shops. It connects with Goodge Street on the east and with the north side of Cavendish Square and Wigmore Street on the west, thus providing a useful relief thoroughfare to the heavy traffic of Oxford Street. Goodge Street still retains its original shabby appearance, and has not so far been invaded by modern buildings. Wigmore Street, on the other hand, is a smart shopping thoroughfare, and extends from Cavendish Square to Portman Square. It derives its name from Wigmore in Herefordshire, whence Robert Harley took his title as Earl of Oxford, Earl Mortimer, and Lord Harley of Wigmore Castle. On the south side of this street is the dry-goods store of Messrs Debenham & Freebody, rebuilt about 1906 and ranking amongst the largest and finest in London. Antique dealers, cafés and establishments devoted to the supply of medical and surgical equipment are also to be found on both sides of Wigmore Street. On the north side is the Times Book Shop and Welbeck Court, a handsome block of shops and offices at the corner of Welbeck Street.

Returning to Oxford Street, after passing Oxford Circus, described during a previous walk, we next come to the extensive drapery store of Messrs John Lewis & Company Limited. It originally consisted of two groups of buildings; the eastern block, from John Prince's Street to Holles Street, formerly the premises of T. J. Harries & Co., which was taken over in 1928 and the western block, which was completely destroyed by enemy action in September 1940. The eastern block was relinquished and is now being developed by The Land Securities Investment Trust Ltd; it comprises a new school on the Oxford Street frontage, a number of new shops and the now familiar tower block of flats and offices rising through nineteen floors to a height of 240 feet. The western block, from Holles Street to Old Cavendish Street and extending back to Cavendish Square, is the magnificent new John Lewis building, which covers an area of 76,500 square feet and was opened on 17 October 1960. Including two basements there are ten floors. The architect was Mr R. H. Uren, F.R.I.B.A. and the cost of the building, including equipment, was 'in the region' of £5 million. Holles Street, together with Cavendish Square, Portland Place, Welbeck Street, as well as Great Portland Street and Great Titchfield Street, forms part of the estate of the Duke of Portland. A section of this estate, including Holles Street, descended to Lord Howard de Walden from the fifth Duke of Portland, who died in 1879.

About forty years ago, desiring to extend his premises to Cavendish Square, the late Mr John Lewis converted the two corner houses into shops without the consent of Lord Howard de Walden, who objected to shops being opened in Cavendish Square. Thereupon an order was obtained from the court by Lord Howard de Walden calling upon Mr John Lewis to reinstate the residential premises at the corner of Cavendish Square. But relying upon passive resistance, and refusing to obey the order of the court, Mr John Lewis, then eighty years of age, was committed to prison for contempt of court. Mr Lewis's broadsheets about his controversies with his landlord used to be exhibited in his window at the corner of Oxford Street, and were one of the curiosities of London. This eventually resulted in an action against him for libel which, however, was settled upon amicable terms. Mr John Lewis, who died in 1928 at the great age of ninety, started his business as a small shop in 1864 with six assistants and a window space of twenty feet. Since then times have changed and business premises are now allowed in Cavendish Square, which, like Hanover Square and Berkeley Square, has lost its purely residential character. The former chairman of the company, Mr John Spedan Lewis, reorganized the firm on a partnership basis in 1930, so that all his staff now have an interest in the business. The cleared site of the western block was loaned to the Government during the second World War for public exhibitions of war-time industry.

Number 24 Holles Street was the birthplace of Lord Byron in 1788, and formed part of the destroyed premises of Messrs John Lewis & Company Limited, who have a Byron plaque in one of the Holles Street windows of their new premises. During the period of shortage of timber and other building materials, the Ministry of Works would not authorize the rebuilding of shops and stores destroyed in the bombing. Messrs John Lewis and Company, however obtained a licence to erect, as a temporary measure, a series of one-storey shops on the site of the western section of their premises which had been destroyed on the night of 17 September 1940.

Cavendish Square, laid out in 1717, takes its name from Lady Henrietta Cavendish Holles, together with the adjoining Henrietta Street and Holles Street. It stands directly opposite Hanover Square on the south side of Oxford Street, which is approached through Harewood Place. On the south side of the square facing Holles Street is a statue of Lord George Bentinck. On the west side of Cavendish Square is a handsome block of flats, erected on the site of an old gloomy mansion called Harcourt House, wherein resided the fifth Duke of Portland. On the north side is the convent of the Holy Child Jesus. On the arch connecting the two wings is a fine Madonna and Child by Jacob Epstein. Harley Street, built about 1770, leading from Cavendish Square to Marylebone Road, and Wimpole Street, running parallel, are largely inhabited by consulting physicians and specialists. Wimpole Street was so named after Wimpole on the borders of Hertfordshire and Cambridgeshire, originally the country seat of the Harleys, Earls of Oxford.

Proceeding farther along Oxford Street, after passing the establishment of John Lewis, we next come to that of D. H. Evans Limited. It formerly consisted of two blocks of buildings separated from each other by Old Cavendish Street. Both of them had a considerable frontage to Old Cavendish as well as to Oxford Street, but after the western block had been rebuilt in 1936 the eastern block was sold to John Lewis. The magnificent new store of D. H. Evans covers the island site at the western corner of Oxford Street and Cavendish Street. It also has frontages to Henrietta Place and Chapel Place. It escaped damage in the blitz of 1940 and was the first store in London to install escalators up and down to all its six floors. On the opposite side of Henrietta Place is the Royal College of Nursing and the building of the Royal Society of Medicine. At the corner of Henrietta Place and Cavendish Square is the Cowdray Club for Ladies, a handsome building with a stone façade erected in 1936. Farther along Oxford Street are the premises of Marshall & Snelgrove, another large drapery store, between Vere Street and Marylebone Lane, which was established in 1837. In Vere Street is the attractive little church of St Peter, formerly called the Marybone Chapel, built by Edward Harley 2nd Earl of Oxford in 1722 to the designs of James Gibbs. It is now a Chapel of Ease to All Souls, Langham Place.

Marylebone Lane, leading to High Street, Marylebone, is interesting as having originally been the main approach to the small village which as late as 1700 was still nearly a mile distant from the nearest part of the metropolis. It was formerly called Tyburn, and derived its name from the small rivulet called Tyburn Brook, which ran from Hampstead through Regents's Park, Oxford Street, St James's Park, and Tothill Fields into the Thames. Notice how quaint little Marylebone Lane twists and turns regardless of the surrounding geometrically laid out streets and squares, clearly showing that it was once a pathway running alongside the old Tyburn Brook. It is supposed that when its church was removed to another spot near the same brook it was renamed St-Mary-at-the-Bourn, which was afterwards corrupted to Marylebone. The extension of the metropolis in this direction followed upon the construction of Cavendish Square. By 1739, Maitland states, there were 577 houses in the parish and thirty-five persons who kept coaches. In 1811 there were already 8,476 houses containing a population of 75,624, and as the old church had long since become inadequate for the requirements of the parish the present church at the corner of the High Street and Marylebone Road was completed and opened in 1817. On the triangular site at the corner of Oxford Street and Marylebone Lane now stands Stratford Court, a ten-storeyed building containing 104 small flats. It covers the site of the old Marylebone Watch House pulled down in 1935 which until 1920 had served as the Town Hall, and the famous bookshop of Messrs Bumpus who have removed to new premises in Baker Street. The ground floor houses one of the Dolcis shoe stores. The High Street is now a busy thoroughfare, lined with good-class family shops which have been largely rebuilt during the past forty years.

On the east side of the High Street, close to Weymouth Street and Beaumont Street, once stood the famous Marylebone Gardens, which until 1790 were a splendid public pleasure resort equalling Vauxhall Gardens. The grounds were still surrounded by pastures and hedgerows until the middle of the eighteenth century, and extended from Marylebone Lane almost as far north as Marylebone Road, being bounded by what is now Harley Street on the east. The gardens closed down in the autumn and reopened in the spring each year. On one occasion Doctor Johnson went there with a friend who wanted to witness a display of fireworks. Unfortunately the evening turned showery and the management were unable to provide the entertainment. The crowd were very disappointed and particularly Doctor Johnson, who was cross and behaved like a child, and forgot he was a philosopher. He contended that it was merely an excuse on the part of the management to save their crackers for a more distinguished company. Some young fellows who overheard the doctor's remark obliged him by creating a disturbance, and thereupon attempted to ignite the fireworks. This, however, proved abortive, because the fireworks were too wet and refused to go off, whereupon the disappointed company departed.

But we must resume our travels once more along Oxford Street. After passing Marylebone Lane we next come to Stratford Place, a cul-de-sac built in 1775 Lord Mayor's Banqueting House, which was pulled in 1737. Here the by Edward Stratford, afterwards second Earl of Aldborough, on the site of the Lord Mayor and Members of the Corporation used to dine after their periodical visits to the Bayswater and Paddington Conduits, which then supplied the City with water. A large portion of Stratford Place has been rebuilt without altering the original style of the frontages but some of the latest buildings erected on the west side are faced with Portland stone. On the east corner of Oxford Street is a branch establishment of the Westminster Bank, and on the west corner are the handsome new premises of Messrs Lilley & Skinner Limited, the boot manufacturers, facing Davies Street immediately opposite. Stratford Place is closed by Derby House, formerly the residence of the Earl of Derby, and unt il 1955 occupied by Messrs Hutchinsons, the well-known publishers. It is now occupied by the Oriental Club, who were previously in Hanover Square; their house flag, an elephant on a green and yellow ground, now flies over Stratford Place. Between Bird Street and James Street stood until 1940 a large C. & A. drapery store. Messrs Penberthy and Company, who were in the next block of buildings have recently moved to 187-193 Oxford Street, on the south side. Mandeville Place, at the top of James Street, consists of a double row of large mansions leading into Thayer Street, and contains the Mandeville Hotel. On the west side is Royds House (G. S. Royds Ltd) a new building on a bomb-damaged site. The Trinity College of Music on the same side is the subject of proposals for a new seven-storey college which will include a concert hall, large music library and more than thirty sound-insulated practice-rooms.

Duke Street leads to Manchester Square, begun in 1776 and completed in 1788, and so named after the Duke of Manchester, to whom the square itself owes its origin. On the north side of the square is Hertford House, formerly Manchester House, built in 1776, now housing the Wallace Collection of pictures, furniture, and porcelain, bequeathed to the nation by Lady Wallace on condition that the Government should provide a special museum to house it in the centre of London. Hertford House was accordingly purchased and reconstructed for that purpose at a cost of £100,000 and was opened to the public in 1900. A recent acquisition is an elegant public drinking fountain of French manufacture which may be seen in the forecourt of Hertford House. It is representative of at least a hundred such fountains that were presented to the City of Paris by Sir Richard Wallace. This particular example formerly stood in the City Road, near Mr Micawber's Windsor Terrace, and was presented to the Wallace Collection by the old Borough of Shoreditch. How it managed to cross the Channel appears to be a mystery that may never be solved. At the north west corner of Manchester Square, overlooking the stately Hertford House, is the new E.M.I. House, its six floors rising to a modest 80 feet above ground level.

Occupying the whole of the large island site between Duke Street, Oxford Street, Orchard Street, and Somerset Street is the popular store of Messrs Selfridge & Company Limited. A feature of this building, which has a frontage of about five hundred feet to Oxford Street, is the long row of stone columns above the ground floor, at intervals of about twenty feet, reaching to the fourth floor. The first portion of the Selfridge store was opened in 1909, but it has since been enlarged to more than double its original size by absorbing the extensive shops of Messrs T. Lloyd & Company Limited, which until 1923 stood on the corner of Orchard Street and Oxford Street, as well as several other smaller shops in the same block of buildings. The entire building as it now appears was completed in 1928 by the addition of the central wing containing the mnia entrance to the store over which is a clock and a peal of bells. The Selfridge store was damaged in the great air raids of 1940 and again in 1944 when its numerous windows were smashed by flying-bombs.

It is now more than half a century since the late Mr Harry Gordon Selfridge, whose name is now familiar all over the world, decided to settle down in London and begin life all over again. He had amassed a great fortune as a partner in the famous Marshall Field store in Chicago. Idleness to a man of his active spirit was irksome and impossible so that instead of retiring a happy man with every prospect of a long and enjoyable life in front of him, he sold his interest in the Marshall Field store and founded the great new store in Oxford Street. In those days the fashionable quarter of Oxford Street, or what is now known as 'The Ladies' Mile', ended at Marylebone Lane and its western end was still a shabby thoroughfare with old and faded shops. Many people doubted whether another store in this street could succeed, but Mr Selfridge, attracted by the cheapness of the ground rents here compared with those of the West End, decided to make this bold experiment. Since those now far off days, the tide of fashion has spread westwards to Marble Arch. Various large multiple shops have followed Mr Selfridge, so that today the west end of Oxford Street has altered out of all recognition compared with sixty years ago. Mr Selfridge died in 1947 at the age of ninety. About 1934 work was commenced upon the erection of a gigantic annexe to the Selfridge store which was planned to cover the great island site enclosed by Somerset Street, Orchard Street, Wigmore Street and Duke Street. Another piece of land having been given in exchange, Somerset Street has been 'liquidated' and the new extension is now completed. It includes a garage seven storeys high, with accommodation for 1,000 cars, all floors directly connected with the store. Selfridge's (taken over by the north of England firm of Lewis's in 1951) celebrated its fiftieth birthday in 1959 and is at the moment the largest store in the United Kingdom and possibly the largest in the world.

Amongst the houses which were demolished for the extension of the Selfridge store was the Grotrian Hall in Wigmore Street, formerly known as the Steinway Hall and now re-established in Conduit Street.

On the west corner of Orchard Street is Orchard House, a handsome block of buildings which harmonizes admirably with the Selfridge building on the opposite corner. The greater part of this building is now occupied by Messrs Marks & Spencer Limited, one of the largest multiple stores, and a branch of the National Provincial Bank. On the south side of Oxford Street at the corner of Lumley Street formerly stood St Saviour's Church, erected by the Association in Aid of the Deaf and Dumb. It was opened in 1880, and the site was given by the Duke of Westminster. This church was pulled down in 1924, and a new building erected on this site which contains offices and shops. Between Lumley Street and Balderton Street, opposite Selfridges, now stands Keysign House, a block of shops and offices nine storeys high and faced with Portland stone. It was erected in 1939. Now for sale is the striking red-brick King's Weigh House Congregational Church in Duke Street, which is at present used as the Protestant Chapel of the United States Navy. It takes its strange title from the original church, which was founded on the site of the King's Weigh House on Cornhill in 1622.

Orchard Street, leading to Portman Square, has been widened on the east side and this was completed in 1936. Portman Square was commenced about 1764, but was not completed until 1785. Montagu House, which has been destroyed in the blitz, stood by itself at the north-west corner. This was originally the residence of Mrs Montagu, a kind-hearted lady famous for her literary talents and for her custom of regaling all the little chimney-sweepers of London every May Day in her house and garden. Mrs Montagu died in 1800 aged eighty. Montagu House was finally the residence of Lord Portman, the ground landlord, but since its destruction the space serves as a large car park. A recent proposal to erect a twenty-eight-floor hotel on the site is meeting with stiff opposition from the local residents. The hotel would be nearly 300 feet high.

Once among the more fashionable squares in the West End, Portman Square ranked second only to Grosvenor Square as a favourite place of residence. Today it is almost doomed. All the original houses which lined the east side were demolished as long ago as 1927, when Orchard Court, flats and shops, took their place. On the south side, new office buildings accommodate *inter alia,* the Portman Building Society, the Registry Office of the Jockey Club and National Hunt Committee, Weatherby & Sons and the Brewer's Society. Demolition of the west side has begun; the last house to be occupied was No 27.

The bulldozers have had to hesitate on the north side, however, for although there is a block of modern flats at No 15 and a further 64 in the luxury category on the north-east corner, No 20 at the north-west end is Home House. Built by Robert Adam in 1777 for the Dowager Countess of Home, it was acquired by Samuel Courtauld in 1932 and dedicated by him to the use of the Arts. This, the finest example of an Adam house, with its beautiful staircase and exquisite decoration, is now the Courtauld Institute (University of London) for teaching the history of art.

The long line of thoroughfares, almost as straight as a ruler, extending from Hyde Park to Clarence Gate, Regent's Park through South Audley Street, Grosvenor Square, North Audley Street, thence across Oxford Street, through Orchard Street to Portman Square, is continued by Baker Street, a fine broad thoroughfare of highly-dignified appearance mostly built between 1785 and 1800. It derives its name from a Mr William Baker who assisted Mr Portman in developing his London estate. Amongst its distinguished residents were Mrs Siddons, the famous actress, Lord Lytton, the novelist, who was born here, Cardinal Wiseman, who died at Number 8 on 15 February 1865, and William Pitt, who lived at Number 14 from 1800 to 1806. Mrs Siddon's house has now been replaced by a block of flats called Chalfont Court, in the hall window of which may be seen four small stained-glass panels of Shakespeare, Milton and Spenser which came from Mrs Siddons' house. On the west side of Baker Street occupying nearly the whole of the long row of houses between Blandford Street and Dorset Street, formerly stood the large furniture and clothing establishment of Messrs Druce & Company, and in the same terrace stood the Portman Rooms, which were used for public dances and social gatherings. For over forty years the

Portman Rooms housed the waxwork exhibition of Madame Tussaud's, prior
to its removal to Marylebone Road. This side of Baker Street has shared in the
general havoc created in this quarter by Hitler's bombs. Here nearly the entire row
of houses between Blandford Street and Dorset Street including the store of Messrs
Druce & Company and the famous Portman Rooms were destroyed in the great
air raid of 10 May 1941. This site was cleared and for several years utilized as
a car-park. It is now covered by a new block of offices principally occupied by
Marks & Spencer Ltd and the Metal Box Company. It was in this section of
Baker Street, according to one of several conflicting theories, that Number 221b
was situated, where Mr Sherlock Holmes, Sir Arthur Conan Doyle's famous
character, had his rooms. Messrs Druce & Company continue their business as
estate agents and contract furnishers and decorators at new premises on the east
side of Baker Street – exactly opposite the site of their once-famous 'Baker
Street Bazaar'.

On the east side of Baker Street, at the corner of Robert Adam Street is
St Paul's Church, originally the chapel to the Portman Estate. At the east corner
of Dorset Street is a handsome block of shops and offices with a row of stone
columns above the ground floor. It afterwards became the headquarters of the
Imperial War Graves Commission but many years later was vacated by the
Government and is now occupied by a commercial firm. The northern section of
Baker Street was formerly known as York Place, but some thirty years ago the
London County Council altered the name of the entire thoroughfare to Baker
Street. This is obviously a wise plan, which should be copied, with a view to
avoiding confusion, in other London streets which are called by two or more
different names, as, for instance, in the case of Southampton Row and Woburn Place.

Thirty years ago York Place was entirely a residential street, but after the
first World War and the renaming of this thoroughfare one house after another
was converted into shop premises, so that it now differs but little from the rest
of Baker Street. On this side of the street is the Classic Cinema erected in 1938
which has a distinctive façade of stone. The Bedford College for Ladies, one of
the most important in London, and affiliated to London University, formerly
occupied the house on the east side of York Place in which Cardinal Manning
resided. The college has now been removed to the west side of Regent's Park,
close to the Inner Circle. York Place Mansions, a distinctive block of shops and
flats on the west corner of Baker Street and Marylebone Road, lost its three top
storeys in the blitz but has since been repaired. One of the finest buildings in
Baker Street is Abbey House, head offices of the Abbey National Building
Society, on the west side at the corner of Melcombe Street. This is a building of
red brick with stone dressings. The central section of this building is adorned by
a lofty clock-tower 150 feet high which lends majesty to the long vista of buildings
in Baker Street. It was formally opened on 18 March 1932 by the late Mr Ramsay
MacDonald, then Prime Minister.

So well established and extensive is the popularity of Sir Arthur Conan
Doyle's stories of Sherlock Holmes, that the great detective is still very much

alive to many readers in all parts of the world. Since No 221b Baker Street, numerically at least, now lies within Nos 217-223, covered by Abbey National House, numbers of letters addressed to Mr Holmes and his friend, asking for photographs, autographs or advice, still arrive at the Building Society offices and, after due acknowledgement are added to the bulky files (which we have been allowed to inspect) under 'Holmes, Sherlock'. Though this may offend the serious Holmesian student, who would reject the suggestion that the rooms shared by Holmes and Watson were in *Upper* Baker Street (as it then was), what is the poor postman to do with letters addressed to 221b Baker Street?

With its long straight streets and fine vistas Marylebone may aptly be described as first cousin to Berlin as it was before the last war, both in respect of the width of its streets and the height of its buildings. Such thoroughfares as Baker Street, Wigmore Street, and Great Portland Street bear a striking resemblance to the long vistas of the Friedrichstrasse, the Leipzigerstrasse, and the Charlotten-strasse in the German capital, and if Marylebone streets were the best that London had to show, it could even then claim to rank as a very fine city.

Mr Thomas H. Shepherd in his *London in the Nineteenth Century,* published in 1829, says: 'The extension and improvement of the metropolis in this princely parish and district within the memories of not very aged people, has been more rapid and surprising than those of any other country in Europe. They present to the astonished spectator, so magnificent are the buildings and so tasteful the scenery, more the appearance of the newly-founded capital of a wealthy state, than one of the suburbs of an ancient city'.

Mr Shepherd's remarks, of course, apply chiefly to the vicinity of Regent's Park, but could he come to earth again and revisit this quarter of the metropolis at the present day, what would he say to the wonderful improvements which have taken place here in recent years? Well might he exclaim 'Marvellous Marylebone' when contemplating the endless rows of stately new buildings now lining almost the whole of the north side of Oxford Street, Great Portland Street, Portman Square, Cumberland Gate, Marylebone Road, and St John's Wood.

Gloucester Place, running parallel to Baker Street on the west side, consists of large well-built private houses, faced with yellow brick turned black by the London soot and fog. Two large blocks of flats, namely Ivor Court and Rossmore Court, have been erected at the junction of Gloucester Place, Rossmore Road, and Park Road. Gloucester Place was built more or less at the same time as Baker Street, and a distant view of the heights of Hampstead can be obtained from both of these streets on a clear day.

On the south side of Oxford Street is Hereford House, erected in 1928 for Gamage's West End store, but afterwards acquired by a group of Insurance Companies for Trade and Industrial Exhibitions and now consisting of shops and flats. On the opening day in September 1930 no less than 100,000 people visited this Gamage store. But its later history was less happy, and in less than a year the company went into liquidation. The ground floor now houses a large C. & A. drapery store and one of the Monseigneur Theatres. The upper storeys of this huge building, which is eight storeys high, and is faced with red brick, consist of flats. Hereford Gardens, demolished in 1928, consisted of a row of large mansions faced with red brick, very similar in appearance to those of Grosvenor Gardens. It extended from the back of Park Lane to Park Street, and the small garden which separated the mansions from Oxford Street gave this locality the atmosphere of some quiet corner in Tunbridge Wells. As compensation for the loss of this small garden, a widening of the roadway was carried out in 1930 in this part of Oxford Street opposite Hereford House. On the corner of Park Lane was one of Stewart's Restaurants. It has been reopened under different management; the once popular Marble Arch Pavilion Cinema has also gone. Between Park Street and North Audley Street is a new range of shops below the 17-floor Park House of Stewart & Lloyd's.

Of late years the western end of Oxford Street has been changed out of all recognition by the erection of mammoth buildings like Mount Royal and the neighbouring Cumberland Hotel on the north side and by Hereford House on the south side. The gigantic Mount Royal building covers the large rectangular site bounded by Oxford Street, Old Quebec Street, Bryanston Street and Portman Street and was erected in 1933-34. Its eight upper storeys contain 750 small service flats run on the lines of a hotel with accommodation for 1,200 people, and its main entrance is in Bryanston Street. It has a sixteen-foot-wide promenade surrounding the top floor resembling the promenade deck of the *Empress of Britain*. Its Oxford Street front was previously occupied by a long row of small shops mostly built in the early years of the nineteenth century when the small skopkeeper reigned supreme. Here also stood the old Marble Arch Cinema, one of the first to be opened in London. Nearly half the shops of the Mount Royal building now house the large and handsome store of Messrs Thomas Wallis & Company Limited, who have migrated to the West End since the destruction of their former establishment in Holborn. It also has a long frontage to Portman Street.

The large gloomy mansions which until 1927 stood on the two corners of Great Cumberland Place opposite the Marble Arch have been replaced by magnificent new buildings. On the east corner site, extending from Great Cumberland Place to Old Quebec Street and back to Bryanston Street, now stands the huge Cumberland Hotel erected by Messrs J. Lyons & Company Limited, designed by F. J. Wills, F.R.I.B.A., and opened on 12 December 1933. It contains a thousand rooms, all fitted with private baths. It has absorbed the site of the old underground station together with the former Marble Arch Hotel, and is directly connected with the new station by a subway. Attached to the hotel is the new Cumberland Corner House which has its own separate entrance. Cumberland Court on the opposite corner of Great Cumberland Place is a handsome block of shops and flats erected in 1929. It is of the same elevation and design as the Cumberland Hotel and is also faced with Portland stone.

Next to Cumberland Court at the junction of Edgware Road is the new building which, with a 23-storey tower of offices, also includes showrooms, shops and a new Odeon Cinema to replace the well-known Marble Arch Odeon which opened in 1928 with Al Jolson's pioneer talking film, *The Singing Fool*. The Marble Arch quarter is blossoming out into one of London's greatest centres of both business and pleasure. The large shops, new cinemas and the gigantic Cumberland Hotel and various attractive restaurants and tea-rooms have made it as popular as the West End. The orators of Hyde Park who draw large crowds to Marble Arch add to the scene of animation. Great Cumberland Place, built between 1800 and 1810, was named after the hero of Culloden, unfairly called the Butcher. It is a fine broad thoroughfare leading to Bryanston Square, named after Bryanston in Dorsetshire, and is admirably suited for the erection of large blocks of residential flats whenever the demand arises for increased accommodation of that kind. ATV House, a new building for Associated Television Ltd has recently been erected in Great Cumberland Place.

Bryanston Square, once called Millionaire Square, and the neighbouring Montagu Square were built between 1810 and 1815 on a spot known as Ward's Fields (which had previously contained a wretched cluster of hovels known as Apple Village) by a Mr Potter, formerly a chimneysweep in the locality, who had amassed a fortune. In Bryanston Square, the little fountain, erected in 1862 by the friends of William Pitt Byrne, sometime proprietor of The Morning Post, should not be overlooked, for the 125-word eulogy is, like its subject, a model of its kind.

Edgware Road, forming a part of the old Watling Street, runs diagonally from the Marble Arch to Cricklewood with scarcely a curve for the entire distance, and thence on to Hendon, Edgware, and St Albans. It is one of the broadest thoroughfares leading out of the metropolis, and might aptly be termed the Gateway to the North-west. From the Marble Arch to Praed Street it is a good-class thoroughfare, but farther north it traverses a poor but improving quarter extending from Chapel Street to the fringe of Maida Vale. So much rebuilding took place in the years preceding the last war that the west side was altered out of all recognition. The increased elevation of the new buildings erected of late years has given a new dignity to this important metropolitan artery. Dingy rows of houses and shabby shops have given way to stately new blocks of shops and flats which present an unbroken line from Marble Arch to Burwood Place.

On the east side at the corner of Bryanston Street is A. T. V. House, the main entrance of which is in Great Cumberland Place, already mentioned. The handsome building at the corner of Seymour Street which has a long frontage to Edgware Road was formerly the large drapery store of Messrs Cozens & Company Limited, who retired from business in 1940. During the second World War it became the American Red Cross Mostyn Service Club but is now miscellaneous shops and offices called 'Marble Arch House'. With the expiration of various leases, a fine new quarter is gradually developing in this immediate vicinity. In Nutford Place was until recently the remnant (tower only) of a church dedicated in 1845 to 'St Luke the beloved physician as a thank-offering for mercies vouchsafed by Almighty God to the inhabitants of this district at a time of visitation by cholera.'

Turning now to the west side of the Edgware Road and starting from Marble Arch, we first pass the Victory Ex-Services Club, formerly the Connaught Club, at the south corner of Seymour Street, which was founded in 1908 by Lady Hope for young men in limited circumstances. In this capacity it proved a failure and after a short period of existence came under new proprietorship and then enjoyed a successful career. The section which fronted Edgware Road, which consisted of shops, was destroyed in the air raids of 1940 when the secretary of the club, Col. Appleyard, was killed in his office. During the second World War, the Connaught Club was taken over by the American Red Cross Columbia Club and became the largest service club in Great Britain. Opposite the Victory Ex-Services Club is Westchester House which together with the adjoining Grosvenor Mansions erected in 1932 forms a long terrace of high-class shops and flats extending along Edgware Road from Seymour Street to Connaught Street. 'The Mitre' tavern, on the north corner of Seymour Street has been re-named 'The King and Queen', adopting the sign of another establishment in the Harrow Road, which was recently demolished.

The neighbouring island site between Connaught Street and Kendal Street is now covered by Connaught Mansions and a vast new block of shops and flats called Portsea Hall. This is faced with red and yellow brick and is a stately building of eight storeys completed in 1938. Its central section stands back in a recess above the ground floor and its two side wings form a bay. From Burwood Place to Sussex Gardens are the new super-luxury flats called 'The Water Gardens'; three 18-storey towers, a 10-storey block and a crescent of houses enclose private gardens with pools (complete with goldfish), fountains, trees, etc; which, the agents suggest will 'produce an atmosphere of tranquillity, insulated from the traffic of the Edgware Road and Marble Arch'. Between Sussex Gardens and Star Street is Cambridge Court, a block of shops and flats erected in 1932 which has replaced a row of shabby houses and shops. Outside Lloyd's Bank, at the corner of Star Street, is a milestone which still tells us we are 'Half a mile from Tyburn Gate'. Tyburn was used as a place of execution from time immemorial until 1783, and the triangular gallows stood there from 1571 to 1758. The first recorded execution took place in 1196. At the junction of Edgware Road and Chapel Street is a new seventeen-storey office block with a large Marks & Spencer's store occupying the street level.

Half a mile north of Marble Arch the Edgware Road is intersected by Sussex Gardens on the west and Marylebone Road on the east, but to achieve this the Marylebone Road after having pursued a generally straight course for nearly a mile, suddenly makes a curious turn to south-west. Works now proceeding will rectify this lapse and a straightened Marylebone Road will cross the Edgware Road a little further north and, by means of a flyover and a roundabout now under construction, make a flying junction with the important Harrow Road. Marylebone Road calls for special notice. Extending from Edgware Road to Great Portland Street, it comprises the western portion of the original New Road between Islington and Paddington, and is about one mile in length.

71 Sir Alfred Gilbert's Shaftesbury Memorial Fountain, topped by the aluminium figure of Eros, dominates Piccadilly Circus.

72 Piccadilly Circus at night.

73 Sometimes mistaken for Lord Nelson, the Duke of York stands on a column 124 feet high.

74 Chester Terrace, one of the famous Nash terraces in Regent's Park, newly restored.

75 Carlton House Terrace, built by Nash in 1831, on the site of the old Carlton House.

76 The Athenaeum Club in Waterloo Place. On the pavement edge is a horse-block erected for the Duke of Wellington in 1830.

77 Burlington Arcade, Piccadilly, in 1828.

78 Burlington Arcade today.

79 Train's Street Railway, near Marble Arch, 1861.

80 Piccadilly in 1886; site of the Ritz Hotel.

81 Albany, Piccadilly, in 1830.

82 An aerial view of Buckingham Palace, London home of H.M. the Queen, which is now overlooked by the tall buildings on the Stag Brewery site, Victoria.

83 The London Hilton, western Europe's largest luxury hotel.

84 The footbridge over the lake in St James's Park, which replaced the old suspension bridge in 1957.

85 *The Economist* building in St James's Street,

86 Boodle's Club (1765) and *The Economist* building of 1964.

87 Brooks's Club (1788) in St James's Street.

Commencing from Edgware Road, on the north side of Marylebone Road, are Hyde Park Mansions and Oxford and Cambridge Mansions, extending through to Chapel Street, and comprising several large blocks of flats, some of which are dated 1887. Beyond Chapel Street we next pass the building of the former Marylebone Public Baths on the south side, opposite Lisson Grove, now used as Council offices, opened in January 1850, the Samaritan Free Hospital for Women and Children, opened in 1890, and the Western Ophthalmic Hospital at the corner of Enford Street. The new Marylebone Public Baths and Hall are in Seymour Place and were erected in 1935. On the north side of Marylebone Road is the Church Army Women's Hostel, formerly the Nurses' Home of Queen Charlotte's Hospital until it was removed to Goldhawk Road, and at the corner of Lisson Grove the St Marylebone Grammar School, instituted in 1792 as The Philological School. Just beyond is the former Hotel Great Central. Opened in 1899, this fine hotel was owned by the Frederick group and during the first World War was utilized as a hospital. It is now the headquarters offices of British Railways. Marylebone Station, also opened in 1899, was the London terminus of the former Great Central Railway Company, now British Railways (London Midland Region). The Great Central was the last of the leading railway companies to extend its system to the metropolis, and to make room for this new station Harewood Square was swept away, together with much poor-class property in the vicinity of Lisson Grove.

The Great Central building has for a worthy neighbour the head offices of the National Cash Register Company. This is a handsome building of six storeys faced with Portland stone and completed in 1936. Its architects were Messrs Stanley, Beard and Bennet. The neighbouring row of old houses between Balcombe Street and Upper Gloucester Place have since been pulled down and the site is now occupied by the new sixteen-storey Castrol House, a glassy-looking affair which contrasts violently with the handsome Town Hall opposite.

From here to Baker Street, Marylebone Road is bordered by an almost continuous range of fine modern buildings and includes an extensive widening of the roadway by incorporating its original long front gardens. This improvement was carried out in 1932, and has given Marylebone Road the appearance of a stately Continental boulevard. On the south side of the road is Marylebone House, a nine-storeyed block of office serected in 1939 between Knox Street and Wyndham Street. It is now the offices of British Home Stores. Next to it is the fine building of the North-West District Permanent Building Society. This was erected in 1938 and is eight storeys high with a façade of red brick with stone dressings.

At the west corner of Gloucester Place is the new Marylebone Town Hall, a fine building in the classic style, adorned with a Corinthian colonnade and a lofty clock-tower. It was opened in March 1920, having been designed by Sir Edwin Cooper, and replaced the old Town Hall in Marylebone Lane, opened in 1825. A large annexe on the west side extending to Upper Montagu Street and the new public library were opened in 1940. Between Gloucester Place and

Baker Street are the Bickenhall Mansions, a long block of flats, seven storeys high, erected in 1897.

Opposite Bickenhall Mansions two fine new blocks of shops and flats called Berkeley Court and Dorset House, ten storeys high, have been erected on the island sites between Upper Baker Street and Gloucester Place. Berkeley Court erected in 1928 contains a branch of Lloyds Bank and a roof-garden covering an area of one acre. Its architect was Mr W. E. Masters. In connexion with this improvement, Glentworth Street and Clarence Gate Gardens have been opened up into Marylebone Road by a new street running parallel to Baker Street between Dorset House and Berkeley Court. The stately Dorset House at the corner of Gloucester Place was completed in 1935, at a cost of £500,000, and includes a large underground garage. It is ten storeys high faced with red brick and divided into several wings radiating from the centre. It was designed by Messrs J. P. Bennet & Son.

On the large site extending from Upper Baker Street to Allsop Street is Chiltern Court, a very imposing building erected by the Metropolitan Railway Company in 1927-29 above Baker Street Station. It is seven storeys high, faced with Portland stone, and contains shops and high-class flats, together with an attractive arcade connecting Upper Baker Street with Marylebone Road, and a branch of the Midland Bank at the corner of Baker Street. Its architect was Mr Charles W. Clark. In this building Arnold Bennett, the novelist, died on 27 March 1931. The Metropolitan Railway from Paddington to Farringdon Street, the first underground line to be constructed in London, was opened on 10 January 1863, and the extension line from Baker Street as far as Swiss Cottage on Easter Monday 1868.

Adjoining Baker Street Station is Madame Tussaud's Waxwork Exhibition, founded in 1854. The present building also included a cinema and a restaurant which replaced that which was destroyed by fire in 1925 but the cinema was demolished in 1940 by bombs. On the site of the cinema a Planetarium has now been constructed. This unique and popular feature was opened to the public early in 1958. Opposite Chiltern Court is another large block of flats called Portman Mansions, with a long frontage to Marylebone Road, and beyond is Marylebone Parish Church, designed by Thomas Hardwick and consecrated in 1817. It has a portico supported by Corinthian columns and was erected at a cost of £70,000. Inside, the Browning Chapel recalls the clandestine marriage of Robert Browning and Elizabeth Barrett on 12 September 1846, and the Browning Study Groups of Winnipeg, Canada, presented a commemorative window in 1946. The site of the old church in the village High Street is now a Garden of Rest, in which is recorded the burial of Charles Wesley, who wrote many hymns, James Gibbs, the architect and Allan Ramsay, the painter; also, the marriage of Richard Brinsley Sheridan and the baptism of Lord Byron and Nelson's daughter Horatia. On the same side of the road are the Headquarters of the Methodist Missionary Society, a red-brick building eight storeys high, erected in 1939. From 1840 to 1850 Charles Dickens lived at Number 1 Devonshire

Terrace, a large house with a garden extending to the Marylebone Road. It was but recently pulled down and on the site now stands Ferguson House, a block of miscellaneous offices. On the wall is a sculptured stone panel, about eleven feet by eight, depicting 'The Inimitable' and showing various characters from the six books Dickens wrote while living here. Beyond the High Street is Devonshire Place, leading to Wimpole Street, and on the large site facing Marylebone Road, between Devonshire Street and Harley Street, a new building, seven storeys high, was completed in 1933 for the London Clinic and Nursing Home Limited. Here the building line has been set back for the widening of Marylebone Road to link the Harrow Road Flyover with Euston Road. On the east corner of Harley Street is an ornamental building erected by the Westminster Bank.

Close to Devonshire Street in former times stood the Manor House of Marylebone, then situated within the royal park. In the days of Queen Elizabeth I it was well stocked with game, and it is recorded that on 3 February 1600 the Ambassadors from the Emperor of Russia and the Muscovites rode through the city of London to Marylebone, and there hunted at their pleasure. The manor house, which was built in the reign of Henry VIII, was pulled down in 1791 to make room for Devonshire Place.

On the north side of Marylebone Road, opposite the London Clinic and Nursing Home Limited, is Harley House, another fine block of flats, faced with Portland stone, extending from Harley Street to the Royal Academy of Music. The latter building, which was removed here from Hanover Square, is a very ornate structure of red brick with stone dressings. Old Harley House, which stood on the site of the present block of flats of that name, was a detached residence with a small lawn in front, surrounded by a high brick wall with an entrance in a side street running towards Regent's Park. In 1856 it was rented for a year by the Queen and Royal Family of Oudh, with their army of 110 retainers.

At the corner of Albany Street is Holy Trinity Church, built from the designs of Sir John Soane, and now the headquarters of the Society for Promoting Christian Knowledge. It also contains a tower in two sections, and is quite as imposing as the parish church on the other side of Marylebone Road. At the back of this church now stands an immense block of flats called the White House which covers a large island site. It was erected in 1935 and is built on the radiating principle with several wings diverging from the central section. It is faced with concrete and contains a restaurant, a swimming-pool and squash-racquet courts. East of Albany Street, Marylebone Road is continued by Euston Road, the north side of which as far as Hampstead Road is remembered as a shabby collection of miscellaneous little shops, odd restaurants, sanitary engineers, metal workers and nondescript premises which, though important in themselves, offered nothing of interest to the ordinary passer-by who, though he walked from Osnaburgh Street to Hampstead Road every day of his life, would be puzzled to describe what he saw. All this has now been demolished and replaced by a range of new shops and flats, set back to provide a widened road with six lanes of traffic, culminating at Hampstead Road with a 400 ft office tower of

36 floors. At the busy junction of Euston Road with Hampstead and Tottenham Court Roads, where the volume of traffic passing through is more than 35,000 vehicles per 12-hour working day, a four-lane underpass has been constructed for east-west traffic at an estimated cost of £1,135,000.

Albany Street, which takes its name from the Duke of York and Albany, is a very depressing thoroughfare at the back of Regent's Park, which leads to Camden Town. It contains spacious barracks on the east side, occupying, together with the drill-ground and the outbuildings, a space of nearly eight acres. There has been some talk of pulling down the barracks and disposing of this extensive site for the erection of blocks of flats, but so far nothing definite has been decided upon. There being nothing of interest to detain us in this dreary locality, we will now continue our travels along the north side of Regent's Park to St John's Wood.

It would be a simple matter to deal with St John's Wood by saying that it consists almost entirely of blocks of flats — and that is probably the general impression; but there is a certain fascination about the district that precludes such discourtesy, and it is not difficult still to find numbers of dignified houses with attractive gardens within the seclusion of high walls that give pleasure to the passer-by.

That part of the forest of Middlesex now known as St John's Wood was in the manor of Lilestone (Lisson), and in the time of Edward I was a gift from Otho, son of William de Lilestone to the Knights Templars, and later passed to the Knights Hospitallers of St John of Jerusalem, when it became St John's Wood and has so remained ever since. In 1732 the estate was in the possession of Lord Chesterfield (of the *Letters*) who sold it to Henry Samuel Eyre, and some of it is still owned by the Eyre family.

At the junction of Wellington Road and Prince Albert Road is St John's Church (previously the St John's Wood Chapel), with its burial ground long since converted into a public garden. The other side of this ground is overlooked by St John's Wood High Street, formerly a poor district known as Portland Town. Evidence of this can be seen in Allitsen Road (late Henry Street) where on an old house it is just possible to decipher 'Portland Town Association for United Work among the Poor — entirely unsectarian', and in Chalbert Street nearby is the St Stephen's Portland Town Institute, the gift of Lady Howard de Walden in 1898. All traces of Portland Town and its poverty finally disappeared when the Woronzow Almshouses of 1836 in St John's Wood Terrace — the gift of a Polish nobleman — were completely rebuilt in 1962, and each of the 44 elderly ladies who occupy them now has a modernized selfcontained home. At one time, elderly people of both sexes were accommodated here, but the Matron in charge prefers the present arrangement, and (with a curious glance at your present scribe) expressed the opinion that 'some old men are not capable of keeping their places clean'.

Further along the Terrace is the former Connaught Chapel, with a massive Corinthian portico and pediment, now used as a commercial television studio.

At the west end a group of dwellings recently erected by the former Marylebone Borough Council, true to the artistic tradition of the neighbourhood, have names such as Turner, Cotman, Opie, Wilkie, etc.

Facing St John's Church is Lord's Cricket Ground, covering an area of about seven acres. The present ground was moved here early in the nineteenth century from Dorset Fields where Thomas Lord opened his first ground in 1787, a site which is now covered by Dorset Square. The ground now holds some 34,000 spectators, and an additional feature of interest is the Cricket Museum, opened by the Duke of Edinburgh in 1953. The oldest building at Lord's was The Tavern, built in 1868; an innocent suggestion that it looked rather shabby caused something of a sensation, for it appears that the Members of the Marylebone Cricket Club regarded it with considerable affection and resented any attempt to tamper with it. Nevertheless, in October 1966 it was demolished and a new Lord's Tavern was built and opened in June 1967. This building stands a few yards to the south-west of the old site, upon which a new stand, called the Tavern Stand, has been erected.

Opposite Lord's are three new blocks of 11-storey flats appropriately named Lord's View — from the upper floors and balconies the residents have an excellent view of the cricket.

St John's Wood Road leads to Hamilton Terrace, a fine broad thoroughfare running parallel with Maida Vale, with many elegant houses and St Mark's Church, a handsome edifice in the Early English style of architecture designed by Thomas Cundy in 1847.

In Acacia Road, opposite Grove End Road, the first cabmen's shelter to be erected in London was opened by the Hon. A. Kinnaird, M.P., in 1875. Unfortunately there is no trace of this shelter now; there is merely a 'Cab Rank for One Cab' and a telephone perched on the wall. The need for such shelters has diminished, for the modern 'cabby' is not exposed to the weather like his predecessor of Victorian days. On Ordnance Hill are the St John's Wood Barracks, erected in 1832 as the 'Riding House Department of His Majesty's Ordnance'. The King's Troop of the Royal Horse Artillery and a number of horses are now quartered there, and it is among their special duties to fire gun salutes on Royal Birthdays, State Visits and other ceremonial occasions.

At the corner of Acacia Road, where Wellington Road becomes Finchley Road is St John's Wood Underground Station. This replaces two earlier stations — St John's Wood Road, which was near Lord's and Marlborough Road. It is strange that, while so many of the large houses that we once admired in Wellington and Finchley Roads have been demolished, the disused old Marlborough Road Station building still survives. In the adjacent Queen's Terrace is 'Ye Knights of St John', a tavern with a sculptured sign on the front of the house depicting the Knights on horseback smiting the infidel.

Opposite the station, by Grove End Road stood, from 1821 until 1928, the Eyre Arms Hotel. The grounds were sometimes the scene of balloon ascents in the early days of aeronautics and the hotel became the headquarters of the

Belsize Boxing Club, started in the eighties by Messrs Bettinson and Fleming who founded the National Sporting Club. The large Wellington Hall adjoining the Eyre Arms was frequently used for dances and other social functions; the seven-storey Eyre Court now stands on the site. Across the road is All Saints, the parish church, which contains several memorials to various members of the Eyre family.

In Grove End Road is the hospital of St John and St Elizabeth, founded in Bloomsbury in 1856, and further south the St John's Wood United Synagogue, dedicated by the Chief Rabbi, Dr Israel Brodie, on 29 September 1963. At No 44, on the other side is the large studio-mansion of the Victorian artist of Dutch descent, Sir Laurence Alma Tadema. Said to be one of the oldest houses in 'The Wood', one can still see many glazed tiles with the monogram L.A.T. set in the walls. A pillared pergola (attributed to Jean Jacques Tissot, a previous tenant) leads through the large garden to the entrance hall — with *Salve* over the doorway — and at the topmost point of the building is an iron weathervane in the form of a palette and brushes.

At the junction with Abbey Road is a memorial to Onslow Ford, R. A. (1852-1901), and a large house in Abbey Road is now the E.M.I. Recording Studios, where the usual cluster of enthusiastic young autograph hunters varies in size according to the popularity of the recording star inside.

At the Abbey Road Baptist Church is the Abbey School for the English Language, which provides tuition for missionary candidates and theological students from other countries. It was in the vestry of this church (built in 1864) that the Abbey Road Building Society was formed on 8 March 1874. It is further chronicled that in excavating for the building of this church two ancient wells were discovered, and upon reference to early records it was found that on this spot once stood the Abbey of St John of Jerusalem, whence come the names 'Abbey Road' and 'St John's Wood'.

It is customary to deplore the fact that St John's Wood is not what it used to be — which of course, is quite true — and applies equally to most other parts of London; nevertheless, it is not difficult to discover that there is still ample evidence of that special charm which has always been associated with St John's Wood or, as the journalist of an earlier day loved to call it, "The Shady Grove of the Evangelist".

Seventeenth Walk

From the Bank to Shoreditch, Hoxton, Spitalfields, Whitechapel, Bethnal Green, Mile End, Victoria Park and Stepney

Our route is from the Bank of England by way of Threadneedle Street and Bishopsgate, past Liverpool Street Station. Between Liverpool Street Station and Shoreditch High Street, Bishopsgate, or Norton Folgate, as it was originally named and part of it is still called, was formerly a very narrow thoroughfare, which was a great hindrance to the heavy volume of traffic in this part of the City, A part of Norton Folgate was widened on the west side in consequence of the extension of Liverpool Street Station, but the complete widening of this thoroughfare from Liverpool Street Station to Shoreditch was not completed by the City Corporation until 1910. As a result of this improvement the London County Council were enabled to extend their tramways from Shoreditch almost up to the doors of Liverpool Street Station.

On the west side of Norton Folgate, now lined by modern buildings, formerly stood the City of London Theatre, built in the year 1837 by Mr George Honey, an actor. It was eventually pulled down for the extension of the Great Eastern Railway from Shoreditch to Liverpool Street, which was cut through the stage and part of the auditorium. What still remained of the theatre became the Central Hall. Between Middlesex Street and New Street on the east side, is a handsome new police station with a façade of stone, six storeys high with its two top floors set back from the building line. Many of the old houses on this side of Bishopsgate between Middlesex Street and Shoreditch High Street were destroyed in the air raids of 1940 and have been removed.

Between Commercial Street and Bethnal Green Road is the old terminus of the Eastern Counties Railway, which later became the goods station of British Railways (Eastern Region). Unfortunately, it was completely destroyed by fire in December 1964. Great Eastern Street, nearly opposite and leading to Old Street, is a broad thoroughfare, opened on 12 October 1876, and together with Commercial Street provides direct access from Bloomsbury to Whitechapel and the London Docks.

The metropolitan borough of Shoreditch extended from Bishopsgate to Old Street on the west, and from Finsbury to Hackney and Bethnal Green on the north and east. It is now part of the London Borough of Tower Hamlets (which revives an old name). It was originally a village on the old Roman northern road, but is now a continuation of Bishopsgate. Shoreditch, or Soerdich, derives its name from the old family of the Soerdiches, Lords of the Manor in the time of Edward III. In the Shoreditch High Street is a veneer warehouse, until recently a well-known tavern, 'The Jane Shore'. On the wall of the entrance is one of those excellent paintings on glazed tiles that were such a popular feature of Victorian pubs. This large picture shows Edward IV meeting his mistress Jane Shore in the goldsmith's shop that her husband kept. That Shoreditch derived its name from Jane Shore and that she died in a ditch are quite unreliable traditions. The High Street, which extends from Norton Folgate to Kingsland Road, was considerably widened on the east side in 1877, and is now one of the leading business thoroughfares of East London though most of its buildings have disappeared in the air raids of 1940. On the east side the large establishment of Messrs Jeremiah Rotherham, known in the trade as 'Jeremiah's', the wholesale drapery warehousemen, has been destroyed and a new building, Anlaby House has replaced it. On part of the site now occupied by their present premises, the new Shoreditch Telephone Exchange was built in 1956. Next door formerly stood the London Music Hall which was pulled down in 1935, since when this site has remained vacant. Another notable building now standing in Shoreditch High Street is the huge bacon factory of Messrs Thomas Lipton & Company Limited. This is a building of eight storeys which covers a large site on the corner of Bethnal Green Road, erected about 1932.

Great Eastern Street formerly contained the premises of the ill-fated National Penny Bank, which started business on 1 January 1878, when some 233 persons opened accounts. The foundation-stone of this building was laid by the Lord Mayor in May 1877, and it was the first to be specially erected as a penny bank, and was open for business every evening. About seventy years ago the National Penny Bank suspended payment and went into liquidation. Many similar banks were established in Great Britain during the nineteenth century.

At the corner of Shoreditch High Street and Hackney Road is St Leonard's Church, a handsome brick edifice with a Tuscan portico and a tall steeple, erected in 1735 by George Dance, the elder. Like St Paul, Covent Garden, St Leonard's is known as The Actor's Church, for among the theatrical people buried here are James Burbage, who in 1576 built in Shoreditch the first English playhouse — known as 'The Theatre'. Also his son Richard, who 'created' the parts of Hamlet and Richard II. Richard Tarleton, one of Queen Elizabeth's players and Will Somers, jester to Henry VIII are others among this distinguished company. The churchyard is now used as a public garden. The parish stocks and whipping-post are preserved in the churchyard. Against the railings may be seen the Victoria Diamond Jubilee Fountain, the gift of the readers of *Little Folks,* 1897. Holywell Street, a turning on the west side of the High Street leading to Curtain Road, is built on the site of a huge dump or mound of rubbish accumulated here after the Great Fire of London. It was removed in 1777 to make room for houses and new streets in this locality, and was similar to others formerly existing in Leather Lane, Holborn, and in Whitechapel Road.

In Old Street, west of St Leonard's Church, is the Shoreditch Town Hall on the south side, erected in 1866, and the Police Court on the opposite side, erected in 1905. At the back is Hoxton Square, now a public garden, containing shabby old-fashioned houses used as business premises. In Hoxton Street to the north of Old Street stood until 1940 the Britannia Theatre, once famous as a house of blood-curdling melodrama, and afterwards used as a cinema. It was burned out in an early raid of 1940 and then wrecked by a landmine on 8 December of the same year. It stands on the site of the Pimlico Tavern which was a resort of poets and actors mentioned by Ben Jonson. In 1858 it was rebuilt by Samuel Lane as a splendid new theatre. Under his management and later that of his wife Sara who survived him for many years it became one of the most famous of music-halls but for some years before the second World War it had been a picture-theatre. Amongst its famous artists of by-gone days were Marie Lloyd, Charles Coburn, Albert Chevalier, Dan Leno and Herbert Campbell. Faint traces of the old 'Brit' still survive, for at each side of the space where it stood is a pilaster with a capital of scroll work in which may be seen the 'S. L.' monogram of Mrs Sara Lane.

Hoxton as a slum area is rapidly becoming a thing of the past and dilapidated properties are being replaced by blocks of modern flats, built by the former Shoreditch Borough Council and their successors. In Falkirk Street, which was a particularly undesirable slum, the outstanding building now is a new comprehensive school for 1500 pupils. 'Charles Square, 1771', west of Pitfield Street, was a pathetic collection of decayed 18th century houses which have been superseded by new flats. No. 16, on the north side, is the sole survivor of the period; it originally accommodated the Shoreditch County Court, and is a well-proportioned house with a fine central doorway, over which in its official days was the Royal Coat of Arms. Midway along Pitfield Street on the corner of New North Road is St John's Church, Hoxton, consecrated in 1826. This is a building of stone which has a circular tower with a clock. From 1898 to 1908, the Vicar was the Revd Eric Farrar, M.A., son of Dean Farrar and hero of his fathers' popular book, *Eric, or Little by Little*. Hoxton, which forms a part of the borough of Hackney was once inhabited by the fashionable world, and was famous for its medicinal wells. Already in 1598 it was joined to the City, and Stow describes it as a large street with houses on both sides.

The existing Shoreditch public baths are situated in Pitfield Street, but in Tabernacle Street there were once some baths attributed to the well of St Agnes-le-Clair. Owing to a discovery about 1841, during some excavation work opposite these baths, it has been supposed that they were already celebrated for their medicinal properties in the time of the Roman occupation. At a depth of about fourteen feet below the surface a spring was discovered, and this stream of water was found to pass through an aqueduct composed of Roman tiles, well cemented together, and in an excellent state of preservation. The last record of these baths was an advertisement of 1848 which said they were supplied by a chalybeate spring producing 10,000 gallons every 24 hours. It also included an illustration of the entrance – a Victorian building bearing the strange date of 1502.

The old Shoreditch Vestry was one of the first public bodies to undertake the generation and distribution of electricity and in fact, stands as the pioneer in this respect for the East End of London. In Hoxton Market, near the Pitfield Street Library, is a building of 1896 which was the Combined Electricity and Dust Destruction Undertaking. Burning refuse provided the heat which drove the turbines and generated electricity at the same time. An opening banquet was held in the Town Hall on 28 June 1897 and the Chairman switched on the New Electric Light. In the Library is a bust of 'Charles Bradlaugh, of this Parish' who, as a refractory Member of Parliament was, in 1880, imprisoned in the Clock Tower of the Houses of Parliament. Not far from this spot stood, until 1844, a house which was at one time occupied by Oliver Cromwell, and Queen Elizabeth I also resided in this neighbourhood. The baths are also stated to have been frequented by Charles I and some of the high personages of his court. Furniture making is the principal industry of the Borough of Shoreditch and opposite the Baths in Pitfield Street is a striking building with a portico having four massive Doric columns and a pediment which is now the G.L.C. Technical College for the Furnishing Trades. It was originally 'The hospital and almshouses at Hoxton of the Haberdashers Company under the foundation of Robert Aske'.

Turning our attention next to the opposite side of Shoreditch High Street, just beyond St Leonard's Church to the south of Hackney Road is Columbia Road, in which was situated Columbia Market, built by the Baroness Burdett-Coutts at a cost of £200,000, and opened on 28 April 1869. Unfortunately, it never attracted the public favour, and for a short period the City Corporation took control of the market, but as it could not be made self-supporting they gave it back again to the Baroness Burdett-Coutts in 1874. The building, which was thought to have considerable architectural beauty, was erected in the Gothic style from the designs of Mr H. A. Darbyshire. It was a cathedral-like building with innumerable figures of angels, saints and heroes, lavishly decorated with crocketing, foliation and biblical and other uplifting texts. For many years a landmark for miles around, it was latterly dwarfed by surrounding multistorey Council flats and was finally used as a depot and workshop by the London County Council. It should have been preserved as a beautiful 'folly', but it has now been demolished, and Council dwellings stand in its place.

On the site occupied by Columbia Market and the buildings forming the square stood a foul colony of squalor and disease, consisting of wretched low tenements and hovels, called Nova Scotia Gardens. It was situated in the midst of pestilential drains and dust-heaps, and was one of the most squalid areas in London. Thanks to the benevolence of Lady Burdett-Coutts the whole of this foul rookery was swept away, and in its place four large blocks of model dwellings were erected, forming the square known as Columbia Buildings. These buildings, earlier in date than the Market, have since been superseded as more modern accommodation becomes available. In Bethnal Green, the memory of Angela Georgina, Baroness Burdett-Coutts will, ere long, survive only in Angela Street, Georgina Gardens and Baroness Road — *while they last*.

Other slums in the worst parts of Shoreditch had already been cleared away in 1843 for the construction of Bishopsgate Terminus, in the vicinity of Bethnal Green Road. But there still remained another terrible rookery between Shoreditch Church and Bethnal Green Road, now covered by the Boundary Street Estate, which was a shame and a reproach to this part of the metropolis. It comprised an area of about fifteen acres, and was bounded on the north by Virginia Road, on the east by Mount Street, on the south by Old Nichol Street, and on the west by Boundary Street, from which the modern estate takes its name.

Three centuries ago the whole of this area formed a part of the garden of the nunnery of St-John-the-Baptist, Holywell, founded by Sir Thomas Lovel. Old Nichol Street and the streets which then ran parallel to it, New Nichol Street, Half Nichol Street, Vincent Street, and Mead Street, are said to have been constructed about the time of Nelson's great victories and to have been named after his admirals. At the time of their demolition in 1893-95 these streets were slightly less than a century old. In addition to these streets there existed a large number of small courts entered under the houses, and built generally over what had once been the gardens or yards of the original houses.

Whatever might have been the original character of this neighbourhood, it had by 1880 become one of the worst rookeries in the East End of London, as regards the character both of its houses and of their occupants. This area, which formed the nucleus of the parish of Holy Trinity, contained a population of 5,700 inhabitants. The entire parish, although numbering 8,000 inhabitants, possessed no church, and all services were held in a long room over a stable in Old Nichol Street. In this street alone there dwelt at one time no fewer than sixty-four ticket-of-leave men. Street rows between rival groups of the inhabitants who acknowledged a 'Royal Family of the Nichol' and those who acknowledged a pretender were frequent. Morality was at its lowest ebb, and the courts running off the main streets were the harbours of shoplifters, thieves, and ruffians of the lowest type. Only their inhabitants dared venture down these courts, which were a veritable sink of iniquity and forcing-house of crime.

Nevertheless, the vicar of Holy Trinity, the Rev. Osborne Jay, who was appointed in 1886, secured a marvellous hold on the people. He built mission premises, including a club-room and gymnasium, with a church above, and also established a lodging-house which competed successfully with the most famous of the filthy and verminous lodging-houses in this area. The ground floors of these wretched hovels were so constructed as to be twelve to eighteen inches below the street level, and no house possessed such a thing as a front door. No repairs were ever carried out, and what backyards had ever existed had nearly all been roofed in and occupied as additional houses. This sordid story has been graphically told in Arthur Morrison's book *A Child of the Jago*.

In 1890 the London County Council decided to step in and remedy this state of affairs under a recently-passed Housing Act, and deeming that no half-measures could adequately deal with such an area, they decided to undertake the clearance and rebuilding of the whole of this congeries of alleys and courts by razing the entire area to the ground. From that time onwards it became popularly known as the Condemned Area, and starting from 1891 the old streets were demolished bit by bit, and wide new streets constructed in their place, containing new blocks of flats to rehouse as many people as was consistent with a due regard to health and sanitation.

An avenue sixty feet wide, named Calvert Avenue, planted with trees, now leads from the High Street, Shoreditch, to a central open space or circular garden called Arnold Circus, from which other streets, fifty feet wide and also planted with trees, radiate to the limits of the new estate. During the rebuilding operations a well, supposed to be one of those belonging to the ancient nunnery, was discovered in Old Nichol Street. The new buldings have provided accommodation for between five thousand and six thousand persons in flats varying in size from one room to six rooms. So conveniently situated and nicely laid out is the Boundary Estate that many people would doubtless prefer it to Fulham or Barnsbury as a place of residence.

Let us now return to High Street, Shoreditch, and passing Bethnal Green Road, a wide thoroughfare leading to Cambridge Heath Road, continue our travels along Commercial Street to Spitalfields. This thoroughfare, about half a mile in length, connecting Shoreditch with Whitechapel High Street and continued by Leman Street to the London Docks, was constructed in 1845-46. Like so many other new streets it failed at first to attract speculative builders, and for some time after its opening none of the building sites were taken up. In 1863 the Peabody buildings at the corner of Folgate Street were erected. These are five storeys high and contain a number of shops fronting Commercial Street. The rents were fixed at such a low figure as to place these rooms within the means of those whose wages were no higher than from twelve shillings to twenty-two shillings per week, but no tenant was allowed to sublet his rooms under any pretext whatever. Also in Commercial Street is the tobacco factory of Messrs Godfrey Phillips Ltd. Over the main entrance is a very fine statue of Sir Walter Raleigh by Benno Elkan. Sir Walter wears a suit of armour and, appropriately, carries a tobacco plant in his hand. Another, rather insignificant, statue of Raleigh is (temporarily) in Whitehall.

About half-way along Commercial Street, at the corner of Brushfield Street, is the new Spitalfields Market or London Fruit Exchange, owned by the Corporation of London, which was opened by Queen Mary in December 1928. The market buildings alone cover an area of seven acres, the largest combined fruit, vegetable and flower market in the world though, in amount of trade, it is second to Covent Garden. The buildings are all comparatively modern. When the London Wool Brokers found that the old Wool Exchange in Coleman Street, City was to be demolished, they moved to Spitalfields and the Fruit Brokers, who use only one of their two auction rooms, leased the other to the Wool Brokers. The Spitalfields building was then renamed The London Fruit Exchange and Wool Exchange. Spitalfields derives its name from the St Mary's

Spital or Hospital founded in 1197 in the parish of St Botolph Without, Bishops-gate. It originated in the great extension of the metropolis which arose out of the calamity of the Great Fire of London, owing to people having been forced to seek refuge in the suburbs and in Southwark whilst the City was rebuilding. Thus a great number of additional workmen were attracted to the capital as the work proceeded, and most of them afterwards made it their settled abode. Owing to these circumstances nearly the whole of Spitalfields was built, and it became a good, if not fashionable, neighbourhood until the 19th century exodus began. Thus we find in this area whole streets of early 18th century houses, still dignified, but shabby and deteriorating, many of them now used as workrooms for the tailoring trade.

Spitalfields afterwards became the home of the Huguenot immigrants after their expulsion from France in 1685 on the revocation of the Edict of Nantes. Stow says, 'God's blessing is surely not only brought upon the parish by receiving poor strangers but also a great advantage hath accrued to the whole nation by the rich manufacturers of weaving silks and stuffs and camlets, which art they brought with them.' Their large-windowed houses could be seen in Seabright Street, Cheshire Street and others. In Sclater Street ('This is Sclater Street 1773' – says an inscription on the wall), a few derelict weavers' windows where they placed their looms – about four times the width of a normal window – can still be seen. Sclater Street is the present-day 'Club Row' – the Sunday morning market for cage birds and dometic pets of all kinds.

Spitalfields still contains some fine old houses once inhabited by the more prosperous of the merchant weavers, more suggestive of Bloomsbury than of East London. Their large gardens contained mulberry-trees in the Huguenot days, when the silkworms were fed on the home-grown leaves. In the once-prosper-ous Church Street, nearly every occupant used to keep his carriage. Opposite Brushfield Street, which has undergone an extensive widening, is Christ Church, a noble building with a magnificent portico and a tower built in 1725-29 from the designs of Hawksmoor. One of his three East End churches, Christ Church Spitalfields is being restored. It seems that the trouble is not solely war damage, but also decay and old age. Its churchyard is now a pleasant public garden. Spital Square, midway between Bishopsgate and Commercial Street, continued by Lamb Street, has been largely obliterated by the street improvements which have been carried out here in recent years. Only the houses on the north side now remain; those on the south side were demolished for the extension of Spitalfields Market. It was a somewhat gloomy red-brick square of the early Georgian period and marked the site of the old hospital. In Spital Yard is the house where Susannah Annesley, mother of John Wesley, was born on 20 January 1669.

On the east side of Commercial Street, to the north of Christ Church, stood until about 1934 the Cambridge Music Hall, formerly a popular East End place of entertainment. The curious little almshouses in nearby Puma Court were erected in 1860 'for the poor inhabitants of the liberty of Norton Folgate'. The courtyard is dotted with massive stone vases. Between Christ Church and Whitechapel High Street, crossing Commercial Street, is Wentworth Street. Here we are in the heart of the densely-populated Jewish quarter of the East End of London. We almost seem to have taken leave of everything English and entered a foreign city. We might just as well be in some street in Warsaw or Cracow. Wentworth Street is a *daily* market, not Sunday mornings only, like the better-known Middlesex Street, formerly called Petticoat Lane, of which it is a branch. Middlesex Street runs north-west from High Street, Whitechapel, to Bishopsgate. The greatest part of it is now occupied by modern warehouses. Its name was altered from Petticoat Lane in July 1846 but people still continue to call it by its original name.

For a hundred years or more Petticoat Lane has been famous for its crowded Sunday market of second-hand clothes, boots and shoes and various other articles. In the bad old days it was said that you could lose your watch at one end of the lane and buy it back at the other end. The section which leads out of Whitechapel High Street has been destroyed in the early raids of 1940 and on 29 December of that year the large clothing factory of Messrs Hollington's was the centre of a fire which spread far and wide. Four years later, in November 1944, a rocket which landed in the parallel thoroughfare of Goulston Street caused twenty-three deaths and increased the devastation behind Middlesex Street. Between Middlesex Street and the north side of Houndsditch a large demolition of courts and alleys was carried out about twenty-five years ago and on this site now stands Commerce House, a fine block of shops and offices, and the wholesale warehouse of Messrs H. Lotery & Company Limited. Here, as in the City and the West End, the new London is rising, with irresistible energy, on time-honoured sites, and sets us wondering whether in the course of time the East End will develop into some high-class business quarter as important in a different way as even Westminster or the Strand.

The southern portion of Commercial Street, extending from Whitechapel High Street to Christ Church, Spitalfields, was carved out of Essex Street, Rose Lane, and Red Lion Street in 1845 at a cost of £120,000. In Essex Street was a mansion occupied by the Earl of Essex, the favourite of Queen Elizabeth I, which was three storeys high. Another large mansion, which was a palace where Queen Elizabeth occasionally resided, stood near Elliston Street. Both of these were removed in 1844 to make way for the construction of Commercial Street. Some of the houses thus demolished were notorious dens of infamy, and included the worst part of Wentworth Street. In a thoroughfare called Ewer Street stood the Catherine Wheel public-house, once a rendezvous of Dick Turpin and his comrades, who sallied forth from here to Epping Forest. Another Turpin adventure belongs to the 'Red Lion' tavern opposite Aldgate East Station. In 1738 Dick Turpin stole from a farmer near Epping a mare called 'White Stockings' and stabled her at the 'Red Lion'. When he and his fellow highwayman Tom King came to fetch her, the constables also arrived. There was a struggle, and Turpin cried, 'Shoot, Tom or they'll get us!', but in the confusion Turpin shot King, who died almost immediately. Behind a glass case in the bar of the 'Red Lion' is an old signboard illustrating the incident, and also the key of the stable where 'White Stockings' was concealed. Duval Street, a turning on the west side of Commercial Street next to Spitalfields Market, formerly called Dorset Street, was the scene of the last of six murders committed in 1888 by Jack the Ripper, whose identity has remained a complete mystery. Because of the skilled character of the knife-incisions made by the murderer in every crime committed it is popularly supposed that they were the work of some mad surgeon or doctor. All the former houses on the north side of Duval Street were pulled down for the new Spitalfields Market. It now has a long frontage to this street, which has been much widened.

On the east side of Commercial Street, not far from Whitechapel High Street, is Toynbee Hall, an important social service centre, where Oxford and Cambridge graduates and professional people explore at first hand the problems of poverty and share the existence of the people around them. In 1867 Denison, an Oxford student who had been deeply impressed with the gulf existing between the rich and the poor in London, took lodgings near the London Hospital in order to share the life of the poor in this district. His example was followed by others, so that by 1874 it had become the custom for a few Oxford graduates to spend part of their vacation in the neighbourhood of St Jude's, Whitechapel, and to join in the good work of the parish. Canon Samuel Barnett, the vicar of St Jude's, founded Toynbee Hall in 1884 as a memorial to Arnold Toynbee, who had died in the previous year. Canon Barnett was the first Warden of the Settlement. In the great raids of 1941, the valuable Toynbee Library was destroyed by incendiary bombs. The theatre was also badly damaged, but this was reopened in 1964 and is now a drama centre for Inner London. Evening classes continue under the auspices of the Inner London Education Authority, but it is the social and welfare services that are the major work of Toynbee Hall.

In Leman Street, leading to the London Docks, is the huge building of the Co-operative Wholesale Society Limited, and the Sailors' Home, both on the east side of the street. Whitechapel High Street, which we now enter, provides quite a welcome surprise to the stranger to these parts. Of all the great arteries leading out of the metropolis, this is perhaps the most spacious and the most picturesque. Strype refers to Whitechapel as 'a great thoroughfare, being the Essex Road and well resorted unto, which occasions it to be the better-inhabited and accommodated with good inns for the reception of travellers, and for horses, carts, coaches and wagons'.

For all practical purposes the Whitechapel boulevard may be said to commence from Houndsditch and the Minories, but thence to the City boundary at Middlesex Street it is known as Aldgate High Street, after which it assumes the name of Whitechapel High Street from Middlesex Street to Brick Lane. Whitechapel Road commences east of Whitechapel Churchyard and Brick Lane. The Jewish settlement in the East End, which centres principally round Aldgate, Whitechapel, and Brick Lane, is the largest colony in London, and has inhabited this quarter for many years. It consists mostly of working people employed in tailoring and dressmaking, who in the past have poured into London in their thousands from Poland, Russia, and the Baltic countries. Street after street and district after district became occupied almost entirely by Jews, and this occasioned bitter complaints from the old inhabitants, especially those whose businesses suffered as a result.

Before the construction of Commercial Street the ground in the rear of Aldgate Church bore that aspect of squalid poverty which caused the visitor to shudder as he reflected upon the extremes of wealth and want which a century ago were a feature of this great metropolis. In 1845 much of this squalid property was swept away and a new metropolitan market was erected at the back of Aldgate Church by Andrew Kennedy Hutchison for the convenience of the Jewish population in this district. According to Strype, 'Both sides of Petticoat Lane were hedgerows and elm-trees with pleasant fields to walk in, insomuch that some gentlemen of the Court and City built their houses here for air'.

The north side of Aldgate High Street contains the Three Nuns Hotel, mentioned in Defoe's *Journal of the Plague Year*, and rebuilt in 1880. The south side had long been famous for its collection of butchers' shops, but they have given place to a length of new road which provides a one-way traffic diversion for west-bound vehicles; a formidable array of railings compels any pedestrian who wishes to cross the road to use the devious subways. For over 300 years hay wagons from Essex and Hertfordshire used to occupy the Whitechapel High Street from early morning to late afternoon on three days of the week, until the Hay Market was abolished in 1928. In the Whitechapel Library is one of those attractive paintings on tiles (about five feet by four) picturing this Hay Market scene in 1788; this was on the wall of the entrance to one of the many taverns along the road and, fortunately, was saved when these buildings were demolished in 1963 to make way for the traffic roundabout just mentioned. With a little imagination, the fragrance of new-mown hay might also be recaptured a little further east, by Stepney Green, where 'The Hayfield' tavern stands at the corner of Hayfield Passage. A new Aldgate East Station has been constructed at the junction of Whitechapel and Commercial Roads with a pedestrian subway. This was opened in 1939 and has replaced the former St Mary's Whitechapel Underground Station. In both Whitechapel Road and Mile End Road, whole rows of houses have been destroyed or damaged beyond repair by bombs. This may afford scope for the erection of higher buildings better suited to the great width of this spacious London throughfare.

The streets on the south side of Whitechapel High Street were built on the site of Goodman's Fields, a part of a farm belonging to the abbey of the Nuns of St Clair. The principal ones are Leman Street, Mansell Street, and Prescott Street, and according to Strype these streets were already inhabited in 1720 by thriving Jews. Leman Street forms a continuation of Commercial Street, and leads to the London Docks on the east side and the St Katherine Docks on the west.

At the junction of Commercial Street and Leman Street is the entrance to Commercial Road, a broad thoroughfare constructed in 1800 near Whitechapel in order to provide direct access from the City to the newly constructed West India Docks. It was cut across what was previously known as Stepney Fields, which became rapidly built over as a result of the formation of these new docks. In 1802 it was extended to the East India Docks. It originally terminated at Church Lane, at which point the traffic had to turn to the right and pass round by Whitechapel Church in order to reach Aldgate. In May 1870 it was extended from Church Lane to Leman Street at a cost of £250,000, and opened by Sir John Thwaites, Chairman of the Metropolitan Board of Works.

The last church of St Mary in Whitechapel High Street was erected in 1875, and crowned by a tall spire. The cost, amounting to £12,000, was defrayed by Mr Octavius Coope, M.P. for Middlesex. It was destroyed in the air raids of 1940, leaving only the tower and fragments of the nave walls. But in the early morning of 14 July 1945, a stroke of lightning split the topmost six feet of the spire down the centre and one half crashed to the ground. A month later, a demolition squad of four workmen removed the dangerous spire, which fell in pieces inside the shell of the church. The old church of St Mary Matfellon dated back at least to the early fourteenth century, though the name 'Matfellon' was not given to it until about the year 1428. In the churchyard was an open-air pulpit but this was also destroyed in the blitz. The churchyard has now been grassed and seats provided for the public, while a narrow rectangular path marks the outline of the bombed church. In the church wall at the corner of Whitechurch Lane is a (dry) drinking fountain erected in 1860 'by one unknown, yet well known'. Whitechapel was originally a portion of Stepney and derives its name from the white walls of the chapel of ease which stood on the site of the old church.

Osborn Street, opposite Whitechapel Churchyard, which has lost many of its buildings in the blitz, leads to Brick Lane, a long narrow thoroughfare extending to Bethnal Green Road and Virginia Street.

On the west side of Brick Lane is the brewery of Messrs Truman, Handbury & Buxton. Most of the better shops are situated nearer to Whitechapel High Street, the poorer ones being located at the northern end of the lane. Bethnal Green Road was originally continued by Church Street, a turning out of Shoreditch High Street, but in 1879 it was opened up into Shoreditch opposite Great Eastern Street, as a new direct thoroughfare from east to west. The opening ceremony was performed by Sir James M. Hogg, Chairman of the Metropolitan Board of Works. The former borough of Bethnal Green extended from Shoreditch on the west to Poplar and Victoria Park on the east, and from Stepney on the south to Hackney on the north and is now part of the new Borough of Tower Hamlets. It was originally a hamlet in the parish of Stepney, from which it was separated in 1743. By 1742 it had a population of 15,000 crowded in the narrow streets and courts of its southern and western quarters and this had increased by 1787 to 23,000. The name of Bethnal is a contraction of Bathon Hall, a family named Bathon having resided here in the reign of Edward I. The original hamlet was centred round the Green in Cambridge Heath Road. At the dawn of the nineteenth century it still consisted largely of open fields, and according to a map of London in 1799, most of the streets came to a finish about half-way between Brick Lane and Cambridge Heath Road. Bethnal Green appears to have finally lost its rural character between 1820 and 1830, during which decade a great extension of the metropolis took place in every direction.

Retracing our steps along Brick Lane to Whitechapel Road, we note Rivoli Garage, which recalls the blitzed Rivoli Cinema on the south side of the street which stood next to St Mary's, Whitechapel, Underground Station. It occupied the site of Wonderland, a famous East End boxing resort, which was destroyed by fire about forty years ago. No. 34, at the corner of Fieldgate Street, is the Whitechapel Bell Foundry, where bells have been cast for nearly 400 years; among them the $13\frac{1}{2}$ ton Big Ben, the famous Bow Bells, the eight bells of Westmister Abbey — the earliest of which was cast at Whitechapel in 1853 — and hundreds of others all over the world. Farther east is the London Hospital, founded in 1740, when a house was opened in Prescott Street for sick and wounded seamen, watermen, and dock labourers. In December 1758 a Charter of Incorporation was obtained, and the present building erected, from the designs of Mr B. Mainwaring. A new wing was added in 1866 and another in 1876 and the hospital, now the largest in England, contains accommodation for nearly a thousand patients. The hospital is to be rebuilt on very elaborate and up-to-date lines as soon as circumstances permit. At the back is the large church of St Philip, Stepney, built at the expense of the Rev. Sidney Vatcher, one of its vicars, on the site of a church which dated from 1818.

Until early in the nineteenth century the site immediately to the west of the London Hospital was occupied by a huge dump which was known as the White-chapel Mount. It was stated to be 329 feet long and 182 feet wide, and was considerably higher than the adjoining London Hospital. From the summit an extensive view of the former villages of Limehouse, Shadwell, and Ratcliff could be obtained. The construction of the East and West India Docks early in the nineteenth century caused roads to be made through the low marshy fields extending from Shadwell and Ratcliff to Whitechapel. Cannon Street Road, leading from Whitechapel Mount to St-George's-in-the-East, so increased the value of the land on each side of it, that the Corporation of London decided to take down the Mount. This occurred in 1807-08, and Mount Terrace, and East Mount Street were then built on that site, thus marking the spot where the Mount stood.

The Mount owed its origin to the earth thrown up from various trenches dug for the defence of London in the Civil War of 1642. After the Great Fire of London, a large portion of the debris from the streets at the east end of the City was piled upon the Mount, and later its height was further increased by the accumulation of rubbish from newly-erected buildings. A report was spread at the time that the ruins from the Fire of London had been thrown over a deep pit where the bodies of persons who had died in the Plague of 1665 were deposited, but neither any human remains nor any objects of interest or value were discovered during the removal of the Mount. The cartloads of earth which were removed after many weeks of labour were carefully examined with that object in view.

On the north side of Whitechapel Road, which also contains the principal shops, stood until 1940 the Pavilion Theatre at the corner of Vallance Road, which was principally devoted to Jewish drama. It was originally built for a floorcloth factory, but in 1828 it was converted into a commodious house of entertainment. On 10 February 1856 it was destroyed by fire, but was rebuilt in the following year. The southern end of Vallance Road leading from White-chapel Road to Bethnal Green Road has been destroyed in the air raids of 1940 and so also has the Pavilion theatre. Hughes Mansions, a block of flats in Vallance Road completed in 1929, was destroyed in March 1945 by one of the last of Hitler's rockets that fell on London. Of its ninety-three flats, sixty were completely destroyed and had to be demolished. One hundred and thirty-one people were killed and forty severely injured. Hughes Mansions were named after Councillor Mary Hughes, J.P., of the housing committee and daughter of the author of *Tom Brown's Schooldays*. Nearly opposite the London Hospital is Whitechapel Station, formerly the terminus of the Metropolitan District Railway. In 1902 this line was extended for a distance of two miles beneath the Mile End Road to Bow Road and Campbell Road Junction, from which point it runs alongside the Tilbury and Southend line, now British Railways (Eastern Region), to Barking and Upminster. By 1905 the entire underground railway system in London had been converted to electricity.

Cambridge Heath Road, the dividing line between Whitechapel and Mile End Road, formerly owned to the title of Dog Lane, and runs northward through Bethnal Green to Hackney. Just beyond Bethnal Green Road on the east side is the Bethnal Green Museum, opened in June 1872 by the Prince of Wales, afterwards King Edward VII, as an eastern branch of the Victoria and Albert Museum. The original village green, covering seven acres, which adjoins the Museum, has been converted into a pleasant public garden, and close by on the same side of the road is the former Bethnal Green Town Hall. Standing on the Green facing Bethnal Green Road is the church of St John which was designed by Sir John Soane and consecrated in 1823. It was damaged by fire in 1871 and has since been enlarged. It has a thick square tower with a clock surmounted by a turret. The church, which looks much older than it actually is, was badly damaged in the blitz, but its exterior walls and massive tower escaped destruction. In Cambridge Heath Road many shabby houses have been removed by bombs, but on one large site at the back of Messrs Mann, Grossman & Paulin's White-chapel Brewery several fine new blocks of London County Council flats are now completed. These have frontages to Cambridge Heath Road and Lisbon Street and are five storeys high. At the corner of Bethnal Green Road and Cambridge Heath Road is the new Bethnal Green Underground Station, opened in 1947. During the second World War, before the opening of the extension from Liverpool Street to Stratford, this station was used as a large air-raid shelter. This was the scene of a disaster which occurred on the night of 3 March 1943. Following an air-raid alert some 1,500 people surged forward to the entrance to the shelter. This caused a sudden pressure on those who were already descending the nearby dark stairway and a woman holding a child fell down. In a matter of seconds there was an immovable mass of bodies against which people above were forced by the pressure from behind. One hundred and seventy-three men, women and children were killed and sixty-two injured.

Mile End Road claims to be the widest thoroughfare in London, and what were originally bare and very broad strips of pavement have now been adorned with gardens and shrubberies. A long stretch of this wide pavement known as Mile End Waste is a Saturday street market. It was here that William Booth, founder and first 'General' of the Salvation Army, 'commenced his work of salvation' in July 1865. This is commemorated by a bust of the General by George Wade, which was unveiled in 1927 by John Scurr, a Roman Catholic M.P. for Stepney. At the corner of Cambridge Road, now renamed Cambridge Heath Road, are the Trinity Almshouses, the quaintest group now left in London. They are constructed on a seventeenth-century plan behind an enclosing wall and spiked railings that screen them from the public view. They were built in 1695 for twenty-eight decayed masters and commanders of ships or their widows, on land given by Captain Harvey Mudd of Ratcliff, who was an Elder Brother of the Trinity House. Badly hit by bombs, they have been restored to their original condition, but with modernized interiors.

Sidney Street, opposite Cambridge Heath Road, leading to Commercial Road, was the scene of the celebrated siege of criminals on 3 January 1911. Late on the night of 16 December 1910 the tenant of the house next door to Number 119 Houndsditch, occupied by Mr Harris, a jeweller, heard strange sounds and tappings at the back of his own premises. He gave the alarm, whereupon the attention of the police was directed upon three houses, Numbers 9, 10, and 11 Exchange Buildings, which backed on to Houndsditch. A police cordon was then drawn round the buildings, and Sergeant Bentley knocked at Number 11. The door was opened by one of the criminals, named Gardstein, whereupon Bentley placed his foot across the threshold. Almost immediately Bentley and Sergeant Tucker were shot dead. Afterwards Gardstein was accidentally wounded by one of his own friends, and was found dead on the following day in a house in Grove Street, together with a number of papers, which threw light on the other criminals. These included the ringleader, known as Peter the Painter, Fritz Svaars, and a third man called Joseph.

At midnight on 2 January 1911, information was obtained that the latter two had forced their way into the room of a woman living at Number 100 Sidney Street, and had there taken refuge. At daybreak the two fugitives were called upon to surrender. A fusillade then took place, in which Inspector Leeson was mortally wounded. A detachment of Scots Guards was then brought up, which began a process of sniping at the windows and roof of the house. The house caught fire, and later charred remains, identified as those of Svaars and Joseph, were discovered amongst the ruins. Beyond these two men, no other participants in the earlier crime were ever punished. Three firemen were injured. Among those present was Sir Winston Churchill, who, as Home Secretary, superintended the operation. The notorious Sidney Street was flattened by bombs, but today it is a splendid new housing estate, with open spaces and fresh air that were never known there before.

On the north side of Mile End Road, beyond Cleveland Street, is the brewery of Messrs Charrington & Sons, erected in 1847, the Tower Hamlets Mission, the Mile End Cinema, formerly the Paragon Theatre, and a Supermarket in what was previously the imposing drapery store of Messrs T. Wickham & Sons, with an extensive frontage to Mile End Road, built in a style which will invite favourable comparison with similar establishments in the West End.

Further along on the same side of the road was the People's Palace, standing on the site of the Almshouses and School founded by Francis Bancroft, a benevolent Alderman and Draper of the City of London. The almshouses 'for 24 old men' were built in 1735-7 and the school 'for 100 poor scholars' began to function in 1738. The bequest is administered by the Drapers' Company. In 1884 the site was acquired for the building of the People's Palace, which was opened by Queen Victoria on 14th May 1887, and the boys of Bancroft's School were temporarily lodged at Tottenham while their present school at Woodford Wells, opened in 1889, was being built. The People's Palace buildings and the East London College are now part of London University and known as Queen Mary College. A new building extends from Grantley Street across Bancroft Road to join the earlier buildings. It is the Queen Mary College Faculty of Engineering and the foundation stone was laid by Queen Elizabeth the Queen Mother, Chancellor of the University of London, on 5 June 1956. Across the road is the large L.C.C. Ocean Estate, consisting of sixty-two blocks of flats, yellow brick with concrete balconies, all having salt-water names such as Atlantic, Biscay, Caspian etc. East of Mile End Road is Bow Road, lined with old-fashioned houses, once inhabited by well-to-do tradesmen. Bow Church, standing in the middle of the road, was built in the time of Henry II, and was made parochial in 1740. This beautiful church, including the upper portion of its massive square tower, was damaged in the air raids of 1940, but it has been handsomely restored and is again open. Also in the middle of the road, overlooking the public conveniences, is a statue of Mr Gladstone with outstretched hand pointing to the 'Way In'. The shabby houses which until recently flanked the south side of Bow churchyard have now been pulled down and replaced by Greater London Council flats. On the north side of Bow Road not far from Bow Church is the Poplar Town Hall, a plain red-brick building of five storeys erected in 1938. It has no claim to distinction or beauty and is more suggestive of a warehouse than a public building. Near this spot, until 1953, stood the fountain erected in 1872 to record the part played by Bryant & May and their work people in securing the abandonment of a Match Tax proposed by a Chancellor of the

Exchequer of the period. Just east of Bow Church a considerable widening of Bow Road with the introduction of a flyover is proceeding, which will improve the northern approach route to the Blackwall Tunnel.

Burdett Road, leading from Mile End Road to Limehouse and the West India Docks, contains the East London Tabernacle, opened in February 1872 at a cost of £12,000, and providing accommodation for about three thousand people. It was bombed, but completely rebuilt and reopened in 1957. Grove Road, the continuation of Burdett Road northwards from Mile End Road, leads to Victoria Park, one of the largest and finest in London. It was formed between 1842 and 1847 at a cost of £50,000, which was defrayed out of the purchase money received from the Duke of Sutherland for the Crown lease of Stafford House, St James's (now Lancaster House), sold in 1841 for £72,000. Victoria Park serves as an open space for the densely-peopled districts of Bethnal Green and East London, and is one of those places which no student of London life should miss seeing. All kinds of popular amusements are provided for; there are three lakes for boating and bathing, an open-air swimming-bath, several gymnasiums, flower gardens, shrubberies, a bandstand, a palm-house, an open-air theatre, a tea-house, and a large ornamental fountain presented by the Baroness Burdett-Coutts in June 1862. By way of contrast to this leviathan of drinking fountains which is sixty feet high, just outside the park, in Lauriston Road stands a very modest little fountain, 'From L.S. and B.S. 1881. To commemorate 25 years of happy married life.'

Near the western entrance to Victoria Park, in what was then called Bonner's Field, on the banks of the Regent's Canal, stood the house of Bishop Bonner at Bethnal Green, which was pulled down about 1850. Bonner's Field was the scene of the Chartist Riots of 1848. On the east side of Bonner Road, leading to Old Ford Road, is the City of London Hospital for Diseases of the Chest the foundation-stone of which was laid by the Prince Consort on 25 June 1851. In this neighbourhood, at the time of the formation of Victoria Park, a wretched village of hovels was swept away, formerly known as Botany Bay, from so many of its inhabitants having been consigned to another place bearing the same name. The Old Ford estate round about Victoria Park was largely developed in 1855, when small parcels of land were eagerly bought for upwards of £6,000. On the north side of Victoria Park is Hackney Common, also called Wells Common, an open space of about fifteen acres. This is now flanked on its east side by a long row of attractive London County Council flats, with sun balconies affording particularly agreeable views, which were erected between 1945 and 1949.

Returning again to Mile End Road, on the south side nearly opposite the Mile End Brewery is Stepney Green, leading to the High Street, and St Dunstan's Church. The Green itself, which is a long narrow strip of ground in the centre of the road, has been converted into pleasant public gardens laid out with paths and bordered with shrubs. The area of the parish of Stepney, which is now in the Tower Hamlets borough, is so great because it was once mostly a wild heath called Stibenheath. It extends from the City boundary to Poplar from west to east and from the Thames to Bethnal Green from south to north. The village of Stepney proper consisted, as late as 1700, of only a few houses other than places of entertainment. On Sundays and at Easter and Whitsun holidays vast crowds of Londoners then resorted here to eat Stepney buns and to regale themselves with ale and cider. Looking upon its dull grey streets to-day it is difficult to realize that Stepney was once a lonely heath.

The ancient church of St Dunstan is situated midway between Mile End and Commercial Roads. It is practically an unchanged fifteenth-century edifice in the likeness of a rural church of that period, and whilst all around has altered, it alone preserves its rural aspect. The churchyard, covering over seven acres, surrounds the church, and in 1871 was converted into a recreation ground by the late Metropolitan Board of Works at a cost of £3,000. It was opened to the general public in August 1872. Though St Dunstan's Church has escaped destruction in the great blitz, the streets round it have been wiped out. The new east window in the church records, in coloured glass, the surrounding devastation. White Horse Road, leading to Commercial Road, overlooks the east side of the recreation ground, and is used as a street-market. Here the rows of costers' stalls afford a picturesque contrast to the old-world appearance of the churchyard.

Commercial Road, which traverses the densely-peopled quarters of Limehouse and St-George's-in-the-East, is also a busy shopping thoroughfare. On the north side stood until 1940 the extensive drapery store of the London Co-operative Society, one of the largest in the East End, but this too was destroyed in the blitz. In Arbour Square just off the north side of Commercial Road is a distinctive-looking block of flats, with sun balconies, six storeys high. Raine's School on the east side of the square is a handsome five-storeyed building with a façade of red brick.

On a part of one of London's most-bombed areas, in Poplar, the London County Council has developed a new estate at a cost of £1,600,000, called Lansbury after the late Mr George Lansbury, first Commissioner of Works in the second Labour government. Here flats, houses, schools and a shopping centre have been erected. The London County Council bore the main cost, including the purchasing and clearing of the site which covers thirty acres, but the Festival of Britain authorities contributed substantially towards the cost of buildings which were the 'live architecture' section of the 1951 Festival.

Eighteenth Walk

The Port of London, Shadwell, Limehouse, Isle of Dogs, Poplar, Canning Town, West Ham, Woolwich, Greenwich, Deptford and Bermondsey

In this chapter we propose to describe the various docks and the region covered by the Port of London. That London is the third largest port in the world is a well-known fact, but comparatively few Londoners are aware of its real magnitude. This is partly because so much of it is behind walls and partly on account of the winding character of the River Thames, which breaks the continuty of its docks. In Liverpool on the other hand, where the River Mersey is very wide and follows a straight course, the docks extend in an unbroken line for several miles, and can therefore be seen to great advantage.

From an aeroplane it is possible to see all the docks of London at one time, even including Tilbury when visibility is good. When seen from the air they resemble a series of lakes spread out at intervals between Tower Bridge and North Woolwich. The area now administered by the Port of London Authority extends from Teddington to 22 miles beyond the Nore, a total distance of about 90 miles, but the inner Port of London may be said to begin at London Bridge and finish at North Woolwich.

During the war, the Port was never closed to ordinary mercantile traffic, though a small proportion was diverted to Liverpool, Bristol, Glasgow and west-coast ports. Enormous damage was caused to the various docks and ware-houses by enemy action. On 7 September 1940, some 350 planes attacked in two waves east of Croydon up to the Thames estuary in an attempt to destroy the docks. They were met over Kent and East Surrey but a number broke through and were engaged over the capital. On this day, though not for the first time since 1666, Londoners saw flames leaping up from various points in the crowded and densely-populated districts of Dockland and Woolwich. The sky was lit up for three days by the great fires which raged in the Wapping and Rotherhithe districts of the East End. The blitz destroyed a third of the enormous warehouse area in Dockland. Yet by the middle of 1945, London as a port had already recovered its trade to a surprising extent. At a cost of five hundred casualties, no less than 106 million tons of shipping passed through London. Only nine years after the day when the Thames was turned into a river of fire, the Port of London was already back in its old exalted place. Though not all that was destroyed has by any means yet been replaced, nine hundred ships a week are now carrying nearly sixty million tons of merchandise a year in and out of London's river. This great waterway from the sea to the heart of this great metropolis is once again the mercantile hub of the world.

Starting out our travels from the Tower Hill, our route is by way of East Smithfield. The surroundings are gloomy, and not exactly comparable to those of Piccadilly, but they are full of historical interest.

The St Katharine Docks, which first call for notice, extend from Tower Hill on the west to Thomas More Street on the east, and are bounded on the north by Upper East Smithfield. The cover an area of twenty-three and a half acres. To make way for the St Katharine Docks, the first stone of which was laid on 3 May 1827, nearly a whole parish, comprising 1,250 houses and the old hospital of St Katharine, was pulled down. No less than 11,300 inhabitants were moved in clearing the ground for the new docks, of which Mr Telford was the engineer, and which were publicly opened on 25 October 1828. The construction of the St Katharine Docks provided employment for 2,500 men for two years, and the total cost was £1,700,000. The soil excavated at St Katharine's, was conveyed by water to Millbank and utilized to fill up the reservoirs of the Chelsea Water-works Company, on which land a considerable portion of South Belgravia was built by Mr Cubitt. Near St Katharine's Hospital, down by the river, stood the great breweries which supplied beer to the English armies in the Low Countries in the days of Queen Elizabeth I. All the warehouses of the St Katharine Docks which back on to East Smithfield were destroyed or badly damaged in the blitz of September 1940 and some of them have been razed to the ground. These docks are now only used by small craft and dredgers, but when the war damage has been made good, the Port of London Authority have plans for the moderniza-tion of these docks, but that will depend upon future requirements.

To the east of the St Katharine Docks, separated only by Nightingale Lane, now renamed Thomas More Street, are the London Docks, which extend east-wards to Shadwell, The first and largest of these docks was opened on 31 January 1805. They cover an area of one hundred acres and cost £4,000,000. Extensive new tea warehouses were opened in 1845, and in 1858 two new locks were constructed, 60 feet wide, together with a new basin 780 feet long by 450 feet wide. The London Docks are the great depot for the storage of wines, spirits, and tea. In 1864 the St Katharine and London Docks were amalgamated.

The construction of the various London Docks was not carried out without much opposition, for it is on record that the cargo of a large vessel was often delayed five or six weeks before it was delivered. Before the docks were built, goods were put into lighters at Blackwall and conveyed to the old-fashioned quays near London Bridge, and after a long delay, occasioned sometimes by the Customs officials themselves, they were finally removed to the different warehouses in the City. In those days river robbery was a thriving trade, and it was said that many a fortune was made by this systematic plunder. No wonder, then, that an outcry was raised by carmen, porters, waterside labourers, and lightermen, who profited considerably by the difficulties attending the removal of merchandise, and that from Wapping to Westminster the whole riverside populace was up in arms against the coming of the docks. In 1800 it was estimated that there were 11,000 riverside robbers making depredations to the value of half a million pounds a year.

In 1831 the average number of British ships and vessels of all kinds in the Thames and the docks was estimated at 13,444, including 3,000 barges and 2,288 small craft engaged in the inland trade. At that time it was stated that the East India Company's ships alone carried more cargo than all the vessels of London combined had done a hundred years previously.

On the south side of the London Docks is Wapping High Street, and on the north side East Smithfield is continued eastwards by St George's Street, now renamed the Highway, leading to Shadwell High Street. St George's Street was the modern name bestowed upon the notorious Ratcliff Highway.

The original hamlet of Ratcliff contained 1,150 houses in 1794, of which 455, together with 36 warehouses, were destroyed by fire on 23 July of that year. This fire consumed more houses than any one conflagration since the Great Fire of London in 1666. It was caused by the boiling over of a pitch-kettle at a boat-builder's, whence the flames spread to a barge loaded with saltpetre and other stores. It then spread to several other vessels lying near by which could not be removed owing to the low tide. The blowing up of the saltpetre in the barge carried the flames to the saltpetre warehouses of the East India Company, which were blown up, raining fire on all the adjacent buildings. The south-west wind directed the flames to Ratcliff Highway, which caught fire on both sides. Towards Stepney almost every building was destroyed, until, having reached an open space, the fire was brought to a standstill. Several hundred families were rendered homeless, and the Government sent 150 tents from the Tower, which were pitched on an enclosed piece of ground adjoining Stepney Churchyard. A subscription for the relief of the sufferers was opened at Lloyd's Coffee House.

In 1811 Ratcliff Highway was startled by a series of murders which for the moment filled all London with terror. Mr Marr, the first victim, kept a lace shop at Number 29. At about midnight on Saturday, 7 December 1811, after having sent his servant-girl out to purchase some oysters for supper, he was found murdered behind the counter, together with Mrs Marr, the shop-boy, and a child in the cradle. Very little, if any, money was missed from the till. Other crimes followed. On 19 December, Williamson, the landlord of the King's Arms public-house in Old Gravel Lane (now renamed Wapping Lane), together with his wife and female servant, were also murdered. The author of these crimes, a sailor named Williams, was eventually captured at a sailors' boarding-house, where a knife stained with blood was afterwards found hidden. The wretch hanged himself in prison the night of his arrest. His body was placed on a platform in a high cart and driven past the houses of Marr and Williamson. A stake was then driven through his breast and his carcass thrown into a hole dug for that purpose in Cannon Street Road.

In Dock Street is St Paul's Church for Seamen, with a fine weathervane of a three-masted ship, and just off the Highway is the church school in the middle of Wellclose Square, erected on the site of a Danish church which stood here from 1696 to 1869. Thomas Day, the eccentric author of that deadly classic *Sandford and Merton,* lived here. Wellclose Square once contained the Royalty Theatre, built by John Palmer, the actor, and opened in April 1826. It was succeeded by the Brunswick Theatre, which was built in seven months and opened on 25 February 1828. Three days later it collapsed during a rehearsal, killing ten people. A number of eighteenth century houses still survive here, though in pretty poor condition. In North East Passage, at that angle of the Square, a stone on a derelict little cottage proclaims that in 1806 it was 'Metilda Place'. Adjacent in Swedenborg Square stood a Swedish church where Emmanuel Swedenborg was buried. It was demolished in 1908 and his body removed to Uppsala. This Square is being developed, and 137 homes are to be built by the Greater London Council. The shops in the Highway, of which only a few now remain, cater principally for the requirements of sailors, and here Charles Jamrach, the founder of the firm of dealers in wild animals, set up in business about 1840. Most of the shops in the Highway have been destroyed by bombs and are now in ruins. Cable Street, which runs parallel to the Highway, has also been badly damaged.

In Cannon Street Road is the church of St-George's-in-the-East, built in 1714-22 by Nicholas Hawksmoor, and one of the so-called 'Fifty new churches of Queen Anne' (of which only twelve were built). The parish of St-George's-in-the-East was detached from that of Stepney in 1727. As a result of the 'No Popery' agitation in 1860, disorderly scenes occurred almost every Sunday in the church of St-George's-in-the-East, in which the congregation shouted, 'No Popery', and interrupted the church services. In order to put a stop to these riots it became necessary to admit the police to the church to maintain order. In May 1941, St George's was destroyed by incendiary bombs and for 17 years a hut within the remaining walls, known as 'St George-within-the-Ruins', served the parish. The approach and façade of the old building remain, and a new church, built inside the shell of the old one — very light and bright, with modern furnishings — was re-dedicated by the Bishop of London in April 1964. The space previously occupied by the galleries has been adapted to provide accommodation for the clergy, and the Crypt is now an up-to-date church hall. The churchyard, in which is the family vault of Henry Raine, brewer and founder of Raine's School, is a public garden.

Farther along the Highway is Wapping Lane, leading to Wapping Station, from which point the Thames Tunnel runs underneath the river to Rotherhithe. It was projected by Sir Marc Isambard Brunel and begun on January 1825, but an inundation caused the work of construction to be suspended for seven years. The tunnel, which cost £600,000, was eventually opened for foot passengers on 25 March 1843. The crown of the tunnel is 16 feet below the river bed. It has sloping approaches and includes two arched passages 1,200 feet long, 14 feet wide and 16½ feet high, divided by a wall 4 feet thick, with sixty-four arched openings. In 1866 it was sold for £200,000 to the East London Railway Company, whose line was opened for traffic on 10 April 1876. Electrified in 1913, it is now part of the Underground system. Before that time annual fairs used to take place in the Thames Tunnel, and in 1853 some forty thousand persons visited the fair, upon which occasion the tunnel was brilliantly illuminated.

In former times the ill-famed streets and dangerous alleys of Wapping were unsafe even in the daytime, and the Tower Hamlets once disgorged their lawless inhabitants to witness an execution on Tower Hill. In 1879 the High Street, Wapping, was widened by setting back portions of both the northern and southern sides, commencing from the eastern side of the entrance to the Wapping Basin and terminating near the entrance to the St Katharine Docks. Nearly all of Wapping High Street has been destroyed in the blitz and some of its warehouses razed to the ground. Its remaining houses are mostly empty and waiting to be pulled down. At the back of the High Street near the entrance to the London Docks are several blocks of flats with courtyards and balconies erected by the London County Council before the last war.

In the 'forties of the last century hired vagabonds used to tout at every wharf and public-house on the neighbourhood of the London Docks. Their call, although perhaps not so openly made as that of an omnibus conductor, only varied inasmuch as America was substituted for Charing Cross or Paddington. These men took passengers for almost anything they could get, not caring whether they had stores to last the voyage, or whether they would starve before they were half-way across the Atlantic. It was a sorry sight, and the law had no power beyond that of making a few arrangements that would contribute to the comfort of the poor passengers.

Beyond the East London Railway the Highway continues, here formerly named High Street, Shadwell, once one of the poorest and most densely-peopled districts in East London. The sordid conditions which once prevailed here have been depicted by Mr John Martin, schoolmaster and poet, the author of *John Bull and his Island*. He remarks that 'London is indeed an ignoble mixture of beer and Bible, of gin and gospel, of drunkenness and hypocrisy, of unheard of squalor and unbridled luxury, of misery and prosperity, of poor, abject, shivering, starving creatures, and people insolent with happiness and wealth'. The people followed daily the same dull round of existence, the only variation to which they could look forward being that of hard drinking. At four years old the children could swear like troopers, and were very often taught to do so by their parents. Thanks to the higher standard of living and the more even distribution of wealth, coupled with better housing conditions and improved education, the reproach levelled against London by Mr John Martin has been largely removed in our own day. On the south side of the Highway, adjoining Shadwell Basin, is the interesting little church of St Paul, Shadwell, originally built in 1656, but rebuilt in 1820 to the designs of F. A. Walters. In the shady churchyard are the graves of sea-captains and ships' masts are to be seen just over the wall.

In 1720 Jane Randolph, daughter of a merchant seaman, was born in Shadwell. In 1739 she married Peter Jefferson in Virginia, and in 1743 became the mother of Thomas Jefferson, third President of the United States.

Occupying the site of the former Shadwell Fish Market is the King Edward VII Memorial Park, attractively laid out with bowling greens, playgrounds and flower gardens, comprising seven and a half acres. It was opened in 1922 and its riverside promenade affords a most interesting view of the shipping in the Thames and of the Surrey Commercial Docks on the opposite side of the river. The Shadwell Fish Market was closed during the first World War and never reopened.

Adjoining the King Edward VII Memorial Park is the Rotherhithe tunnel for vehicular and pedestrian traffic, constructed by the London County Council at a cost of over £2,000,000 and opened in 1908. It has a diameter of thirty feet and runs obliquely under the Thames, the northern approach road beginning near Stepney East Station, and the southern approach road at Lower Road near Rotherhithe Station. The tunnel and its approaches are about a mile and a quarter in length. One of London's shorter bus routes, the No. 82 service, runs through the tunnel between Stepney and Rotherhithe. Above the approach in Branch Road is an arch, the cast steel segments of which formed the cutting edge of the shield used in the construction of the tunnel.

From here the road was continued by Broad Street and Medland Street, but these names have dissappeared and it is now called The Highway right up to the Regent's Canal Dock. In Stepney Causeway is the first of Dr Barnardo's homes for destitute children, opened in 1866. To-day the organisation has 156 homes and branches all over the United Kingdom and three in Australia.

A short walk along Commercial Road will bring us to the former Stepney Town Hall close to which is St Anne's Church, Limehouse, designed by Hawksmoor between 1712 and 1724. It was erected at a cost of £35,000 and contains a clock-tower 130 feet high. On Good Friday 1850 this church was destroyed by fire. On that morning the inhabitants were alarmed by the loud and irregular ringing of the church bells, and as the crowds flocked to the spot they discovered that the roof of the church was on fire and the entire building enveloped in smoke. The flames spread with such rapidity that before a single fire-engine could be got to work the roof had fallen in, and in a very short time the interior was consumed, leaving only the bare walls of the church. The tower was saved, although it had been damaged internally. The roof and fittings were renewed after the fire, and further alterations were made in 1891.

Beyond St Anne's Church, which is a busy traffic centre, Commercial Road is continued by the East India Dock Road, leading to Blackwall and Poplar. The West India Dock Road forks to the right, and the corner site where these two roads meet is occupied by the Eastern Hotel. Here the King of Siam took luncheon upon the occasion of his visit to the East End half a century ago. Burdett Road, a fine broad thoroughfare leading northwards to Mile End Road and Victoria Park, was constructed in 1862 and is named after the Baroness

Burdett-Coutts. Salmon Lane, running in the direction of Stepney Green, is crowded with small shops and costers' stalls. Close by, in Commercial Road, is the building of the British Sailors' Society Empire Memorial Hostel for Seamen.

Turning next into West India Dock Road, on the left stood the East London Seamen's Mission and adjoining was the Asiatic and Overseas Home, erected in 1857 at a cost of £15,000, and providing accommodation for 230 inmates. The foundation-stone was laid on 31 May 1856 by the Prince Consort. Before that time the Lascars, who were cast ashore at the Port of London to await fresh employment, averaging some two thousand to three thousand yearly, and who could not speak English or any other European language, fell victims to all kinds of sharpers. Thus they were quickly relieved of all their money and left in helpless destitution. Gambling and other vices were the ruin of hundreds, and some became street beggars, whilst others took to thieving, passing forged coins, or introducing parcels of smuggled tea and tobacco and other contraband goods. Since those days more stringent laws have been enacted for the general protection and assistance of seamen generally, and there are now many admirably-managed Sailors' Homes and boarding-houses in London and other commercial ports. Both of these excellent establishments were destroyed by bombs and a new Police Station and some business premises stand in their place.

At the bottom of West India Dock Road under the railway bridge is The Railway Tavern, once known to seafaring men all over the world as 'Charlie Brown's'. It was celebrated for the collection of antiques, curios, freaks and monstrosities which has unfortunately been dispersed since the death of the genial Charlie in 1932.

Many of the side streets of Limehouse were inhabited almost entirely by Orientals and contained foreign restaurants and drinking-shops hardly suitable for unaccompanied tourists. Limehouse Causeway, Penny Fields, and the neighbouring alleys were popularly known as Chinatown. Here the population consisted of Chinese, Lascars, Maltese, and a few Japanese. Here also one might dine in rather unusual but interesting surroundings on such Oriental delicacies as sea slugs, birds' nests, and sharks' fins. Since the war, however, the clearance made by the bombs has robbed Chinatown of much of its oriental glamour.

Pennyfields, a long narrow street at the end of West India Dock Road was the centre of London's Chinatown. In pre-war days, imagination primed with the vivid stories of novelists and journalists, one would venture through Pennyfields after dark with mixed feelings of bravado and apprehension, scarcely daring to look at the dimly-lit oriental 'joints', most of which one assumed to be opium dens inhabited by sinister almond-eyed Asiatics.

Today Pennyfields has been transformed. A splendid street of modern Council flats has replaced the old squalor and not one of the dingy little houses and dirty old shops remains. A development of the most drastic and praise-worthy kind – but, Goodbye, Chinatown!

Much slum-property in this locality, including the whole of Limehouse Causeway, was destroyed in the great blitz of September 1940, but already the new Stepney is rapidly arising on the cleared bombed sites. The new Limehouse Causeway, which has been much widened, is now almost built up with Greater London Council flats. These are five-storeyed buildings which stand back from the roadway in gardens and are faced with red and yellow brick. In West India Dock Road is West India House, the first post-war block of flats in Stepney, completed in November 1946 and formally opened by the then Premier, Clement Attlee, later Earl Attlee. On the other side of Commercial Road, another new quarter is rapidly arising on the bombed sites between the Regent's Canal and St Dunstan's Stepney Church. This is bounded on the north side by Ben Jonson Road and includes Carr Street and Conder Street, where several five-storeyed blocks of flats with sun balconies have been erected of similar design to those at Shadwell. Some smaller three-storeyed blocks have also been built as well as some two-storeyed houses for single families. Between Ben Jonson Road and Mile End Road is the Ocean Estate which covers forty acres and was acquired by the London County Council before the second World War. The remaining portion of this area was secured in 1945 by a compulsory purchase order because during the war so many houses had been completely destroyed or badly damaged. The redevelopment scheme for this area comprises 1,382 dwellings in blocks of flats and cottages in mixed development. The cottages will overlook green spaces while the flats will have forecourts and gardens. Four of the blocks will be eight storeys high and there will also be a shopping centre and market, public houses, communal buildings and a nursery school.

The long-term plans of the Greater London Council for the new Stepney which are to cost £15,000,000 cover some 1,500 acres of Stepney and Poplar for town-planning purposes, but most of the money will be spent in buying land for the layout of five or six new quarters. Each of these will house from six thousand to ten thousand people and form a new riverside town on up-to-date lines. The area involved is roughly that bounded by Whitechapel Road and Mile End Road on the north, Leman Street on the west and the Thames and docks on the south and east. It is designed to provide flats and houses to accommodate 136 people per acre. There will be rows of two-floored terrace houses and blocks of flats varying from two to ten storeys high. The houses are intended for large families and persons living alone. There are to be playing-fields, public gardens and tennis-courts, and each quarter will have its own shopping centre. There will also be a central area of stores, shops, cinemas and theatres. Special areas will be reserved for the many large and small industries which form part of the life and work of Stepney, but these will be separated from the residential quarters. The west end of Stepney where Whitechapel and Commercial Road meet will form the chief industrial district.

The West India Docks, projected by Robert Milligan, an eminent West India merchant who died at Hampstead in May 1809, were the first commercial wet docks ever constructed in the Port of London. Although Milligan was one of those who 'projected' these docks, Alderman George Hibbert, who became the dock company's first chairman, was accepted as the leading spirit in the enterprise. They were built by the engineer William Jessop, cover an area of 242 acres, and were begun in 1800. The first stone was laid by William Pitt in July 1800, and the docks were partially opened in August 1802. They are situated on a peninsula formed by the River Thames and known as the Isle of Dogs, and at first consisted of two docks, one for imports and the other for exports. To the south was the so-called City Canal, three-quarters of a mile long, cutting off the great bend of the river, and which in 1829 the West India Dock Company purchased from the Corporation of London. This was afterwards widened and converted into the South Dock and allotted to the wood and timber trades.

The East India Docks at Blackwall, originally constructed by the East India Dock Company, were opened on 4 August 1806 and consist of an inner and an outer dock. They were designed by John Rennie and Ralph Walker, the well-known engineers of that period. Later these two companies were amalgamated under the title of the East and West India Dock Company, and by the time the Port of London Authority came into being in 1909 all of the various docks companies, with the exception of the Millwall Docks and the Surrey Commercial Dock Company, had become united under the title of the London & India Dock Company. The great archway surmounted by a large model ship, which formed the entrance to East India Dock, was demolished in 1958 in connection with the widening of the approach to the new Blackwall Tunnel.

The Millwall Docks, now connected with the West India Docks, were opened on Saturday, 14 March 1868, and were constructed by the Millwall Docks and Land Company. The whole extent of the land purchased was 204 acres, of which 52 were allotted to dock accommodation and 152 to wharves and warehouse accommodation. At first only 35 acres were devoted to the docks, the remaining third of the ground being uncompleted until the requirements of trade called for such increased accommodation. The name of Millwall is derived from seven windmills which stood on the wall built here to keep the Thames from overflowing at high tide.

It was at Millwall that the famous steamer *Great Eastern* was built between 1857 and 1859. This gigantic vessel of 22,000 tons was up to that time the largest ever built since Noah's Ark. No other ship exceeding 5,500 tons was then in existence. On Whit Monday 1859 the *Great Eastern* was visited by enormous crowds of holiday makers. She laid the first transatlantic cable from Valentia to Newfoundland, starting on her journey from Sheerness on 30 June 1866. After an existence of over thirty years, the *Great Eastern* was finally broken up at Birkenhead in the eighteen-nineties. No other ship as large as the *Great Eastern* was constructed before the early years of the present century. Her maiden trip to New York took ten and a half days.

The Isle of Dogs formerly consisted of rich pasture land and when our kings had a palace at Greenwich they used it as a hunting-ground and are supposed to have kept the kennels of their hounds in this marsh. These hounds frequently made a great noise and this led our seamen to call it the Isle of Dogs, though at that time it was not an island but a peninsula. The former City Canal was constructed here in 1799-1800 to enable vessels in their passage up the Thames to avoid the circuitous and inconvenient journey round the Isle of Dogs. Before the construction of the West India Docks this peninsula was reckoned one of the richest tracts of agricultural land in England, for not only were the largest cattle raised here, but the grass was esteemed a restorative for distempered cattle, and beasts turned loose to graze here soon fattened and grew to a large size. A tunnel for pedestrians only, constructed in 1902, connects Millwall with Greenwich.

The former metropolitan borough of Poplar, between Limehouse and West Ham, was originally a hamlet of Stepney and obtained its name from the large number of poplar-trees that once grew there. Poplar Chapel, in East India Dock Road, is now the church of St Mathias, and is surrounded by four acres of lawns and shrubberies, including tennis-courts and greens. In 1866 it was made the church of the new ecclesiastical parish of St Mathias, and the exterior was then remodelled. Poplar Chapel was erected between 1650 and 1654 on land given by the East India Company and was rebuilt in 1776. After the construction of the East and West India Docks the population increased rapidly, and by 1841 Poplar already contained thirty thousand inhabitants. Its population in the 1951 census was 73,544. To meet the shortage of church accommodation a new chapel was built in 1848 by the Wesleyan Methodists to accommodate 1,500 persons. St Stephen's Church, which is also in the East India Dock Road, was opened in 1867 and accommodates 950 people. Poplar Hospital, in the same road, was opened in 1835, but has long since been rebuilt. It was badly damaged in the great blitz of 1940. The original building was the old Custom House at the entrance to the East India Dock gates.

Branching southwards from this corner is the approach to the Blackwall Tunnel, opened in 1897 and built at a cost of £1,500,000. It provides free communication for pedestrians and vehicles between Blackwall and East Greenwich. The tunnel is 6,200 feet long but only about one-fifth of it is actually under the bed of the river. The external diameter is twenty-seven feet and the internal twenty-three feet. The number of vehicles using the tunnel is upwards of one million per annum. To relieve congestion in the tunnel, the construction of a second Blackwall Tunnel, about 250 yards further downstream and roughly parallel with the original one, has now been completed.

The new tunnel was opened by the Leader of the Greater London Council on 2nd August 1967, and the work had occupied about seven years and cost £8 million. As the new tunnel opened the old one was closed for overhaul and widening; when this is finished, one-way traffic will be introduced, southbound vehicles using the new tunnel and those northbound, the old.

Before the construction of the East India Docks there was already a shipyard and a wet dock at Blackwall, capable of accommodating twenty-eight East Indiamen and sixty Greenland sloops together with storehouses and every convenience. The shipyard and appendages were afterwards purchased by Sir Robert Wigram and the dock was sold to the East India Company. Beyond the

East India Dock is Bow Creek, where the River Lea flows into the Thames. Poplar High Street, which runs parallel to the East India Dock Road, is a long narrow street of shabby houses and shops practically all of which have been destroyed in the earlier air raids of 1940. But a widening was begun at its western end before the war and two great blocks of flats were erected which have escaped destruction. These are Willis House on the north side and Dolphin House on the south side.

The Queen's Theatre, the well-known music-hall in Poplar High Street, built in 1873, was closed in 1956; in 1958 there was a proposal to re-open which failed to materialize. It has since been demolished and nothing now remains of a theatre whose stage was graced by theatrical notabilities from Sir Henry Irving to Gracie Fields. Affection for the old 'Queen's Poplar', where one could enjoy a 'robust' music-hall performance from the comfort of the bar at the back, was by no means restricted to the local patrons. A combined visit to the Queen's and Charlie Brown's was always a good evening out until one closed and the other changed hands.

After passing Blackwall the East India Dock Road runs alongside the boundary wall on the north side of the East India Dock and leads to the wide new bridge over the River Lea, connecting Poplar with Canning Town, built in 1933 to replace the former narrow iron bridge. This portion of the East India Dock Road was formerly quite narrow, but in 1908 the boundary wall of the docks was set back and the width of the roadway practically doubled in order to make room for the extension of the tramways of the London County Council from Blackwall to Canning Town. Here, on a large bombed site, new three-storeyed blocks of London County Council flats have been completed, with their frontages turned away at right angles to the East India Dock Road. There is also a large five-storeyed block which stands back at the top of a spacious court-yard. Shortly after crossing the River Lea we come to Canning Town Station opposite which is the narrow Victoria Dock Road, close upon a mile long, which leads to the Victoria Dock. In order to provide improved access to the Victoria and Albert Docks a wide new road called Silvertown Way was opened in 1934. This commences at Canning Town and provides direct access to the Victoria Dock without passing through the narrow and congested Victoria Dock Road. It was cut across some of the worst slums in Canning Town and the section which crosses the entrance to the Victoria Docks at Tidal Basin is built on a concrete viaduct.

Opened in 1855, and named after the ruling sovereign, the Victoria Dock was built to meet the requirements of the rapidly expanding trade of the Port of London, which had increased by no less than 35 per cent within the previous two years. The site of this dock had remained up to that time a deserted tract of land extending from Bow Creek to Gallions Reach, known as the Plaistow marshes, and adjoining the North Woolwich Railway. It consists of a long wet dock with an entrance from the river a little below Bow Creek, and has a water area of eighty acres with nearly four miles of quayside accommodation. At the east end it is connected with the Royal Albert Dock. The Victoria Dock was the first dock in the Port of London to be connected with the railway systems of the country and was also the first to be equipped with hydraulic power for working machinery.

The capital of the original company was £1,000,000 and unlike present-day conditions the local rates at that time were low and enabled the new docks to compete with rival establishments on very favourable terms. The result was that in 1856 the Victoria Dock Company sold land at fifty shillings per foot on the south side of the dock, commanding the use of both the dock and the Blackwall Railway, which had become highly valuable for the timber trade, and for which they had paid only a trifling sum a few years previously. The Company was empowered to provide pasture accommodation for the large number of Scottish and foreign cattle landed here for the supply of the metropolis.

However, with the construction of the Victoria Dock the new and unlovely neighbourhood known as Canning Town, now forming a ward of the great borough of Newham, sprang up with the rapidity of a budding Chicago, and very soon covered this entire locality with densely-populated streets, where hitherto there had been nothing but open fields. Many taverns were erected in the vicinity of the Victoria Dock Road, notably the Victoria Tavern, the Essex Arms the Bell and Anchor, the Lord Nelson, and the Prince of Wales. One of the first to be erected bore the sign of the Excavators' Arms. But bombs have played havoc with Canning Town and have removed practically all the remaining slums in this quarter and large sites have been cleared of their debris. This applies especially to the Tidal Basin quarter where already a large number of streets and new house have been constructed since 1946 on a much-improved scale. At the cessation of hostilities in 1945, West Ham claimed to be London's most bombed borough, and plans to become a garden city within the next twenty years with tree-lined streets, modern homes and parks. The Tidal Basin quarter is the first to be rebuilt and several hundred of the three thousand homes which it will contain are already built and occupied.

On the north side of Barking Road stood Holy Trinity Church, opened in 1867, but completely destroyed by bombs; Rathbone Street, nearly opposite, which leads in the direction of the Victoria Dock Road, once contained a densely-crowded street market nearly half a mile long, but its shops and houses have nearly all been destroyed in the blitz. It was thronged with people who appeared every bit as happy and contented in their surroundings as do those of Bond Street or Oxford Street. On a Saturday morning Rathbone street, like Petticoat Lane, was almost completely choked with its long double line of stalls, its many sightseers, and its crowds jostling each other in their endeavours to get near the stalls. Very little of Rathbone Street remains, but a long range of some thirty or more shops, set back from the main road, have been built. In the space between the shops and the Barking Road the market stalls have been reinstated. Canning Town takes its name from one of the principal local employers, and the neighbouring district of Silvertown was named after a Mr Silver's factory at North Woolwich.

After 1851 West Ham, which up to that time had been a place of small importance, grew with such rapidity that it soon became known as 'London over the Border', meaning, of course, London across the Lea. It was formed into a municipal borough in 1886 and includes Stratford, Plaistow, and Forest Gate. Now linked with East Ham in the borough of Newham, it is a great industrial centre, and in addition to the Victoria Docks it contains the shops of British Railways (Eastern Region) at Stratford, and soap, sugar and various other manufacturing establishments. Except in the densely-peopled quarter of Canning Town, now blotted out by enemy action, most of the streets have been planned with due regard to the necessity for light and fresh air. The Town Hall, which is situated in Stratford Broadway, is a handsome stone-fronted building in the Italian Renaissance style, with a lofty tower, opened on 7 July 1869. It cost £20,000, including the site. Close by is St John's Church, with a tall spire, erected in 1834 at the junction of the Broadway and Romford Road. In the churchyard is a memorial to the Protestant Martyrs burned at Stratford during 1555 and 1556. Most of the largest shops are also centred in Stratford Broadway, including those of Messrs Boardmans Ltd the large firm of drapers. Among many London cinemas closed recently was the Stratford Gaumont, seating 2,464 people, which when opened by the Mayor of West Ham in 1927 was the largest in Europe. The Theatre Royal in Angel Lane is the headquarters of the Theatre Workshop company founded by Joan Littlewood.

In 1820 Stratford itself was still a straggling village, but there were some good houses there with large gardens. At Maryland Point was situated Stratford House, the seat of Lord Henniker, with extensive gardens. This house was built by a gentleman who founded an estate in the former colony of Maryland in the United States and who was also proprietor of these houses. From that circumstance they were named Maryland Point. Between 1934 and 1939 an extensive widening of Stratford High Street was carried out between Bow Bridge and Stratford Market Station. This necessitated filling in a canal which formed the western channel of the River Lea. A part of the widened road has been converted into a dual carriageway with a wide kerb down the centre, but the work has not yet been completed. When this has been done, London will have a fine wide exit all the way from Aldgate to Stratford Broadway.

Close to the recreation ground in West Ham Lane is All Saints' Church, boasting a considerable antiquity and containing a square Gothic tower. It affords a marked contrast to the depressing streets by which it is surrounded. West Ham Park, to the east of All Saint's Church, was jointly purchased by Mr John Gurney and the Corporation of London for £25,000, each contributing £10,000 towards the total cost and the remaining £5,000 being raised by local subscriptions. This park, which was opened in July 1874, contains seventy-seven acres, and was formerly the seat of the Gurney family. After the death of Samuel Gurney, the Quaker banker and philantropist, in 1856, it was thrown on the market as a building site, but was happily saved from the hands of the speculative builder and secured as a public open space.

The Royal Albert Dock, to which we will now turn, was opened on 24 June 1880 by H.R.H. the Duke of Connaught, and was constructed by the London and St Katharine Dock Company at a total cost of about £2,200,000. It is considerably over a mile in length and flanked on both sides by large sheds. Together with the Victoria Dock it forms an enclosure two and three-quarter miles long, containing a water area of over 182 acres and more than nine miles of quays. Between two thousand and three thousand men were employed on the construction of the Albert Dock, and the four million cubic yards excavated were raised seventeen feet, the marsh having previously been seven feet below high water, and the quays being six feet above. The dock was sunk through peat soil containing the remains of forest trees, in which were found a few horns of deer and relics of prehistoric man. A canoe twenty-seven feet long was also discovered in the excavations and was removed to the British Museum. Below the stratum of peat the engineers encountered a bed of rich washed gravel, which lies above the chalk. The peat and portions of the gravel were utilized to raise the surface of the quays. Gravel was left for the bed of the dock and other gravel dug out was mixed with Portland cement from the Medway, thus forming blocks of concrete for building the walls of the docks. The gates are of stone and the floors of the entrance passages are of brick.

The King George V Dock which adjoins the Royal Albert Docks on the south side is 4,578 feet long and 710 feet broad at the widest point. It contains a water area of sixty-four acres and over three miles of quays. There is also a drydock 750 feet long and 100 feet wide. It was constructed by the Port of London Authority at a cost of over £4,000,000, and was opened by King George V on 8 July 1921.

The Seamen's Hospital at the Victoria and Albert Docks was opened by King Edward VII, when Prince of Wales, in June 1890. The foundation stone was laid on 15 July 1889 by Prince George, afterwards King George V. To the south of the Victoria and Albert Docks are Silvertown, a manufacturing district, and North Woolwich, which, although on the north side of the Thames, is actually in the County of Kent. The territory immediately north of the Royal Albert Dock is situated in the borough of East Ham, but unlike the fringe of the Victoria Dock still consists partly of open fields extending in the direction of Beckton Road. Farther north is the East Ham and Barking by-pass road leading to Dagenham, where new houses are gradually invading this hitherto desolate neighbourhood.

East Ham, now a large suburb of London, in the borough of Newham, is of very modern growth, the population in 1891 having been under twenty-nine thousand. The Town Hall, erected in 1902, a fine redbrick building with a lofty clock-tower, is situated in the Barking Road, at the south corner of the High Street, adjoining the Municipal College. The streets are well planned and there are several parks and open spaces in the vicinity of Barking Road. The leading Shops are in High Street North, between Barking Road and Manor Park. Little more than a century ago East Ham was noted for its rich market gardens and was inhabited by poor Irish labourers who cultivated the crops of potatoes and vegetables.

Proceeding along High Street South, we next pass the Central Park on our right and then Beckton public park further on. After crossing the eastern entrance to the Royal Albert Dock at Manor Way Station we come to the North Woolwich Ferry. Beckton contains the extensive works of the North Thames Gas Board, and here also the northern outfall sewer empties itself into the Thames. The southern outfall sewer is on the opposite side of the river at Crossness, a short distance lower down.

Once a reproach to the metropolis, the main drainage system of London to-day comprises the most efficient and costly scheme for the sewerage of a great city which has ever been accomplished. Great extensions have been made in recent years, the supplementary works almost equalling the original scheme in their magnitude. The London County area alone contains 370 miles of sewers, and their capital cost has amounted to over £13,000,000.

In addition to the free ferry for pedestrian and vehicular traffic there is a convenient tunnel for pedestrians only, approached by a lift and a staircase. This was begun on 23 August 1876, in consequence of nine men having been drowned on a foggy morning while crossing to their work in a boat, but was not completed until 1912.

We will now walk through the tunnel, or cross by the ferryboat (the three new vessels are diesel-operated) which will bring us into the centre of Woolwich, close to the High Street, and make the return journey to the City by following the south side of the Thames. The former borough of Woolwich, which includes Plumstead and Eltham, now comes under Greenwich. During the first World War, thousands of houses were built for munition workers on the Well Hall estate by the London County Council. The leading shops, including the immense Woolwich Arsenal Co-operative Stores, are in Powis Street, a smart and lively thoroughfare leading from the High Street to Beresford Square and in Hare Street leading to the pier. To the west of Powis Street is the Dock Yard, established in the reign of Henry VIII and said to be the oldest in the Kingdom. To the east is the Arsenal, for many years a centre for the design, manufacture and testing of armaments, but the range of modern arms is such that some of the research is carried out in other places with less population. Though much of its normal work is still here, part of the Arsenal area has been developed as an industrial estate and some parts are occupied by private industries. The Town Hall is in Wellington Street which leads steeply up on to Woolwich Common. It is a handsome building of red brick and stone designed early in the present century by Brumwell Thomas, architect of the City Hall at Belfast. Its façade has numerous circular columns and at the corner is an ornate and lofty clock-tower. Another fine building is that of the Woolwich Equitable Building Society, in General Gordon Place, which has a stone façade. Beneath General Gordon Place run the trains of the Southern Region. It was formerly an open cutting, in pre-electric days known locally as 'The Smoke Hole'.

In the parish churchyard of St. Mary, Woolwich is the grave of Tom Cribb, the famous pugilist. One regrets the disappearance (due to the improvement of the river front) of the memorial to the five sinful children who, in 1831, were drowned while playing on the ice on the Sabbath day.

On the north side of Woolwich Common, which comprises an area of 159 acres, are the Royal Artillery Barracks, with a façade that was once described as '1200 feet of Georgian elegance'. On the east side is the Royal Naval Tactical School, formerly the Royal Military Academy. The Rotunda on the west side of the Common, a circular building nearly forty yards across, was designed by Nash and contains an interesting military museum. The whole of the Woolwich Garrison is in process of redevelopment and many of the older barrack buildings have been removed to make way for modern structures. At Eltham Palace, of which little remains except the banqueting hall, Henry VIII and Queen Elizabeth I spent several years of their childhood. It has a moat crossed by a fifteenth-century bridge.

Plumstead, to the east of Woolwich, is a most unattractive suburb, and except for its open spaces has little to commend it as a place of residence. The church of St Nicholas, with its seventeenth-century square tower, has been displaced since 1864 as the parish church by St Margaret's, built in 1858. The open spaces include Plumstead Common, Bostall Heath, acquired for the public in 1877-78, and Bostall Woods, acquired in 1892, comprising altogether about 134 acres. Bostall Heath is a favourite holiday resort with Londoners and commands a splendid view over the river. Beyond Bostall Heath, in the new London Borough of Bexley, are the ruins of Lesnes Abbey, founded in 1178 by Richard de Lucy. It was dedicated to St Mary and St Thomas the Martyr — possibly as an atonement by de Lucy for the part he had taken against Becket. It was suppressed by Wolsey in 1524, having then less than seven inmates (the qualifying number to avoid suppression). The site was acquired by the L.C.C. in 1936 and opened as a public park. Behind is Abbey Wood, and not so many years ago, local residents complained that the nightingales kept them awake at night. Woolwich Arsenal football ground, once in this district, is now located at Highbury. Another pleasant spot is Shooter's Hill Park, purchased for the public in 1921 and also known as Castle Wood. It contains twenty-two acres, and includes Severndroog Castle, a triangular tower built in 1784 in honour of Sir William James, who took Severndroog, a pirate stronghold on the Malabar coast in 1775. Below the tower, which is almost concealed by trees, is a beautiful terrace garden commanding extensive views over the south-eastern suburbs and the Surrey hills.

Until the middle of the nineteenth century Plumstead Marshes formed a great alluvial district containing many thousands of acres of land, five miles in length and one and a half miles in width. They were intersected by hundreds of miles of open ditches and contained extensive swamps of stagnant water. At that time no provision whatever had been made for drainage, and many of these ditches, which were dangerous to health, had not been cleaned out within the memory of living men. The Plumstead Marshes were hotbeds of malaria and were the cause of much illness amongst the inhabitants of Woolwich. The inhabitants

343

were mostly poor people and the parish church was then a mile and a half away from the centre of the population, then numbering ten thousand, and could only accommodate four hundred parishioners. Plumstead Marshes are now traversed by the southern outfall sewer, which enters the Thames at Crossness opposite Dagenham beach. This great undertaking was completed and formally opened by King Edward VII, when Prince of Wales, on 4 April 1865.

From Woolwich Ferry to Greenwich is an uninteresting journey of about three miles across the Greenwich marshes. A more agreeable way is along Shooter's Hill Road which flanks the south side of Woolwich Common and leads through Charlton to Blackheath Common and Greenwich Park. Almost continuous with Woolwich Common on its north-west side are Charlton Park, Maryon Wilson Park and Maryon Park, together providing about three hundred acres of open space.

The Woolwich Road is continued by Trafalgar and Romney Roads and passes between the Greenwich Hospital and the Royal Naval College on the river side and the Royal Hospital School on the south side. The Greenwich Hospital and Royal Naval College is a long range of buildings with an imposing frontage to the river, and occupies the site of an old royal palace used as a residence by successive sovereigns from the early part of the fifteenth century down to the time of the Commonwealth. Henry VIII and his daughters Elizabeth and Mary were born here, and here also the young King Edward VI died. Charles II commenced to rebuild the palace in 1667 from designs by Inigo Jones and Webb, but only the west wing was then completed. Building was resumed under William III and Anne by Sir Christopher Wren and in 1705 the edifice was converted into a hospital for superannuated seamen. It no longer serves this purpose, for when the system of indoor pensions expired in 1869 the building were mostly adapted to the needs of the College, which was opened in 1873. On the opposite side of Romney Road is the Queen's House, begun in 1617 and intended by James I as a palace for his Queen, Anne of Denmark, who died in 1619. The building remained unfinished until Charles I commissioned Inigo Jones to complete it for *his* Queen, Henrietta Maria. It was finished in 1635 and is the oldest and most beautiful of the present buildings. The Queen's House was occupied by the Royal Hospital School for over 100 years until 1933 when the school moved to Suffolk. In 1937 it was reopened by H. M. King George VI as the National Maritime Museum, and displays a splendid collection of pictures, models of ships, ships' figureheads, Nelson relics and other exhibits illustrating our maritime history.

At the dawn of the nineteenth century the population of Greenwich was fourteen thousand and by 1871 had increased to forty thousand. Today it has absorbed most of Woolwich to become the new borough of Greenwich with a population of 231,130. As recently as 1813 there were trees standing in the very centre of the town at the junction of London Street and Church Street, and it contained many respectable houses inhabited by gentlemen and retired servicemen. In Church Street, much damaged, but now restored and open, is the church of St Alphege, which contains the tombs of General Wolfe and Thomas Tallis, the sixteenth-century church musician. It is dedicated to St Alphege, who was martyred here by the Danes in 1012. The church was destroyed by lightning in 1718 and then rebuilt. Dr Johnson resided in Church Street, next door to the Golden Heart, where he had taken apartments when he first left his native town of Lichfield for London. Above the 16-columned entrance to Greenwich Market, erected in 1831, is inscribed 'A false balance is an abomination to the Lord, but a just weight is His delight'.

Overlooking the Thames in the immediate vicinity of the Royal Hospital were some noted waterside hotels, which became celebrated for whitebait and public dinners. These included the Ship next to Greenwich Pier, the Crown and Sceptre, and the Trafalgar. On the morning of 1 November 1941, the Ship Hotel received a direct hit from a bomb which wrecked the building. On the site of the old Ship now stands another ship, the famous wool clipper, *Cutty Sark*, a museum piece now permanently in dry dock. The Ship Hotel was celebrated for its whitebait dinners. Here also the Judges met every year for a fish dinner and Ordnance barges brought the distinguished guests from London. The original building was sold by auction in 1908. The whitebait were caught in the Thames and skilfully cooked within an hour or two and served at table. The Ship Hotel was also very popular among travellers by river steamers. In Nevada Street, at the foot of Croom's Hill, is the disused Parthenon Theatre of Varieties, variously known as the Greenwich Hippodrome, Barnards, and in 1868, Crowder's Theatre. Closed for many years, it is now being restored and will re-open as a local repertory theatre.

South of the Hospital is Greenwich Park, a royal domain of 185 acres laid out by Charles II. Crowning a hill in the centre was the Royal Observatory, the first stone of which was laid by Flamsteed on 10 August 1765. The building stands 160 feet above low-water mark. The time-ball descended precisely at 1.0 p.m. and the correct time was then telegraphed to all the most important towns. The Observatory has now been removed to Hurstmonceux in Sussex. The Observatory building, now known as Flamsteed House, has recently been reopened as a public museum. A very fine distant view of St Paul's Cathedral and the City of London can be obtained from the hill in Greenwich Park, and one can easily realize that Greenwich, when it was a small town distant four miles from London, must have been as attractive to the holiday-maker of Dr Johnson's time as Richmond is to the present-day pleasure seeker. The park is crossed by the wide tree-lined Blackheath Avenue at the northern end of which is a bronze statue of General Wolfe presented by the Canadian Government in 1930 and designed by Dr Tait McKenzie, a Canadian sculptor. Close to the avenue is a handsome teahouse and there is a boating-pool at the foot of the hill.

Adjoining Greenwich Park on the south is Blackheath Common, comprising 267 acres. It was secured for the public as a place of recreation under the Metropolitan Commons Act of 1866. Here Wat Tyler in 1381 and Jack Cade in 1450 marshalled their hosts and here likewise have taken place many highway robberies. The Common is said to derive its name from its bleak situation. The game of golf was introduced here to an unappreciative southern public by James I. The common, which is breezy and commands delightful views, reminds one somewhat of Tunbridge Wells, a comparison which also applies to the village which is situated in a hollow called Tranquil Vale. The district of Blackheath, which contains a population of 6,500, is one of the most agreeable of London suburbs. All Saints' Church is a handsome Gothic edifice with a tall spire erected in 1859 from the designs of Mr B. Ferrey.

After following the road across the common we turn down Blackheath Hill, and then come to Deptford Broadway. Situated immediately west of Greenwich, Deptford was originally a large town detached from London and divided into Upper and Lower Deptford. It was anciently called Deepford and West Greenwich, from which town it is separated by Deptford Creek, and later became a borough until extinguished by the 1963 Act. The town, which has always been a rather dirty and uninviting place, nevertheless contained many good houses in former times. The High Street, leading from the Broadway towards the foreign-cattle market, is a narrow but rather picturesque street traversing a densely-populated neighbourhood. At No. 146 was the Friend's Meeting House, where Peter the Great, Czar of Russia worshipped in 1697-8, when he was staying at John Evelyn's house. Between the High Street and Church Street is St Paul's Church, a handsome building of stone in the Romanesque style which has a pillared Tuscan porch of semicircular plan with a flight of steps round it. The church, designed by Thomas Archer, was restored in 1856 and again in 1883. On cleared sites in Tanner's Hill opposite Deptford High Street a row of a dozen very old shops still survives. Deptford was once famous for its noble dockyard, which employed a large number of men and was commenced by King Henry VIII in 1513.

Here Captain Drake docked his ship, the *Golden Hind,* which was visited by Queen Elizabeth I on 4 April 1581. Her Majesty dined on board and after dinner conferred the honour of knighthood on the captain. Here, also, Peter the Great studied navigation. He rented the house of Mr John Evelyn, called Sayes Court, adjoining the Dockyard, to which it had direct access through a private entrance. In April 1869 the dockyard was closed by the Government as a measure of economy, but the Royal Army Victualling Yard was still retained, The Town Hall, which is a handsome building, is situated in New Cross Road; it is decorated with sculpture symbolic of the town's naval history and crowned by an elegant weather-vane in the form of a three-masted man-o'war. The proscenium arch of the adjacent Broadway Theatre (now demolished) used to have the device of a ship's prow supported by anchors. Not far from here there occurred one Saturday morning in November 1944 in New Cross Road the second worst bomb disaster of the war when a V2 bomb fell here, killing 168 people and seriously wounding 108 others. Outside several of the larger shops there were queues of people waiting to buy their weekend food and other household goods when at ten minutes past twelve without a second of warning this busy street was converted into a shambles. Between seventy and eighty bodies were recovered from the large Woolworth store alone, and so great was the force of the explosion that the entire store with all the people in it were hurled into the basement together with hundreds of tons of masonry. On the west side of Evelyn Street, leading from the High Street to Rotherhithe, is Deptford Park, a small open space of about ten acres on the north side of the Surrey Canal. It contains a children's playground and an open-air gymnasium.

The direct route from Deptford Broadway to the City is by New Cross Road, Old Kent Road, Great Dover Street, and the Borough High Street to London Bridge, but for purposes of sight-seeing, we propose to follow the alternative road through Deptford High Street, Rotherhithe and Bermondsey. At the end of Evelyn Street, situated on the curved peninsula between the Pool and Limehouse Reach, are the Surrey Commercial Docks, occupying a land and water area of about 376 acres, and principally used for timber and Canadian and North American produce. The oldest of these is the Greenland Dock, built in 1699, which originally comprised an area of ten acres, and was then called the Howland Dock, after the family owning the land in Rotherhithe on which this dock was built. It was the first wet dock ever built in London and had a windscreen of trees but no warehouses around it. Afterwards it was adapted for the whaling trade and hence its change of name to Greenland Dock. The entrance is nearly opposite that of the Millwall Docks and the King's Arms stairs on the Isle of Dogs. Later it was taken over and enlarged by the Commercial Dock Company, which constructed five new docks here in 1826.

The Surrey Docks, built in the 'seventies of last century by a separate company, were planned by Messrs Bidder at a cost of £100,000, and include the Albion, Canada, and Quebec Docks, with a tidal basin at Rotherhithe Street opposite King Edward VII Memorial Park at Shadwell. In August 1875 the excavation for the new tidal basin laid bare a forest bed six feet from the surface. Among the trees in the peat were found bones of the great ox. Subsequently the two dock companies became merged into one concern under the title of the Surrey Commercial Docks Company. In 1904 the Greenland Dock was entirely reconstructed and is now capable of accommodating ships of about 10,000 gross registered tonnage. The critical factor is the size of the Greenland Entrance Lock.

Close to the Greenland Dock is the Surrey Docks Station in the Lower Road, which, with Plough Road and Rotherhithe Street encircles the Surrey Commercial Docks. This neighbourhood is very similar in character to that of Wapping and Limehouse on the opposite side of the river. Practically all the houses on the south side of Rotherhithe Street and in the immediate vicinity of the Surrey Commercial Docks were destroyed in the great blitz of September 1940 and except some newly-erected blocks of London County Council flats little remains of this once-crowded quarter. Prior to 1770 Rotherhithe was chiefly inhabited by seafaring persons and tradesmen whose business depended on seamen. In former times it was also called Redriff. On 1 June 1765 upwards of two hundred houses were destroyed by a disastrous fire which occurred at

Rotherhithe. Near the entrance to the Greenland Dock stood the Dog and Duck Tavern, which derives its name from a barbarous pastime of our ancestors, the hunting of ducks in a pond by spaniels.

In Rotherhithe Street, close to the East London Railway tunnel, is St Mary's, Rotherhithe, church, dedicated to the Virgin Mary and erected in 1739 on the site of an earlier church which had stood there for over two hundred years. This is a building of red brick and is crowned by a tall spire. The churchyard is now a public garden. At the junction of Lower Road and Jamaica Road is the southern approach to the Rotherhithe and Shadwell tunnel, and close by in Lower Road was the Rotherhithe Town Hall, which, with the Hippodrome Variety Theatre on the other side of the road, was completely destroyed in the blitz. Facing Jamaica Road and near the entrance to Rotherhithe Tunnel is the Norwegian Seamen's Church of St Olaf. This handsome red brick building, opened by the Crown Prince (now King) Olaf in 1927, has a weather-vane in the shape of a Viking ship.

Southwark Park, which is approached from the west side of Lower Road and also from Jamaica Road, was opened on Saturday, 26 June 1869, at a cost of £55,000. It is beautifully laid out and covers sixty-three acres. Its amenities include a lake for boating and swimming two and a half acres in extent, richly wooded and crossed at its northern end by a picturesque stone bridge, a flower garden, bowling green and playground. The land was mostly purchased from Sir William Gomm and the park was declared open by Sir John Thwaites, Chairman of the Metropolitan Board of Works. It is eventually intended to enlarge Southwark Park by extending it to the Thames not far from St Mary's Church, Rotherhithe, and to construct a lido overlooking the river.

Our route from here to the Tower Bridge is through Bermondsey by way of Jamaica Road, Dockhead, and Tooley Street. Bermondsey, which includes the parish of Rotherhithe, was formerly a metropolitan borough of 60,661 inhabitants, situated between Deptford, Camberwell, and Southwark. It is the centre of the leather trade and is largely inhabited by dock labourers and others employed locally. Its Town Hall is situated on the north side of Spa Road. Bermondsey is said to derive its name from Beormund, the Saxon lord of the district, and from 'eye', an island, a suitable description of the locality near the river, which was once intersected by numerous small streams and ditches. It is supposed to have been a marshy island when the tide was out and a wide expanse of water when it was in, until gradually it was reclaimed through succeeding centuries and turned to practical use.

Despite the densely-populated area of present-day Bermondsey, the descent to Tooley Street from London Bridge indicates the low-lying character of the land. Tanneries and rope-making factories abound here. The parish church of St Olave, which was pulled down some thirty years ago, stood on the north side of Tooley Street near London Bridge, and with the exception of its southern side was concealed from public view. Bermondsey once possessed an abbey, adjoining which was a large field anciently used by the neighbouring inhabitants as a pasture ground for their horses and cattle, and which was called Horsedown or Horselydown.

The waterside division of Bermondsey was intersected by several streams or watercourses. Upon the south bank of one of these, between Mill Street and Shad Thames, now called St Saviour's Dock, stood a number of very ancient houses called London Street, which was amongst the fastnesses of Jacob's Island. This was rendered familiar to the public by Charles Dickens in *Oliver Twist*. Here, across one of the bridges in Mill Street, could be seen the inhabitants of the houses on either side lowering from their back-doors and windows buckets, pails, and domestic utensils in which to haul the water up. Crazy wooden galleries, common to the back of half a dozen houses, with holes overlooking the slime underneath, windows broken and patched, with poles thrust out to dry the linen which was never there, rooms so small and filthy and so confined that the air seemed too polluted even for the dirt and squalor which they sheltered, wooden chambers thrusting themselves out above the mud and threating to fall into it, dirt-besmeared walls and decaying foundations, all ornamented the banks of Folly Ditch, Jacob's Island.

Jamaica Road, which lost many of its houses in the blitz of 10 May 1941, is so named from an inn called the Jamaica, which once stood in this immediate locality. Three years later, on 15 June 1944, Numbers 123-69 were completely destroyed by a flying bomb. In Dockhead between Jamaica Road and Tooley Street a Roman Catholic church built in 1835 was destroyed in a raid of 1940. A new church, designed by Prof. Goodhart-Rendel, was opened in May 1960. The Jamaica Inn was formerly a palace of Oliver Cromwell and in his time had extensive grounds. This house was pulled down in 1843. On the south side of Jamaica Road, at the northern end of Spa Road, is the parish church of St James, Bermondsey. It is a spacious building of brick and stone in the Greek style, designed and built by James Savage in 1829, and now threatened with demolition because, having accommodation for 1,600 worshippers, it is much too large for present day requirements. On the other side of the road is the L.C.C. Dickens Estate of twenty blocks of flats, each having names such as Bardell, Copperfield, Dombey etc. The Bermondsey Borough Council also have erected several large blocks of dwellings in Abbey Street, and more are going up. Abbey Street, on the south side of Jamaica Road, leads to Long Lane and Bermondsey Street, at the corner of which is the church of St Mary Magdalen, dating back to not later than 1538. The tower was repaired and beautified in 1830. Bermondsey has been the centre of the leather trade for 250 years, and the market, which is in Weston Street on the north side of Long Lane, was established on this site about the year 1833. On the corner of Leathermarket Street and Weston Street is the London Leather, Hide and Wool Exchange building of 1878. In Long Lane is an old tavern with the sign of 'Simon the Tanner'. Although there is less leather dressing in Bermondsey than formerly, one can still catch an occasional odd smell, not only of hides, but of vinegar from the six gigantic storage vats of Messrs

Sarson's in Tanner Street, while a different aroma is offered by a bacon-curing factory in Long Lane.

Absurd though it may appear to our readers, an attempt was made in the latter part of the eighteenth century to make Bermondsey a fashionable watering-place. Although that part of the district near the river was so close and filthy, there were pleasant fields stretching away towards the Old Kent Road. The meadows near the Abbey were still green and market-gardens still abounded. In 1770 a chalybeate spring was discovered in some grounds adjoining Grange Road, whereupon the owner induced water-drinkers and lovers of fashionable promenade to resort there. Thus Bermondsey Spa for a brief period became a favourite suburban watering place like Hampstead. In 1853 a company was formed to construct new docks close to Spa Road Station, which were to have been called the Wellington Docks. The entrance was to have been opposite the St Katherine Docks. The capital was £1,000,000 and the docks were to have covered 180 acres, of which sixty were to be water and capable of admitting the largest steamers.

With a view to relieving the enormous pedestrian traffic of London Bridge, a tunnel under the Thames from Tower Hill to Tooley Street was opened for foot passengers in April 1875. It was constructed in less than twelve months at the remarkably low cost of £16,000. It was designed by W. Barlow and is about sixty feet below the surface of the river. After the opening of the Tower Bridge the tunnel was closed and is now used by the Metropolitan Water Board to connect up the water supplies of North and South London. A circular brick building, which was the entrance, can still be seen on Tower Hill.

At the time when the Tower Bridge was first opened there was no suitable connexion between the approach from Tooley Street and the Old and New Kent Roads. Various plans for a new street were considered by the London County Council, but much delay occurred in arriving at any decision, as many as four different schemes having been placed before the Committee. In the direct line between Tooley Street and Bermondsey New Road the church of St Mary Magdalen and its recreation ground stood in the path. Eventually the Committee adopted the scheme for a street sixty feet wide from Tooley Street to the south-western end of Bermondsey New Road, passing to the east of the recreation ground of St Mary Magdalen church, and curving round its south-eastern angle into Bermondsey New Road, which was also widened to sixty feet. The length of the new thoroughfare, which terminates at the junction of the Old and New Kent Roads, is 3,600 feet. It was constructed at a cost of £400,000. In March 1902 the London County Council decided to name this thoroughfare Tower Bridge Road. New blocks of flats have been erected at the back of Long Lane and Abbey Street in connexion with local slum clearances and in Druid Street which flanks the Southern Region Railway. Many others have also been erected on the Arnold Estate. In Bermondsey Square, at the junction of Long Lane and Tower Bridge Road, the famous Caledonian Market from Islington, which was closed during the last war, has been given a new home and is open on Fridays only.

We have now conducted our readers all round the Port of London and the adjacent districts of this great metropolis, but no account of the Port would be complete which did not include a description of the Tilbury Docks, situated twenty-six miles below London Bridge. They were opened in 1886, and, like all the other docks, were privately owned until the formation of the Port of London Authority. They cover a land area of 675 acres and a water area exceeding 104 acres. For thirty years the Tilbury Docks underwent no change or modernization, but eight years after taking control the Port of London Authority extended the main dock. More recently they have constructed a new entrance lock and dry dock, and a passenger landing-stage and baggage-hall. The latter was formally opened by Mr Ramsay MacDonald, then Prime Minister, on 16 May 1930.

During the war period, Tilbury Docks, although scarred, did not suffer so greatly from bombing as the other docks. Early in the war one or two buildings were demolished and in 1944 an isolated incendiary attack destroyed the Tilbury Hotel, which commanded a fine view of the Thames opposite Gravesend. Tilbury is in the forefront of Port of London development. Here the P.L.A.'s major expansion and modernisation plans are taking shape and a new branch dock, part of which is already in use, is being built to accommodate big modern ships.

Nineteenth Walk

Southwark and Lambeth, including Borough High Street, St George's Circus, Waterloo Station, County Hall, St Thomas's Hospital, Lambeth Palace, Vauxhall and Kennington

Southwark and Lambeth may properly be regarded as the nucleus of South London in much the same way as the Cities of London and Westminster form the centre of this great metropolis on the north side of the Thames. Like them both Southwark and Lambeth command special interest by virtue of their antiquity and their historical associations.

In former times, when London Bridge alone spanned the Thames, and Southwark High Street was the only exit from the metropolis on the south side of the river, this thoroughfare was famous for its numerous inns. These became the common pleasure-ground of travellers and of the citizens of London and the surrounding villages, for, in addition to the inns, several theatres were located in Bankside between London and Blackfriars Bridges. So many inns were to be found in the High Street that Thomas Dekker, a seventeenth-century satirist, spoke of the entire street as being 'a continued ale house with not a shop to be seen between red lattice and red lattice, no workers but all drinkers'. This was because the coaches from Dover and the southern counties unloaded their passengers on the Surrey side of the Thames at a time when the narrowness of London Bridge, the only bridge over the river, barred them from London proper.

The ancient and historic borough of Southwark – always known as 'The Borough' – was quite different from any ordinary suburb. Until modern times the district possessed no industries such as tanning and brewing, which now flourish in this immediate locality. The Borough and Newington Butts were formerly under the jurisdiction of the City Corporation, and were called Bridge Ward Without, until Southwark became an independent Parliamentary Division. Until 1763 an annual fair was held at Southwark on 7 September, which was opened by the Lord Mayor and Sheriffs riding in procession from the City.

Many of the twenty-three inns which were once located in the Borough High Street and its immediate vicinity were of considerable size and stood back from the roadway, with large wooden gates for protection. They had tiers of timbered galleries on three sides, with connecting bedchambers overlooking a cobblestone yard. One of these was the Bear, at the foot of London Bridge, which was demolished about the middle of the eighteenth century for the widening of old London Bridge. Others were the Tabard, the George, the White Hart, the Queen's Head, the King's Head, and the Catherine Wheel. The Southwark inns had room between them for between two hundred and three hundred guests, and on an average nineteen public conveyances started out from them daily.

Dickens wrote in *Pickwick,* 'In the Borough there still remain some half-dozen old inns which have preserved their external features unchanged, and which have escaped alike the rage for public improvement and the encroachments of private speculation. Great rambling queer old places with galleries and passages and staircases wide enough and antiquated enough to furnish material for a hundred ghost stories'.

The whole of these inns, including the White Hart, demolished in 1889, have long since disappeared, with the exception of the George. And of the George only the south side, with one balconied fragment, now remains intact, as the north and east sides of the yard have been appropriated for railway goods sheds. There are plans for widening the Borough High Street and the east side is 'under review', but assurances have been given that The George will not be disturbed. The old High Street, Southwark, before it was swept away about 1830, was the narrowest thoroughfare leading into London. Various gabled and plaster-fronted houses were then demolished to make way for the new southern approach to London Bridge. This and the corresponding northern approach cost £1,000,000 or more than double the bridge itself, and nearly all the buildings on the west side of the Borough High Street were demolished for this great improvement.

In rebuilding the west side of the street Southwark Cathedral, the third largest church in London, was left open to view on its eastern side, which had remained hidden for centuries with the exception of the upper portion of the tower. The sum of £45,000 had been expended shortly before on the restoration of the tower, which is 150 feet high, and upon the east end of the church. This work was carried out in 1818 under the supervision of Dr George Gwilt, F.S.A.

St Saviour's, which is second only in interest to Westminster Abbey itself, was originally the church of the Augustine Priory of St Mary Overie, and was founded by Mary Audrey or Overy, a ferry-woman (probably legendary) who, long before the Conquest or the existence of any bridge over the river, devoted her earnings to this purpose. She was buried within the walls of the church. The building was formally inaugurated as a cathedral for the diocese of South London on 3 July 1905 by King Edward VII, and was afterwards further renovated at a cost of £40,000. John Harvard, founder of the famous university in the United States, was baptized here on 29 November 1607, his father being then a churchwarden. To mark the tercentenary of his birth the Chapel of St John, north of the chancel, was restored in 1907 by sons and friends of Harvard University, and a memorial window inserted. A fine memorial to William Shakespeare, whose theatre, the Globe, stood close at hand, was erected in 1912.

The southern approach to London Bridge, which will form our starting-point, is now spacious and of sufficient width to suit the requirements of its traffic, but all traces of its original picturesque appearance have long since vanished. In June 1854 a Gothic clock-tower, resembling a market cross, with a canopied niche, was erected in the centre of the roadway, which gave a picturesque architectural appearance to this locality. It was designed by Mr Arthur Ashpitel, F. S. A., but had to be removed owing to the construction of the railway to Charing Cross and is now at Swanage. Funds would not permit of the erection of the intended statue of the Duke of Wellington. Before the construction of the Charing Cross Raiwey the northern section of the Borough High Street had been renamed Wellington Street.

In Tooley Street, leading to Bermondsey, stood St Olave's Church, which was pulled down about 1930. It commemorated the sainted Olaf, King of Norway, who, with Ethelred destroyed in 1008 the Bridge of London, which was then in the hands of the Danes. The church was rebuilt on the site of another one by Flitcroft, a pupil of Kent, in 1736-40. In August 1843, a fire occurred in Tooley Street which attacked the tower of St Olave's Church, burnt out the roof and ceiling, and melted the peal of bells, which fell from the belfry. Topping's Wharf was burnt down in the same fire. In the past, Southwark has been the scene of several great fires. On 26 May 1676 some five hundred dwelling-houses were destroyed in a great fire which occurred here, including the older portions of the Tabard, the Queen's Head, White Hart, King's Head, and Green Dragon Inns. But for the Great Fire of London which occurred ten years previously this could have been considered the worst fire that had yet occurred in London.

On Saturday, 22 June 1861, Tooley Street was the scene of another fire, the most extensive which London had witnessed for more than a century. It continued to burn until the Sunday morning and involved a loss of about £2,000,000. It started in a warehouse belonging to Messrs Scovell & Company. Many engines arrived on the spot without delay, but, no water being obtainable from the mains, the majority of them remained idle for quite an hour, until water could be obtained from the plugs. By that time the fire had spread to eight warehouses, and before it could be got under control many more were ignited and their contents destroyed.

By nine o'clock the adjoining Chamberlain's Wharf had been reduced to ashes and the fire had spread to several schooners filled with barrels of oil, tallow, and tar, which could not be floated into the middle of the river, owing to the very low tide at the time. The burning barrels of tar formed a line along the burning banks of the river for about a quarter of a mile, and it could almost literally be said that the Thames was on fire. Later the wind shifted and carried the flames in an eastward direction, and several more warehouses were speedily enveloped in the flames. The fire then spread to Tooley Street, and gutted still more warehouses, including Hay's Wharf, Cotton's Wharf, and the branch Custom House.

It was three o'clock on Sunday morning before the fire was got under control, and even then the ruins continued to smoulder for a long time. The length of the fire was a quarter of a mile, from St Olave's Church to Mile Lane and

Humphrey's new wharf. The depth of the fire between Tooley Street and the river was about three hundred yards. The most awful view of the fire was to be seen from London Bridge, which on Saturday night was thronged with large numbers of the inhabitants of the metropolis coming to see a spectacle such as might never be witnessed again.

Thousands of spectators took up their positions on the quays, wharves, and sundry vessels, on the tops of church steeples, and in the gallery of the Monument. No such mass of flame and heat had ever been known before, even during the Great Fire of London in 1666. Soon after midnight an immense mass of wall facing the river fell outwards with a hideous crash, revealing a most appalling scene. During the whole of Sunday and Monday smoke and flames broke forth from amongst the ruins. On Sunday the Prince of Wales, afterwards King Edward VII, visited the scene of the fire, which broke out almost exactly opposite the Monument, where on 2 September 1666 the Great Fire of London had started. On the wall of Number 33 Tooley Street is a memorial to James Braidwood, Superintendent of the London Fire Brigade, 'who was killed near this spot in the execution of his duty' during this great fire. He is also commemorated in Braidwood Street, nearby.

Adjoining Tooley Street is the spacious approach to the stations of the South-Eastern and the Brighton lines, now British Railways (Southern Region). A third station, that of the former London and Greenwich Railway, occupied the eastern part of the site now covered by the South-Eastern section but that line was taken over by its larger neighbour.

The London and Greenwich Railway was the first line to be constructed in the metropolis, and ran from London Bridge Station to Deptford, from which place it was afterwards extended to Greenwich. It was commenced in 1834 and opened as far as Deptford by 1837. A peculiarity of this line is that it was constructed on a viaduct composed of 878 arches, each of 18 feet span, 22 feet high, and 25 feet in width from side to side. It runs in a straight line from London Bridge to Deptford, where it crosses the Ravensbourne river, now called Deptford Creek. At the time it was opened it was intended to construct a branch line from the main line at High Street, Deptford, to the riverside, where there was a pier for the embarking and landing of passengers by steam vessels. During the first eleven months the line carried 456,750 passengers, or an average of 1,300 a day. A few years later this railway track was greatly widened in order to provide space for the lines of the London and Brighton and the South-Eastern Railway Companies. A further widening was carried out in 1902 by the South-Eastern Railway Company in order to cope with the ever-increasing volume of passenger traffic.

The London Bridge Station of the Brighton Railway, which was also that of the Croydon Railway Company, was already opened by 1840, but in 1845 these two companies were amalgamated. The width of this station was doubled in 1853 in order to cope with the increase of the Company's suburban traffic and that occasioned by the opening of the Crystal Palace. Several buildings were pulled down to make room for this improvement, and in 1861 the Bridge House

Hotel, adjoining London Bridge Station, was opened. It contained about 150 rooms, but was never very popular with visitors to London, and after an existence of about thirty years was closed down. The building was then used by the Southern Railway Company as general offices.

The early raids of 1940 played havoc in this immediate locality. Both the Brighton line and South-Eastern Stations were badly damaged including the roof, the façade and the Bridge House building, which has been demolished as have many houses in St Thomas Street and those at the back which extend to Bermondsey Street and Weston Street.

The old terminus of the South-Eastern Railway was located at Bricklayers' Arms, near the Old Kent Road, and was opened to passenger traffic on 1 May 1844. The line was extended to London Bridge in 1851, after which Bricklayers' Arms became a goods station. The natural character of the land upon which this immense station was erected had previously made it unsuitable for building operations. In earlier times Bricklayers' Arms had been a travellers' resting-station, familiar to all coaches bound for the south-eastern districts which called here to pick up passengers from the north-west parts of London.

In August 1851 the South-Eastern Railway Company opened a shopping arcade at London Bridge Station, but this speculation proved a failure owing to the high rentals asked for the new shops. The Greenwich Station was on the east side of the South-Eastern Station, and the arcade, which was similar to the old Lowther Arcade in the Strand, was 150 feet long, with a basement in Tooley Street, above which it had an elevation of sixty feet. This was divided into three storeys, the upper elevation being on a level with the railway, and the lower part in Tooley Street forming a range of ordinary shops. The front of the arcade was designed in the Italian style.

In 1863, when the South-Eastern Railway Company extended its lines to Cannon Street and Charing Cross, the London Bridge Arcade was demolished and a viaduct constructed on its site. This is continued by the box-girder bridge built across the Borough High Street, which forms the approach to London Bridge Station. The bridge is composed of a long and a short iron girder, the former 207 feet long and the latter 176 feet, the difference being caused by the curve made by the line at this spot. No uglier structure could well have been devised, and it was said at the time that the expenditure of a few hundred pounds, or no more than the cost of a Lord Mayor's banquet, could have given London a bridge which might have been an ornament to this approach to the metropolis. Strong opposition to the disfigurement of London by such unsightly railway bridges was in fact raised by the Metropolitan Board of Works in 1863, who proposed that the matter should be placed before Parliament.

At that time the extensive buildings of St Thomas's Hospital stood between the Borough High Street and London Bridge Station. It had been rebuilt in massive style about the same time as London Bridge, and a new north wing had been added, the site of which cost £41,000, or at the rate of £55,000 an acre. Requiring a small portion of their ground, the South-Eastern Railway then requested St Thomas's Hospital to sell them one sixteenth of an acre for £20,000 The Railway Bill before Parliament was vigorously opposed by the Hospital but finally the Company got their Act.

The Hospital authorities then demanded that the South-Eastern Railway Company should take all or none of the hospital, and after protracted litigation the Company were compelled to purchase the entire property, and St Thomas's Hospital was then removed first to Walworth and later to its present attractive site opposite the Houses of Parliament. The ground of the original hospital cost the South-Eastern Railway £74,000 an acre, and comprised altogether nearly four acres. The site of the old Southwark Town Hall close by had recently been let at £500 per annum.

Close to Tower Bridge Road, and overlooking the track of the Southern Railway, was the church of St John, Horsleydown, one of fifty new churches ordered to be built by Act of Parliament. It was completed in 1732, had a square tower with a tall spire which looked like a miniature Nelson's Column. The church was destroyed in the blitz; the walls that remain are rapidly being overgrown with creeper, which makes them quite a picturesque ruin.

At the back of St Saviour's Cathedral is the Borough market for fruit and vegetables. This busy market was instituted in 1756 in place of stalls in the congested High Street, which, in their turn had, in 1551, replaced a market on London Bridge. Clink Street, a narrow, dark lane between tall warehouses, which adjoins the market, commemorates the prison which the bishops used for the confinement of 'Such as should babble, frey or break the peace.' Winchester House, which once stood between St Saviour's Cathedral and the river, was built in 1107. It was the old palace of the Bishops of Winchester, and a 14th century rose window of about 15 feet diameter still survives (without glass, of course) in a stone wall of the palace which is embodied in a warehouse that has been built on the site. An end of this wall can be seen from Clink Street. In Stoney Street, behind St Saviour's Cathedral, connecting with Clink Street and leading to the riverside, stood several old houses belonging to the period of Queen Elizabeth I. When making the approaches in 1865 to the new railway bridge carrying their line into Cannon Street, the South-Eastern Railway were obliged to demolish these houses. One of these was the George Inn, with a gable-end front and projecting windows. Between the twelfth and sixteenth centuries this locality was occupied by licensed houses of immoral reputation until they were suppressed by law during the reign of Henry VIII. These included the Globe, Rose, Hope, and Swan Taverns, and the Paris or Bear Garden on Bankside.

Southwark Street, leading from the Borough High Street to Blackfriars Road, is a fine broad thoroughfare about the same width as the west end of Queen Victoria Street, to which it bears a certain resemblance. The section between the Borough High Street and Southwark Bridge Road was opened for traffic on 28 July 1862, but the entire street as far as Blackfriars Road was not completed until 1864. Southwark Street was very rapidly built over and lined with ware-

houses and other large commercial buildings. The east end of the thoroughfare
runs into the Borough High Street with a bold curve nearly opposite the street
leading to Guy's Hospital. The Midland Bank on the south corner of the street
adjoining the Borough High Street stands on the site of the old Southwark Town
Hall erected in 1793 and demolished in 1859. On the opposite side of the street,
next to the railway bridge, is Central Buildings, formerly the Hop Exchange,
which was partly destroyed by fire in 1918. It was opened on 16 October 1867
at a cost of £50,000, and occupies over an acre of ground. The columns of the
imposing entrance have capitals which are clustered with hops and their foliage,
a pleasantly appropriate *motif* that is repeated in the iron balustrades to the
galleries of the upper floors with the addition, at intervals, of shields charged
with the White Horse of Kent.

Like most other new London thoroughfares Southwark Street is provided
with a subway for the gas and sewer mains, and must be ranked amongst the
leading metropolitan improvements carried out during the nineteenth century.
The total cost of Southwark Street was £597,000. Facing the eastern end of the
street stood the Talbot Inn, situated in the Borough High Street, originally called
the Tabard Inn. It was renamed the Talbot after the Great Fire of London, and
was itself destroyed by fire in 1873.

Within a few yards of the eastern end of Southwark Street is the site of the
Globe Theatre on Bankside which was associated with William Shakespeare
from 1598 to 1613. This is commemorated by a bronze tablet fixed to the wall
of Courage's Brewery, formerly Barclay, Perkins, on the corner of Park Street
and Bankside. Bankside itself is a long narrow thoroughfare running from Clink
Street to Blackfriars. Its north side is open to the Thames for most of the way
and commands fine views of St Paul's Cathedral and the other side of the river.
The Bankside Electric Power Station has been erected on the south side of the
street despite strong opposition. However, none would deny that it is a handsome edifice, built in conformity with the proposed south side embankment.

In November 1862 Sir Joseph Bazalgette suggested the construction of an
embankment on the south side of the Thames from London Bridge to Vauxhall,
which he thought would not cost any more than the construction of Southwark
Street and the Albert Embankment. However, the opposition from the wharves
on the south side of the Thames and other vested interests proved much too
powerful to give this scheme any prospect of realization beyond the new termination of Waterloo Bridge on the Festival of Britain site.

Close to Southwark Bridge Road, occupying twelve acres of ground at Bankside, is the famous brewery long known by the name of Barclay, Perkins.
A smaller brewery stood on this site over two centuries ago, belonging to
a Mr Halsey, who, on retiring from the business with a large fortune, sold it to
the elder Mr Thrale. This gentleman left the property to his son, the friend
of Dr Johnson, who, from 1765 until his death, lived at the house in Southwark
and at Mr Thrale's villa at Streatham. In 1781 Thrale died, and as he had no
sons his executors, of whom Dr Johnson was one, sold the brewery jointly to

Mr Barclay and Mr Perkins, the latter of whom had been the superintendent of the brewery, for £135,000. A great portion of the original premises was destroyed by fire in 1852, but was rebuilt almost immediately, with all the advantages of improved machinery. As already mentioned, it is now Courage's Brewery.

Guy's Hospital, in St Thomas Street to the south of London Bridge Station, owes its foundation to Thomas Guy, born in 1645, son of a coal merchant at Horselydown, who became a Lombard Street bookseller. The original building dates from 1728 and the east and west wings and the chapel in which the founder, Thomas Guy, is buried were added later. The east wing was severely blitzed in 1940, but plans have been prepared for the rebuilding of the entire hospital. The first stage of the rebuilding scheme was completed when the eleven-storey 'New Guy's House', with 378 beds, ten air-conditioned operating theatres and all up-to-date equipment was opened recently.

Retracing our steps once more to the Borough High Street, a short distance beyond Guy's Hospital on the east side stood the White Hart Hotel, pulled down in July 1889 after it had long ceased to be an inn. It had a court surrounded by old balustraded galleries. On the same side of the High Street, by Long Lane, stood the Marshalsea Prison, used from before 1377 until 1842 for political prisoners and afterwards for debtors. The prison was finally demolished in 1849, but a considerable section of the high prison wall, backing on to St George's churchyard (now a public park) can still be seen. The Marshalsea is the scene of several chapters of *Little Dorrit*. It was here in 1824 that John Dickens and family were resident in respect of a debt of £40. Lant Street, where Charles Dickens lodged to be near the family, is now quite demolished. Until very recently, however, it was possible to identify one—*even two*—houses that claimed to have sheltered the youth who in later years, when writing *Little Dorrit*, would recall his visits to the Marshalsea.

Farther south, on the west side of the Borough High Street, stood the Queen's Bench Prison, largely used for debtors, and for persons charged with libel and contempt of court. It was situated at the angle of Borough Road and Scovell Road, and some grim tenements, Queen's Buildings, now occupy the site of Mr Micawber's 'Place of incarceration'. It contained 224 rooms, and was surrounded by a brick wall fifty feet high. Within the walls were several pumps yielding pure spring water, a coffee-house, two public-houses, with shops and stalls for the sale of various commodities. The number of persons moving to and fro or engaged in various amusements had quite the opposite appearance to what might have been expected from a place of incarceration.

Debtors were allowed to purchase what were called 'the rules', which enabled them to have houses or lodging outside the walls within a prescribed area of about three miles in circumference. These liberties were purchasable at so much per cent on the amount of the debts, and against good security to the governor. Day rules could also be obtained permitting the prisoner to go out upon certain conditions. Thus the Queen's Bench became the most popular debtors' prison in England. Persons enjoying the rules sometimes lived in luxury for years, in defiance of their creditors, while in other cases large properties were thus preserved to their innocent heirs. The Queen's Bench Prison was demolished in 1880, but it is said that some small remnant can still be identified.

Until about 1880 the Borough High Street between St George's Church and Newington Causeway was known as Blackman Street. St George's Church, which is situated at the busy traffic junction of Long Lane, Tabard Street, Great Dover Street, and Borough High Street, was built by John Price between 1733 and 1736, at a cost of £9,000, on the site of an earlier church. It is dedicated to St-George-the-Martyr, the patron saint of England. The exterior is of brown brick with stone dressings, and the building is crowned by a lofty eight-sided tower. It is known as Little Dorrit's Church. Inside, there is a fine oval ceiling in plaster, restored in 1952 and the pulpit, with a handsome curved stairway, stands on four very tall columns. Somewhere in the churchyard, Edward Cocker, the 17th century mathematician ('according to Cocker') is buried.

Tabard Street, for centuries known as Kent Street, calls for special notice. It was the main highway to the south-east of England before the construction of Great Dover Street early in the nineteenth century, and was formerly the centre of a large slum area. Commenting on Tabard Street, Smollett remarked that 'it would be for the honour of the Kingdom to improve the avenue to London by way of Kent Street which is a most disgraceful entrance to such an opulent city. A foreigner in passing this beggarly and ruinous suburb conceives such an idea of misery and meanness as all the wealth and magnificence of London and Westminster are afterwards unable to destroy.

Towards the close of the eighteenth century Kent Street presented a scene of squalor and destitution unequalled even in St Giles's. It was very long and ill-built, and gipsies, thieves, and doubtful characters were to be found in almost every house. Human beings, asses, pigs, and dogs frequently shared a single room. Kent Street was then the only road existing as a northern continuation of the Old Kent Road, and at the junction of these two roads stood a cross pointing the way to Bermondsey Abbey. In 1809 the new thoroughfare of Great Dover Street was constructed parallel with Tabard Street from St George's Church to the Old Kent Road. The New Kent Road, at first called Greenwich Road, which crosses the Old Kent Road, links the Elephant and Castle with Tower Bridge Road, and was formed by the Kent Road Trust at the beginning of the eighteenth century.

The Tabard Street of the present day reveals a starting contrast to that earlier scene. Acres of slums and mean streets have been swept away by the London County Council on the east side of the road, between Tabard Street and Long Lane. These have been replaced by a large new recreation ground surrounded by four-storey blocks of well-built artisan dwellings faced with red brick. This is the Tabard Garden Estate. Altogether the improvements carried out by the London County Council in the Tabard Street area are scarcely less spectacular than those effected in the condemned area in Shoreditch in the nineties of the last century.

Completing a triangle with the Borough High Street and Great Dover Street is Trinity Street which, with its Trinity Square and Merrick Square display a uniformity and well-kept appearance that is quite distinctive. In front of Holy Trinity Church stands the oldest outdoor statue in London. Said to represent King Alfred the Great and date from the 14th century, it is believed to be one of several statues that originally stood in Westminster Hall.

Large areas in both Southwark and Bermondsey were destroyed in the great blitz of 1940 and this applies especially to the west side of Great Dover Street and the quarter in the triangle enclosed by Newington Causeway, New Kent Road and Great Dover Street. Here rebuilding is in active progress and since 1945 many fine new blocks of County Council flats have been erected, notably in Harpur Street, Falmouth Street and on the north side of New Kent Road. Many rows of houses have also been destroyed in the Old Kent Road, which, like Mile End Road, is one of the widest thoroughfares leading out of London. The Old Kent Road was always a road of character and though it has suffered many changes, it is perhaps the familiar names of the old taverns that best recall its earlier days. The Dun Cow, like the Road itself subject of a popular song many years ago. The Kentish Drovers, a favourite halting-place for cattle dealers and said to have been there some 250 years. The Thomas A'Becket, at the corner of Albany Road, marks the shrine of St Thomas A'Watering, where pilgrims rested on their way to Canterbury. On the other side of the road are The World Turned Upside Down and The Bricklayers Arms. These are but a few of the best known among many. At Number 108 are the old-established premises of Messrs Edgington & Co. Ltd, specialists in tents, flags, marquees and suchlike, who describe themselves as 'Tent Makers since Trafalgar'.

The Licensed Victuallers' Asylum in Asylum Road, a turning out of the Old Kent Road, was founded in 1826 by Mr J. P. Hodgson, a distiller of Finsbury. It occupies six acres of ground, and a new Albert wing was added to the building in 1858, the first stone of which was laid on 23 June by the Prince Consort, who was a patron of this institution. Today, the buildings are no longer occupied by the Licensed Victuallers, who have moved to Denham. They have also taken with them the impressive marble statue of the Prince Consort, which formerly stood in the middle of the lawns. The buildings have been taken over by the Camberwell Borough Council who have modernized the interiors to provide much needed housing accommodation. In addition to electric lighting and heating, an extension along the rear of each block adds a bathroom, washbasin and indoor toilet to each dwelling. The Chapel, in the centre of the group, was severely damaged by bombs and is to be rebuilt as a small hall or theatre for this little community. In this vicinity a whole new quarter has been developed, and is centred round Friary Road and Green Hundred Road. Here are wide streets containing new rows of five-storeyed blocks of flats with balconies and spacious courtyards, some of them already erected before the last war.

The Borough High Street is continued by Newington Causeway, a wide thoroughfare of small interest which leads to the busy crossroads known as the Elephant and Castle, but invariably called 'The Elephant'. Six leading thoroughfares converge on this great traffic centre which is by far the most congested in South London.

The Elephant and Castle Improvement Scheme, commenced by the London County Council, is now nearing completion. The famous tavern of that name has been demolished and the whole area transformed. From the traffic point of view, it is now a very large roundabout; for pedestrians, of course, there is a rabbit warren of subways with directions to the 'east side' of this road and the 'west side' of that, and although there are little diagrams at the entrance to each subway, it is down below that the stranger feels the need of a map and compass. However, instead of the usual 20 or 30 steps down and up again which plague elderly people in other parts of London, most of the subways at the Elephant are reached by gentle slopes, called 'rampways', which are much appreciated.

A speciality of the whole scheme is the covered shopping centre on three levels with a galleried arcade, ventilated and heated to a controlled temperature.

The massive bronze elephant with a circular castle on his back, after braving the storms and sunshine of many years on top of the old tavern, now stands under cover, warm and dry, among a hundred or more shops; an 'unveiling ceremony' by the Minister of Labour took place in March 1965.

Above ground, Draper House, Sherston Court and Wollaston Close are new 'skyscraper' buildings to replace the hundreds of houses displaced by bombs and/or the new development. The London College of Printing with 15 floors, was opened by Sir Isaac Hayward in 1964; adjoining is a workshop block, well equipped with machinery. Alexander Fleming House, on the Newington Causeway side, is occupied by the Ministry of Health and, above a block of new shops, Castle House provides accommodation for offices of the Greater London and Southwark Borough Councils.

There is a new Underground Station for the Northern Line, but on the other side of the merry-go-round the old Bakerloo station with the South London Press above seems to be the only pre-war building left. As a centre-piece, a London Transport electricity sub-station with shiny aluminium panels is said to be named after Michael Faraday.

The Elephant and Castle is not the only tavern that has disappeared; another prominent establishment was the Rockingham, and The Black Prince is missing from the Walworth Road. The Hampton Court Palace is still open in Crampton Street and among the reinforcements are the Butts, The Pineapple, The Charlie Chaplin, The Hand in Hand and the Gibraltar, at least one of which restores the name of an earlier sign. The original Elephant and Castle hostelry stood between the junction of Walworth Road and Newington Butts. The latest contribution to the conviviality of this district is a new Elephant and Castle tavern, opened at Christmas 1966, but on the site of the old Rockingham at the New Kent Road – Newington Causeway Corner. Next to this is a new Odeon Cinema standing almost, but not quite, where the huge Trocadero Cinema stood. So complete is the transformation in this area and such is the South

Londoner's appreciation of modern architecture that a young lady on a bus approaching the Elephant said to her friend, *It's like the End of the World down here now, ain't it?* In Newington Butts, the massive six-columned portico of the Metropolitan Tabernacle survived the bombing and stood out among the desolation like a South London Parthenon. The building behind was destroyed but has now been rebuilt in a brick and concrete manner quite unsuited to its handsome Corinthian frontage. This was originally the famous tabernacle built for the popular preacher, Charles Haddon Spurgeon, at a cost of £30,000 and opened on Good Friday, 5 April 1861.

About half-way down the Walworth Road on the east side is the Southwark Town Hall, erected in 1864 and enlarged in 1902. It is a plain red-brick building, quite unpretentious for this large metropolitan borough though the modern extensions for the health departments are quite attractive. On the wall is a maxim, 'The health of the people is the highest law'. Walworth, now a poor neighbourhood, was originally a village in the parish of Newington Butts, and in 1820 was described in current works on London as containing many good houses inhabited by citizens connected with public affairs whose happiness arose from alternate bustle and retirement. Next to the Town Hall is the Public Library and the small but most interesting Cuming Museum, the nucleus of which was the private collection of Henry S. Cuming and his son Richard, residents in Kennington Park Road. The collection, which is rich in items of local interest, was bequeathed to the borough in 1902. The museum was closed by enemy action in 1941, but reopened in 1959.

Passing East Street, the popular street market, Walworth Road continues to Camberwell. The former Borough of Camberwell, which included Dulwich and Peckham, is now, with Bermondsey, in the enlarged Borough of Southwark with a total population of 311,160. It derives its name from a stream of limpid water situated in the grounds of the former Grove House, which flowed into the canal at Fountain Cottage. The old parish church of St Gile's, Camberwell, was destroyed by fire in 1842 and was replaced by the present Gothic edifice, which was completed in 1844, and has a spire 207 feet high. Camberwell Green was formerly the scene of an annual fair held in August, much to the annoyance of the local residents, who tried in 1832 to do away with it as a public nuisance. However, as it was a manorial right, as well as a source of revenue, it was suffered to remain until 1855, in which year it was abolished. In that year the manorial rights in the green were purchased by a subscription raised among the principal inhabitants of the district. The green was then laid out as a new park and opened to the public on 26 April 1859. The short Wren Road at Camberwell Green is so named because Sir Christopher Wren is believed to have lived there during the rebuilding of St Paul's Cathedral. A similar claim has also been made regarding two houses in Bankside, Southwark and another in Botolph Lane, City.

Retracing our steps to the Elephant and Castle, a walk through London Road will bring us to St George's Circus, another great traffic centre where six thoroughfares meet, including the Blackfriars, Waterloo, and Westminster

Bridge Roads. It formerly contained a clock-tower which was presented to the borough by Messrs Rowland Faulkner and Frederick Faulkner in 1907, but this has since been removed in order to relieve the traffic congestion. It superseded the former obelisk erected on this site to the honour of Brass Crosby in 1771, who was confined to the Tower of London by the House of Commons for fulfilling his duty as a magistrate. The obelisk has been removed to the grounds of Bethlem Hospital, now the Imperial War Museum. On three sides of the base of the obelisk are inscribed the distances to Westminster Hall, London Bridge and Fleet Street. As these measurements were made from its former position in St George's Circus, they are no longer quite correct. Since St George's Circus is now a 'roundabout' with a large circular lawn in the centre, perhaps the obelisk could be restored to its rightful place again without hindrance to traffic. This is a suggestion that a local history society might consider. Facing Newington Butts in the former churchyard of the parish church of St Mary, now a public garden, is a handsome clock-tower erected in 1877 by Mr R. S. Faulconer, a churchwarden of the parish, to mark the site of the original church said to date back to Saxon times. The last church erected in 1792 was removed in 1876 to Kennington Park Road but this fine edifice was destroyed in the air raids of 1940 on a Sunday when several people were killed in the church. The massive square tower remains and forms an entrance to the new and very handsome church, in yellow brick, built on the site of the old one.

Until the dawn of the nineteenth century the whole of the triangular space known as St George's Fields, situated between Westminster Bridge Road and Blackfriars Road, was a marsh, and was also the scene of the 'No Popery' riots of 1780. St George's Fields were named after the adjacent church of St-George-the-Martyr, and were once marked by all the floral beauty of meadows uninvaded by London smoke. During the Fire of London many of the poorer inhabitants took refuge in St George's Fields which were intersected by dirty ditches. The Fields were much resorted to by itinerant preachers, who in the time of the Stuart sovereigns were not allowed to hold meetings in London. They also abounded with beer-gardens, where working-folk met to drink and pass a pleasant hour.

With its broad thoroughfares radiating fanwise from St George's Circus and the Elephant and Castle, St George's Fields constitutes an excellent piece of town-planning, and no American city could wish to be designed upon better lines. To a large extent this happy result is due to the great bend in the river between Southwark and Lambeth, which has caused the various roads leading from the Thames bridges to meet at St George's Circus. Thoroughfares such as Blackfriars Road, Lambeth Road, and Westminster Bridge Road remind one very much of Dublin, which is a city of wide streets and magnificent distances. If all London had been planned like St George's Fields the problem of its traffic congestion would be reduced to a bare minimum. So many shabby streets and houses have been destroyed by enemy action in this immediate locality that it is safe to predict that within another few years' time a handsome new quarter will cover the entire district of St George's Fields.

Blackfriars Road was mostly built between 1770 and 1800, and was long known as Great Surrey Street. It is broad and perfectly straight, and about two-thirds of a mile in length. Stamford Street, running at right angles to Blackfriars Road opposite Southwark Street, leads to Waterloo Road and dates from the beginning of the nineteenth century. Before the construction of the first Blackfriars Bridge there was a ferry near this spot for the conveyance of traffic across the river. Farther down the same side of the road is The Cut, formerly the New Cut, mainly occupied by costers' stalls, which, with its continuation, well-known as Lower Marsh, leads direct to Westminster Bridge Road. The New Cut was so named from its being the direct line of communication from Blackfriars to Westminster Bridge Road. Many buildings in Blackfriars Road and The New Cut have been destroyed by bombs. Some attractive new County Council blocks of flats have been erected in Baylis Road and Frazier Street at the back of Lambeth Lower Marsh. Others are still in course of erection. On the south side of Stamford Street is Dorset House, a splendid example of modern commercial architecture. This is the headquarters of Iliffe's, the publishers. It was designed by Mr L. A. Culliford, F.R.I.B.A., is nine storeys high and faced with Portland stone.

Next to Stamford Street is Christ Church, Southwark, which was destroyed by incendiary bombs on the night of 17 April 1941. On one of the lawns in the churchyard a large cross is laid out in stones to mark the place where the grass was scorched when the burning cross fell from the roof of the church. A completely new church has been built, with a special function as an Industrial Mission for young people employed in this largely commercial and industrial area. It seats about ninety people and at the back of the church is a hall with a stage, dressing rooms, kitchen, canteen, projection room and shower baths—everything that the modern youngster requires in his community centre. The partition between the church and hall can be opened up to accommodate a larger congregation when required. The whole building cost £80,000, and was paid for by War Damage compensation and a grant from the trustees of the Charity of John Marshall, who founded the original church in 1671.

On the east side of Blackfriars Road, near the river, is the former terminal station of the London, Chatham and Dover Railway, now used as a goods station. It was erected while the old Blackfriars Bridge was still in course of demolition, and was opened in 1864. Being a large station it was capable of accommodating an enormous traffic, and before the line was extended to Ludgate Hill the station was devoted to the suburban traffic of Brixton, Dulwich, Peckham, Herne Hill, and South London generally. The railway bridge, which is 1,216 feet in length, was constructed in 1863-64 to take four lines of railway.

On the west side of Blackfriars Road, near St George's Circus, stood, until 1935, the Surrey Music Hall. Originally a theatre, it shared with the old Elephant and Castle Theatre the claim to be the home of what used to be called 'Transpontine Melodrama', but was destroyed by fire on 30 January 1865 and rebuilt within twelve months. The fire occurred during the final scene of the Pantomime called 'The Investigation in the Forest of Fancy', but the audience, not being very large, soon dispersed, and nobody was hurt. Shortly afterwards the theatre was a mass of flames and nothing was saved except the money in the box office. In less than an hour the building had been burned to the ground. The first theatre on this site was known as the St George's Fields Circus. It was built in 1782 by Charles Dibdin, the author of *Tom Bowling* and many other sea songs; in 1805 it was burned to the ground like its successor. The second theatre was opened in 1806. The site has been acquired for an extension of the Royal Eye Hospital. Close by is Peabody Square, built in 1871, which contains sixteen blocks of artisan dwellings enclosing two quadrangles, which communicate with each other. They occupy the site of the old Magdalen Hospital on the west side of Blackfriars Road. A notable building which also stood in Blackfriars Road was the Ring, originally the Surrey Chapel, built in 1783 by the Rev. Rowland Hill who preached here for nearly fifty years from a pulpit in the centre. In 1910 it became a centre for boxing and in 1928 was visited by the Duke of Windsor when Prince of Wales, accompanied by the late Sir Harry Preston. It was twice bombed in 1940 and its ruins were cleared away in 1941.

Waterloo Road, which is not quite so wide as Blackfriars Road, was constructed at the same time as Waterloo Bridge, in about 1816. At the corner of the Cut is the rebuilt Royal Victoria Hall, commonly known as the Old Vic, where Shakespeare is played to crowded houses. It was badly damaged in the air raids of 1940 but was re-opened on 14 November 1950. It stands on the site of the Coburg Theatre erected in 1816-18 and in the 'eighties and 'nineties of last century was used for variety entertainments. On the same side is the Union Jack Club for soldiers and sailors, founded as a memorial to the members of both Services who lost their lives in the South African and Chinese Wars. St John's Church, which was damaged in the blitz of 1940, was built in 1823 and has a portico and six Doric columns. It had accommodation for two thousand people and was rebuilt for the Festival of Britain. Nearly all the old buildings in Waterloo Road have also vanished in the blitz except those between Stamford Street and the river, which were pulled down to make way for the 1951 Festival of Britain and to provide a better approach to the new Waterloo Bridge. A roundabout has been laid out at the junction of Waterloo Road, Stamford Street and York Road. Several fine buildings already line the east side of Waterloo Road, including Cornwall House, headquarters of the London Telecommunications Region, the Royal Waterloo Hospital and a fine nine-storey block of offices called Waterloo House erected in 1938 on the south corner of Stamford Street.

Waterloo Station, the largest and finest terminus in Great Britain, together with its approaches, covers the greater part of the land enclosed by York Road, Waterloo Road, Lambeth Lower Marsh, and Westminster Bridge Road. The fine entrance archway, which stands on a raised position overlooking Waterloo Road, is a memorial to the 585 of the Company's employees who fell in the first World War. A sloping roadway provides access to the station from Westminster Bridge Road, and another leading to York Road is for departing traffic.

The original terminus of the former London and South-Western Railway was situated at Nine Elms, Vauxhall, but its distance from the centre of London was a source of complaint from suburban passengers. Vauxhall itself was still a suburb, and the inconvenience was only partially remedied by the omnibus, steamboat, and cab. In consequence the London and South-Western Railway extended their line to Waterloo, which, although the distance was barely more than two miles, was a very costly undertaking, involving an outlay of £800,000. When opened in 1848 Waterloo Station had only three platforms and a service of fourteen trains a day. However, it was only intended as a temporary station, and the permanent building was completed shortly afterwards, with its principal façade and entrance in York Road. Previous to 1844 the site of Waterloo Station had been vacant ground occupied by hay-stalls, cow-yards, and dung-heaps. The great expense of constructing the short extension from Nine Elms to Waterloo was due in large measure to the six bridges which had to be built across Wandsworth Road, South Lambeth Road, Vauxhall Road, Lambeth Palace Road, Lambeth Butts, and Westminster Bridge Road. Twenty houses on the west side of Westminster Bridge Road and in Upper and Lower Marsh, Lambeth, were pulled down for the extension of the line in April 1847, after which the work progressed very rapidly.

One crossing at Miles Street, South Lambeth, was built in record time. It was a skew arch, very difficult to build, as it was 48 feet wide on one side and only 38 feet wide on the other, forming a curve of 54 feet span. It required for its completion ninety thousand bricks, but notwithstanding its peculiarities this immense arch of brickwork was begun, pointed, dressed, and completed in the incredibly short time of forty-five hours.

The present magnificent station, which was rebuilt between 1900 and 1921, covers two and a quarter acres, and has twenty-one platforms with a normal service of 1,200 trains a day. It is greatly superior to all other London termini and the nearest approach to a really perfect railway station. All its platforms face the spacious entrance hall which has seats for hundreds of waiting passengers and can accommodate large crowds of travellers without the confusion or discomfort which exist in most other great railway termini. It was formally opened by Queen Mary on 21 March 1922, King George V being confined indoors at the time with a cold. The reason why the reconstruction of Waterloo Station was spread over such a long period was because the former London and South-Western Railway provided the necessary funds out of annual earnings, instead of borrowing fresh capital. During the war its glass roof was badly damaged by enemy action but has since been repaired. The old offices of the Southern Railway at the corner of York Road were destroyed in the blitz and have been demolished. A new subway with escalators has been constructed which provided direct access from inside Waterloo Station to the Palace of Culture erected for the 1951 Festival of Britain, which it was expected would be visited by 100,000 people daily. These escalators later gave direct access to Waterloo Air Terminal, now demolished.

The Bethlem Hospital in Lambeth Road, now removed to its new quarters at West Wickham, was a fine building nearly seven hundred feet long, consisting of a centre and two wings. A lantern cupola added by Smirke in 1838 rises from the centre of the building, which is four storeys high and chiefly constructed in brick. It was erected at a cost of £100,000 and provided accommodation for a thousand patients. In 1853 two large annexes were added at the rear of the main building. With its grounds, the building occupies an area of fourteen acres. It was transferred here from Moorfields in 1815, and at that time was considered to be the finest hospital building in Europe. Bethlem Hospital, founded in Bishopsgate as long ago as 1247, is the oldest charitable institution in the world for the treatment of mental patients. In 1930 the grounds of Bethlem Hospital were purchased by the late Lord Rothermere as a gift to South London, laid out as a public open space and renamed the Mary Geraldine Harmsworth Park. Two wings of the former hospital have been pulled down, and the main building now houses the War Museum.

Another important building in Lambeth Road is the Roman Catholic Cathedral, commenced in 1840 and opened in 1848, but which still lacks its central tower. It was designed by Pugin, and at that time was the largest Roman Catholic church in England. It was consecrated with great pomp and ceremony on 4 July 1848, and here Cardinal Wiseman was enthroned as the first Archbishop of Westminster. The building is situated close to the spot where the 'No Popery' riots took place in 1780. Unfortunately the Cathedral was destroyed in the great blitz of 1940 but it has now been completely rebuilt. Off China Walk, is the famous Lambeth Walk, a lively street market which has given its name to a popular dance. Although some of its houses have been destroyed in the blitz, it retains its picturesque character, even though all around it is rapidly changing and a new quarter is arising on the blitzed sites.

In Westminster Bridge Road, also a very wide throughfare, is Christ Church, once a handsome Gothic edifice with accommodation for 2,500 people. It stands at the junction of Kennington Road, and was opened in 1876 at a cost of £60,000. It was built to replace the old Surrey Chapel rendered famous by the preaching of Rowland Hill. The tower and spire were built with American contributions as a memorial to Lincoln, and the stonework is ornamented with the Stars and Stripes. Christ Church was hit by a bomb in the air raids of 1940 and the building was damaged beyond repair, though the steeple or Lincoln Tower, as it is called, still stands. A new church of quite modern design has been built and appears to be embodied in a six-storey block of offices called Lincoln House. This gives the unusual effect of a nineteenth century church spire apparently rising from a twentieth century office building. Westminster Bridge Road once contained a very popular house of entertainment much patronized by Londoners in the 'fifties and 'sixties of the last century, Astley's Royal Amphitheatre, which afterwards became Sanger's Circus. The building has long since been swallowed up in the improvements effected in this part of London. It was started in 1768 as an open riding school, and was converted into a theatre

88 The 14th century Jewel Tower Abingdon Street, Westminster.

89a Westminster Abbey and (left of Abbey) St Margaret's, Westminster, Central Hall and Big Ben.

89b Westminster Abbey floodlit.

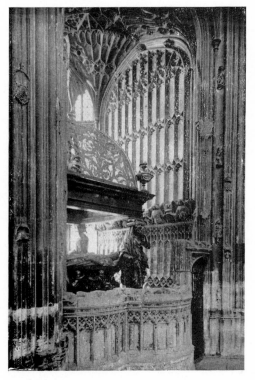

90 Henry VII Chapel, Westminster Abbey.

91 Parliament Street in 1896.

92 The Millbank Penitentiary in 1829; the site of the present Tate Gallery.

93 Westminster Cathedral.

94 Statue of William Huskinsson, M.P. in Pimlico Gardens.

95 The Royal Aquarium, on the site of the present Central Hall, was opened in 1876 as a place of general amusement. It was demolished in 1902.

96 Scotland Yard, old and new. In the foreground (right) are the old buildings and just left of centre is the new headquarters building (skyscraper, with many blinds drawn) of the Metropolitan Police.

97 Trams finally disappeared from the London streets on 5th July 1952.

98 The symbol of Stag Place among the new buildings on the ten-acre site of the old Stag Brewery, Pimlico.

99 Above Lambeth Bridge and the Houses of Parliament stands the 390-foot Vickers House.

100 The Metropolitan Police moved into this new Scotland Yard building in Victoria Street early in 1967.

101 The modern E.M.I. House in Manchester Square overlooks the stately Hertford House, home of the Wallace Collection.

102 After many years in the City Road, this fountain now stands in the forecourt of the Wallace Collection.

103 The new Odeon Cinema, Marble Arch and its adjoining 24-storey block of offices.

104 Marylebone Gardens about 1761.

in 1780. It was destroyed by fire in 1794 and again in 1803, and was rebuilt in 1843.

On the river front, at the north corner of Westminster Bridge Road, backing on to Belvedere Road, is the County Hall, the headquarters of the Greater London Council. The building was designed by Sir Ralph Knott, an old boy of the City of London School and a pupil of Sir Aston Webb. The river façade of the County Hall consists of a crescent-shaped centre with wings, and is built in the English Renaissance style, although it has a Flemish appearance. It opens on to an embanked promenade for foot passengers, and contains about nine hundred rooms.

For many years the various departments of the London County Council were housed in different buildings scattered about the metropolis, and the absence of any proper home for London's central governing authority was a standing reproach to the capital of the British Empire. The construction of the County Hall led to bitter party warfare between the Moderate and the Progressive members of the Council.

The site for the first portion of the County Hall was cleared and the piles driven into the river-bed between 1909 and 1912, but the actual construction was only begun in 1912, when King George V laid the foundation-stone. During the excavations for the County Hall in the summer of 1910 the workmen unearthed a Roman galley of oak, 50 feet long by 16 feet wide. This was carefully removed to the original London Museum at Lancaster House, where it is still below stairs. Building operations were suspended during the first World War, when the partly-completed building was requisitioned by the Food Ministry. The County Hall was finally completed and opened by King George V in 1922. The total cost of the building eventually amounted to £3,000,000, and after an interval of over twenty years the new northern wing was completed in 1933, several years after the death of its architect.

Even this gigantic building was not large enough to house all the various departments of the London County Council under one roof, and it was decided to erect at a cost of £1,000,000 a large annexe on the other side of Belvedere Road to cover the great island site bounded by Westminster Bridge Road, York Road and Chichele Street. Work on this annexe, which consists of two twin buildings, was begun in 1936. These are eight storeys high and faced with Portland stone with their main frontage to York Road. The two top storeys above the main cornice are built partly in the sloping roof and the two buildings are connected by a triple archway and a bridge which crosses the central approach roadway. Pieces of granite from the old Waterloo Bridge have been incorporated in the bridge. Some of the former slums in and around York Road were conveniently removed during the last war by bombs and those which still remained have now all been pulled down to make way for the 1951 Festival of Britain site which we have described in our eighth walk.

The London County Council was generally admitted to be the largest and most efficiently managed municipal governing authority in the world. It superseded the old Metropolitan Board of Works created in 1855 to watch over the requirements of London, and its 118 councillors were first elected on Thursday, 17 January 1889. On 21 March 1949 it celebrated its Diamond Jubilee. It has often been said that if Parliament ceased to talk for twelve months the country would suffer no inconvenience, and many people would probably be glad. On the other hand, if the London County Council ceased work for a few days indescribable chaos would result, and the health of London would be seriously jeopardized.

On the opposite corner of Westminster Bridge Road the County Hall has for a worthy neighbour St Thomas's Hospital, which also boasts an extensive frontage to the river. It stands on eight and a half acres of land reclaimed from the river between Westminster Bridge and Lambeth Palace, for which the hospital paid £100,000. The first stone was laid in May 1868 by Queen Victoria, who also opened the building on 21 June 1871. The Hospital consisted of seven detached blocks of buildings, four storeys high, 125 feet apart, and raised on lofty foundations. The total cost of the buildings was £500,000.

In 1862, as we have seen, the South-Eastern Railway bought the former buildings of the hospital, and in 1863 the Governors of St Thomas's approached the Governors of Bethlem Hospital with a view to the purchase of the latter's site for the new St Thomas's Hospital. Upon these overtures being rejected, St Thomas's chose the present site on the Albert Embankment for their new home. The buildings have a frontage of 1,700 feet to the Thames and a depth of 250 feet. The style of architecture is Palladian, with rich facings of coloured brick and Portland stone. The reason for building St Thomas's Hospital in detached blocks was to avoid the necessity of treating more than a comparatively small number of patients in the same building. In 1902 a new wing was constructed at the back of the main buildings, close to Westminster Bridge Road, for the accommodation of the nurses, but this was destroyed in the air raids of 1940. The three blocks of the hospital next to Westminster Bridge were also badly damaged but much of the damage has been repaired.

St Thomas's Hospital is to be entirely rebuilt and Stage One has already been completed. The Addington Street diversion of south-bound traffic and the re-alignment of Lambeth Palace Road at its northern end enabled the hospital to acquire land upon which they have built a new East Wing comprising a 4-storey block containing accident and emergency departments with a suite of operating theatres, connected with a 12-storey tower having ward accommodation for 200 beds. Stage Two of the rebuilding is expected to commence shortly with the demolition of the northern half of the hospital.

The footway from Westminster to Lambeth Bridge in front of St Thomas's Hospital was opened to the public in March 1868. A short walk along it will bring us to Lambeth Palace, which has been the residence of the Archbishops of Canterbury for seven centuries. It is entered by a Gothic gatehouse of red brick, the lower floor of which was once used as a prison, near the parish church. It was rebuilt by Cardinal Morton about 1490. The Lollards' Tower at the west end of the chapel was erected by Archbishop Chichele about 1430, and here the followers of Wycliffe were tortured and imprisoned. The chapel was built about 1245 by Archbishop Boniface, and the Hall, 83 feet by 38 feet, by Archbishop Juxon, who attended Charles I to the scaffold. It now contains the valuable library of thirty thousand volumes founded by Archbishop Bancroft's will in 1610.

Ten acres of the grounds are loaned to the Greater London Council and maintained for public use under the name of the Archbishops' Park. Adjoining the south gateway of the palace is St Mary's Church, which contains the graves of six archbishops. It has a Perpendicular tower, which was restored in 1906. Costly restorations and additions to Lambeth Palace were carried out in 1847-48 by Dr Howley, Archbishop of Canterbury, involving an expenditure of nearly £80,000. St Mary's Church was rebuilt in 1851 and opened by the Bishop of Winchester on 3 February 1852. All but the clock-tower of the old church was pulled down, the accommodation of the building having become inadequate. Unusual in an Anglican church is the semi-circular marble baptistry below floor-level, with descending steps for 'total immersion'; a memorial to the Archbishop Benson that has seldom been used.

The Albert Embankment, extending from Westminster to Vauxhall Bridge, was constructed at a cost of £909,000, and was named after the Prince Consort. The first stone was laid by Mr William Tite, M.P., on 28 July 1866, and the official opening ceremony was performed by Sir John Thwaites, Chairman of the Metropolitan Board of Works, on 24 November 1869. To make way for this improvement some picturesque old houses with wooden balconies, with their backs to the river, were demolished in 1867. These fronted a narrow thoroughfare called Fore Street, which was the nucleus of the original riverside village of Lambeth. On the large key site at the south-east corner of Lambeth Bridge now stands Lambeth Bridge House, a large building of nine storeys faced with white brick and completed in 1940. It is at present the headquarters of the Ministry of Works. Next to it are the new offices of Messrs Doulton & Sons, the well-known firm of sanitary engineers. On the adjoining site is the distinctive building erected in 1934 by Messrs W. H. Smith & Sons, the well-known firm of newsagents founded in 1848. It has a frontage of 200 feet to the river, is faced with stone and is crowned in the centre by a handsome clock-tower rising to a height of 150 feet, from which the hours can be flashed at night across the London sky. On the neighbouring site now stands the great new headquarters of the London Fire Brigade, a building of nine storeys erected in 1936 which has a long frontage to the Albert Embankment. The London Fire Brigade celebrated its centenary in 1966 – which was also the anniversary of the Great Fire of London. The Brigade now serves the whole of the Greater London area of 620 square miles, with its population of 8 million, and in addition to attending outbreaks of fire, has a special branch to deal with fire *prevention*. Farther along extensive blocks of offices have been erected on the sites of blitzed houses.

Vauxhall derives its name from the Manor of Faukeshall, or from Fulke de Bréauté, a mercenary follower of King John. The famous Vauxhall Gardens were situated at the back of the present Albert Embankment, not far from Vauxhall Bridge. They were a place of public resort from the reign of Charles II for two hundred years until they were abolished on 25 July 1859. The gardens were formed about 1661 and were at first called New Spring Gardens, to distinguish them from Old Spring Gardens at Charing Cross. The price of admission was 1s. up to the summer of 1792, after which it was raised to 2s. Later it was raised to 4s., but after 1840 it was again reduced to 1s.

Opposite the main entrance was a magnificent Gothic orchestra and a rotunda, where the band used to play in wet weather. There were numerous recesses or small pavilions where suppers and other refreshments were provided. Champagne was 8s. a bottle, red port or sherry 2s. a bottle, and ice was sold at 6d. for two pounds. As many as fifteen thousand lamps were used at one time to illuminate the grounds, and sixteen thousand persons have attended here in one evening. The Gardens were opened every evening at five o'clock, from about the middle of June to the end of August. By the reign of William IV the gardens were already on the decline and were no longer patronized by the upper ten thousand, and by 1851 they had become the resort of the rabble. The contents of the gardens were sold by auction in the autumn of 1859.

On 3 August 1802 the French aeronaut Garnerin, with his wife and a Mr Glassford, ascended in a balloon from Vauxhall Gardens. When at a considerable height they sent down a cat on a small parachute, which came to the ground in perfect safety. The passengers themselves descended at Frognal Place, near Hampstead.

At Vauxhall Cross, one of the most congested traffic centres of South London, where five great thoroughfares converge, a new by-pass was completed in 1938. On the east side of South Lambeth Road is Vauxhall Park, which, incidentally, has no connexion with the defunct Vauxhall Gardens. This park, which is some ten acres in extent, was formerly occupied by Carroun House. At 'The Lawn', near Vauxhall Park, lived Henry Fawcett who, although blind, was a professor of Economics at Cambridge and in 1880 became Postmaster-General. Until recently, a statue of this remarkable man, by George Tinworth, a local sculptor, stood in Vauxhall Park, but the space it occupied was required for other purposes, so the statue has gone. However, Lawn Lane, at the side of the park recalls the site of his house, and there is another memorial to the blind Postmaster-General in the Victoria Embankment Gardens, opened by the Prince of Wales, afterwards King Edward VII, on 8 July 1890. The late Metropolitan Board of Works, the Lambeth Vestry, and the Charity Commissioners jointly contributed £36,000 towards the purchase money of £43,500, the balance being raised by voluntary subscriptions. The cost worked out at £4,300 per acre.

A short walk along Harleyford Road will bring us to Kennington Oval, the ground of the Surrey Cricket Club. It covers an area of nine acres on the site of the park of Sir Noel Caron, a Dutch Ambassador to England in the seventeenth century. It was opened as a cricket ground on 16 April 1846, and is now held on a lease from the Duchy of Cornwall. Kennington Oval is now almost surrounded by newly-erected blocks of London County Council flats, all of which are five storeys high and provide a free view of the Surrey County cricket matches to the fortunate tenants. Some of the flats were badly damaged in the air raids of 1940 and so also was the neighbouring Archbishop Tenison's Grammar School, but these have all since been repaired.

At the corner of Kennington Park Road is the Oval Station, of the former City and South London Railway, now merged into the vast system of London Transport. The original line from King William Street to Stockwell, three and a quarter miles in length, was the first tube railway to be opened in London. The construction of this line occupied four years and the cost was £200,000 per mile. It was opened on Tuesday, 4 November 1890, by the Prince of Wales, afterwards King Edward VII. Ten years later this line was extended to Clapham Common and in 1926 to Morden.

Lambeth, which has taken in part of the former Borough of Wandsworth, has a population of 340,762, which makes it the largest among the new London boroughs. It extends from the Thames to Norwood and from Southwark to Wandsworth. Kennington Park, at the junction of Camberwell New Road, was originally a common, but was enclosed by iron railings in 1853 and converted into an ornamental park. About the same time the old Kennington turnpike-gate, which stood near this spot, was removed. What appears to be a keeper's lodge on the west side of Kennington Park is a pair of cottages bearing the date 1851 and the familiar initials V. and A. They were model working-class dwellings of a design approved by the Prince Consort, who showed them in the Great Exhibition of 1851 in Hyde Park. Though they were doubtless ideal homes then, today they give an impression of being rather cramped and dark inside; they are generally used as changing rooms for netball players in the park.

Until the 'sixties of the last century there were no less than 117 toll-gates within six miles of Charing Cross, mainly owned by vested interests. They were a blot upon metropolitan civilization and the most odious of taxes. Londoners then submitted to the exactions of some 250 tax-gatherers with whose appointment they had nothing to do, and who, besides performing no service in return, were a public nuisance. In France, America, and even in the Isle of Man, there were no toll-gates in existence, and England was distinctly behind the times in that respect. Kennington, Camberwell, and their companion gates on the south side of the Thames were removed on 18 October 1865, and by the following November the whole of the gates in South London, numbering sixty, were removed, with the exception of Dulwich Gate, and 108 miles of roads emancipated. Nowadays the idea of long lines of motor-buses held up at these toll-gates would provide most amusing material for our imagination to play with.

Kennington Park Road, leading to Newington Butts and the Elephant and Castle, still contains a number of old-fashioned Georgian houses. A great feature of this neighbourhood in the middle of the last century was the Surrey Zoological Gardens. They were situated between Kennington Road and Walworth Road, and were first opened to the public in August 1831. They were fifteen acres in extent, and second only in importance to the Regent's Park Zoological Gardens. They contained a lake, facing which was a music hall affording accommodation for ten thousand persons, modelled on the lines of a huge winter garden. The grounds were adorned with flower-beds, pathways, undulating lawns, Italian terraces adorned with statuary, Swiss chalets, grottoes, fountains, and cascades. They were one of the most beautiful gardens ever adapted for open-air entertainments. The orchestra could accommodate a thousand performers, and was on an upper storey, the front of which was hung by iron rods from a strong truss above. In February 1878 the Surrey Gardens were sold for building purposes, and their site is now covered by several uninteresting streets about forty feet in width.

The whole of the west side of Kennington Park Road between Harleyford Road and Kennington Road is now lined with five-storeyed blocks of flats, some of them with shops on the ground floor. So many blocks of flats have been erected hore and in the neighbouring streets that these new London County Council estates have almost assumed the dimensions of a large new village or small town. In Kennington Lane is Imperial Court, a large Victorian structure with an impressive portico approached by steps; originally the Licensed Victuallers' School, it is now the headquarters of the N.A.A.F.I. Opposite is the extensive Duchy of Cornwall estate, a 'model village' with the Prince of Wales' Feathers' emblem much in evidence. Black Prince Road nearby gives a clue to the early ownership of this manor, which was confirmed by excavations within the Kennington Lane-Sancroft Street-Cardigan Street triangle. This voluntary 'dig' was undertaken by local archaeologists between 1965 and 1967, and parts of six buildings belonging to the Palace built by Edward the Black Prince between 1346 and 1362 were found. St Mark's Church was one of the churches said to have been built to commemorate the Battle of Waterloo and its vicarage was the birthplace of Field-Marshal Lord Montgomery, whose father was the vicar. St Mark's was built on the site of a gallows where many Jacobites were executed. The church was damaged in the blitz of 1940, but has since been repaired. The Assembly Rooms next to the Horns Hotel in Kennington Road have also been destroyed in the blitz. The Horns Hotel is now closed.

Camberwell New Road, opened in 1820 from Kennington Common to Camberwell Green, resulted in a saving of nearly two miles and a half in the distance from Westminster into Kent. At the back of Brixton Road another large colony of London County Council flats covers both sides of a new street between Vassall Road and Mostyn Street. This has been named Gosling Way after Alfred Gosling, a former socialist M.P. for Whitechapel who died in 1930. Brixton Road, the Oxford Street of South London, contains some of its largest shops. The biggest store, the Bon Marché, is owned by the John Lewis Partnership Limited, but its sister store, Quin and Axten Limited, was destroyed in the blitz. The shopping centre begins at Stockwell Road and extends for half a mile southwards to Acre Lane. It once contained a wide open space which was used as a street market, but this was abolished in 1935 to allow for a widening of the roadway at a cost of £13,000. The shabby houses which previously lined the east side of the road have been replaced by a row of handsome new buildings. Lambeth Town Hall at the foot of Brixton Hill is a handsome building of red brick with stone dressings erected in 1908. An extension which faces Acre Lane was opened by Queen Mary in 1938. Its lofty clock-tower is a prominent landmark of Brixton Hill. On the opposite side of Brixton Road is a public garden called the Tate Library Garden.

The South London tramways, formerly owned by London Transport and and now all replaced by motor-omnibuses, were opened from Westminster to Brixton Kennington and Clapham in May 1870, and those from Blackfriars Bridge to St George's Circus, Lambeth Road, and along Kennington Road in September 1871. The lines to East Greenwich and Blackheath Hill were also opened in the same year. The whole of the South London tramway system, comprising about sixty miles of lines, was electrified by the London County Council from 1903 onwards. The last horse trams (Tower Bridge to Rotherhithe) were withdrawn in 1915.

Twentieth Walk

Muswell Hill, Hornsey, Highgate, Hampstead, City Road, Islington, Highbury, Holloway, Camden Town etc.

In our sixth walk we took in the City Road as far as Old Street. Thence this road continues in a north-westerly direction as far as the Angel at Islington, and thus forms a suitable point of departure for our present walk.

City Road is a broad thoroughfare, now consisting largely of factories and warehouses. It was projected in 1760 by Mr Robert Dingley. Harrison described it in 1776 as 'an easy and pleasant communication from the eastern parts of the City to all the roads between Islington and Paddington and from thence down to Oxford Road and the Great Western Road, thus avoiding the necessity of travelling three miles over the stones'. The City Road, which is one mile in length, was then regarded as one of the handsomest in England, and was maintained in proper repair by the tolls levied on horses and carriages. For many years after its construction it remained on the fringe of the country. Until the construction of the City Road, Aldersgate Street with its continuation, Goswell Road, was the principal thoroughfare connecting the city with Islington.

At one time the City Road was the scene of rivalry between competing omnibus companies, and in 1842 cases of furious driving frequently occurred in Islington and Holloway. Keen competition then existed between the omnibuses of Mr Wilson and Mr Colson, and more than once the lives of passengers were endangered as a result. The driver of an omnibus called the Hope was charged with manslaughter for running over and killing a man in the City Road. One of the witnesses declared that the Hopes and the Favourites drove down the City Road at the rate of twelve miles an hour, a pace slow enough for a mechanically-propelled vehicle under proper control, but highly dangerous for horses racing in a crowded thoroughfare. As a general rule the offenders of those days were only fined a few shillings, and this rarely produced any change in their subsequent behaviour.

On the north side of the City Road, not far from the Angel, stood until 1940 the Church of St Matthew, opened on 11 April 1848. It was situated in Oakley Crescent, then only recently completed, which runs parallel with the main road way. The church was destroyed in the air raids of 1940 and has been completely demolished. The Islington Borough Council have built new flats on this site. Three houses, one of which was the Vicarage of St Matthew's, are all that is left of Oakley Crescent. In Garden Row, close to the City Road, are the Palmerston dwellings, erected in 1866 by the Improved Industrial Dwellings Company, consisting of three blocks of buildings five storeys in height.

Like most of the other great roads leading out of London, the City Road had its toll-gate, and there was another one at Islington. These were abolished on 1 July 1864, when some fifty miles of turnpike roads on the north side of the Thames were freed of toll obstruction, including the Notting Hill, Kensington, Hammersmith, Kilburn, Camden Town, Holloway and Hackney gates.

At the top of the City Road, close to the Angel, running parallel to the High Street, Islington, is Colebrooke Row. It was built in 1768, and here Charles Lamb resided after 1825, upon retiring from City life at the East India House on a pension of £450 per annum. His cottage, now Number 64 Duncan Terrace, still stands. Alfred Street nearby has been renamed Elia Street. In 1796 Lamb resided with his sister in Chapel Street, Pentonville. Until the middle of the last century the New River passed along Colebrooke Row, after which time it was covered over. The delightful gardens between Colebrooke Row and Duncan Terrace now form a public recreation ground which affords a pleasant contrast to the ugliness of the surrounding neighbourhood.

The Angel, Islington, is perhaps the busiest traffic centre in the north of London. Not only is it situated at the junction of St John Street, Goswell Road, City Road, and Pentonville Road, but it is likewise the point on which several of the great northern roads converge. The Angel has been established for upwards of two centuries as an inn or licensed house, and in olden times was the special resort of salesmen, farmers, and graziers attending Smithfield Market. It was first rebuilt in 1819 and again early in the present century. In 1922 it was acquired by Messrs J. Lyons & Company Limited, and converted into a restaurant. However, it is now unoccupied. From an old coaching inn to a Lyons Corner House, for over two hundred years there was an 'Angel' at Islington. Today there is not. The other buildings which form this junction are old and shabby, but since the direct road which is to connect the Eastern Avenue with the Western Avenue via Pentonville Road and Euston Road is to pass across this congested area, it is highly probable that a large circus or roundabout similar to that designed for the Elephant and Castle in South London will form part of the rebuilding scheme. A few doors along the High Street are the remains of the Islington Empire Cinema, which recently celebrated the centenary of its opening in 1860 as The Royal Philharmonic Hall, but better known to everybody as The Grand Theatre. Among the artistes who took part in the opening performance at the Philharmonic was the Irish comedian Sam Collins, who later founded Collin's Music Hall at Islington Green. A glance through old Grand Theatre programmes of the 'nineties reminds us that theatrical knights Sir Henry Irving, George Alexander, Johnston Forbes Robertson, Martin Harvey, Gerald du Maurier and Seymour Hicks were among the many famous players who brought their west-end companies to the old 'Grand'. The façade of the main entrance in the High Street, with columns, pediment and a pair of classical-looking ladies still stands, though the building behind has been completely demolished.

Between the fork of St John Street and Goswell Road is Owen's School, founded in 1613 by Dame Alice Owen. Mistress Owen, when a girl in Islington, narrowly escaped death from an arrow which pierced the hat on her head. In gratitude for her deliverance she founded the school which bears her name. The bequest is administered by the Brewers' Company.

Further south is Northampton Square, built about 1830 and occupying the site of what was once a pipe field or ground covered with wooden pipes, belonging to the old New River Company before the introduction of iron pipes enabled them to build over this and similar adjoining sites. In Rawstorne Street are several blocks of buildings bearing the arms of the Brewers' Company ('In God is all our trust'). Some of them date back to 1871, but although the exteriors show signs of age they have been modernized inside and the rents are said to be still 'very reasonable'. On the north corner of Wyclif Street, formerly Ashby Street, where now stands the imposing modern building of the City University, Northampton House formerly stood. For many years prior to 1802 it was a private asylum, and here was confined Richard Brothers, the sham prophet. Afterwards it became a private residence, but it was originally a mansion of the Earls of Northampton, whose titles provided names for most of the adjoining streets, and on whose family estates they were erected. Inaugurated by Royal Charter in 1966, the City University has for its Chancellor the Lord Mayor of London; it will therefore be unique in having a new Chancellor each year. On the south corner of Wyclif Street, then Ashby Street, stood the unique Memorial Church of the English Martyrs, having many statues outside and inside, individual memorials to many who suffered in the sixteenth century fires at Smithfield. The church was irreparably damaged during the war, and on the site the Finsbury Borough Council have built a fourteen-storey block of flats called Wyclif Court. King Square, to the east of Goswell Road, was erected about the same time as Northampton Square. It has now been completely altered, with tall new Council dwellings and a public garden in the centre of the square. St Barnabas Church on the east side of the square which was also damaged is a building with a portico supported by four columns and has a tower crowned by a spire.

With the addition of the borough of Finsbury, the new London Borough of Islington has an area of 3,678 acres and a population of 260,410. The population in 1801 was only 10,202, but in 1821 it had increased to 22,417. By that time Islington was described as a large and populous place, superior both in size and appearance to many considerable country towns, and the air was considered remarkably beneficial. The fact that several main roads starting from the Angel diverged towards various parts of the city, made Islington a most convenient place of residence for those people whose occupations called them to London in the day-time at a period when there were no omnibuses or practical means of conveyance other than walking.

Previously Islington had been noted for its agricultural land, where many hundreds of cows were kept for supplying the metropolis with milk, for which commodity it had been famous for centuries. In 1754, 28,602 oxen and 267,565 sheep passed through the Islington turnpike. After the discovery of Sadler's Wells, or New Tunbridge Wells as it used to be called, Islington Spa soon became famous with hypochondriacs, and by 1700 it was in high favour with the public. In 1733 the Spa had become so fashionable that Princesses Amelia and Caroline frequented the gardens daily in June of that year, and the nobility came here in great numbers. The gardens continued in public favour from 1683 until after 1811.

Another famous pleasure resort was White Conduit House, situated on the north side of Pentonville Road, not far from Islington High Street. It was so named from a white stone conduit that stood at the entrance. The gardens were handsomely laid out, and there was a reservoir in the centre, as well as tea-rooms for the entertainment of visitors. The site of White Conduit House and its gardens is now covered by slums and dreary streets, some of which have mercifully been removed by bombs. This applies especially to Collier Street, Cumming Street and Donegal Street where large bombed sites have been cleared of their debris. Chapel Market, a busy shopping centre and street market at the back of the blitzed area, has escaped almost unharmed. White Conduit Street, a turning off Chapel Market, commemorates the site of White Conduit Gardens. In the neighbouring Chapel Place are some new blocks of flats which were erected before 1939. Several other fine blocks have also been erected on the west side of Barnsbury Road and on the corner of Copenhagen Street. Islington High Street is rather elusive; on its west side it extends from the Angel to Liverpool Road and Upper Street. The east side, however, soon disappears behind Upper Street buildings and later becomes Camden Passage. This narrow footpath has, like Carnaby Street, undergone a complete change of face and the former squalid little alley now abounds with antique shops, and on Saturdays, stalls of a similar category, the quality of the whole area ranging from genuine antiques to junk. At No. 45 in the Passage, Alexander Cruden, author of the Complete Concordance of the Holy Scriptures, died on 1st November 1770. Two hundred yards to the west of the former White Conduit House is the tunnel carrying the Regent's Canal through Islington. It is about nine hundred yards long and follows a perfectly straight course terminating close to Colebrooke Row. Its height is 18 feet, including 7 feet 6 inches of water, and its width is 17 feet. The depth of the necessary cutting, as well as the number of houses which stood in the line of the canal, made it impracticable to continue it through Islington as an open course.

Islington Green, situated at the junction of the High Street with Upper Street and Essex Road, contains a statue of Sir Hugh Myddelton of New River fame, erected in 1862 near the corner of Upper Street and Essex Road. On the north side of the Green was Collins' Music Hall. In its earliest days, such was the propriety of its entertainment that it was known as 'The Chapel on the Green', but during its last years of existence, the Chapel put on nude shows. A fire in an adjoining timber yard put an end to all performances in 1958, though the bar below, which had a rare collection of old playbills, autographed photographs of celebrities of the Variety stage etc. continued until 1963, when all these mementoes were sold by auction and the famous music hall founded by Sam Collins in 1863 gave way to the commercial building that now stands in its place. A notable building on the west side of Upper Street is the former Agricultural Hall, opened on 13 December 1862. It has a second entrance in Liverpool Road, and before the last war was used for all kinds of exhibitions, particularly those of a commercial character. It is now a department of the General Post Office. Farther north on the opposite side of Upper Street is St Mary's Church, the successor to one or more churches occupying the same site. It has a handsome tower surmounted by a spire of Portland stone. The foundation-stone was laid by James Colebrooke, the largest landed proprietor in the parish, on 28 August 1751. Badly damaged in 1940, the body of the church was rebuilt and reopened in 1956, though the handsome tower and spire survived.

In Dagmar Passage is the Little Angel Theatre, the headquarters of John Wright's Marionettes, the only permanent public puppet theatre in England. Regular performances for both adults and children have been given since 1961 in this little theatre which, formerly a temperance hall, has seating for 100. Close to St Mary's Church is the new Islington Town Hall, erected in 1921. It is a spacious building with a façade of Portland stone, but its appearance might be greatly enhanced by the addition of a lofty clock-tower.

Upper Street, leading to Highbury Station and Holloway Road, is the principal shopping thoroughfare of Islington, and is about a mile in length. Its buildings are very old-fashioned and shabby in appearance, and the great majority of them would look all the better for redecoration or a cleaning with the steam brush. No rebuilding ever takes place in Upper Street, and compared, for instance, to Brixton Road in South London it is a great disappointment to the casual visitor to these parts, and suggests that almost anything is good enough for the people of North London. Many buildings at the northern end have been destroyed or damaged by bombing including the façade of Highbury Statiin and some houses opposite in Compton Terrace which were demolished by a flying bomb in August 1944. Compton Terrace is flanked by a pleasant public garden extending for some distance along Upper Street. In the centre of Compton Terrace is the Union Chapel which is crowned by a tall and handsome Gothic tower. Founded in 1799, the present building dates from 1877. Highbury Corner is now a grassy roundabout centred with a 15-storey block of flats. A little passage near the North London station proudly bears the stately name of 'Hampton Court, N1.'

Essex Road, which has no claim to distinction, was called Lower Street from time immemorial until late in the nineteenth century. Here a cattlemarket was established in 1833 by John Perkins of Bletchingley in Surrey, who, intolerant of the dirt and cruelty of the old Smithfield Market in the City, and the nuisance and danger of driving vast herds of cattle through the crowded London streets, projected this new market in the north of London. It was built at a cost of £100,000, and opened on 18 April 1836, but so strong was the popular acceptance of old abuses, that this excellent new market proved an utter failure and was soon closed. It covered nearly fifteen acres on the east side of Essex Road close to Balls Pond Road, and was enclosed by a brick wall ten feet high, with vast sheds on all sides.

Another interesting feature of Essex Road or Lower Street, as it was then called, was Fisher House, a spacious mansion situated nearly opposite the east end of Cross Street. It was built early in the seventeenth century by Sir Thomas Fisher, and had very fine grounds. In 1845 it was demolished for local street improvements, but for some time previously it had been uninhabited. Many houses on both sides of Essex Road were destroyed in the great blitz of 1940. Large bombed sites have been cleared and one of them at the corner of Essex Road and New North Road is now covered by four-storeyed blocks of London County Council flats. This includes a long row of new shops which has been set back from the old building line in Essex Road. Cross Street, between Essex Road and Upper Street, contains a picturesque row of Georgian houses built on a raised pavement. In Canonbury Square, between Upper Street and Essex Road, is Canonbury Tower, a rugged brick structure over sixty feet high, which is said to have been built by Prior Bolton of St Bartholomew's about 1520, but which now houses a repertory theatre.

Highbury Station, at the northern end of Upper Street, was reconstructed and opened in 1873 in place of a primitive wooden building erected here twenty-four years earlier. Between Upper Street and Caledonian Road, situated in the parish of Holy Trinity, Islington, is the district of Barnsbury. It takes its name from Ralph de Berners, to whom the manor of Isledon was granted by the Bishop of London in the thirteenth century. Until about 1842 it was known as the Caledonian Fields and the Barnsbury Fields, and was little better than a mere waste dotted with cottages and huts. The fields were notorious as a centre of brutal sports, and the habits of the population were generally of that low order then commonly found on the borders of a great city.

As if to scare such evil-doers, in 1840 the Model Prison, containing a thousand cells, was erected in the Caledonian Road at a cost of over £84,000. To-day it is more commonly known as Pentonville Prison, although it is located in Barnsbury. Several modern blocks of workmen's dwellings have been erected on the east side of Caledonian Road, close to the prison, which bear the names of Scottish celebrities such as Burns, Wallace, and Scott. After the erection of the prison a big clearance took place of all the old cottages and huts, which was followed by the construction of wide streets and houses for the middle classes upon these sites.

During the course of this walk, we shall encounter several of the Squares which are such an attractive feature of the Islington landscape. One of the largest, though not strictly square in shape, is Thornhill Square, lying east of the Caledonian Road. The well-kept garden in the centre and the large expanse of sky overhead give an impression of space and light that tempts one to envy people who live in Squares. In Thornhill Crescent at the north end is St Andrew's

Church, which at the time of its building was one of the largest churches in the suburbs. Among other large Squares nearby, Gibson Square, between Liverpool Road and Upper Street, is the oldest; the house fronts are rusticated stucco and the garden is pleasant. The neighbouring Milner Square is impressively high, for the houses go to four storeys and a basement. The garden is now covered with asphalt and paving for use as a children's playground, but there are a few shrubs round the edges. Milner Square was originally built on a uniform plan, with brick pilasters, painted balconies, porches and cornices in two colours. These decorations were modified in 1935 and it is now a shabby old Victorian Square, but when first built it may well have been suggestive of Belgravia rather than Islington. Gibson and Milner Squares were laid out between 1835 and 1840, and were named after Mr Milner Gibson, the ground landlord, afterwards M.P. for Ipswich and President of the Board of Trade. Lonsdale Square on the west side of Liverpool Road is much smaller and contains handsome Gothic houses fronted with grey brick greatly superior to others in this locality. Thornhill Square, Barnsbury Square and Richmond Gardens between Caledonian Road and Liverpool Road are now public gardens which relieve the monotony of the surrounding streets. Arundel Square, now also a public garden, lies just off the north side of Offord Road, a shabby street which descends steeply into Caledonian Road. Mention should be made of the two 'loops' attached to the corners of the west side of Barnsbury Square. One of them, Mountford Crescent, is an attractive little cul-de-sac with semi-detached villas. The public garden is well-wooded, but one or two factories spoil the general appearance of this otherwise pleasing Square. Of Arundel Square, through which the old North London line runs, one can only say that it is in poor condition and much broken up. An end wall on the west side is dated 1860. Richmond Avenue shows us a terrace of houses with unusual decoration, the entrances being flanked by sphinxes with miniature 'Cleopatra's Needles' behind them; the doors and window frames also have embellishments of the kind we associate with the Egyptian Room of the British Museum.

In Liverpool Road on a large site on the south corner of Laycock Street are six handsome blocks of flats called Lewis Buildings. These are built in parallel rows with courtyards in between the blocks. They are faced with red brick with stone dressings and have bay windows. Externally they bear the appearance of high-class West End buildings. At the northern end of Liverpool Road is the Mersey housing estate of the Greater London Council covering one and a half acres and acquired during the last war.

Cloudesley Square, farther south, just off the west side of Liverpool Road, forms part of the Stonefield Estate, which was left by a Roman Catholic gentleman named Cloudesley, in the time of Henry VIII, to the Catholic Church for the salvation of his soul by means of annual masses, and also to provide a dole for a certain number of poor people of the parish of St Mary, Islington. The large Holy Trinity Church, built in the style of King's College, Cambridge, occupies most of this Square—which is not a very big one. A plaque on the wall tells us that 'During the air-raids of the Great War the crypt of this church was used as a shelter for 2,000 people. In the midst of peril we came to no harm.' Caledonian Road which connects Islington with Holloway is so named from the Caledonian Asylum founded in 1815 and now removed to Bushey, for children of Scottish parents. From King's Cross as far as the bridge over the North London Railway it is a squalid thoroughfare with long drab rows of three-storeyed houses and small shops, few of which it would seem have ever been cleaned or decorated. Some of the most dreadful streets on either side have been happily removed by bombs. This has been followed by the clearance of a large bombed site just off the west side of Caledonian Road, bounded by Copenhagen Street, York Way, the Regent's Canal and Treaty Street. Here the Islington Borough Council have erected fine new four-storeyed blocks of flats with wide courtyards, balconies and playgrounds, which is like an oasis in the midst of this desert of slums. Directly opposite this new estate and opening into Copenhagen Street are several parallel streets of mean dwellings owning to the names of Delhi Street, Outram Street and Havelock Street. One wonders how India and her great generals came to be commemorated by such squalid surroundings. This is London in its most forbidding aspect, for whereas the East End is picturesque and varied, the King's Cross district of North London is without any open spaces or redeeming features.

On the west side of Caledonian Road is the Metropolitan Cattle Market, erected in 1854-55 in Copenhagen Fields after a long parliamentary struggle with the Corporation of London. Copenhagen House was pulled down in 1853 to make way for the new cattle-market, and, together, with the grounds, was purchased for £65,000. The house was at least two centuries old when it was demolished, and is said to have derived its name from the fact that a Danish Prince or Ambassador resided here during the Great Plague. The market, which was opened by the Prince Consort on 13 June 1855, covers thirty acres, and is said to have cost £445,000. Fifteen acres are enclosed, providing space for 7,600 bullocks, 40,000 sheep, 1,400 calves, and 900 pigs, and in the centre is a clock-tower. The architect was Mr Bunning. A part of this ground formerly contained a popular public market but this was closed down during the second World War, and despite vigorous pleas advanced by the former stall-holders and the general public the City Corporation declined to reopen the market which has now moved to Bermondsey. The 32-acre site of the market is now being developed by the Greater London Council who are building 271 dwellings on The Stones, as it used to be called. The dominant clock tower will be retained. Another feature of the market is that there was a 'pub' at each of the four corners; they were the Lamb, Lion, White Horse and Black Bull, of which the last has been demolished, but the first three still survive.

At the northern end of Upper Street, near the junction of Holloway Road and St Paul's Road, is Highbury Fields, a small public park of twenty-seven and a half acres, shaped like a triangle. It was acquired in 1885 at a cost of £60,000, one-half of which was contributed by the Vestry of Islington. Overlooking its eastern side is Highbury Place, built between 1774 and 1779. At that time it overlooked the hills of Highgate and Hampstead, and here died, amongst others, the celebrated Mr A. Newland, chief cashier to the Bank of England. He was the son of a baker in Castle Street, Southwark, where he was born on 25 April 1730. He died on 21 November 1807, and was buried in Islington Church. Highbury Terrace, on the west side, was built before the year 1820, and Highbury Barn was then a noted tavern with tea-gardens, much frequented by Londoners in the summer.

In 1850, when the district north and east of Highbury Fields was still open country, an attempt was made to secure this ground as a public park for Islington. The scheme, which was projected by a Mr Lloyd, was to appropriate five hundred acres of ground, including some two hundred acres now covered by the villas of Highbury Grove and Highbury Vale. The proposed park was to have extended from Highbury to Green Lanes and from Stamford Hill to Holloway, and to have included an ornamental lake of some fifty acres. The main entrance was to have been in Highbury Place.

The cost was estimated at £200,000, and the project had already received the support of the Prince Consort, Lord Robert Grosvenor, Lord Ashley, and Lord Carlisle. It was urgently pointed out at the time that, unless the land could be secured immediately, it would be covered with buildings in less than twelve months. But, alas, the necessary funds were not forthcoming, and the builders were too rapacious to feel any sympathy for the project of preserving this ground as a public park.

On a part of this land stood Highbury House, on high ground about a mile north of Islington Church, which was supposed to have been the site of a Roman camp. This mansion was the property of Mr John Dawes, and was erected by him in 1781 at a cost of £10,000. It had some seventy-four acres of park and shrubberies. Had this ground been secured for a public park for the north of London, it would have been a most delightful resort, and one can only regret that such a valuable opportunity was lost for ever.

The district which has arisen on this site, now generally known as Highbury, was built in 1859 and 1860. It contains an imposing group of large villas in spacious gardens extending a mile and a half one way and about a mile from east to west, and might aptly be described as the Mayfair of Islington. Such large houses are out of fashion nowadays, partly owing to the servant problem, and many of the Highbury villas have been divided up into flats and others converted into boarding-houses and private hotels. Some of these villas have been destroyed by bombing, notably in Grosvenor Avenue, where the London County Council erected several blocks of flats on their new Highbury estate. This covers an area of nearly five acres and will eventually consist of ten five-storey blocks and two four-storey blocks of a slightly different pattern. In Highbury New Park, a tree-lined thoroughfare ending at Clissold Park, many of the villas are as fine as those of Hamilton Terrace, St John's Wood, and when first built must have been inhabited by people of considerable wealth. At the corner of Highbury New Park and Highbury Grove, the dreaded Truant School is now Highbury County School. On the high ground between Gillespie Road and Avenell Road is the ground of the Arsenal football club which has large and distinctive grandstands on the east and west sides. This is the remains of the former grounds of Highbury House. Included in this locality is Christ Church, Highbury, which is situated at the junction of Highbury Hill and Highbury Grove and was opened on 16 November 1848 by the Bishop of London. It is a handsome edifice with accommodation for six hundred persons, and was erected at a cost of £6,000. In front of the church is a clock-tower presented to the former Islington Vestry in 1897 by Alfred Hutchinson to commemorate the Diamond Jubilee of Queen Victoria.

Holloway, which forms the northern section of the borough of Islington, originally consisted of two hamlets known as Upper and Lower Holloway, so named from the hollow way to the south of Highgate. The latter place was once famous for its cheese cakes, which until the beginning of the nineteenth century were regularly hawked through the streets of London by a man on horseback. Upper Holloway contains many small villas, formerly inhabited by retired and well-to-do Londoners. Holloway Road, which is very wide, contains some excellent shops, including the old-established departmental store of Jones Brothers, now owned by John Lewis Partnership, and one of the largest in North London. At the corner of Tufnell Park Road is a large Gaumont Cinema which was badly damaged in the blitz, and close to Parkhurst Road is the Marlborough Picture Theatre. Farther along Holloway Road are several blocks of London County Council flats erected about 1934 which stand back from the roadway in gardens. They cover the triangular site between Holloway Road, Caledonian Road and the Great Northern Line of British Railways.

Holloway Prison, erected on land belonging to the Corporation of London, is situated on the north side of Parkhurst Road. It was opened in October 1852, and covers ten acres within a boundary wall eighteen feet high. It is reserved for female prisoners, and is built in the castellated style of architecture, and was designed by Mr Bunning at a cost of £100,000. The main front is 340 feet in length, and is faced with Kentish Rag and Caen Stone. It is built on the radiating principle, with four wings diverging from one centre and two additional wings in front of the others. The design of the Central Tower is said to have been based on that of Caesar's Tower, Warwick Castle. Among its habituées, Holloway Prison is always known as 'The Castle'.

Camden Road, a broad residential thoroughfare, was constructed in the early part of the nineteenth century to connect Camden Town with Islington. Previously the want of a direct road had been a source of great inconvenience to the inhabitants of these populous districts, as the only means of communication was by the circuitous route of King's Cross and the New Road or by Camden Villas and Holloway. Camden Road forks to the right at the junction of Parkhurst Road and terminates at Holloway Road, at the corner of Caledonian Road. n Brecknock Road and Carleton Road five-storeyed blocks of flats have been erected by the London County Council on their Tufnell Park Estate. This covers over five acres and was acquired in 1937 under a compulsory purchase order. This land had previously been occupied by large suburban villas.

Opposite Parkhurst Road, at the corner of Holloway Road and Seven Sisters Road, is the well-known Nag's Head Tavern, a traffic centre almost as famous to Londoners as the Angel or the Elephant and Castle. Seven Sisters Road was constructed in 1832, prior to which time there was no thoroughfare connecting Holloway and Hornsey with Tottenham. The southern end of Seven Sisters Road is a busy shopping street, but the central portion skirts the south side of Finsbury Park and traverses a good-class residential district. Finsbury Park Station, at the corner of Stroud Green Road, was the former terminus of the Piccadilly Underground Line, but in 1934 it was extended to Southgate and Cockfosters. The High Barnet and Mill Hill East branches have been absorbed by the Underground system.

Finsbury Park, opened in 1869 at a cost of £95,000, comprises 120 acres, and was in the nature of a consolation prize to North London for the loss of the projected park at Highbury Hill some twenty years earlier. Finsbury Park was formed out of Hornsey Wood, adjoining which stood Hornsey Wood House, a public-house and a popular place of entertainment. For some time previous to the demolition of the house its grounds were used for pigeon shooting. The lake is an oblong sheet of water surrounded by pleasant walks, and contains one or two islands. There is also an Open Air Theatre. Finsbury Park was opened by Sir John Thwaites, Chairman of the Metropolitan Board of Works, but how it ever came to be so named is a mystery, since it has nothing in common with the former borough of Finsbury, which is over two miles distant from the park. Perhaps it was due to the fact that the new park was originally intended to serve the crowded district of Finsbury.

To the north of Finsbury Park lies the extensive district of Hornsey, which is almost entirely a product of the last seventy years. Until 1870 few villages near London had retained so rural a character as Hornsey. It now includes the populous suburbs of Crouch End and Muswell Hill within its municipal area. The population, which in 1881 was only 5,673, had increased by 1951 to 97,600. In 1816 it was described as a pleasant village five miles from London, through which the New River flows, and as a favourite resort of its good citizens. The parish church lies at some distance from the old village in a valley, now covered with houses, near Hornsey station. It can be easily seen from the neighbouring heights, but is of modern origin and only dates from 1888. It is built in the Gothic style of architecture and replaced an earlier structure dating from about the year 1500, which was pulled down in 1832, except the old tower which still remains. In the churchyard is the tomb of Samuel Rogers, the 'Banker Poet', author of The Pleasures of Memory. He was born at Newington Green in 1763 and died in 1855. The former Hornsey Town Hall in Crouch End Broadway is a building of red brick crowned by a lofty clock-tower and was erected at a cost of £120,000. It was opened by the Duke of Kent in 1935 and it includes a large assembly hall for public use. The clock-tower, however, has no clock; probably because it is so close to the familiar Clock Tower in the Broadway which was erected in 1895 as a tribute to Henry Reader Williams, J.P. for his services to the district.

Crouch End, which lies to the west of Finsbury Park, is a fashionable district of Hornsey, and contains some good shops in its Broadway. Christ Church, erected in 1863 in the Gothic style, was enlarged some ten years later. The new Hornsey Central Library, erected at a cost of £277,000, was opened by Princess Alexandra on 5 March, 1965.

Muswell Hill, situated to the north of Crouch End, derives its name from a well on the top of the hill belonging to the fraternity of St John of Jerusalem in Clerkenwell, who built a dairy here next to a large farm. The water of this spring was deemed a miraculous cure for scrofula and the shrine of Our Lady of Muswell Hill became a centre of pilgrimage in the Middle Ages, people coming here laden with their offerings and buoyed up with great hopes of a cure. Muswell Hill with its fine residences and high-class shops and nearby open spaces can almost claim equality with the best parts of Hampstead and Highgate, and, being some 350 feet above sea level, commands extensive views in the direction of Hornsey and the Alexandra Palace. St James's Parish Church in Muswell Hill Road, a once noble edifice with a tower crowned by a tall spire, was burnt out in the war. It was one of the first churches to be rebuilt completely and, what is rare, exactly as before, with a magnificent new organ. Coldfall Wood, north of Creighton Avenue, is a densely-wooded open space and beauty spot covering the steep northern slope of Muswell Hill. It is little known except among local residents.

At the foot of Highgate Hill is the Archway Tavern, situated at the junction of Archway Road and Highgate Hill, and close by is the Archway Station of the Northern Underground Line. Highgate Hill forms a part of the ancient road from Islington to Highgate, which was constructed by one of the hermits of the Highgate hermitage, who had the gravel excavated from the top of the hill where the ponds are now situated. Highgate derives its name from the High Gate or gate on the hill which from time immemorial had been the toll-gate of the Bishop of London. It had been erected in 1386.

The high gate was an arch, with rooms overhead, extending from the Gate House Tavern to the old burial-ground. The rooms were approached by a staircase in the eastern buttress, and immediately prior to the removal of the gate in 1769 were occupied by a laundress. The inconvenience caused to heavy traffic, which was compelled to pass through the yard in the rear of the tavern, led to the removal of the arch.

Archway Road to the east of Highgate Hill, now forming a part of the Great North Road, was the first great by-pass road to be constructed near London. The steep acclivity of Highgate Hill caused great inconvenience to the traffic proceeding from London, and the new road was therefore constructed in 1808 at enormous expense, branching off at the Archway Tavern near Whittington's stone. The new by-pass road was carried on by a tunnel through the hill for a distance of about three hundred yards, passing to the north-east of Highgate Village, and rejoining the Great North Road between the fifth and sixth milestones. This great undertaking was completed in the latter part of 1809, and the tunnel, 24 feet high and 22 feet wide, was arched with brick, but on the morning of 13 April 1812 some of the brickwork gave way. About noon the ground above the tunnel was seen to crack and settle, and during that and the following day the whole arch, which had been carried for a distance of 130 yards, fell in. Not a single person was injured, although on the preceding Sunday several hundred people had visited the works out of curiosity.

As a result of this accident an open road was afterwards formed on the line of the tunnel, with a greatly reduced gradient, and an elevated archway was constructed to carry Hornsey Lane over the new thoroughfare. In those days the view over London from the pathway of this bridge was very fine in the clear atmosphere of the early morning. The archway was first opened to the public on 21 August 1813. The toll-gates were then removed from the old Highgate Road to the archway itself. In 1897 the old archway was replaced by a new iron bridge across Archway Road. Highgate Archway was probably London's first flyover. In 1906 Highgate Hill was the scene of a disastrous tramway accident. The brakes of one of the electric cars failed to function, causing it to rush down the hill and to collide with the car in front, several persons losing their lives. In the angle of Highgate Hill and Archway Road is the extensive Whittington Hospital which is under the jurisdiction of the N. E. Metropolitan Board. Whittington College, a group of almshouses for elderly ladies, administered by the Mercers' Company, stood at the foot of Archway Road, whence it had moved from the City in 1828. In 1966 the inmates moved to new quarters at Felbridge Place, Surrey. They were accompanied by the charming little statue of their founder, with his staff and bundle (but no cat), which stood in the grounds.

About three-quarters of a mile up Archway Road, on the east side, at the junction of Muswell Hill Road, are the Highgate Woods, maintained by the City Corporation as a public open space, comprising altogether 120 acres. They are situated on both sides of Muswell Hill Road, that on the west side being known as Highgate Wood, and that on the east as Queen's Wood. There is a picturesque tea-chalet in Highgate Wood and another in Queen's Wood, which covers the steep slope leading down the hill towards Crouch End. Queen's Wood is a beautiful spot with winding paths traversing its wild and dense woodland. Adjoining it and forming practically a continuous open space are the so-called Playing Fields bounded by Shepherd's Hill and Park Road. From here a fine view is obtained of the distant Alexandra Palace across the valley. From Highgate Woods crossing Archway Road, a short walk through Southwood Lane will bring us to the top of Highgate High Street, near the junction of Swain's Lane and West Hill. Until about 1920 Holly Lodge, the beautiful residence of the late Baroness Burdett-Coutts, stood in this immediate vicinity, but the grounds have been built over and are now covered with good-class houses. Holly Village in Swain's Lane was originally built for the work-people employed on her ladyship's estate in 1845. It was a model village, and the garden suburb of that time, but is now occupied by wealthier residents. The church of St Anne close to Swain's Lane was opened on 10 May 1853. Highgate High Street contains old-fashioned houses and shops which give it the appearance of a small country town. On the west side of Highgate Hill is the Roman Catholic Church of St Joseph which is crowned by a large copper dome, weathered to a beautiful bright green.

On the southern slope of Highgate Hill, extending to Swain's Lane, is the beautiful Waterlow Park, comprising twenty-nine acres, and presented as a free gift to London by Sir Sidney Waterlow on 12 November 1889. The offer was made to Lord Rosebery as first chairman of the newly-created London County Council, who were gratified with this most generous and unexpected birthday gift. Sir Sidney Waterlow, who had been Lord Mayor of London, had previously rendered great services to London by constructing workmen's dwellings in Finsbury, which proved so popular that he afterwards formed a company to construct more blocks of dwellings. The mansion of Waterlow Park, Lauderdale House, is so named after the Duke of Lauderdale, minister of Charles II, who installed Nell Gwyn there. It was built on a terrace about 1661 and is now used as a tea and refreshment house. Down in the hollow of Waterlow Park is a beautiful sheet of water with richly-wooded banks.

Adjoining Waterlow Park is the old Highgate cemetery, opened in 1839 and comprising about twenty acres. The new cemetery is on the opposite side of Swain's Lane. At the top of Highgate Hill, in North Road is Highgate School, standing in spacious grounds. To the left, past the Gatehouse tavern, is the attractive old village, with The Grove, Pond Square and West Hill. In South Grove is St Michael's Church, a well-known landmark for many miles around — which is confirmed by a 'Level with the top of the cross of St Paul's' mark just inside the porch. The remains of the poet Samuel Taylor Coleridge lie here, having recently been removed from the Chapel of Highgate School. A picturesque old tavern, The Flask, claims the date of 1663, while Georgian houses are the rule rather than the exception. Between Hampstead Lane and Parliament Hill Fields is Kenwood, now a public park, covering two hundred acres. The mansion was built by Robert Adam in the time of George III, and many of the fine trees were planted under the direction of the first Lord Mansfield. The grounds are hilly and contain a lake, and afford all the sylvan seclusion of some remote country mansion. At first only 120 acres of Kenwood were secured for the public in 1922, but chiefly through the generosity of the late Lord Iveagh in 1927 the whole of Kenwood became public property. The mansion, which was damaged during the last war, contains a superb collection of paintings bequeathed to the nation by Lord Iveagh.

Parliament Hill Fields, to the south of Kenwood, comprising 265 acres, were bought in 1886-88 for £307,000, a huge sum of money, but the purchase was essential if the beauty of the adjoining Hampstead Heath and the view from it towards London was to be preserved. Otherwise we should by now have been looking down on to the roofs of a densely inhabited suburb from the heights of Hampstead Heath. The origin of the name of Parliament Hill has not yet been traced, but the usual story is that some of the Gunpowder Plot conspirators adjourned to this eminence on 5 November 1605 to get a good view of the blowing-up of the Houses of Parliament. The land was purchased from the owners of the Mansfield estate and Sir Spencer Wilson, one-half of the cost having been contributed by the Metropolitan Board of Works, £50,000 by the Charity Commissioners, £46,000 by public subscription, £30,000 by St Pancras, £20,000 by the Hampstead Vestry, and £5,000 by Marylebone. From the top of the hill, which is 320 feet high, is an extensive view in every direction, including the churches of Hampstead and Highgate and the distant Surrey Hills. A short distance from the summit is an artifical mound called Boadicea's Grave now concealed in trees and undergrowth. It is ten feet high and nearly forty yards across and is surrounded by a dry ditch. It is believed to be a grave of the early Bronze Age and possibly four thousand years old.

Adjoining Parliament Hill Fields and Kenwood are the celebrated Highgate Ponds, now a popular bathing resort of Londoners in the summer-time. They were originally designed to supply the north of London with water, a scheme which was promoted in 1690 by William Paterson, founder of the Bank of England. Paterson's plan was to collect the springs of Ken or Caen Wood, as it was then called, near the source of the Fleet River, into ponds or reservoirs. These sufficed to provide Hampstead and Kentish Town with water until the New River Company drove them out of business. To-day these five ponds form a pleasant feature of this large open playground of North London, and here the scenery looking towards Kenwood and Hampstead Heath is delightful.

From Kenwood a walk of about a mile and a half along Hampstead Lane and Spaniard's Road will bring us to the top of Hampstead Heath. On the north side of Hampstead Lane is Hampstead Garden Suburb, a highly exclusive new quarter of large houses standing in spacious gardens which has been developed between the two World Wars. The various roads radiate from the Central Square with its Institute and the parish church of St Jude, by Sir Edwin Lutyens. The houses are of several different kinds and size, for one of those interested in the scheme was Dame Henrietta Barnett who, being the wife of the Warden of Toynbee Hall, had ideas of social reform and intended that the suburb should include smaller houses for people of low income as well as the well-to-do. The suburb is strictly residential and the absence of shops, restaurants or entertainment is sometimes thought to be a disadvantage. A considerable area of land in this quarter is occupied by the Highgate Golf Club. The Spaniard's Inn stands in a fine romantic spot and is associated with the exploits of Dick Turpin. Opposite The Spaniard's is the old 18th Century Toll House which, to the surprise and dismay of all good motorists, has recently been renovated instead of, as they hoped, demolished. Its continued existence certainly narrows the road at that point and in the view of the pro-demolition party constitutes a 'serious traffic hazard', while the Hampstead Heath Protection Society interpret this 'bottleneck' as a safety-valve which prevents motorists from using the road across the Heath as a race-track. The delightful walk along the Spaniard's Road between Jack Straw's Castle and The Spaniards—nearly 400 feet above sea-level—has *always* been a pleasant evening and weekend 'promenade'; but recent proposals to cut a *motorway* across the Heath have not encouraged confidence in the possibility of preserving a non-functional old toll-house—or a promenade. The hilly slopes of the Heath on both sides of Spaniard's Road are wild and overgrown with brambles on the ridges, and filled with pools in the sandy hollows. This picturesqueness is the result of the old sand diggings on the Heath many years ago. The appearance of this road between Hampstead Village and the Spaniard's Inn resembles an embankment; this is due to the gravel having been dug away on either side of it.

Sand diggings on the Heath for many years brought in a handsome addition to the income of the Wilsons, Lords of the Manor, who claimed autocratic right in this wild expanse. Hampstead Heath supplied the fine red and silver sand greatly in demand some eighty years ago for sanding the floors of public-houses. It was sold at from 2*s*. 6*d*. to 6*s*. a load, and, according to a then prominent resident, in carting away the sand they were taking with it the climate, the drainage and the health of the neighbourhood.

A handsome viaduct of red brick and terracotta carries the roadway across the pond in East Heath. This was built by the Lord of the Manor as a carriageway to a house he intended erecting in the days when it was hoped to convert the Heath into a building estate.

In February 1867, when the Metropolitan Board of Works entered into negotiations with Sir Thomas Maryon Wilson for the purchase of Hampstead Heath, that rapacious individual valued his rights at the preposterous figure of £5,000 per acre for what he claimed as his building land. His 240 acres at that price would have brought him in a sum of £1,200,000, but needless to say Sir John Thwaites, the chairman of the Board, deemed it useless to continue the negotiations. Already in 1856 Sir Thomas Maryon Wilson had applied for a Bill in the House of Commoms giving him power to enclose Hampstead Heath, but this was strenuously opposed by the surrounding districts at a public meeting held in the St Pancras Vestry Hall on 21 April 1856. In 1866 he actually began to build on the Heath, but he died in 1870 and was succeeded by his brother, Sir J. M. Wilson, who sold his rights to the Metropolitan Board of Works in October 1870 for the very moderate figure of £45,000. In January 1872 the Board took formal possession of the Heath, and the Hampstead Vestry gave a luncheon to celebrate this happy event.

Before that time the great majority of Londoners knew no more of the beautiful lanes and walks within an hour's omnibus ride of the Bank of England than they did of New Zealand or Brazil. About fifty years ago another eighty acres of land were added to Hampstead Heath on the north-west side by the Eton College Trustees, who have been owners of 320 acres of agricultural land in this district since the days of Henry VI. Golders Hill Park, which is contiguous with Hampstead Heath, was acquired for the public in 1905. The mansion, which was destroyed in the air raids on London, was formerly the residence of Sir Spencer Wells, physician to Queen Victoria. The combined purchases of Hampstead Heath, Parliament Hill Fields, Kenwood, and Golder's Hill Park, which are all contiguous, has provided London with an open space of well over eight hundred acres, an area exceeded only by Wimbledon Common, Richmond Park, and Epping Forest. Close to the Heath in North End Road is the Bull and Bush Inn which was the frequent resort of Addison and his friends.

The charming old town of Hampstead is built in a tortuous irregular fashion on the slope of the hill leading up to the Heath. It includes the fairly broad High Street, consisting largely of old brick houses converted into shops and business premises, narrow byways, courts and passages, and streets and lanes bordered with shady elms and limes. It is quite the most rural and old-fashioned of the semi-suburban districts of the metropolis, and its narrow roads leading to secluded spots are so hidden from the turmoil of the town that you might still imagine yourself in some old-fashioned country town. It is quite different from the ordinary London suburb inasmuch as it has not been invaded by any of the large multiple stores except a Woolworth store. The modern blocks of flats which have been erected in this locality blend admirably with their oldworld surroundings, notably Greenhill on the west side of the High Street which consists of several blocks built on a high bank in gardens at the corner of Prince Arthur Road. Behind the 'King of Bohemia' in the High Street, the disused buildings of the old Hampstead Brewery remain—their trade mark was a colourful highwayman—and in Heath Street one is surprised to find a tavern with the unusual sign of 'The Cruel Sea'—so far inland and about 400 feet above sea-level!

Hampstead was once a favourite spa and pleasure resort, ranking high for the number and variety of its medicinal waters, two of which were discovered by a Mr Goodwin, a skilful practitioner of this neighbourhood. One of these was reputed to be a purgative saline similar to that of Cheltenham, and the other was sulphurous water. In the reign of Henry VIII Hampstead was merely an obscure hamlet inhabited by washerwomen, and here the clothes of the nobility, gentry, and chief citizens used to be brought from London to be laundered. Towards the commencement of the seventeenth century it became a fashionable watering place, teeming with amusements and dissipation. Concerts were held at the so-called Long Rooms, raffles took place at the Wells, and races on the Heath. The waters were pronounced equal to those of Tunbridge Wells, and so highly were their qualities assessed some 250 years ago that they were sent in flasks to London and retailed in different parts of the city.

Like Tunbridge Wells in former times, Hampstead held certain attractions for the wealthy, idle, and sickly, and its waters provided the thinnest of excuses for having a good time amid the society of people who were not really ill but only crowded together to make the wheels of fashionable life turn faster. But this was not surprising because the town-dweller of those days must have felt the same urge to get away for a change of air from the hot and smelly streets of medieval

London in summer-time as we who in our own age migrate to the country or the seaside. There were no facilities then for long-distance travelling. Houses of entertainment and dissipation started up on all sides; fairs were held in the Flask Walk, and the Well Walk and Church Row became the fashionable promenades of the town. Flask Walk, which runs eastwards from the High Street, is a straggling thoroughfare planted with trees. Here an annual fair of riotous character was held. Flask Walk and Well Walk are still popular with London residents, but nowadays no attention is paid to the virtues of the Hampstead waters, and the Wells Ball Room was eventually converted into a chapel.

In 1811 the population of Hampstead was only 5,483 and the number of its houses 904, whereas prior to its absorption into the new Borough of Camden, it was a large metropolitan borough of 97,710 inhabitants extending from Marylebone to Hendon and from Willesden to Highgate. On a clear day such places as Windsor Castle, Leith Hill, and Box Hill were formerly visible from certain parts of Hampstead, but the growth of the suburbs has long since obliterated such views. Keats lodged in Well Walk in 1817-18, and afterwards lived at Lawn Bank, at the foot of John Street, Hampstead. The house is now the John Keats Museum, and the road has been re-named Keats Grove.

Church Row, the hub and centre of old Hampstead, was built in the time of Queen Anne and is a survival of the old semi-rustic condition of affairs with dull red-brick houses of the urban type originally set down amidst the country. At the end of it is the church of St John, built in 1747. This is a brick building with a tower and a spire. In the churchyard is buried John Constable, the eminent landscape painter; one of his favourite subjects, a group of trees by the Spaniards Road, is still known as 'The Constable Firs'.

Of late years the spread of London has almost converted Hampstead Heath into a park, as the rural fields to the north of Golder's Green, Hendon, and Edgware have now become covered with new suburbs. This, however, has in no way altered its wild and rustic character. Whitestone Pond at the top of the Heath, close to the High Street, is 440 feet above sea-level, and the air is so bracing that you almost feel as though you were by the sea. Here children bathe, paddle and sail their boats or enjoy rides on the donkeys, whilst their parents repose in deck-chairs. The scenery is charming, with views across the densely-wooded vale to the Hertfordshire Hills on the north side and over London and St Paul's Cathedral to the Surrey Hills on the south side. At the corner of Spaniard's Road and North End Way is Heath House standing in about two and a half acres of wooded grounds which remained empty for several years (now occupied) and which it is intended to add to Hampstead Heath. This would provide an excellent site for a picturesque tea-house or chalet, an attraction which is missing from Hampstead Heath. Here also a tower, perhaps a hundred feet high, might be erected so that an all-round view might be enjoyed at a height of over five hundred feet, which would include Windsor Castle on a clear day. The tower would be concealed all but the top part by the trees and foliage. On the wall of some flats at the top of East Heath Road is a diagrammatic plaque showing that the height at that point is 435 feet above sea level. Near the White-stone Pond is the famous inn known as Jack Straw's Castle which takes its name from one of Wat Tyler's lieutenants and was much frequented by Charles Dickens. 'Jack Straw's' was recently rebuilt with a weather-boarded front and crenellated parapet. At the bottom of the Vale of Health, close to Parliament Hill Fields, are the Hampstead Ponds, used for boating and bathing. Several large blocks of flats have been erected in East Heath Road, in striking contrast to the old-fashioned houses of Well Walk, but the finest houses are situated on the west side of the Heath and in Fitzjohn's Avenue, a fine wide residential thoroughfare bordered with trees leading from Heath Street down to Swiss Cottage.

The more modern quarter of West Hampstead is centred round Finchley Road and West End Lane, and was mostly built between 1890 and 1905, but since the opening of the Underground Railway to Hampstead and Golders Green in 1907 the town has rapidly spread in the direction of Hendon and Finchley. The principal shops are located in Finchley Road between Swiss Cottage and Frognal Lane, and in West End Lane. With its fine shops and many artistic modern houses standing back in their own private gardens, Finchley Road must be considered one of the finest of the great main arteries leading out of London.

For five years during the second World War Northways, a block of flats situated at the junction of College Crescent and Finchley Road, was requisitioned by the Government and became the secret headquarters of Britain's submarine service. Here the Navy came in 1940 headed by Admiral Sir Max Horton, who planned the offensive off the Norwegian coast and also in the Mediterranean. A part of the basement was taken over and converted into an emergency operations centre, but tenants of the flats remained in undisturbed residence above this vital part of Britain's war machine. On 26 September 1945, the submarine service returned to its peace-time headquarters at Gosport.

To the east of Fitzjohn's Avenue and Swiss Cottage is the residential quarter of Belsize Park, extending to Haverstock Hill. It is built principally on the site of Belsize House and its grounds. This mansion was pulled down in 1854 and during the two previous centuries had been a feature of that delightful upland district extending to Hampstead. The beautiful park was then cut up and converted into a London suburban villa district, including a fine modern church.

Adelaide Road, also containing large houses, leads to Chalk Farm Road at its junction with Haverstock Hill. In Regent's Park Road is the Chalk Farm Tavern, once a farm-house on the estate of Chalcotts, a name corrupted to Chales Farm, and afterwards to Chalk Farm. The old building was pulled down in 1853 and the existing tavern was then built. Up to that time Chalk Farm had been a country district, and here was some of the most charming scenery to be found near London, extending from Chalk Farm to Hampstead and from Hampstead to Highgate, consisting of sloping fields and woods, including the Belsize, Chalcotts, and Eton College Estates. Chalk Farm was a favourite spot for duels in the earlier half of the nineteenth century, and at the back of the Chalk Farm

Tavern was a row of trees where duellists used to retire to settle their differences.

When this country was cut up for building in 1853 it was suggested that a boulevard a hundred yards wide, with rows of trees, and lined with elegant villas, should be constructed through these estates from Primrose Hill to Hampstead Heath. If this could have been done it would have formed one of the grandest pieces of urban scenery in the kingdom. But unfortunately it was too late, for Eton College had already laid out its fields to the back of Chalk Farm. Chalcotts was being built over, and the Dean and Chapter of Westminster had planned the imposing new villa town of Belsize which intersected the proposed boulevard.

Some attractive villas had already been erected prior to 1853 in Adelaide Road, on land belonging to the former London and North-Western Railway. From here a walk down Chalk Farm Road will bring us to Camden Town, at the busy junction of the High Street and Camden and Kentish Town Roads.

To the east of Haverstock Hill, which contains many large old-fashioned houses and crescents, was the Tailors' Asylum, built for the relief of aged and infirm journeyman tailors, and opened in 1843. This institution was founded on 10 February 1837, and the first stone of the new building was laid by the Marquess of Salisbury on 31 May 1842. The building has now gone and in its place stands Montague Tibbles House, a St Pancras Borough Council block of dwellings. In Ferdinand Street, a turning on the east side of Chalk Farm Road, new eight-storeyed blocks of flats with balconies have now been completed with narrow lawns in front. These have been erected by the St Pancras Borough Council and are among the finest of any that have been built in St Pancras during the post-war years.

Camden Town, forming the central portion of the former borough of St Pancras, is another busy traffic centre, being the junction of the bus routes from Holloway, Highgate, Hampstead, Tottenham Court Road, and Holborn. The construction of the now defunct North London tramways was begun in October 1870 from Holloway Road near the Nag's Head along the Camden Road to St Pancras and Camden Town, and thence to Euston Road. The entire tramway system of North London was electrified by the London County Council in 1906-08, but is now operated by diesel buses.

Camden Town, which was begun in 1791, was named after Lord Camden, the ground landlord, who was created a peer in 1765, taking the style of Baron Camden of Camden Place, in Kent. The following year he became Lord Chancellor. In 1791 this land, which was then in Kentish Town, was let for building 1,400 houses, and here a few years later the pleasant fields were mapped out for streets. Several builders then set to work, but little development took place until about 1804, except in Camden High Street, which was originally called Southampton Place.

The uniformly-built houses with shops at the southern entrance to Camden High Street display a marked contrast at the present day to the former village simplicity of the Southampton Place of a century and a half ago. Close to the spot where now stands the statue of Richard Cobden erected in 1868 by public subscription, was the turnpike gate, adjoining which there was a weighbridge for determining the amount of toll to be charged. Practically all traces of the small houses and shops which lined Camden High Street in 1793 have been obliterated. The densely-populated quarter of Kentish Town to the north of Camden Town, extending to Highgate, is said to derive its name from its foundation by Walter and Thomas de Cantilupe, and to denote a vulgar appellation of Cantilupe Town, of which that great family were the original owners. For many years the principal industries of Kentish Town have been railways and the manufacture of pianos and their component parts; Brinsmead, Broadwood, Challen and Cramer were among the familiar names in the district. While some of the pianoforte factories have been diverted to other purposes, the railways remain, and several goods and locomotive depots still draw on Kentish Town for their personnel. The extensive engine sheds and goods depot of the former Midland Railway cover a large area west of Kentish Town Road bounded approximately by Holmes, Grafton and Gordon House Roads, and much of the immediate neighbourhood is accordingly very shabby and most depressing. That it was not always so, and once had claim to rural charm, was revealed when recent excavations in the goods yard unearthed a little stream enclosed in a wooden culvert. This would explain the adjacent Spring Place—hitherto regarded as a romantic misnomer—and enquiries among local residents produced further evidence of bygone watercress beds and green fields.

To the south of Camden High Street is Mornington Crescent, built early in the nineteenth century, and in front of which until 1926 was a semicircular garden overlooking Hampstead Road. The former Carreras factory at Mornington Crescent has now been rebuilt and re-named 'Greater London House'. On the wall of No. 247 Hampstead Road at the corner of Granby Street, until it was demolished recently, was a plaque inscribed: 'Here was Wellington House Academy where Charles Dickens was educated, 1824-6'. A few doors further south at No. 263, the house still stands where George Cruikshank who illustrated some of Dickens's books, lived and died. Opposite Greater London House is Harrington Square, which was partly destroyed in the blitz, and here a large bombed site is now covered by a new block of flats erected by the St Pancras Borough Council. Ampthill Square and Oakley Square on the east side of Hampstead Road contain large houses of the early Victorian style, erected about 1840, with porticoes and faced with yellow brick. The rebuilding of Euston Station may have its effect on Ampthill Square.

To the west of Hampstead Road is Cumberland Market, now converted to a children's playground. Large housing developments by the St Pancras Borough Council have taken place around the old market and much bomb-damaged and slum property has been demolished. Handsome blocks of flats and a shopping centre have replaced dilapidated houses, but more remains to be done between Hampstead Road and Albany Street. Between Drummond Street and Euston Road the building line on the east side of Hampstead Road formerly narrowed into a dangerous bottleneck which exercised a stranglehold on the traffic coming from Tottenham Court Road. In order to provide space for the London County Council tramways in 1906 the building line was set back a considerable distance and brought into conformity with that of the wider portion of Hampstead Road.

At the junction of Hampstead Road with Seymour Street is Crowndale Road, on the north side of which is the Working Men's College, founded by Frederick Denison Maurice in 1854. Crowndale Road leads into Pancras Road, originally known as Fig Lane. A walk through this street will bring us to Goldington Crescent and St Pancras old church, dating from about 1180. It was enlarged in 1848 by taking the open space occupied by the old square tower into the body of the church. A spire was then placed on the south side of the building. Seven acres of the burial-ground with the adjoining burial-ground of St Giles's, overlooking Pancras Road, were converted into a public garden in 1877, the rest being acquired by the Midland Railway. Close by formerly stood the old St Pancras town hall and public library, which were destroyed in the air raids and have since been razed to the ground. It was a gloomy-looking building of red brick without any claim to distinction. St Pancras Square, which dates back to 1847, was the first block of workers' flats built in London. It was erected by the Metropolitan Association for Improving the Dwellings of the Industrial Classes founded in 1841. The dwellings were a show place and were visited by the Prince Consort in 1848. Other notable visitors who came to see this early experiment in social welfare included Gladstone, Charles Kingsley, Lord Shaftesbury, Charles Dickens and the Duke of Wellington. St Pancras Square has vanished completely and its site is now used by the St Pancras Borough Council as a building-materials depot. St Pancras derives its name from a youthful nobleman of Phrygia who suffered martyrdom at Rome by order of Diocletian.

Until about two hundred years ago St Pancras was a spa containing mineral springs, which attracted many visitors, and in those days the Fleet River flowed past the church. Not only were digestive troubles alleged to be removed by a cure at St Pancras, but even leprosy, scurvy, and cancer. Mr Richard Bristow, a goldsmith of Bride Lane, Fleet Street, advertised in 1730 delivery to any part of London of either the St Pancras or the Bristol waters at six shillings per dozen bottles. St Pancras Wells boasted a pump room and a house of entertainment in 1730, together with an uninterrupted view of the Hampstead and Highgate Hills, as well as of the lesser elevation of Primrose Hill. The site of St Pancras Wells is now occupied by British Railways (Midland Region), and it would be difficult to indicate the exact spot where it once stood.

The former borough of St Pancras, of 2,694 acres now joins with Hampstead of 2,265 acres and Holborn, the smallest of the 28 old boroughs – only 405 acres – to form the new London Borough of Camden, with a total population of 243,954.

Twenty-First Walk

Hyde Park and Kensington Gardens

Hyde Park has an area of 360 acres, and is joined on the west to Kensington Gardens, with 275 acres, and on the south-east to the Green Park, which, in turn, adjoins St James's Park, thus forming a continuous series of parks extending from the Horse Guards to Kensington High Street for a distance of two and a half miles.

From an historical point of view Hyde Park ranks foremost amongst the great metropolitan parks of the world, and one might justly claim that its history is that of the British Nation. It was formerly the Manor of Hyde, belonging to the ancient abbey of Westminster. When that monastery was dissolved by Henry VIII the King took this ground for a hunting park, and there were still stags and deer to be found here in the reign of Queen Elizabeth I. Under William III and Queen Anne some thirty acres of Hyde Park were taken for the gardens of Kensington Palace, and about 250 more by Caroline, Queen of George II. Queen Caroline once asked Sir Robert Walpole what it would cost to enclose the whole of the three Royal Parks for the exclusive use of the Court. That wise minister answered, 'Madam, it would cost you three crowns, those of England, Ireland, and Scotland', whereupon Her Majesty thought no more of this design.

After having been enclosed with deer fences from a very early period, Hyde Park was first walled in with brick in the reign of Charles II, and with an open iron railing in the reign of George IV. In 1550 the French Ambassador hunted in Hyde Park with the youthful King Edward VI, and by the reign of Charles I it had become celebrated for its foot- and horse-races round the Ring. In Cromwell's time the Park was famous for its musters and coach-races, and it first became fashionable for its drives and promenades in the reign of Charles II.

In the eighteenth century Hyde Park was a favourite rendezvous for duellists, and here the Duke of Hamilton fought Lord Mohun on 15 November 1712. Both men were killed, Lord Mohun falling into the ditch upon his back, and the Duke of Hamilton falling severely wounded. On 16 November 1763 a duel took place between John Wilkes and Samuel Martin, M.P., on account of an article which appeared in *The North Briton*. They fought near the Ring, and Wilkes was wounded in the abdomen.

Barely two hundred years ago no one would have dared to walk from Kensington to the City after nightfall. At Hyde Park Corner a bell was rung at seven and at nine o'clock, and people wishing to journey to the City assembled at the call and proceeded in a body in order to be comparatively safe from the attacks of highwaymen. Small groups of men were often stopped by robbers and sometimes passengers were attacked by gangs of young fellows fresh from the public-houses. But after George II had been stopped and plundered one night on his return from hunting, the very next morning a troop of armed horsemen was established to police the public streets, and these latter constituted a portion of the nucleus out of which our present-day Metropolitan Police Force has been evolved.

At the beginning of the nineteenth century a part of Kensington Gardens was still wilderness and swampy ground, and it is recorded in the minutes of the Board of Green Cloth in the year 1798 that a pension of £18 per annum was granted to Sarah Gray for the loss of her husband, who was accidentally shot while the keepers were hunting foxes in Kensington Gardens. Hyde Park was still a deer park and as rural and solitary as Windsor Forest still is at the present day. Unlike its opposite number, the Bois de Boulogne in Paris, Hyde Park stands within a huge city and not two miles outside. Only a century ago Hyde Park stood on the border of market gardens now covered by the streets of South Kensington.

The Marble Arch, or Cumberland Gate, already noticed in another chapter, and which we will make the starting-point of our travels, replaced some handsome iron gates erected here in 1822 at a cost of £2,000. The first gate which stood on this site was erected in 1744 at the expense of the inhabitants of Cumberland Place, and was at first generally known as Tyburn Gate.

It was a mean brick building comprising an arch with side entrances and wooden gates, and was the scene of a fight between the populace and the military at the funeral of Queen Caroline, as a result of which two people were killed by shots from the Horse Guards on duty. In the following years this unsightly gate was taken down. It was replaced in 1760 by the Tyburn Turnpike House, which stood until 1829 in the position previously occupied since 1571 by the Tyburn triangular gallows.

Tyburn was used as a place of execution from time immemorial; the first recorded execution there took place in 1196. Near the entrance to Edware Road, on a large triangular refuge in the middle of the road is a circular stone inscribed: 'The site of Tyburn Tree'. Numerous criminals were executed here down to 1783 when Newgate gallows replaced that of Tyburn. Here were hung the bodies of Oliver Cromwell, Ireton and Bradshaw, torn from their graves in Henry VII's Chapel in Westminster Abbey on the first anniversary of the death of Charles I after the Restoration. Other famous names include Jack Sheppard (1724), Jonathan Wild (1725) and Catherine Hayes, who was burnt alive for the murder of her husband by the mob who, in their indignation, would not wait for the hangman. It is said that two hundred thousand people witnessed the hanging of Jack Sheppard.

Inside the park facing the Marble Arch is the famous Speakers' Corner which is principally monopolized by orators and street-corner preachers. Here one may spend a most amusing half-hour listening to sermons on religion and politics, and on the proposed solutions of the leading problems which confront mankind generally. Confined to reasonable limits not calculated to cause a breach of the peace, such demonstrations may be regarded in the light of safety valves, as well as a free entertainment for the onlookers. Until the latter half of the nineteenth century such meetings were not tolerated in the public parks; on Monday evening 23 July 1866, an attempt was made by the Reform League, in defiance of the police authorities, to hold a meeting in Hyde Park. This resulted in great confusion, much damage to public property, and many severe casualties.

Processions were formed at several points with flags and bands, which marched to Hyde Park. On their arrival at the Marble Arch they found the gates closed and strong bodies of police guarding them. Admission was formally demanded and refused. An enormous crowd then gathered in Park Lane, Piccadilly, and Bayswater Road, and effected an entrance into the park at each of these places. For several hundred yards the railings were torn down, and thus thousands of people got into the park. The police charged them and used their truncheons, but all in vain, for more than fifty thousand people had succeeded in entering, and although the police charged them again and again they could not be driven out. Several arrests were made, a company of the Foot Guards were marched into the park with fixed bayonets, and a troop of Horse Guards patrolled the principal avenues, but people succeeded in remaining in the park until a late hour. A meeting was held at which resolutions were passed denouncing the sins of the Government. Nobody was killed, but many were injured, including forty police officers, the latter by the stones and brickbats which were hurled at them. The destroyed railings were replaced by temporary wooden ones.

At that time Hyde Park was still infested nightly by bands of thieves and ruffians, who preyed upon defenceless pedestrians without the slightest inter-ference by the park-keepers or the police. Several gross outrages were perpetrated here in the dark after the destruction of the railings, including robberies and indecent assaults. In our own day we are still confronted with the problem of Hyde Park after dark, though police supervision is much more efficient and improved lighting has recently been introduced.

During the general strike in May 1926 the roadway inside the park leading from the Marble Arch to Victoria Gate was used as a depot for the milk supply of London. Here the lorries were drawn up two deep, and thousands of them came and went as fast they could be unloaded, and thus an adequate supply was maintained for the public requirements. The gates of the park were guarded by special detachments of police, and nobody was allowed to enter without a pass. A comfortable canteen and resting-place were provided for the lorry drivers by the Y.M.C.A.

During the second World War the section of Hyde Park between the Marble Arch and the Serpentine became an armed camp bristling with anti-aircraft guns, trenches, barbed wire and balloon emplacements. Many unexploded bombs fell in both Hyde Park and Kensington Gardens. These danger spots were enclosed by barbed wire and crossing the park became something of an adventure as you never knew when you might have to retrace your steps or make a long detour to arrive at your destination. One very fine Saturday afternoon in August 1940 during the Battle of Britain a German aircraft was shot down in Hyde Park but before the excited crowds of onlookers had any opportunity of looking at it, the wreckage was quickly removed by a fleet of lorries. In the autumn of 1941 the railings of Hyde Park were removed for the war effort and have now been in part replaced by wire netting.

The drive leading from the Marble Arch to Hyde Park Corner was called the Ring Road, but later became the East Carriage Drive, and is now the south-to-north road of the dual Park Lane. In the eighteenth century the Ring was the central resort of fashion. It then had an uninterrupted view of the Surrey Hills and of the heights of Hampstead and Highgate. Near this spot Oliver Cromwell, whilst driving his own coach in the park, met with an accident. His horses ran away and got out of control. Cromwell was thrown off the coach and fell upon the pole between the wheels and, his feet becoming entangled in the harness, he was dragged for a considerable distance. However, he escaped with a few bruises. Opposite Mount Street is the Ring itself, now a circular fountain surmounted by a modern group of sculpture. It occupies the site of an ugly circular reservoir built about 1725 by the Chelsea Waterworks and formerly surrounded by a low wall and iron railings, owing to its having been much frequented by would-be suicides. The reservoir was abolished in 1861. Grosvenor Gate was built in 1725 on the petition of Sir Robert Grosvenor, who obtained leave to erect the gate and form a carriageway to be kept in repair at his own expense. Between Stanhope Gate and Apsley House a private enclosure of seven acres formerly for the use of the owners of the houses in Park Lane and Piccadilly has now been merged into Hyde Park. It was first proposed by John Fordyce, Surveyor-General, that this triangular piece of ground between Apsley House and Park Lane should be enclosed and laid out in gardens with houses suitable for wealthy families. At first, owing to popular outcry, this scheme was shelved but was eventually carried out. Of late years all of the distinguished families have vacated these mansions, some have been demolished in connection with roadway improvement, others are now let for offices.

The statue of 'Achilles' close to Hyde Park Corner was erected 'by the women of England to the Duke of Wellington and his brave companions in arms, on 18 June 1822, by command of King George VI'. The statue was cast by Sir R. Westmacott, R.A., from cannon taken in the victories of Salamanca, Vittoria, Toulouse, and Waterloo, the cost being defrayed by a subscription of £10,000 raised among the ladies. It is popularly supposed to represent Achilles, but is actually a copy of one of the figures on Monte Cavallo at Rome.

Between the statue of 'Achilles' and the open screen gateway is the entrance to Rotten Row, the fashionable ride of London, which is a mile long. The odd name of Rotten Row is said to be a corruption of Route du Roi. Here riders are to be seen exercising at all hours of the morning, before and after breakfast. The old royal route from the palace of the Plantagenet kings at Westminster to the royal hunting forests was by what is now called Birdcage Walk, Constitution

Hill, and Rotten Row. In 1853 the equestrian road in Rotten Row was widened to double its former width by the Department of Woods and Forests. The carriage-drive was a famous sight during the season in Victorian days, and is still a favourite rendezvous for motor-cars.

After passing Albert Gate, opened on 9 August 1845, and so named as a compliment to the Prince Consort, we come to the Dell on our right, forming the head of the Serpentine. A sheet of dirty water which flowed from a waterfall in connexion with the east end of the Serpentine once faced Albert Gate. This was entirely filled up in 1844.

The Serpentine was created by Queen Caroline in 1730 by enlarging the bed of the Westbourne stream, together with several ponds, into a wide straight canal. Though termed the Serpentine the lake in Hyde Park is shaped more like a parallelogram, but its slight bend in the centre was deemed sufficient to justify the name of Serpentine. Its surplus waters, entering an underground passage, form an artificial cascade over rocky stones which were arranged about the year 1817. The original cost of the Serpentine was estimated to have been £6,000, but actually amounted to £20,000. Robert Walpole is said to have furnished Queen Caroline with the greater part of the money required, without the King's knowledge. Work on the formation of the Serpentine was begun in October 1730, when some two hundred men were employed to construct a dyke or dam across the valley of the Westbourne. The soil thus excavated was used to raise the mound at the south-east end of Kensington Gardens.

In 1814 Hyde Park was the scene of the Regent's Fête, held in commemoration of the centenary of the House of Hanover on the British throne, and likewise in honour of the visit of the Emperor of Russia and the King of Prussia, following on the allied victories in the Napoleonic Wars. The festivities were begun on 12 August, and included a representation of a sea fight on the Serpentine, together with the blowing up of a fire-ship. This idea is said to have come from the future George IV. First a couple of frigates were engaged, then the Battle of the Nile was imitated, and finally there was a brilliant display of fireworks. The fair lasted for a week, and during that period side-shows, booths, and swings were allowed in the park. Again in 1815, after the battle of Waterloo, Hyde Park was made the centre of rejoicings.

The Serpentine was not always the delightful sheet of water it is now. Up to 1855 two branches of the Ranelagh sewer, running from Hampstead and Kensal New Town, united in a stream a little north of the Harrow Road, and, passing through a sewer from Gloucester Terrace, entered the head of the Serpentine near Bayswater Road. Until this state of affairs was remedied by diverting this sewage into a main sewer, the water of the Serpentine remained polluted.

In January 1849 a meeting was held at the Cadogan Institute, Sloane Street, with the object of calling public attention to the filthy state of the Serpentine and the nuisance caused by it to the neighbouring districts. The chair was taken by Dr Copland, who remarked that he had seen many unhealthy rivers on the coast of Africa, but none of the waters of which were so polluted and contained so much animal and vegetable matter as the Serpentine. All that was required to generate disease of the most fatal kind was a tropical heat, and even in this climate, he added, the effect of such a large volume of filthy water must prove very destructive. The bottom of the river was covered to a considerable depth with thick black mud and the water was impregnated with sulphur and ammonia, the two ingredients most prominent in filthy drains and cesspools. Bathing in such conditions was considered dangerous, and rowing ought not to have been indulged in, since the black mud was stirred up by the action of the oars, thus liberating a greater quantity of noxious gas. A young nobleman had recently been seized with malignant fever after rowing upon the Serpentine, and this had been attributed to the filthy exhalations from the water. 1849 was the date of the first of two serious outbreaks of cholera in London. The second was in 1854. Both were attributed to polluted water.

A resolution demanding the cleansing of the Serpentine was carried, and it was stated that some months previously a petition signed by two thousand of the residents in the neighbourhood of Hyde Park had been presented to the Commissioners of Woods and Forests. Another deputation was therefore appointed to wait upon the Commissioners of Woods and Forests, as result of which the work of draining the Serpentine was commenced in February 1849.

Again in 1858 attempts were made to purify the Serpentine by throwing in large quantities of lime, and this caused the eels and other fish to rush to those places where the water was clear, thus exposing themselves to easy capture. As soon as this fact became generally known immense crowds assembled by the waterside, defying all efforts of the park-keepers to clear the gardens. At the head of the lake, near Marlborough Gate, was a dirty duck-pond one foot deep, into which the Ranelagh sewer periodically discharged its contents. This evil was finally removed in 1860, when the sewage was diverted into a new channel, and work was commenced on the permanent purification of the Serpentine by means of filtration. The duck-pond was then transformed into the present delightful Italian garden, together with the filtering basins and fountains and other ornamental works sculptured by Mr John Thomas, who designed many of the carvings on the Houses of Parliament. In addition to medallions of the young Queen Victoria and Prince Albert, the balustrading of the Italian Garden displays frequent V. & A. monograms, and the statue of Dr Jenner, who discovered vaccination, occupies a prominent position.

Ever since it was first created the Serpentine has been a popular resort of bathers. On account of the numerous accidents which occurred here, George III in 1794 gave a plot of land on the northern bank, where the Royal Humane Society erected a house for rendering first aid to drowning persons. This structure was replaced in 1844 by a later building designed by Mr Decimus Burton. It was destroyed by a 'doodle-bug' during the war.

As a result of the efforts of the late Mr George Lansbury, First Commissioner of Works in the second Labour Government, a handsome bathing pavilion was erected in 1930 on the south side of the Serpentine, and here mixed bathing in the summer-time is allowed at all hours of the day at a small charge. This venture has proved immensely popular, and was known as 'Lansbury's Lido'. There are plenty of row-boats for hire and being nearly a mile long the Serpentine offers the best substitute for the Thames for an hour's pleasure cruising. Singularly enough small motor-launches have never been allowed here, although trips round the Serpentine would no doubt prove a great attraction to Londoners and holiday-makers during the summer months.

Between the Serpentine and Rotten Row, extending from the Knightsbridge Barracks to Alexandra Gate, is the Exhibition Ground of 1851, and here games may now be played. No historical account of Hyde Park would be complete without a reference to the first great exhibition ever held in this country, which during the twenty-four weeks of its existence was visited by upwards of six million people, and of which the receipts totalled over £400,000. The Crystal Palace erected in Hyde Park was designed by Sir Joseph Paxton, and after serving its purpose was removed to Sydenham between 1852 and 1854.

On Thursday, 1 May 1851, in perfect weather, the Great Exhibition was opened by Queen Victoria and the Prince Consort at twelve o'clock. The long stream of carriages which had been following without interruption along the whole line of the route from Long Acre and Piccadilly Circus started at half-past nine. From a calculation made by the *Morning Chronicle* it was said that if all the carriages had been placed in a single line they would have extended over a distance of twenty miles. Of the vehicles which arrived at the park gates up to twelve o'clock, there were 1,050 state carriages, 1,500 hackney carriages and cabs, 800 broughams, 600 post-chaises, 300 clarences, and 300 other vehicles. Already by six o'clock in the morning, the hour fixed for the opening of the park gates, streams of carriages were pouring in from all parts of the metropolis and surrounding districts. Omnibuses conveyed passengers to the Exhibition from Kennington and other parts of South London for the low fare of twopence.

The only houses from which a view of the procession could be obtained were those in Grosvenor Place and Hyde Park Corner. The roof of Apsley House was fully tenanted and also that of the park-keeper's lodge. The windows of the newly-erected front of Buckingham Palace were filled with persons attached to the Royal Household, the centre balcony being occupied by the younger princes and princesses attended by several ladies. The Royal Procession consisted of eight carriages, that of the Queen being drawn by two horses and remaining open to enable the people to see her to advantage. The other carriages were occupied by the Lords and Ladies-in-Waiting, the Lords of the Household, the Maids of Honour, and some of the ladies of the suite of the Princess of Prussia. The Duke of Wellington was early in attendance, arriving with the Marchioness of Douro about ten o'clock; that day being also his birthday he received a great ovation. There were some fifteen thousand exhibitors, one-half of whom were British.

Thirty-six years before the Great Exhibition, the most famous of living Englishmen had brought to a conclusion the most furious and desolating war ever recorded up to that time in European history. It left the nation a legacy of an enormous national debt, international jealousy and hatred. But peace gave the nations leisure for work. A few years of peace and security produced a wonderful change, and by 1825 Europe had begun to recover. The debt of this country, though found to be a burden, was discovered to be one which the trade and industry of the people would enable them to bear. Hatred of the French and all other foreigners was consigned to oblivion.

Great progress took place between 1830 and 1850. Railways were established, making this country seem like one huge metropolis, and Europe like one large country. This had made nations understand one another better than before, and had broken down to a certain extent the ancient barriers of jealousy and exclusiveness. At that time it was said that if nations had previously known as much of one another as they did then, there would have been no battles of the Nile, Trafalgar, Leipzig, or Waterloo.

But in the light of subsequent events, we see that the apostles of universal peace on earth and goodwill towards all men cried victory too soon, The Crimean War followed, and during the first World War of 1914-18 the exhibition ground in Hyde Park was utilized as a drilling-ground. Here were trained some of the flower of the British soldiers who successfully met the onslaught of the Prussian Guard at Contalmaison and on the Somme in 1916. During the second World War the exhibition ground was covered by a huge dump built from the debris of bombed buildings. Afterwards its material was utilized for building additional air-raid shelters and various other war-time requirements. By 1942 it had all been cleared away. Bowling greens have now been laid out at the western end of the exhibition ground. Saddled with a national debt more than ten times as great as that of 1815, the British people are once again proving equal to the occasion, just as they did after the Napoleonic Wars.

A short walk past the exhibition ground will bring us to Alexandra Gate and then to Kensington Gardens. Here the carriage-drive is continued past the Albert Memorial as far as Queen's Gate, where it comes to an abrupt end. The handsome entrance gates to Kensington Gardens, opposite Queen's Gate, 150 feet in length, were erected in 1858. The former entrance to the gardens was close to the old barracks of Kensington, which were then pulled down, and the new entrance was made at the commencement of the carriage-way leading to Rotten Row and Hyde Park corner. As a result of the demolition of the old barracks facing Kensington Gore, over a quarter of an acre was added to Kensington Gardens.

Midway between the Alexandra and the Queen's Gates is the Albert Memorial, completed in 1872 and inspected by Queen Victoria. The structure is crowned by a lofty spire of rich tabernacle work in gilt and enamelled metal, terminated by a cross rising to a height of 180 feet. Beneath the vast canopy or tabernacle is a colossal statue of the Prince Consort, designed by Foley. The steps to the Memorial are constructed of grey granite from Castle Wellan in the Country of Down, but a portion of them are from the Dalbeattie Quarries in Kirkcudbright. The lower range of steps fronting the south side, some two hundred feet in length, is of granite from Penrhyn in Cornwall, whilst the blocks which terminate them are capped with pink granite from Isle of Mull.

The Memorial contains four large groups of sculpture at the corners of the basement pyramid of steps, representing Europe, Asia, Africa, and America. On the projecting pedestals of the clustered granite columns are marble groups representing Agriculture, Manufacture, Commerce, and Engineering. The Memorial was constructed on the model of an Eleanor Cross by Sir Gilbert Scott, at a cost of £120,000, and from start to finish took about twenty years to complete. The statue of the Prince Consort in the Albert Memorial was not unveiled until March 1876. The structure has been renovated three times, in 1902 and again in 1930 and 1950.

Kensington Palace, situated at the western end of the Gardens, was originally Nottingham House, the seat of Heneage Finch, Earl of Nottingham and Lord Chancellor of England, whose son, the second earl, sold it to King William III for £18,000 very soon after his accession to the throne. Reconstruction was carried out by Sir Christopher Wren for William and Mary in 1691 and additions to the building were made by William Kent in the reign of George I. Close to the Palace is the Orangery designed by Sir Christopher Wren and erected in 1705. It is a building of red brick which stands upon a platform of stone. The origin of its name remains unexplained. Outside the Palace is a statue of Queen Victoria sculptured in 1893 by Princess Louise who resided here for many years. In the grounds on the south front of the palace is a bronze statue of William III by Baucke. William III and Queen Mary, Queen Anne, her husband Prince George of Denmark, and George II, all died at this palace. Queen Victoria was born here in 1819. The palace itself, although in Kensington, is attached to the City of Westminster. It is a plain red-brick building of homely appearance, two storeys high, but without any pretension to architectural magnificence. Leigh Hunt described Windsor Castle as a place to receive monarchs in, Buckingham Palace to see fashion in, and Kensington Palace a place to take tea in. Between the Broad Walk and the Palace is a beautiful Dutch garden with a lily-pond. The majority — but not all — of the exhibits forming the London Museum are to be seen in several rooms of the State Apartments. They will ultimately be re-assembled when the new museum building in the Barbican is ready.

When purchased by William III the gardens attached to Kensington Palace did not exceed twenty-six acres, and in 1691 they were described as not great, nor abounding with fine plants. Queen Anne added some thirty acres, which were laid out by her gardener Wise. At that time the eastern boundary of the gardens was approximately in the line of the handsome Broad Walk. The Broad Walk is fifty feet wide, and is lined on both sides by rows of stately elm-trees, and extends from Palace Gate to Bayswater Road. To the east of the Broad Walk is the Round Pond, situated in a direct line with Kensington Palace and having an area of seven acres. It is a favourite spot for sailing model yachts, and frequently skating can be indulged in here after two or three days of frost, when ice is still too thin on the deeper waters of the Serpentine. Some way off is a huge equestrian statue by G. F. Watts, twelve feet high, representing Physical Energy, a replica of the central portion of the Rhodes Memorial on the slope of Table Mountain at Capetown. Near the Serpentine is the statue of Peter Pan by Sir George Frampton, R.A. Very popular with children (as it was meant to be), the bronze figures of rabbits, mice and snails are polished bright by the affectionate caresses of little hands. Between the Round Pond and the Long Water, directly facing Kensington Palace, is a fine double row of elm-trees forming a wide grassy avenue similar to that of the Home Park at Hampton Court. Here you might imagine yourself right out in the country or in the Long Walk of Windsor Great Park. Near the Victoria Gate is the Dogs' Cemetery created by the Duke of Cambridge who, in 1180, when Ranger of Hyde Park, obtained permission for his wife to bury a pet dog there. Other burials followed and in time the number of small tombstones erected there made it a sizeable cemetery.

The roadway between Hyde Park and Kensington Gardens crosses the Serpentine by a five-arched stone bridge built by Rennie in 1826, and on the Kensington Gardens side is a handsome refreshment pavilion, faced with red brick and stone, built in 1930, which has replaced a rustic tea-house that previously stood on this site. This, in its turn, has recently been closed and superseded by a more modern, but less attractive refreshment pavilion (with Bar) on the other (i.e. Hyde Park) side of the road, opened in 1964. That portion of the Serpentine situated in Kensington Gardens goes under the name of the Long Water, and, being beautifully wooded, affords a most delightful view from the Serpentine bridge. The Serpentine, together with the Long Water, covers an area of fifty-three acres. In 1816, Harriet Westbrook, wife of the poet Shelley, committed suicide in the Long Water.

On the north side of the Serpentine is a fine carriage-drive known as the Ladies' Mile, extending to Hyde Park Corner, which was greatly widened in 1852. Close to the bridge is the powder magazine, beyond which is the building of the Royal Humane Society and the boat-house. A small island adorns the centre of the Serpentine, midway between the bridge and the Dell at the eastern end. To the north of the Serpentine are the Rangers' Lodge, the tree-embowered police station, and the Ring tea-house which forms a popular addition to the attractions of Hyde Park.

In 1925 an official Bird Sanctuary was opened a few hundred yards west of the Rangers' Lodge, which is a memorial to W. H. Hudson, writer and field naturalist. A panel by Epstein of Rima, a character in one of Hudson's books, erected at the bird-bath was at first the target of much ridicule, and on two occasions was tarred and feathered. It has now been railed off, to discourage further damage.

Beyond the Serpentine, just behind the carriage-drive, is the bandstand, where military bands play every afternoon and evening during the summer months. In 1930 near Grosvenor Gate a magnificent carillon of bells constructed for the Government of New Zealand was temporarily set up in a square tower in order to give Londoners an opportunity of inspecting it before it was shipped to Wellington. There it is now set up as a War Memorial to the men of New Zealand who laid down their lives in the first World War.

As the result of a demonstration organized by the 'hunger marchers' in Hyde Park on Thursday, 27 October 1932, numbering some two thousand, serious disorders occurred near the Marble Arch. Clashes took place between groups of unemployed and strong forces of mounted and foot police. These occurred both inside and outside Hyde Park and spread to Edgware Road, Seymour Street, and Bryanston Street, where large numbers of windows were smashed. A great crowd of people gathered, railings in the park were laid flat, and traffic for the time being was completely disorganized in this area. A considerable number of people were injured, including police-officers who were assailed with stones and missiles of various kinds and were compelled to use their batons against the demonstrators. Some fourteen men were arrested, and this was followed on 1 November by the arrest of Mr Wal. Hannington, the leader of the hunger marchers, who was sentenced to imprisonment.

On 20 July 1933 Hyde Park was the scene of a mass protest against the persecution of the Jews in Germany. This was attended by some fifty thousand people, and, by agreement, many Roman Catholics took part in the procession and cooperated which the Jews in their protest. Nearly every Jewish shop, street stall, and refreshment bar in the East End of London was closed for the occasion, both the proprietors and their employees joining in the great procession to Hyde Park.

Twenty-Second Walk

Hyde Park Corner, Knightsbridge, Brompton Road, Sloane Street and Belgravia

Until after 1820 Hyde Park Corner, which will form the starting-point of this walk, was regarded more or less as the western limit of the metropolis. The toll-gate which then stood at the junction of the roads close to St George's Hospital, was removed in 1825; Belgravia had not yet come into being, and to the south-west were the Five Fields, extending from London to Chelsea, intersected by mud-banks and occupied by only a few sheds.

Knigshtsbridge was then the first village out of London, but was already joined to it by the row of rather good houses, then called Knightsbridge Terrace, extending from Hyde Park Corner to Wilton Place. On the south it was also joined to Chelsea by the long row of houses extending the full length of Sloane Street. It was a shabby straggling village, consisting principally of one long street forming part of the great western road, extending from Wilton Place as far as the Knightsbridge barracks. In former times Knightsbridge had a reputation for salubrious air, and this was the reason for its selection in 1733 as the site of St George's Hospital.

The derivation of the name of Knightsbridge is somewhat obscure, but like many other places it has its legend. The story goes that two knights leaving London to wage war for some holy purpose had a quarrel. They fought on the bridge which spanned the little River Westbourne, whilst their companions watched the struggle from its banks. Both of them, so the legend tells, fell in mortal combat, and ever after the place was called Knightsbridge to commemorate their fatal feud.

Still a shabby quarter of the metropolis as recently as eighty years ago, the transformation of Knightsbridge, since 1890, into an opulent district consisting mainly of handsome shops, luxury hotels, and huge block of modern residential flats, almost invites comparison with that of some great city in the United States or South America.

Starting from St George's Hospital we pass the extensions to the Hospital, and then the site of the Alexandra Hotel, which was the first of any importance to be erected in this part of the metropolis. It was erected in 1863 and covered a site previously occupied by about six houses in St George's Place. It contained 150 rooms and was so named in honour of wedding of King Edward VII when Prince of Wales and Princess Alexandra. The hotel was struck by a bomb in April 1941 and the building was razed to the ground. Agriculture House, the headquarters of the National Farmers' Union and kindred organisations has been erected on the site. Here the houses stand back from the road and have deep basement areas in front of them. Wilton Place, the first turning on our left, leads to Wilton Crescent and St Paul's Church, a handsome Gothic edifice with a Perpendicular tower, erected at a cost of £13,000. The first stone was laid on 4 November 1840, and the church was consecrated on 1 May 1843. The site upon which it stands was originally an exercising ground belonging to the foot barracks, and was given by the Duke of Westminster, who also contributed £500 towards the cost of the building. The above reference to the 'foot barracks' explains Barrack Yard, a narrow passage off Knightsbridge leading to the back of St Paul's Church. At the end is the picturesque and popular tavern 'The Grenadier', which has a sentry-box outside (securely padlocked against souvenir-hunters).

Wilton Place, built in 1872, occupies the site of a cow-yard, into which there was a narrow entrance from the main road, and Wilton Crescent was commenced in 1826 by Mr Seth Smith. In Motcomb Street is 'The Pantechnicon', a massive building adorned with ten great Greek Doric columns, the furniture warehouse of Seth-Smith Bros., dating from 1830. Inside the doorway a pair of stuffed lions are posted; nothing less than lions could guard such a building. Until 1841 a house stood at the west corner of Wilton Place, which had to be removed in order to provide a wider entrance to that thoroughfare from Knightsbridge. Here a Mrs Dowell carried on business for many years as a tobacconist. This good lady conceived a great fancy for the Duke of Wellington, and was continually figuring out some fresh plan whereby to express her regard for him. She used to send him patties, cakes, and other similar delicacies, and as it became useless to attempt to defeat the old woman's perseverance, everything was taken in. To such an extent did she develop this mania that she regularly laid a place for him at her dinner table, never abandoning the hope that one day the Duke of Wellington might actually call and honour her with a visit.

Between Wilton Place and William Street, opposite Albert Gate, the roadway formerly narrowed into a bottleneck, and in 1902 the London County Council carried out a considerable widening by setting back the building line to seventy feet. This, however, has proved inadequate, as this part of the main road is still too narrow for the requirements of its greatly increased traffic. The terrace of shops and flats extending from Wilton Place to William Street has superseded the former St George's Place, and was erected in 1903-04. The buildings are five storeys high, and faced with red brick and stone, but the style of architecture gives them a heavy and old-fashioned appearance. Mr Liston, one of England's most famous comedians, resided in St George's Place from 1829 until his death in 1846.

The large block of shops and flats on the opposite side of the road, known as Parkside, is nine storeys high, and was built in 1906. It replaced a long row of old-fashioned shops and houses erected about 1790, extending from opposite Wilton Place to the French Embassy. On a portion of this site stood Holy Trinity Chapel, anciently attached to the Abbey of Westminster. It was rebuilt in 1860, and afforded accommodation for 650 people. It was sixty-five feet high, and enjoyed the unusual distinction of having public-houses on both sides as neighbours. On that account it was jocularly nicknamed Heaven between two hells; both these taverns were owned by the Ecclesiastical Commissioners. That on the west side, called the White Hart, was demolished in 1899, together with two other houses, to make room for the extension of the French Embassy. The other one, known as the Queen's Head, together with the chapel itself, was pulled down in 1905.

The tall mansion at the east corner of Albert Gate is the French Embassy, the Ambassador living at Kensington Palace Gardens; it was built by Mr Cubitt and sold to Mr George Hudson, the railway king, for £15,000. That on the opposite corner was also built by Mr Cubitt, for Captain Leyland, as well as the adjoining house now occupied by the Westminster Bank. When first erected these two monster buildings became the target of London wits, who nicknamed them Gibraltar and Malta, because they were so large that they could not be taken. They are built on Crown land purchased in 1843 from the Dean and Chapter of Westminster in order to open up this new entrance to Hyde Park, and a part of which was leased for ninety-nine years to Mr Cubitt.

Albert Gate occupies an arched surface over the bed of the Westbourne, which was previously open at this spot and crossed by two bridges, one just inside the park erected about 1734, and the other spanning the main high road. The Westbourne stream, long since converted into a sewer, was occasionally a source of annoyance to the inhabitants of Knightsbridge, and in 1768 overflowed its banks, causing great damage to some of the neighbouring houses, Again in January 1809 it overflowed to such an extent it covered the neighbouring fields, giving them the appearance of a lake. The water was so deep that for several days passengers were rowed from Chelsea to Westminster by Thames boatmen. In 1820 there was still neither draper's nor butcher's shop between Hyde Park Corner and Sloane Street, and only one in the whole locality where a newspaper could be bought. The only regular conveyance to London was by stagecoach, the roads were dimly lighted by oil, and modern paving was only to be seen along the south side of the main road. On the site of Albert Gate stood the Cannon Brewery, a large ugly brick building, and here also at an earlier period stood a row of mean dwellings with open cellars and a filthy court at the western end. These were pulled down in 1804 to make way for the new brewery, which was in turn demolished in 1841. After that this ground remained unoccupied for ten years, until the erection of the two large mansions at the corner of Albert Gate in 1852. From an architectural standpoint they were not considered imposing, but they were then the tallest buildings in London, towering like two bullies high above all their neighbours. To-day 'Gibraltar' and 'Malta' are considerably exceeded in height by the adjoining Hyde Park Hotel.

On Friday, 12 May 1854, Queen Victoria attended a Bal Costumé given by the French Ambassador, Count Walewski, at the Embassy in Albert Gate. The circumstance of a British Sovereign paying a friendly visit to the Minister of another Power was at that time so unusual as to excite a more than ordinary degree of public interest. It indicated a new *entente cordiale,* and the mutual resolution of the two great nations of Great Britain and France to stand by one another in their struggle with Russia in the Crimean War, which resulted in the victory of the allies and the Peace of Paris in 1856.

The immense and imposing Hyde Park Hotel erected by the Liberator Building Company is another of the Jabez Balfour palaces. Completed in 1890, it was originally designed as a block of flats and was named Hyde Park Court, but it was converted into an hotel in 1900. It is ten storeys high, faced with red brick and stone, and capped by several turrets forming a prominent landmark when viewed from Hyde Park. The row of Georgian houses which stood back in long gardens on the west side of the Hyde Park Hotel long survived the great changes which took place in this neighbourhood in later years, but were quite out of harmony with their changed surroundings. This valuable site was sold in 1935 for the princely sum of £500,000 but it seems that the purchaser, Mr Ernest Leopold Payton, then managing director of the Austin Motor Company Limited, who died in February 1946, was unaware that, being Crown property, its development was subject to certain restrictions which did not allow the erection of commercial showrooms. For that reason this valuable site covering one and a half acres remained derelict for seven years with the upper storeys of the houses defaced with unsightly advertisement boards. The houses were finally pulled down in December 1942 and on this site an enormous block of offices called Bowater House has been built. One side is occupied by the Bowater organisation and the other by miscellaneous firms. Between and underneath them a new thoroughfare into Hyde Park, called Edinburgh Gate, has been made. On the park side of the building stands a bronze group which was the last work of Sir Jacob Epstein. It was commissioned by Land Securities Investment Trust to be a decorative feature on this side of Bowater House and was presented by them to the Ministry of Works for erection in the Royal Park.

William Street, opposite Albert Gate, leading to Lowndes Square, was built about 1830. Until 1930 it consisted entirely of private houses, but those on the east side have now been converted iinto shops. Occupying the site between William Street and Seville Street is the ornate drapery establishment of Messrs Woolland Brothers Limited, a six-storey building faced with Portland stone. It stands on the site of an old mansion called Spring Gardens. The garden itself is mentioned by Pepys as World's End, a drinking-house near the park, and it formed the grounds of an old mansion on the north side of Lowndes Square which was only pulled down in 1828. This building, it is understood, will be demolished and replaced by a tower block comprising an hotel and shops.

Harvey Nichols & Company occupy the block of buildings extending from Seville Street to Sloane Street. It is six storeys high and faced with red brick. A handsome new wing facing Sloane Street was added to this establishment in 1923. These two rows of shops between William Street and Sloane Street were formerly known as Lowndes Terrace, and superseded a row of old-fashioned houses two storeys high, with pleasant gardens in the front and rear, giving the roadway quite a rural appearance. These were pulled down in 1823.

Lowndes Square was commenced in 1836-37 by Mr Cubitt, who procured a lease of this ground from Mr William Lowndes, J.P., but the square was not completed until 1849. The Lowndeses were a well-known Buckinghamshire family from Chesham, where they owned large estates. Well over a century ago the Mr Lowndes of that day was asked by a neighbouring landowner who greatly coveted a portion of his estate in Buckinghamshire if he would give it him in exchange for an equal portion of land in what was then the village of Knightsbridge. The request was granted, and upon the land thus acquired now stands some of the finest house property in London. Mr Lowndes thus became possessed of an estate yielding at the time of his death a revenue of nearly £60,000 a year.

Both the east and west sides are now partly lined with new blocks of flats, seven storeys high, of uniform design and faced with yellow brick with stone dressing. The largest of these is situated at the northwest corner of the square between Harriet Street and Seville Street and was erected in 1934. Two new blocks on the east side sandwiched between some of the older town houses give one a fair idea of how Lowndes Square will eventually look when it has been entirely rebuilt.

At the corner of Lowndes Street and Cadogan Place is a distinctive new block of flats with a semicircular façade. This is ten storeys high and faced with stone and white brick and its corners are so rounded off that the maximum light reaches the main rooms. Several houses in this immediate locality, notably in West Halkin Street and in the south end of Sloane Street, were destroyed in in the air raids of 1940.

At the junction of Knightsbridge and Brompton Road stood, until 1933, an equestrian statue of Field-Marshal Lord Strathnairn, designed by Onslow Ford and erected in 1895. It was cast from guns taken in the Indian Mutiny. It has now been removed. Here also the one-way-traffic system has been introduced, and close to this spot the boundaries of the City of Westminster, Kensington, and Chelsea converge and the northern portion of Chelsea, which includes the whole of Sloane Street, forms a narrow wedge between the City of Westminster and the Royal Borough of Kensington.

The triangular site between Knightsbridge, Brompton Road, and Knightsbridge Green is occupied by an immense block of shops and flats, eight storeys high, called Park Mansion, erected between 1900 and 1902. A very ragged collection of old houses and shops previously stood on this site, which up to that time possessed no great value. A feature of this great building is the arcade of shops connecting Knightsbridge with Brompton Road.

Facing Knightsbridge Green was Tattersall's, the great sporting rendezvous and auction-mart for horses, erected in 1864, and with the yards behind it occupying nearly two acres of ground. The front consisted of a central gateway and two side entrances, and two wings built of yellow brick with Portland-stone dressings. The original establishment at Hyde Park Corner stood on the site of the grounds of the old Lanesborough House at the back of St George's Hospital. Tattersall's alas, is no more. Large blocks of offices now occupy this historic site. However, a new tavern, called 'Tattersall's' is there to remind horse-lovers of 'Tatt's'.

Knightsbridge Green, a triangular strip of ground at the back of Park Mansions, facing Brompton Road, is said to have been one of the plaque pits used to bury the dead during the great epidemic of 1665. Adjoining Park Mansion, is the Normandie Hotel, situated on the west side of Knightsbridge Greeen. It was erected in 1912 and displaced a number of poor shops and houses which had previously stood on this site.

Continuing along Knightsbridge, we next come to Trevor Street and then Trevor Place at the corner of which is a large building now used as a depot by Daimler Motors Limited. It was originally the celebrated Princes Skating Rink, which was much frequented by fashionable society before the first World War, but is now defunct. At the corner of Trevor Street, on the site of the 'Trevor Arms', is Mercury House, a new twelve-storey office building.

Trevor Place and Trevor Street lead to Trevor Square, so named from Sir John Trevor, who had a house on that site. It was built about 1818, and is a relic of the vanished Knightsbridge of a century ago. Trevor Square should prove a favourite spot for the erection of modern flats when there comes a further demand for them in this part of London. Near Trevor Square stood the famous oilcloth factory of Mr Baber, said to have been the earliest ever established. It was erected in 1754 by Nathan Smith, but was destroyed by fire in 1794. It was rebuilt the following year, and again in 1824, when it presented a remarkable appearance owing to its great height. It contained a clock over which was placed a figure of Time cut in stone. The site of this factory is now occupied by a block of flats called Albert Mansions.

On the opposite side of the road, next to the Knightsbridge Barracks, is another extensive colony of flats called Wellington Court, extending to Hyde Park, and adjoining which is a court and gateway leading into the park opposite the Serpentine. The recent Household Cavalry Barracks were completed and first occupied in May 1880 by the Royal Horse Guards, removed from the Albany Street barracks. They were built of red brick and stone, forming an irregular oblong, with the officer's quarters overlooking the old Exhibition Ground in Hyde Park. At the time these barracks were considered very up to date and well appointed. They were completely demolished in 1966 and new barracks, to the design of Sir Basil Spence, are to be erected on the site.

Opposite the Knightsbridge barracks is Rutland Gate, consisting of a terrace of houses commenced in 1838 and completed in 1856. Rutland House, a large red-brick mansion, was pulled down in 1833 and the grounds sold for building, but the large detached house which formerly stood on the east side of Rutland Gate, built by John Sheepshanks, a distinguished patron of British art, was not pulled down until 1901. A large block of flats, called Rutland Court, now stands on the site of the house and its grounds, overlooking Hyde Park. To the south of Rutland Gardens is Montpelier Square, erected in 1837 between Knightsbridge and Brompton Road.

Nearly opposite the western end of Rutland Gate, built in the roadway, formerly stood an old inn of very bad repute called the Half Way House. An unusual array of stabling, troughs, pigsties, etc., was built along the roadway in a very unsightly manner. Being in a lonely situation, it was at one time a resort of highwaymen and footpads. When this house was purchased by the Government in 1846 at a cost of £3,500 and pulled down, a secret staircase was found built in the wall leading from a small chamber in the western part of the house to the stables. Many a villain was reputed to have escaped by this passage when pursued by police officers. On 2 April 1740 the Bristol Mail was robbed in this immediate vicinity by a man on foot, who took the Bath and Bristol bags and, mounting the post-boy's horse, rode off towards London. On 30 November 1774 two men named Lane and Trotman were executed at Tyburn for robbing the Knights-bridge coach. The purchase money paid for the Half Way House included a sum of £470 15s. 10d. paid to the Dean and Chapter of Westminster for their interest in the premises.

West of Rutland Gate is Prince's Gate, so named after the Prince of Wales, afterwards King Edward VII, who opened it in 1848. It is said to stand on the highest plot of ground between Hyde Park Corner and Windsor Castle. The eastern terrace of the houses opposite, which overlook the park and back on to Ennismore Gardens, was completed in 1851, and the western block, which extends to Exhibition Road, in 1855. All the houses of the eastern terrace but one have been pulled down, including the former Ethiopian Legation, and on this site a new block of luxury flats seven storeys high was erected in 1938. This is faced with yellow brick with stone dressings but was interrupted in the centre by one large house which remained obstinately between the two sections. Between these two terraces was Alford House, an admirable mansion of red brick with high roofs and terracotta ornaments, built by Lady Marion Alford, which has now been pulled down. Listowel House, built about 1770, which stood on the adjoining site, was a pleasant mansion with a conservatory and was also known as Kingston House. It stood in private grounds behind a high brick wall and was at one time the residence of Elizabeth Chudleigh, Duchess of Kingston, who was tried for bigamy at Westminster Hall. From 1842 until its demolition in 1937 it was owned by the Listowel family. When first built, it stood alone in the fields with only Rutland House and the notorious Half Way House as its neighbours. On this site behind a private drive fronting Kensington Road now stands Kingston House, an eight-storey block of luxury flats faced with red brick completed in 1938.

To the south of Kingston House is Ennismore Gardens, built by a Mr Elger on land belonging to the Earl of Listowel, from whose second title the Gardens are named. They were commenced in 1848 and completed in 1855. A stone marking the 'Boundary of Mr Elger's freehold land' is set in the wall of the coachhouse next to the 'Ennismore Arms'. This, in its earlier days, was a 'coach-men's pub' and stands at the corner of Ennismore Mews. It was bombed in 1940 and has been rebuilt in modern style. All Saints Church, at the upper end of the gardens, is now the Russian Orthodox Patriarchal Church of the Assumption. Ennismore Gardens and Prince's Gate are ornate examples of the Victorian style of house-building in fashion among people of means during the 'forties and 'fifties of the last century. There have been some changes here, with the appearance of a 12-storey block of flats. Three other adjacent buildings look like flats, but are described by the agents as 'houses'. The district between Knightsbridge and Brompton Road was mostly built between 1820 and 1850 on land which had previously been occupied by nursery gardens, and was originally termed Bromp-ton New Town. It had been a rustic hamlet to which the Londoner and his spouse used to resort for an afternoon's enjoyment. Here the Gothic church of Holy Trinity to the south of Ennismore Gardens was opened on 6 June 1829, the foundation-stone having been laid in October 1826.

Close to Holy Trinity Church is the Brompton Oratory, a fine specimen of Italian Renaissance built from the designs of Mr H. Gribble, and opened by Cardinal Manning in 1884, though the façade and dome were not added until 1897. The nave is the widest in England, with the exception of those of West-minster Cathedral and York Minster. The organ contains upwards of four thousand pipes. In the Oratory grounds, overlooking Brompton Road, is a statue of Cardinal Newman, who seceded to the Roman Catholic Church in 1845, and introduced the Institute of the Oratory to England. The present building replaced the temporary church opened on 22 March 1854, which was built in the simplest manner and could accommodate 1,200 persons.

To the east of the Oratory is Brompton Square, once the residence of famous actors and composers, including Mr John Baldwin Buckstone, Mr Edward Fitzwilliam, Mr George Colman, and Mr William Farren, who took his farewell at the Haymarket Theatre in 1855. These are forgotten names today: but two houses display the blue L.C.C. plaque—one recording the residence of Francis Place, Political Reformer, and at No 6, Stéphane Mallarmé, poet, *stayed* in 1863. The houses, which belong to the Georgian period, are of yellow brick, and are typical specimens of the Bloomsbury style.

Nearly opposite the Oratory on the south side of Brompton Road, are two red-brick blocks of buildings erected in 1886. These have been erected on the site of two rows of small uniform brick houses called Michael's Place, built in 1786, but which at first proved a failure owing to their being so far out of town. Michael's Place was railed off from the main Brompton Road and consisted of forty-four houses. It was a building speculation of Michael Novosielski, who died at Ramsgate in 1795. Number 13 was occupied by his widow for some years after his death. Michael's Grove, which has been renamed Egerton Terrace, led to Brompton Grange, which was pulled down in 1843 and its spacious grounds covered by a crescent of new buildings. The Grange was constructed by Novo-sielski for his own residence. The whole of this property, now consisting of high-class residences, was rebuilt in the 'eighties of last century, and Brompton Crescent has been renamed Egerton Crescent. Hidden behind the magnificence of Egerton Crescent is Crescent Place, an attractive little group of eight two-storey houses with small front gardens, and in the fork between the south end of Brompton Road (which is really the beginning of Fulham Road) and Egerton Crescent is the large and high-walled Mortimer House, Tudor-style in red brick with patterns in blue brick and 'Hampton Court' chimneys.

Brompton Road a century ago was a quiet suburban road with private houses on both sides, forming a part of the main thoroughfare from London to Fulham. The north side of Brompton Road was then called Brompton Row and consisted of fifty-five respectable-looking houses of more or less uniform appearance. Some of these are still standing, but from Knightsbridge Green to Trevor House, No 100, Brompton Road, all are new buildings except Princes Court, which dates from 1934. This is a gigantic block of shops and flats which stands on the corner of Lancelot Place opposite Harrod's stores. It is a handsome building of ten storeys faced with red brick with stone dressings. The central section above the ground-floor shops stands back in a bay or open court giving most of the flats a clear view of Brompton Road.

The south side of the road formerly went under the name of Brompton Grove and Queen's Row. The former extended from Hans Road, then called Queen Street, as far as Yeoman's Row. Various good-class residences standing back in their own front gardens then lined the Grove, including one called Grove House, which was the residence of Sir John Macpherson, Bart, a member of the Supreme Council of Bengal, and afterwards of Mr Wilberforce, who resided here in 1823. The site of this house, which was pulled down in 1846, now forms the entrance to Ovington Square. Queen's Row, erected about 1770, comprised the row of houses between Sloane Street and Hooper's Court and beyond as far as Hans Crescent, then called New Street, and was named after Queen Charlotte. These houses were built on a raised pavement with steps in front, since abolished, very much after the style of those still remaining on the opposite side of Brompton Road.

About 1870 a great change came over this neighbourhood; Brompton Road began to lose its suburban appearance, and shops, mostly of a humble character, were built over the front gardens of the houses on the south side. Brompton Road became an abode of fast-living people, and ladies objected to walking down there by themselves. But it was too near Hyde Park and the West End to remain under a cloud for any length of time, and with the rebuilding of the adjoining Cadogan Estate, Brompton Road was changed into highly respectable shopping thoroughfares.

Nothing now remains of the original buildings which lined the south side of Brompton Road. Some of the houses between Sloane Street and Hooper's Court were rebuilt between 1897 and 1900, but practically the whole of the long row of new buildings, half a mile in length, extending from Lloyd's Place past Hans Crescent to Sloane Street and thence along Knightsbridge as far as Wilton Place, was rebuilt between 1901 and 1905. During those years so much reconstruction was taking place that Brompton Road presented a scene of devastation equalled only by that of Regent Street between 1923 and 1925.

The premises of Messrs Harrods Limited cover the island site enclosed by Brompton Road, Hans Crescent, Basil Street, and Hans Road. This immense building, which has a frontage of about an eighth of a mile to Brompton Road, is six storeys high, faced with terracotta, and crowned in the centre by a great dome. The four upper storeys consisted originally of a large colony of luxury flats called Hans Mansions but these were abolished many years ago and the additional floor space merged into the stores. Escalators up and down to all floors have since been erected. Recently the extensive frontage to Basil Street has been reconstructed on the most modern lines.

Harrod's stores, now possibly the most fashionable shopping resort in the kingdom, started in a small way, and when Mr Harrod opened his first small grocer's shop here in 1848 lit by paraffin lights, Brompton Road was a poor street lined with costers' stalls on Saturday nights. Two other shops were added at a later date, and within a few years the whole of the shops between Hans Crescent and Queen's Gardens had been absorbed into the stores. Later the business was converted into a limited company and greatly extended. The new buildings in Basil Street were erected about 1895, and in 1902, when the Brompton Road side was rebuilt, the building line of Brompton Road at the corner of Hans Crescent was set back some distance. Queen's Gardens, which was only a cul-de-sac, was then demolished in order to provide an unbroken frontage to Brompton Road between Hans Crescent and Hans Road. In 1948 Harrod's stores celebrated the centenary of their foundation and a replica of the original small shop was put on exhibition on the ground floor of the present building.

In August 1944 all the windows of Harrod's stores fronting the Brompton Road were smashed by a flying-bomb which also demolished a newly-erected public-house and several adjoining buildings on the opposite side of the road. Between Princes Court and Knightsbridge Green the north side of Brompton Road narrowed into a bottleneck. This has now been removed and a new line of shops built. The road has been widened to ninety feet including the footpaths, each of which is fifteen feet wide. Brompton Road carries a heavy volume of traffic which has increased since the Cromwell Road exit from town was completed.

Between Hans Crescent and Sloane Street formerly stood the large drapery store of Messrs Gooch Limited, which had an entrance to Knightsbridge Underground Railway Station at the corner of Hans Crescent. During the second World War this store closed down and its buildings were taken over by the Government. It has since been derequisitioned and converted into a block of shops and offices. In 1935 a new Underground station was opened at Knightsbridge with entrances at Sloane Street and Hans Crescent. At the corner of Hooper's Court is the Basil Street Hotel, and a few doors nearer Sloane Street a handsome arcade of shops connecting Brompton Road with Basil Street.

Strolling down fashionable Sloane Street or through the opulent Hans Crescent and Basil Street, with their elegant shops and blocks of flats, few people would imagine that little more than seventy years ago this neighbourhood was a collection of slums and mean streets. Hans Crescent went under the two names of New Street and Exeter Street, and Basil Street was then called North Street. In those days Sloane Street was a respectable thoroughfare and nothing more, whereas today it almost rivals Bond Street as a fashionable centre of shopping. A notable establishment in this immediate locality is the Hans Crescent Mansions, which, together with the Cadogan Rooms, occupies a choice position in Hans Crescent, opposite Harrod's stores, between Sloane Street and Brompton Road.

Little rebuilding has so far taken place on the north side of Brompton Road, but on account of their proximity to Hyde Park such places as Montpelier Square, Trevor Street, Raphael Street, and Trevor Square should in time afford great possibilities for the erection of high-class residences or blocks of flats.

Thirty years ago Beauchamp Place, on the south side of Brompton Road, consisted of dingy houses of a most unsightly appearance, but on account of the rise in the value of property on this immediate neighbourhood since the first World War, nearly all of these houses have been fitted with shop-fronts. Four or five small steps lead up to each doorway and add to the attraction of these little shops, which are now occupied by antique-dealers, artists, and high-class dressmaking establishments, so that today Beauchamp Place can claim to rank as a good-class thoroughfare. Together with Pont Street it forms the most direct route between South Kensington and Victoria Station. Pont Street is a handsome thoroughfare of modern redbrick mansions constructed by the owners of the Cadogan and Hans Place Estate and opened to traffic in March 1878. It takes its name from a bridge over the Westbourne stream. At the west end of Pont Street stood until 1950 the ruins of the Scottish church of St Columba, a modern building crowned by a square tower. This church was destroyed in the air raids of 1940 but has now been rebuilt. The foundation-stone of the new church, which also includes a public hall, was laid on 4 July 1950 by the Queen Mother. Hans Place, on the north side of Pont Street, contains a pleasant garden surrounded by high-class residences, as does Cadogan Square to the south of Pont Street, constructed in 1880 and one of the most attractive London squares.

Pont Street, Cadogan Square, and the neighbouring streets were erected on the site of a large private mansion called the Pavilion, standing in twenty-one acres of private grounds. In the year 1777 Mr Holland took a lease of a hundred acres of land called Blacklands from Lord Charles Cadogan. This area is now covered by Sloane Street, Cadogan Place, Ellis Street, Hans Place, Sloane Square, Sloane Gardens, and several minor thoroughfares. The buildings were begun at the commencement of the American War of Independence, owing to which their progress was much impeded. In 1787 an Act of Parliament was obtained for forming and keeping in repair the streets and public highways within the district of Hans Town, as this new quarter was then called.

When Mr Holland took this lease from the Lord of the Manor he reserved for himself twenty-one acres of ground, upon which he erected an elegant house. This was the Pavilion, which was afterwards purchased from the executors of Mr Holland by Peter Denys, from whom the property afterwards passed to Lady Charlotte Denys. The Pavilion consisted of three sides of a quadrangle open to the north. The approach was from Hans Place through a handsome pair of iron gates leading up through an avenue of elm-trees to a portico supported by four Doric columns. Facing the south side of the house was an extensive lawn, on the west side of which was an ice-house surrounded by imitation ruins of an ancient priory, built of stone-work brought from the demolished residence of Cardinal Wolsey at Esher. The grounds were surrounded by lofty trees and shrubberies in such a fashion as to convey the impression that they were of greater extent than was actually the case. Adjoining the lawn was a fine sheet of water. To remind us of Henry Holland's mansion is the narrow Pavilion Road, less than 50 yards west of, and parallel with, the whole length of Sloane Street. It consists almost entirely of garages, some with mews-type flats above.

Most of the houses then lining the west side of Sloane Street have been replaced by modern buildings during the past sixty years, but many facing Cadogan Gardens are still standing between Pont Street and Sloane Square. Here new blocks of flats such as Grosvenor Court, Sloane House, Cadogan House, and Dorchester Court, have been erected of late years, but most of the new buildings in Sloane Street are situated at the northern end, including a bloc of shops and flats nine storeys high called Knightsbridge Court. Sloane Street, Hans Place, and Sloane Square are named after the Lord of the Manor, Sir Hans Sloane. At the corner of Pont Street, overlooking the private gardens opposite, is the Cadogan Hotel. Number 50 Sloane Street between Hans Crescent and Pont Street is another tall block of shops and flats erected in 1935. On the east side of Sloane Street opposite Knightsbridge Court is Richmond Court, a towering block of shops and flats erected in 1937-38. It is eight storeys high and is faced with yellow brick and over the shops in Sloane Street is an awning which provides a covered walk in bad weather. On this site covering Numbers 187-201 Sloane Street previously stood a long row of Georgian houses with high-class shops on the ground floor. Three of these that survived until recently at the corner of Harriet Street have been replaced by a shiny new building. Shelton House on the same side of Sloane Street and Hugo House are other notable buildings erected here of late years.

Cadogan Gardens, extending for the greater part of the east side of Sloane Street, is more than a quarter of a mile long, and is perhaps the largest private enclosure in London. It is sufficiently large to be termed a small park, and contains delightful walks and a large number of tennis courts. It is overlooked on the east side by Cadogan Place, a long row of five-storeyed mansions with portico balconies, and no more choice place of residence could well be desired by the wealthy Londoner. At the north end of the gardens, on the corner of Sloane Street and Cadogan Place, a new eighteen-storey hotel, the Carlton Tower, was opened by Mr Maudling, President of the Board of Trade, on 4 January 1961. The building, which rises to a height of 200 feet and has 328 rooms, was completed in eighteen months – six months ahead of schedule. The Carlton Tower is a venture of the Hotel Corporation of America. The north garden of Cadogan Place, from the Carlton Tower to Pont Street, was closed for a few months in 1966 during the construction of a two-floor underground car park with accommodation for about 350 cars.

The fine quarter of Belgravia situated between Sloane Street, Hyde Park Corner, and Grosvenor Place was known until 1824 as the Five Fields. A short distance to the east of Sloane Square the Westbourne rivulet then flowed in a narrow stream to the Thames. In 1825 Mr Thomas Cubitt, the builder, began the development of the Five Fields, where previously no one would build because of the clayey swamp, which retained much water. The Fields were then the terror of foot-passengers proceeding from London to Chelsea after nightfall, and here also duellists formerly met to decide their quarrels.

On the site of what is now Cliveden Place, leading to Eaton Square, there used to be a bridge fording the Westbourne which was about fourteen or sixteen feet wide with a wall on both sides to prevent passengers from falling into the narrow rivulet. It was continued by the King's Private Road, now forming a part of King's Road, Chelsea, and leading across the Five Fields to Buckingham Palace. In Cary's map of London dated 1810, this bridge figures under the name of Bloody Bridge, doubtless on account of the robbers and thieves who then infested the Five Fields. Adjoining this bridge was an inn called the Coach and Horses. Here Mr Crouch, cook to the Earl of Harrington, was attacked on the night of 17 September 1753 by two highwaymen. Upon his showing resistance, they fired two pistols at him, after which he was beaten to death. Cliveden Place between Sloane Square and Eaton Square was struck by a bomb in an air raid of 1944 which made a huge cavity in the centre of the road and demolished several houses on the north side.

Finding that the subsoil consisted of gravel topped by clay to an inconsiderable depth, Mr Cubitt removed the clay and manufactured bricks from it. He then made up the ground with soil excavated in the construction of the St Katherine Docks, which was brought up the Thames on barges and dumped at Millbank. By building upon the substratum of gravel he tranformed this spot from the most unhealthy into one of the most salubrious in the metropolis, to the immense advantage of the ground landlord and to London as a whole. This plan adopted by Mr Cubitt has proved one of the most perfect adaptations of the means to an end to be found in the records of the building trade. The Act of Parliament enabling the Five Fields to be drained and the level raised was obtained by the Duke of Westminster in 1826.

The rise of Belgravia began in 1827-28 with the construction by Mr Thomas Cubitt of Belgrave Square from the designs of George Basevi. It covers an area of ten acres and is 740 yards in circuit. Being on a low level, the ground floors of the houses in Westbourne Terrace on the opposite side of Hyde Park, which are seventy feet above the Thames at highwater mark, are at the same height as the attics of those in Belgrave and Eaton Squares. The houses of Belgrave Square are four storeys high, faced with stucco, and greatly superior to those erected in the previous century. In the late 19th century Belgrave Square was described as 'London's most aristocratic quarter, and occupied by the heads of the highest nobility, and many foreigners of distinction'. In the changed conditions of today the aristocratic residents are somewhat reduced, but there is a possible increase in the number of distinguished foreigners, for the diplomatic representatives of several foreign countries are located in Belgrave Square.

Many of the Belgravia streets are named after the Grosvenor family and their possessions. Belgravia itself derives its name from the village of Belgrave in Leicestershire, where the Grosvenor family have one of their estates. Eccleston Street gets its name from a place in Cheshire of that name, Halkin Street takes its name from Halkin Castle, Flintshire, and Eaton Square is named after Eaton Hall, in Cheshire, the principal seat of the Duke of Westminster.

The junction of Hobart Place with Grosvenor Place and Gardens is a notorious spot in history as having been the scene of a double tragedy which occurred in June 1823, when a young man murdered his father and then committed suicide. At that time it was still the custom to bury a suicide at crossroads within the parish of the death, with a stake driven through the body. On this occasion the site selected for the interment was at the junction of Hobart Place with Grosvenor Place and Gardens, exactly opposite the grounds of Buckingham Palace. This incident caused so much annoyance to King George IV, who resented its occurring so close to the entrance of his intended new palace, that the custom of burying suicides at crossroads was abolished by Act of Parliament on 8 July 1823. Grosvenor Place was built in 1767, during the Grenville administration, and it was because of of Grenville's refusal to pay the £20,000 asked for the site that George III was unable to prevent this row of houses from being built to overlook his palace grounds. Before that time the Lock Hospital, which was pulled down in 1846, stood alone on that spot. The streets running from Grosvenor Place before the construction of Belgravia were terminated by high mudbanks which formed a boundary over which no traveller ever cared to venture. One of the houses at the north end of Grosvenor Place, which was rebuilt in 1868, was occupied by the Duke of Northumberland after the sale of his house in the Strand.

Lord Grosvenor gave £30,000 for the Five Fields, and Lord Cowper, who also wished to buy them, sent his agent for that purpose, but he came back empty-handed. Upon being reprimanded by his lordship, the agent said, 'Really, my lord, I could not find it in my heart to give £200 more than they were worth.' Afterwards Mr Cubitt offered a ground rent of £60,000. Lowndes Square and Chesham Place mark the one field which belonged to the Lowndeses of Chesham.

A few words relating to Mr Thomas Cubitt, who, next to Nash, has the best claim to be regarded as the Napoleon or the Baron Haussmann amongst London town-planners, may here prove of interest to our readers. In his nineteenth year

Mr Thomas Cubitt was working as a journeyman carpenter. He then made a voyage to India and back as captain's joiner, and on his return to London, with his savings commenced business in the metropolis as a carpenter. In about six years he erected large workshops upon a slice of ground in Gray's Inn Road. About 1824 he contracted with the Duke of Bedford for the ground upon which Tavistock Square and Gordon Square, with Woburn Place and the adjoining streets, now stand. In the same year he contracted with the Duke of Westminster and Mr Lowndes to cover large portions of the Five Fields and adjacent ground, this resulting in Belgrave Square, Lowndes Square, Chesham Place, Eaton Place, Eaton Square, and other ranges of houses. He subsequently contracted to cover the vast open district lying between Eaton Square and the Thames, now called Pimlico or South Belgravia.

His works, which were established at Thames Bank, were destroyed by a fire in which Mr Cubitt lost £30,000. When he was informed of the calamity his reply was. 'Tell the men they shall be at work again within a week and I will subscribe £600 towards buying them new tools.' Mr Cubitt, who died in 1856, had two brothers, Alderman Cubitt, twice Lord Mayor, and Lewis Cubitt, who was the architect of the Great Northern Railway terminus.

Eaton Square is of oblong shape and covers an area of fifteen acres, extending from Hobart Place to Cliveden Place. Being a good quarter of a mile in length, with the wide main thoroughfare from Grosvenor Place to Sloane Square running through the centre, Eaton Square, like Euston Square, is far more suggestive of a park-like boulevard than of an ordinary London square. It is crossed from north to south by Belgrave Place and Lyall Street, thus dividing the so-called square into six sections, which might more appropriately be termed gardens. The ground floors of the houses on the north side of Eaton Square are completely covered by heavy porticoed balconies, somewhat resembling those of Carlton House Terrace, overlooking the Mall. Facing the east side of the square is St Peter's Church, erected in 1826. Under the portico is a memorial stone: 'Here in this porch died Austin Thompson, Vicar, killed by enemy action on the night of 16th April 1941 whilst firewatching'.

During the second World War whole terraces of large town houses in Eaton Square were requisitioned by the Army and have now been vacated. Practically all the houses have now been repaired and redecorated, and the Square, now once more occupied by private tenants, has regained much of its pre-war glory.

Chester Square, to the south of Eaton Square, has an area of five acres and extends from Eccleston Street to Elizabeth Street. On the west side is St Michael's Church, erected in 1847 in the Gothic style and crowned by a tall spire. This church is associated with the weekly broadcast services by the late Canon W.H. Elliott.

Unlike Mayfair and Marylebone, Belgravia has largely retained its residential character, though new blocks of flats have invaded Lowndes Square and Chesham Place. Recent developments in this quarter of the metropolis have been mainly confined to Grosvenor Gardens and Buckingham Palace Road, where many new

buildings have been erected of late years. Turning east we now come to Buckingham Palace Road, rendered somewhat depressing by the quarter-mile wall of
Victoria Station.

At the west corner of Eccleston Street and Buckingham Palace Road is a large
garage erected in 1928 on the site of several Georgian houses, and at the corner
of Elizabeth Street on the site of an unimposing row of Georgian brown-brick
houses now stands the huge Victoria Coach Station. Completed in 1931, it
contains a glass roof so that the loading bays are protected from bad weather.
During the day, accommodation is provided for 140 coaches moving in and out,
forty of them under cover. Amongst other prominent features, the building
contains a tower, a large booking-hall, a buffet, a cafeteria, and a first-class
restaurant with a floor so laid that it can be used for dancing. On the opposite
side, just by Ebury bridge, is the interesting Airways Terminal with its coach-bays
and direct access to a special railway platform. The square tower of this building
with its large clock is a landmark of considerable prominence.

Provision has also been made in this district for the requirements of the working
classes. At the junction of Ebury Street and Pimlico Road two large blocks of
dwellings to accommodate two hundred families were opened in November
1870. A large party was present at the ceremony, including the Duke of Cambridge, the Earl of Shaftesbury, and Sir Sydney Waterlow. Other blocks of
workmen's dwellings, including Walden House, were erected on the north side
of Pimlico Road close to Buckingham Palace Road, and between 1930 and 1935
several fine blocks of flats were erected by the Westminster City Council between
Ebury Bridge Road and the Grosvenor Canal. In Pimlico Road is St Barnabas's
Church, with a tall spire, consecrated by the Bishop of London on 11 June 1850.
On the bombed site bounded by Ebury Street, Pimlico Road and Ebury Square
the Duke of Westminster has erected four seven-storey blocks of flats, known
as the Cundy Street Flats.

A short walk through Ebury Street will bring the traveller to Victoria Station,
a convenient spot to end our tour of this district.

Twenty-Third Walk

The Royal Borough of Kensington and its Neighbours

The Royal Borough of Kensington is to a certain extent overshadowed by the more central districts of London, but on account of its splendid streets, great shops, and noble public buildings, it excels in magnificence many of the leading capitals of Europe and America. Now joined with Chelsea, it takes in Sloane Street on the east and extends to the West London Extension Railway in the west, northward to the Harrow Road at Kensal Green and down to the Thames in the south. The new borough covers an area of 2,951 acres.

The name of Kensington appears to be of doubtful origin. The most probable derivation is from the Saxon *Kyning's-tun*, meaning King's Town.

Kensington, from which London could be reached on horseback in an hour, and which was reputed to be fairly healthy, began to increase in population towards the end of the reign of Queen Elizabeth I. Notwithstanding the prohibition placed upon building within ten miles of London in 1620, and the ordinance that every new house was to have four acres of ground, Kensington increased rapidly in favour and in population. During the outbreak of the Great Plague in 1665, people found it a very convenient place to which they might retire from London. By the reign of William III it had become the most fashionable of all the outlying suburbs of London, and many large houses such as Campden House, Noel House, Aubrey House, and Bullingham House were erected here.

This was partly due to the fact that King William III ennobled the town with his court and royal presence, thereby attracting notable people to Kensington. Writing in 1705 Bowack tells us that there was an abundance of shop-keepers and all sort of artificers in Kensington, which even then made it appear more like a part of London than a country village. He also states that with its dependencies it was about three times as large as Chelsea in number of houses, and that in summertime it was extremely well filled with lodgers, for the pleasure of the air, walks, gardens round it, to the great advantage of its inhabitants.

Several newer Kensingtons, not really Kensingtons at all, such as North Kensington, once called the Potteries, West Kensington, which forms a part of the borough of Hammersmith, and South Kensington, which is partly within the confines of the City of Westminster, have grown up around the old Court suburb.

Selecting Hyde Park Corner as a convenient starting-place for our tour of Kensington, our route is by way of Knightsbridge, past Sloane Street and the site of the Knightsbridge Barracks, and thence along the Kensington Gore, this part of which is now called Kensington Road, to the High Street. Already more than a century ago an unbroken line of buildings extended from Hyde Park Corner in the direction of Kensington as far as the Half Way House. Between that point and Kensington there was a certain amount of open ground, but there were large houses situated at frequent intervals along the main road, such as Listowel House, Gore House, Noel House, and Colby House, so that even then Kensington seemed to be virtually joined to London. In former times, owing to the unsettled and ill-protected nature of the country, these large suburban houses were surrounded by high and substantial walls.

After passing Prince's Gate we come to Lowther Lodge, at the west corner of Exhibition Road, formerly the residence of Mr Lowther and now the head-quarters of the Royal Geographical Society. The house, which has been enlarged, is a pleasing specimen of the architecture of the late Mr Norman Shaw.

A hundred yards farther west is the Royal Albert Hall, one of the largest halls in the world, the design of which was originally suggested by the Prince Consort and afterwards carried out by General Scott. The building resembles a gigantic ellipse roofed over by a glass dome, and is capable of holding about eight thousand persons. The foundation-stone was laid on 20 November 1868 by Queen Victoria, who also opened the building on 29 March 1871. It measures 200 feet in length, 160 feet in width, and 140 feet in height, and is lined with seats rising step-fashion in the manner of a Roman circus. The cost of the building, about £200,000, was defrayed by selling the boxes in the first tier, seating ten persons, for £1,000 each, and those in the second tier, seating five people, for £500 each.

The architectural merits of the various South Kensington buildings have been severely criticized, more especially the Albert Hall and the Albert Memorial. At the present time the exterior of the Albert Hall is looking very shabby and urgently in need of a cleaning.

Though frequently used for political demonstrations, boxing contests, and other public gatherings, the Albert Hall is still principally famous for musical performances on a large scale. The magnificent organ, built by Willis and after-wards reconstructed, has nearly nine thousand pipes, and the platform will accommodate 1,100 performers. The appearance of the Albert Hall is greatly enhanced by the adjacent Albert Hall Mansions, situated next to Lowther Lodge. Erected in 1881, these mansions afford the eye a measure for the vast size of the Albert Hall. West of the Albert Hall, in the modern idiom, is the recently erected eight-storey Royal College of Art.

Between the Albert Hall and Queen's Gate is Hyde Park Terrace, a row of large old-fashioned houses faced with stucco, which was erected many years before the development of the neighbouring Gore estate and then formed one of the principal features of the high road to Kensington. At the top of Queen's Gate, facing Kensington Gardens, is a statue of Field-Marshal Lord Robert Napier of Magdala, erected in 1869. Ignoring for the time being the district of

South Kensington, with its many public buildings, we next pass a row of stately mansions called Hyde Park Gate, among which No 28 was Sir Winston Churchill's London home, where he died on 24 January 1965, at the age of 90, and then come to Palace Gate, which forms the northern end of Gloucester Road. On the east corner is a handsome block of flats called Thorney Court, erected in 1907 on the site of a stone-fronted villa of the same name. The buildings, which are seven storeys high and faced with red brick, stand back in a private garden from the main Kensington Road. Adjoining Thorney Court is a large mansion which was formerly the residence of Sir John Everett Millais. At the junction of Gloucester Road with Palace Gate on the east side, is a quiet square called Kensington Gate, built about the year 1847. On the corner site once stood a handsome private mansion which until its demolition in 1937 was occupied by the Peruvian Legation. It has been replaced by a block of flats.

At one time a toll-gate stood across the main road where Thorney Court now stands, and behind the walls of Kensington Gardens there were cavalry barracks. Gloucester Road originally known as Hogmore Lane, derives its name from the Duchess of Gloucester, who built a villa here, in which she died in 1807. The Princess Sophia, her daughter, sold the villa to George Canning, and here his son, the future Governor-General of India, was born in 1812. At the eastern corner of Hogmore Lane, where now stands Thorney Court, was a public-house called the Campden Arms, and on the western corner stood Noel House, the residence of Mr George Aust.

Next to Palace Gate comes De Vere Gardens, built on the site of a livery stable and riding school which existed behind a row of small houses called Craven Place, which has long since disappeared. De Vere Gardens consists of terraces of large houses, some of which have been converted into private hotels. Prominent amongst these are the De Vere Hotel on the eastern side, at the corner of Kensington Road, and the Prince of Wales Hotel farther down on the other side of the road. Robert Browning lived at Number 29 De Vere Gardens from 1887 to 1889 and from there his body was taken for interment in Poets Corner, Westminster Abbey.

On the opposite side of Kensington Road, between Palace Gate and the High Street, a wonderful improvement was carried out in 1929 by setting back the railings of Kensington Gardens a considerable distance and removing the cab-rank to the middle of the roadway. Previously it had narrowed into a bottleneck at this point, which was both unsightly and inconvenient to the large flow of traffic to and from Kensington High Street.

Victoria Road, next to De Vere Gardens, forms the centre of a new quarter built between 1840 and 1851, and contains Christ Church, consecrated in 1851. Notice the charming Victoria Grove with its verandahs and Albert Mews with the Prince Consort's head on the keystone of the arch. Houses in Victoria Road and Douro Place were destroyed in the air raids of 1940 and in August 1944 a part of Prince of Wales Mansions fronting Kensington Road was also destroyed by a flying-bomb. This great building was one of several blocks of flats which were requisitioned to house the twenty-five thousand refugees evacuated from Gibraltar in 1940, who had been removed from this building only a few days before it was bombed. A large new hotel which was completed for the Festival of Britain has been built on the site. After passing Prince of Wales's Terrace, we next come to Kensington Court, a collection of artistic houses and flats mostly designed by Mr John Stevenson. The majority of them are faced with red brick or terracotta and have tall sloping roofs. In the centre is a square garden.

Until 1873 two picturesque old buildings, Colby House and old Kensington House, stood on a portion of this site. The seven acres of land occupied by the house and grounds were obtained by the demolition of old Kensington House and the mansion of Sir Thomas Colby, the miser, and of the adjoining group of small houses. To the south stood a rookery of slums consisting of Jennings Buildings, Russel Place, Tavern Yard, and New Court. It was an Irish colony and had been a nuisance to the parish for years previously. On this site Mr Albert Grant, a millionaire who gave Leicester Square garden to London, erected in 1873 a magnificent mansion called Kensington House, and arranged for the displaced tenants to be housed in some new industrial dwellings at Notting Hill. This mansion, which was said to have cost £250,000, was designed by Mr James Knowles and took four years to complete.

It was screened off from Kensington High Street by a massive chocolate and gold iron railing pierced by gates from which a carriage-drive led up to the main entrance. The high road was widened at this spot and the dreary wall which formerly stood on the opposite side of the road was replaced by open iron railings providing a view of Kensington Palace.

Kensington House, which was said to have been the largest private residence in London, contained upwards of a hundred apartments, some of them of the most magnificent proportions and exquisite decoration. Along the whole of the south or garden front ran a marble terrace 220 feet long, with three flights of steps. The grounds were beautifully laid out and banked up with gigantic trellis-work so as to prevent anybody overlooking from the adjacent houses. There was an Italian garden, an orangery, an aviary, a skating rink, a bowling alley, and an ornamental lake with two miniature islands.

But like many other noted millionaires, Mr Albert Grant eventually got into financial difficulties, and his magnificent new home was never occupied by him. After he became bankrupt the mansion was put up for sale, and though it cost its owner £250,000 to build, it was finally disposed of for the paltry sum of £10,461. It was demolished in 1883, only ten years later, and Kensington Court was erected in its place.

Kensington High Street, which we now enter, is one of the finest shopping centres in the metropolis. Seventy years ago it still retained the appearance of some large country town, but the rapid growth of London in this direction, together with extensive rebuilding and street widenings, has transformed the High Street into a second Oxford Street but with none of the latter's vulgarity. As the result of an extensive widening on the north side between St Mary Abbot's

Church and Kensington Gardens, carried out in 1902 by the London County Council, the picturesque shops which formerly stood here have been replaced by large modern buildings. Prominent amongst the vanished shops was that of Messrs Herbert & Jones, one of the oldest confectioners in London, who used to make gingerbread from a recipe given by Queen Caroline of Anspach. Another interesting house was the Civet Cat Tavern, which stood on the east corner of Church Street. Some years after being rebuilt it was converted into a branch of Barclay's Bank. The old sign of 'Ye Civet Cat' still hangs on the wall.

The huge Royal Palace Hotel, eight storeys high, situated at the corner of Kensington Gardens, together with the adjoining Empress Rooms, erected in 1890, stood on the site of the King's Arms Tavern, burnt down on 10 June 1857, and well known to readers of *Henry Esmond*. The hotel, Empress Rooms and adjoining Bodega Tavern, plus two double-fronted shops have now been demolished. On this site now stands the new £5,000,000 Royal Garden Hotel, the largest British hotel to be built in London since the war. From fourth floor below ground to the roof, 125 feet above ground level, there are 14 floors, 500 bedrooms and four restaurants. The hotel overlooks Kensington Gardens and Hyde Park on two sides and the management emphasise its unique position on the edge of 'Millionaire's Row'. Between Church Street and Kensington Gardens is a noble road of private mansions, called Kensington Palace Gardens. It is not available for commercial traffic. To make room for this road, which connects Kensington High Street with Notting Hill High Street, the old barracks at Kensington, together with the Grapes public house, were removed in January 1840. At that time it was called Queen's Road but to-day it is popularly known as 'Millionaires' Row'. Nearly all the mansions at the northern end which stand back in spacious gardens are in the Italian style of architecture with various façades of stone, stucco and grey brick. Those at the southern end, which go under the name of Palace Green, are more modern and faced with red brick with stone dressings. Many notable people, including foreign ambassadors and wealthy financiers and business magnates, have resided at Kensington Palace Gardens. Most of the houses were requisitioned by the Army during the second World War. Number 13 is now the Soviet Embassy while other embassies are in the same road; in fact the whole length of the Gardens now has a decidedly diplomatic flavour about it.

Young Street, on the south side, nearly opposite Kensington Church Street, was built by Mr Young, an eminent builder in the time of James II, and here at Number 13 Thackeray lived for a considerable part of his life. The house, now Number 16, still stands and is occupied by a firm of architects. Young Street leads to Kensington Square, dating back to before 1689 and also built in the reign of James II. It was originally called King's Square. On the west corner of the High Street and Kensington Church Street is St Mary Abbot's Church, a magnificent example of the Gothic style of architecture, rebuilt between 1869 and 1881. The previous church erected in 1696 was condemned in 1868 by two architects as being unsafe to be used for public worship and was therefore pulled down in 1869. This church was considered by Bishop Blomfield to be the ugliest in London. It was erected in the reign of Henry I and dedicated to St Mary, and being annexed in 1111 to the Abbey of Abingdon, it received the additional title of Abbot's and was thenceforth called St Mary Abbot's. It originally possessed a Gothic stone tower, but this was afterwards taken down and a square brick tower with a clock and wooden turret erected in its place. King George III contributed £350 towards this work. The new church possesses an architectural dignity more in keeping with the splendid Court Suburb or Royal Borough of Kensington. The vicar of the parish, Archdeacon Sinclair, gave a donation of £1,000 towards the erection of the present building, which cost upwards of £35,000, and is crowned by a lofty spire. St Mary Abbot's Church was damaged in 1944 by a flying-bomb but its Gothic tower and spire escaped unharmed.

A granite column at the junction of the High Street and Kensington Church Street, erected in 1902 as a memorial to Queen Victoria, has been removed to the large circus at the entrance to Warwick Gardens. Kensington Church Street, leading from St Mary Abbot's to Notting Hill High Street, was formerly called Church Lane, and in recent years has been considerably widened on the east side from Kensington High Street as far as the junction with Vicarage Gardens. The wall fronting the Kensington Barracks has been set back to the new line of frontage. The new buildings erected here include that of the North Thames Gas Board, three blocks of flats called Church Close, York House, and Vicarage Court on the east side, and on the west side Newton Court and Winchester Court at the junction of Church Street and Vicarage Gardens. In August 1944 Kensington Church Street at its junction with Vicarage Gate was laid waste by a flying-bomb which demolished several shabby old houses on both sides of the street. The neighbouring Carmelite Church was completely destroyed but has now been rebuilt, while both Newton Court and Winchester Court were badly damaged.

The continuation of Kensington Church Street, formerly Silver Street, narrows into a bottleneck close to Notting Hill High Street. Until 1864 one of London's numerous toll-gates was situated at the junction of Silver Street and Campden Street. Between Kensington Church Street and Palace Gardens Terrace is the Mall, which contains model dwellings erected in 1868 by Sir Morton Peto to supply a long-felt want in providing housing at a moderate rental.

Returning to the High Street, Kensington, after leaving Kensington Church Street we next pass on the north side the Kensington Town Hall, opened in 1880 at a cost of £55,000, including the site, and considerably enlarged about 1900. Behind the Town Hall, on the wall of St Mary Abbot's Parish Schools, is another pair of those quaint schoolboy and schoolgirl figures, of which, surprisingly, quite a number still survive in various parts of London. The adjoining Library buildings were originally used as the offices of the former Vestry, but were let to the Library Commissioners in 1889. They have now been vacated as the Library has moved to the magnificent new building in Hornton Street which was opened by Queen Elizabeth the Queen Mother on 13 July 1960. The new building, of red brick and stone, extends from Hornton Street to Campden Hill Road and is the largest municipal library in the London area, having accommodation for about 600,000 volumes.

The whole of the frontage of the opposite side of the High Street, extending from Young Street to Wright's Lane, a distance of nearly a quarter of a mile, is occupied by the three great allied stores John Barker, Derry & Toms, and Pontings. All three of these establishments are owned by the first-named company. Barker's store was founded in 1870 as a small establishment by Mr John Barker, who seceded from Mr William Whiteley, of Westbourne Grove.

The main Barker store covers the site between Young Street and King Street, now renamed Derry Street. The eastern section was rebuilt after a disastrous fire which occurred in November 1912 at the corner of Young Street. On the south side of what was formerly Ball Street, at the rear of the main building, a large new block was added in 1934. Ball Street was a superfluous thoroughfare, which has now been built over. By way of compensation a much-needed widening was carried out on the south side of the High Street which is now completed. The rebuilding of the main block between King Street and Young Street was commenced in 1935 and by 1939 had been completed, and the block at Young Street corner is now also finished. The new Barker store is a fine building which is fitted with escalators up and down to all floors. The centre section is crowned by a square tower which forms a prominent landmark when viewed from Kensington Gardens.

The adjoining establishment of Derry & Toms which was acquired by John Barker & Company in 1920, extends from Derry Street to the Underground Station in the High Street. This store, rebuilt between 1928 and 1932, has a bold façade adorned with stone columns. Here the building line of what was formerly the narrowest part of the High Street has also been set back to the same line of frontage as the neighbouring Barker stores. A wide and noble High Street, Kensington, one of the show thoroughfares of London, rivalling Oxford Street in splendour, had long been the great ambition of Sir Sydney Skinner, the managing director of John Barker & Company. He died in 1941, but lived to see his wish fulfilled. A notable feature of this building is the Derry Gardens, which have been laid out on the roof a hundred feet above the High Street and cover an area of over an acre. This modern equivalent of the Hanging Gardens of ancient Babylon contains matured trees and lawns, a river, waterfall and bridges, Spanish pergolas and cloistered Tudor walks. There is also a Sun Pavilion where morning cocktails and afternoon teas are served. A small charge is made for admission. The Ponting store is separated from that of Derry & Toms only by the wide arcade of the Underground Railway Station, and covers the greater part of the east side of Wright's Lane, formerly occupied by Scarsdale House and its extensive garden.

Wright's Lane takes its name from Gregory Wright, who built the houses at the south end about 1774. West of Wright's Lane, on the site now occupied by a handsome row of shops and flats extending as far as the Adam and Eve

Tavern, formerly stood Kensington Terrace, a row of large houses separated from the main road by a cobblestone pavement. They had long back gardens, which occupied the extensive ground now covered by the huge blocks of flats in Iverna Gardens, and were pulled down in 1892. Adjoining Iverna Court on the west side of Wright's Lane is one of the newly-erected Christian Science churches. In Iverna Gardens is the pretty little Armenian Church, erected in 1922 by Caloust Sarkis Gulbenkian in memory of his parents. Kensington Close at the southern end of Wright's Lane is an extensive block of flats, seven storeys high, completed in 1939. It covers the site formerly occupied by the National Home for Crippled Boys.

Allen Street, the next thoroughfare west of Wright's Lane, is named after a Mr Allen, who, about 1820, built these houses in the modern style, faced with stucco. The row of houses in the High Street on the east side called Bath Place was pulled down in 1908 and the present handsome terrace of shops between Allen Street and the Adam and Eve Tavern erected on that site.

On the north side of the High Street, opposite Wright's Lane, is Hornton Court, a magnificent block of shops and flats erected in 1905 on the site of a portion of the long row of buildings called Phillimore Place. It contains a fine terrace garden on the first floor, and extends from Hornton Street to Campden Hill Road. The space formerly occupied by the front gardens of the original terrace of houses has been allocated entirely to the widening of this section of the High Street, giving it the appearance of a noble boulevard. The Phillimore Terraces, of which there were four, once extended from Holland Park to Hornton Street, and were erected about 1787 by William Phillimore, whose father, Robert Phillimore, held a lease of this land. Because of a swag of drapery carved on a stone high up in the face of each house, they were nicknamed Dishclout Terrace. The range of buildings comprising the three remaining Phillimore Terraces was pulled down in 1931 and new blocks of shops and flats erected in their place. These include Phillimore Court, Stafford Court, and Troy Court which have been set back to the line of Hornton Court and have thus transformed the High Street into a splendid thoroughfare after the fashion of the widened Marylebone Road.

The district of Campden Hill, situated on the north side of the High Street, is one of the most agreeable residential quarters in the metropolis. It is built on ground rising to a height of over 130 feet above the Thames, and contains several large mansions with extensive grounds, which give this neighbourhood somewhat the appearance of a rural district far removed from the centre of London. Agryll Road, Phillimore Gardens, and the southern end of Campden Hill Road are covered with large houses built in the 'sixties of last century, but the old-world mansions at the top of Campden Hill, standing in extensive park-like grounds, have been ruthlessly destroyed.

These handsome residences, which included Holly Lodge, Cam House, Thorpe Lodge, Thornwood Lodge, Moray Lodge, and Aubrey House, were tenanted by people of such exalted rank that this district used to be nicknamed

105 Bust of General Booth, founder of the Salvation Army, on Mile
End Waste.

106 An alcove from the old London Bridge, demolished in 1832.
It now stands in Victoria Park, Hackney.

107 East End street scene in 1905: stalls, shoppers and passers-by in Bethnal Green Road.

108 'Petticoat Lane' (properly Middlesex Street) on a Sunday morning.

109 A block of flats in Bethnal Green, and some of the houses in Baroness Road which they replace.

110 A Pearly King in Petticoat Lane.

111 The building of the steamship *Great Eastern* at Millwall, 1857.

112 One of the diesel-engined ferries which have replaced the coke-fired vessels at Woolwich. They carry 1000 passengers and 200 tons of vehicles.

113 The Port of London Authority building in Trinity Square.

115 The Royal Naval College, Greenwich.

114 Historic Southwark. A surviving wing of the George, one of the last of London's galleried coaching inns.

116 Southwark Cathedral, formerly the church of St Mary Overie.

117 A new Odeon Cinema at the New Kent Road side of the Elephant and Castle. Part of the shopping precinct is seen on the right of the picture.

118 The Imperial War Museum, formerly the Bethlem Hospital.

119 The Talbot in 1831. Better known by its original name, the Tabard, meeting-place of Chaucer's Canterbury pilgrims.

120 Ruins of the former Winchester Palace, Southwark, in 1800.

121 St Olave, Tooley Street, 1830. This church was demolished in 1928.

122 Tooley Street after the fire of 1861.

123 Kennington Toll gate on Derby Day, 1828.

'the Dukeries' by the neighbouring inhabitants. In Holly Lodge Macaulay spent the last years of his life until his death on 28 December 1859. It is now used by the students of the Queen Elizabeth College. Aubrey House, mentioned above, stands in a secluded corner on the site of Kensington Wells, an eighteenth century spa. Thorpe Lodge remains as the library and common-room of the new school referred to below. Cam House and Moray Lodge have been demolished. Between these various houses are walled lanes for pedestrians only, and here one can enjoy a pleasant ramble, away from the noise and din of passing motor-cars. In Campden Hill Road, standing on high ground, is a palatial block of flats called Campden Hill Court, opposite to which is the Queen Elizabeth College of General and Domestic Science (University of London). At the top of the hill is the Grand Junction reservoir of the Metropolitan Water Board, but the tall chimney attached to the engine-house can hardly be described as an ornament to this neighbourhood. In the porch of St George's Church in Aubrey Walk is a notice: *Please close the door—to keep the cats out.* In Duchess of Bedford's Walk, a turning on the east side of Phillimore Gardens which is a secluded and quiet locality, are two handsome new blocks of flats called Campden Hill Gate. These are of red brick with stone dressings and the gardens at the back have such a rural appearance that you might imagine they were miles away from the centre of London. In 1946 during the acute shortage of housing accommodation Campden Hill Gate, after being vacated by the Government, was invaded by squatters and so also was Abbey Lodge, Regent's Park. They remained in possession for several weeks before they could be dislodged. A housing scheme of the London County Council to urbanize the Campden Hill area by erecting blocks of flats caused serious misgivings among Kensington residents; protest meetings were held and a Campden Hill Preservation Fund was inaugurated. However, instead of flats, the L.C.C. have built at the junction of Campden Hill and Holland Walk a huge school, with accommodation for more than 2,000 scholars—who are drawn from the surrounding districts of North and South Kensington, Hammersmith, Shepherds Bush, Notting Hill etc. Occupying $8^1/_2$ acres of ground, the school was opened in September 1958. The building cost about £680,000 and the equipment another £58,000. Among the mansions demolished in this area—each of which was a 'country house in town'—was Moray Lodge, well-known in the 'eighties as the residence of Mr Arthur Lewis, senior partner in the Regent Street firm of Lewis & Allenby. Mrs Arthur Lewis was Kate Terry, one of that gifted theatrical family that is still represented on the London stage of today. Their musical productions at Moray Lodge, at which Sir Arthur Sullivan frequently assisted, were known as *The Moray Minstrels*. More modern buildings are being erected in this once attractive district which has now completely lost the quiet seclusion which was its principal charm.

Campden House, situated between Sheffield Terrace and Gloucester Walk, was built about 1612 and was for five years the residence of Queen Anne when Princess of Denmark. Towards the close of the eighteenth century the house became a boarding-school for young ladies, but was afterwards converted again into a private residence. On the site of its grounds, which extended to Kensington Church Street, a number of red-brick houses, together with a large block of flats called Campden House Court, were erected in 1897.

On the east side of Hornton Street a long row of modern red-brick residences, built in 1904, has replaced the Georgian brown-brick houses which had previously stood on that site. The building line was then set back a few feet in order to widen the sidewalk. The adjoining Independent Chapel, which until about 1929 stood at the corner of Hornton Place, was built in 1793. This site is now covered by a new block of flats.

Standing on high ground, close to Holland Park Avenue, is Campden Hill Square, formerly called Notting Hill Square, affording a fine view from the houses on its southern side. One of these, called Tower Cressy, was a weird-looking mansion, with a stuccoed front resembling stone, five storeys high, from the top of which a magnificent bird's-eye view of London could be obtained. This was erected by Thomas Page, the architect of the 1857 Chelsea Bridge, and named in honour of the Black Prince, whose emblems adorned the exterior of the building. It was said that a clause in the lease required the tenant to hoist a flag every year on the anniversary of the battle of Cressy. This strange building has been demolished and several new houses now stand in its place. To the west of Campden Hill Square is Holland Walk, which skirts Holland Park and passes over the top of Campden Hill to High Street, Kensington. It is for the use of foot-passengers only, and being nearly a mile long, forms an ideal walk for nursemaids with children and perambulators. Seats are provided at frequent intervals for the use of the public. Holland Walk is so rural in its appearance that it is difficult to realize that one is so close to the centre of London.

Holland House, which next claims our notice, is a famous example of Jacobean architecture. The centre building and turrets were erected by John Thorpe in 1607 for Sir Walter Cope, though doubts have been expressed regarding the attribution to Thorpe of this and some other buildings. At that time the mansion was known as Cope Castle. Later it was extended for the first Earl of Holland, husband of Cope's daughter. Joseph Addison died here in 1719, three years after his marriage to the widow of the third Earl of Warwick and Holland. The house was bought by Henry Fox, who was created Baron Holland in 1763, and on the death of Lady Holland, widow of the fourth baron, in 1889, the property passed by purchase to the Earl of Ilchester, a descendant of Henry Fox's brother. Holland House narrowly escaped destruction from a fire which occurred in January 1871, and during the second World War it was badly damaged by bombing. Holland Park and the House were acquired by the L.C.C. in 1952 and the grounds, in which exhibitions of sculpture are frequently held, have been opened to the public. The poet Samuel Rogers was a frequent visitor to the house and an alcove in the grounds is inscribed: — 'Here Rogers sat and here for ever dwell With me those Pleasures that he sang so well'. Holland House is being restored, while immediately adjacent a large youth hostel has been built known as the King George VI Memorial Hostel.

Holland Walk terminates opposite Earl's Court Road, to the east of which is the rebuilt Roman Catholic Church of Our Lady of Victories. This was adopted by Cardinal Manning as his pro-cathedral for the diocese of Westminster until the opening of Westminster Cathedral in 1903. It stands back behind some small shops fronting Kensington High Street which were rebuilt before the war. It is a lofty Gothic structure of the Early English type completed in 1869, but its façade is almost concealed from the main street. The church was destroyed in the early morning of 13 September 1940 by fire and oil-bombs during an air raid. This handsome church has now been rebuilt. One morning in August 1944 the western section of Kensington High Street was hit by a bomb with devastating effect. Several shops close to Earl's Court Road were completely demolished. Troy Court on the opposite side of the road was severely damaged and the two small lodges at the entrance to Holland Walk were also destroyed. In a Lyons teashop which was crowded during the lunch hour when the bomb exploded, about a dozen people were killed, including members of the staff of the Ministry of Aircraft Production who were quartered at Oakwood Court.

Earl's Court Road was formerly called Earl Street, and little more than a century ago its buildings came to a finish at Pembroke Square. The remaining portion was then called Earl's Court Lane, and is now covered by large houses, shops, and blocks of flats extending to Old Brompton Road. Some delightful villas with long gardens which stood on the south side of Pembroke Road between Earl's Court Road and Pembroke Gardens were pulled down in 1935 to make way for Chatsworth Court and Marlborough Court, two large blocks of flats. Pembroke Square is made most attractive by the premises of Messrs. Rassell's, the florists and nurserymen. Facing Earl's Court Road, plants and flowers decorate the forecourt of the charming creeper-covered old house, and their tree and flower-filled gardens behind occupy a large part of the enclosure in the middle of the Square. In the Spring, this rustic little bit of Kensington is surprisingly pretty.

At the south-east corner the former 'Pembroke Arms' has been re-named 'The Hansom Cab'. Re-fitted with leather-upholstered seats and cushions, the interior displays an interesting collection of sepia photographs of the hansom cab era and is lighted by lamps of the kind carried by the 'gondolas of the London streets'. The very special feature, however, is to be found in the dining-room where, suspended above the tables, is a *real hansom cab* (of uncertain vintage).

After passing Earl's Court Road we come to the Kensington Cinema, now an Odeon, on the main Kensington Road, opened in 1926. It occupies a part of the site of Leonard Place, a terrace of four-storeyed brownbrick houses erected early in the nineteenth century. The remaining houses were pulled down about 1929 and a new block of shops and flats called Leonard Court has been erected on this site.

Leonard Place and the long range of houses just beyond, called Earl's Terrace, as well as Edwardes Square at the back of the terrace, were originally designed by a Frenchman named M. Changier as a building speculation. This venture proved a failure, and after having spent over £100,000 on the work, M. Changier went bankrupt and returned to France, leaving the unfinished houses in the hands of the creditors. These were afterwards completed and soon became a popular centre of residence. In 1910 Earl's Terrace was the scene of an interesting battle between the owners of the estate and the Kensington Borough Council. The houses are separated from the main thoroughfare by a private road which runs in front of them, parallel to the Kensington Road. With the intention of building over the private road, the owners of the estate erected barriers at both ends. The Kensington Borough Council, however, questioned their right to do so, and claimed a right of way for the public. As fast as the barriers were erected the Council proceeded to pull them down again. Eventually the Kensington Borough Council emerged as victors, and the scheme to build over the private road was abandoned. Owing to the slump in the demand for flats which then prevailed, no offer for the site of Earl's Terrace was forthcoming, and as a consequence these old houses were modernized and redecorated and let on new leases. Edwardes Square was so named from the family name of Lord Kensington.

On the opposite side of the Kensington Road, between Holland Lane and Melbury Road, is Melbury Court, a handsome block of shops and flats erected in 1928 on land originally forming a part of Holland Park. That site had been on offer for building purposes for many years previously, and the back portion was utilized as a school for golf. Melbury Road, leading to Oakwood Court and Addison Road, was a haunt of successful Victorian artists, for among these large red-brick mansions, several have commemorative plaques marking the residences of, among others, Holman Hunt, Sir Luke Fildes and Sir Hamo Thornycroft, the sculptor. G. F. Watts lived at No 6, which only recently disappeared to be replaced by a modern building, and No 9, The Tower House, once noted for its original interior decoration, having long been threatened with demolition, is now undergoing considerable restoration. Off Melbury Road, in Holland Park Road is the large house and studios of Lord Leighton, P.R.A., who lived there for 30 years until his death in 1896. A notable feature which the artist added later is the Arab Hall, with its colourful decoration of old Persian tiles, stained-glass windows and central pool of water with a trickling fountain. Acquired by the Royal Borough in 1926, the house is open to the public.

Oakwood Court, comprising several large blocks of flats seven and eight storeys high and extending to Addison Road, was mostly erected between 1900 and 1903, but one large block situated on the north side dates only from 1927. In the centre of the road is a small square garden. Oakwood Court has recently been continued towards Holland Park by the newly-formed Ilchester Close, consisting of high-class detached nonbasement houses. Together with Oakwood Court these furnish a typical example of the new London which is rapidly coming into being at the present time. A new thoroughfare called Abbotsbury Road which runs parallel to Addison Road was opened up between Melbury Road and Holland Park Avenue in 1938. The land required for its construction was taken from Holland Park.

A few years ago the district between the High Street, Kensington, and the West London Extension Railway retained its old-fashioned and monotonous appearance, but of late years many of the gloomy houses on the main Kensington Road have been replaced by modern buildings. On the west side of Warwick Gardens, on a site extending to Kensington and Warwick Roads, are several fine blocks of flats called St Mary Abbot's Court, erected between 1926 and 1934. Others called Kenton Court and Eastbury Court have been erected on the opposite side of Kensington High Street, between Addison Road and the West London Railway's bridge. The houses between Melbury Road and Addison Road, known as St Mary Abbot's Terrace, have all been demolished and new houses, shops and flats have been built on the site. Warwick Gardens and Warwick Road are named after the Earls of Warwick, the former owners of Holland House.

Kensington Crescent, an old-fashioned row of private houses which stood back from the main Kensington Road in a private drive between Warwick Road and the West London Extension Railway, was pulled down in 1933 for a proposed annexe to the Olympia. The scheme failed to mature and this extensive site covering seven acres remained empty for the next fifteen years. In 1948 it was sold for the erection of Charles House, a new building designed by Mr A. S. Ash at a cost of £930,000 which is leased to the Government. This great structure, now completed and occupied, which is nine storeys high and faced with yellow brick, consists of two open quadrangles enclosed by three plain, narrow wings facing the main Kensington Road. Here a widening of the roadway at the junction of Warwick Road and Kensington Road was carried out some years ago.

We will now turn down Addison Road, with its large villa residences standing in their own roomy gardens, especially No 8, covered with glazed blue, green and white tiles designed by Halsey Ricardo in 1906 and then, crossing Holland Park Avenue, pay a brief visit to the district of North Kensington. Until 1864 one of London's numerous toll-gates stood nearly opposite to the southern end of Addison Road, at the junction of the Kensington Road, and there was another one at the northern end of Addison Road. On the east side, close to Melbury Roads, is St Barnabas's Church, erected in the Perpendicular style, with four cupolas, and opened in 1830.

Holland Park Avenue, forming a part of the main Uxbridge Road, is a fine broad thoroughfare lined with trees on both sides. Opening crescent-wise on to the south side are two broad roads containing handsome detached villas faced with stucco like those of Belsize Park. The back gardens of the first of these roads overlook Holland Park Avenue, and those of the other one back on to Holland Park itself. Some of these large houses, which were built in the 'sixties, have now been converted into private hotels, flats and maisonettes, but on account of its quiet and pleasant situation this neighbourhood has retained its original popularity. These houses have been built at the expense of Holland Park, which formerly extended as far as the Uxbridge Road.

The Norland division of Kensington, situated to the north of the main Ux-bridge Road, is an important section of the old manor of Notting Barns. Before the dawn of the nineteenth century this district was almost uninhabited, and down to the time of Queen Elizabeth I and long after was covered with woods, heath, and scrub. In those days the view from what is now the top of Holland Park Avenue must have been very agreeable. Norland Square and Royal Crescent, facing Holland Park Avenue, were erected in 1845 on the site of Norland House, the residence of Mr C. Drummond, the banker. Holland Park Hall, opposite Royal Crescent, built in 1908, was originally a skating rink, but is now used as motor-car showrooms. To the north of Uxbridge Road is a district formerly known as the Potteries, which was very squalid, but the erection of Royal Crescent and Norland Square effected a considerable improvement in that locality. The site of the North Kensington Potteries is indicated by a red-brick kiln which pro-jects through the wall of the old pottery yard on to the footpath in Pottery Lane. It is preserved by the Borough Council as an interesting relic. In St James's Square at the end of Addison Avenue is St James's Church, consecrated in 1845. On a large bombed site at the back of this square bounded by Wilsham Street, Sirdar Road, Becher Street and St Ann's Road, several three-storeyed blocks of workers' flats have been erected by the Kensington Borough Council. These have Dickensian names, such as Carton, Estella, Nickleby etc.

Opposite Holland Walk is Ladbroke Grove, a fine broad thoroughfare which passes over a high knoll and leads due north to Harrow Road. On the knoll stands St John's Church, a building in the Gothic style, crowned by a tall spire, It was consecrated in 1845 and stands on the site where Notting Hill farmhouse originally stood. After the demolition of the farmhouse this site was occupied for a short time by a racecourse called the Hippodrome, which also included the ground now covered by Clarendon Road, Westbourne Park Road, Portobello Road, and Ladbroke Square. Racing men made a strong a fight to save it, petitions were got up on both sides, and an Act of Parliament was demanded for shutting up the public right of way.

The main entrance to the Hippodrome was at the junction of Kensington Park Road and Ladbroke Road, and Portobello Road marked its eastern boundary. It was a delightful walk through the lanes of this neighbourhood, the whole country being then open, with only a few farms here and there. On the north side Hampstead was visible, and Harrow-on-the-Hill on the north-west side. The Hippodrome only flourished as a racecourse from 1837 to 1841, because the deep clay of Notting Hill was unsuited for running except at certain seasons, and the land was gradually encroached upon by the constant growth of the metropolis in this direction. Hippodrome Place recalls the racecourse. Ladbroke Grove and Ladbroke Square derive their name from Richard Ladbroke, son of a Lord Mayor of London, who was a banker and owned property here in the eighteenth century.

Notting Hill, or Kensington Park, as it is sometimes called, is a handsome quarter of the Royal Borough of Kensington, well laid out with broad streets, squares, and crescents. Prominent amongst these are Ladbroke Square, Stanley Crescent, Ladbroke Gardens and Kensington Park Road, all containing large houses of the type which was fashionable in the mid-Victorian era, with stucco fronts and large porticoed balconies. Many of these have since been divided into flats and maisonettes. In Kensington Park Road is the handsome church of St Peter, Notting Hill, built in 1856. There is still some uncertainty regarding the name of the architect; it was probably Thomas Allom, or Hallam, or perhaps Allason. Just behind is Portobello Road, which is one of the sights of London on a Saturday, when the lower part of the road is lined on both sides with stalls displaying antiques of a very miscellaneous character, and crowded with prospective customers. The church of All Saints, with St Colombs in Talbot Road, was damaged by bomb blast, but has now been repaired. Many houses have also been destroyed in Westbourne Park Road. The district of Bassett Road, Oxford Gardens, Cambridge Gardens and St Quintin's Avenue farther to the north contains a more modern type of house. This quarter also contains the Roman Catholic College of St Charles, the St Marylebone Hospital, and the Kensington Memorial Recreation Ground. On another bombed site near St Charles's Square, the Kensington Borough Council have built small blocks of flats of the maisonette type containing three storeys.

Along the east side of Kensington Park Road are several fine blocks of flats erected in 1935. Pembridge Square contains handsome Victorian villas, most of which have been converted into flats and private hotels. On the north-west corner now stands Vincent House, a seven-storeyed building erected in 1938 which contains a residential club and flats.

Notting Hill Gate on the busy main Uxbridge Road forms a kind of second Kensington High Street, being to the northern half of Kensington what the Kensington High Street is to the southern portion. But it is inferior to the latter as regards the style of its shops. In 1900 a widening of the south side was carried out between Kensington Church Street and the Mall. It was formerly known as Kensington Gravel Pits and received its name from the gravel pits lying between it and the town of Kensington. The principal street along the north high road was three-eighths of a mile long, and the village enjoyed excellent air and was enlivened by the passing of mail coaches, stages, and wagons every hour. In 1844 there were only two shops in the village above one storey high, and close to the turnpike gate were the village pump and the village pound.

The district to the north was very rural, and until the beginning of the nineteenth century had undergone little change for ages. Although it was scarcely three miles from London, the traveller could imagine himself in the most remote part of the country. The main road passing through this locality is now represented by Latimer Road. At the end of Pottery Lane was a colony of pig-keepers, and every house had a collection of pigs in its yard. A number of carts filled with tubs passed daily to London gathering refuse from hotels and mansions to provide food for the large families of pigs gathered here. During the outbreak of cholera the inhabitants suffered severely. In those days the main road was a very rough thoroughfare, cut through the fields which were the only means of approach. Brickfields and pits on either side rendered it dangerous on dark nights.

The constriction caused by the narrow Notting Hill Gate or High Street has recently been removed by opening out the cross-roads at this busy junction, and the road between Kensington Palace Gardens and Ladbroke Terrace has been widened to 85 feet for a distance of about 700 yards. The north end of Kensington Church Street has been widened to 65 feet and Pembridge Road has been widened at its southern end. The clearance of buildings to effect this has created new frontages for development. To the north new shops and offices and flats and maisonettes comprising 145 dwellings are grouped in three and six-storey blocks facing Pembridge Road and the widened Notting Hill Gate has an eighteen-storey tower rising above the shops to a height of 176 feet. New buildings to the south include a new 'Hoop' public house, shops and offices in a four-storey block facing Notting Hill Gate and a parade of shops fronting Kensington Church Street which terminates in a five-storey block of flats above the shops. A twelve-storey block of offices above shops has been set back from the road to link the other two blocks.

The London Transport Executive has undertaken a complete reconstruction of the two underground stations which have been made into one interconnecting station, the main concourse of which lies below the widened road. The two entrances to the station, one on each side of Notting Hill Gate, together with the concourse provides a pedestrian subway under the main road. The cost of the total improvement, including property requisitioned for rehousing displaced people, is estimated at £3,000,000.

Close to Notting Hill Gate yet another poor quarter formerly existed. This was a rookery of overcrowded and filthy houses known as Campden Place. It comprised two side streets, Pitt's Cottages and Anderson's Cottages, which contained altogether fifty separate houses of the poorest description. This land belonged to the parochial charities, having been purchased on 18 June 1651 from Thomas Coppen for the sum of £45. In 1868 the parish authorities obtained possession of this slum and the place was then cleared. On this site has since arisen the handsome Clanricarde Gardens built by Messrs Goodwin & White on a ninety-nine years' lease. The neighbouring Linden Gardens form a pleasant retreat leading out of Notting Hill Gate which has no other outlet and contains handsome residences standing in private gardens. Many are now private hotels and maisonettes.

We will now turn down Kensington Palace Gardens at the other end of Notting Hill Gate, and after skirting the south side of Kensington Gardens visit the splendid quarter of South Kensington mostly built between 1862 and 1877. The area enclosed by Queen's Gate, Kensington Gore, Exhibition Road, and Cromwell Road, comprising about 120 acres, forms the Gore Estate, purchased by the Government out of the profits derived from the Great Exhibition of 1851. The receipts left a profit of £186,000 in the hands of the Commissioners, and when in 1856 a great part of Kensington Gore came on the market, that sum was increased by a grant from Parliament and £300,000 was spent on the purchase of the Gore House Estate. The greater part of it is situated in the parish of St Margaret's, Westminster, although the Victoria and Albert Museum and the Natural History Museum are both in the Royal Borough.

The Committee of the Great Exhibition of 1851 still functions, and deals with the administration of funds, properties and investments resulting from the show that delighted our great-grandparents.

Gore House, the residence of Lady Blessington, stood approximately on the site where the Albert Hall now stands. The original idea was to erect either a new National Gallery or some building connected with the fine arts upon this ground. After being acquired by the Government the ground was rapidly cleared of the previously-existing buildings and then surrounded by noble roads, upon which first-class mansions sprang up as if by magic, equal to the finest in Belgravia. As these houses possessed a superior drainage, purer water, and stood on a more gravelly soil than the fashionable mansions of the older quarters of London, it was predicted that a large new quarter second to none would soon be added to the metropolis.

Before the Great Exhibition of 1851 South Kensington consisted of dairy farms, market gardens, and orchards fenced with park railings. The first houses to be constructed were those at the eastern end of Cromwell Road in 1856, one of which was rented by Prince Jerome Bonaparte. From the Victoria and Albert Museum, then called the South Kensington Museum, what is now Exhibition Road was cut through some delightful spots, which were at that time described as very picturesque. To the west of the Gore Estate, terraces stretched towards Kensington.

Queen's Gate, on the west side of the Gore Estate, was called Prince Albert Road when first laid out, but after the erection of the new gateway opposite into Kensington Gardens, its name was changed to that of Queen's Gate. This noble thoroughfare is a hundred feet wide and extends from Kensington Gardens to Old Brompton Road, a distance of about three-quarters of a mile. With its long rows of stately mansions and blocks of residential flats it presents an imposing vista, perhaps equalled only by those of Portland Place, Marylebone, and Westbourne Terrace on the opposite side of the park. Queen's Gate stands on the site of Brompton Park, the retreat of some famous actors, including Mr Webster, a former lessee of the Adelphi Theatre. A block of flats at the northern end of Queen's Gate close to Prince Consort Road was destroyed in an air raid which took place in March 1944.

The Natural History Museum in Cromwell Road stands on the site of the International Exhibition building in 1862, which was designed by Captain Fowke, R.E. The main entrance was in Cromwell Road, and there was a second entrance from the former gardens of the Royal Horticultural Society to the rear of the Exhibition grounds. This great exhibition, originally proposed by the Prince Consort, was opened on Thursday, 1 May 1862, in brilliant weather after some morning rain. On account of the recent death of the Prince Consort and the absence of the Prince of Wales, afterwards King Edward VII, in the East, there was no Royal opening. The doors were opened at 10.30 a.m., and amongst those present were the Queen's Commissioners, the Lord Mayor and Sheriffs, the Archbishop of Canterbury, Lord Palmerston, the Earl of Derby, the Duke of Cambridge, the Crown Prince of Prussia, the Lord Chancellor, and the Speaker of the House of Commons. The exhibition was declared open by the Duke of Cambridge.

The Natural History Museum, as it is generally called, houses the natural history collections of the British Museum. The building is 675 feet long and consists of a central hall with two lateral wings, each 233 feet long, and was designed by Sir Alfred Waterhouse. It was erected at a cost of £150,000. The towers rise to a height of 192 feet. The building is Romanesque in style, and the terracotta façade is greatly admired. Its erection occupied the years from 1873, to 1880, and the building was opened in 1881. Opposite the Natural History Museum, at the corner of Queen's Gate and Cromwell Road, Baden-Powell House has been built 'as a living memorial to the Founder of the Scout Movement and a meeting place and hostel for the Boy Scouts of the World'. Also in Cromwell Road is the large new building of the Institut Français.

The gardens of the Horticultural Society, Kensington, were opened on 5 June 1861. Before that time they had been located at Chiswick, and they are now at Wisley, in Surrey, having been presented by Sir Thomas Hanbury in 1903. The Society has about thirteen thousand fellows, members, and associates, and, after examination, grants diplomas to gardeners.

Up to March 1859 the sum of £312,000 had been spent by the Royal Commissioners and the Science and Art Department on the Kensington Gore Estate. In 1871 another International Exhibition was held in new buildings erected at the back of the Albert Hall, and from that year until 1886 these exhibitions were held annually at South Kensington. The terrace at the back of the Albert Hall then overlooked the exhibition grounds and formed a most imposing vista when seen from the farther end of the central walk. Between 1883 and 1886 the series of exhibitions included the Fisheries, the Health, the Inventions, and the Colonial and Indian Empire Exhibitions. The last mentioned, held in 1886, was visited by 5,373,120 persons, and was the last exhibition which took place at South Kensington.

In 1887 the two fine thoroughfares, Imperial Institute Road and Prince Consort Road, were constructed across the site of the exhibition grounds from Exhibition Road to Queen's Gate. The Imperial Institute Road is ninety feet wide, and on the north side was the Imperial institute, with a façade 704 feet long. It was designed by Mr T. E. Colcutt as a National Memorial to Queen Victoria's Jubilee of 1887, and its lofty central tower is a landmark for miles around. The building occupied almost the entire length of Imperial Institute Road, and the foundation-stone was laid by Queen Victoria on 4 July 1887.

The Imperial Institute is now called the Commonwealth Institute and the Indian Museum became the Commonwealth Museum. Colcutt's building, however, has been demolished though, protests having been registered, the central tower, 280 feet high has been preserved, and is now known as Queen's Tower. West of the tower, the ground has been cleared for development, while on the east side is the new Civil Engineering wing of the City and Guilds College, adjoining the main building in Exhibition Road which was rebuilt in 1963 on the site of the original building, opened in 1884. The Commonwealth Institute has moved to a new position at the lower end of Holland Park Gardens, opposite Earl's Court Road. On this site of $3^1/_4$ acres a new building with a copper roof of unusual design has been erected. The new building — 'The Commonwealth Under One Roof' — was opened in the autumn of 1962.

The greater part of the opposite side of Imperial Institute Road is occupied by the Imperial College of Science and Technology, erected between 1900 and 1906 from the designs of Sir Aston Webb. A new building for the department of Bio-Chemistry adjoins the west side, and was opened by the Chancellor of the University of London, Queen Elizabeth the Queen Mother, in 1965. At the back of the Imperial College of Science and Technology is the Science Museum, until recently the Cinderella of the State museums. It was established in 1856 as a branch of the South Kensington, now the Victoria and Albert, Museum. The Patents Museum was added in 1884, and in 1909 the combined collections were reconstituted as the Science Museum and made a separate institution. Measures were then taken for the provision of a new building, which was begun in 1913, but the first World War holding up construction, the first or eastern section was not completed until early in 1928. The new Science Museum was designed by Sir Richard Allison, and is a ferro-concrete structure of four floors marked by a handsome elevation of Portland stone with columns of the Ionic order. On the west side the new building adjoins the old, in which the Science Library is housed.

Next to the Science Museum in Exhibition Road and designed by John H. Markham is the new building of the Museum of Practical Geology, which was removed here from its old home in Piccadilly in 1934 and officially opened on 3 July 1935. It is a handsome building faced with Portland stone and forms a notable addition to the imposing collection of colleges and museums centred at South Kensington. In 1933 this building was utilized for the World Economic Conference. This was formally opened by King George V on 12 June 1933 and was attended by 166 delegates of sixty-six nations.

Adjoining the buildings of the Imperial College of Science and Technology in Prince Consort Road is the Royal College of Music, designed by Sir Reginald Blomfield and opened in 1894. The foundation-stone was laid by the Prince of Wales, afterwards King Edward VII, on 9 July 1890. Here musical training is provided for some five hundred pupils. On the opposite side of Prince Consort Road is the immense block of flats called Albert Court, occupying nearly the whole of the site between Exhibition Road and the Albert Hall. The frontage to the west of the Albert Hall is occupied by the Union building to the Imperial College of Science and the adjoining church of Holy Trinity, close to Queen's

Gate. This beautiful church was G. F. Bodley's last design and contains a memorial to that architect. The late Canon Hannay, who wrote several novels under the name of George A. Birmingham, was vicar here for some fifteen years. In the south aisle may be seen an example of the decorative needlework which was the hobby of that distinguished actor the late Ernest Thesiger, who died in 1961 at the age of 82. On the west side of Exhibition Road, built on some vacant land at the back of Lowther Lodge, are some handsome blocks of flats completed in 1929. The opposite side of the road is lined by several imposing terraces of large Victorian houses with porticoed balconies but their uniformity is now broken by a large ten-storeyed block of flats erected in 1937 which faces Imperial Institute Road.

Directing our steps down Exhibition Road on the east side, and noticing the new church of the Latter Day Saints (Mormons) and, at No 55, a memorial plaque to the victims of the Hungarian Rising of 1956, we reach the Mathematical Section of the Royal College of Science, completed in May 1872 from the designs of Captain Fowke, R.E. Along the central portion of the front is a handsome Italian arcade supported by a range of columns with terracotta sculptures designed by Mr Godfrey Sykes to represent the seven ages of man. There is also an upper arcade projecting a little from the top storey of the building. The walls are of red brick and the cornices and window-dressings are of terracotta. Like the Albert Hall, the exterior of the Royal College of Science is urgently in need of renovation.

The noble Victoria and Albert Museum, immediately adjoining, stands on twelve acres of ground, purchased at a cost of £60,000, originally comprising the Hale House Estate. Temporary buildings were opened here on 24 June 1857, and designs for the permanent buildings in Cromwell Road were prepared by Captain Fowke in 1865, but the work was not actually proceeded with until 1899. The new buildings, with a frontage to the Cromwell Road of 720 feet and to Exhibition Road of 275 feet, were designed by Sir Aston Webb, P.R.A. They are in the Renaissance style, with domes and towers, and are faced with red brick and stone dressings. The foundation-stone was laid on 17 May 1899 by Queen Victoria, assisted by King Edward VII, then Prince of Wales, and the new buildings were opened in state ten years later by King Edward VII and Queen Alexandra, on 26 June 1909.

Thus South Kensington has developed in the course of time into what is really a university of art, science, and technology, and with its museums contains the most extensive range of similar buildings to be found in any city in the world. As a piece of urban scenery it is second only to Westminster, both in respect of its public buildings and the width of the roads which permit them to be seen to such great advantage. Thronged during the lunch hour with students of almost every nationality, Exhibition Road presents a scene closely resembling that of Oxford or Cambridge. Although the streets of South Kensington are exceptionally wide they are exempt from the monotony which characterizes the modern quarters of Paris, Berlin, and New York. There is nothing mean or commonplace about South Kensington for, unlike North Kensington, it has few slums and its beautiful square gardens, public buildings and spacious thoroughfares like Queen's Gate, Exhibition Road and Cromwell Road give majesty and distinction to this splendid quarter of London.

At the eastern end of Cromwell Road, opposite the Victoria and Albert Museum, is Thurloe Place, now lined with tall buildings and shops, including Dalmeny Court and the extensive Hotel Rembrandt. Until 1908 a row of detached cottages stood on this site, including the Bell and Horns Tavern at the corner of Fulham Road, dating from the period when this was a quiet suburban road on the outer confines of the metropolis. The Bell and Horns Tavern was itself rebuilt in 1856, previous to which time it had been a place of very picturesque appearance. Alexander Square, at the back of Thurloe Place, was built between 1827 and 1830. Thurloe Square contains some fine large town houses.

Cromwell Road, a fine thoroughfare about a hundred feet wide and one mile in length, extends from Brompton Road to Earl's Court Road, and is continued as far as Warwick Road by West Cromwell Road. It was originally called Cromwell Lane, after one of Cromwell's sons, who once lived there. The project of making Cromwell Road the main gateway to the West of England was hindered ever since its construction by strong local opposition and even more so by the presence of the West London Railway, which acted as a barrier to its extension westwards. But in 1936 a joint Parliamentary Bill was obtained by the London and Middlesex County Councils for the construction of a wide new road nearly four miles long to connect Cromwell Road with the Great West Road at Gunnersbury at a total estimated cost of £2,500,000. Its completion has been delayed by the war but the new Cromwell Road Bridge over the West London Railway was completed and opened to traffic by the end of 1941. This connects West Cromwell Road with Talgarth Road opposite West Kensington Station. It carries a double roadway leading into North End Road. The viaduct which carries it over the railway was bombed in 1940. Opposite South Kensington Station a large roundabout has been formed by the demolition in 1935 of Onslow Crescent. Its garden now forms the island in the centre. The site of Onslow Crescent is now covered by a large eight-storeyed block of shops and flats called Melton Court erected in 1938.

Facing the triangular open space at the corner of Exhibition Road formerly stood a large island block of houses which remained untenanted for upwards of thirty years as the result of great slump in house property which occurred in this part of London during the closing years of the last century. Before its demolition in 1937 it was occupied for many years by the French Institute which was then removed to a handsome new building in Queensberry Place. This site was bought for the erection of the intended new National Theatre but after the war the Cromwell Road site was exchanged for another near Waterloo Bridge on the cleared south bank of the Thames. Some of the large houses facing the Natural History Museum are now private hotels and others are used as business offices. The west end of Cromwell Road, which also consists largely of private hotels, was not constructed until after the International Exhibition of 1862, and west of Gloucester Road was still market gardens until after 1870. By 1890 the whole of the vast area between Gloucester Road and the West London Railway had been covered with large town houses.

In Sydney Place, connecting South Kensington Station with Fulham Road, is a large block of shops and flats called Malvern Court at the corner of Pelham Street. In the adjoining Onslow Square is St Paul's Church, completed on 24 December 1860. In 1908 strong complaints were made by the residents of Onslow Square about the noise made by the new motor-omnibuses, which had just invaded this district. Various leading articles enlarging upon the 'bitter cry of Onslow Square' appeared at that time in the London newspapers. Onslow Square, the estate of the Earl of Onslow, was built on the site of a lunatic asylum with extensive grounds. Harrington Road, which runs parallel to Cromwell Road, contains the former Queen's Gate Hall, now a Christian Science church, and the Norfolk Hotel. In August 1944 Harrington Road was laid waste by a rocket-bomb which damaged Queen's Gate Hall and several large houses on the north side and the Naval and Military Hotel on the south side, now replaced by a block of flats. The entire block of houses lining the east side of Stanhope Gardens was also wrecked, leaving only the façades and bare walls. They have now been replaced by an interesting range of some twenty new four-storey houses, with balconies, railings—and even basements, to harmonise with the surrounding property.

In Gloucester Road, now a busy centre of hotels, flats, and shops, are Bailey's Hotel, opened in 1876, close to the Underground Station, the Alwin Hotel near Cromwell Road, St Stephen's Church close to Cornwall Gardens, and St George's Court, a large modern bloc of shops and flats. In the noble Queen's Gate Terrace is the South Kensington Hotel, which, like Bailey's Hotel, is owned by Empire Hotels Limited. A great impetus was given to the development of South Kensington by the extension of the Metropolitan Railway from Gloucester Road to Westminster Bridge on 24 December 1868. In order to get this line ready for the Christmas traffic nearly three thousand men were employed day and night during the last month of the work. By 1870 Kensington had become completely joined to the metropolis by fine new houses and streets on every side. Some of the old villas at the southern end of Gloucester Road and also in Hereford Square and Brechin Place were destroyed by a rocket-bomb in 1944.

Harrington Gardens, Courtfield Gardens, and Collingham Gardens, to the south of Cromwell Road, were erected about 1877, and the more modern houses and blocks of flats in Barkston and Bramham Gardens after the demolition of Earl's Court House about 1887. In Collingham Road is St Jude's Church, a handsome edifice which contains a memorial to Sir Henry Lytton, the Savoyard, with the text: *The fear of the Lord maketh a merry heart.* Earl's Court House was formerly the residence of John Hunter, the great anatomist. That site is now covered by large blocks of flats facing the east side of Earl's Court Road, and by Bramham and Barkston Gardens. After Hunter's death in 1795 his house was bought and occupied successively by four or five different owners, most recently by the family of Mr Gunter, the London confectioner. On the opposite side of Earl's Court Road was the Gunter Estate, comprising about sixty acres, long since covered with buildings. The original hamlet of Earl's Court is situated in the triangle enclosed by Earl's Court Road, Cromwell Road, and Hogarth Road.

Earl's Court Station, a great traffic junction of the London Underground Railways, was first opened in November 1871, and is the converging point of the Wimbledon, Richmond, Ealing, and Piccadilly lines. That between Earl's Court and Hammersmith was opened on 9 September 1874, and the extension from Earl's Court to Walham Green and Putney on 1 March 1880.

In Warwick Road is the principal entrance to the Stadium which was erected on the site of the former Earl's Court Exhibition grounds, which superseded those of South Kensington. The American Exhibition of 1887 was the first one to be held at Earl's Court, and the series was continued from that year until 1914. During the first World War Earl's Court grounds and buildings were requisitioned for Government service. Afterwards they remained empty for many years, but were purchased in 1935 by a company who have erected on this site the largest indoor stadium and exhibition hall in Europe at a cost of £1,250,000. This was opened in 1937 and contains seating accommodation for twenty thousand people. It is a steel and concrete building of two storeys covering eighteen and a half acres and is held on a lease of ninety-nine years granted by the London Passenger Transport Board. It is over 150 feet high and has a second entrance in Lillie Road on the other side of the West London Railway. The building is largely used for exhibitions and for notable events such as the Motor Show. At first it was not a financial success and a receiver was appointed in 1938. During the second World War it was requisitioned by the Government.

A prominent landmark of Earl's Court Exhibition for many years was the Great Wheel erected in 1894, which followed upon the construction of that erected at the World's Fair Exhibition in Chicago, which it exceeded in size. A journey round the Earl's Court Wheel occupied twenty minutes. On one occasion it got stuck, with the result that the passengers were compelled to pass the night on the Wheel before they could be liberated. However, they received £5 each as compensation for their enforced captivity. The Great Wheel was finally dismantled in 1907. Nevern Square which lies between Earl's Court Road and Warwick Road was hit by a rocket-bomb in July 1944 which reduced nearly half of the square to ruins. The two blocks on the corner of Nevern Road were completely demolished but they have now been rebuilt and the square has almost resumed its pre-war appearance.

Philbeach Gardens, leading out of Warwick Road, contains St Cuthbert's Church, which on Good Friday, 1898, was the scene of an anti-ritualist demonstration by Mr John Kensit, who had to be forcibly ejected from the building. The church was badly damaged in the air raids of 1940 but is now rebuilt. Opposite the southern end of Warwick Road is the West Brompton Cemetery, extending from Richmond Road to Fulham Road and covering an area of forty acres. It was laid out by the West London and Westminster Cemetery Company, incorporated in 1840, and the burial-ground was consecrated on 12 June 1840. Adjoining Brompton Cemetery is the Princess Beatrice Hospital which was rebuilt and extended about 1934.

Opposite Earl's Court Road are Redcliffe Gardens and Redcliffe Square, a handsome quarter of large houses erected between 1869 and 1872. Redcliffe Gardens stands on the site of Walnut Tree Walk, and Finborough Road, with Ifield Road, skirting the east side of Brompton Cemetery, was formerly known as Honey Lane. Lillie Road, the western continuation of Old Brompton Road, is named after Sir John Scott Lillie, who owned the adjoining land when this thoroughfare was first opened. Many houses in the Redcliffe Square quarter have been destroyed in the blitz and their sites cleared for rebuilding. Redcliffe Square has been acquired for a public garden.

Coleherne Court, an extensive colony of flats facing Old Brompton Road between Redcliffe Gardens and the Grove, was erected between 1901 and 1903 on the site of Coleherne House and the adjoining Hereford House. At the back of the flats is a pleasant garden. Coleherne House was at one time the residence of Lady Ponsonby, the widow of Major-General Sir William Ponsonby, K.C.B., who was killed at the battle of Waterloo on 18 June 1815. Farther along, opposite Collingham Road, is the Boltons, an oval enclosure formed by two crescents with St Mary's Church in the centre and clustered around which are some pleasant semi-detached residences with large gardens.

Twenty-Fourth Walk

Chelsea, Battersea Park, Fulham, Hammersmith and Shepherd's Bush

At the dawn of the nineteenth century Chelsea was described as a large and populous village situated about three miles from London, which, by virtue of the great increase in the number of its buildings, might be said to resemble a large town. It is said to derive its name from the river shore, being like the chesil, which the sea washes up, composed of sand and pebble-stones. It then contained close upon twenty thousand inhabitants, and whilst it was indirectly connected with London by the long line of houses on the west side of Sloane Street, extending to Knightsbridge and thence ot Hyde Park Corner, it was separated from it on the east side by the Five Fields, situated between Sloane Square and Grosvenor Place. The subsequent rise of Belgravia, laid out by Mr Thomas Cubitt between 1826 and 1831, resulted in Chelsea becoming a part of the west end of London. Now joined with Kensington under the new title of 'The Royal Borough of Kensington and Chelsea'.

Starting on this walk at Hyde Park Corner, our route is by way of Knightsbridge and Sloane Street. In Sloane Terrace, on the east side of Sloane Street, is the First Church of Christ Scientist, London, a handsome building faced with Portland stone and crowned by a tall stone tower. At the south end of Sloane Street, near the square, is Holy Trinity Church, a building of the Gothic Revival period, erected in 1830, and rebuilt about 1890. The frontage to Sloane Square consists of a centre flanked by two wide towers terminating in octagonal spires.

The centre of Sloane Square itself has been repaved with flagstones, somewhat after the manner of Trafalgar Square, and is planted round the sides with plane-trees which have now almost reached maturity. There is also an attractive fountain with a large octagonal basin. In the centre is a bronze nude on a pedestal, the sides of which are decorated with reliefs showing Charles II and Nell Gwynne in dalliance. When first laid out towards the end of the eighteenth century, Sloane Square was an open space, simply enclosed with wooden posts connected by iron chains. Here boys frequently played cricket, and Queen Charlotte's Royal Volunteers assembled and marched off in military fashion to Hyde Park, accompanied by an excellent band.

On the east side of the square, adjoining the Underground Railway Station, is the Royal Court Theatre, opened in January 1871, and replacing a chapel built in 1818. An earlier theatre had formerly stood on this site. The booking-hall of the Underground Station, which had only just been rebuilt before the last war, was completely wrecked during an air raid in November 1940. The south-west corner of Sloane Square and King's Road, now occupied by Lloyds and Barclays Banks, was rebuilt about 1891, but the block of shops and flats called Wellesley House at the south-eastern corner was not completed until 1906. Wellesley House and the adjoining Wyndham House are largely occupied by William Willett Ltd, Estate Agents. On the wall is a memorial plaque to William Willett (1856-1915) originator of Daylight Saving ('Summer Time'). The latest development in bank architecture is to be seen at the rebuilt branch of Barclay's Bank. Gone is the massive stonework and heavy furnishings with marble pillars and frosted glass. Instead, the windows are large sheets of plain plate glass extending from ceiling height to floor level with glass doors to match. This is now a familiar pattern of bank rebuilding. Previously a row of some half a dozen old houses had stood upon this site. The Royal Court Hotel, a red-brick building on the north side of the square, was erected about 1895. The houses on the west side were pulled down to make room for Messrs Peter Jones, the largest drapery store in Chelsea. The original store was a three-storeyed red-brick building, which was pulled down and the new six-storeyed structure put up in its place between 1935 and 1937. It belongs to the John Lewis partnership. This store is noteworthy for its modern concrete cantilever construction, permitting the windows of all storeys to be in a continuous horizontal line with apparently no support. Actually the building is erected with large internal columns with outspread cantilever arms supporting each floor; this method permits the maximum of light and air to enter the building. It is generally considered to be an outstanding example of store architecture.

Sloane Gardens and Lower Sloane Street, to the south of Sloane Square, are now lined with red-brick houses, erected between 1891 and 1895 on the site of shabby rows of old buildings which, formerly a poor neighbourhood, was transformed into a rich one, but a shabby terrace of houses and shops, which still lines the east side of Lower Sloane Street between the Chelsea Barracks and Sloane Gardens, will convey a fair idea of what it was like some seventy years ago. They are gradually being demolished and the five that now remain have been so smartly redecorated that, with the new buildings at each end, this terrace can no longer be disparaged as 'shabby'.

King's Road, to which we will return later, is the central thoroughfare of Chelsea. Originally it was only a footway through fields, for the use of farmers and gardeners, but after the restoration of Charles II it was found to be a convenient way for His Majesty to get to Hampton Court Palace, and was therefore converted into a coach road.

On the south side of King's Road, extending to Cheltenham Terrace, is the former Duke of York's School, founded in 1801 for the support and education of the sons of soldiers, and removed to Dover in 1909. In that year a considerable widening of this part of King's Road was effected by setting back the railings of the school grounds. The building is now the headquarters of several Territorial Regiments. In Lower Sloane Street at the corner of Turk's Row is the Rose and

Crown Tavern, rebuilt in 1933 after an existence of some two hundred years. Its upper five storeys now form a modern block of flats.

A century ago what is now the western end of Pimlico Road, running into Lower Sloane Street further south, was then called Jew's Row. At that time it was a centre of depravity as bad as any part of the East End of London, but it was confined to this small area. An unsightly collection of buildings which then occupied the ground between Turk's Row and Jew's Row has long since been demolished, and the site is now covered by two new streets called Sloane Court East and Sloane Court West, consisting of modern blocks of flats.

In Jew's Row stood the famous Chelsea Bun House, a one-storeyed structure with a colonnade projecting over the footpath. It was especially popular on Good Friday, when as many as fifty thousand people are said to have come here to buy buns, and 240,000 buns were sold. George II and Caroline of Anspach were fond of driving down to fetch their buns, and this practice was continued by George III and Queen Charlotte, who set the fashion for everyone else. The Chelsea Bun House enjoyed the favour of the public for more than a century and a half, but in 1839 the proprietors foolishly killed the goose that laid the golden eggs by rebuilding the old house, with the result that no one came any more.

Proceeding along Royal Hospital Road, formerly known as Queen's Road, we come to the principal entrance to the world-famous Chelsea Royal Hospital built by Sir Christopher Wren. It was originally a theological college, the first stone of which was laid by James I in 1609. The building progressed very slowly, however, and in 1681 was conveyed to Sir Stephen Fox for £13,000, in order to build a new hospital. The foundation-stone of the new building was laid by Charles II in 1682. The hospital was completed in 1690, and the total cost of the building was £150,000. The Hospital stands in large and attractive gardens, extending to the Thames and covering a part of the site of the old Ranelagh Gardens. The frontage to the Thames consists of a centre and two wings of red brick with stone dressings. The buildings comprise three courts, two of which form spacious quadrangles, whilst the third is open to the river. In the centre of the front quadrangle is a statue of Charles II by Grinling Gibbons. Accommodation is provided for 558 inmates, and there are also many out-pensioners. During the second World War, thirty-two large bombs fell in this area. Early in 1941 the Infirmary was destroyed by a mine, and in 1945 a rocket demolished the residences of several officials. A new Infirmary building has been completed. In the grounds in front of the Hospital is an obelisk erected in 1853 to the memory of the officers and men of the XXIVth Regiment who fell at Chillianwalla during the second Sikh War.

Ranelagh Gardens, a celebrated place of amusement in the second half of the eighteenth century, was opened annually in April and closed in July. Many people used to go there by river, for the gardens extended to the Thames. The chief attraction of Ranelagh was the Rotunda, an elegant wooden building on the lines of the Pantheon in Rome, designed by Mr William Jones, architect to the former East India Company, and erected in 1740. Here vocal and instrumental concerts were given, and the interior was tastefully fitted up with recesses for taking refreshment.

The fare to Ranelagh from London by hackney coach was one shilling, and the price of admission to the grounds half a crown. Already in 1770 the road from Ranelagh to London by way of St James's Park and Buckingham House was lighted all the way with lamps, but even so, there was a well-armed patrol between Ranelagh and Hyde Park Corner, as well as a guard at the back of Chelsea College. Ranelagh House itself originally belonged to the Earl of Ranelagh, but on his decease the estate was sold, and a large part of the gardens converted into fields.

Chelsea Bridge Road, forming the eastern boundary of the Royal Hospital grounds, was constructed in 1853 to connect Lower Sloane Street with the new Chelsea Suspension Bridge. The latter was opened on 30 March 1858, and was crossed for the first time on 18 March by the Prince of Wales, afterwards King Edward VII, and the Prince Consort. The cost of the bridge was £85,319, but having proved inadequate for the requirements of its present-day traffic, it was closed in March 1935 for reconstruction. The new bridge, which was opened in 1937, is considerably wider than its predecessor. The Chelsea Barracks on the east side of Chelsea Bridge Road were erected in 1861-62 at a cost of £100,000, and were designed to accommodate a thousand men. The trenches for the building were opened on 5 November 1860, the sixth anniversary of the battle of Inkerman. A hundred years later, in 1960, the barracks were completely demolished. A new building, the foundation stone of which was laid by the Duke of Gloucester in June 1960, has now been completed; it has accommodation for two battalions of Foot Guards, and cost over £2,000,000.

Grosvenor Road, the riverside embankment between Chelsea Bridge and Vauxhall Bridge, was constructed in 1857, but the more imposing Chelsea Embankment to the west, along which we will now proceed, was formally opened in May 1874 having cost £133,000 to construct. The opening ceremony was attended with much less pomp than that of the Victoria Embankment. A spacious pavilion was erected at the eastern end of the new Embankment, accommodating a thousand visitors, quests of the Metropolitan Board of Works, including members of the City Corporation and Members of Parliament. The foundation-stone of the Chelsea Embankment was laid in August 1871 by Colonel Hogg. The roadway is three-quarters of a mile in length, and nine and a half acres of land were reclaimed from the river.

In the reign of Charles II this part of the river, which is called Chelsea Reach, was so fashionable as a rendezvous for pleasure-boats and barges that it became known as 'Hyde Park on the Thames' or 'Pall Mall afloat'. Being the widest reach anywhere west of London Bridge it was eminently suitable for grand aquatic displays, which were attended by dukes and duchesses and a throng of fashionable society.

Near the western end of the Chelsea Embankment is the Royal Albert

Suspension Bridge, commenced in 1870 and opened to the public without ceremony in August 1873. The bridge is 710 feet long and 40 feet wide including the footways, and connects Oakley Street, Chelsea, with Battersea Park Road. Oakley Street, built in the' fifties of the last century, is a fairly broad thoroughfare leading to King's Road and consists of long rows of large yellow-brick houses with porticoed balconies. By way of Sydney Street, a little farther down on the north side of King's Road, it provides a direct route from Battersea Park to South Kensington.

A well-known resident of Oakley Street was the rich and eccentric Dr John Samuel Phene, LL.D., F.S.A., F.R.G.S., etc., who lived at No 32. Descendent of an Italian family who occupied a large chateau at Savenay on the Loire, he built at the corner of Upper Cheyne Row, opposite his house, what he intended to be a fascimile of the French chateau, but it was never completed. The building, known locally as 'Gingerbread Castle', was decorated with all sorts of curious ornaments — statues, carvings, heraldic shields, cherubs, gargoyles, mermaids, mottoes and inscriptions of various kinds. These could all be seen on the outside of the building, but according to reports by the very few people who had been privileged to enter, the inside was even more fantastic in its decoration.

Dr Phene, who was also the first to plant trees in the streets of London, died in 1912 at the age of 89, and his Chelsea chateau was demolished in 1917. He is remembered by Phene Street and the 'Phene Arms' tavern, and Margaretta Terrace, which he built in 1851, is named after his wife, who left him soon after their marriage.

Cheyne Walk, built in 1708, now forming the western continuation of the Chelsea Embankment, extends to Lots Road, and is so named from Charles, Lord Cheyne, once Lord of the Manor. Among the many brick-fronted, eighteenth-century houses, with carved doors and wrought-iron gates, are two handsome modern houses, the Clock House and the Swan House, the works of Norman Shaw. The latter house commemorates the Swan Tavern, which served as a goal for the London watermen who rowed from London Bridge for Doggett's coat and badge, and also as a place of jovial entertainment for Samuel Pepys. George Eliot (Mrs J. W. Cross) died at Number 4 Cheyne Walk on 22 December 1880. Cheyne Row was long the residence of Thomas Carlyle, who lived here for forty-seven years, from 1834, until his death in 1881. Opposite the opening to Cheyne Row is a statue of Thomas Carlyle by Boehm, and further to the east in Cheyne Walk Gardens, is a memorial fountain (dry) to Dante Gabriel Rosetti, opposite No 16 where he lived.

To the east of Cheyne Walk, near the junction of Royal Hospital Road with the Chelsea Embankment, is the Physic Garden of the Apothecaries' Society. In 1734 Sir Hans Sloane granted the freehold of this property upon various conditions, including one that the Society should deliver 50 dried specimens of plants every year to the Royal Society until the number reached 2,000. A marble statue of Sir Hans by Rysbrach, stands in the garden. Since 1899 it has been maintained by the Trustees of the London Parochial Charities and is now used for research work in connexion with the Imperial College of Science.

Parallel with the river at the corner of Old Church Street stood Chelsea Old Church, built early in the fourteenth century, and practically demolished by enemy action in April 1941. When the debris was cleared, a large portion of More's chapel, including the fourteenth-century roof, was found to be almost intact. Five fire-watchers were killed in the church during this incident. The original church, being in a state of decay and too small for the large congregation of the town, was partly demolished in 1667, and rebuilt much as it appeared at the time of its destruction, with a new steeple and a peal of six bells. Against the south wall of the chancel stood the monument erected to himself by Sir Thomas More in 1532. Happily this historic church has now been rebuilt and was re-consecrated by the Bishop of London, in the presence of Queen Elizabeth the Queen Mother on 13 May 1958.

Returning to King's Road and proceeding in the direction of Sloane Square, we pass Manresa Road where, next to the public library, the former Polytechnic building (opened in 1895) is now the Chelsea College of Science and Technology; there are also new buildings for the School of Art, and Lightfoot Hall, a student's hostel. In Dovehouse Street is the Chelsea Hospital for Women, and at the corner of Sydney Street was the Chelsea Palace of Varieties (erected 1905) recently a television studio, but demolished in 1966. In Sydney Street is Chelsea New Church, erected in 1820. The square tower is 142 feet high and the church is built in imitation of the Gothic style of the fourteenth century. The cost of the building was £30,000. In this church Charles Dickens was married to Catherine Hogarth on 2 April 1836. After the completion of St Luke's Church many new streets were laid out in Chelsea, notably Sydney Street, then called Robert Street, Jubilee Place, opened in 1809, Blenheim Street, and Wellesley Street. Because of a murder committed there over a hundred years ago, the name of Wellesley Street was changed to Chelsea Manor Street. Blenheim Street has been renamed Astell Street.

Opposite Sydney Street is Chelsea Town Hall, a red-brick and stone building of 1886, extended in 1906-8. Across the road, facing Royal Avenue is a new development; about 50 yards behind the normal King's Road frontage is Ranelagh House, a new building of flats and offices with shops below which, being set back from the bustle and traffic, forms a small edition of the 'shopping precinct'.

On the south side of King's Road, a few doors east of Oakley Street, is the Six Bells Tavern, a distinguished-looking house with a Tudor façade. Beyond the Town Hall some modern buildings have been erected between Manor Street and Flood Street. At the back of King's Road is an immense block of flats erected in 1930. It is called Swan Court, and extends from Flood Street through to Manor Street. Quite a lot of widening has been carried out in recent years in King's Road, between Beaufort Street and Sloane Square, but much still remains to be done, notably between Jubilee Place and Anderson Street where the roadway narrows into a bottleneck.

Wellington Square and the wide Royal Avenue leading to Chelsea Hospital contain large Georgian town houses which have retained their popularity to the present day. In Tite Street, at the western end of Royal Hospital Road, adjoining the grounds of Chelsea Hospital, is the Victoria Hospital for Children. The building, which was converted to its present use in 1866, was formerly known as Gough House. It was built by John, third Earl of Carbery, at the commencement of the eighteenth century. The estate was afterwards acquired by the Gough family, and later the house became a school for young ladies. Sir Richard Gough, who died in 1727, was an eminent London merchant who had amassed a large fortune in India.

Until after 1815 Chelsea boasted a common, which in ancient records was called Chelsea Heath. It was bounded on the north by Fulham Road, on the south by King's Road, on the east by Blacklands Lane, now Draycott Avenue, and on the west by Pond Place. Here certain houses, farms, and cottages had a right of pasturage for forty cows and twenty heifers. To attend these there was always a cow-keeper whose business it was to mark the cattle, drive home the cows at night to their several owners, and to impound all cattle unmarked or any horses which broke into the common or were found there. After 1674 the common was closed by the consent of Charles Cheyne, the Lord of the Manor. About 1810 the Lord of the Manor, the rector, and other proprietors let the common on building leases, and it was then covered with streets lined with small private houses.

This later became a poor neighbourhood, but some fifty years ago an attempt was made to convert it into a prosperous one by carving the wide new thorough-fare called Sloane Avenue out of the former Keppel Street and cutting Draycott Place through from Marlborough Road (now Draycott Avenue) to Sloane Avenue. At first considerable developments took place, a number of fairly large town houses were erected in Sloane Avenue and the western end of Draycott Place, and Cadogan Court, a large block of flats built in Draycott Avenue. Nevertheless acres of ground which had been cleared of old houses remained unsold, and to such an extent did this new quarter fail to realize the hopes that were placed in it that for more than twenty years not a single new house was erected here.

Gaping and half-demolished slums could be seen leading out of Sloane Avenue, and Draycott Place entirely failed to respond to the dignity of its aristocratic new title. Since 1928 this quarter has been fully built up, and some semi-detached houses now stand on the east side of Sloane Avenue, and two immense blocks of flats have been built on either side of Whitehead's Grove. That on the south corner, Sloane Avenue Mansions, is faced with concrete and was erected in 1933, whilst that on the north corner, Nell Gwynne House, which is a much larger building, was completed in 1937. It is faced with red brick and has a spacious open courtyard in the centre which forms the main entrance from Sloane Avenue. Both these buildings are ten storeys high and have second frontages to Draycott Avenue. On the west side of Sloane Avenue now stands Cranmer Court, erected in 1934, and it covers the greater part of the island site bounded by Sloane Avenue, Whitehead's Grove, Elystan Street and Petyward. The buildings are of red brick and nine storeys high. On the side facing Sloane Avenue is a row of shops which extend through to the first quadrangle. Cranmer Court was badly damaged in the air raids of 1940 but has since been repaired. A group of small red-brick Tudor-style houses called the Gateways has been erected on the opposite side of Whitehead's Grove, opening on to courtyards in the manner of ancient almshouses. On this side of Sloane Avenue is another vast ten-storeyed block of flats called Chelsea Cloisters. This opens on to a spacious courtyard and was erected in 1937-38. It covers most of the island site bounded by Sloane Avenue, Makin Street, Elystan Street and Ixworth Place. In Draycott Avenue on the east side is a large site which is bounded by Rosemoor Street, Rawlings Street and Denyer Street, It was cleared of its slums many years ago but remained vacant until after the second World War. On this site the Chelsea Borough Council completed several fine blocks of flats to house 216 families. These are six storeys high and faced with red brick and are built round an open courtyard.

A walk through Sloane Avenue will bring us to Fulham Road opposite Pelham Street, which leads direct to South Kensington Station. At the corner of Draycott Avenue and Fulham Road is the Admiral Keppel, a famous tavern which once had tea gardens. The original house was demolished in 1856 and the present much larger tavern erected in its place. Before they were amalgamated in 1965, Fulham Road was the dividing line between the boroughs of Chelsea and Kensington. Pelham Crescent on the north side, with gardens fronting the main Fulham Road, has retained its original Georgian houses, but its gardens are now overlooked on the south side by large new blocks of shops and flats. These include Thurloe Court, and the adjoining Pelham Court, completed in 1933. Thurloe Court was badly damaged by enemy action but has lately been rebuilt. On the north side beyond Pelham Crescent is the Brompton Hospital for Diseases of the Chest, an Elizabethan-style structure comprising a centre and wings. The building has a frontage of about two hundred feet and occupies a piece of ground covering three acres. The foundation-stone was laid by the Prince Consort in 1841.

On the opposite side of the road is the Cancer Hospital, now renamed The Royal Marsden Hospital, erected in 1851. It is built of plain white brick alternating with bands of red brick, with keystones and cornices of terracotta. Farther along is the Chester Beatty Research Institute which is situated close to the Jews' Burial Ground at the east corner of Old Church Street. The latter was purchased in 1813 by a society of Jews and opened in the same year. It was designed for the interment of the families of those who had subscribed the purchase money. The opposite corner of Old Church Street and Fulham Road, now occupied by a large tavern of the same name, is called Queen's Elm, and is traditionally said to derive its origin from the following incident. Queen Elizabeth I was out walking with Lord Burghley, and being overtaken by a heavy shower of rain took shelter under an elm-tree growing on this spot. After the shower was over she said, 'Let this henceforth be called the Queen's Tree'. Trafalgar Square, now renamed Chelsea Square, to the east of Old Church Street, was laid out in the year 1812, and once contained Georgian houses, all of which have now been pulled down, the ones on the south-west corner being the last to go. They have been replaced by modern (very expensive) red-brick villas.

After leaving Queen's Elm we pass a long row of modern shops and then come to Elm Park Gardens, consisting of two parallel rows of large Victorian houses backing on to spacious private grounds. The houses on the south-western side, which are of more recent construction, directly face the gardens, from which they are separated by a roadway. Elm Park Gardens was built in the 'seventies of last century upon the site of the grounds of Chelsea House, which fronted the south side of Fulham Road and comprised an area of thirty-two acres. Originally built by John Appletree, Chelsea House afterwards became the residence of the Duke of Wharton. Here a manufactory of raw silk was established by patent about the year 1721 and the grounds planted with mulberry-trees. This venture, however, proved a failure, and was therefore abandoned. No less than two thousand trees had been planted here, and it was the intention of the owners to plant many more if the industry had paid its way. Rows of large town houses in Elm Park Gardens which were requisitioned during the second World War were later taken over by the Chelsea Borough Council, and were converted into flats and maisonettes to accommodate people with high incomes.

Cranley Gardens, opposite Elm Park Gardens, leading to Gloucester Road, contains a similar type of house. On the east side is St Peter's Church, opened in 1868, and crowned with a tall spire. The adjoining Evelyn Gardens, on the west side of Cranley Gardens, contains some pleasant modern houses with red-brick frontages. At the corner of Fulham Road and Drayton Gardens is the Forum Cinema which was erected in 1930, and as Fulham Road narrows into a bottleneck at this point the opportunity was taken of setting back the building line for a considerable distance at the west corner of Drayton Gardens. Let us hope that this widening will be continued in the near future towards Gilston Road. Directly opposite Drayton Gardens is Beaufort S reet, along which we will now proceed, and after crossing King's Road once again, come to Battersea Bridge.

Beaufort Street, south of King's Road, has been completely rebuilt in modern times, and consists largely of blocks of dwellings faced with red brick. It stands on the site of Beaufort House, a large mansion which was reputed to have been the site of the house of Sir Thomas More, who purchased an estate in Chelsea about the year 1520, and resided here after his resignation from the Chancellorship in 1532. The actual site of Sir Thomas More's house had nevertheless remained in doubt, and the Rev. Dr King, one of the vicars of Chelsea Old Church, remarked, 'As seven cities in Greece contended for the birthplace of Homer, so there are no fewer than four houses in this parish which lay claim to Sir Thomas More's residence'. Beaufort House is the most generally accepted site. Formerly the mansion of the Duke of Beaufort, it was purchased in 1736 by Sir Hans Sloane for £2,500 at a public sale and was pulled down in 1740.

The present Battersea Bridge, designed by Sir Joseph Bazalgette at a cost of £143,000, was opened by Lord Rosebery on Monday, 31 July 1890. It is forty feet wide, of which twenty-four feet are allotted to the roadway and eight feet to each of the two sidewalks. By 1883 the old bridge, which was an unsightly timber structure, had become so unsafe that it had to be closed to traffic. A temporary footbridge was erected and the old structure demolished. Erected between 1766 and 1771, the old bridge, twenty-eight feet wide, was built by John Earl Spencer and other subscribers at the small cost of under £18,000, including the approaches.

Before resuming our travels westwards, we will turn once more into Cheyne Walk and at the corner of Danvers Street and Cheyne Walk we pass the famous Crosby Hall, erected in Bishopsgate in 1466 and removed to its present site in 1910; the oak roof and oriel windows are among the finest examples of that century. It now forms part of an international hall of residence and clubhouse, under the British Federation of University Women, for women graduates studying in London.

Between Crosby Hall and the Church, are the new Roper's Gardens, laid out in 1964 on the site of buildings destroyed by a parachute mine in April 1941. The site of these gardens formed part of the marriage gift of Sir Thomas More to this daughter Margaret on her marriage to William Roper in 1521. Among lawns with seats and shelters is a bronze nude, *Awakening*, by Gilbert Ledward, R.A. (1888-1960).

Crossing the Albert Bridge, we enter Battersea Park, which was originally known as Battersea Fields, and was occupied mainly by cabbage-planters and asparagus-growers. The land was purchased about 1828 by the Marquess of Westminster, who afterwards leased it to Mr Cubitt, the builder. This gentleman conceived the idea, in view of the rapid growth of London, of converting these swampy marshes into a park for the people. His scheme was submitted to the Metropolitan Improvement Commissioners, who strongly recommended it for the consideration and support of the Government. As a result, an Act of Parliament was passed in 1846 to enable the Commissioners to purchase 320 acres of land at Battersea to be utilized partly for building houses and villas, the Commissioners being authorized to advance a sum not exceeding £200,000. Negotiations also took place with other owners of land, and eventually £232,620 was expended on the property, with an additional sum of £51,000, for laying out the park, by a system of annual grants from 1853 to 1858 from the Parliamentary Committee and the Commissioners of Woods and Forests. Some 185 acres were set aside for the park, and 101 acres remained to be sold for building purposes. By December 1848 work in the formation of Battersea Park was in active progress. Up to that time the ground had been cultivated to the very limits by industrious allotment-holders, agriculturalists, and market-gardeners, but the frontage next to the Thames was cut up into numerous small properties and for years had been put to no productive use; when the tide ran high the water overflowed into the adjacent lands. Considerable difficulties were experienced by H.M. Office of Woods and Forests in completing the purchase of the riverside frontage, as private enterprise had already stepped in and anticipated the future movements of the Government.

The result was that several of the owners commenced embanking their respective frontages. Barges were employed daily to convey the sweepings of the streets of London to Battersea, whence they were deposited on the embankment. When first deposited the soil was particularly soft and slushy but soon consolidated and formed a good substantial stratum. The embankment itself is about five feet above high-water mark, seventy or eighty yards in width, and traverses the whole of the river frontage of Battersea Park. In Battersea Fields the Duke of Wellington fought a duel with the Earl of Winchelsea in 1829.

The formation of Battersea Park involved the disappearance of the Tivoli Tea Gardens and pleasure grounds, which were closed on 22 August 1853, and possession was also obtained of the Red House Tavern and its grounds. In its palmy days, the Red House formed a second Vauxhall Gardens, and attracted quite a number of aristocrats to Battersea, but eventually it became a hotbed of drinking, gambling, donkey races, and fortune-tellers. The common rights of St Mary, Battersea, were abolished upon payment of £1,500 as compensation. Battersea Park, now one of the most beautiful in the metropolis, also contains a large expanse of lake constructed in 1860, and a sub-tropical garden of four acres. About 1896, during the early days of cycling, Battersea Park became for a short time the fashionable rendezvous for London society, who used to frequent the place for cycling before breakfast. That part of Battersea Park nearest the river is now occupied by the Festival Pleasure Gardens.

On the east side of the park are the tracks and yards of British Railways (Southern Region), which are screened from view by an ornamental wall, and close by, overlooking the Thames, is the gigantic new Battersea electric power station. For many years the land on the south side of Battersea Park remained more or less derelict, but in May 1885, the Albert Palace was erected on the site now covered partly by the Battersea College of Technology, which was opened on 24 February 1894, and partly by modern blocks of flats. It was originally built for the Dublin Exhibition of 1872, and re-erected here with substantial additions and improvements. The Albert Palace specialized in high-class musical entertainments, and contained a very fine picture gallery. The venture never proved a success, and in 1886 the Albert Palace Company collapsed, after which the building and grounds passed in to the hands of Mr William Holland. Still proving a complete failure, the building was pulled down about 1894, after having remained closed for several years. Half a mile of large five-storeyed blocks of flats in Prince of Wales's Drive now line the entire south side of Battersea Park; and Albert Bridge Road, on the west side of Battersea Park, likewise contains some good-class houses.

At the junction of Prince of Wales's Drive and Surrey Lane is Battersea Bridge Road, along which we will now direct our steps. The original village of Battersea, or Peter's Eye, which was situated at the bend of the river to the west of Chelsea Reach, is said to have derived its name from a corruption of St Peter's Island as in ancient times it belonged to the Abbey of St Peter at Westminster. The manor house, which was formerly the seat of Lord Spencer, was a venerable structure with forty rooms on one floor. The greater part of the house was pulled down in 1798, the last remaining portion being re-erected in Philadelphia. This building in turn was pulled down in 1819. The parish church, a picturesque brick building with a square tower and a spire, which faces the river, was rebuilt in 1777 and replaced an earlier structure which had stood on the same site for centuries. Near the church in Vicarage Crescent stands Old Battersea House, which has been scheduled as an ancient monument. Built in 1699, it is one of the finest examples of Sir Christopher Wren's domestic architecture. In addition to furniture and pictures there is a splendid collection of pottery by the late William de Morgan (author of *Joseph Vance*). Mrs A. M. W. Stirling, author of several books of historical interest, who lived at Battersea House, was a sister of Evelyn de Morgan the artist, many of whose paintings are to be seen here. Mrs Stirling, a gracious and gifted lady, who gradually converted her home into a private museum, died in August 1965, within two weeks of her 100th birthday. The Vicarage, Battersea, was the home of Edward Adrian Wilson, the Antarctic explorer (1872-1912). In the High Street is Sir Walter St John's School (*Rather Deathe than False of Faythe*), founded in 1700, and A.D. 1600 is the date claimed by Ye Olde Castle Tavern on the other side. 'The Castle' was completely rebuilt in 1965, and a stone recording the event tells us that in 1600 the price of Mild Ale was 4s a barrel (about $^1/_4$d a pint), but by 1965 has risen to 1s 5d a pint (of which 7d is Excise Duty). During the rebuilding, a crock of early 19th century gold and silver coins, valued at about £250, was found in the footings of the old tavern. Battersea is now part of the borough of Wandsworth. Though it is cursed with mean streets and slums, many of them have been removed by Hitler's bombs leaving bombed sites for future redevelopment. A fine new housing estate has been developed by the London County Council on the south side of Wandsworth Road centred round Union Road and several wide roads on the sloping ground leading up to Clapham Road.

We now recross the Thames Battersea Bridge and turn to the left along the western end of Cheyne Walk. A short walk brings us to Lots Road, and the generating station of the Underground Electric Railways of London. The dreary streets situated between Lots Road, King's Road, and Cheyne Walk are mostly built upon the site of Cremorne Gardens, which until finally closed in 1877 was one of London's principal summer pleasure resorts. Many houses have been destroyed in this quarter by bombing and large sites have been cleared of their debris. The Cremorne Estate was originally known as Chelsea Farm, and in 1751 became the property of the Dowager Countess of Exeter. It devolved in 1803 to Viscount Cremorne, after whom the property was named. The natural beauty of its situation afterwards led to the grounds being opened to the public, and when the splendour of Vauxhall was on the wane, it occurred to some enterprising individual to open a rival establishment higher up the river in a more bracing air. Cremorne covered sixteen acres. It was much gayer than Vauxhall even on its most brilliant nights, and splendid displays of fireworks were given here. Amongst other attractions were a theatre, a circus, an outdoor orchestra, grottoes, and dining-hall. The gates of Cremorne Gardens (1845-1877) are preserved in Tetcott Road.

In the summer of 1845 numerous balloon ascents were made from Vauxhall and Cremorne Gardens by a Mr and Mrs Green, who came to earth in such places as Epping Forest, Plumstead, Highgate, Shepherd's Bush, and Croydon. A later attempt at aerial navigation by a Mr de Groof resulted in disaster, for when the apparatus was suspended beneath the car of a balloon, and the machine was liberated, it immediately collapsed owing to some defect in its construction, and fell to the ground with a terrible crash, instantly killing its unfortunate occupant.

The district to the north of King's Road, extending to the West London Railway, was formerly known as Little Chelsea. Until about 1860 it still remained more or less a rural hamlet in its general character. It commenced west of Chelsea Park, now Elm Park Gardens, and had its centre in Fulham Road, at the corner of Beaufort Street, leading to Battersea Bridge. On 16 April 1765 Mr James House Knight, of Walham Green, returning home from London was robbed and murdered on the Fulham Road in the vicinity of Little Chelsea. A reward of £50 was offered for the discovery of the murderers, and on 7 July following two Chelsea pensioners were committed to prison charged with the murder on the evidence of their accomplice, another Chelsea pensioner, whom they had threatened to kill as the result of a quarrel which took place between them.

The accused were tried, found guilty, hanged and gibbeted, one nearly opposite Walnut Tree Walk, now renamed Redcliffe Gardens, and the other at Bull Lane, a quarter of a mile farther on, which connected the main Fulham Road with King's Road, by the side of the former Kensington Canal, now covered by the West London Railway. In those positions the bodies of the murderers hung in chains for some years, to the terror of benighted travellers and market gardeners passing here of an early morning bound for Covent Garden, until one day a drunken frolic caused the removal of this painful and useless exhibition. Many houses in this district have been destroyed or damaged in the blitz of 1940, notably in Gunter Grove, Ifield Road and Finborough Road.

At Park Walk and Milman's Street, about two hundred yards west of Beaufort Street, the King's Road bends in zigzag fashion to the left and then to the right, forming what was originally a dangerous corner but was considerably widened about forty years ago. Near the King's Road end of Milman's Street is the mid-eighteenth century Moravian Burial Ground, a tree-shaded square enclosure divided into four equal parts by two bisecting paths. The small gravestones are laid horizontally in regular rows; the married men in one section, the bachelors in another and the married and single women similarly separated. A short half-mile farther on past the World's End Tavern is the bridge over the West London Railway, which separates Chelsea and Fulham.

The West London Railway follows the track of the former Kensington Canal, which ran from Battersea Bridge to Hammersmith Road, and was designed to provide a connecting link between the railways north and south of the Thames. The canal, which was two and a quarter miles long, was opened on 12 August 1828, and was a hundred feet wide and capable of affording a passage for craft up to a hundred tons burden. It was built at a cost of £40,000 to convey water to Kensington and its income from wharfs, tonnage, etc., was estimated at £2,500 per annum. Similarly a canal was constructed in 1724 by the Chelsea Waterworks Company from the Thames near Ranelagh to Pimlico, to provide water to Westminster, Chelsea, and the West End of London. This canal was abolished to make way for Victoria Station. The first section of the West London Railway from Willesden Junction to Addison Road, now Kensington (Olympia), the former terminus, just north of Hammersmith Road, was opened in 1844, but the extension to Chelsea and Battersea, which involved the filling up of the old Kensington Canal, was not completed until 2 March 1863. By the 'Nell Gwynne Tavern', near Chelsea Creek, a short turning leads to Sandford Manor House which is probably over three centuries old. Believed to have been a country residence of Mistress Nell Gwynne, it has a good sized panelled hall and a square well staircase built exactly in the centre of the house. In the back garden is a mulberry tree said to have been planted by 'Poor Nelly'. Purchased by the Imperial Gas Company in 1824, the house, now the property of the North Thames Gas Board, is used as a private residence by members of their staff.

Following the King's Road for a short distance beyond the West London Railway, we next come to Walham Green, formerly a populous village or hamlet, but now densely built over. Prior to 1688 it was known as Wansdon Green, this name being derived from the Manor of Wendon. It was then a triangular plot of ground on the north side of Fulham Road, upon which donkeys used to graze and children to play cricket. The main King's Road skirts Eel Brook Common, but the shopping centre of Walham Green is the Broadway, situated in Fulham Road, reached by way of Harwood Road, at the corner of which is the Town Hall. Now that Fulham is in the borough of Hammersmith, the former Fulham Town Hall is now known as the 'Old Town Hall'. Opposite was the Granville Theatre of Varieties, now regrettably closed, and used for other purposes. North End Road is Fulham's busiest shopping centre and includes one of London's most lively street markets.

The church of St John in North End Road was built after the design of Mr Taylor upon a filled-up pond. The foundation-stone was laid on 1 January 1827, and the church was consecrated by the Bishop of London on 14 August 1828. Close to the Broadway stood the Butchers' Almshouses, the foundation-stone of which was laid by Lord Ravensworth on 1 July 1840. In 1921 the inmates moved to their new building, appropriately named Smoothfield, in the Staines Road, Hounslow. The Samuel Lewis Trust Dwellings of 1922 now stand on the Walham Green site. Until late in the last century stood the mansion called Purser's Cross, the residence of Mr John Ord, and afterwards of Lord Ravensworth. It was approached from the south side of Fulham Road shortly after passing Walham Green by carriage gates connected by a brick wall. It contained a curious garden planted and laid out in 1756 by Mr John Ord; this garden produced some of the finest specimens of trees in the kingdom. The mansion was visited by Queen Victoria and the Prince Consort in 1840, after which its name was changed for some unknown reason to Percy Cross.

Wandsworth Bridge Road, to the south of Walham Green, leads to Wandsworth Bridge, first opened in October 1873. Having become too narrow for the requirements of its traffic, the original bridge was pulled down in 1834 and replaced by the present handsome new structure of three arches which was opened for traffic in 1938. North End Road, leading to Lillie Road and West Kensington, follows the line of the original hamlet of North End, which consisted of a line of residences extending more than a mile in length, from Walham Green Church to Hammersmith. Market gardens skirted both sides of the road, and the gardener's cottages were very old. Amongst the noteworthy houses in this locality was Mount Carmel, formerly Hermitage Lodge, which stood at the corner of Lillie Road and North End Road, and which was originally built as stables for the residence of Foote the dramatist and comedian. His house stood on the opposite side of Lillie Road, and was surrounded by a large garden enclosed by high walls, but it has been pulled down and replaced by modern shops.

On the east side of North End Road, close to Lillie Road, Beaufort House stood in eight acres of ground, until about 1900. It was used as the headquarters of the South Middlesex Volunteers and was the meeting place of the London Athletic Club. This ground is now covered by several streets of two-storeyed houses. In Fulham Road, adjoining the West London Railway, is Stamford Bridge Football Ground, home of Chelsea, the First Division Club. Set in the walls of the railway bridge are stones marking the parish boundaries of Kensington, Chelsea and Fulham.

Little more than a century ago the entire parish of Fulham consisted of fertile and highly-cultivated market gardens, and it was said that at least one-half of the vegetables and fruits sold at Covent Garden were grown in this and the adjoining parishes. In addition to those we have already named, Fulham then contained many handsome villas and country seats. Fulham House, situated near Parson's Green, was the residence of the Lords Stourton, and afterwards of William Sharpe, who first brought the slave trade into disrepute. He died there in 1813 in his seventy-ninth year. Munster House was traditionally said to have been a hunting seat of Charles II, and was afterwards occupied by J. W. Croker, Secretary to the Admiralty.

But no other quarter of the metropolis has been so ruthlessly spoiled as Fulham, and London can show no place more cheerless or depressing than the district which lies between North End Road, Greyhound Road, Lillie Road, Dawes Road, and Munster Road. This is as mean as anything to be seen in the East End or the north of London. Much of it was destroyed, both in the early raids of 1940 and in 1944 by rocket-bombs, notably in Lillie Road and Star Road where large bombed sites have been actively developed by the Fulham Council. Among those in Lillie Road is the tall 'Clem Attlee Court', consisting of maisonettes, each of two floors — so that the numeration runs: — first, third, fifth etc. Across the road is the new Normand Park Primary School. The monotony of this part of Fulham is relieved by Queen's Club Gardens, which is like an oasis in the midst of a desert. This is a large square garden surrounded by four-storeyed blocks of flats faced with red brick which might have strayed here from South Kensington. It was built about 1897 and includes a tennis club. Mr Charles G. Harper in his work *A Londoner's Own London* says that places like Earlsfield, Tottenham, and Edmonton have been built to yield an immediate profit and designed to herd as many houses and people per acre as possible. Thus they have become joyless abodes inhabited mainly by artisans and clerks living in long monotonous streets with very small gardens. He forgot, however, to include Fulham amongst these delectable places. No one, he says, lives there from choice, but only for the sake of cheapness. Some fine new blocks of flats have been erected of late years by the Fulham Borough Council on the south side of Fulham Road not far from Parson's Green Station and one large new block of flats has been erected since 1946 on the corner of Fulham Road and Fulham Park Gardens called Arthur Henderson House. Near the junction of Fulham Road and New King's Road is the Fulham Pottery — 'Founded by John Dwight, Scholar & Master Potter, 1671'. The kilns are still there, though today there is not so much 'throwing' of clay, but a considerable output of modelling clay for artists and others and clay 'candles' for filtering apparatus. John Doulton, founder of the Doulton Pottery, served an apprenticeship here.

The only other feature of interest in this neighbourhood is Fulham Palace, situated close to the Thames near Putney Bridge. For upwards of eight centuries it has been the summer residence of the Bishops of London, though the oldest of the existing buildings dates back only to the reign of Henry VII. The Palace and walls were surrounded by a moat which has now been filled in. The present Putney Bridge, opened in 1886, has replaced a wooden structure built in 1729 from a design by a celebrated surgeon named Cheseldon. In 1934 an extensive widening of Putney Bridge was carried out by the London County Council to cope with the enormous increase in the traffic to this part of London. Fulham High Street, once a picturesque village street, was extensively widened on the west side in 1908 between Fulham Road and Putney Bridge. Most of this frontage is now covered by Parkview Court, a large six-storeyed block of shops and flats erected in 1934. The parish church of All Saints, close to the bridge, is an ancient building of stone with a conspicuous embattled tower. Adjoining the grounds of Fulham Palace is Bishops' Park, which contains attractive bowling greens, a tea-house, a paddling-pool and a sand-pit for the amusement of children; and a riverside promenade nearly half a mile long. East of Putney Bridge are the grounds of the Hurlingham Club, and several newly-erected blocks of flats called Rivermead Court overlooking the Thames and private gardens. The grounds of the Hurlingham Polo Club have been acquired by the London County Council, part for one of their new housing estates and part for a park.

A walk or an omnibus ride through Fulham Palace Road, half-way along which we pass the Fulham Cemetery and the adjoining recreation ground, will bring us to Hammersmith Broadway. Down to the year 1834 Hammersmith was a part of the parish of Fulham, but since that time it has become a separate parish, and now extends from Kensington on the east to Chiswick on the west and alongside the Thames from Crab Tree to Chiswick.

The parish church of St Paul, situated in Queen Caroline Street near the junction of Hammersmith Broadway and Bridge Road, was originally a chapel of ease, and was built in the reign of Charles I at the cost of Sir Nicholas Crispe, a wealthy citizen of London, and consecrated in 1631. On the west wall of the Church is a fine bronze bust of King Charles I, presented by the faithful Sir Nicholas, whose heart rests in an urn just below. Since that time it has undergone extensive repairs on different occasions. In 1864 it was restored and enlarged, and will now accommodate a thousand people. In the churchyard is the grave of Richard Honey, carpenter, and George Francis, bricklayer, 'who were slain on the 14th August 1821, while attending the funeral procession of Caroline of Brunswick, Queen of England.' This incident is referred to in our twenty-first walk. The present Hammersmith Suspension Bridge, opened in the summer of 1887 by Prince Albert Victor, Duke of Clarence, replaced an earlier suspension bridge erected in 1827, the first to be constructed in London on the suspension principle. It was designed by Mr Tierney Clark, at a cost of about £80,000. The roadway, which was sixteen feet above high-water mark, was suspended by eight chains arranged in four double lines, but was only twenty feet wide. The existing bridge, although an equally handsome structure, suffers like its predecessor from the drawback of being absurdly narrow for the requirements of its traffic, and it speaks very little for the judgment of our minucipal authorities in 1887 that they failed to realize that a much wider structure would later become imperative. Mr W. Tierney Clark, C.E., F.R.S., died in 1852 and his memorial on the north wall of St Paul, Hammersmith embodies an outline of the earlier Hammersmith Bridge.

In 1939 rebels of the Irish Republican Army who were seeking to create trouble between Britain and the Irish Free State attempted to destroy Hammersmith Bridge by planting a time-bomb. This however was discovered and courageously removed by a passer-by who threw the bomb into the river.

Hammersmith Broadway, which is the meeting-point of six thoroughfares, is quite the busiest traffic centre anywhere west of Hyde Park Corner. Here omnibus routes converge from all parts of London, and at week-ends, owing to its being the principal western exit from town, the volume of motor-car traffic is enormous. In 1908 Hammersmith Broadway was considerably widened in order to provide room for the electric tramways to Shepherd's Bush laid down by the London County Council to create increased facilities for visitors to the newly-opened White City. These have now been replaced by diesel-buses. The former Hammersmith Town Hall opened in 1897 by the Duke and Duchess of Fife, a handsome red-brick and stone building with a central clock-tower, has been demolished.

The Underground Railway Station is on the south side, and the Metropolitan Railway Station is situated on the opposite side of the Broadway, close to Beadon Road. The new and larger Town Hall, erected between 1937 and 1940, is on the south side of King Street at the corner of Nigel Playfair Street. This is a splendid square building of three storeys with a flat roof and façade of red brick with stone dressings. Its south front, which faces the Thames, flanks the Great West Road extension which runs parallel to King Street. Next to the Town Hall overlooking the river are several distinctive blocks of workers' flats. Some fine new six-storeyed blocks with balconies and faced with red brick have recently been completed by the Hammersmith Borough Council between King Street and Hammersmith Bridge Road near the Great West Road extension. This leads from West Cromwell Road, through Talgarth Road and Colet Gardens where it leaves the ground and, avoiding the Broadway, rises to cross Queen Caroline Street (unpleasantly close to St Paul's Church) by a flyover. The flyover, more than half a mile long, is of pre-stressed concrete supported on central columns, and was opened in November 1961. The extension then runs parallel to King Street past the new Town Hall and south of St Peter's Square via Hogarth Lane to join the original Great West Road at the Chiswick Floyver, which was opened on 30 September 1959 by film star Jayne Mansfield. An extensive roundabout system has been introduced at Hammersmith which includes a completely new thoroughfare from the east end of the Broadway to Fulham Palace Road. This new approach is called 'Butterwick' after the eighteenth-century mansion of that name—a remnant of which can be seen as part of the London Transport bus garage opposite St Paul's Church. Other improvements at Hammersmith Broadway seem to indicate that here, as elsewhere, the pedestrian is rapidly losing his cherished priority on the road. For his 'especial safety' new subways have been constructed. Access to these subways is obtained by descending anything from twenty-six to twenty-nine steps; at the other end, of course, there is a similar number of steps to climb. Hammersmith is well provided with places of amusement. There is the Gaumont Palace in Queen Caroline Street and also the Regal Cinema in King Street next to the new Town Hall. In Beadon Road is the Lyric Theatre and in Hammersmith Road the King's Theatre of pleasant memories, now replaced by a commercial building.

As indicated in our Fifth Walk, the massive Black Bull which stood over the entrance to the offices of Messrs. Bull & Bull in King Street was removed when the building was demolished. It is pleasant to record that the bull has been repainted and re-erected in the forecourt of the Ravenscourt Arms between Weltje Road and Vencourt Place. Enquiries about this almost life-size beast reveal that it was modelled by Obadiah Pulham of Woodbridge, Suffolk in the early 19th century and transported to London *by sea* for duty as the sign of the 'Black Bull' Inn, Holborn until 1904, when the inn was demolished. Thanks to the late Sir William Bull, Bt., M.P. for Hammersmith, the animal was preserved as already described, and has now survived a second demolition.

Early in the nineteenth century Hammersmith boasted several good houses inhabited by gentry and persons of quality, but these have long since been pulled down, cut up into smaller tenements, or been replaced by large factories, etc. One of these, called Brandenburgh House, was built early in the reign of Charles I by Sir Nicholas Crispe at a cost of £23,000. It stood near the river about a quarter of a mile east of Hammersmith Bridge. It was plundered during the Civil War in August 1647, when the parliamentary army was stationed at Hammersmith and General Fairfax took up his quarters here. In 1792 it was sold to the Margrave of Brandenburgh-Anspach, who died in 1806. Many alterations were then made to the mansion, which was renamed Brandenburgh House. Later it was occupied by the unhappy Queen Caroline, wife of George IV, who here kept up her rival court pending her trial in the House of Lords. When the Bill of Pains and Penalties was abandoned, the tradesmen of Hammersmith who enjoyed her custom illuminated their houses and the populace cheered and made bonfires in front of Brandenburgh House. Less than a year after the death of Queen Caroline, on 7 August 1821, the remains of Brandenburgh House were sold by auction, the mansion was pulled down, and a large factory erected on its site.

Between King Street and the River Thames is St Peter's Square completed, in 1839, and consisting of forty-three houses built in sets of three, which gives them the appearance of detached villas. An engine-house in the centre formerly supplied the houses with water from an artesian well 310 feet in depth. Facing the square on the east side is St Peter's Church, consecrated in 1829, which has a portico and four columns and is crowned by a clock-tower. King Street, the principal shopping thoroughfare of Hammersmith, forms part of the main western road out of London and was widened about forty years ago between Cambridge Road and Shaftesbury Road. The eastern end, however, which is a one-way street, still remains too narrow for the requirements of its traffic.

In the Mall, which runs westwards from Hammersmith Bridge to Chiswick, are some modern blocks of flats at the foot of the bridge. The Mall was once the fashionable part of Hammersmith, and is divided into the Upper and Lower Malls by a narrow creek crossed by a wooden footbridge known as the High Bridge, which was erected by Bishop Sherlock in 1751. 'The Doves', a seventeenth century tavern that claims to be the scene of the opening chapter of William de Morgan's *Joseph Vance*, still stands at the beginning of the Upper Mall. Nearby is Kelmscott House, where William Morris set up his printing press in 1891. The Mall is shaded by tall elm-trees planted over two hundred years ago by the widow of Charles II, Queen Catherine, who resided here for some years during the summer season.

We return to the Broadway and proceed in an easterly direction along Hammersmith Road, passing Rowton House on the south side erected in 1897 and one of the first hostels of this kind in London to provide cheap living-accommodation for single men of the working class. Almost adjoining is Nazareth

House of the Convent of the Little Daughters of Nazareth, a tall Gothic building of secluded appearance, three storeys high, and standing in grounds screened from the road by a high wall. Immediately opposite is the gigantic Latymer Court, erected in 1934, which when first built was claimed to be the largest block of shops and flats in Europe. It stands on the site of a long row of suburban villas with spacious front-gardens.

Beyond Nazareth House on the same side of the road is St Paul's School, removed here from the City in 1884 and standing in sixteen acres of land purchased by the Mercers' Company in 1877. The buildings were designed by Sir A. Waterhouse, R.A. Field-Marshal Lord Montgomery was educated at St Paul's School. During the second World War the school was transferred to Easthampstead Park, Wokingham, and its buildings in Hammersmith Road were requisitioned by the Government. Adjoining the grounds of St Paul's School at the corner of Colet Gardens is the Red Cow Tavern, rebuilt in 1897. The original inn was over two hundred years old when pulled down, and was famous in the old coaching days. At the corner of Edith Road, the church of St Mary, West Kensington, having been destroyed by bombs, has now been rebuilt.

East of St Paul's School is a tall building erected in 1930 containing the laboratories of Messrs J. Lyons & Company Limited, the caterers. Cadby Hall, the headquarters of this well-known firm, is on the opposite side of Hammersmith Road and occupies the entire frontage between Brook Green and Blythe Road. Leading out of North End Road on the south side of Hammersmith Road is Fitz-George's Avenue, lined with tall blocks of flats. On a portion of this land once stood North End House, situated in private grounds. It was demolished in 1929 and large blocks of flats called North End Court were then erected on this site.

The so-called district of West Kensington, which is not in the Royal Borough, but is situated in Hammersmith, is centred round North End Road, and extends from the West London Railway to the vicinity of St Paul's School. It includes the streets on the opposite side of Hammersmith Road between Olympia, Addison Road Station and Shepherd's Bush Road, and consists mainly of good-class streets and houses which have sprung up since 1880. A great impetus was given to this neighbourhood by the coming of St Paul's School and the extension of the Metropolitan District Railway from Earl's Court to Hammersmith in 1874, which led to the development of West Kensington from the hamlet of North End. The opening, in 1906, of the Piccadilly Line Tube Station at Baron's Court also furthered the development of West Kensington. This quarter was badly damaged by enemy action during the second World War. On the east side of North End Road are several modern blocks of workers' flats erected before the last war by the Fulham Borough Council. Baron's Keep in Gliddon Road near Baron's Court Station is a very large four-storeyed block of flats built round an open quadrangle, West Kensington Court on the corner of North End Road and the Cromwell Road Extension is a large seven-storeyed block of flats erected in 1937 and faced with red brick.

In North End Crescent, just beyond West Kensington Station, stood 'The Grange', a Queen Anne House that was the home of Samuel Richardson, author of *Pamela* and 'the Father of the English novel', also the pre-Raphaelite artist, Sir Edward Burne-Jones. There was considerable discussion when the Fulham Borough Council announced their intention to pull it down. Although (it was reported) a private gentleman had offered to purchase the property and restore and preserve it, 'The Grange' was duly demolished, and on the site now stands a block of council maisonettes – called 'Samuel Richardson House'.

Olympia, which is situated on the north side of Hammersmith Road, adjoining the West London Railway, was erected in 1886 by the National Agricultural Hall Company. The original buildings had an area of four acres. The grand hall, two and a half acres in extent, is one of the largest in the kingdom, and is covered by one span of iron and glass 450 feet long by 250 feet wide, or nearly half as large again as the Agricultural Hall. The opening exhibition in December 1886 was that of the Paris Hippodrome, for which purpose the French artists brought over a staff of three hundred, an orchestra of seventy, and no less than 250 performing animals. Various other exhibitions followed, such as 'Venice in London' and 'Constantinople in London', but for many years Olympia proved a complete failure.

The subsequent development of the motor industry retrieved the fortunes of the company, and from 1910 onwards the Motor Show was held here annually, until removed to Earl's Court. The Horse Show, the Military Tournament, and the Ideal Homes Exhibition are now held at Olympia, as well as the Bertram Mills Circus. A considerable extension of the building was carried out in 1923, which involved the demolition of several rather fine houses in Hammersmith Road. This proving insufficient to meet the increased demands for accommodation by motor-car companies, a further large annexe in Hammersmith Road was added in 1928. This has a fine elevation, which introduced the German modernist style into England with great success.

From here a walk either through Blythe Road, past the immense buildings of the Post Office Savings Department, or by way of Brook Green farther west, will bring us to Shepherd's Bush Road. Brook Green Common is a pleasant open space which extends along Brook Green Road from Blythe Road to Shepherd's Bush Road. From here a short walk northwards brings us to Shepherd's Bush Green. This triangular open space was acquired for the public by the Metropolitan Board of Works in 1872. Until about 1860 Shepherd's Bush was still a rustic hamlet, but it is now a busy traffic and shopping centre, completely absorbed into the metropolis. The railway between Shepherd's Bush and Hammersmith, joint Great Western and Metropolitan, was opened on 1 July 1864.

Until 1890 there stood on Shepherd's Bush Green an ancient thatched cottage, which was hired and inhabited by Miles Syndercombe in January 1657 for the purpose of assassinating Oliver Cromwell, who discovered the conspiracy and had Syndercombe arrested, tried, and condemned to death. He remained a prisoner in the Tower until the morning appointed for hanging him, when he was found dead in bed. It was believed that he had taken poison secretly brought to him by his sister the night before. Near the Green on the east side of Shepherd's Bush Road is a gigantic ten-storeyed block of flats called the Grampians, erected in 1937. One-way traffic is in operation round Shepherd's Bush Green.

On the west side are the Gaumont Cinema and the Shepherd's Bush Empire, now a television studio, and in Uxbridge Road the parish church of St Stephen, consecrated by the Bishop of London on 11 April 1850. Running northwards in a direct line with Shepherd's Bush Green is Wood Lane, which leads to the White City Stadium and Wormwood Scrubs Common. First opened in May 1908 for the Franco-British Exhibition by King Edward VII, accompanied by the French President, M. Fallières, the White City was quite the largest and most magnificent exhibition ground ever seen in London down to that time. It was laid out on a very imposing scale, and the Court of Honour, with its lake and illuminated cascade, was the most beautiful place of its kind ever seen in London. Other leading features were the Stadium, the largest in London before the construction of that of the Wembley Exhibition, and the Garden Club building situated in the Élite Gardens. Annual exhibitions were held at the White City during the summer months from May to October, but upon the outbreak of war, in 1914, it was taken over for Government service. Afterwards, except for an occasional indoor exhibition, mostly confined to the long galleries connecting Uxbridge Road with Wood Lane, the White City remained derelict for many years. In 1936 fifty acres of its grounds were acquired by the London County Council as a housing estate. Nevertheless it seems a pity that London should be permanently deprived of such a resort during the summer months notwithstanding our fickle climate, and also having regard to the fact that open-air cafés such as one can enjoy in all Continental capitals are conspicuous in London by their absence.

On the north side of the White City is the new Western Avenue, here called Westway, designed as a by-pass road starting from Wood Lane to connect with the main Oxford Road near Gerrard's Cross. Its completion was delayed for many years until it was finally opened through to Gerrard's Cross in 1943. Centred round Westway is an immense new artisan quarter erected by the London County Council between the two World Wars. It extends from Wood Lane towards East Acton, and forms a part of the borough of Hammersmith. Amongst other features of this quarter are a public library on Western Avenue, an open-air swimming-bath at Wormholt Park, the Savoy Cinema, a large roundabout and a handsome shopping centre near the junction of Westway and Old Oak Road.

The housing estate at the White City is the largest for municipal flats ever planned by the London County Council and its pre-war cost was estimated at £1,437,000 and provided for 2,286 dwellings containing 7,290 rooms including 312 flats of a new type. All blocks are five storeys high and provide accommodation for eleven thousand people. There are also schools, public buildings and children's playgrounds. Here a fine new quarter, a sort of working-man's

Kensington of fine wide streets, is rapidly covering all of the remaining unbuilt land in this locality, and there are no better-housed workers in any other city in the world. The new blocks of flats have long frontages to Westway and Bloem-fontein Road with various roads running parallel and at right angles to Westway. This new quarter bears a distinctly Continental appearance and one wonders whether the London County Council decided to copy pre-war Berlin when drawing up their plans for developing this estate. This quarter is enlivened by the football ground of the Queen's Park Rangers in Ellerslie Road and by the White City Stadium mainly given over to dog-racing and boxing. On the adjoining Cleverly Estate between Wormholt Park and Old Oak Road are some handsome three-storeyed blocks of flats erected by the Peabody Trust.

To the north of the Government prison is Wormwood Scrubs Common, a large open space of 194 acres, purchased in December 1876 by the Government for over £52,000. Formerly called Wormholt Common or Scrubs it was originally a wood and consisted of two hundred acres, of which about sixty were enclosed. In 1812 a lease of this common was taken by the Government for a term of twenty-one years at a rental of £100 per annum, for the purpose of exercising the two regiments of the Life Guards. The money was to be divided equally between Fulham and Hammersmith, but the copyholders were to continue to enjoy the usual privilege of turning out their cattle to graze.

In 1876 the Government offered the land free of cost to the Metropolitan Board of Works. This handsome offer was gladly accepted, but the Government stipulated that Wormwood Scrubs should be preserved as an open space for the benefit of the public under the Commons Act and not be converted into a park.

On an area of thirteen acres in Wood Lane, covering part of the site of the Franco-British Exhibition of 1908, is the new B.B.C. Television Centre. Its studios are the first the B.B.C. has had which have been designed and built expressly for television programmes, all other B.B.C. studios have been adaptations of existing buildings. The principal building, the circular Main Block, contains a series of studios radiating from a ring set round a central garden. A circular runway provides for the rapid movement of heavy scenery and properties between the adjacent scenery block and the studios. Close at hand is everything for the comfort and convenience of the performers—dressing rooms, wardrobe accommodation, make-up, hair-styling, baths, showers, tea bars etc.

The departmental and administration offices are on the upper floors. The main block covers an area of $3^1/_2$ acres, nearly twice the area covered by St Paul's Cathedral. There are seven major studios and two presentation studios. The architect of the Television Centre is Mr Graham Dawbarn, C.B.E.

Twenty-Fifth Walk

Paddington, Bayswater, Maida Vale, Kilburn, Willesden, Cricklewood, Hendon and Golder's Green

PADDINGTON, NOW part of the new City of Westminster, was in the early years of the nineteenth century the most distant village completely united to London. Fifty years earlier it was already joined to the capital by a long line of buildings on the east side of Edgware Road, and in 1783, on a map of London by Carington Bowles, Edgware Road north of the New Road, now called Marylebone Road, figures under the name of Paddington, although the village itself was situated to the west of Edgware Road.

Paddington is said to derive its name from the Saxon *Paedings-tun*. In ancient times King Edgar is reputed to have given lands at Paddington to the monks of Westminster, and these lands were claimed in later ages by the Bishop of London and the Dean and Chapter of Westminster as their share of the spoils of the Convent of Westminster. Hence today a large part of Paddington is owned by the Ecclesiastical Commissioners.

As recently as 1820 Paddington, although joined to the metropolis, still possessed many rural spots which appeared as secluded as though they had been a great distance from town. The small population of Paddington was wholly absorbed in agriculture; although they lived at so short a distance from the two rich towns of London and Westminster, they made no greater advances in civilization than did those who lived in the remotest village in England.

Opposite the Marble Arch, which will form the starting-point for this walk, is the junction of Oxford Street and Edgware Road, and here stood the Tyburn Gate until 1829. Although the entire east side of Edgware Road from Hyde Park to Paddington had been covered with streets and buildings at the dawn of the nineteenth century, no building operations of any importance were commenced on the west side until about 1820. Thus Paddington formed for many years the outer limit of the metropolis, and as late as 1830 was still regarded by many people as a rustic village.

But although Edgware Road itself remained unbuilt on the west side between Paddington village and Hyde Park, a village somewhat resembling the unsightly bungaloid growths with which we are so familiar in our own day had arisen in the fields a short distance to the west of Edgware Road. Thus Lysons, writing of Paddington in 1794, says that, this parish being chiefly church land, there had been but little increase of buildings till about 1790, since which time nearly one hundred small wooden houses had been erected a little north of Tyburn turnpike.

These cottages were let at from £7 to £12 per annum, and were inhabited principally by journeymen artificers who worked in London, forming with their families a colony of about six hundred persons. This colony of cottages, built nearly opposite George Street, partly on ground where now stands the sumptuous Park West block of flats, was called Tomlin's New Town. After 1816, as the result of a Building Act obtained by the Bishop of London, these journeymen artificers had to vacate this land in order to make way for the construction of Connaught Terrace and better houses for the rich. During the winter evenings the muddy roads which led to these cottages were in total darkness. No provision had of course been made for the effective drainage or sanitary arrangements of these cottages, built in the open fields and occupied as fast as they were completed. They were sought after by the poor as a kind of country retreat, but were in fact breeding-centres of disease, filth, and misery. At the dawn of the nineteenth century, the Bayswater Road, once you passed Tyburn Gate, was a lonely road with rarely a house for the next mile until you came to Craven Hill.

Bayswater Road today, together with Oxford Street, is the straightest of all great London thoroughfares and runs for two clear miles without a curve. If you stand on the refuge in the centre of the roadway at Victoria Gate on a clear day you can easily spot the two turrets of Albion House in New Oxford Street which are more than two miles distant.

In 1795 there were still upwards of 1,100 acres of grass-land in Paddington, of which only eighty-five were arable or garden land, and for a long time the tenants of the Bishop of London's estate at Paddington were as celebrated for the quality and quantity of their milk as they now are for the number and the size of their houses. Within the short space of twenty years a city of palaces had sprung up on the Bishop's Estate, and one of our leading railways, the Great Western, had opened its terminus here, from which were carried to and from this great city a larger number of human beings in one year than could be found in all England only a short time before.

Tyburnia, properly speaking, comprises the quarter situated in the triangle bounded by Bayswater Road, Sussex Gardens, and Edgware Road. As we have already seen, the long terraces of ugly brown-brick houses, four storeys high, which once lined the west side of Edgware Road, have been mostly pulled down these last few years, and have been replaced by modern buildings like the Connaught Club, Grosvenor Court Mansions, Portsea Hall and Park West. Thus much of the new grandeur of Marylebone and Great Cumberland Place is spreading to the other side of the Edgware Road. Park West, a vast new colony of flats, already noted in our sixteenth walk, also has extensive frontages to Kendal Street and Burwood Place.

The streets leading out of Edgware Road are for the most part very gloomy, with long rows of brown-brick houses, but those opening on to Bayswater Road and Hyde Park are more modern, with stucco-fronted houses quite as fine as any to be seen in Belgravia. Land in this neighbourhood, which was let for £12 per annum in the early part of the eighteenth century, was producing a rental of £12,000 a year by 1845, and the manors of Paddington and Westbourne, which once produced but a trifling sum, were yielding a rental to the Ecclesiastical Commissioners of £50,000 per annum. Most of the streets of this quarter were built during the reign of William IV and all of them were completed by 1849 but, doubtless on account of its association with public executions, the name of Tyburnia never seems to have been popular with its inhabitants, so that to-day it is more commonly known as Hyde Park. Like Belgravia and Mayfair, it still retains its original high-class character, but before the second World War much rebuilding had already taken place in this quarter.

In 1860 Mr George F. Train was granted permission to lay down a trial tramway line from the Marble Arch along the Bayswater Road, and this event was celebrated by a public banquet at St James's Hall. The line, however, proved a nuisance to the inhabitants of this district, mainly on account of the raised lines, which hindered the free circulation of the traffic. As a result the Metropolitan Board of Works in July 1861 resolved by a large majority that the Bayswater Road Tramway should be removed, and Mr Train was given until 4 October to carry out their instructions.

Connaught Place, the terrace of large houses between Edgware Road and Stanhope Place erected about 1816, is shielded from Edgware Road by an attractive screen of pillars with a wrought-iron gate. Several of the houses, which have massive porches, are the offices of Schweppes Ltd, the mineral-water firm. Between Stanhope Place and the Chapel of the Ascension stood until March 1944 the Tyburn Convent which together with some adjoining houses was destroyed in 1944 by a rocket-bomb. A new Shrine of the Sacred Heart and Tyburn Martyrs has now been completed; a commemorative stone was laid by Cardinal Archbishop Godfrey on 10 December 1961.

Just beyond Stanhope Place is a burial-ground enclosed and consecrated in 1764 on land vested in the Bishop of London, about one acre in extent, and rented by the parish of St George's, Hanover Square. On the west side is the grave of the Revd Laurence Sterne M. A., author of *Tristram Shandy* and *A Sentimental Journey*, who died in 1768. The Chapel of the Ascension which faces Bayswater Road is in ruins through bombing. In 1901 the shabby houses which stood on both sides of the chapel were replaced by modern red-brick houses and by a handsome block of flats faced with terracotta, overlooking Hyde Park. Sandwiched between two of these new red-brick houses, curiously enough, is one of the many houses claiming to be the smallest in London. It measures no more than five feet in width. Farther along, on the two corners of Albion Street, are two bold blocks of flats of uniform design erected in 1935-36 called Albion Gate. These are seven storeys high and faced with yellow brick with stone dressings.

Hyde Park Street, a few paces farther west along Bayswater Road, leads to Hyde Park Crescent, formerly Southwick Crescent, named after Southwick Park,

Hampshire, the property of the Thistlethwayte family, formerly joint lessees of the Paddington Manor. Here many of the original large town houses with deep basements were pulled down between 1934 and 1939 and replaced by non-basement labour-saving houses which are so much in demand at the present time. These are only three storeys high and have replaced five-storeyed houses with basements. They are built of yellow brick without any external ornamentation. The new Hyde Park Crescent looks far too like Dagenham and is totally unworthy of the character of this quarter of London. Hyde Park Crescent, faced by St John's Church, together with Cambridge Square, Norfolk Crescent, and Oxford Square, form an oval-shaped island midway between Edgware Road and Hyde Park, a piece of town-planning which would have done credit to Mr Cubitt.

Hyde Park Gardens, which we next pass, is a fine terrace of large four-storeyed houses standing back from the main Bayswater Road, from which it is separated by a private enclosure with gardens in front. It was built about 1845 and was formerly called Hyde Park Terrace, and is a fine example of the type of mansions inhabited by the very wealthy classes in the early Victorian period. In the road at the back of Hyde Park Gardens are the stables and mews belonging to the houses. During the second World War, Hyde Park Gardens was taken over by the Ministry of Aircraft Production, but after some members of the staff quartered at Oakwood Court had been killed in a tea-shop in Kensington High Street by one of Hitler's rocket-bombs in August 1944 the Ministry was removed to Harrogate. This quarter of London contains several spacious squares including Hyde Park Square, Cambridge and Oxford Squares, and Gloucester and Sussex Squares, where until 1840 all was open market gardens. These are still bordered by large Victorian mansions except Gloucester Square which has been partly rebuilt. Its east and west sides are now lined with new non-basement houses of red brick with stone dressings three storeys high. Architecturally they are greatly superior to the unsightly new houses of Hyde Park Crescent. During the last war many houses in this district were taken over to provide accommodation for the United States Expeditionary Force and Hyde Park Crescent and the various squares served as drilling-grounds for the troops. The Victoria Tavern in Strathearn Place has an interesting display of Victorian relics, souvenirs and furniture. Upstairs, in the Edwardian Gaiety Bar, one may sit in the stalls — or even a box — rescued from the Gaiety Theatre in the Strand when it was pulled down in 1957.

Close to Hyde Park Gardens is Victoria Gate, forming the entrance to the roadway between Hyde Park and Kensington Gardens leading to Exhibition Road and opened in 1854. Westbourne Terrace, nearly opposite Victoria Gate, a handsome avenue leading north to Bishop's Road, derives its name from the Westbourne brook which ran from Kilburn between Paddington and Bayswater into the Serpentine. It was built between 1847 and 1852, and is lined on both sides by rows of large five-storeyed houses faced with stucco, many of which have been converted of late years into flats and maisonettes. The Westbourne brook, now converted into a sewer, was at the commencement of the ninetenth century a favourite resort for young fishermen, and was once the centre of a beautiful valley. Until 1840 cricket was played on the site of Westbourne Terrace. Next to Lancaster Gate Underground Station, the new Lancaster Hotel stands on the site of the former 'Crown' tavern at the corner of Lancaster Place.

Facing Sussex Gardens or Grand Junction Road, as it was previously called, is the parish church of St James's, built in 1843 and rebuilt by G. E. Street, architect of the Law Courts, in 1881. It is built in the Gothic style, with a tower and spire, and provides accommodation for a thousand people. Of melancholy interest is the memorial window to five schoolboys who died in 1890 'from drinking impure water while on a walk together in the neighbourhood'. Sussex Gardens, the continuation of Marylebone Road, is really a boulevard, and was constructed about 1828. Still following the Bayswater Road we come, after passing Westbourne Terrace and the parallel thoroughfare called Gloucester Terrace, to Lancaster Gate, a long range of buildings divided into two sections by the opening which leads to Christ Church. Lancaster Gate was completed in 1866 and is a beautiful piece of town-planning, as well as a fine example of the architectural improvements carried out in the metropolis during the mid-Victorian period. A special feature of the façade of these terraces is formed by the balconies, with their range of columns, which give a most imposing appearance to the long row of houses.

To-day Lancaster Gate is no longer the abode of the very wealthy, for many of the houses have been converted into large private hotels. Its uniformity is broken by Barrie House, a ten-storeyed block of flats at the west corner of the wide roadway leading to Christ Church erected in 1936-37. In 1938 another block of flats of a similar design to Barrie House but not so high was erected in the centre of the eastern terrace of Lancaster Gate. Lancaster Gate stands on the site of Hopwood's Nursery Ground and the Victoria Tea Gardens, famous for running matches and sporting meetings, and was the last slice of open land on the Bayswater Road to be covered with buildings. Christ Church, which stands back from the main road in the centre, is a noble Gothic edifice with a lofty tower and spire which shows to great advantage when viewed from the Long Water in Kensington Gardens. The top part of the spire which was damaged in the blitz has been taken down.

On the east side of Lancaster Gate is Craven Terrace, now lined with shops, leading to Craven Hill, on which was formerly a pleasantly situated hamlet. The former inequality of the ground level was removed by filling up the low ground where the Westbourne brook once ran from north to south. This estate was owned by Lord Craven, a nobleman known for his humane exertions during the Great Fire and the Great Plague. Observing the difficulties which attended the burial of infected corpses in 1665 he gave a piece of land in the parish of St-Martin's-in-the-Fields as a burial-place for use during any future epidemics. About the year 1720, when Carnaby Market and other buildings were erected on the Craven Estate, the land he had given was exchanged for a field now covered by Craven Gardens on the Paddington Estate, which, if London should ever again be visited by a plague, will still be available for its intended use. This quarter was badly damaged in the great blitz of 1940, three shops and houses in Craven Terrace were reduced to a huge mound of rubble which stretched half-way across the street and the neighbouring Barrie Street was struck by a land-mine which destroyed every house in the street including two large private hotels and a public-house. The street was closed for nine months while the damage was being repaired. Three seven- to ten-storey blocks of G.L.C. flats—Carroll, Gilray and Garson Houses—now occupy the site that was Barrie Street. A bomb which fell one night in Bayswater Road wrecked the water- and gas-mains forming a crater in the centre of the road which became a deep pond. A passing motor-car crashed into it, but the driver escaped and his car was retrieved on the following morning. Traffic had to be diverted to Lancaster Gate for several months while the roadway was being repaired. Maitland Court, a large block of flats erected in 1932 at the corner of Lancaster Terrace near St James's Church, was also damaged but has since been repaired.

Craven Hill, to the east of Craven Gardens, leads to Praed Street and Paddington Station, in front of which is the Great Western Royal Hotel, opened in July 1852, a handsome building designed by Brunel and containing over 150 rooms. Before that time the hotels in the northern and western district of London were very inadequate for the requirements of visitors to the metropolis. Until 1856 the Great Western Royal Hotel stood out alone in a neighbourhood of poor buildings and humble shops, but the clearance effected by the extension of the Great Western Railway led to important improvements, notably in Craven Road. The two top storeys of the Great Western Royal Hotel were damaged in 1944 by a bomb but these have since been repaired. The title 'Royal' was bestowed on the hotel after an occasion when King Edward VII lunched here on his way to Windsor.

The original terminus of the Great Western Railway, now British Railways (Western Region), was in Bishop's Road, but was only intended as a temporary provision, without any attempt at ornamentation, pending the construction of a magnificent new terminus. The Great Western Railway from London to Bristol was begun in 1835 and opened as far as Maidenhead in 1838 but the entire line to Bath and Bristol was not completed until June 1841. Paddington Station was the joint work of Mr Brunel and Mr M. D. Wyatt. The office buildings, facing Eastbourne Terrace, partly destroyed in the blitz, are 580 feet long, and the platforms under the curved roof are 700 feet long. The roofing consists of three spans, each 50 feet in width. The centre span is 54 feet high, and the side divisions 46 feet. Notwithstanding its age Paddington Station can still invite favourable comparison with our most modern railway termini. As a result of the extension and improvements carried out at Paddington Station in 1933, Bishop's Road Station, used for suburban traffic, has now been merged into Paddington Station. During the last war this was a favourite target of the *Luftwaffe* but being in a sheltered situation in a hollow, Paddington Station escaped serious damage.

All the houses on the opposite side of Eastbourne Terrace have been pulled down. These were almost entirely private hotels, some of them of rather doubtful character. New blocks of offices have now risen along the Terrace. One large block is occupied by the Metropolitan Regional Hospital Board, another by the Midland Bank and other offices, a third is Williams House. Towering above the rest is C.J.B. House of seventeen storeys. Telstar House at the top includes a new 'Prince of Wales' tavern.

On the opposite side of Praed Street is the Metropolitan Railway Station, which is connected by subway with Paddington Station. The Metropolitan Railway was the pioneer London Underground Railway, and was opened from Bishop's Road, Paddington, to Farringdon Street on 10 January 1863. On the opening day over thirty thousand persons travelled over the line, and from nine o'clock in the morning until past mid-day it was impossible to obtain a place on the City-bound trains at any of the intermediate stations. The carriages were then mere open trucks. In the evening the returning crowds from Farringdon Street were equally great. In the course of a twelvemonth the number of passengers carried amounted to nearly 9,500,000, or more than three times the population of London at that time.

On 3 October 1868 the section of the Inner Circle from Paddington to Kensington High Street and Gloucester Road was opened. In the following year the western extensiin from Paddington to Hammersmith was completed, and within the first three months of its opening 1,600,000 passengers were carried on that line. In November 1871 the two stations of Royal Oak and Westbourne Park on the Great Western Railway were opened. This enabled passengers from all districts served by the Metropolitan Railway to transfer to the Great Western Railway main line at Westbourne Park without being compelled as formerly to proceed to Paddington.

In 1915 the Baker Street and Waterloo Railway was extended to Paddington, Maida Vale, and Willesden Junction, thus providing direct communication with the London & North Western Railway, and in 1917 this was extended to Watford Junction. To-day, London Transport carries nearly 3,000 million passengers by train, bus and coach in the course of a year, covering a total of 8,000 million passenger miles.

Paddington Station, although now so conveniently linked with all parts of London, is the most remote of all from the actual centre of the town, and when first built was virtually on the fringe of the metropolis. This was because in the pioneer days of the railways the Commissioners who were appointed to investigate the subject resolved that no railway should be permitted to come within the limits prescribed by them on the north side of the Thames, so as not to interfere with the comfort or the property of the inhabitants. Various schemes had previously been submitted by the different railway companies without reference to any uniform plan of development, and the Commissioners had deemed it desirable that a connection between the various railways entering London on the north and south sides of the river should be effected by a railway encircling the metropolis, crossing the Thames at some point west of Vauxhall Bridge, and not coming into the centre of the town. They also recommended a connection between the various railways and the docks as part of this scheme. In later years this restriction was modified, and the southern railways were allowed to come into Victoria, Charing Cross, and Holborn Viaduct, whilst the Great Eastern Railway was permitted to extend its line to Liverpool Street.

British Railways have long-term plans for improving Paddington Station and are now rebuilding their destroyed offices in Eastbourne Terrace. At the back of a bombed site in Praed Street facing the Great Western Royal Hotel is Talbot Square, a cul-de-sac of large town houses which opens into Sussex Gardens. Some of the houses on the north side of the square were demolished in the air raids of 1940 and for a time a new view of the Great Western Royal Hotel was opened up from Sussex Gardens. A new block of flats called Stephen Court now occupies the blitzed site. Talbot Square, Norfolk Square, Sussex Gardens and many of the neighbouring terraces contain a great number of private hotels for which this part of Paddington is well-known to the out-of-town visitor.

Bayswater is the title given to the vague district between the north side of Hyde Park and Notting Hill Gate. The name is derived from the so-called Baynard's Watering, that is, source of water supply for the house of Baynard, which once occupied this locality. Baynard was the ancient Lord of the Manor.

The running streams and gravelly soil of this neighbourhood were at one time very suitable for growing watercress, and as recently as 1825 there were several cultivators here. Close to what is now Craven Hill stood until about 1820 an ancient stone-built conduit house, constructed and maintained by the Corporation of London to supply the City with water, which was conveyed underground in leaden pipes made in Holland to Cheapside and Cornhill.

Bayswater has always been a favourite abode of foreigners of every nationality, who have settled here particularly during the second World War. Many of its shops are owned by foreigners and its restaurants are amongst the best of any in London. It also contains quite a lot of good residential hotels.

Between Lancaster Gate and Queensway are several imposing thoroughfares, notably Leinster, Porchester, Queensborough, and Inverness Terraces. Some of the large town houses in these roads have been turned into private hotels. Queen's Road, now renamed Queensway, which next claims our attention, leads from Kensington Gardens, nearly opposite the Broad Walk, to Westbourne Grove. Little more than a century ago it was a country lane traversing the district known until the reign of William IV as Westbourne Green. Until 1830 this was one of the most beautiful rural spots for which the parish of Paddington was renowned. The hamlet of Westbourne Green or Tybourn was situated near the Royal Oak Tavern, then a rustic inn, but long since rebuilt. It stood approximately on the site of Porchester Road and the Great Western Railway near Royal Oak Station adjoining Harrow Road. It contained a mansion called Westbourne Place, the residence of Samuel Pepys Cockerell, the architect, situated on rising ground commanding a fine view of Hampstead and Highgate, as well as the village of Paddington, with its elegant church. No other part of London could be seen, and it was possible to forget one's proximity to the busy metropolis. The Westbourne Manor House stood on the high ground opposite the Military Hospital in Harrow Road and its site is now covered by the spacious Sutherland Avenue and its tributary streets.

Opposite was the secluded cottage and grounds once inhabited by Mrs Sarah Siddons, the famous actress, who afterwards moved to Baker Street. The cottage was demolished to make way for the Great Western Railway. Mrs Siddons, who died on 8 June 1831, in her seventy-sixth year, is buried at Paddington Church. The Westbourne Estate was formerly the property of Mr Isaac Ware, who started life as a chimney-sweep and afterwards studied architecture and became the editor of various professional publications. With materials brought from the Earl of Chesterfield's house in Mayfair, which he was employed to build, he erected the mansion called Westbourne Place.

Until 1831 Queensway was called Blackman Lane, and contained a row of small houses on the west side close to Kensington Gardens, which were afterwards converted into shops. These were pulled down in 1928, and this site is now covered by two seven-storeyed blocks of shops and flats called Queen's Court and Princess Court erected in 1932-33 by London Properties Limited. Queen's Court contains an ice-skating rink which is open to the public. Queensway, together with Westbourne Grove, must be considered the leading shopping centre of Paddington. Occupying the whole of the west side of Queensway from Porchester Gardens to Redan Place is the huge store of Messrs William Whiteley. Although a considerable portion of this store always has been housed in Queensway, next to Redan Place, the main buildings were located until 1911 in Westbourne Grove. In that year the entire establishment was removed to the new buildings in Queensway, which were erected on the site adjoining the original premises near Redan Place. In order to complete the new store the old Queen's Road premises were pulled down and rebuilt in 1925. On the site of the new Whiteley buildings erected in 1911, close to Porchester Gardens, stood the Paddington Swimming Baths, then considered to be the finest in London. They were erected by the former Paddington Vestry and opened in June 1874 by the Lord Mayor. The new Paddington baths and the adjoining Porchester Hall erected in 1929 are situated at the northern end of Queensway.

On 6 August 1887 Whiteley's premises in Queen's Road were destroyed by fire. The old building, which was fronted with York stone, was five storeys high and had a frontage of three hundred feet. The value of property destroyed was estimated at £525,000, of which only a small portion was covered by insurance. The various offices in London had declined to insure Mr Whiteley because four fires had already taken place on his premises since 1882, and a fire which occurred in June 1885 had burnt out four of his shops and involved them in a loss of £350,000. Mr Whiteley suspected rivals of having resorted to incendiarism. The present store is one of the largest and most spaciously planned in London and is crowned in the centre by a large dome. William Whiteley was a Rochdale man who in 1863 started business in a fancy-drapery shop at Number 31 Westbourne Grove, which in those days was sarcastically known as Bankruptcy Row. By 1876 he had already acquired fifteen adjoining shops and was employing two thousand persons. In 1899 the business was converted into a limited company with a turnover exceeding £1,000,000. In 1907 Mr Whiteley was shot dead by Horace George Rayner who was under the impression that he was his illegitimate son. Founded in 1863, Whiteley's was the pioneer of the great London stores. Opposite Whiteley's is a newly-erected block of luxury shops and flats called Inver Court. The northern section of Queensway from Westbourne Grove to Porchester Road was formerly a shabby street called Pickering Place. On the east side at the corner of Bishop's Bridge Road is the Queen's Cinema and at this end of Queensway are two eight-storeyed blocks of flats, Ralph Court on the east side and Arthur Court on the west side. In Porchester Road is another called Peter's Court with shops on the ground floor. All three of these buildings were erected by London Properties Limited between 1934 and 1937.

Kensington Gardens Square, on the south side of Westbourne Grove, contains large town houses mostly converted into flats and private hotels and the same thing applies to the neighbouring Leinster Square and Princes Square. In Moscow Road, a turning out of the west side of Queen's Road, and in Palace Court, leading to Kensington Gardens, are several modern blocks of flats, the principal of which is called Moscow Court. Orme Square, which faces Bayswater Road, was built about 1815, and is named after a Mr Orme, a Bond Street print-seller, who purchased the ground upon which this square is built. In the square stands a mysterious double column surmounted by an eagle. Close to Orme Square is St Petersburg Place, also erected about 1815, which, together with Moscow Road and Coburg Place, commemorate the visit of the allied sovereigns to London in 1814. At the west corner of Queensway and Bayswater Road is the Coburg Court Hotel, partly erected above the Underground Railway Station. This was badly damaged by a bomb in August 1944 which completely destroyed the adjoining Patrickson Hotel, the site now being occupied by a new block of flats called Caroline House.

In Victorian days it was the custom during holiday time to draw the blinds, shutter the windows, and cover up the furniture in the large houses during the months of August and September, when people left town. The few who remained behind concealed themselves from the view of their neighbours and lived in the dark sooner than let it be known that they had not left town with the rest. Paddington and Kensington were like cities of the dead, and an old joke was that whilst the family was on the Rhine the ottomans were all in Holland. The passing of some four-wheeler cabs loaded with the luggage of a family returning from the seaside was the signal for hungry-looking, down-and-out men, who would frequently chase it for miles to the door of the house in the hope of earning a few pence by assisting in the unloading of the luggage. Nowadays things have changed completely. Americans and foreigners visit London in large numbers during August, and the various motor-coaches bring provincial visitors in their thousands. We no longer have a dead season, and many of the former town houses have been converted into maisonettes or large private hotels which keep open all the year round.

On the west side of St Petersburg Place is St Matthew's Church which is crowned by a tower with a tall spire and on the opposite side of the road is the new West End Jewish Synagogue. At the corner of Moscow Road and Ilchester Gardens is the Greek Church.

Westbourne Grove, as recently as 1852, was a quiet street consisting of detached cottages with gardens in front, and at the Queensway end was an open nursery garden rich in dahlias, geraniums, etc. During the 'eighties of last century Westbourne Grove was one of the most fashionable shopping centres in London and as Whiteley's was the pioneer of the great London stores, that was hardly a matter for surprise. The virtual departure of Messrs Whiteley from Westbourne Grove deprived that thoroughfare of much of its former glamour; in later years it has been eclipsed by the High Street, Kensington, and Brompton Road as a popular centre of shopping. But to-day a new king has succeeded Mr Whiteley. This is the great furnishing establishment of Frederick Lawrence Limited which now occupies eleven of the former Whiteley shops and four others on the opposite side of Westbourne Grove. Hatherley Court, a seven-storeyed block of flats in Westbourne Grove Terrace erected in 1936, covers a part of the site of a long row of shops which once formed the now defunct drapery store of Messrs William Owen & Company Limited which closed down about 1920. Its frontage to Westbourne Grove is now occupied by the Westbourne Park Building Society. At the corner of Westbourne Grove and Chepstow Place was the large fur store of Bradley & Sons, the building now being occupied by several Ministries.

Bishop's Road, now renamed Bishop's Bridge Road, is the eastern continuation of Westbourne Grove, and, after crossing the Great Western Railway and the Paddington Canal, leads to Harrow Road, close to the original village of Paddington. An interesting feature of Bishop's Road is the stately church of Holy Trinity on the north side, crowned by a tall spire. It was erected in 1845 to accommodate the residents of this great new neighbourhood which had grown up with such surprising rapidity, partly owing to the construction of the Great Western Railway terminus, and partly to the westward movement of fashion and wealth. The site upon which Holy Trinity Church stands was originally a deep hole which had been left at the junction of Bishop's Road and Westbourne Terrace. This was caused by the roads having been raised by the Great Western Railway Company, by special agreement with the owners of the state, when the railway bridges were built. So deep was this hole, according to railway Mr William Robins's *Paddington Past and Present,* dated 1853, and so unfitted was it for the site of a church, that the parishioners would have been money in pocket if the Vestry had rejected the free grant of this site offered by the Bishop of London and had bought land somewhere else. At Number 26 Bishops Bridge Road, now a grocer's shop, Charlotte Brontë stayed in 1848. At that date it was a private house, Number 4 Westbourne Place, and the home of her publisher,

Mr George Smith of Smith, Elder & Co., who lived there with his mother.

On the south side of Bishop's Bridge Road an extensive housing scheme, designed to provide new homes for nearly nine thousand people, has recently been completed. The site comprises nineteen-and-a-half acres which before the war was covered with stucco-fronted Victorian mansions and villas. The project, which took many years to carry out, provides 1,873 new dwellings including one hundred houses and flats of every size from one to four bedrooms. Twenty-five six-storey blocks have been erected on the site of the old houses and provision has been made for restaurants, nursery schools, communal laundries and two public houses. The site extends from Inverness Terrace across Porchester Terrace to Gloucester Terrace and includes the long terrace of houses on the south side of Bishop's Bridge Road which were the last to be demolished. On the other side of Bishop's Bridge Road a large site on the corner of Porchester Road has been cleared of its old houses and shops extending to Porchester Square. This site was understood to be reserved for the erection of a new Town Hall for the Borough of Paddington; but now that Paddington is in the City of Westminster the space is likely to remain as a car park for a little longer.

Close to the Great Western Railway Goods Station, the Paddington or Grand Union Canal unites with the Regent's Canal, thus providing direct water communication with the Thames at Limehouse. The Regent's Canal was constructed between 1812 and 1820 to provide an easy means of conveyance from the Thames of coals, stone, timber, and other heavy goods which had previously been conveyed across the town, to the great annoyance of the public.

The Paddington Canal, which commences at the dock at the back of Paddington Station, was opened in 1801 and joins the Grand Union Canal at Bull Bridge, in the vicinity of Southall, in Middlesex. Rather more than a century ago a passenger boat used to leave the Paddington Dock every day during the summer months, at eight o'clock in the morning, for Greenford Green and Uxbridge, returning in the evening. Breakfast was provided on board. The fares were most reasonable, being one shilling for six miles, eighteenpence for ten miles, and half a crown for the complete voyage to Uxbridge. After passing Wormwood Scrubs Common an uninterrupted view could be obtained of the Surrey Hills, including the spire of Streatham Church, the tower of Croydon Church, the heights of Headley, Box Hill, and the still more distant tower of Leith Hill.

On the opening day, 10 July 1801, no less than twenty thousand people came to Paddington to welcome the mighty men who had so altered this hitherto quiet village. Unfortunately, as time went on, the banks of this canal were used for stowing not only dirt and ashes, but the filth of half London, which was brought to 'stinking Paddington', as it was then nicknamed.

The original village of Paddington lies between Harrow Road and Edgware Road, and whatever its claims to rustic beauty may have been in the past, it is now a dreary spot, hedged in principally by slums and only relieved by the Green and the adjoining public garden. The church of St Mary, rebuilt in 1788-91 near the site of the earlier church at a cost of £6,000, has a portico of the Doric order.

The foundation-stone was laid on 20 October 1788. On the Green is a fine statue by Chavalliaud of Mrs Siddons, seated, as the Tragic Muse; it was unveiled by Sir Henry Irving in 1897. The old Town Hall which stood next to the Green on the north side of Harrow Road, was demolished in 1966. In St Mary's Terrace on the site of a row of houses which was destroyed in an air raid of March 1944, a fine new block of workers' flats has been erected by the Paddington Borough Council. This backs on to Paddington Green and has been named Fleming Court after Sir Alexander Fleming who discovered penicillin.

The first horse-bus service, operated by George Shillibeer, was introduced in 1829 and ran from Paddington to the Bank, via the 'Angel'. The bus had 22 seats and was drawn by three horses, harnessed abreast. It is generally accepted, though one authority disagrees, that the Paddington starting point was 'The Yorkshire Stingo' in the Marylebone Road, a celebrated tavern which, unfortunately, was demolished quite recently. At No. 185, next door, are the new headquarters of The Church Army, founded by the Revd Wilson Carlisle.

The section of Harrow Road from Edgware Road to Bishop's Bridge Road will form part of the new thoroughfare which is to connect up Marylebone Road with the Western Avenue at Wood Lane. A start on the widening of Harrow Road has been made near Edgware Road. A part of this scheme involves the construction of a new street opposite Harrow Road between Edgware Road and Marylebone Road and a large roundabout and flyover at this busy junction as mentioned in the Sixteenth Walk.

On the north side of Praed Street, which leads from Edgware Road to Paddington Station, is St Mary's Hospital, established in 1843. The foundation-stone of the original buildings was laid by the Prince Consort on 28 June 1845, they were opened on 13 June 1851. The hospital was rebuilt in 1903, and is now faced with red brick and stone. A Medical School and Pathological Institute by Sir Edwin Cooper, A.R.A., was added to the hospital about fifteen years ago. Praed Street takes its name from Sir John Praed, a director of the Grand Union Canal in the early part of the nineteenth century. This street, though it has always been shabby, is enlivened by the constant stream of travellers on their way to and from Paddington Station. Many old houses on the north side are being demolished between North Wharf Road and Paddington Station on both sides of St Mary's Hospital for an extension of its buildings and thus Praed Street is gradually losing its poverty-stricken appearance.

To resume at the Harrow Road Flyover. For the next half-mile, the Edgware Road still retains its humble character until it crosses the Regent's Canal, beyond which it becomes Maida Vale. In its south-westward direction the canal follows an open course and, flanked by Blomfield Road and Maida Avenue resembling the canal-lined streets of Bruges or Rotterdam, finds itself in quite a picturesque setting which many years ago acquired the title of 'Little Venice', though recent building developments threaten the validity of that description.

Built mostly between 1830 and 1840, Maida Vale was formerly called Edgware Road, of which it is actually a continuation but in 1868 its name was altered at the special request of its residents to Maida Vale instead of Kilburn Road, as originally intended by the Metropolitan Board of Works. It is a fine broad thoroughfare about a mile in length, extending from the Regent's Canal to Kilburn High Road.

While the eastern side of Maida Vale, except for a row of houses beyond Abercorn Place, gave way to blocks of mansion flats many years ago, on the Paddington side large stucco-fronted villas standing well back from the road with large front gardens survived until quite recently. The challenge to the monopoly of these well-to-do residents began in 1938, when Dibdin House on the corner of Carlton Vale was erected by the Ecclesiastical Commissioners, to house 230 families that had been displaced by slum clearance in other parts of Paddington, of which they were ground landlords. Post-war development on a large scale by the former Paddington Borough Council has replaced the remaining villas on this side with large buildings of flats and maisonettes ranging from six to seventeen storeys in height. Being adjacent to Sutherland and Elgin Avenues, these new 'Houses' sustain the nominally Scottish atmosphere of this part of Maida Vale with names such as Edinburgh, Braemar, Falkirk etc.

To the west of Maida Vale, between Harrow Road and Kilburn Park, is another handsome quarter of Paddington, containing many wide streets and avenues lined with large private houses and blocks of flats. Those between Sutherland Avenue and the Regent's Canal are about eighty years old. Most of the houses here are similar to those of Bayswater and Kensington, but those centred round Sutherland Avenue, Lauderdale Road, and Elgin Avenue are of much more recent construction and consist largely of non-basement houses and blocks of flats. Little more than fifty years ago a large part of the ground upon which these newer houses have been built was still open land, although it had long since become surrounded on every side by streets and houses stretching towards Kilburn and Harrow Road. Two fine thoroughfares, Sutherland Avenue and Elgin Avenue, connect Maida Vale with Harrow Road, and running diagonally between them is Lauderdale Road, consisting almost entirely of modern four-storeyed blocks of flats faced with red brick. Many blocks of flats have also been erected in Elgin Avenue, but semi-detached houses have been mostly built is Ashworth Road and Biddulph Road, connecting Elgin Avenue and Lauderdale Road. At the junction of Clifton Gardens and Warrington Crescent is the handsome Gothic church of St Saviour's, with a square tower.

This pleasant quarter of the town has the advantage of being very accessible from the West End by means of the Bakerloo Tube. This part of London suffered severely from air raids during both World Wars and much damage was done to property, notably in Warrington Crescent, Elgin Avenue and Randolph Avenue, as well as in the vicinity of Abbey Road, St John's Wood, and near Lord's Cricket Ground. To the north of Elgin Avenue is the Paddington Recreation Ground. It was purchased for £33,000 and is bordered on the south and west sides by four-storeyed blocks of flats. This is attractively laid out with flower gardens, bowling greens, a race-course, a children's playground and a large refreshment pavilion. In Kilburn Park Road is St Augustine's Church, a handsome Gothic edifice crowned by a tower with a lofty spire. At the corner of Kilburn High and Priory Road is the Kilburn Empire, which is now a cinema.

Kilburn, the district to the north of Maida Vale, was once famous for a spring of mineral water belonging to a drinking house called Kilbourn Wells. The house, with its adjoining grounds, was situated close to the turnpike gate at the southern end of what is now the very busy shopping thoroughfare of High Road, Kilburn. It stood on the site of a hermitage which was afterwards converted into a nunnery called Kilburn Priory, of which nothing now remains. In the eighteenth century Kilburn Wells, being only two miles distant from Oxford Street or a morning's walk from the centre of London, was a favourite resort of visitors, who came here to drink the waters and to indulge in refreshments, music and dancing. A printed brochure on the water, described by an eminent physician, was given gratis to people visiting the wells. The Old Bell Tavern, long since rebuilt, marks the site of the original house in Kilburn High Road. The mineral spring stood close to the site now covered by the Kilburn station of British Railways (Midland Region). The turnpike gate at the southern end of the High Road, Kilburn, was abolished in 1868.

Until after 1870 Kilburn was situated on the fringe of the metropolis and consisted principally of one long street forming a part of the main Edgware Road. The whole of the vast territory on the east, extending to Finchley Road and Hampstead, was then open country, and the great urban district of Willesden on the west was non-existent. High Road, Kilburn, is one of the most lively shopping centres of semi-suburban London and together with Shoot-up Hill and Cricklewood Broadway, forms the boundary line between Brent and Camden. It is about three-quarters of a mile long and contains many excellent shops, the largest of which is the extensive drapery store of Messrs B. B. Evans on the east side. Near the junction of Kilburn High Road and Willesden Lane now stands the Gaumont State Cinema, one of the largest in London. It was erected in 1936 and is crowned by a lofty square tower. Higher up is the Kilburn Grange Cinema, at the back of which is a small public park, formerly the private grounds of a mansion called the Grange. This is tastefully laid out with flower gardens, tennis courts, a children's playground and a girls' gymnasium.

A century ago Willesden, then called Wilsdon, was a retired village five miles from Oxford Street, and a favourite walk was then from Kilburn Wells through Willesden Lane, passing by Brondesbury House, the former seat of Lady Salisbury and afterwards of Mr Coutts Trotter. Another very pleasant walk was from the Paddington Canal to Willesden by way of Kensal Green.

The district of Kensal Green is situated on the north side of Harrow Road, but the famous cemetery of that name is on the opposite side, within the area of the Royal Borough of Kensington. It was formed in 1832 by a joint-stock company and comprises about seventy acres of ground between the Grand Union Canal and British Railways (Midland Region), with its entrance-lodge and gateway in the Harrow Road. The necessity of providing cemeteries out of town was already keenly felt by 1832, and no sooner was Kensal Green Cemetery opened than other companies were formed to construct cemeteries at Highgate, Norwood, Nunhead, and various other places outside of inner London.

Kensal Green Cemetery, which contains upwards of fifty thousand graves, is modelled on the lines of the famous Père-Lachaise Cemetery in Paris. Amongst the notable people interred here are Leigh Hunt, Thackeray, Tom Hood, Anthony Trollope, John Leech, and the Duke of Cambridge. On the west side of the cemetery is the Roman Catholic burial-ground, opened in 1860, and here Cardinal Wiseman is interred; he died at his residence in York Place, Baker Street, in February 1865. Between Harrow Road and Kilburn Lane is the Queen's Park Estate which was laid out in the early eighteen-seventies and developed on total-abstinence principles by the Artisan Labourers and General Dwellings Company. All its streets have names following the alphabet from A to Z and its main avenues leading out of Harrow Road are numbered from one to six. There are no public-houses on this estate. Many of its houses were destroyed or damaged in the great blitz of 1940. On a large bombed site at the corner of Ilbert Street and Peach Street the Paddington Borough Council have erected four six-storeyed blocks of workers' flats.

To the north of Harrow Road, in the district of Kensal Rise, is Queen's Park, opened in 1887 and containing an area of thirty acres surrounded by modern suburban houses. It was formerly the ground of the Queen's Park Rangers Football Club and was conveyed by the Ecclesiastical Commissioners to the Corporation of the City of London by whom it was laid out at a cost of £3,000. The park is richly wooded and bands play here during the summer months. Chamberlayne Road, opposite Ladbroke Grove to the west of Queen's Park, has been extended through to Willesden High Road, and thus affords direct communication between Holland Park and Willesden Green. In this quarter of Willesden are the ancient parish church of St Mary, where Charles Reade, author of *The Cloister and the Hearth* and many other novels is buried, the King Edward VII recreation ground, opened in 1909, which contains an open-air swimming-bath, and the beautiful Roundwood Park. This has a steep hill in the centre and covers an area of twenty-six acres. It was opened on 11 May 1895 by Sir Ralph Littler, Chairman of the Middlesex County Council, at a cost of £26,000. The district of Harlesden, forming the south-western portion of Willesden, is centred round Harrow Road, and contains some of the principal shops, but the finest houses are situated at Brondesbury, Willesden Green, and Cricklewood.

Having been planned on garden-city lines, and formerly one of the most rustic spots in London, the residential thoroughfares of Willesden are of a very pleasant character, and for the most part lined with trees. There are also many large blocks of flats, notably in Sidmouth Road, Donnington Road and in Walm Lane near Willesden Green Station including some high-class shops. Close to Dollis Hill Station is the beautiful Gladstone Park, which is reached either by

Anson Road or Dollis Hill Lane. It was formerly the suburban retreat of Lord Aberdeen, and was frequently visited by Mr Gladstone, after whom the park is named. It has an area of a hundred acres, and contains an open-air swimming-pool, a bandstand, public tennis courts, and bowling greens. It is situated on steeply rising ground from the top of which a panoramic view is obtained of north-west London and in the direction of Hampstead Heath. The mansion is used as a refreshment- and tea-house.

In Dollis Hill Lane which flanks the north side of the park are St Andrew's Hospital and a large block of newly-erected flats called Neville Court built round an open quadrangle. The park was opened by Lord Aberdeen on 25 May 1901. Its cost was £51,300, and a further £8,000 for laying out the grounds. The Middlesex County Council and the Hendon and Hampstead Councils contribut-ed towards the cost. The district of Neasden, to the west of Gladstone Park, contains the Eastern Region and London Transport railway depôts and also an excellent golf course near the North Circular Road.

The handsome suburb of Cricklewood is divided into two parts by the Edgware Road, which here goes under the name of Cricklewood Broadway, and is lined on both sides with high-class shops for a distance of about half a mile. The west side is in the borough of Brent whereas the east side is in Camden and Barnet. The Crown Hotel, tastefully rebuilt in 1889 with a terracotta frontage, stands back on the east side some distance from the roadway, and is now the terminus of some of the motor-omnibus routes. Farther along on the same side of the road is the Cricklewood skating rink. Fifty years ago Cricklewood stood where the London houses began to get fewer, and ended in the open country, but since the first World War much building has taken place farther north in the direction of Hendon. Cricklewood owes its rapid development to the motor-omnibuses, which made Edgware Road their principal centre during the pioneer days of close on sixty years ago. It is also connected with Hendon and Edgware by motor-omnibus. In Chichele Road, leading to Willesden Green, is St Gabriel's Church, the principal one in this district, and in Ashford Road is a huge block of flats called Ashford Court erected in 1937.

Between Cricklewood and West Hendon a number of factories have been erected on the Edgware Road, some of which greatly disfigure the landscape. On the west side are the extensive garages of London Transport, about half-way between Cricklewood and the Welsh Harp Inn. The Brent Reservoir, a large lake known as the Welsh Harp, has been a favourite resort of Londoners for generations. It was formed in 1838 by enlarging the bed of the River Brent to feed the Grand Junction Canal. In the old days boating, bathing and fishing could be enjoyed. The craze for sun-bathing has been freely indulged in on the shores of the Welsh Harp lake, but on account of the objections raised by the local inhabitants the apostles of this pastime have been compelled to seek accommodation elsewhere. On the south side of the lake is a recreation ground, at the back of which now runs the new North Circular Road connecting Finchley with Wembley. A portion of the lake has been drained and the land adjacent to Edgware Road developed for building. On that account this locality has lost its former rural and picturesque appearance. The old Welsh Harp Inn was pulled down in 1937 and rebuilt on very up-to-date lines and factories are gradually being erected in this section of the Edgware Road. A second arm of the Brent Reservoir at Silk Bridge at the Hyde farther up Edgware Road has also been filled in. London has spread rapidly in this direction. A scheme is on foot at the present time to convert the Welsh Harp lake into a permanent holiday resort for Londoners. There is another recreation ground on the north side of the lake which together with the adjoining Woodfield Park would be incorporated into the scheme.

After passing the Welsh Harp we come to the busy West Hendon Broadway, sixty years ago a country road boasting scarcely a single house, and now a busy shopping thoroughfare extending for half a mile along the main Edgware Road. About half-way up on the east side is Station Road which leads past Hendon Station to the Burroughs, the quaint title given to one of Hendon's main streets. Around the heart of the village much building has taken place of late years, but the old Perpendicular-style parish church of St Mary, situated on a hill-top, still overlooks large stretches of meadow-land. It was partly rebuilt in 1827, and is noted for its battlemented tower and ancient roof. Its square Norman font is the finest example in Middlesex. Hendon Church is the burial-place of Sir Stanford Raffles, the founder of Singapore, to whom a memorial has been erected in the tower. Hendon Hall, now a private hotel, was the home of Garrick, who owned the Manor. The signboard of the Chequers Inn, near the Church, gives us a familiar quotation: *If you want to get somewhere else, you must run twice as fast as that.*

Hendon, which derives its name from Heandune or Highdown, was a scattered village sixty years ago, but since the opening of the Underground Railway to Golder's Green in 1907 and in 1923 to Hendon and Edgware, it has assumed the proportions of a large town. Hendon was incorporated as a Borough in 1932, but is now, with West Hendon, in the new London Borough of Barnet. The Town Hall and the Public Library are situated near the Burroughs and their architectural style blends admirably with the surrounding property. Close to the Town Hall is the new Hendon Technical College, a handsome building which has a façade of yellow brick with stone dressing and is crowned in the centre by a small clock-tower. On the south side of Queen's Road is Hendon Park, which is beautifully laid out with tennis courts and putting greens. Brent Street, leading to Golder's Green Road, is the leading business thoroughfare, but a handsome new shopping centre and the large Gaumont Cinema have also been erected round Hendon Central Station. An Odeon Cinema has been erected in Brent Street which on its west side is partly flanked by the picturesque Green leading up to the corner of Queen's Road. A feature of Hendon is Brent Park which has been laid out on the North Circular Road and through which flows the River Brent. It is narrow but densely wooded and extends from Golder's Green Road to Bridge Lane. Hendon is now completely joined to Golder's Green by large numbers of new houses and roads admirably laid out in garden-city fashion between the two World Wars.

Golder's Green, which owes its original development to the opening of the Hampstead tube railway, is a most attractive suburb. It is situated on the northern heights between Hampstead and Hendon, near the beautiful Golder's Hill Park. With its beautiful homes and fine avenues, Golder's Green is a garden suburb of which any great city might feel proud, and Golder's Green Road, the main business thoroughfare, contains many fine shops which would be a credit to Oxford Street. Close to the wide crossroad, next to the Underground Railway Station, is the Golder's Green Hippodrome, one of the finest theatres outside Central London, which is visited by the leading touring companies. Being so conveniently situated next to the Underground Station it is much frequented even by Londoners accustomed only to visiting West End theatres. This is also a busy terminus of several omnibus routes controlled by London Transport.

At Child's Hill, a short distance south of Cricklewood Lane, is the entrance to the new Watford by-pass road which here goes under the name of Hendon Way. Here several attractive blocks of flats, namely Vernon Court, Wendover Court and Moreland Court, with frontages in the Tudor style, have been erected of late years, which being situated on high ground command extensive views in the direction of Hendon and Edgware.

First Drive

A Tour of the North-Eastern Suburbs

This tour is intended to embrace those north-eastern suburbs which have not already been included in our previous chapters, but as it covers too much ground for an ordinary walk it is best made by omnibus or motorcar. Making Shoreditch Church our starting-point, we proceed along Kingsland Road. Between Shoreditch Church and the overbridge of the North London Railway, a much-needed widening of the roadway was carried out in 1930 by setting back the building line on the west side. Previously the road had only been wide enough to accommodate three lines of traffic, including a single tramway track, thus causing great congestion at this busy traffic centre. At the lower end of Kingsland Road, several boot and shoe factories have their warehouses, but a little further along on the east side we are reminded that one of the principal industries of this part of Shoreditch is the manufacture of furniture. In the vacated almshouses of the Ironmongers' Company on the east side of Kingsland Road, founded by Sir Robert Geffrye, the Master, early in the eighteenth century, is now the Geffrye Museum. It contains a collection illustrative of domestic art, consisting of furniture, woodwork and fixtures preserved by the London County Council from demolished buildings.

Beyond Old Street, Kingsland Road becomes a broad straight thoroughfare and leads to Dalston. To the east is Haggerston, once a hamlet in the parish of St Leonard's Shoreditch, but now an extensive quarter of factories and small houses stretching from the north side of the Hackney Road to Dalston and eastwards to Mare Street and London Fields. It is mentioned in Domesday Book under the name of Hergotestane and as late as the seventeenth century consisted only of a few country residences. Queen's Road, now renamed Queensbridge Road, which runs from north to south through this quarter is a fine wide thoroughfare of good semi-detached villas. At the 'Fox' tavern, Haggerston Road and Middleton Road enter the east side of Kingsland Road together; the manner in which the roadway dips suddenly and then rises again while the footways at the side remain at their normal level is quite picturesque – until one realises that the depression was made merely to provide sufficient clearance under the low bridge carrying the North London Railway. From this point northward the Kingsland Market stalls occupy one side of the road on Saturdays.

London Fields, close to Mare Street, Hackney, and comprising an area of twenty-six and a half acres, is the nearest open space to the City on the east side of London, and as such was subjected to very rough treatment in its earlier days. At the time when Hackney was inhabited by many wealthy citizens London

Fields was chiefly devoted to sheep grazing. In Rocque's map of 1745 the thoroughfare at the south-west of the Fields is shown as Mutton Lane. The memory of its former inhabitants is preserved at the present day by the two thoroughfares called Sheep Lane and Lamb Lane on the east side of London Fields. With the increase of the population the use of the Fields became much more general, and in course of time the surface was worn so bare that the four months of close time were not sufficient to enable the grass to grow again. In dry weather the Fields became a hard, unsightly, and dusty plain with a few isolated patches of turf, and in wet weather a dismal swamp. It was the resort of the riff-raff of East London, and here the most dissolute practices were carried on. Cockshies were put up and the scenes were similar to those of a common fair. Happily this is now a thing of the past, and by systematic fencing it has become possible to preserve the turf.

The modern public-house at the south corner of London Fields stands on the site of an ancient tavern called the Shoulder of Mutton, dating back at least to 1731. Its present name is the Cat and Mutton, which is supposed to be a corruption of the older title. On the signboard is the doggerel verse:

Pray, Pussy do not claw
Because the mutton is so raw;
Pray, Pussy do not tear
Because the mutton is so rare.

A little further south the Regent's Canal is crossed by the Cat and Mutton Bridge.

On the west side of Kingsland Road, to which we will now return, half-way to Dalston and adjoining the Regent's Canal, stood until 1852 Balmes House, which, together with its estate, had been a place of note for upwards of three centuries. Originally called Baumes, this house was built about 1540 by two Spanish merchants named Baulm and was pleasantly situated in the midst of gardens and grounds laid out in the geometrical style of the sixteenth century. On one occasion Charles I, with his Court, was entertained here, in tents erected in the garden, by Sir George Whitmore, who occasionally resided here when Lord Mayor in 1631-32.

Tradition says that about the year 1680 a man was found drowned in a moat which at that time surrounded the house, and that the body having been brought to the churchwardens of Shoreditch parish they refused to receive and inter it. Thereupon an application was made to the parochial authorities of Hackney, who received the body and buried it at the charge of the parish. Owing to this circumstance the house and estate were afterwards claimed as being in the parish of Hackney, where it has remained ever since. The mansion was built of brick and had two storeys with dormer windows in a high-pitched roof. Until the close of the eighteenth century it had a walk planted with fruit trees, and the house and moat were supplied with water from an ancient well adjoining Canonbury House in Islington.

In the early part of the nineteenth century the house was used as a private asylum, and the estate became the property of Richard Benyon de Beauvoir. After 1852 the land attached to the mansion was covered with streets and a new square of houses, the new district being called De Beauvoir Town. Whitmore Road, adjoining the Regent's Canal, was originally a carriage-drive leading to Balmes. Here and to the south of the Regent's Canal much slum property was destroyed in the blitz of 1940. Facing Phillipp Street is the Haggerston Branch Library; on the staircase wall hangs a *very* large oil painting called *The Finding of Jane Shore,* by the Hon. Lewis Wingfield.

The streets between Kingsland Road and Southgate Road, extending northwards to Dalston, are wide and very well laid out with large detached two-storey houses with gardens, so that whatever its original social status may have been, there are still many far worse places in which to live than De Beauvoir Town. Forming the centre of this quarter is De Beauvoir Square, which is bordered by Gothic houses and contains St Peter's Church, a pseudo-Gothic edifice erected about the year 1830. The north end of De Beauvoir Road, before the school in Tottenham Road was built, was crossed at right angles by Ball's Pond Road, which connects Kingsland Road and Dalston with Essex Road, Islington.

Dalston, formerly spelt Dorlston, is a hamlet in the parish of Hackney and comprises the houses on either side of Ball's Pond Road and Dalston Lane. In 1774 it was described as a small but pleasant village near Hackney. Now a part of London, and an important railway junction, it was once famous for its nursery gardens, some of which were still cultivated as recently as 1860.

Many houses at the back of Ball's Pond Road were destroyed in the air raids of 1940 and large sites on the north side have been cleared for re-building. Here the Islington Borough Council have erected several new blocks of flats in Kingsbury Road and Boleyn Road.

A few words relating to the part played by the North London Railway, now merged into British Railways (Midland Region), in the development of the metropolis may here prove of interest. Opened in 1851, the railway then ran from Fenchurch Street via Bow, Homerton, Hackney, Dalston, Highbury, and Barnsbury to Camden Town, where it linked up with the London and North Western Railway. At that time there were still open fields adjoining the Tower Hamlets Cemetery, including Bow Common, which is now built over and partly covered by Burdett Road. From here a distant view could be obtained from the train of the East India Docks and the Surrey and Kent Hills. North of Bow Road there was still open country, and on the right was the newly-formed Victoria Park. There was also an extensive view on the left over the Hackney Marshes, with the wooded Essex scenery in the background. (The writer of the account upon which this is based was travelling with his back to the engine). By the end of 1851, which completed the first six months of working, the number of passengers carried was nearly a million and a half. With the opening of the line from Bow to Poplar and the West India Docks in 1852, the North London was completed, except for the short branch from Dalston to Broad Street which came much later, in 1865, to provide its own City terminus. Homerton, now a thickly-populated quarter, was then a retired village, formerly a district of the parish of Hackney, but afterwards formed into a separate parish. Here a new church had been built in 1847 by Mr Ashpitel. This is St Barnabas, Homerton, which was badly damaged during the war, but has now been repaired and re-opened. Berger Road, near the Church is named after the German chemist (originally Steigenberger) who came to this country in 1760 and founded the Berger paint manufactory. Leading into Homerton High Street is Sutton Place; with a terrace of late Georgian houses culminating in Sutton House, a Tudor mansion where lived the founder of the Charterhouse, Thomas Sutton.

Hackney was still a picturesque locality, and in Kingsland large tracts of land belonging to Mr W.G.D. Tyssen, Lord of the Manor, were then being laid out for building detached villas of the better class. Caledonian Road, farther west, was then being rapidly lined with houses, streets, and squares, and the Model Prison at Pentonville, erected a few years earlier, still stood in the midst of open fields. By 1851, however, it had become almost surrounded by houses.

After passing Dalston Station we come to Kingsland High Street, which, together with Stoke Newington Road and High Street, forms a busy shopping thoroughfare about a mile long, extending north to Stamford Hill. Just off Kingsland High Street on the east side is Ridley Road, at the entrance to which is a wide opening that serves as a street market. In St Mark's Rise, off Ridley Road is the handsome parish church of St Mark, erected in 1866-70, to the design of Chester Cheston Jnr., though the tower with its unusual feature—a circular barometer, half way up—was a later addition by Edward L. Blackburne. Often referred to as the 'Cathedral of the East End', St Mark's is the largest parish church in London, and has an estimated seating capacity for a congregation of 2,000. The stained glass windows are considered to be of special interest. Kingsland is supposed to have derived its name from a royal residence or mansion on Stoke Newington Green, traditionally said to have been frequented by Henry VIII when indulging in the pleasures of the chase. Other Tudor associations not far from the Green are King Henry's Walk, Boleyn Road and Wolsey Road, while at the east side of Clissold Park is Queen Elizabeth's Walk. Until about the middle of the eighteenth century it contained a hospital for lepers, which was annexed after the Reformation to St Bartholomew's Hospital, and was used as a sort of out-ward for that institution. At the corner of Stoke Newington Road and Amhurst Road the West Hackney Church was completely destroyed in the blitz of 1940. A new church, dedicated to St Paul and designed by Mr N. F. Cachemaille-Day has been built on the site and was opened in March 1960.

Stoke Newington is now included in the new Borough of Hackney. Already in the *Ambulator* of 1774 it is described as 'a pleasant village near Islington where a great number of the citizens of London have built houses and rendered it extremely populous, more like a large flourishing town than a village. The church', says the writer, 'is a low Gothic building belonging to the Dean and

Chapter of St Paul's. Behind the church is a pleasant grove of tall trees where the inhabitants resort for the benefit of shade and a wholesome air.' This refers to the still surviving Ancient Mother Church of Stoke Newington, a very old building to which the south aisle was added in 1563. It is probable that a church has occupied this site since Anglo-Saxon times.

The name of Stoke Newington denotes the new village or town built on the borders of a wood. In the words of Walford's *Old and New London,* our land is full of Stokes, and wherever there is a Stoke we may be sure there was once a wood. The wood in which Stoke Newington was situated formed part of the great Middlesex forest. In 1835 it consisted principally of the one long street already mentioned, which extends from Kingsland Road to Stamford Hill on the high road from London to Cambridge, and at that time contained a population of 3,500 inhabitants. Branching off on the western side near the centre of the town is Church Street, leading to the parish church and Green Lanes. Alderman Pickett, who instituted the great improvements in the Strand near Temple Bar, is buried in the churchyard, together with his son and daughter.

Nos. 187-191, Stoke Newington High Street are three early eighteenth century houses of melancholy interest that have deteriorated considerably since they were vacated by the W.V.S. and some other offices formerly located there.

At the corner of Church Street opposite Albion Road, is the handsome Town Hall, of the bygone borough, opened on 3 July 1937. This is a building of yellow brick with stone dressings and circular columns on the ground floor. It has replaced the old Town Hall in Milton Grove. Albion Road leads to Newington Green, a large square which is gradually losing its old-world charm. However, the Newington Green Church, on the north side, erected in 1708, is still active in the Unitarian interest and on the west side of the green is the China Inland Mission, founded by Dr J. Hudson Taylor in 1865 to send missionaries into the Chinese interior. Since the Chinese Communist Government took over in 1949 the mission work has been continued in other parts of the Far East. Appropriate texts in Chinese characters decorate the main entrance. In Yoakley Road the Stoke Newington Borough Council have erected three new blocks of dwellings, one of them a nine-storey building. The Yoakley Almshouses have gone and the old 1830 Meeting House of the Society of Friends (Quakers) has been replaced by a new building.

On the other side of Church Street; facing the old Church, is the relatively modern church of St Mary built in 1858 from the designs of Sir G. Gilbert Scott. The spire was not completed until some thirty years later. Adjoining the older church is Clissold Park, which in the mid-nineteenth century was known as Crawshay's Farm, the property of an irascible old gentleman named Crawshay who had two daughters. The curate of the parish at that time was the Reverend Augustus Clissold, and he fell in love with Mr Crawshay's elder daughter, who reciprocated the curate's effection, much to the annoyance of her father, whose dislike of parsons was intense. Despite the old gentleman's threats of physical violence, the young couple bided their time, and when death put an end to all opposition they were married, and the name of both the daughter and the farm was changed to Clissold. Clissold House, now a refreshment centre in the park, is an elegant structure of 1830, with a portico supported by six doric columns. A disused drinking fountain attached to a side wall bears an inscription that seems to hint at tragedy; 'In memory of three sweet sisters aged 1, 3 and 4 years, daughters of Wilson Yeates Esq., interred at Horton Bucks, 1834.' It was erected by their sister in 1893. The park extends westward as far as Green Lane and covers an area of 55 acres. On the north side of Church Street is Abney Park Cemetery, laid out about 1840 on the site of the grounds of the mansion of Sir Thomas Abney, a member of the Fishmongers' Company and a distinguished Nonconformist. He was knighted by William III and became Lord Mayor of London in 1700. His daughter, Miss Abney, ordered by her will that after her death the estate of Abney Park should be sold and the proceeds distributed amongst charities and given to the poor. It was sold to Mr Jonathan Eade and later became a college for youths of the Wesleyan Society, until it was pulled down in 1845. It was to Abney House that Dr Watts, author of many well-known hymns, went to stay for a few days as the guest of Lady Abney. He died there in 1748, a still welcome guest, having extended his visit to 36 years! A plaque on the corner of Defoe Road marks the site of the house where Daniel Defoe lived and where *Robinson Crusoe* may have been written. It is also claimed n Yorkshire that part, at least, of *Robinson Crusoe* was written at the 'Rose and Crown' Inn, Halifax. While several prominent literary figures are associated with Stoke Newington, the local celebrity is undoubtedly Daniel Defoe. His bust stands in the hall of the local library and in Green Lanes, opposite Church Street is the 'Robinson Crusoe' tavern; the customer standing at the bar counter is likely to be as surprised as Crusoe himself, for should he happen to glance at the floor he will see the footprint of Man Friday on the linoleum!

Stamford Hill, the continuation northwards of Stoke Newington High Street, is a fine broad thoroughfare about a mile in length, bordered with good-class houses and modern blocks of flats.

At the summit of the hill, not far from the High Road, Tottenham, Stamford Hill joins the old Cambridge Road, which passes through Hackney by way of Mare Street and thence through Lower and Upper Clapton. That part of Hackney situated next to Stoke Newington and Clapton contains large houses and well-planned streets, notably Amhurst Road, leading from Stoke Newington High Street to Hackney Station and Mare Street, and although Hackney Station is closed, it is still an important road junction and continues to figure on the destination blinds of the buses. Downs Park Road on the east side leads to Hackney Downs, a pleasant open space of forty-two acres which is higher than any other spot within the same distance from the City. A high proportion of Jewish people inhabit this quarter of London.

Hackney Downs was one of the lammas lands of Hackney, and formerly included the playground of the handsome school of the Grocers' Company on the southern side. The enclosing of this land caused serious disturbances, and

124 Statue of Sir Hugh Myddelton, Islington Green.

125 Whittington's stone, Highgate Hill, has no authenticity, and the cat less!

126 Hampstead Heath: the viaduct or 'Red Arches'.

127 A famous tea garden: Highbury Barn Tavern in the early 19th century.

128 Highgate Village, about 1800.

129 Chalk Farm Tavern, once the meeting place of duellists. It was demolished in 1853.

130   Haverstock Hill as it appeared in 1830, showing, on the left, Steele's cottage.

131   The Pavilion, Hans Place, in 1800. It was pulled down in 1879.

132 Knightsbridge in the 1890s.

134 The new public library in Horton Street, Kensington.

135 The Royal Garden Hotel, Kensington, stands on the site of the famous Royal Palace Hotel.

133 Sloane Square.

136 Cheyne Row, from Chelsea Old Church, about 1840.

137 St Mary Abbot's Church, Kensington, before being rebuilt in 1869.

138   The BBC Television Centre in Wood Lane, near the White City.

139   Originally the sign of the Black Bull Inn, Holborn, this massive beast is now in Hammersmith.

140   Statue of the great tragic actress Sarah Siddons, Paddington Green.

141 Paddington Canal in 1820.

142 Clissold Park, Stoke Newington.

143 This fifteenth century building stands near the church in the village of Walthamstow, E. 17.

144 Valentines, the 18th century mansion of Valentines Park, Ilford.

145 Section of pillar from the old G.P.O., St Martin's-le-Grand, now at Walthamstow.

on 11 December 1875 the wooden posts and iron railings set by the Lord of the Manor as an assertion of his rights were pulled down by the indignant inhabitants, who strongly resented this encroachment on their rights. But the Lord of the Manor gained the day, so that the passing of the commons under municipal control has been a decided benefit to Hackney.

On the west side of Mare Street, south of Graham Road, are the Hackney Empire (recently a television studio) and the Town Hall, the third erected in Hackney, a handsome square building with a stone façade opened on 3 July 1937. This stands to the west of an earlier Town Hall opened on 20 September 1866 of which the foundation-stone was laid in November 1864 by Mr Tyssen Amherst, the Lord of the Manor. On the opposite side, near the junction of Mare Street with Amhurst Road, at No 354 Mare Street, is a building inscribed, 'Hackney Old Town Hall'; it was the first of Hackney's Town Halls, and is now occupied by the Midland Bank. Opposite Well Street, 195 Mare Street is a well-preserved house dating from the early eighteenth century which in 1849 was opened as an institution for the shelter and reform of penitent female prisoners on their discharge from criminal gaols. It was called the Elizabeth Fry Refuge, as a memorial to that famous Quaker lady who devoted her life to prison reform, and was known as 'the female Howard'. The house is now the New Lansdowne Club.

Hackney new church, St John-at-Hackney, at the corner of Mare Street and Lower Clapton Road, was commenced in 1792 and consecrated on 13 July 1797, but the steeple and the entrance porticoes were not built until the years 1812 and 1813. The old church was pulled down in 1798, but the tower, which is of very picturesque appearance, has been preserved in the churchyard. This is now tastefully laid out as a public recreation ground. The 13th century tower of the old church survives because it was thought that the eight bells were too heavy for the new building—and the parishioners were reluctant to lose their peal of bells. However, it was discovered later that their fears were groundless and the bells were re-hung in the new church in 1854. The new church, which was erected from the designs of Mr Spiller at a cost of £28,000, was severely damaged by fire in 1955; it was rebuilt and re-consecrated in 1958. In former times, when the nobility were scattered over the metropolis, Hackney was distinguished for its fine mansions, but these eventually became lodging-houses and tenements or were pulled down. It was said to have been the first village near London that provided carriages for occasional passengers, hence the origin of the name Hackney carriages; but this claim is disputed.

The new London Borough of Hackney, which includes the former boroughs of Stoke Newington and Shoreditch, has an area of 4,814 acres, with a population of 255,930. Mare Street, which is the leading shopping thoroughfare, was extensively widened about 1904 by the London County Council, but the roadway still narrows into a tiresome bottleneck at the junction of Amhurst Road and Mare Street near Hackney Station. In Amhurst Road, a fine wide avenue leading to Stoke Newington Road, are many distinctive blocks of flats standing back in gardens and covering sites formerly occupied by large villas. In Pembury Road, which leads from Amhurst Road up on to Hackney Downs, is a large housing estate now covered with five-storeyed blocks of flats of an attractive design. These were mostly completed shortly before the last war and some of them face the south side of Hackney Downs. Another estate was developed on a part of Hackney Marshes on the north side of Marsh Hill, a continuation of Homerton High Street. This was formerly a public Recreation Ground but in 1937 after much bitter controversy it was surrendered to the London County Council in exchange for another open space in the same neighbourhood so that the Council might provide much-needed housing accommodation. The marshy character of this land necessitated pile-driving to provide suitable foundations for the new blocks of flats.

Lower Clapton Road, along which we will now proceed, is continued by Upper Clapton Road, and here are a number of good-class houses. On the east side of the road, near the point where it joins Stamford Hill, is Clapton Common which is bordered by trees and old-fashioned villas in spacious gardens. Nearby, in Castlewood Road is the very ornate Cathedral Church of the Good Shepherd, with winged animals symbolising the Evangelists at the four corners of its tower. Once known as the Church of the Agapemonites it achieved notoriety in 1902, when the Rev. H. J. Smyth Piggot informed his congregation that he was the 'Messiah'. This claim, which caused violent demonstrations in the neighbourhood, resulted in his being unfrocked and, with the members of his 'Abode of Love', he retired to Spaxton, Somerset, where he died in 1927. Sloping down from Clapton Common is Springfield Park, a beautiful open space, comprising an area of thirty-two acres, extending to the River Lea, where boating can be enjoyed. It was acquired for the public at a cost of £40,000 and opened on 5 August 1905. The park is richly wooded and contains an ornamental lake, flower gardens, tennis courts and bowling greens. Between Springfield Park and Moresby Road is a large colony of flats built round a spacious open quadrangle which provides a large children's playground. The buildings, which are all five storeys high, were erected before the last war by the Hackney Borough Council. Some air-raid shelters erected in the quadrangle have been usefully converted into sheds for perambulators.

Noticing the Skinners' Company's School for Girls at the summit, and descending the sloping ground to the north of Stamford Hill we enter the extensive area of Tottenham which, with Hornsey and Wood Green, is in the new Borough of Haringey. The main street or High Road is very broad, and lined with straggling houses and shops. Tottenham has grown very rapidly during the past forty years. In the centre of the town is a large triangular enclosure called the Green, close to which is the High Cross, which has stood here from time immemorial. It originally consisted of a column of wood, but this was taken down early in the seventeenth century, when the present octagonal column was erected in its place by Dean Wood. The column is of brick, but was given a coating of stucco in 1809. In 1952, the High Cross was found to be no less than nineteen inches out of the perpendicular; it has since been corrected.

To the west of the High Road, near Bruce Grove Station, is Bruce Castle, which takes its name from a castellated mansion, the residence of Robert Bruce, father of the Scottish king of that name. It was rebuilt in the latter part of the seventeenth century, and is a good specimen of Elizabethan domestic architecture. In more recent times it was converted into a metropolitan school for boys by Rowland Hill, who died in 1879, aged eighty-four years. Bruce Castle, now a museum, is owned by the Borough Council, and its grounds have been turned into a public park. The museum, in addition to items of local interest, has a Post Office collection which maintains the association of the building with Sir Rowland Hill. From here, Risley Avenue leads to the Roundway, a wide new semi-circular thoroughfare which has a double road with grass verges down the centre. This forms the southern approach to the great Cambridge arterial road around which a large new quarter has sprung up of late years.

The parish church of All Hallows is situated on a slope a short distance north of Bruce Castle, and is an ancient building in the Gothic style of architecture, surrounded on three sides by a rivulet called the Moselle, which rises at Muswell Hill. In the Churchyard of All Hallows, a friend of Sir Walter Scott, James Hogg, the unlettered shepherd who was also a poet, is recalled by a gravestone inscribed, 'Margaret Lydia, daughter of the Ettrick Shepherd'; she died in 1847 aged 22. On the main High Road was an almshouse for eight people founded in 1596 by a Spaniard named Sanchez, who was confectioner to Philip II, and the first ever known in this country. He became a Protestant and died in 1602. Near the Cross was another row of almshouses, founded by Nicholas Richardson in the early part of the eighteenth century. It is unfortunate that these ancient almshouses should have been pulled down, one for a block of flats, the other for a departmental store; the Spanish señor is not forgotten, however, for the department store is named 'Sanchez House'. To the east of the High Road, Tottenham, is the football ground of the Tottenham Hotspur Club.

On the west side of the Green is the former borough's Town Hall, a building of red brick with stone dressings surmounted by a clock-turret. On the opposite side of the Green is the Prince of Wales Hospital, a handsome five-storeyed building of red brick. Near Broad Lane is Page Green which at one time contained a group of seven elm trees, thought to have been planted there by seven sisters of a Tottenham family in the early eighteenth century. These were replaced on 2 March 1886 by seven new trees planted by the seven daughters of Mr Hibbert, a local butcher. The Seven Sisters were ultimately dispersed when Page Green was made into an air-raid shelter during the last war. From here about a mile along Seven Sisters Road brings us to the housing estate at Woodberry Down. This covers an area of sixty-four acres and is one of the largest in the Metropolis. It is on high ground and consists principally of five-storeyed blocks of flats, but it also contains four eight-storeyed blocks with sun-balconies overlooking wide strips of garden. A Primary and large Secondary School have been built and a riverside promenade by the New River has been arranged, but owing to the presence of so many children on the estate and the proximity of two large reservoirs in addition to the New River, the promenade is closely fenced and barbed-wired. We now turn into Green Lanes which leads down past Finsbury Park to the busy shopping centre of Harringay. On the east side we pass Northumberland House, a group of new L.C.C. buildings which include some ten-storey blocks of flats and altogether provide 219 new homes. They replace an earlier Northumberland House which, charmingly situated with lawns sloping down to the New River, had a splendid gateway surmounted by the Percy Lion. The house was recently demolished by the L.C.C. and the lion was dealt with by the local marksmen. There is little reliable information available regarding this building. Dating from about 1825, it seems to have had an unbroken history of use as a private asylum. There is no known connection between the house and the Percy family and it was probably called Northumberland House as a compliment to a Duke of Northumberland who was connected with the Lunacy Commissioners.

Further on is the huge Harringay Arena, once famous for circus performances and championship boxing contests; the arena is now closed and is used for storage purposes. Adjoining is the Harringay Stadium, a popular greyhound racing track. Duckett's Common on the west side of Green Lanes is an open space of six acres which is so named from a farmer of that name who lived in this vicinity. Round the corner, off Turnpike Lane begins Haringey Passage, the curious footway that runs between the houses and crosses the middle of all the nineteen roads from here down to Harringay Park Station; an unusual, but useful arrangement. North of Turnpike Lane, Green Lanes temporarily becomes High Road, Wood Green, which is a good shopping centre. The parish church of St Michael stands prominently at the junction of Bounds Green Road and Jolly Butchers Hill. Wood Green, now in the new borough of Haringey, was formerly a small borough of 1600 acres, with a modern Town Hall, built as recently as 1958.

The principal building of interest in Wood Green is undoubtedly the Alexandra Palace and Park. The original Palace was opened in May 1873, but was entirely destroyed only two weeks after its formal opening, by a fire which broke out in the roof of the central hall. The Palace was rebuilt on the same site and again opened on 1 May 1875. At the turn of the century this great building and the grounds of 280 acres were purchased by the combined efforts of neighbouring local authorities, who appoint a Board of Trustees for its management.

The main feature of the Palace is the Great Hall, which is 387 feet long and 184 feet wide and capable of accommodating 14,000 people, and Grand Concerts and Organ Recitals were popular in earlier days. Schoolboy memories recall a collection of coloured plaster statues of the Kings and Queens of England that were dispersed about the hall. Today the hall is frequently used for trade exhibitions, professional examinations, flower shows, dog shows, etc., and is famous for its organ, a masterpiece of Willis, the organ builder. Other parts of the building are used by the B.B.C. Television News Centre, and the tall mast rising from the roof is a conspicuous landmark; from the terrace, over 300 feet above sea-level, there are fine views across London, well into the counties south of the Thames, and adjoining the Park is the popular 'Ally Pally' race-course.

Edmonton, two miles north of Tottenham, but joined to it by continuous streets, is a place of considerable antiquity. Entering Edmonton at Fore Street, one of the principal shopping centres, one sees extensive municipal housing development, first the Snells Park area, with imposing nine-storey blocks of flats as the outstanding feature. 'The Bell' at Edmonton has always been associated with Cowper's *Ballad of John Gilpin,* but any nostalgic enthusiast wishing to drink to the immortal memory of that 'citizen of credit and renown' will have to go elsewhere, for 'The Bell' was demolished in 1964; perhaps to the 'Angel' — formerly 'The Blue Bell' — at the crossroads, which is a rival claimant as the tavern where Gilpin and his wife *should have* dined. A little northwards is an important road junction where the North Circular Road meets the old Hertford Road. Close by in Silver Street is Pymmes Park which covers 53 acres and is laid out with lawns, flower gardens and a lake. The mansion was accidentally destroyed by fire during the last war. In the reign of Queen Elizabeth I it belonged to Lord Burghley. On the east side we see what is perhaps the most imposing modern municipal housing project, the Fore Street Redevelopment site adjoining the Town Hall, a battlemented building with large transomed windows, which looks a little out of place against the modern development. To the left we find Edmonton Green which, with its disused level crossing, daily market stalls, and occasional old building, has a distinctly rural atmosphere. If we deviate here and turn westwards along Church Street we come to the Parish Church of All Saints, a large edifice in the perpendicular style, and here in the churchyard, are buried Charles Lamb and his sister Mary, who lived for a while in the cottage nearby now known as Lamb's Cottage. Inside the church is a double memorial to Charles Lamb and William Cowper, erected in 1892 by the London and Middlesex Archaeological Society. Cowper, as far as is known, was never in Edmonton. A plaque in Church Street marks the site of the cottage in which John Keats served his apprenticeship (1811-15) to Mr Hammond, a local surgeon. Across the road, a little schoolhouse, decorated with the figure of a schoolgirl, is described as 'A structure of Hope founded in Faith on the basis of Charity 1784'. Turning eastward along Bury Street West to regain the Hertford road we pass an attractive late Tudor or early Jacobean house known as Salisbury House, recently restored by the Borough Council as an Art Centre.

Beyond Edmonton the long line of houses fronting the Hertford Road straggles out to Ponder's End and Enfield Highway, nearly as far as the bus terminus at Waltham Cross, but as these districts consist mainly of factories, shops and small houses they afford nothing of interest to the tourist, except that Angel Place, a little row of cottages near 'The Angel' should be noted and an interesting terrace of nearly 30 early Victorian — perhaps earlier — houses stands on the right of the Hertford Road, between Monmouth and Bounces Roads. With a pediment and flat pilasters at intervals, the terrace is complete from end to end.

On the left, Southbury Road leads past the Ponders End Bus Garage to Enfield Town, now joined to the metropolis by houses lining the main road through Wood Green and Palmers Green.

It is intersected by the New River, and contains a spacious market place, on one side of which is the ancient grammar school and parish church. The finest shops are located in busy Church Street to the west of the market place. The parish church is an embattled building of stone in the Perpendicular style with a western tower. At the back of the church beside the New River which winds through the town is an agreeable recreation ground comprising twenty-four acres of gardens and trees. On the other side of Church Street is the spacious Green. A picturesque feature of Enfield is the pretty Gentleman's Row, bordering the New River at the west end of Church Street. Among its old cottages is one claiming Charles Lamb as a past resident. The mansion known as the Tudor Palace was demolished in 1927, but valuable parts of the interior were rescued by a local resident and are preserved in a specially built annexe to his house in Gentleman's Row.

The favoured residential quarter of the town is situated on a ridge running westward, and here many fine modern houses have been erected of late years commanding extensive views towards Epping Forest on the east and Hadley Wood and Potter's Bar on the west. Enfield was once famed for its Chase, a large tract of woodland filled with deer. When King James I resided at Theobalds it was well stocked with deer, but during the Civil Wars it was stripped of its game and timber and let out in farms. At the Restoration it was again planted with woods and stocked with deer. Enfield Chase was disafforested by an Act of Parliament in 1779. It originally comprised an area of 8,349 acres. Many of Enfield's industries are located on the east side of the Cambridge Road, and at Enfield Lock is the Royal Small Arms Factory, erected in 1856, where the celebrated Enfield rifles were made. At the west end of the town is the Ridgeway from which Hadley Road forks to the left and leads to Trent Park, which was given by George III to his favourite physician, Sir Richard Jebb, and named after Trent in the Tyrol where he had saved the life of the King's brother. It was afterwards sold to the Earl of Cholmondeley and later to Henry Lushington and then to Sir Philip Sassoon who made it into a palace of luxury. The greater part of the mansion, which is of brick, was rebuilt about 1894. It is approached by a double avenue of limes from the Southgate Road. The grounds cover an area of a thousand acres and the house with its stately terrace faces a beautiful lake of several acres. At one period it was occupied by the Ministry of Works, but it is now used as a teachers' training college. Cockfosters, which lies to the south of Trent Park, is the terminus of the Piccadilly tube railway. Around here a new shopping and residential centre was developed between the wars.

A little more than a mile north of Enfield is Forty Hall, an estate of over 260 acres, acquired for the public in 1951. The 17th century mansion, built by Sir Nicholas Raynton, a former Lord Mayor of London, has some fine plaster ceilings, while the grounds and lake make a beautiful setting. On the way up

Forty Hill, from the 'Goat' tavern, there are several houses contemporary with the Hall which are worth notice in passing.

We will now return by way of Green Lanes, Wood Green, and West Green Road to Tottenham, and then, after crossing the High Road opposite the junction of Seven Sisters Road, proceed along Ferry Lane and Forest Road, past the extensive reservoirs of the Metropolitan Water Board, to Walthamstow and Epping Forest. Farther north in the Lea valley between Ponder's End and Chingford is the great King George V Reservoir which is a mile and a half long and half a mile wide. It has been constructed to meet the demand of the ever-increasing population of London's eastern suburbs for an adequate water supply. South of the 'King George', another reservoir, the William Girling, with a capacity of 3,493 million gallons, was opened in 1951. The borough of Waltham-stow received its municipal charter in 1929 from the Right Hon. J. H. Thomas, the Lord Privy Seal in the Labour Government. It contained a population in 1956 of 117,800, and now forms a part of the London Borough of Waltham Forest. The most important part of the town is situated between Lea Bridge Road and Forest Road, to the north of Hackney Marsh, now a public recreation ground.

Walthamstow is predominantly residential, though many industries are also represented, and owes its growth and development to the construction of the branch line of the Great Eastern Railway, now British Railways (Eastern Region), to Chingford. Before that time it was a pleasant rural suburb containing a number of large houses and gardens. These have now disappeared, and in their place have arisen miles of two-storeyed houses and semi-detached villas of various grades. It enjoys an excellent railway service to the City, and situated as it is on the margin of Epping Forest, it is one of the healthiest districts of the metropolis. The principal business thoroughfares are Hoe Street, High Street, and Wood Street, Forest Road and the Highams Park area. On the north side of Forest Road near Hoe Street now stands the splendid new Walthamstow Town Hall, the neighbouring Assembly Hall, and the imposing South-West Essex Technical College. The buildings, completed in 1940, stand some distance from the main road on open ground which the Walthamstow Borough Council have laid out as public gardens at a cost of £7,000. The Town Hall and the Assembly Hall are faced with stone and the South-West Essex Technical College has a handsome façade of red brick. No finer range of public buildings can be seen in any other suburb of London. Well worth the effort is the steady climb from here up to Hurst Road to the parish church of St Mary on Church Hill—probably the highest ground in the district—and old Walthamstow Village. Facing us in Church Lane is a long timber-framed building of the 15th century, and among the little shops below is an antiquarian bookshop which is perfectly harmonious in such a setting; the others are not quite so much in the period. Near the alms-houses founded in 1527 by George Monoux, a former Master of the Drapers' Company, is the Walthamstow Local History Museum in the old Vestry House, dated 1730. That this was once the parish workhouse is disclosed by the grim inscription over the door:

'If any would not work
neither should he eat'.

A massive relic in the foreground is the upper portion of one of the Ionic columns of the old General Post Office building in St Martin-le-Grand, which was demolished in 1912; this section is about six feet in height. Some old school buildings and mature little cottages complete this fascinating corner of busy Walthamstow. In Lloyd Park is The Water House, at one time the home of William Morris the nineteenth century artist, poet and craftsman. In 1950 it was opened as the William Morris Museum by Lord Atlee, then Prime Minister and member for Walthamstow West. Besides numerous examples of Morris wallpapers, textiles and furniture and a number of books from the Kelmscott Press there is a large collection of pictures by various artists, with special emphasis on the work of the late Sir Frank Brangwyn, R. A.

From here a journey of one mile through Forest Road will bring us to the roundabout at the junction of the North Circular Road and Woodford New Road at the southern fringe of Epping Forest. The southern extremity of the Forest includes the popular Wanstead Flats with Leytonstone on the west side, and Snaresbrook and Woodford on the east side. In Hollybush Hill is the Royal Wanstead School for Boys, one of whose Governors was the late Sir Winston Churchill. The girls' section is at Sawbridgeworth.

Between Walthamstow and Stratford is Leyton, formerly a borough which included the district of Leytonstone, situated close to the southern limits of Epping Forest. Little more than seventy years ago it was a mere hamlet; it is supposed to have derived its name from its proximity to the River Lea, and resembles Walthamstow in its general character. The old parish church of St Mary, rebuilt except for the tower in 1821, contains a memorial to John Strype, the historian and antiquary, who was its vicar for sixty-eight years, and who was buried here in 1737.

Strype was a prolific writer and the best known of his numerous works is probably his edition of Stow's *Survey of London* in 1720. Described as a 'painstaking and honest, but dull and unmethodical writer', it is said that he probably spent the first 50 years of his life collecting the material for the voluminous works which he gave to the world in the succeeding 40 — for he lived to the age of 94.

St Mary, Low Leyton, although so much rebuilt, is full of interest, having been well 'documented' by an enthusiastic incumbent some years ago. In 1962, excavations were made in an endeavour to discover the crypt which was believed to be under the church. Digging at the west end of the nave revealed, not the crypt, but a large vault, which the old Vestry books show was dug in 1711 at the request of Sir Gilbert Heathcote, sometime Lord Mayor of London. The vault was wide and deep, for Sir Gilbert had a large family; however they never occupied the vault for they moved away to Derbyshire. But when this 'large room' as the Vestry book calls it, was uncovered in 1962, one solitary leaden coffin lay on the floor; on the lid was inscribed, 'Thomas Sherwood, died 1742, age 79'.

ia, and was
the Epping
as the result
stined to be
out from its
ed incentive
increasing
nclosure in
during the
ing Lords
he Epping
e City of
ent in the

who first
eedom of
g animals
g himself
e support

ation of
eath, Mr
housand
and an
ue than
e decree
nounced
inst the
twenty
re thus

warm.
a large
grand
at the
nated.
close
1880
usand
breed-
itted.
from
gers,
ction

me to be buried there remains a mystery!
nstead Flats, a large open space of grassland'
e north and to the City of London Cemetery
te with a small island in the centre. North of
ied on the western side, is the beautiful Wan-
and purchased by the Corporation of London
nteenth century by Sir Josiah Child, a wealthy
y the River Roding, are screened by splendid
he rooks keep house. Wanstead House, which
in 1715 by his son Richard, first Earl Tilney.
th Portland stone, 300 feet in length, and 70 feet
e of the finest houses in Europe, and was con-
ld be seen in Italy. It was adorned by a portico
1820 Wanstead House was pulled down.
e former Borough of Wanstead and Woodford,
inhabitants, lies to the east of Epping Forest,
dford, and is the starting-point of the new Eastern
s it is also called. This skirts the northern fringe
ins the main Colchester Road at Gallows Corner,
Borough of Havering.
will now explore, is one of the finest recreation
haps the largest and most beautiful domestic park
orld. It comprises an area of about five thousand
ead Flats and Wanstead Park, six thousand five
s from Leytonstone and West Ham on the south
ng on the north, a distance of about eleven miles.
orest which commences at Whipps Cross is narrow,
, and in shape somewhat resembles the tail of a kite,
nd Buckhurst Hill it expands into dense coverts of
rspersed with grassy glades and rough 'bottoms' well
ws again towards Epping Town, beyond which is the
f three hundred acres. The Forest widens out to half
Cross Road and Snaresbrook and the scenery becomes
a large lake, with thickly-wooded banks, divided into
good fishing and boating. On the eastern fringe of this
another which is called the Eagle Pond and is flanked by

edible that within a dozen miles of the Bank of England
act of country so sequestered that it might be far distant
perhaps on Saturdays and Sundays, when holiday-makers
ily to stroll off the main roads to find complete tranquility
as dealt gently with the countryside in this part of Essex,
proclaimed by someone as Rip Van Winkle Land. Certainly
of England on the fringe of London.

Epping Forest was dedicated on 6 May 1882 by Queen Victo[
specially visited by the Queen in response to an invitation from
Forest Fund Committee, which had secured this open space only
of almost incredible efforts. The rapacity of the land-robber was de
a feature of the nineteenth century, when London began to push
ancient limits and the rapid development of the great city gave increas
to the desire for the illegal appropriation of land which was rapidl
in value as the population became denser. The progress of illegal e
Epping Forest was greater between the years 1851 and 1871 than
whole of the previous 250 years. From 1871 onwards the encroac[
of Manors had to meet the formidable opposition of two bodies,
Forest Fund Committee and the Commissioners of Sewers for t
London, as well as a Commission of Inquiry appointed by Parlia[m
same year.

But it was a poor villager of Loughton named Thomas Willingal[
set the ball rolling by his fight for the rights of the people to the f[
Epping Forest. He earned a scanty living by collecting wood and grazin
there, but in the middle of the last century, already an old man, he flu[
into the battle for the preservation of this beauty-spot and enlisted th
of the City Corporation.

The result of the protracted litigation conducted by the Corpo[
London and other interested parties, such as Mr Francis George H[
Frederick Young, and Mr William George Smith, was that the three
acres to which Epping Forest had shrunk by 1851 were nearly doubled
expanse of pleasure-ground was secured for London of greater val
untold gold for the teeming millions of the greatest city in the world. Th
of the Court of Chancery in the well-known Corporation suit was pro[
in November 1874, when the Master of the Rolls gave judgment aga
enclosers and spoilators of the forest lands. All enclosures made within
years previous to 14 August 1871 were declared illegal and 2,600 acres w[
recovered by the City of London Corporation.

The weather on the Saturday of the dedication ceremony was bright and
Many thousands of people went out to the Forest, and the day was to
extent observed as a public holiday in the East of London. In the evening a
display of fireworks was provided by Messrs C. T. Brock & Company
back of the Royal Forest Hotel, the grounds of which were likewise illum[

The cost of freeing Epping Forest for the public, for ever, amounted t[
of £40,000, nearly half of which was absorbed in legal expenses. In Marc[
Mr E. W. Roberts, a member of the City Corporation, sent a gift of ten tho[
fish to stock the waters in Epping Forest, on condition that a proper close
ing season should be observed and that Sunday fishing should not be perm
Dark-brown fallow deer run wild, and a few small roe deer were introduced
Dorsetshire in 1883. Rabbits are numerous, and a certain number of ba[
foxes, squirrels, and weasels are also found here. The best of the wooded s[

of the forest is situated on high ground between Loughton on the east and Chingford on the west, and includes Monkwood, north-west of Loughton, and Epping Thicks, north-west of Theydon Bois. In 1930 Knighton Wood, thirty-seven acres in extent, was added to Epping Forest. This adjoins an isolated section of the Forest called Lord's Bushes between Woodford and Buckhurst Hill.

Connaught Water, in the heart of the Forest, near the well-known Queen Elizabeth's Lodge on the road to High Beech, is a favourite resort of boating and fishing parties, and covers an area of seven acres. It also bears two islands, and before its transformation by the Corporation of London was a dismal swamp known as the Forest Pool. Connaught Water was named after the late Duke of Connaught, Ranger of the Forest.

Chingford, on the west side of the Forest, with a population in 1951 of 48,300, has grown enormously of recent years. It was described a century ago as being so agreeably situated for retirement that the most remote distance from the metropolis could hardly excel it. It occupies a fine situation, and building developments have been carried out with due regard for the amenities of the neighbourhood. The town contains a handsome modern church and a green; the old church of All Saints, formerly an ivy-clad ruin, was restored in 1929-30 and is now again in full use. The Royal Forest Hotel is a handsome red-brick building in the Tudor style, with grounds adjacent to the Forest and is now a busy terminus of several lines of omnibuses operated by London Transport. At the back of the hotel are the links of the Royal Epping Forest Golf Club. Higham's Park, a new residential suburb, lies to the south of Chingford and may be regarded as an extension of Walthamstow. Higham's Park itself is a narrow section of Epping Forest half a mile long and forming its western boundary. It is a charming spot in the centre of which is a beautiful fishing lake surrounded by densely-wooded banks.

The east side of Epping Forest is bordered by the straggling suburbs of Woodford, Buckhurst Hill, and Loughton, all of them consisting principally of good-class houses, built with due regard to the choice character of this locality. Many of the older residences are surrounded by large gardens. Woodford, the principal suburb bordering Epping Forest, is contiguous with Wanstead and extends eastwards to the Chigwell Road. The unrestricted growth of Greater London threatens to convert even Epping Forest into an enclosed park surrounded by straggling suburbs unless this is halted by the Green Belt. The extension of the Central Line of the London Underground to Epping and Ongar which was opened in 1949 now provides rapid access to the City and the West End.

At the north-east corner of the new Borough of Redbridge is Hainault Forest, consisting of eight hundred acres of grassland with copses here and there and also a small lake. Like Epping Forest it once formed part of the ancient Forest of Waltham, all the remaining four thousand acres of which, except Crabtree Wood, near Chigwell Row, were disafforested in 1851-52. Hainault Forest was purchased for the public by the London County Council and local authorities in 1903, at a cost of £21,830, and opened in July 1906. Many new trees have since been planted which have now almost reached maturity and in course of time it will doubtless rival Epping Forest in beauty. From here we now proceed along Romford Road, which leads past the Recreation Ground and then skirts the west side of Hainault Forest up a steep hill to the ground of the Hainault Forest Golf Club. Here we turn to our right and continue along Forest Road which leads in two miles to a roundabout at the crossroads at Barkingside High Street and Fairlop Road. Barkingside, little more than fifteen years ago a quiet village, is now a thriving suburb of Ilford. Its spacious High Street is flanked on both sides by rows of shops, and there is also a large cinema.

From here a journey of a little over a mile brings us to Gant's Hill Circus where a large new roundabout has been constructed at the busy traffic junction of Eastern Avenue, Woodford Avenue, Cranbrook Road and Perth Road. In the centre is the new Underground Railway Station of the Central Line Railway from Liverpool Street to Newbury Park, Woodford, Epping and Ongar. Gant's Hill Station has been copied from the Moscow Underground Railway and instead of the usual two tunnels has a single large pillared and vaulted hall 140 feet long, 21 feet high and 73 feet wide with the rails at each side. Here also is a busy shopping centre, including the Odeon Cinema at the corner of Perth Road. In Eastern Avenue is the recent 12-storey office building 'Thames House', and near the Valentine Hotel 'Arodene House' combines shops and offices. From Gant's Hill Circus it is a little more than a mile through Cranbrook Road Ilford Broadway. About half-way on the east side we pass the beautiful Valentine's Park covering 136 acres and noted for its wooded lakes and flower gardens. The eighteenth century mansion, now occupied by the borough housing department, has a number of portraits of members of the Holcombe and Ingleby families, former residents. The Great Vine at Hampton Court is reputed to have been grown from a cutting taken from Valentine's in 1769. Beyond Valentine's Park, Cranbrook Road continues to Ilford Broadway.

Ilford, a residential and industrial suburb seven and a half miles from Liverpool Street, includes Seven Kings, Chadwell Heath and Barkingside. Formerly a borough with a population of 177,760 in 1962, it is now part of the 248,596 population of the new borough of Redbridge. In recent years extensive building has taken place round the new Eastern Avenue and towards Newbury Park Station on the north side of the town, but it is now considered that, owing to the lack of available land, further building development in Ilford is likely to be very restricted. Ilford is perhaps the most attractive suburb on the eastern side of the metropolis, and will invite favourable comparison with Ealing or Wimbledon on the western side in the matter of high-class houses and shops and public parks. The High Road, over a mile long, forming a part of the main Romford Road, extends to Seven Kings, and is lined on both sides with good shops, and includes the Town Hall, a handsome building of stone in the Renaissance style, the Central Library, and the church of St Mary, built in 1831, which has a tower with a spire. Ilford was a part of Barking parish until the year 1888. Local industries include the manufacture of chemists' supplies, electronic equipment and components, plastics etc., while the research laboratories and administration offices of the old-established photographic firm of Ilford Ltd cover a large area in Roden Street. Many houses in Ilford were destroyed by rocket-bombs, also a bank and a Gaumont cinema in Cranbrook Road. In January 1945 a V2 rocket fell behind the stage of the Ilford Hippodrome bursting a water-tank above the stage which drenched the orchestra. Nevertheless they went on playing to the performance of 'Robinson Crusoe'. The Hippodrome has been replaced by a new office block, supported by 'The Black Horse' at one end, and 'The Hope Revived' at the other. All Ilford's war-damaged sites have now been rebuilt, as well as that part of the High Road involved in what is known locally as The Great Fire—a conflagration that destroyed a considerable number of shops in 1959.

Beyond Ilford the suburban area extends through Seven Kings, Goodmayes, and Chadwell Heath, to the ancient market town of Romford, in the borough of Havering—the easternmost of the new London boroughs. Romford contains a number of picturesque old houses and inns situated in the spacious market-place and in the High Street which has been considerably widened at its western end. The charter for Romford market dates back to the time of Henry III, and here on Wednesdays, Fridays and Saturdays is held the ancient street market when both sides of the Market Place are crowded with stalls. Another interesting feature of Romford is the handsome parish church of St Edward the Confessor built in 1849 which is the modern successor to an ancient church built in 1410. It is crowned by a spire 162 feet high. The narrow streets of the old town inevitably present a traffic problem, but there are proposals for a Ring Road to divert traffic from the centre, which if approved, may save the picturesque weather-boarded old Golden Lion Hotel at the tight corner of narrow North Street and the High Street. To the east of Ramford are the pleasant new garden suburbs of Gidea Park and Squirrel's Heath which have extended rapidly of late years.

In this direction, one mile from the centre of the town, is the beautiful Raphael Park opened in 1904 and presented to the town by Sir H. H. Raphael, Bart. Beyond Gidea Park we shortly come to the roundabout at Gallows Corner where the main Colchester Road is crossed by the Eastern Avenue and the Southend arterial road. About a mile and a half beyond Gallows Corner on the north side of the Colchester Road is the Harold Hill housing estate of the Greater London Council. This is divided into two sections, each planned to contain a population of fifteen thousand. Shopping centres are provided for both areas around which are grouped three-storeyed blocks of flats and dwellings for old people. There are eleven school sites covering no less than 121 acres, and playgrounds for children so arranged as to avoid the necessity of crossing any major road. Paynes Brook runs from north to south through the estate and the centre of a public park. The industrial quarter near the main Colchester Road has been separated from the residential section. The estate is near Harold Wood Station and is well served by the electric trains now running from Liverpool Street.

South-east of Romford lies Hornchurch, a town with claims to Roman antiquity which gaves its name to the extensive Urban district of Hornchurch of over 30 square miles, since it was joined with Romford to form the Borough of Havering. Unlike its neighbours, the majority of the residential development at Hornchurch has been by private enterprise. The parish church of St Andrew in Hornchurch is the mother church of those in many surrounding parishes including St Edward's, Romford. An unusual feature of St Andrews is that the east wall is crowned by a bull's head instead of a cross; of several different explanations one suggests that it is emblematic of the tanning industry which once flourished in Hornchurch for some hundreds of years. At Rainham, the Parish Church of SS Helen and Giles dates from the 12th century and is a remarkably complete example of Norman work. Near the church is Rainham Hall, a small but dignified house of red brick with stone dressings, built in 1729 and now the property of the National Trust. It has a splendid porch and doorway with Corinthian columns and the wrought iron gates are contemporary with the house. At All Saints, Cranham, are buried the remains of General James Oglethorpe, the founder of Georgia. One of the best known establishments in the district was the R.A.F. Station, Hornchurch. From here many of the pilots whose names were famous during the Battle of Britain made their sorties and their names are commemorated in the streets of the New Elm Park Estate. The R.A.F. Station was dismantled in 1963. Although mainly residential in character and served by three trunk roads and three rail routes, there is much industrial activity in the South Hornchurch and Rainham area. At the Upminster terminus of London Transport, the Executive have constructed, as part of their reorganization, a large area of sidings, and an extensive covered depot building. The central area around Hornchurch High Street has been developed as a modern shopping centre and the civic buildings are concentrated near to the High Street where old houses are giving place to buildings of modern design. Despite its rapid development Hornchurch retains vast areas of Green Belt.

To the south of Goodmayes and Chadwell Heath is Becontree, forming the northern section of the immense garden suburb of Dagenham, erected by the London County Council after the First World War. As recently as 1921 Dagenham was a mere village and a part of a straggling parish of 6,556 acres situated on the eastern fringe of London, with a population of under ten thousand. Since that year over 26,000 houses have been built, extending over an area of about 2,000 acres, with a Civic Centre developing near Becontree Heath.

Until its recent amalgamation with Barking, Dagenham was an elongated borough stretching some eight miles from Hainault Forest in the north down to the Thames, with a maximum width of about three miles, narrowing to less than half a mile near the Eastern Avenue. There is a tendency to assume that Dagenham is an entirely new area that owes its existence to the Ford Motor Works and the large estate of Council houses, but south of Dagenham East Station is the old village. The church of SS Peter and Paul here was very much rebuilt in 1800, but retains its 13th century chancel, and opposite is the 15th century Cross Keys Inn, with low ceilings and Tudor fireplaces.

Dagenham is famous in history on account of the great breach made here by the Thames in 1700, which laid nearly five thousand acres under water. After many expensive attempts to stop the breach, the landowner abandoned the project as impracticable. However, in 1714 Parliament intervened, and in the following year trustees were appointed who contracted with Captain John Perry, who had been employed by the Czar Peter the Great in his works on the River Don, to reclaim the land. This great undertaking was accomplished in thirteen years and cost £80,000.

Between Dagenham and Hornchurch an enormous dump was built after the first World War from the accumulation of refuse and rubbish deposited here by various local municipal bodies. At frequent intervals strong complaints were lodged by the inhabitants of this district on account of the noxious fumes and gases emitted by the Dagenham dump, but for long afterwards these proved of little avail. Eventually, however, the inhabitants were relieved of the nuisance. The late Mr Henry Ford, the American motor magnate, who had erected immense new works at Dagenham, having inspected the great dump, decided that there was money to be made out of it by utilizing these waste products to generate electricity for his new factory. His works covered an area of six hundred acres, on the banks of the Thames. Mr Ford had already spent £2,000,000 on this factory, and when the works were opened in 1932 they had cost not less than £5,500,000. Here also a jetty had been constructed at a cost of £300,000, enabling ships up to 12,000 tons to load and unload.

From the Chequers Inn, Dagenham, a journey of about two miles, passing Rippleside and a large number of newly-erected houses on both sides of the road, will bring us to the ancient market town of Barking. It is joined to Ilford by continuous houses and streets on the north, and to East Ham and London on the west. Barking is situated on the Roding, seven miles from London, and the various industries represented include the manufacture of heavy machinery, precision tools, food preserves etc. Later in its passage towards the Thames, the River Roding is known as Barking Creek.

In 1901 Barking was made the seat of a suffragan bishopric. It once possessed a magnificent abbey, founded by St Erkenwald in 666. His sister, St Ethelburga, was the first Abbess. Destroyed by the Danes in 870, it was restored by King Edgar and again destroyed in 1541. St Margaret's Church, originally attached to the abbey, is a Norman building with Early English additions, having a lofty tower with a clock and eight bells. At the entrance to the churchyard is the 14th century Curfew Tower with octagonal turrets on each side and in the centre is a pointed arch. Over the gateway is the Chapel of the Holy Rood. It is manifest from old records that this gateway belonged to the abbey and is now the principal relic of its past magnificence. Considerable fragments of the walls, from a few inches to ten or twelve feet in height, remain to give a good impression of the extent of the old abbey. The precinct is now a public park.

Great improvements have been carried out in the town of late years. London Road which formerly terminated in North Street was extended through in 1937 to East Street at its junction with Ripple Road, thus avoiding the necessity of passing by the awkward bend at the junction of North Street, the Broadway and East Street. Here a handsome new parade of shops has been erected. Barking Park in Longbridge Road covers an area of seventy-six acres and through it runs a boating-lake half a mile long amidst rustic scenery. There is also a swimming-pool 165 feet long, opened in 1931. Half-way between Barking and Dagenham in Ripple Road is Eastbury Manor House, an ancient brick mansion in the domestic Tudor style, said to have been built about 1555 by Sir W. Denham to whom Edward VI granted the estate. The buildings form three sides of a quadrangle and include an octagonal tower and a tall stack of weirdly-decorated chimneys. Having been threatened some years ago with demolition it was bought in 1936 and handed over to the National Trust. Leased to the Barking Corporation, it is now used by physically handicapped people five days a week, and the Barking Blind Club, Toc H and other local organisations meet in the building at various times. In the Quaker Burial Ground in North Street Elizabeth Fry, the prison reformer, and other members of the Gurney family, are buried.

Barking, which has been raised to the status of a borough, is a town which has history and personality, and there is even some beauty and romance in its creeks and mud-flats. It is difficult to imagine Barking as a prominent fishing port, but such it was for at least four hundred years until the mid-nineteenth century; the old Town Quay still survives, where today barges may be seen unloading cargoes of timber, brought up the Roding from the Surrey Commercial Docks.

Although more than a million of the inhabitants of London now reside in Essex, or in London over the border, as it used to be termed, a century ago the development of the suburban area was still confined mainly to the western, north-western, and south-western districts of Middlesex. This was because natural obstacles in the shape of unhealthy marshes originally hindered its growth toward the east, and later the poverty-stricken East End rendered it difficult to imagine residential suburbs beyond. Only the wealthy Londoner could then enjoy a suburban retreat, because in the days before cheap and rapid transit it was impossible for the wage-earners to travel a considerable distance between their homes and the places of their employment.

The year 1933 witnessed the completion of the North Circular Road, which . commences at Gunnersbury and encircles the northern half of the metropolis, passing through Ealing, Wembley, Hendon, Finchley, Palmers Green, Edmonton, and Walthamstow to Wanstead. Here it connects with the Eastern Avenue, providing direct access to Southend-on-Sea.

Second Drive

A Tour of the South-Eastern Suburbs

Making Westminster Bridge our starting-point for this excursion, our route is through St George's Road to the Elephant and Castle, and thence along Walworth Road and Camberwell Road to Camberwell Green. Between Camberwell New Road and Brixton Road, and little known except to local residents, is Myatts Park, nicely laid out with flower gardens, tennis courts, bowling greens and a bandstand. It covers twelve acres and was formerly known as Myatts Fields which were noted for their strawberries. It serves as a public park for the densely-populated area of North Brixton. It was presented to the public in 1889 by Mr William Minet.

Denmark Hill, leading southwards from Camberwell Green to Herne Hill and Brockwell Park, derives its name from Prince George of Denmark, the Consort of Queen Anne, who kept a shooting-box here. About half-way up on the right-hand side, opposite Denmark Hill Station, is King's College Hospital, founded at Clare Market in 1839 in connexion with King's College, and moved here in 1913. The foundation-stone of the present hospital was laid in 1909, and in its construction and equipment it is one of the finest in the metropolis. North of the original hospital building a new six-storey erection in the modern style was opened recently; this is the Dental Department and School of Dental Surgery. South of the 1913 building, a new ward block, which will extend up to the railway, is under construction. Adjoining King's College Hospital is Ruskin Park, a beauty spot situated on steeply-rising ground, with an area of thirty-six acres, and so named after John Ruskin, who spent the earlier part of his life at Denmark Hill and Herne Hill. It contains an ornamental lake, bowling greens, tennis courts, and all the amenities of other London parks. It was purchased at a cost of £72,000. A sundial in the park marks the site of a house where in 1842 Mendelssohn composed the popular *Spring Song,* originally called *Camberwell Green.* A number of large old houses are still standing in Denmark Hill, but these are gradually disappearing and being largely replaced by typical red-brick residences of the post-war type. On the opposite side of Denmark Hill, at the corner of Champion Park is 'The Fox on the Hill', a tavern belonging to Messrs Charrington's which was opened in 1959. This is the successor to a hostelry of very ancient origin that stood some 300 yards lower down and was well known as 'The Fox under the Hill'. Building developments downhill caused 'The Fox' to move uphill to its present site, where its sign has been suitably modified to 'The Fox *on* the Hill'. In Champion Park is the Salvation Army International (William Booth Memorial) Training College, with resident accommodation for 400 cadets; it was opened by the late Duke of Kent in 1929.

Running parallel to Denmark Hill on the east side is Camberwell Grove, formerly known as Grove Hill. Here resided Dr John Coakley Lettsom, a well-known Quaker physician, at the beginning of the last century, whose income sometimes amounted to as much as £12,000 a year, and who was as philanthropic as he was wealthy. In his large house at Grove Hill he entertained some of the most eminent men of his time, but adverse circumstances compelled him to part with his delightful mansion some time before his death, and as his town house was not large enough to accommodate them, he also had to dispose of his library and museum. His memory is preserved in Lettsom Street. Although hardly more than three miles distant from Blackfriars or Westminster Bridge, the fine situation of this estate afforded extensive views in every direction over a circumference of two hundred miles. In front of it could be seen the City itself, with Hampstead and Highgate in the background, with Harrow-on-the-Hill and Windsor Castle on the west, and Essex, Shooter's Hill, and Greenwich on the east. On the south the view was shut in by Sydenham Hill and Norwood. Chelsea formed a prominent feature in the landscape. A sheet of water flowing from a spring on the summit of the hill adorned the grounds. This district is now covered with modern villa residences, but some of them have been destroyed by a bomb. Near the top of the hill, at Number 188 Camberwell Grove, was born in 1836 the Rt. Hon. Joseph Chamberlain, M.P., Colonial Secretary and advocate of 'Protection' and 'Tariff Reform' in the earlier years of the present century. Another famous native of Camberwell was Robert Browning, who first saw the light of day in South-ampton Street (now Southampton Way) in 1812.

At the corner of Camberwell Grove is the Mary Datchelor Girls' School, founded by the munificence of Miss Mary Datchelor who, like John Stow, is buried in the church of St Andrew Undershaft in Leadenhall Street. For more than a century after her death in 1725, the Charity was administered for the benefit of the parishioners of St Andrew's, in accordance with her wishes. By 1871, however, the value of the bequest had so greatly increased that the Charity Commissioners decided that part of the fund should be devoted to the foundation of a school for girls in the parish. But social conditions in the City of London had also changed, and it was found that if the school were established in the parish there was only *one* girl eligible to be a pupil! So the Camberwell site was purchased and, with Miss Caroline Edith Rigg as Head Mistress—a position she was to hold for forty years—the Mary Datchelor School opened in 1877 with thirty pupils. Today, with 650 pupils and modernized buildings, it is recognised as one of the foremost scholastic establishments in South London. The school is now a 'voluntary aided' Grammar School with Governors appointed by the Clothworkers' Company and the Greater London Council. At the top of Dog Kennel Hill near East Dulwich Station are several handsome five-storeyed blocks of flats erected by the London County Council between Albrighton Road and Quorn Road. From here we return to Denmark Hill, which is continued by

Herne Hill and leads us to Brockwell Park opposite Herne Hill Station. This was originally the property of Joshua J. B. Blackburn, who offered seventy-eight acres of this ground in August 1889 and allowed the Committee six months to raise the sum of £120,000 required for its purchase as a public park. The price was considered very moderate compared with the £4,300 per acre paid for Vauxhall Park. The Charity Commissioners granted £25,000 and the London County Council and the South London Boroughs also contributed. Lambeth contributed £20,000, Camberwell £6,000, Southwark £5,000, the Ecclesiastical Commissioners £500, and the park was opened by Lord Rosebery, Chairman of the London County Council, on 6 June 1892. The formal celebrations were marred by a sad incident. After the termination of Lord Rosebery's speech Mr Bristowe, M.P. for Norwood, was seized with a fit, from which he never rallied, and expired from heart disease. It was largely due to the efforts of Mr Bristowe, who personally guaranteed £60,000 of the purchase money, that Brockwell Park was secured for the public.

For a number of years the owner retained the other fifty acres of Brockwell Park, but this also was eventually acquired, at a cost of £64,500, and opened to the public on 28 February 1903, thus increasing the area to 128 acres. Adjoining the 'Old English Garden' on the north side of the park is a small building that was originally the chapel to the estate. There is also a large lake available for bathing since made into a fine open-air swimming-bath. Theatrical performances take place during the summer months. The mansions which was damaged by bombing during the last war now serves as a refreshment- and tea-house. Dulwich Road, on the north side of the park, and its continuation Brixton Water Lane, lead to Brixton Hill, and Tulse Hill, on the west side, leads to West Norwood.

Close to Brixton Water Lane, between Tulse Hill and Brixton Hill, stood Raleigh House, a valuable suburban estate which was cut up for building in 1887. The estate contained a fine mansion and about twelve acres of grounds, through which in olden times a pretty stream called the Effra flowed amongst pleasant woods and meadows. It was originally intended to purchase Raleigh House for a public park at a cost of £4,000 per acre, but about the same time Brockwell Park was offered, and as it had a much larger area and could be purchased for the very moderate figure of £1,600 per acre, as against the £4,000 per acre asked for Raleigh House and its grounds, it was decided to purchase Brockwell Park instead. At the corner of Brixton Hill and Effra Road is St Matthew's, the parish church of Brixton. Its façade is adorned by large Greek Doric pillars and a tower at the east end. St Matthew is another of the four so-called 'Waterloo Churches' in Lambeth, popularly believed to have been built by the authority of Parliament as a thanksgiving for the victory of Waterloo. In the forecourt of the Central Library is a bust of Sir Henry Tate, the donor; among the shrubs lies the foundation stone of the old Brixton Theatre, 'laid by Henry Irving, May 3rd 1894'. The theatre was demolished in the blitz and an extension to the Library now stands in its place.

In Brixton Hill, leading to Streatham, there are still many large houses on the east side standing back from the roadway in their own long front gardens – surely the longest front gardens in London – but as they are neglected by their respective tenants and have been left to revert to a wild state, the Lambeth Borough Council have a scheme to make a mile-long woodland walk which would extend from St Matthew's to the top of Brixton Hill. This idea would be copied from that of Lord Street, Southport, which would then have to look to its laurels. There is no immediate cause for anxiety in Southport, however, as this attractive boulevard is still among the things to come. The old houses on the west side of Brixton Hill are gradually disappearing, and business premises, shops, and flats have been erected in their place, between Brixton Water Lane and the Lambeth Town Hall. Halfway up Brixton Hill, in Blenheim Gardens is the Brixton Windmill. Built in 1816 and owned by Joshua Ashby & Son, millers, it was in full working order until 1862. The sails or 'sweeps', always the first part of a windmill to go, were removed in 1864 and for at least another fifty years the mill continued working under power provided by steam, and later gas, engines. As promised, the old mill tower, which is solidly built of fourteen-inch brickwork, has been preserved and furnished with new sweeps and the little two and a half acre site in which it stands is now a public garden. Almost at the top of Brixton Hill on the west side, just off the main road, is the well-known Brixton Prison, built in 1820, and planned in the form of a crescent, with the governor's house in the centre. At first it was used exclusively for female convicts sentenced to transportation and penal servitude, but in 1853 it was purchased by the Government since when it has been reserved for male prisoners including those on remand awaiting trial at the criminal courts.

Coldharbour Lane, at the foot of Brixton Hill, leads us back again to Camberwell Green, and from here we will next proceed eastwards through Church Street and Peckham Road to Rye Lane, passing the Town Hall of the late Borough of Camberwell on the way. Next to it the former Guardians' offices, built in 1905, display a sundial with the reproachful motto, 'Do today's work today'. Peckham, formerly a small village, increased greatly in population between 1820 and 1840, since which time it has been more or less joined to the metropolis. Until 1827 an annual fair was held at Peckham on 21, 22 and 23 August, following immediately upon that of Camberwell, but, growing to be a nuisance, like most other fairs, it was abolished in that year, Between the two World Wars several large five-storeyed blocks of London County Council flats were erected on both sides of Peckham Road. These stand back from the footpath in strips of gardens. Many buildings in this locality were destroyed in the blitz of 1940 and by rocket-bombs in 1944.

The original village, situated mid-way between Camberwell and New Cross, now a busy shopping quarter, is centred round the High Street and Rye Lane, leading southwards to Peckham Rye Common, Honor Oak, and Forest Hill. At the corner of Rye Lane is the extensive department store of Messrs Jones & Higgins Limited, one of the largest in South London. Rye Lane, bordered on both sides by attractive shops, leads to Peckham Rye Common. The name of Rye given to Peckham signifies a common or an untilled ground. The Rye has been used as a recreation ground from time immemorial, and mention is already made of it in documents of the fourteenth century. In 1890 Peckham Rye Common was extended by the purchase of the adjoining Homestall Park, a lovely resort situated on rising ground. The Borough of Camberwell contributed £20,000, the London County Council £18,000, and the Charity Commissioners £12,000 towards its purchase price of £51,000. The original common was sixty-four acres in extent, and the additional area acquired was forty-nine acres. Rye Lane and its tributary streets were badly damaged in 1944 by Hitler's rocket-bombs as were East Dulwich Road, Lordship Lane and the east side of Peckham Rye Common.

Barry Road, on the west side of Peckham Rye Common, leads to Lordship Lane and beautiful Dulwich Park. The latter, containing an area of seventy-two acres, was presented to the former Metropolitan Board of Works by the Governors of Dulwich College, on condition that the Board would lay it out as a park for the public. This arrangement was confirmed by Parliament, and the park was laid out at a cost of £33,000 and opened by Lord Rosebery on 26 June 1890. Amongst its attractions are a richly-wooded lake, tennis courts, a band-stand, a carriage drive, a horse ride, an aviary and an open-air theatre.

Dulwich College lies to the south of Dulwich Park, on the west side of College Road. It is a very handsome edifice of red brick and terracotta with much enrichment in the ornamental Italian style of the thirteenth century, and was erected between 1866 and 1870 from the designs of Charles Barry, Junior, at a cost of over £100,000. It consists of three blocks and has accommodation for seven hundred boys. The present building replaced the earlier ones founded in 1619 by Mr Edward Alleyn, who named it the College of God's Gift. He was an actor in the reign of Queen Elizabeth I, and the principal performer in many of Shakespeare's plays. The original building is about a quarter of a mile distant from the new College, and was designed by Inigo Jones. The eastern wing was built in 1939-40.

Edward Alleyn's bequest has been modified from time to time to suit changing circumstances. One detail of his bequest seems to have stipulated that the surname of the Master of the College should always be Alleyn or Allen. Though this condition must sometimes have been difficult to satisfy, the Master from 1721 to 1941 was James Allen, who bequeathed certain properties to the College, the income from which was to be used for the education of boys and girls in Dulwich. The Dulwich College Act of 1857, however, restricted his bequest to girls only, and the James Allen's Girls' School in East Dulwich Grove is the handsome building to which the school moved in 1886. With 500 pupils, the school has since been several times enlarged, and the grounds extended to some 20 acres.

The Dulwich Picture Gallery, attached to the College, is in Gallery Road, some distance north of the present college buildings and near the charming Dulwich Village. The Gallery is open to the public and contains an interesting collection of pictures. A most unusual feature of the building, which is a typical design of Sir John Soane, is that it embodies a mausoleum in which are deposited the remains of Sir Peter Francis Bourgeois R.A. and of Noel Joseph Desenfans and his wife, founders of the Gallery in 1811. It is not generally known that there is also a fourth sarcophagus in the mausoleum. It is unoccupied, and is believed to have been intended for the architect himself, but Sir John Soane rests with his wife in Old St Pancras Churchyard.

Dulwich itself is perhaps the most beautiful of South London suburbs, and, unlike most others, which have no ancient or separate existence to which they can lay claim, it possesses a history. Moreover, its restfulness and beauty are secured by the great stretches of Dulwich Park and by the grounds and playing-fields of the College. The roads are wide, many of the older houses have splendid grounds, and the regulations of the College and Estate Governors, to whom most of this land belongs, are of such a character that the country-like aspect of Dulwich seems likely to be permanently assured. In the very middle of the district, on the road from Herne Hill to the Crystal Palace, is Dulwich Village, to this day almost as secluded as a country hamlet, and even yet existing as a separate entity. Dulwich Common still retains the old toll-gate where motorists are charged sixpence each time they pass through and drovers with cattle, sheep or ducks at 'tenpence per score'. Until she retired in 1958, the tolls were collected by an elderly lady who is said to have performed this duty for fifty-seven years. To the south of Dulwich College on the west side of College Road is the Kingswood Estate of the Greater London Council which covers an area of thirty-seven acres held by Dulwich College under the Royal Charter from 1619 until the middle of the last century. This consists of Kingswood House and the grounds. Here thirty seven 'Houses', containing flats, maisonettes and cottages have been built. Kingswood House, the grey stone castle-like mansion with a fine staircase and some good oak panelling, is the community centre of the estate and includes a branch of the Camberwell Public Libraries. Totalling nearly 800 dwellings, the settlement has its own little group of shops.

From here we will re-cross Dulwich Park and turn south along Lordship Lane and London Road, where we next pass the Horniman Museum and Gardens, situated on a hill close to Lordship Lane Station (now closed). The Museum contains objects of historical and archaelogical interest, including collections of insects, carved furniture, enamels, armour, and toys. It was presented to the public by Mr E. J. Horniman, and the surrounding grounds of fifteen acres, which were opened to the public in 1901, have been laid out as a park.

The adjoining suburbs of Forest Hill and Sydenham comprise a very large and favourite residential district. They crown the western side of the ridge of hills upon which the Crystal Palace was built, and form part of the extensive metropolitan borough of Lewisham. The main roads are bordered with trees and are very wide and picturesque, with plenty of space between the houses. Every variety of residence is to be found in this district, from the mansion surrounded by several acres of private grounds to the maisonette and flat or the newly-erected house of post-war type. In Round Hill, Upper Sydenham is an unusual garden ornament, consisting of the spire of the Wren church of St Antholin Watling Street. Brought here when the church was demolished in 1875, the spire still remains, though Round Hill House has gone. It is hoped to reinstate this City relic as a centre-piece of the group of new houses being built by the Lewisham Borough Council.

Turning northward from Dartmouth Road, Honor Oak Road will bring us to One Tree Hill, which rises steeply to 315 feet above sea level.

> 'Hate me! I often roll down One Tree Hill!
> Love me! I'll join you there!'
> *The Sorcerer*

A public park since 1905, One Tree Hill, despite its name, is well covered with trees and shrubs; the tradition regarding its name is that Queen Elizabeth I is supposed to have rested there and refreshed under an oak tree at the summit of the hill which became known as the 'Oak of Honour'. The original tree perished long ago; there have been several successors the last of which, protectively railed in, still survives.

At the top of the hill, among the trees, is the church of St Augustine, consecrated in 1874. There is an unreliable story that the Revd S. Baring Gould, at one time resident in the district, wrote *Onward Christian Soldiers* as a marching hymn to assist local churchgoers in their ascent of the hill. No attempt has been made to convert One Tree Hill into a conventional park; the scenery here is wild and similar to Hampstead Heath, and the views from the summit in clear weather embrace Tower Bridge, St Paul's Cathedral, the Houses of Parliament, etc., with the heights of Hampstead and Highgate in the background.

North of Honor Oak Park, and close to Peckham Rye Common, is Nunhead Cemetery, which has an area of fifty acres; it was consecrated in 1840. Between the cemetery and Peckham Rye Common is the underground Beachcroft Reservoir of the Metropolitan Water Board, which took three years to construct at a cost of £230,000 and was opened in 1909. It has a capacity of sixty million gallons. From Nunhead Station it is about half a mile to Queen's Road, which is the continuation of Peckham High Street, and leads past the junction of Old Kent Road to New Cross Road. At the top the steeply-rising ground to the south of New Cross in the quarter known as Hatcham is the small but lovely park called Telegraph Hill. It has a flower garden, tennis courts, bowling greens and a bandstand, and the park is divided into two sections by Kitto Road. From here a fine view is obtained of the Thames and the Isle of Dogs. Telegraph Hill is so named from an old Admiralty semaphore which is said to have signalled the news of Waterloo from here. After passing New Cross Gate Station we come to the junction with the Lewisham Way, leading to the centre of that town, about a mile and a half to the south-east of New Cross.

Lewisham, once the third largest borough in area of the County of London, was a century ago an attractive village with the Quaggy River, a branch of the River Ravensbourne, running alongside its main street. With the land rising gently on either side of the stream, it was then a very pleasant rural district, but, as in most of the other outlying suburbs of London, the green fields which once hemmed it in have long since been covered with streets and houses; however the stream is still very much in evidence along the east side of the High Street. There are two familiar landmarks at prominent points in the High Street; the Obelisk, originally a drinking fountain, erected in 1866 at the foot of Lewisham Hill, and the better known Clock Tower, at the junction with Lee Bridge, marking the diamond jubilee of Queen Victoria. For the greater part of the busy stretch between the Clock Tower and the Odeon Cinema, there are no pedestrian crossings and the pavement on both sides of the High Street is fenced in to prevent people from crossing the road; a most inconvenient method of ensuring the safety of the pedestrian. The old parish church dedicated to St Mary was pulled down in 1774 and replaced by the present building. It is a plain oblong structure of stone, with a square tower at the west end and a portico on the south side supported by four Corinthian columns. The principal shops are situated in the High Street and at the busy junction of the Catford, Lee, Greenwich, and London Roads.

The Town Hall, which is situated at Catford, is a building of church-like appearance erected in 1874 and enlarged in 1900. It was extended in 1932 and occupies an island site on the main road and is surrounded by shops. The new extension was formally opened by King George V in 1932. Other notable buildings were the Colfe Almshouses, destroyed by bombs and removed in 1956 and the Grammar School founded in 1652 by the Rev. Abraham Colfe, Vicar of Lewisham from 1610 to 1657. The school also was severely damaged by a flying bomb in 1944 and a completely new building has now replaced it. The Colfe Charities are administered by the Worshipful Company of Leathersellers. A narrow lane turning out of the main road by the side of the parish church leads to Ladywell, formerly a twin village of Lewisham, and now forming a part of the municipal borough. It possesses a long narrow recreation ground running parallel to the main Catford road covering fifty acres which is traversed by the Ravensbourne stream. On the high ground to the west and reached from Vicars Hill is the breezy recreation ground called Hilly Fields which covers forty-five acres. From the summit of the hill fine views are obtained of Lewisham town, the hills of Kent, and also of Blackheath and Shooter's Hill.

The populous quarter of Catford to the south, now forming a considerable portion of the borough of Lewisham, was little more than sixty years ago almost unknown and scarcely built upon. Since 1900 its development has been almost continuous, and it has now spread to the village of Southend, on the road to Bromley, and beyond to the large suburb of Downham, erected shortly after the first World War by the London County Council on similar lines to Dagenham and East Acton. It is named after Lord Downham, Chairman of the London

County Council in 1919. At Southend Village is a picturesque millpond where children paddle and sail their boats.

Returning north to the Lee High Road we pass through the modern quarter of Hither Green, consisting principally of small red-brick houses and some fairly good shops, and constituting the eastern portion of the borough of Lewisham. The suburb of Lee is built principally on the rising ground sloping up towards Blackheath, but the more modern portion extends eastwards in the direction of Eltham. The parish church, dedicated to St Margaret in 1841 near Blackheath, is a Gothic building with a tower and spire. Just across the road is the old tower and graveyard of the previous church. Dr Edmund Halley, the Astronomer Royal who discovered the comet named after him, is buried there. Beyond Eltham the straggling suburban area extends to Bexley, which gives its name to a new London Borough of nearly 16,000 acres. It includes the suburbs of Bexleyheath and Welling on the road to Dartford. Bexley old village with its ancient Norman church in the High Street lies one mile to the south. Hall Place, comprising over 160 acres, has been purchased by the Bexley Council for a public park. The mansion is famous for its association with the Black Prince whose ghost is said to appear in the grounds. The town has improved very much of late years, the main Dover Road has been widened in places and unsightly rows of mean houses have given way to fine new terraces of shops, notably in Welling High Street. On the south side of the Dover Road is the beautiful Danson Park, the grounds of which were originally laid out by Capability Brown with flower gardens, woods and a large lake. It is now a public park; the mansion was at one time a museum.

Midway between Lee and Eltham is the splendid new Sidcup by-pass road, constructed in 1923, one of the widest leading out of the metropolis. It is about five miles long and rejoins the main Folkestone Road a short distance to the south of the village of Foot's Cray. Many houses have been erected at the northern end, and entirely new quarters have rapidly sprung up in the vicinity of Mottingham and New Eltham. The old main road traverses the pleasant suburb of Sidcup, which contains many good-class houses and some excellent shops in its long narrow High Street. This is being gradually widened and here some fine new terraces of shops have been erected. From here Elm Road leads westwards across the new by-pass road to Chislehurst, a delightful suburb situated on the brow of a hill surrounded by commons and woods.

Facing the western fringe of Chislehurst Common is Camden Place, an Elizabethan mansion named after Camden, the antiquary, who lived here from 1609 until 1623. It was the home of Napoleon III from 1871 until his death in January 1873, and is now a golf club. The Emperor and his son were buried in the Roman Catholic Church near the parish church, but their bodies were subsequently removed to the mausoleum built by the Empress Eugénie at Farnborough, where she herself now lies. Opposite the gates of Camden Place is The Cedars, where William Willett, the originator of 'Daylight Saving' lived. On the Common close by, is a Runic Cross, 27 feet high, erected in 1880 to the memory of the

Prince Imperial, son of Napoleon III, who was killed when serving with the British Forces in Zululand in 1879. There was also a statue of the Prince at Woolwich Common, but this was removed to Sandhurst recently.

The parish church of St Nicholas dates from the fifteenth century, but only the north part is in the Perpendicular style of that period, the rest being chiefly modern. The family of the Walsinghams, who resided for several generations at Chislehurst, are interred in the church. From the High Street the main road leads across Chislehurst Common, Royal Parade and St Paul's Cray Common to Petts Wood, a delightful stretch of wild woodland. It is so named after the Petts family of Thames ship-builders in the days of the wooden walls, who owned this estate. It was secured in 1927 by the National Trust as a memorial to William Willett. Elmstead Wood, between Grove Park and Chislehurst, covering sixty-one acres, has also been acquired as a public open space. The entrance to the famous Chislehurst Caves is at the Bickley Arms, near the west end of Chislehurst Common. These consist of a remarkable labyrinth of passages running in every direction, and are the remains of a chalk mine supposed to have been worked as early as Roman times by means of shafts sunk from the surface. Parties are taken through the caves at frequent intervals, and prior to starting, the guide distributes half-a-dozen lighted hurricane lamps among responsible-looking members of the party—which add to the sense of adventure. During the second World War the caves were used for air-raid shelters. Within Mottingham Park were the buildings of the Royal Naval School, opened by King George V, when Duke of York, on 17 July 1889. The buildings now house Eltham College. Beyond Petts Wood the Chislehurst Road leads in about two miles to the thriving suburb of Orpington. Its narrow and picturesque High Street, which is now avoided by the new by-pass road, is gradually being widened. Here several fine new blocks of shops have been erected. Orpington was noted for its poultry farms where the famous Buff Orpingtons were bred. The town is situated amidst very agreeable Kentish scenery. About a mile and a half to the north of Orpington on the west side of the by-pass road is the St Paul's Cray Housing Estate of the London County Council. This is situated between St Mary Cray Station and the Sidcup by-pass road with an additional small area south of the railway. It consists chiefly of two-storeyed houses but there are also a number of three-storeyed blocks of flats, a shopping centre, four school sites, and a community centre. In the centre of the estate is Hoblingwell Wood which is a public park for the estate. From Orpington a journey of about five miles by way of Station Road, Crofton Road, Farnborough Common and Bromley Common will bring us to the old market town of Bromley, now the civic centre of the London Borough of Bromley which, with 38,266 acres or more than 60 square miles, has the largest area of all the 32 new boroughs. It has absorbed Beckenham, Orpington, Penge and parts of Chislehurst and Sidcup. Of late years so much building has taken place towards the north that Bromley is now joined to London by Downham, Southend Village, and Catford. The main London Road has been much widened for the greater part of the distance between Bromley and

Southend Village, and here many new rows of good-class shops have been erected. Bromley Town is built on the summit of a hill and contains several features of interest, including the former palace of the Bishop of Rochester, in the well-kept grounds of which is a chalybeate spring known as St Blaise's Well. The palace is a brick house situated above the railway near the South Station, and when seen from the road has the appearance of a large homely mansion. It is now a Teachers' Training College, known as Stockwell College. King Edgar gave the manor in the year 700 to the Bishop of Rochester and here also a 'college' was erected by Dr Warner, Bishop of Rochester in the reign of Charles II, for twenty poor clergymen's widows, who were made an annual allowance of £20, while the chaplain received a remuneration of £50 a year.

Next to the Palace grounds just off the High Street is a public recreation ground called The Queen's Garden. The main street passes through the Market Place, which was widened in 1932 when the ancient red-brick Town Hall, a building in the French style which covered an island site, was pulled down. The High Street, which leads down to the South Station, has also been extensively widened and converted into a double roadway with flower beds down the centre. The old parish church of St Peter and St Paul on Martin's Hill lies to the west of the Market Place up a short by-road but was completely destroyed in the air raid of April 1941. Only the floor and the tower of the church remained. The church has been entirely rebuilt and the foundation-stone was laid by H. M. the Queen when Princess Elizabeth in October 1949. Here the wife of Dr Johnson is buried. Below the church the northern slopes of Martin's Hill have been laid out as a recreation ground, which has fine views over the Ravensbourne Valley. The Crystal Palace towers, now demolished, were formerly a prominent feature of the landscape. This is a charming spot with scenery so richly wooded on both sides that you might imagine yourself far away in the country. A part of Martin's Hill surrounding the War Memorial has been laid out as a public pleasure garden. A commemorative plaque is affixed to the site of No 47 High Street, where H. G. Wells was born in 1866. Bromley extends southwards from the centre of the town through the populous district of Bromley Common for two miles, both sides of the Farnborough Road being lined with good-class houses.

Leaving Bromley High Street we now turn west, and, proceeding along Beckenham Lane, past the rising suburb of Shortlands, come to Beckenham. Shortlands is associated with the names of Grote, the historian, and Dinah Maria Mulock (Mrs Craik), author of *John Halifax Gentleman,* both of whom resided here. It was also the home of Sir Josiah Stamp, afterwards Lord Stamp, the famous economist and a director of the London, Midland and Scottish Railway from 1924 to 1941. Beckenham is a smart modern suburb with wide roads and excellent shops, and the original village still retains some of its old-time features in some quaint old timbered houses and shops, including the 17th century George Inn. The parish church of St George, a large building erected between 1886 and 1903 replaced the previous church which was demolished in 1885. The 13th century lych gate of a still earlier church is still in use. Beckenham has a fine Town Hall, built in 1932, which is now used by the Borough Engineer and other departments of the new borough. Beckenham Place Park on the north side of the town is a beautiful expanse covering three hundred acres on the southern slope of Beckenham Hill. Here the scenery is similar to that of Richmond Park. The mansion is used by the Foxgrove Golf Club.

Beyond the High Street the main Beckenham Road leads to Penge and the Crystal Palace Grounds. Until the middle of the last century Penge was a rural hamlet famous for its woods and fine trees. In those days people came here who wanted to live right out in the country, but after the removal of the Crystal Palace to this district from Hyde Park in 1854, and the opening of the railway from London Bridge Station, it became a popular residential suburb. The principal shops are situated on the main Beckenham Road, leading up to the southern entrance to the Crystal Palace grounds, and in Anerley Road. Prominent at the corner of High Street and Penge Lane are the 48 cottages of the Royal Watermen's Asylum.

The Crystal Palace, constructed mainly of glass and iron, was originally the home of the Great Exhibition of 1851 in Hyde Park. Designed by Sir Joseph Paxton, it was then intended merely as a temporary building, but a very general desire on the part of the general public to preserve the Crystal Palace on its original site found expression in two public meetings held in April 1852, and later at a crowded meeting held at Exeter Hall, at which the Earl of Shaftesbury took the Chair. Certain alterations and extensions were then proposed by Sir Joseph Paxton, with a view to converting it into a winter garden and adapting it to other scientific purposes. Finally the building was purchased by a private company, who re-erected it on its present site at Sydenham Hill. The first pillar was erected there on Thursday, 5 August 1852 by Mr Samuel Laing, and the building was opened on 10 June 1854 by Queen Victoria.

Erected at a total cost of £1,500,000, the Crystal Palace was without doubt the most magnificent and costly building of its particular kind that had ever been built; the upkeep of it cost as much as £60,000 a year. The main building, exclusive of wings and colonnades, was 1,850 feet long, and was composed of 9,642 tons of iron and twenty-five acres of glass. When the Crystal Palace was removed to Sydenham the central transept was made much higher, and the north and south transepts and the two towers were added. The towers were each 282 feet high, or 80 feet higher than the Monument and 98 feet higher than Nelson's column in Trafalgar Square. When erected in 1856 these towers were considered a most extraordinary engineering feat, but the first attempt to construct them proved a failure and involved the company in a great loss. When all but completed they were found to be insecure, and would neither carry the weight intended for them nor sustain the vibratory shock of the ascending and descending water, and therefore they had to be pulled down again. The fountains used to rise to a height of two hundred feet, and surpassed those of Versailles.

Before the first World War the Crystal Palace, like so many other undertakings of this kind, was in danger of insolvency and public subscriptions were raised for it. Largely as a result of the efforts of the Earl of Plymouth the palace became the property of the nation in June 1920. The Festival of Empire Exhibition of 1911 was held in the grounds of the Crystal Palace, and in 1914 it was taken by the Admiralty as a recruiting and training centre for the Royal Naval Division and other units. Here over 125,000 men were trained, and at the conclusion of that war the building was utilized as one of the great centres for demobilization.

Sir George Grove and Sir August Manns did much to foster good music at the Crystal Palace, and from 1857 onwards the Triennial Handel Festival was held in the central transept. The palace was a great attraction at holiday time, and was also a centre for Dog Shows, Brass Band Contests, and various exhibitions. Amongst its permanent attractions were a cinema, a weekly programme of dirt-track cycling, and on Thursdays during the summer months a display of fireworks. Before the opening of the Wembley Stadium the Cup Final was played here.

Unhappily the Crystal Palace was destroyed on the night of 1 December 1936 in the most spectacular fire seen in Britain for many years. This started about eight o'clock in the evening near the Egyptian Room and spread with such amazing rapidity that within half an hour the great building was ablaze from end to end. Ninety engines and five hundred firemen were engaged in fighting the flames, which rose to a height of three hundred feet. The cause of the fire was never discovered. Only the two towers escaped destruction but these were taken down in 1941 because they afforded a conspicuous landmark to enemy planes.

During the second World War the grounds were again used for martial purposes, after which they were largely derelict until 1952 when the London County Council took over and began the task of clearance and re-development. The Park of 70 acres, with its lake, gardens and prehistoric monsters (dating from the 1850's) was restored in 1953. A 40 acre site has been reserved for use as an exhibition centre, and a further 36 acres is being developed as The Crystal Palace National Recreation Centre, of which the Sports Hall—which includes a swimming bath and indoor arena—Stadium and King George VI Memorial Hostel are already in use.

The district of Upper Norwood, being very bracing, contains some good private hotels, such as the old-established Queen's Hotel in Church Road. In 1862 plans were drawn up for the erection of a large hydropathic establishment at Upper Norwood, a scheme which failed to mature. Westow Hill contains some of the principal shops of Upper Norwood, and its continuations westwards, Central Hill and Crown Lane, lead to Streatham Common and form the boundary-line between the boroughs of Lambeth and Croydon. On the north side of Central Hill on steep sloping ground is Norwood Park and below is the uninteresting quarter of West Norwood and the South Metropolitan Cemetery.

Though still sometimes termed a village by its inhabitants, Streatham has all the advantages of a large and handsome suburban town, comprising Streatham proper and the more modern Streatham Hill district to the north. Now in the borough of Lambeth, it was formerly in the metropolitan borough of Wandsworth, and its High Road extends from the top of Brixton Hill on the north to Norbury on the south, for a distance of close upon two miles. It is exceptionally wide at the northern end and is bordered for almost its entire length by smart shops, cinemas, theatres and ultra-modern blocks of flats. This gives Streatham the most Continental appearance of any of the larger London suburbs. The leading shops extend along the High Road, between Streatham Hill and Streatham Stations, for a distance of about a mile, and will invite favourable comparison with those of the best suburbs of London. On the west side, about mid-way between the two stations, is the large departmental store of Messrs Pratt Brothers Limited, now forming one of the John Lewis Partnership group of stores. On the opposite side of the road is the Public Library and the Odeon Cinema. The parish church of St Leonard, rebuilt in 1830, is situated near the junction of Streatham High Road and Mitcham Lane, where there is a small recreation ground. Here the Streatham High Road was widened in 1933 when a handsome new terrace of shops was erected. Streatham Public Baths, largely used for dances and private social gatherings, is situated close to Streatham Station, Southern Region.

Farther north on the west side of Streatham Hill is the handsome Streatham Hill Theatre, which has seating accommodation for about two thousand people. It was opened in 1929, and is perhaps the finest of any to be seen outside the West End of London. It was damaged in the air raids, but has now been rebuilt; at the time of writing it is described as a 'Bingo Casino'. Here also are the Locarno Dance Hall and a fine terrace of shops and flats known as Telford Court. On the same side of the road is the Gaumont Cinema which has seating accommodation for 2,500 people. On the east side of the road are several large blocks of shops and flats. These include Streatham Court and a distinctive row of shops and flats called 'The High'. This was erected in 1938-39 and over the footpath is a glass awning which affords cover in wet weather. Also on this side of the High Road near Streatham Hill Station are two tall blocks of shops and flats called Streatleigh Court and Corner Fielde and just beyond is another called Pullman Court with an approach from the main road through a spacious open quadrangular garden tastefully laid out with shrubberies. Close to the Common is the Streatham Ice Rink, accommodating six thousand skaters, which claims to be the largest in London. To the east of the High Road is the Leigham Court Estate, containing attractive modern houses planned amidst gardens and tennis courts, extending towards Tulse Hill and West Norwood.

To the west of Streatham Hill is Tooting Bec Common, which, together with Tooting Graveney Common, has an area of 218 acres. These two open spaces were acquired for the public between 1873 and 1875, and are now under the control of the Greater London Council. Tooting Bec is so named from having been a dependency of the famous Abbey of Bec in Normandy. To the north of the Common is a pleasant residential quarter of wide roads bordered with trees and large houses in gardens called Clapham Park extending towards Brixton, notably King's Avenue, which is more suggestive of some fine garden city far removed from London than of a district hemmed in on all sides by busy modern suburbs. Some of its larger houses have given way to new blocks of flats.

Streatham Common, which lies to the south of the town, is situated on rising ground, extending towards Norwood, and covers an area of sixty-six acres. About twenty years ago it was enlarged by the grounds of the Rookery, which has now become public property. Streatham was once a spa with medicinal springs that were a favourite resort of many wealthy London citizens in search of health. The springs were discovered in about 1659, but are believed to have dried up; the remains of one of the wells can still be seen in the Rookery Gardens.

Continuing southward, we cross the Norbury Brook and pass Norbury Station. The main London Road here is a wide thoroughfare lined with terraces of shops and flats. The road from Westminster Bridge to Croydon through Kennington, Brixton, Streatham, and Norbury forms one of the exits from the metropolis, of which it is possible to speak with the highest praise. It is wide throughout its entire length, and unspoilt by any of those unsightly bottlenecks and ragged hamlets which are a feature of so many of our great main arteries leading out of the metropolis, particularly on the west side.

Branching south-west at Thornton Heath where the pond, once a landmark reminding one of the rural past, has now been filled in, is the Croydon by-pass road, which skirts the west side of the town at the top of the valley and rejoins the main Brighton Road at Purley. Much building has taken place on this new road since the construction of Croydon Airport, formerly the terminal station of the Continental air services, which is situated on the west side, about mid-way between Thornton Heath and Purley. The old aerodrome at Waddon having become too small for the ever-increasing air traffic, more commodious buildings were erected in 1927. On 15 August 1940, during the Battle of Britain, the Germans made a great mass attack, employing over a thousand aeroplanes as compared with the five hundred to six hundred used on previous days. In the evening, between twenty and thirty dive-bombers made a sudden attack on Croydon aerodrome dropping a number of bombs on and around the target. One aerodrome building was demolished and a number of people buried in the debris. Bombs also fell on an adjoining housing estate, and a number of people were killed in this raid, but it was a sad day for the *Luftwaffe*, for of the German bombers taking part in the attack on Croydon and for whom the *Luftwaffe* had prepared a banquet to celebrate their triumphant homecoming, it is doubtful if one ever returned to its base. After the war, Croydon Airport was for some time used as storage space by motor car dealers with cars on their hands, and rows and rows of these vehicles were to be seen there. Today the ground has been cleared and a housing development is in progress. Named (after an adjacent park) Round Shaw Estate, a proportion of the 407 acre area is earmarked for the erection of houses and flats to accommodate 1,842 families—951 for the Greater London Council and 891 for the London Borough of Sutton. A large area will be available for a library, shops and recreational open spaces. With the 'industrialised' method of building, concrete components are pre-cast by the contractors on the site. Some of the dwellings are already occupied, and it is expected that 21 houses will be handed over each week until the estate consists of a community of nearly 7,000 people.

From Thornton Heath a journey of about a mile along the London Road through a busy suburban area will bring us to West Croydon station and the central portion of the town. On the east side of London Road is the handsome Congregational Church crowned by a tall spire. Croydon originally consisted of two parts, namely, the old and the new towns, each of which was about one mile in length. Today, it would be more correct to divide this town into *three* parts, the third being the extensive re-development area east of Park Lane, which might be called the 'ultra-modern' town. The old town is situated on a low plain near the source of the River Wandle, which, after passing underground for a short distance through the town, flows through Wandle Park on its course to the Thames. On the edge of the park is the parish church of St John the Baptist, a Perpendicular Gothic building of stone and flint designed by Sir G. Gilbert Scott and erected on the site of the old church which was destroyed by fire in 1867, though its 15th century tower—as so frequently happens—has survived. Near the church are the remains of the Old Palace, for centuries the residence of the Archbishop of Canterbury. Now occupied by a girls' school, the surviving buildings include the Great Hall, Tudor Chapel, Norman Undercroft, and a room called Queen Elizabeth's Bedroom. After giving up the Old Palace, the archbishops had, until 1896, a residence at Addington, now the Royal School of Church Music.

The new town is centred round the High Street, which was originally nothing more than a bridle-path over the fields. Being situated on higher ground and on a more direct course than the old road, it became the main road to Brighton and the south, and the surrounding district was rapidly built over. Here are located the Whitgift Hospital and the principal shopping centre of the town.

During the latter part of the second World War Croydon became the worst bombed area in the kingdom. No less than forty-five thousand houses were damaged by 141 flying-bombs that hit the town. When seen from the air Croydon presents a patchwork of bright terracotta formed by the replaced roofs of the damaged houses. The work was carried out with such rapidity that by the end of 1945 over £4,500,000 had been spent in bringing tolerable comfort to the householders, thus providing a heartening picture of how quickly Britain was recovering from her wounds. The damage was mainly confined to residential quarters and the side streets. Croydon's main thoroughfares, including North End, the High Street and George Street escaped almost undamaged.

Although now joined to London, and as metropolitan as Kensington, Croydon still prefers to regard itself as a detached town outside the metropolitan area. Seventy years ago the centre of the town from West Croydon Station to South Croydon was still one long narrow street, except a portion of the High Street, which had been widened on the west side in 1895. Since then North End has been widened between West Croydon Station and the Whitgift Hospital, and an extensive widening of the southern end of the High Street ending at the Swan and Sugar Loaf Hotel had also been carried out. George Street, leading from the High Street to East Croydon Station, has also been widened, but the Whitgift Hospital, which stands at the corner of George Street and North End, forms an obstacle to the complete widening of these two streets.

Some thirty-five years ago the Croydon Corporation intended to demolish the Whitgift Hospital for very necessary street improvements, but were prevented from so doing, partly through local opposition, but principally because the scheme had been vetoed by Parliament. The Whitgift Hospital was erected and endowed between the years 1596 and 1599 by Archbishop Whitgift as 'an abiding-place for the finding, sustenation and relief of certain maymed, poore, needie or impotent people'. A schoolmaster was also appointed at a salary of £20 per annum to teach the children of the poor of Croydon, gratis. The Archbishop's gift increased greatly in value, and in 1881 the trust was reconstituted and another school founded, but the old hospital is still an almshouse. The Trinity School of John Whitgift, which was an impressive building in North End, was erected in 1781 to the design of Sir Arthur Blomfield, and was demolished in 1965. On this important 10-acre site office blocks of eight to twenty storeys, shops and a multi-storey garage are to be built. The school has moved to Shirley Park.

A widening of Crown Hill from the south side has been commenced by rounding off the building line at the corner of the High Street and a handsome new building has been erected on this site. A similar rounding-off on the north corner of Crown Hill has been achieved and the new Barclay's Bank building, opened in January 1961, has been set back to give effect to the widening. The Town Hall in Katherine Street is a noble block of buildings faced with red brick and stone in the Renaissance style, erected in 1893-94 at a cost of £90,000, and is crowned in the centre by a lofty clocktower. It replaced the old Town Hall in the High Street built in 1808, which itself replaced an ancient structure built in 1609.

Croydon, in addition to being a great residential town for Londoners, possesses a number of manufactures, amongst others the making of clocks, and also engineering works, and at one time had markets for corn and cattle. Some of the largest shops, including the two departmental stores of Messrs Kennard's and Messrs Allder's, are situated in North End, but that of Messrs Grant Brothers is on the west side of the High Street. North End, which is half a mile long, is a handsome shopping street and on a Saturday afternoon when it is crowded with shoppers it presents a scene of life and animation unexcelled even by that of Oxford Street in its busiest hours. So large and varied are its shops that no Croydon resident need ever go to the West End of London to find anything he may require. A short distance farther south on the opposite side of the High Street was the Davis Picture Theatre, erected in 1928 and said to be one of the largest in Europe, having accommodation for four thousand people. Celebrated for its Sunday Symphony Concerts, the Davis Theatre, to everybody's dismay, was demolished, and the seven-storey office block Davis House now stands on the site. Further south, Grosvenor House replaces the Grand Theatre, and across the road, the new Green Dragon House takes the name of one of the oldest hostelries in Croydon, which stood there. The Pembroke Theatre and the Eros Cinema have gone, and the Odeon is now the only Cinema (as such) left in central Croydon.

What we have called the third, or 'ultra-modern' part of Croydon is the re-development on the east side of the town, of which the Fairfields Halls may be regarded as the centre. Opened by Queen Elizabeth the Queen Mother in November 1962, they combine under one roof the Ashcroft Theatre, a concert hall, exhibition gallery, restaurant etc. A little further north is the new technical College of Art, opened by Her Majesty the Queen in 1960, which occupy $4^1/_2$ acres and have accommodation for 500 full-time students and many more in the part-time category.

In the remainder of this New Croydon area are a dozen or more commercial buildings of the 'Skyscraper' pattern with which we are familiar in other parts of London, the ground floors of most of them providing new shopping space. St George's Walk, an intersection between Park House and the 24-storey St George's House, is a canopied pedestrian shopping precinct. There are also several new licensed refreshment houses – surely too smart to be called 'pubs' – one of them, 'The Greyhound' recalls the venerable hostelry of that sign in the High Street which was a familiar bus stop years ago. To the student of modern buildings, this concentration of 'monolithic slabs' must be full of interest, for though to the untrained eye they may all look alike, when grouped together as they are here, it is possible to discover subtle variations in their design, and at least one surprise – for hidden away in a cul-de-sac and almost trodden on by the towering giants that surround it, is Wellesley Cottage, a pretty little two-storey dwelling of red brick, hoping to be overlooked.

Purley, which lies two miles south of Croydon Town Hall, has developed during the last fifty years into a flourishing high-class suburb. The best houses, many of which stand in large gardens, are situated on the west side of the main Brighton Road on the hill-side leading up to the Croydon by-pass road. With the great increase of population, many first-class shops have been erected on the main Brighton Road close to its junction with the Croydon by-pass Road and the Eastbourne Road. The erection, some years ago, of the crescent of shops on the Croydon by-pass road at this busy centre resulted in an increase of traffic congestion. An experimental one-way traffic system has now been introduced to overcome the difficulty.

At one time Croydon had hopes of absorbing Purley into its municipal area, but this was successfully resisted by the local inhabitants, who decided in favour of a union with Coulsdon. The new London Borough of Croydon, however, has absorbed both Purley and Coulsdon. The latter town resembles Purley in its general character, but enjoys the advantage of being two miles nearer to the undisturbed country. Many detached houses have been erected with spacious gardens on the slopes of the chalk hills, and of late years some fine shops have also been erected on the main Brighton Road, quite close to two of the stations. The ancient church of Coulsdon is situated about a mile to the south-east, at Bradmore Green, on high ground and amidst beautiful surroundings.

South-west of Coulsdon, the suburban area which is becoming unwieldy has sprawled out into the Chipstead Valley, which is being covered with new houses. East of Croydon the outer suburban area has spread to Addiscombe, Shirley, West Wickham and Hayes. Near Shirley are the Addington Hills, a breezy spot, forming Croydon's largest open space. It is four hundred feet above sea level and was purchased by the Croydon Corporation in 1932.

On the east side of the Purley Valley, about two miles from the centre of Croydon, is the rapidly-growing suburb of Sanderstead. It is situated on high ground rising to an altitude of 550 feet above the sea level, and consists mainly of high-class residences with large gardens. The old village and the parish church are about a mile from the railway station. Attracted by the beautiful surroundings, coupled with the convenient train service of the Southern Region Railway, London is steadily extending her suburban area into the deep and narrow Caterham Valley to the south-east of Purley. In recent years its green contours and wooded crests have been covered with villas, through Kenley and Whyteleafe, and thence the houses straggle beside the main Godstone Road almost as far as the distant town of Caterham, some seventeen miles from Westminster Bridge. The houses lining the sides of the valley are of a superior type, but unfortunately many small, ugly houses were erected at Kenley at the turn of the century. On the east side of the valley, between Kenley and Whyteleafe, is Riddlesdown, a hillside slope of grass and thicket, one of the Coulsdon commons maintained by the Corporation of London, and offering attractions to the holiday-maker similar to those of Hampstead Heath. The main Godstone Road has recently been widened for the greater part of the distance between Purley and Caterham.

On our return journey we first return to Croydon High Street and then proceed along Church Street, Croydon, Epsom Road, and across the by-pass road to Beddington, with its picturesque old church and historic park traversed by the River Wandle. Between this and the adjoining village of Wallington, traces of a Roman villa and other relics were discovered in 1871. The two districts were joined as the Borough of Beddington and Wallington in 1937, but today their civic identity is merged in the London Borough of Sutton. Beyond Wallington, about half-way between Croydon and Sutton, is Carshalton, a picturesque village in the centre of which is a large expanse of water formed by the junction of the Wandle with numerous and copious springs. Close to the parish church is a railed and covered well called Anne Boleyn's Well. Tradition says that as Henry VIII and his Queen, Anne Boleyn were passing on horseback from Nonsuch Palace to visit Sir Nicholas Carew at Beddington, the Queen's horse 'began prancing about at this spot and struck its hoof in the ground, causing a spring to burst forth'. Trout could once be taken from the Wandle at Carshalton, but none have been caught for seventy years. Sir Nicholas Throckmorton, Queen Elizabeth I's minister, had a residence in the village to which he is said to have retired whenever his duties would permit.

Beddington, Wallington and Carshalton are areas covered with houses extending for a distance of about two and a half miles along the main road between Croydon and Sutton, with which towns they are now connected by bus routes. The main road from Croydon enters Sutton town at the junction of the High Street and the Brighton Road. The 'Cock' Inn, a relic of coaching days which stood at the corner, was demolished quite recently, but its old sign still stands at the cross-roads. In recent years Sutton, distant twelve miles from London, has increased rapidly in size, and was formerly joined with Cheam as a municipal borough. The parish church of St Nicholas rebuilt in 1864 is in the Gothic style and has a tower with a spire. The town is almost entirely residential, but contains many attractive shops in its long and busy High Street, which leads up a steep hill and forms part of the old Reigate and Brighton Road. British Railways (Southern Region) has provided an excellent service of electric trains to London by way of Mitcham, and also via Wimbledon, and the town is rapidly extending in the direction of Cheam. The new Sutton by-pass road starts from Green Lane on the north side of the town, and rejoins the main Brighton Road at Belmont, near Banstead Downs.

From Sutton it is a journey of about three miles along the main London Road to Morden, passing first the Green at the bottom of Sutton High Street and then Rosehill Park, a large pleasure-ground with bowling greens and tennis courts on both sides of the main road. Beyond Rosehill Park we come to a large roundabout at the junction of Reigate Road, St Helier Avenue and Bishopsford Road, where there is a handsome terrace of shops and flats and a Gaumont Cinema. Here we reach the splendidly planned St Helier Estate which has been developed by the London County Council since 1927. Thousand of houses have been erected here, most of which stand back in strips of gardens among wide roads and avenues, notably in St Helier Avenue which brings us to Mordenhall Park. This is a lovely domain which was bequeathed to the National Trust by its owner, the late Mr G. S. Hatfield and through which flows a lake fed by the River Wandle. Close to the park centred round Mordenhall Road and London Road is Morden's great new shopping centre and here also is the spacious Underground Station and omnibus terminus of London Transport. Here also terminates the longest tunnel in the world: 17 miles, 528 yards, from East Finchley to Morden, via Bank. The adjoining district of Mitcham is noted for its annual fair, which has been held on 12-14 August from time immemorial. Mitcham was for long also noted for market gardening including the cultivation of lavender and similar herbs. This occupation has, however, almost entirely disappeared and the district is now largely built over. Mitcham Common was one of the earliest homes of golf in England. The lower green has long been famous for its cricket, and here stands 'The Cricketers' Tavern. The church of St Peter and St Paul was rebuilt in 1821 in the Perpendicular style.

From the crossroads at the Upper Green the London Road leads in about two miles to Tooting Broadway. In Mitcham Road is the splendid Granada Cinema, opened in 1931 which has accommodation for four thousand people. Internally it resembles some Continental cathedral with its marble pillared and mirrored foyer, Gothic decorations and stained-glass windows illuminated from behind. Having recently been re-decorated in its original style, it recaptures the palatial luxury which the cinemagoer of the thirties was accustomed to expect for his sixpence, ninepence or one-and-three. In 1928 the London Underground Railways extended their line from Clapham Common to Tooting and Morden. Tooting Broadway is a busy traffic centre formed by the junction of the roads from Clapham, Wandsworth, South Wimbledon, and Mitcham. The High Street, formerly a narrow ragged thoroughfare, was extensively widened about 1904 on the west side to make room for the electric tramways of the London County Council. From here the wide main road to London is continued by Upper Tooting Road, Balham High Road, and Balham Hill, to the south side of Clapham Common. Tooting is a densely-peopled quarter but Balham, which is an important shopping centre, has some good-class houses extending towards Tooting Bec Common. In the High Road, Balham, are several departmental and chain stores, while on the opposite side of the road, at the foot of Balham Hill, is the site of the Duchess Theatre (destroyed by bombing) which has been developed as a housing estate. Ducane Court, on the west side near Balham Station, is a mammoth block of flats erected in 1936 which claims to be the largest in South London. Westbury Court, erected above Clapham South Underground Station, is a bold block of flats facing Clapham Common. Balham High Road lacks the smart appearance of its sister suburb of Streatham, for most of its buildings are badly in need of cleaning.

Clapham Common, an open space of 220 acres, is situated on the west side of the main road to Stockwell and Kennington. It was formerly a desolate morass, but early in the last century it was improved and planted with trees by a subscription raised amongst the local inhabitants. Prominent amongst these was Mr Christopher Baldwin, an active magistrate, who owned an estate of fourteen acres adjoining the Common, which he disposed of for £5,000. The manorial rights of Clapham Common were purchased by the Metropolitan Board of Works in 1877 for £18,000, after which extensive improvements were carried out, including the drainage of the subsoil, filling up of old ditches, formation of new footpaths, and planting a new avenue of trees. Every variety of sport is allowed on Clapham Common, including games on Sunday. The ponds afford special facilities for model-yacht sailing, and bathing is also permitted at certain hours.

For more than a century the Common has been surrounded by good houses, including the former residences of City bankers and merchants. Some of these have long since disappeared, but others situated on the north side have been converted into flats. Clapham High Street, forming part of the main road from Stockwell and Kennington and much bombed during the last war, is less attractive as a shopping centre than either Brixton or Balham.

In Clapham High Street, near The Plough, a tramway depot that was badly bombed and later rebuilt for use by buses became redundant in 1958. It was subsequently taken over by the British Transport Commission and is now the Museum of British Transport. No less than 14 retired steam locomotives are on view, among them the famous streamlined 'Mallard', which established a world speed record for steam of 126 m.p.h. in 1938. Railway coaches included the Royal Saloons built for Queen Victoria and King Edward VII and the handsome Pullman Car 'Topaz'. Omnibuses of the horse, motor and trolley varieties, tramcars and road vehicles may be seen, and a host of small exhibits includes beautiful models, notices, tickets and a variety of surprising transport treasures, Chantrey's colossal statue of James Watt, which crashed through the floor of Westminster Abbey when it was erected there, now stands in the museum among more appropriate surroundings. The Museum is open on weekdays, 10 am to 5.30 pm.

At the entrance to the Clapham North Side Library is a Roman memorial stone, found in the grounds of Cavendish House, Clapham Common in 1907. Believed to date from the first century A.D., its inscription is translated as

"To the shades of Titus Licinus Ascanius. He erected it himself in his own life".

As Cavendish House was the residence of Henry Cavendish, the eccentric scientist, chemist and philosopher, this stone may have been part of his 'collection'.

The most interesting part of Clapham is Old Town. No. 12 is an old house bearing a heraldic shield and crest, with the motto, 'Contentment passe richesse'. The parish church of St Paul, consecrated in 1815, stands on the site of earlier churches, and displays a fragment of a very old brass commemorating William Tableer, who died in 1401. In the north transept is the celebrated 17th century Atkins memorial consisting of five life-size figures, beautifully sculptured in marble representing father, mother, and three children. The vestry contains the large memorial of William Hewer, clerk and friend to Samuel Pepys; it was at the Clapham house of 'W. Hewer', as he is so frequently mentioned in the Diary, that Pepys died in 1703.

As a corollary to the touchingly simple epitaph in the cloisters of Westminster Abbey—'Jane Lister dear childe, 1688', in the gallery of St Paul's, Clapham will be found a memorial to her mother, 'Hannah Lister, deare wife, died the 1st of August 1695 and left six children in teares for a most indulgent mother'. A tablet on the south wall honours John Hatchard, 'nearly fifty years an eminent bookseller and publisher in Piccadilly', who died in 1849 at the age of 80. St Paul's is not a beautiful church, but it is full of interest.

By following the north side of Clapham Common from 'The Plough', with its continuation Battersea Rise, we next come to Wandsworth Common, another large open space, which has an area of 183 acres. It is surrounded principally by good class houses, and extends in a southerly direction from Wandsworth Town towards Tooting.

Although still a comparatively large open space, Wandsworth Common has suffered more in the past from encroachments than any other Metropolitan common. It was acquired in 1871 by a body of conservators from Earl Spencer, the Lord of the Manor, at a time when numerous enclosures threatened to swallow up the whole of this open space. In 1887 it was taken over from the conservators by the Metropolitan Board of Works. When placed under public control in 1871, its surface was bare, muddy, and sloppy after a little rain, undrained, and almost devoid of any trees. To-day it is a beautiful pleasure-ground well planted with trees and its special attractions include a richly-wooded lake divided into two arms where fishing is allowed, also a tea-house and bowling-greens. The Common is divided into two parts by the tracks of British Railways (Southern Region). The two parts are connected by a footbridge known locally as 'The Cat's Back'. One portion of the common was once the resort of gipsy vans and tents. On the west side of the common was the Royal Victoria Patriotic School for Girls, erected as part of the scheme for the relief of the families of soldiers who perished in the Crimean War. The building, a free imitation of Heriot's Hospital, Edinburgh, was designed by Mr Rhode Hawkins, and the foundation-stone was laid by Queen Victoria on 11 July 1857. During the Second World War, the school moved to Hatfield, and the building — soon to be pulled down — is now used as an annexe to the adjoining Spencer Park School.

North of the Common and sandwiched between the tracks of the South Western and Brighton lines, is Emmanuel School for Boys. Founded in 1594 under the will of Lady Dacre, a cousin of Queen Elizabeth, the original school buildings, occupied until 1883, were at Westminster. The present buildings on Wandsworth Common, which include a handsome Chapel, are being modernized and additional accommodation is being provided in accordance with the current needs of a modern day school of 750 boys.

In the angle between Trinity Road and the southern Railway track is Wandsworth Prison, built in 1851 with accommodation for a thousand criminals. It is used for prisoners undergoing sentence for various types of offence, including smash-and-grab raiders and motor-car bandits. Adjoining the prison, between Earlsfield Station and Magdalen Road, is the Wandsworth Cemetery. The unattractive district of Earlsfield and Summerstown to the south-west of Wandsworth Common is mainly an industrial area and is centred round Garratt Lane. Some fine blocks of workers' flats have been erected in Garratt Lane not far from Earlsfield Station opening into a spacious quadrangle. In the reign of Queen Elizabeth I the original hamlet of Garrett consisted of a single house called the Garrett, which was pulled down about the middle of the eighteenth century. The spelling, it will be seen, has since been modified. St John's Road, a busy shopping thoroughfare leading from the north side of Wandsworth Common to West Hill and Clapham Junction Station, includes the large departmental store of Messrs Arding & Hobbs Limited. The buildings extend to the corner of Lavender Hill and are faced with red brick and stone. The original store was completely gutted by fire in 1907. In St John's Hill was the Grand Palace of Varieties, now converted to a cinema.

Wandsworth, once the largest of the 28 metropolitan boroughs, has now lost that distinction, its area as one of the new London Boroughs being reduced to 8,872 acres. The 'village' lies in the valley of the River Wandle between East Hill and West Hill, and the High Street crosses the river by a bridge. The name Wandsworth is a corruption of Wandlesworth, meaning the village on the Wandle. It contained a population of 330,328 in 1951, and includes the districts of Wandsworth proper, Earlsfield, Putney, Tooting, Balham, Streatham, and part of Clapham. Partly wedged in between Battersea and Lambeth but extending all the way from Richmond Park to Norwood, its municipal area is so unwieldy in shape as to suggest that this territory might have been mapped out by the same parties who replanned the map of Europe after the Treaty of Versailles. At the close of the eighteenth century Wandsworth became a resort of Huguenot refugees, who brought several valuable industries to the town of their adoption. Mount Nod, behind the County House on East Hill, is their Burial Ground. The art of dyeing cloth has been practised here since the beginning of the eighteenth century, and various manufactures, such as calico-printing and bleaching, as well as the linseed oil and white lead trades, were already established more than a century ago near the creek at the mouth of the Wandle.

In the High Street are the palatial new Wandsworth Municipal Buildings. These consist of three storeys, faced with Portland stone, built adjacent to the Town Hall, a less pretentious edifice. A series of five stone panels in relief on the High Street elevation illustrate some of the principal incidents and industries in the history of the borough. The Municipal Buildings were completed in 1937 and cover a large island site, in the centre of which is a spacious quadrangle. Opposite the Town Hall is the local Technical College and in Fairfield Street are several fine new blocks of flats. All Saints parish church, near the bridge over the Wandle, dates from the end of the eighteenth century and has a low tower with a clock. To the south of the High Street is King George's Park and Recreation Ground, which skirts the west side of the River Wandle and extends for half a mile towards Earlsfield. Near the entrance to the Park is the Wandsworth Stadium and here also is a large open-air swimming-bath which has been provided by the Wandsworth Borough Council. On the other side of the High Street in Putney Bridge Road is Wandsworth Park which fronts the Thames and extends for a quarter of a mile towards Putney. From here a pleasant view is obtained of Putney Bridge and Fulham Church and of Hurlingham Park on the opposite bank of the Thames. This concludes our tour of the south-eastern suburbs.

Third Drive

A Tour of the South-Western Suburbs

Starting from Hammersmith Broadway, we proceed to Chiswick, by way of King Street, which extends westwards for about three-quarters of a mile as far as Goldhawk Road. At the western end of King Street, approached from Hamlet Gardens, is Ravenscourt Park, with an area of thirty-two acres which was purchased in 1887 for the sum of £58,000, at the joint expense of the late Metropolitan Board of Works and the former Vestry of Hammersmith. The Park extends northwards towards Goldhawk Road, and provides a much-needed open space for this densely-populated quarter of Hammersmith. At the southern end of the park are several blocks of flats called Hamlet Court and the larger King's Court, a ten-storeyed building erected in 1934 at the corner of King Street.

Beyond King Street the Chiswick High Road leads direct to Turnham Green and Gunnersbury, but the old village of Chiswick itself lies about half a mile to the south, with its old and narrow main street running at right angles from the Thames close to the church, which until quite recently could only be reached by walking. Chiswick Mall, which runs along the bank of the Thames, is practically a continuation of that of Hammersmith. It contains Walpole House, which has been the residence of many famous personages, including Daniel O'Connell, and Lingard House, where lived John Lingard, the Catholic historian. Walpole House is believed to be the original of Miss Pinkerton's Academy in *Vanity Fair*, though another house, in Chiswick Square, near the Hogarth Roundabout, also claims to be the place where Becky Sharp threw Johnson's *Dixonary* out of the carriage window. The parish church stands near the river at the western end of the Mall and is dedicated to St Nicholas, the patron saint of fishermen. It dates from about the beginning of the fifteenth century, but various improvements and renovations to the interior were carried out in the latter part of the nineteenth century. There are many memorials in the church, but the interior is so very dark that it is only possible to identify a few of them.

Hogarth died at Chiswick on 25 October 1764, aged sixty-seven, and is buried in the churchyard. His red-brick house in Hogarth Lane, near Church Street, was damaged by a bomb during the war. Its rooms were hung with a collection of 150 engravings, but these were removed and thus saved. It has been restored as the Hogarth Museum. In the western extension of the churchyard are interred Whistler and Sir W. B. Richmond. Hogarth Lane is now part of the Great West Road extension, which only misses Hogarth's house by a very narrow margin indeed. From the roundabout at the bottom of Hogarth Lane, overlooked by the new Chiswick Products building, the Great Chertsey Road leads along

Burlington Lane after which it crosses the Southern Region Railway over a wide new bridge. From here it crosses the Thames to Mortlake by the new Chiswick Bridge. This was formally opened by the Duke of Windsor when Prince of Wales on 3 July 1933. On the same afternoon he opened two more new bridges, at Twickenham and Hampton Court. From Mortlake to Richmond, the Great Chertsey Road is continued by a dual carriageway which is an extensive widening of Lower Richmond Road.

To the west of Chiswick Church, and approached from Turnham Green by Duke's Avenue, is Chiswick House, a former seat of the Duke of Devonshire, which stands almost concealed from view by tall cedars and other trees. The main entrance is in Burlington Lane. It was erected in the reign of George II by the third Earl of Burlington and Cork, from a design by Palladio, and includes a park and pleasure ground covering about 190 acres, extending on the south to Burlington Lane. Chiswick House is associated with Canning and Fox, both of whom died here. In 1814, the Emperor Alexander I of Russia and the other allied sovereigns visited the Duke of Devonshire here, and the house was also occupied for a time by Queen Victoria, Later, after having been a private asylum, the estate, with its beautiful grounds, became public property. Chiswick House, which was also badly damaged during the war by bombing, has been restored by the Ministry of Works. The park is beautifully laid out with lawns, flower gardens, and a long narrow lake with richly-wooded banks which extends right across the park.

On the peninsula formed by the bend of the river, to the south of Burlington Lane, is Grove Park, which contains an extensive range of sports grounds including those of the Polytechnic Institute and the Civil Service, as well as a public sports ground and another one for children. Skirting the river in front of the eastern side of Grove Park are the Chiswick Terraces, which extend from the open-air swimming-bath near Chiswick Cemetery to Barnes Railway Bridge. They are bordered by public gardens containg a rockery and a pergola, which is reputed to be the longest in England. The open-air swimming-bath was opened in 1910.

At Turnham Green, on the main Chiswick High Road, is Christ Church, consecrated by the Bishop of London on 27 July 1843, and surmounted by a lofty spire. It was erected at a cost of £6,000, and will accommodate nine hundred people. At that time Turnham Green was a detached hamlet near Chiswick village, but the establishment of the Royal Horticultural Society at Chiswick in a part of the grounds lying between the mansion and Turnham Green brought increased popularity to Chiswick, which then became a favourite resort and even possessed its own steamboat pier. After the headquarters of the Royal Horticultural Society were removed to South Kensington, visitors to Chiswick, except for the University boat race, became few and far between. Horticultural Place, off Heathfield Terrace, recalls the Society's sojourn here.

The Green is a pleasant open space bordered by good-class houses and several modern blocks of flats. At the corner of Sutton Court Road is the former

Chiswick Town Hall. This is an agreeable residential quarter of villas and also contains many attractive blocks of flats which have been erected of late years in Sutton Court Road and Wellesley Road. Between Chiswick High Road and the Thames this quarter is now traversed by the extension of the Great West Road of which a long section with a double roadway goes from Hogarth Lane to Gunnersbury where it crosses the Southern Region Railway by a handsome new bridge. The remaining section from here to the entrance to the Great West Road is completed by the roundabout and flyover referred to in the Twenty-fourth Walk. Below the new bridge, between the Southern Region Railway and Stile Hall Gardens are several fine new five-storeyed blocks of flats with balconies which are grouped round a well-laid-out garden. This is one of the most agreeable housing estates in Chiswick.

The leading shops of Chiswick are situated on the main High Road between Goldhawk Road and Gunnersbury Station, but most of the old houses facing Turnham Green, which formed the original hamlet, have been pulled down or converted into shops. Nearly opposite the church stood the Chiswick Empire Theatre of Varieties, a handsome building faced with terracotta. On Saturday 20 June 1959 the curtain fell for the last time at the Chiswick Empire, which was soon demolished. An eleven-storey office block with fifteen shops called Empire House now stands on the site. North of Chiswick High Road, adjoining Turnham Green Station, is the small open space of Chiswick Common, which is continued by Acton Green westwards to Chiswick Park Station. North of Chiswick Common is Bedford Park—not really a park—but the name of the very first Garden Suburb, planned by Jonathan T. Carr and begun in 1875, the principal architect being Norman Shaw. Very attractive in their earlier days, the houses, of several designs, are now showing signs of age. The suburb has its own church, bank, shops and a tavern, the 'Tabard Inn'.

Between Chiswick and Kew Bridge is the quaint waterside hamlet of Strand on-the-Green, which is far older than any of its surroundings, and has been gradually hedged in by modern suburbs. Until about the middle of the last century it was just a row of houses looking across to the Surrey shore, but although much else has changed, Strand-on-the-Green remains practically unaltered to this day; it consists of inns, wharves, and respectable old houses overlooking a quay with an eyot in the river. Kew Bridge was opened in 1788 and rebuilt in 1903.

A short distance west of Gunnersbury Station is the flyover junction of the new Great West Road with the Chiswick High Road, and also at ground level, with the North Circular Road leading to Ealing Common. Gunnersbury Park, situated to the north of the Great West Road, and partly skirting Gunnersbury Lane, is now a public park under the joint management of the Ealing and Hounslow Borough Councils. For some twenty-five years it was the home of Princess Amelia, daughter of George II, and latterly of the Rothschilds, and has an area of two hundred acres, containing shrubbery walks, flower gardens, a cricket and football ground, and two lakes. The ground floor of the house is now a museum with souvenirs of the Rothschild family that include a carriage, a coach – and a hansom cab!

Chiswick High Road leads to Kew Bridge Station, where the main roads fork, that to the south leading over Kew Bridge to Richmond, and the other forming the old main west road through Brentford to Hounslow and Bath. On the opposite side of Kew Bridge is Kew Green, around which are grouped a number of old mansions once inhabited by very notable persons. The church of St Anne, situated on the Green, was built in 1714; the churchyard contains the vault of the Duchess of Cambridge and the tomb of Gainsborough, who, though not a resident, expressed a desire to be buried near his friend Joshua Kirby, drawing master to the children of George III, who had died fourteen years earlier, in 1774. They were both natives of Sudbury, Suffolk and now lie side by side. The name of Kew is a corruption of Kay-hough, meaning the road or hough by the quay. Like many other villages near London, it has lost all its distinctive features, with the exception of the Green, and is now a high-class modern suburb.

Old Kew Palace, built in 1631 by a Dutch merchant, Samuel Fortrey, was acquired by George III in 1781 and used regularly as a residence for his family. The palace is open to visitors to Kew Gardens but is not of very special interest. The famous Kew Gardens occupy 288 acres, and were opened in 1840. They are far from being a mere pleasure resort, and are maintained chiefly for purposes of botanic study; in fact, they are an institution of the greatest importance to the domestic and commercial welfare of the Commonwealth, inasmuch as the Directors are the advisers to the Government on all matters concerning plant life. The gardens are now maintained by the Ministry of Agriculture, and trees, plants, and shrubs from all parts of the world may be seen here, either in the open grounds, the conservatories, or in the Great Palm House built in 1848.

Formerly the grounds of old Kew Palace, they were already famous for a botanic garden that had been formed there by Princess Augusta, mother of George III, in 1760. Formerly the ground was a stretch of barren soil, without either wood or water, but princely expenditure overcame all difficulties, and what was once a desert is now a veritable Garden of Eden. The Pagoda was constructed in 1761-62 by Sir William Chambers, and is an imitation of the Chinese Paa. It is 165 feet high, and when first built stood in the centre of the wilderness which formed the upper part of the Gardens. In 1841 these were established as a State institution and, under the control, as first director, of Sir William Jackson Hooker, the great botanist, they attained a foremost rank amongst the botanic gardens of the world. The Palm House in the centre of the gardens was designed by Decimus Burton, as well as the equally fine Temperate House to the south of it. The gardens now extend from the Old Deer Park at Richmond on the south to the Thames on the west, to Kew Green on the north, and to Kew Road on the east. The Old Deer Park contains the Kew Observatory built by Sir William Chambers in 1769, the Mid-Surrey Golf Course and a large public recreation ground fronting the Great Chertsey Road.

We now re-cross Kew Bridge to visit the suburbs on the Middlesex side of the river. We come first to Brentford, long regarded as the County Town of Middlesex, but this was not strictly correct and seems to be a title that was acquired because for many years the County Parliamentary Elections were held there. Today, however, thanks to the recent London Government Act, the County of Middlesex no longer exists! Catherine Wheel Yard, Red Lion Yard and King's Arms Alley are a few of the names that recall the old inns still in thriving business down to the eighteen-thirties when Brentford was the first stage for the coaches from London. A stone pillar near the riverside in Ferry Lane recalls the discovery in 1909 of oak palisades in the river; relics of 54 B.C., when Cassivelaunus and the British tribesmen opposed Julius Caesar at the ford. It also reminds us that in 1016 Edmund Ironside drove Cnut and his Danes across the river, and mentions the Battle of Brentford between the forces of King Charles I and the Parliament in 1642. The long, narrow High Street still contains several old-fashioned shops, the double bow-fronted shops of Messrs Rattenbury being a choice specimen at least 200 years old, though many of the delapidated shops and ramshackle old cottages have been replaced by modern buildings set back to widen the road. Brentford is now the subject of a £50 million development proposal which, if completed will change the character of the ancient town completely. A new building for the County Court was opened in 1963, and on the site of the old County Court in the Half-Acre, a new Police Station and Section House with a twelve-storey tower block providing accommodation for 80 resident police officers, has been erected. Among the attractions of this modern building are central-heated and air-conditioned cells. At the Water Works near the Kew Bridge end of the High Street, diesel and electric pumps have outmoded the 190-foot water tower of 1867 which nevertheless, is being retained as a familiar architectural feature of the Brentford scene.

No. 368 High Street is the unique and interesting British Piano Museum, founded by Mr F. W. Holland, an enthusiastic collector of automatic musical instruments, many of which are displayed in working order, including street barrel organs and reproducing pianos of various kinds. The adjoining disused tavern, the old 'Barge Aground', forms an annexe to the museum and provides storage for additional mechanical musical instruments.

Few will regret the absence of the smell of gas, so long an unpleasant characteristic of Brentford, which disappeared with the demolition of the Gas Works in 1966. One of the oldest in London, gas manufacture had been carried on there continuously since 1821, the works ultimately occupying $8^1/_2$ acres almost equally divided between both sides of the High Street. Leading to the residential part of the town were numerous little alleys between the shops on the north side; few remain now, but one especially remembered was so narrow that if two persons met in the middle, one of them had to retreat—or fight to the death.

Of the two disused churches in the High Street, St Lawrence was the former parish church and has the remnant of a brass to Henry Redman who, as chief mason to Henry VIII, probably took a prominent part in the building of Wolsey's

Hampton Court; there is also a memorial to Thomas Hardwick, the architect. The best of Brentford is The Butts. This is an open, sylvan square with several Georgian houses. Being a quiet open space, it is a heaven-sent place to park a car; at our last visit the score was 91. Boston Manor Park, which is now public property, has handsome grounds, but the Manor House is not open for inspection. The house stands in 40 acres of ground and was restored to its former beauty in 1963, at a cost of about £35,000. Scheduled as an ancient monument, the mansion dates from 1622 and is well known for its fine plaster ceilings. It is now used as the headquarters and training centre of the National Institute for Housecraft.

After passing Brentford town we come to Syon Park, the residence of the Dukes of Northumberland, situated between the main Hounslow and Twickenham Roads and the Thames, opposite Kew Gardens. It has an imposing entrance facing the main London Road, but the mansion itself is entirely removed from observation, except from the towpath near Kew Gardens, by high walls erected at a time when extensive views were deemed inconsistent with the stately privacy affected by people of exalted rank. It is adorned by the Percy Lion with outstretched tail, which was brought here from Northumberland House at Charing Cross after its demolition in 1874. A railed public footpath crosses the grounds between Brentford and Isleworth old village.

Syon House derives its name from a nunnery originally founded at Twickenham by Henry V in 1414, and removed to this spot in 1432. The nunnery was suppressed in the time of Henry VIII and forfeited to the Crown. Here Catherine Howard was confined from 14 November 1541 until 10 February 1542, three days before her execution. Edward VI granted the property to his uncle, the Protector Duke of Somerset, who in 1547 began to build the present house and completed the shell of it. In 1552, after the execution of the Protector Duke of Somerset, Syon House was again forfeited, and was afterwards granted by Queen Elizabeth I in 1603 to Henry Percy, ninth Duke of Northumberland.

To the west of Syon Park, between the Hounslow and Twickenham Roads, lies the residential district of Isleworth, formerly a quiet village. The church, which was unhappily destroyed by fire some years ago, was rebuilt in 1705-06, and has an ancient stone tower which belonged to the former church. This overlooks the Thames opposite Isleworth Ait and on the quay side are picturesque houses including the riverside inn, The London Apprentice. From the upper deck of a Number 37 bus it is possible to look over the wall in St Margaret's Road and get a passing glimpse of the great marble mausoleum in which is entombed the eccentric Earl of Kilmorey, an Irish representative peer who died in 1880, aged ninety-three. Since the recent death of the 4th Earl, the Irish peerage is no longer represented in the House of Lords. From Busch Corner, following the London Road westward we pass Spring Grove House, once the residence of Sir Joseph Banks, the famous botanist, later rebuilt by Andrew Pears of 'Pears' Soap' fame, and now the Isleworth Polytechnic. Half a mile further west Hounslow High Street begins.

In the 17th and 18th centuries, Hounslow was largely dependent upon travellers passing though the town and the many hostelries in the main street provided relays of horses for coaches on the road. Today, the numerous inns and alehouses have been reduced to a few—a very few—highly respectable 'pubs', and the High Street is merely a very good shopping centre, with a high proportion of shoe shops that might challenge the reputation of Oxford Street in that respect. The parish church of Holy Trinity, described as 'plain and ugly, of little or no architectural interest', was burnt down in June 1943 and has been replaced by a new church of pre-stressed concrete which was consecrated in May 1963. A feature of the tower entrance is the pair of angels in polyester resin and glass fibre sculptured by Wilfred Dudeney, F.R.B.S. The Hounslow barracks, erected in 1793, are situated close to the Bath Road, about half a mile farther west, and were at one time occupied by cavalry—hence two local taverns, 'The Hussar' and 'The Light Horse'.

Hounslow Heath lies to the south of the Staines Road and once extended westwards for over five miles, but the greater part is now enclosed. In the eighteenth century it was infested with highwaymen and also with footpads, who made the Heath more dangerous than did the senior branch of the profession and often resorted to murder. From time to time the Heath was scoured by the Bow Street Runners, the detective officers of the early nineteenth century, and though they sometimes rounded up a gang of footpads, they seldom captured any highwaymen. On the main Bath Road, near the barracks, is the church of St Paul, dating from 1874. Half a mile beyond the church the new Great West by-pass road rejoins the old Bath Road and here a large roundabout has been constructed. New buildings erected here of late years include the Traveller's Friend Hotel, a block of shops and a large garage with a massive square tower. Close by and standing back behind a service road fronting the north side of the Great West Road is a long block of flats called Parklands Court erected in 1938. A new shopping centre has also sprung up of late years on the Bath Road opposite Hounslow West Station, and in preparation for a further development of this centre, the 'Earl Haig' tavern, built as recently as 1929, was closed in February 1966. This, a handsome building of red brick with stone dressing, has been replaced by a new one, principally in black stone, and a supermarket. The Great South-West Road, an extension of the Great West Road, provides direct access to the main Staines Road at East Bedfont, three miles farther on. Half a mile west of the Bath Road is the rapidly-developing new suburb of Cranford and also a new housing estate which has been developed by the Heston and Isleworth Borough Council.

Less than a mile beyond Cranford, on the south side of the Bath Road is London Airport, on the site of what was once the village of Heathrow. It covers an area of 2,700 acres and there are five runways, each at least a mile and a half long and a hundred yards wide. The heart of the Airport is the 150 acre Central Terminal Area, consisting of the Control Building, Passenger Building and Queen's Building. The Control Building, with its 127 foot tower, is the nerve-centre of the airport and contains much of the delicate electronic equipment that guides the various aircraft in and out of the airport. The Passenger Building is solely for the use of people arriving or departing by air, and the principal feature here is the 600 foot long Main Concourse or Assembly Hall, which is reached from ground level by a series of escalators. For the convenience of travellers there are banks, shops, travel agencies and adequate catering facilities. The Queen's Building is expressly designed for visitors, for it was realised from the beginning that the airport would attract sightseers – and they are welcome. In the restaurant and bar, the seating is terraced, allowing an unobstructed view across the airport; outside, the roof-top terraces of the building are linked by a bridge with the flat roof of the Passenger Building. The Roof Gardens, with shops, bookstalls and a children's playground, have available space for up to 10,000 people. In 1960, five million passengers passed through the airport and the visitors numbered no less than a million.

The Airport is linked with the outside world by means of a 700 yard tunnel under the runways and the frequent 81b London Transport bus service from Hounslow brings its passengers, via the Bath Road and the Tunnel, right into the centre of the airport. The new M4 motorway is also connected by a spur road which leads directly to the airport tunnel.

On the Bath Road, near the airport, are three new hotels; The Skyway, the Excelsior and the circular Ariel Hotel at the Harlington Road corner, opened by the Minister of Aviation, Mr Peter Thorneycroft, in January 1961. This, the first circular hotel in Britain, is 176 feet in diameter, 48 feet high and has 186 bedrooms. It displaces the picturesque 400 years old Coach and Horses Inn, which, to everybody's regret, was demolished.

The Great West by-pass road between Gunnersbury and West Hounslow, one of the finest arterial roads in the world, was constructed between 1921 and 1924 to provide a new exit for the huge volume of westbound traffic, avoiding the narrow and congested Brentford High Street. It has a total width of 120 feet and a dual carriageway which will accommodate six lines of traffic and there are also cycle paths ten feet wide on either side. It was opened for traffic in May 1924, with the exception of the part situated between South Ealing Road and Boston Road, which necessitated the demolition of a considerable amount of property. This portion was completed in June 1926, and the late King George V drove through the newly-opened road to Ascot races in that year. In March 1965, London's first motorway, the new M4 from Chiswick to Langley, was opened by the Minister of Transport. This £19 million section of $12^1/_2$ miles will eventually be joined up with other sections to provide an unbroken express route between London and South Wales. Much building has taken place of late years on the new Great West Road, and entire new quarters of streets, blocks of flats and semi-detached houses have rapidly sprung up near Osterley Station and round about the hitherto quiet village of Heston. In October 1932, Hounslow, Isleworth, and Heston were formed into one municipal borough, since 1965 joined with Feltham, Brentford and Chiswick to make the new London Borough of Hounslow.

Although it had enjoyed a splendid service of electric trains running direct to the City, the Osterley, or Scrattage district of Isleworth had failed to attract the speculative builder before the construction of the Great West Road and had remained practically virgin ground. At Osterley many good-class shops and villas front the Great West Road, and nearer town on the south side a handsome group of new factories with concrete façades have been erected. Those of the Pyrene Fire Extinguisher Company and others on the south side of the road and the Firestone Tyre & Rubber Company and Messrs Macleans the well-known chemists on the north side, call for special notice. They are faced with concrete and stand back some distance from the roadway behind private lawns, and when seen from the distance look more like the mansions of merchant princes and potentates of some great city of the East than modern factories. Such establishments prove conclusively that the requirements of industry are in no way incompatible with pleasant surroundings. That of the Gillette Safety Razor Company at the corner of Syon Lane, with its lofty clock-tower, looks like a Town Hall or Civic Centre. It was designed by Sir Banister Fletcher and opened in January 1937. The Packard Factory on the south side was hit in 1944 by one of Hitler's rocket-bombs which completely demolished the building. At the corner of Boston Manor Road is the new Turriff Building, headquarters of the Turriff Construction Corporation Ltd and associated companies. Nearer town on the same side of the road is the distinctive Beecham House, erected in 1939 by Simmonds Products Ltd but now owned by the Beecham Group Ltd. This consists of a central block, ten storeys high, with two-storey wings on the east and west sides. In August 1960 Messrs Geo. Wimpey & Co. Ltd acquired the twelve-storey Flyover House, which stands impressively at the point where the Great West Road approaches the Chiswick Flyover. With a floor space of over 100,000 square feet, these premises house the increasing number of staff dealing with the design and procurement of chemical plant and oil refineries throughout the world.

Osterley House, on the north side of the Great West Road, not far from the Piccadilly (former District) Station, formerly the seat of the Earl of Jersey, stands in a large park six miles in circumference and covering about five hundred acres with two large and beautiful lakes, bordered by dense woods. The first house was built by Sir Thomas Gresham in the time of Elizabeth, but about 1700 the estate was bought by Sir Francis Child, whose successor built the present house about 1760. It is 140 feet long and 127 feet wide and was designed by Robert Adam. It is a building of red brick with stone dressings and is adorned in the centre by a double-colonnaded portico of Portland stone. During the second World War it was taken over by the Government but the Earl of Jersey has since presented it to the National Trust. Osterley Park is a wonderful addition to the public open spaces of Greater London. It passed from the Childs to the Earl of Jersey, and its apartments include a fine picture gallery, as well as a number of treasures and works of art. Outside the gates of Osterley Park stands the beautifully-wooded common of Norwood Green, surrounded by groups of rustic houses, with a tiny church at one corner. Despite rebuilding and a new tower added less than a hundred years ago this church still contains much of the original thirteenth to fifteenth century work and several interesting monuments. The village of Heston, now in a built-up area, lies about half a mile to the south, and contains a church situated at the cross-roads, which has every appearance of antiquity, but which was rebuilt in 1886, with the exception of the tower. In the churchyard is the grave of Frederick John White of the 7th Queen's Own Hussars, whose death in 1846 after being flogged was responsible for the discontinuance of that form of punishment in the Army.

From here we return to Hounslow, and after crossing the High Street follow the direct road which leads southwards to Whitton and Twickenham. In the neighbourhood of Whitton is Kneller Hall, a palatial mansion built in 1710 by Sir Godfrey Kneller, the artist, who died here in 1723. Since 1856 it has been the Royal Military School of Music, where the bands of the British Army have been trained, and here band performances take place most Wednesdays from May to September. From Whitton the main road leads past Twickenham Station to the centre of the town at the junction of King Street, York Street, and London Road. In Twickenham is the football ground of the Rugby Union, where international matches are played. Whitton is a new suburb which grew up during the few years preceding the second World War. Its wide High Street consists almost entirely of new terraces of shops erected between 1934 and 1939. After passing the Rugby Union Football Ground, the tall white tower of All Hallows, Twickenham claims our attention. Reference to this Wren church has already been made in the Second Walk, dealing with All Hallows, Lombard Street. Not only was the tower of this City church removed and re-erected here, but also many of the monuments and so much of the furnishings as to read like a catalogue of carved oak, thus: the beautiful reredos, panelling, pews, doors and doorcases, organ in its original case, pulpit and sounding-board, choir stalls, font cover and bread-shelves. There is an old gateway, handsomely carved with a curious design of skulls, bones and cherubs which formerly stood at the entrance from Lombard Street. Finally, the peal of ten bells, originally belonging to St Dionis Backchurch in Lime Street went, when that church was demolished in 1878, to All Hallows, Lombard Street. They have now followed their belfry to Twickenham, where we have the unique instance of an almost complete City church in a residential suburb.

The former old-world riverside village and smart suburb of Twickenham, which includes the districts of St Margaret's, Whitton and Strawberry Hill and Teddington, now form the part of the new Borough of Richmond upon Thames.

Its chief feature of interest is the river, and the reach upon which Twickenham is situated forms a prominent feature in the famous view from Richmond Hill. The parish church of St Mary was rebuilt early in the eighteenth century, and has been several times restored. The tower is said to have been built by William of Wykeham. Alexander Pope and his parents are interred in the churchyard, as well as General Tryon, the last English Governor of New York. Pope's villa was pulled down more than a century ago, and a modern house has been erected on its site. Close to the church is York House, now the offices of the local authority, and formerly a residence of James II, when Duke of York, and his daughters Mary and Anne, who both became Qeens of England.

The weedy shallows and small islands near Twickenham and Richmond are famous for their eels, and in former times parties used to frequent Twickenham to partake of this fish when newly caught. Eel Pie Island, near Twickenham Ferry, and Glover's Island, farther down the river near Richmond Bridge, are favourite resorts of boating parties and pleasure seekers. Twickenham Ferry, operating for hundreds of years and never out of action, has long been associated with the famous song, first published in 1878:—

'Ahoy-ye-ho!, who's for the ferry?
The briar's in bud, the sun's going down
I'll row ye so quick and I'll row ye so steady
And 'tis but a penny to Twickenham Town.'

Today, the fare has increased to the not unreasonable charge of sixpence. The present proprietor has a rare sense of tradition and, despite hints about motor-boats, prefers the familiar old row-boat and, indeed, is building a new one. Casual summer visitors may not realise that there is an all-the-year-round morning and evening rush-hour traffic across the ferry of commuters who find it quicker (and cheaper) than going round by bus. The narrow main thorough-fare of Church Street is situated close to the river, but since the construction of York Street in 1900, which by-passes it on the west, Church Street has been reduced to secondary importance. At the top of King Street, which has been much widened on the east side, is an imposing Odeon Cinema, and a long range of handsome shops. Lebanon Court on the east side of Richmond Road, close to the river, is a distinctive block of flats standing back from the roadway in gardens.

Beyond the Green, and near the point where the Hampton and Teddington Roads converge, is Strawberry Hill. This district takes its name from the villa built in 1747 by Horace Walpole, which was originally a cottage overlooking the Thames, built in 1698 by the Earl of Bradford's coachman and let as a lodging-house. It was afterwards taken by the Marquess of Carnarvon and other persons of note as an occasional summer residence. Subsequently it was let on lease to Mrs Chevenix, the noted toy-woman, from whom it was purchased by Horace Walpole. The humble dwellings which stood here formed the nucleus of the present Gothic mansion, which was gradually erected by Horace Walpole between the years 1753 and 1776. The mansion is now, with its modern additions, a Roman Catholic Institution. Marble Hill Park, on the road leading to Richmond Bridge, comprising seventy acres, has a considerable frontage to the river, and was rescued from the builder in order to preserve the view from Richmond Hill. The mansion, in the Palladian style of architecture, was built in

1724-9 for Henrietta Howard, mistress of George II, later Countess of Suffolk. After a complete restoration, it was opened to the public in 1966. The scenery along the bank of the Thames from here to Richmond Bridge is delightful.

To the south of Twickenham is the adjacent district of Teddington. Anciently Tuddington and Totington, the name is supposed to be a corruption of Tide-end-town, this being the highest point up the Thames at which the tide operates. Teddington Lock also forms the western limit of the Port of London. The chief attraction of the place is the river, for here the boating is very good. Teddington Weir is a favourite resort of anglers and is renowned for fine fish, principally barbel, pike, and carp. The Thames is crossed at this point by a footbridge. The manor of Teddington once belonged to Westminster Abbey, and the church of St Mary, which dates from the sixteenth century, contains some interesting monuments, including a memorial tablet to Peg Woffington, the famous actress, who died here in 1760. Other memorials commemorate Flitcroft, the architect of St Giles-in-the-Fields and Thomas Traherne, 'poet and mystic', who died in 1674. R.D. Blackmore lived in Teddington for forty-two years and there wrote *Lorna Doone* and fourteen other novels. He died in 1900 and is buried in Teddington Cemetery. Teddington was the birthplace of that 'clever young man of the theatre', Noel Coward. The leading shops are situated in Broad Street, close to the railway station, and in the High Street, leading down towards the river. About four miles west of Twickenham on the road to Staines is the rising suburb of Feltham, which has recently had many of its old village shops replaced by a modern shopping 'precinct,' and a valuable acquisition is a new Library. The village green and pond in the High Street survive, but the early 17th century Manor House was demolished in 1966; but except for a few pieces of pottery nothing of special interest has yet been found. Its parish church of St Dunstan's erected in 1802 is a plain building of brick with an embattled tower and a spire. The modern church of St Catherine near the railway station erected in 1880, a building of brick with Bath stone dressings, has a lofty tower with a tall spire added in 1898.

The western side of Teddington is flanked by Bushy Park, an open space of 1,100 acres, containing a fine avenue bordered with chestnut-trees running through the centre past the Diana fountain to Hampton Court Palace, opposite the Lion Gates. The latter, not the most beautiful of their kind in England, were erected in the reign of Queen Anne. Until 1930 the other end of the avenue at Teddington was crowned by a fine mansion standing in private grounds, but, sad to relate, it has now been demolished and the estate cut up into streets with small red-brick houses, and this has completely spoilt the view from the opposite end of the avenue.

Hampton Court, the largest of all the Royal Palaces, originated with Cardinal Wolsey, who took a lease for ninety-nine years in 1515 from the Knights Hospitallers of St John of Jerusalem, of the Manor of Hampton Court. The gift of this palace by Cardinal Wolsey to King Henry VIII did not enable him to retain the royal favour, and his disgrace and ruin are history. Until the reign of Queen Anne, Hampton Court remained the favourite residence of royalty, but has not been occupied by the ruling sovereign since the time of George II. The Palace, which is of red brick, now beautifully mellowed by time, contains about a thousand apartments, of which a proportion, known as Grace and Favour apartments, are occupied by royal pensioners and other privileged persons. The magnificent State Rooms, with their fine pictures, as well as the Courts and the beautiful grounds, are open to the general public. The finest parts of the original building are the Great Gatehouse and the Clock Court, the latter of which contains the famous astronomical clock constructed for Henry VIII. The approach to the Great Gatehouse from the river front has been greatly improved in recent years by the uncovering of the moat and battlemented bridge built by Henry VIII. The Great Hall was built by the same monarch, but the State Rooms, surrounding the Fountain Court, were added for William III by Sir Christopher Wren. Though the tranquil appearance of these grand old buildings in their beautiful setting by the riverside may give the impression that they have slept peacefully through the two hundred years since they were last occupied by Royalty, there is more activity at Hampton Court than the casual visitor might imagine. In June 1964, for example, a Midsummer Night dinner in the magnificent Great Hall marked Shakespeare's 400th anniversary year. Some 430 guests attended and the floor of the hall, long unaccustomed to so much company, was strengthened by the support of heavy baulks of timber erected in the cellars below. April 1965 saw the opening to the public of the beautifully restored group of four rooms known as the Cumberland Suite, which were decorated by William Kent in 1732 and later occupied by that not very attractive son of George II, William Augustus, Duke of Cumberland. These rooms alone are well worth the half-crown we pay to see everything that is to be seen at Hampton Court, but in May 1967, the Ministry of Public Building and Works, in a further effort to please, added to the circuit of the State apartments two more Tudor rooms not seen before; displayed on the walls are three 17th century embroidered tapestries on loan from Buckingham Palace. In passing through, behind the Kings' Guard Room, one gets a furtive glimpse of some unexpected 'back stairs'.

A notable feature of the beautiful gardens is the Great Vine, planted in 1768, which is a famous tree of the Black Hamburg variety and has been known to produce 2,200 bunches in one season. The average crop is now 1,200 bunches of fewer but finer grapes. Adjoining the Lion Gates is the famous Hampton Court Maze, which can easily be traversed if one remembers to follow the hedge on the right when going in and that on the left when coming out. In front of the Palace grounds is the Home Park, bounded on all but the northern side by the Thames, and stretching towards Kingston. It contains an area of six hundred acres, and in the centre is the Long Water and a broad avenue of trees. Hampton Court Palace covers eight acres of ground and the gardens cover forty-four acres.

The old Hampton Court Bridge, which crossed the Thames to Molesey, was pulled down in 1930, having become far too narrow for the requirements of its traffic. The first bridge at Hampton Court, built in 1750, was of wood, the second was built in 1775 and the third, now pulled down, about a century later. The new bridge, which is double the width of the old one, was opened to traffic in 1933 and is a few yards lower down the river than the old bridge and is continued by a wide new road called Hampton Court Way which by-passes the High Street of East Molesey and links up with the Kingston by-pass at Littleworth Common. A large new crescent of twenty shops with flats above has been erected opposite Hampton Court Bridge at the junction of Bridge Road and the by-pass.

Molesey itself, which contains the principal shops and restaurants, together with Hampton Court Station, is a little town not quite worthy of either Hampton Court Palace or the high-class villas by which it is surrounded. Several of the local hotels, notably the Greyhound, opposite the Lion Gates, and the Mitre, overlooking Hampton Court Green, are located on the Middlesex side of the river. A short distance higher up the river is Molesey Lock, the longest on the Thames with the exception of Teddington, and on Tagg's Island, immediately opposite, is the Casino Hotel, a favourite pleasure resort with hotel buildings, a concert hall, boathouse, and plenty of amusements during the summer season. Beyond Tagg's Island is Garrick's Ait and Hurst Park Racecourse, which is no longer used for racing.

We now recross Hampton Court Bridge, and after passing the Green proceed along Hampton Court Road, which flanks the south side of Bushy Park and leads to Hampton itself. The parish church, situated at a bend of the river, is a conspicuous landmark from downstream. It has a tall square tower and was erected in 1830 on the site of an older structure and enlarged and restored in 1888 and 1898. In the lobby is the monument to Sybil Pen (or Pane), nurse to the boy King, Edward VI. East of the church is Garrick Villa, formerly Hampton House, the home of David Garrick from 1754 to 1779. It is separated from the river by the roadway, but is connected by a tunnel supposed to have been designed by Dr Johnson. Amongst other distinguished residents of Hampton was Sir Christopher Wren, who lived here in comparative retirement. The well-known Kempton Park Racecourse, comprising three hundred acres, is situated about a mile west of Hampton, on the main road to Sunbury and Staines.

From Hampton Church we follow the route of the buses, by way of Church Street, High Street, and Wellington Road, through Fulwell, back to Twickenham, and thence past Marble Hill Park to Richmond Bridge. Fronting the Middlesex side of the river are several handsome blocks of flats, situated just below the bridge. The present five-arched stone bridge, built between 1774 and 1777, is a very ornamental structure, but long since had become far too narrow for the requirements of its present-day traffic. It was therefore widened in 1938 to nearly double its former width, but as in Kingston Bridge, which was similarly widened in 1914, the original architectural features have been so carefully preserved that no difference is noticeable when viewed from the river.

The borough of Richmond, situated on the slope of a hill, includes the districts of Kew, Petersham, and a part of Mortlake, with the later addition of Twickenham and Barnes. It derives its name from the fact that Henry VII, rebuilding the palace at Sheen, called it Richmond after his former Earldom of Richmond, in Yorkshire. Its beautiful riverside scenery, its Terrace Gardens, huge park and its proximity to Kew Gardens all contribute to make Richmond London's premier pleasure resort. The streets in the old town are narrow, and some of the houses, including the White Cross Hotel, almost touch the river. Behind this hotel is a row of red-tiled cottages placed end on to the river and just beyond is the popular Castle Hotel, with a stairway and piazza which fronts the Town Hall Gardens. Here stands the War Memorial. Richmond Lock, the lowest on the Thames, is a half-tide lock and was constructed in 1894. The old-fashioned Talbot Hotel in Hill Street, which faced Richmond Bridge, was pulled down and a handsome Odeon Cinema and block of shops erected on its site. A much-needed widening of the roadway has also been carried out at this point. Richmond Town Hall, opened in 1893, a red-brick building with stone dressings in the Renaissance style, is situated near the foot of Hill Street. It was opened on 10 June 1893 by King George V when Duke of York. The finest shops are in the narrow George Street leading to the Quadrant and the railway station. Though not nearly wide enough to accommodate the traffic, George Street was inadequately widened over forty years ago by setting back the buildings a few feet on the western side. On a bombed site opposite Richmond Station, formerly containing the departmental stores of Messrs Breach's which was destroyed in the air raids of 1940, a new block of shops and flats has now been completed. Richmond Station was rebuilt some years ago on a more ambitious scale and is jointly used by British Railways (Southern and London Midland Region) and London Transport. A part of Sheen Road almost in the centre of the town has been widened and here two fine new blocks of shops and flats called Lichfield Court have been erected. Here also is a large Ritz Cinema and immediately opposite is the Queen's Hall which is now a community centre.

Richmond Green lies at the back of George Street and covers twenty acres. It contains Maid of Honour Row, once aristocratic and the home of great traditions. The Richmond Theatre is situated on the east side of the Green, at the back of George Street. The famous old Palace of Sheen once overlooked one side of the Green, and was frequently the place of residence of Queen Elizabeth I, who died there in 1603. In 1649, after the dethronement of Charles I, most of the building were pulled down, and the materials were sold for less than £11,000. Maid of Honour Row itself was only built in the reign of George I, but the houses have been altered to suit present-day requirements. It is a fine old group of red-brick houses facing the Green and adjoining the old gateway to the palace precincts. The original Maid of Honour cheesecakes are said to have been in existence when George II was Prince of Wales and set up a Court of his own in the adjoining Old Deer Park. The cheesecakes are supposed to have been the invention of one of the Ladies-in-Waiting. In a secluded corner at the back of the Old Palace now stands a very ornamental new block of flats called Queensberry

House. The buildings are three storeys high, faced with red brick and grouped round an open quadrangle overlooking the Thames.

The parish church of St Mary Magdalen is situated at the back of the opposite side of George Street, surrounded by narrow streets and alleys, and was rebuilt in the eighteenth century, with the exception of its massive stone tower. Distinguished residents commemorated in the church include Edmund Kean, the actor, James Thomson, poet and author of *The Seasons,* Earl Fitzwilliam, founder of the museum named after him at Cambridge and Miss Braddon, the novelist, best remembered by *Lady Audley's Secret*. Hill Street, leading up to the Terrace Gardens on Richmond Hill, contains some picturesque houses and shops, some of which have been badly damaged by Hitler's bombs. The Terrace Gardens were formerly the property of the Duke of Buccleuch and were concealed behind a tall blank wall. The Duke of Buccleuch's house at Richmond was acquired in 1886 by the former Vestry of Richmond, which obtained legal authority, after an official inquiry by the Local Government Board, to purchase the land and to convert it into a public recreation ground. They were authorized to borrow £15,000 for that purpose from the Public Works Loan Commissioners. The price paid by the Vestry to the Duke of Buccleuch was £30,000, but in consequence of their receiving an offer of £15,000 for the mansion the cost to the parish was reduced to a similar amount. The mansion was built towards the end of the eighteenth century for the Duke of Montagu, from whose family it passed by descent to the Duke of Buccleuch. It was pulled down in 1938 and public gardens laid out on this site which front the river and Petersham Road.

The view from Richmond Hill, embracing seven counties and including Windsor Castle, is one of the finest pieces of domestic scenery in England. Some private houses on the opposite side, facing the Terrace Gardens, have been converted in recent years into private hotels, and are a popular place of residence with City men. The largest of these is the Stuart Hotel, and higher up, near the entrance to Richmond Park, is the old-fashioned Roebuck Hotel, the Richmond Hill Hotel and the Morshead Hotel. About halfway up Richmond Hill, overlooking the Terrace Gardens, are several fine blocks of flats called Richmond Hill Court and Glenmore House which were erected in 1934 on the former site of private mansions. The buildings are six storeys high and erected round an open quadrangle laid out with greens and tennis courts. Below the gardens is a sunken garage.

At the highest point on the hill, opposite the entrance to Richmond Park, is the Star and Garter Home for Disabled Soldiers and Sailors, a beautiful building erected as a Women's Memorial of the first World War. Completed in 1924, it was built by public subscription and designed gratuitously by Sir Edwin Cooper. The former Star and Garter Hotel, which occupied this site, was demolished in 1919, and was a rather pretentious structure with an Italian terrace garden, but when viewed from a distance it looked more like some stately château of the Loire. The house was largely added to between 1780 and 1808, but in the latter year the proprietor failed and died in a debtors' prison. It came under new management about 1810, but the charges were so exorbitant that visitors were frightened away. The hotel was rebuilt in 1864, but was the scene of a fire in 1870. During the 'seventies and 'eighties of last century, when Richmond was still on the fringe of the country, the Star and Garter Hotel was the fashionable resort of parties who came here from town in their carriages, and a day's outing to Richmond at that period corresponded more or less to a day's motor-car run to Brighton in our own time. In later years the hotel went out of favour with the public, and it had already been closed down for some time before the outbreak of war in 1914. Just below the Star and Garter Home is Wick House, the residence of Sir Joshua Reynolds, P.R.A. from 1772 to 1792. The house was rebuilt and equipped by the Order of St John and the British Red Cross as a home for Star and Garter nurses and was opened in 1950.

Richmond Park, a Royal demesne with an area of 2,358 acres, is second only to Epping Forest in point of size amongst the great public open spaces near London. At Robin Hood Gate you have only to cross the Kingston Road to step right on to Wimbledon Common which together with Putney Heath adds another 1,500 acres of continuous open spaces to that of Richmond Park. One of the most beautiful of metropolitan parks, it is undulating, hilly in parts, and consists of oak groves, plantations, and great stretches of bracken fern. Some of the views from the high ground are exceedingly fine, notably that from Broomfield Hill, near Robin Hood Gate. The western ridge of the park forms the escarpment of Richmond Hill, from which glimpses can be obtained here and there of the distant Surrey Hills as far as Dorking Gap. The Queen's Ride leads down past the Pen Ponds to the White Lodge on Spanker's Hill. The Pen Ponds, covering an area of eighteen acres, are well stocked with fish and waterfowl. They are situated almost in the centre of the park and were formed in the time of George II. During the second World War the Pen Ponds were drained but have since been refilled. Spanker's Wood, near the White Lodge, contains a bird sanctuary. Red and fallow deer and herds of cattle roam the park in all directions. From the Sidmouth Plantation near Richmond Gate a view of St Paul's and the towers of Westminster can be obtained on a clear day. Near Roehampton Gate are two 18-hole golf courses. Sheen Gate opens on to Sheen Common, which is little known to strangers.

Once known as Sheen Chase, Richmond Park was enclosed in 1637 by Charles I for hunting purposes. In 1649 the Park was granted to the City of London, but after the Restoration it reverted to the Crown. In 1758 the public right of way between Richmond, Wimbledon, East Sheen, and Kingston was established in the Law Courts by a Richmond brewer named John Lewis. Amonst the Rangers at different periods were the second Earl of Portland, Sir Robert Walpole, and the second Duke of Cambridge. White Lodge was the early home of Queen Mary and here Edward VIII, now Duke of Windsor, was also born on 23 June 1894. Later it became the residence of Lord Lee of Fareham, who presented Chequers to the nation. During the second World War, a large part of Richmond Park was occupied by the Royal Air Force and was closed to the public for six years between 1940 and 1946. During this period a portion of the Park was given over to cultivation.

Between Richmond Park and the river is the village of Petersham, which has retained its old-world appearance and consists of dignified Georgian mansions, a few modest cottages, an inn with tea-gardens, a school with a museum, an old church, and a modern one. In the graveyard of the old church lies Captain Vancouver, the explorer of the north-west coast of America. A tablet to Captain Vancouver has been erected in the church by the Hudson's Bay Company.

The modern church is All Saints, Petersham, a beautiful building in terracotta with a campanile 120 feet high surmounted by a figure of Christ blessing the valley of the Thames. The style of decoration both inside and out would be considered too ornate by present day standards. The architect was John Kelly and the church was dedicated as a memorial to her father, Samuel Walker of Petersham House, by his only daughter, Mrs Loetitia Rachael Warde. By statues, stained glass windows and other memorials, no less than forty saints are recorded.

It was realised at the time of building (1899-1908) that there was no immediate need for a second church in the village, but the declared intention was to build for the future when the anticipated expansion of the district would require another church. That time, it seems, has not yet arrived, for the church has, unfortunately, been closed for some time. Because of its Byzantine interior B.B.C. television recently used the church as the setting for the recording of a play called *The People from Nowhere*.

Petersham Common, which covers the steep slope of Richmond Hill between the Terrace Gardens and Star and Garter Hill, contains a beautiful wood where almost complete solitude can be enjoyed. The adjoining Petersham Meadows which extend from Petersham Road to the river, are much resorted to by holiday makers. They cover forty-nine acres but a further forty-five acres extending along the towpath from Petersham to Kingston are also dedicated for public use as a riverside promenade.

Between Petersham and Kingston near the river is Ham House, built in 1610 and environed by leafy avenues. In 1948 it was presented to the National Trust by Sir Lyonel Tollemache, Bart., and is now used as an annexe to the Victoria and Albert Museum. That avenue leading past the river front of Ham House connects on the east with the longest of them all, which stretches to Ham Common. This neighbourhood is one of the few near London which have so far escaped the attentions of the builder, but south of Ham Common is a built up area which extends to Kingston. The main road from Richmond and Petersham leads past Ham Common to Kingston Station and enters the town close to the main Portsmouth Road.

The Royal Borough of Kingston now includes the former boroughs of Surbiton and Malden & Coombe. Kingston-upon-Thames was already in existence a thousand years ago, whereas Surbiton, its neighbour, which became a borough in 1936 and now has an estimated population of 62,610, is a purely modern suburb created out of nothing by the coming of the railway. According to tradition, at least seven of our Saxon Kings, from Edward the Elder in 900 to Ethelred II in 979, were crowned at Kingston, seated on the Coronation Stone which, mounted on a septangular plinth enclosed within a railed space, stands near the market-place to this day. Close by is the handsome new Guildhall completed in 1935, a circular building of red brick with stone dressings and a massive square clock-tower 122 feet high. It stands on the site of the former Municipal Offices of the Borough Council. Close by runs the little Hogsmill River, crossed at the High Street by the Clattern Bridge, of Saxon origin; it was replaced in 1180 by a stone bridge of three arches, still to be seen. The Market Hall, erected in 1840, was originally the Town Hall before the erection of the Guildhall. Over the south door is a statue of Queen Anne, dated 1706, removed from an earlier building. It is a building of brick with stone dressing in the Italian style. The parish church of All Saints in Clarence Street with its tall tower has some 13th-15th century work. Kingston Bridge, originally constructed in 1828, having long since become too narrow for its traffic, was widened in 1914 to double its original width. This great improvement has in no way spoiled the appearance of the old bridge.

The main road through the town, although it has been widened considerably in places, has always been narrow and congested, especially near the approach to the bridge and at the cross-roads near the market-place. In the past Kingston has been famous for its police traps directed against motorists exceeding the speed limit, and to relieve the prevailing traffic congestion the new Kingston by-pass road, from Robin Hood Gate near Wimbledon Common to Sandown Park near Esher, was completed and opened in 1929. It passes at the back of Coombe Warren and thence above the track of the Southern Railway between Raynes Park and New Malden, after which it leads through Tolworth and Long Ditton and rejoins the main Portsmouth Road near Littleworth Common, a short distance north of Esher.

Surrounded on every side by large residential suburbs, Kingston is a great shopping centre, and its main streets are as crowded in the busy hours of the day as those of Kensington or Croydon. The principal shops are situated in Clarence Street, Thames Street, and the market-place. The huge departmental store of Bentall's, founded in 1867, on the north side of Clarence Street, invites comparison with some of the largest and finest stores in Central London. A massive Jacobean oak staircase, still very much in use, may be seen in the Market Place premises of Messrs Hide's. It is a relic of the old Castle Inn which formerly stood on this site.

Engineering and the manufacture of aircraft, cameras and commercial paints are among the many modern activities of Kingston, but one of the oldest industries in the town, until its recent demolition, was to be found in the Bishops Hall pits and yards of the Kingston Tanning Company, where high grade leather had been manufactured by the oak bark tanning process for over two hundred years. In Penrhyn Road is the Surrey County Hall, a splendid building of three storeys in the Renaissance style and faced with Portland stone. It was erected in 1892, extended in 1928 and further enlarged in 1937. In the centre of the building is a handsome clock-tower. Kingston is well provided with places of amusement with its four large cinemas, and many other social activities. The district of Norbiton, on the main London Road, forms the northern quarter of the town. Below the bridge the river front is skirted by Canbury Gardens, and in the opposite direction by the riverside promenade of Surbiton which is lined with large handsome residences and blocks of flats.

Surbiton itself is a well-planned town of wide avenues bordered with trees, and also has some excellent shops situated in Victoria Road, near the railway station, and in Brighton Road, leading down to the river. The Surbiton embankment overlooks the Home Park on the opposite side of the river, but higher up the view is interrupted by the reservoirs of the Metropolitan Water Board. Returning to the Kingston by-pass and proceeding eastward we come to Tolworth, which is practically an overflow of the residential district of Surbiton. Already a large number of new houses have been erected on the by-pass road and a new shopping centre has been developed close to Tolworth. Two miles beyond Tolworth we come to New Malden, formerly in the borough of Malden & Coombe, but now part of Kingston-upon-Thames. Its main street, Malden Road, which contains a number of excellent shops, lies to the west of the Kingston by-pass road, between Coombe Lane on the north and Old Malden on the south. Many houses and shops in both New Malden and Worcester Park were destroyed or damaged by bombs, but a large number of new flats and maisonettes have been built to replace them. The large 'Decca' factory includes a disused cinema.

From New Malden we turn to the right, and, following the bus route through the suburbs of Raynes Park and Merton, we come to Wimbledon town. Merton, now a rather dreary locality, was once celebrated for its abbey, founded in the reign of Henry I. Here Hubert de Burgh, the able minister of Henry III, took refuge after having been disgraced in 1227. The king ordered him to be put to death, but afterwards relented and restored him to favour. The abbey was demolished after 1680, though in Station Road is a long length of old wall in which is a low arched gateway that has been described as a Norman arch (not forgetting a larger and more imposing Norman gateway from the abbey that has been re-erected in the grounds of St Mary's Parish Church in Merton Park). Behind this wall, beyond a single line of railway and the River Wandle, standing on the site of a calico-printing factory established in 1724, is Liberty's works, where the ancient craft of hand-block printing of fabrics is still carried on.

Passing through Merton High Street, one cannot fail to notice successive roads named Victory, Nelson, Hardy and Hamilton and several tavern signs of a similar kind – all of which remind us of Merton Place – Nelson's 'dear Merton', which he left for the last time on 13 September 1805. On his return from the Baltic in 1801, Nelson, with Sir William and Lady Hamilton, had taken this estate, for which he paid £9,000. The house, which was demolished in 1840, stood on what are now Nelson Grove and Reform Place. The 'Nelson Arms' stands on the site of the entrance gates.

Finally, let us remember an earlier resident, Walter de Merton, founder of the Oxford college, which was originally established at neighbouring Malden in 1264.

Wimbledon has joined with its companion boroughs of Mitcham, Merton and Morden to form the new Borough of Merton—a title chosen, no doubt, on account of the seniority of Merton's ancient history. Wimbledon is of comparatively recent growth and London residents were attracted here by the salubrious climate. The town is divided into two parts, the modern residential quarter being on the hill near the site of the old village and the High Street, and adjoining the Common, whilst the working quarter lies below, mostly to the south of the railway and in Merton. The town is approached from the Common by a steep hill, lined with detached mansions on both sides, leading down to the Broadway and the railway station, and here are located the finest shops and the Wimbledon Town Hall opened in 1931. This is a building of three storeys faced with Portland stone. Externally it is similar to Wandsworth Town Hall. In the Broadway are the Wimbledon Theatre and the Gaumont Cinema. The Wimbledon Football Club ground and the greyhound stadium are situated near the River Wandle close to Summerstown.

The parish church of St Mary, founded in the fourteenth century, was rebuilt in 1786 and 1843. The Common, which is nearly two hundred feet above the sea level, covers an area of a thousand acres, or nearly one-third of the entire municipal area of Wimbledon. It is one of the wildest and most beautiful and invigorating open spaces near the metropolis, and, together with the adjoining Putney Heath, stands in the same relation to the south-western suburbs of London as does Hampstead Heath to the north-western districts. It is of inestimable value to the surrounding districts, and even though it is only an interval, for Wimbledon and other suburbs continue the town farther afield, it is a great blessing that this delightful heath should be retained for all time in a state of nature.

Wimbledon Common was secured to the public in 1871 and in 1922 was enlarged by forty-two acres laid out as a memorial garden to men of the district who fell in the first World War. Close to the windmill, which stands out boldly on the Common, is a deep ravine containing a lovely woodland of hazel, beech, oak saplings, and silver birch, supplemented by an undergrowth of blackberry bushes, brambles, and a dense growth of bracken. Adjoining this hollow is Queen's Mere, a beautiful sheet of water enlarged in 1888 from a smaller pond fed by the Beverley Brook, a little stream rising near Worcester Park, Malden, flowing across Robin Hood Vale through Richmond Park to Barnes and thence into the Thames at Barn Elms. On the Common are also remains of a Celtic earthwork called Caesar's Camp. From 1860 to 1889 Wimbledon Common was the scene of the meetings of the National Rifle Association, since when they have been transferred to Bisley. In Parkside which flanks the east side of Wimbledon Common are many fine villas and large blocks of luxury flats built round open quadrangles, but these are now eclipsed by some eleven-storey buildings recently erected by the Greater London Council.

The district of Wimbledon Park, which lies to the east of the Common, consists mainly of large houses standing in spacious gardens situated in what was a part of the original park, but much of it, including the lake, still remains surrounded by an open space which gives distinction to this district. The west side, which is private, covers a steep and richly-wooded hill sloping down to the lake. This contains the Wimbledon Park Cricket, Golf and Sports Club which has a picturesque chalet near the lake amidst charming scenery. The eastern section of Wimbledon Park is now a delightful Recreation Ground which has been partly laid out by the Wimbledon Borough Council with tennis courts and ornamental gardens with public access to the east side of the lake. Wimbledon Park also contains the headquarters of the All-England Lawn Tennis Club, whose annual international tournaments now form one of the leading events of the London season.

Putney Heath, which adjoins Wimbledon Common on the north, has an area of about four hundred acres. Some of the surrounding villas are more than a century old. One of these, called Bowling Green House, now pulled down, was famous as being the mansion where the great William Pitt died on 23 January 1806 in his forty-seventh year. Here and on other private sites in the midst of Putney Heath blocks of flats erected of late years unfortunately give the Heath a somewhat disconnected appearance. The Green Man Inn, which stands at the northern end of Putney Heath, is a relic of old days and a former abode of highwaymen and footpads. Another relic of bygone days is the old pound for strayed cattle, horses, and sheep.

Situated in hollow to the west of Putney Heath is Roehampton, a name suggestive of wild deer and consisting mainly of secluded mansions and high-class residences once inhabited by famous people. It contains a picturesque inn called the King's Head, and a highly ornate modern parish church with a graceful spire. Nowadays several of the large residences have become institutions of various kinds, and a portion of what was once Roehampton Park is now the site of the Roman Catholic Convent of the Sacred Heart. Some new distinctive blocks of luxury flats have been erected on the west side of Roehampton Lane called Fairacres which stand back in private gardens. On the east side are a number of newly-built detached villas standing back in their own private gardens.

On 29 November 1930 two badgers were dug out of the Convent grounds at Roehampton, the larger of which weighed nearly forty pounds and was so strong that it took two men to capture it. The badgers were believed to have been in the grounds of the Convent of the Sacred Heart since before the first World War, and were removed owing to the fact that they had been burrowing Inder the foundations of the Convent War Memorial and rendered it unsafe. It was supposed that they had originally escaped from Richmond Park in the days before the convent was surrounded by streets of villas and houses. It took three hours to dig down through the labyrinth of tunnels and chambers which the animals had constructed. The secluded charm of Roehampton Village has been disturbed by the recent large scale development of flats and shops by the Greater London Council. This, the Alton Estate, covers 130 acres on the north-east edge of Richmond Park and is one of the largest housing estates in Europe. Consisting of twenty-five 12-storey point blocks, five 11-storey slabs and various other groups ranging from 4 storeys downwards, it accommodates a population of 9,500 and has been described as 'a masterpiece of post-war residential design.'

In Roehampton Lane, which leads down to Barnes Common, is Queen Mary's Hospital, where soldiers maimed in the two World Wars are provided with artificial limbs and trained in handicrafts. In 1915-19 over forty thousand artificial limbs were supplied. During the first World War Roehampton was also a centre for training the dirigible balloon section of the Royal Air Force. Barnes Common, another breezy tract of heather and gorse, having an area of 120 acres, was secured for the public by Act of Parliament. It is traversed by the branch of the Southern Region Railway from Clapham Junction to Putney and Richmond.

The London and Richmond Railway was opened on 22 July 1846, and was then an independent company, with a capital of £260,000. The former South-Western line was used from the original terminus at Nine Elms as far as the point near Clapham Junction where the Richmond and Staines branch of the Southern Railway unites with the main line from Wimbledon and Basingstoke. From here the Richmond Company's line ran through Putney, Barnes, and Mortlake to Richmond town. The Act of Parliament incorporating this company was passed on 21 July 1845, and the new line was constructed in a year and a day. The estimated cost of the works, as laid before Parliament, was £240,000, but the actual cost amounted to only £180,000. The line was built under the superintendence of Mr Locke, Engineer to the South-Western Railway, and was worked by that company, who paid the Richmond Railway two-thirds of the profits.

Barnes, a village which figures in Domesday Book as 'Berne', lies principally to the north of the Common, and it has an extensive frontage to the river, being the base of the loop which it forms here, and which also constitutes the greater part of the Oxford and Cambridge boat-race course from Putney to Mortlake. The district which lies in the bend of the river at the south end of Hammersmith Bridge is called Castelnau and consists mainly of superior-class villas and residences. Close by in Lonsdale Road are the extensive reservoir and waterworks of the Metropolitan Water Board. Just beyond is a public garden with a riverside promenade and on the other side of Lonsdale Road is the Harrodian Club Sports Ground. The old manor-house and grounds of Barn Elms, adjoining Barnes Common and extending from Ranelagh Gardens to the Thames, are now occupied by the Ranelagh Club. Opposite the Red Lion Hotel at the bottom of Castelnau Road is Church Road, which contains the principal shops and leads past the picturesque Green to the High Street. The ancient parish church of St Mary on the east side of Church Road stands back in its small churchyard almost concealed from view. It is a building of flint and stone with a brick tower which dates back to the thirteenth century. Barnes Green is laid out as a public garden and has a large pond in the centre. The chief building of Mortlake, which lies to the west of Barnes village, is St Mary's Church, built of stone and flint, and dating from the fifteenth century. It is situated in the High Street and faces the river opposite Grove Park, Chiswick. Mortlake House was long a residence of the Archbishop of Canterbury. In Mortlake High Street is the famous Watney's Brewery which, since the demolition of the Stag Brewery, Pimlico, shares with Mann's Brewery in the Whitechapel Road the business formerly carried on at 'Stag', and at the junction of Lower Richmond Road and the High Street is Mortlake Green which has also been laid out as a public garden.

Between Mortlake and Richmond Park is the suburb of East Sheen, which is a development of the last sixty years. It consists of well-planned avenues and handsome villas, most of which have sprung up between the two World Wars. It is bordered on the east side by Palewell Common and on the west side by Sheen Common, both of which adjoin Richmond Park. The excellent services of motor omnibuses to the City and the West End have largely contributed to the prosperity of East Sheen, as well as the frequent service of electric trains on the Southern Region Railway to Waterloo. So much building has taken place here that the whole of the vacant land on both the Upper Richmond and the Lower Richmond Roads between Barnes, East Sheen, and Richmond is now completely built upon! On the Upper Richmond Road, east of Priory Lane and the Roehampton polo ground, a great improvement was carried out in 1930 by the construction of a short by-pass road, enabling the traffic to avoid the dangerous and narrow bend in the old road at Priest's Bridge at the corner of White Hart Lane.

Between Barnes Common and Putney is an older district of fine houses, new blocks of flats and villas with spacious gardens, the principal ones being situated in Upper Richmond Road leading to Putney Station and Wandsworth. Ormonde Court and Belvedere Court on the east side have spacious courtyards. From a comparatively small village seventy years ago, Putney has developed into a large and busy suburb. Its crowded High Street forms a convenient shopping centre for the large villa districts by which it is surrounded. Putney Hill, leading up to Putney Heath, was formerly bordered on both sides by handsome houses — almost stately mansions — which are now being demolished with remarkable speed to make way for less attractive, but more densely populated and profitable blocks of flats and similar new construction. At the foot of the hill is 'The Pines' (a stone pineapple surmounts each pillar of the gateway), where the poet Swinburne, for the last 30 years of his life, lived with his friend Theodore Watts-Dunton. It consists of several blocks standing in private gardens with tennis courts and private carriageways. The estate is set amidst ideal surroundings with entrances in Putney Hill and Putney Heath enclosed by gateways. Exeter House, which also faces Putney Heath, is another select block of flats similar to Manor Fields.

At the foot of Putney Bridge on the east side is the parish church of St Mary, which has a fourteenth-century tower. This was restored when the church was

146　Romford Market.

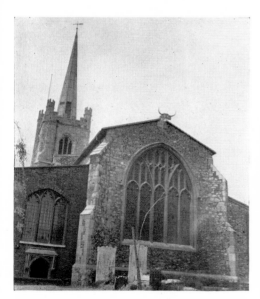

147　Church of St Andrew Hornchurch.

148　Charles and Mary Lamb lived in this cottage in Gentleman's Row, Enfield.

149　Forty Hall, Enfield.

150　The last of old Northumberland House, Stoke
Newington.

151　Christopher Wren's Temple Bar (1672), re-erected in Theobalds
Park, Hertfordshire in 1878.

152   Beech trees in Epping Forest, Essex.

153   Windmill in Blenheim Gardens Brixton.

158   The two-mile long interchange viaduct at Brentford on the M. 4 Motorway.

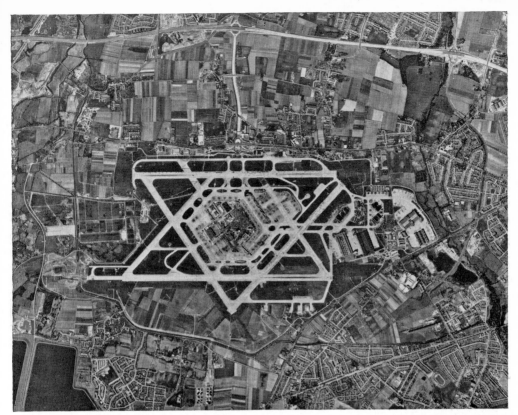

159 London Airport, Heathrow, from 25,000 feet. Across the top of the picture is the M 4 Motorway with the spur road leading, via a tunnel, into the Airport.

160 An aerial view of London Airport (Heathrow).

161 Osterley House, presented to the National Trust by the Earl of Jersey. A mansion of Elizabethan origin, remodelled by Robert Adam.

162 All Hallows, Twickenham, with spire from All Hallows Church, Lombard Street. demolished in 1938.

163 The original Kingston Town Hall (now Market Hall) about 1840.

rebuilt in 1836. Noteworthy is the fan-vaulting of the 16th century Bishop West's Chapel. On the embankment to the west of Putney Bridge are the Star and Garter Hotel and several fine blocks of flats, directly overlooking the grounds of Fulham Palace on the opposite bank of the river. Here also are the head-quarters of several of the leading rowing clubs of London. The widening of Putney Bridge by the London County Council was completed in 1933, the work having occupied a period of about three years.

Fourth Drive

A Tour of the North-Western Suburbs

Shepherd's Bush Green, the terminus of London Transport buses to Hounslow, Ealing and Uxbridge, forms a convenient starting-point for our north-western excursion. Horse tramways were first laid down in 1873 between Shepherd's Bush and Acton, and were opened in June 1874. In 1901 the horse tramways from Shepherd's Bush and Hammersmith Broadway to Acton, Chiswick, and Kew Bridge, were superseded by electric trams and were at the same time extended to Ealing and Hounslow, these being the first electric lines to be laid down in London. An inaugural lunch was given by the former London United Tramways Company at which Mr Balfour, then President of the Local Government Board, was the principal guest. He travelled on the first car from Shepherd's Bush to Ealing. The extension from Isleworth to Kingston and Hampton Court was opened in 1903, and that from Southall to Uxbridge in 1904. The tramways were replaced by trolley-buses in 1936, and from 1960 onward the trolley-buses were superseded by the new Routemaster omnibuses.

Beyond Shepherd's Bush Green the main Uxbridge Road is bordered with shops for a distance of about a mile, as far as Old Oak Road, which leads northwards to the new quarter erected by the London County Council at East Acton. After passing Old Oak Road we come to the Government Building, a large building erected in 1921, standing back some distance on the north side of Uxbridge Road on six acres of ground and containing accommodation for five thousand clerks. This stands in Bromyard Avenue, which takes its name from the Herefordshire village which was the birthplace of John Perryn who, when he died in 1656, bequeathed all his lands in East Acton to pious and charitable uses. Most of the land in Acton Vale fronting the north side of the Uxbridge Road between Old Oak Road and Acton Vale Park remained vacant until after 1935, although the land at the back had long since been covered with streets of small houses. Several blocks of shops and flats were then erected here and since 1945 the Acton Borough Council have erected nineteen four-storeyed blocks of flats on the remaining portion of this land which had previously been occupied by a farm. This housing estate covers nine and a half acres and provided 318 new dwellings. The blocks are planned with their frontages from north to south turned away from the main Uxbridge Road. This system of planning is now adopted on almost every new housing estate because buildings which face east and west get more sun than do those which face north and south.

Acton, which is situated two miles west of Shepherds Bush Green, is a large Area that now forms part of the new Borough of Ealing. It derives its name from

562

Ac-tun—the oak farm, or settlement—because of the large quantity of oak grown in the district. In pre-1914 days, Acton was chiefly remarkable for its laundries, of which it claimed to have 'more than any other single town on earth' and the inhabitants were inclined to boast of the number of distinct and different smells that could be encountered in the neighbourhood. Today it is both a residential and a large industrial centre, and firms in the district manufacture motor cars, machine tools, pianos, meters, precision instruments, sausages and ice cream, biscuits and confectionery. Napier's engineering works, originally in south London, are now at Acton and they have made the British aero-engine as famous as the British car. Acton was a frequent target during the Second World War and many buildings on both sides of the Uxbridge Road were damaged or destroyed.

Acton originally consisted of three villages or hamlets: those of East Acton, a little north of the Uxbridge Road; Acton Town, on the main road; Acton Green, south of the Uxbridge Road. In former times Acton was famous for its three medicinal springs, which were visited by Queen Elizabeth I and which became fashionable in the eighteenth century. Like those of St Pancras and Hampstead, the Acton wells have long since lost their celebrity, fashion having shown a preference for springs of the same character situated at a greater distance from the metropolis. The Assembly Room attached to the wells was afterwards converted into dwellings.

To the west of Acton High Street is Berrymead Priory, which later became the Constitutional Club and is now a social centre and club. It was once a convent of more than forty nuns, and then stood in three acres of grounds. Here also lived Bulwer Lytton, the novelist and statesman. Other prominent residents of Acton were Henry Fielding, the novelist, Richard Baxter, the Nonconformist divine, Sir Matthew Hale, Lord Chief Baron of the Exchequer, and the unfortunate Earl of Derwentwater who was beheaded on Tower Hill for his part in the Jacobite Rebellion of 1715. In a side passage at the end of Chaucer Road may still be seen the east wall and the great iron gates of Derwentwater House, which was built in 1638 and pulled down in the early nineteenth century. Tradition says that the headless body of the young Earl was brought from the Tower through these gates for burial, and they have never been opened since. An obelisk which marked the grave is now in Acton Park. The parish church of St Mary, which stands near the corner of the High Street and King Street, is a building of red brick which replaced the old parish church that was demolished in 1865. The little tower of the earlier church, however, lasted some ten years longer, until the present more lofty one was erected in 1877. The principal shops are situated in the High Street. The handsome Town Hall was completed in 1938 and is a building of red brick with stone dressings on the south side of the High Street at the corner of Winchester Street. It is crowned in the centre by a prominent clock tower. Acton Park, fronting the north side of The Vale, lies to the east of the High Street. In East Churchfield Road are the almshouses endowed by the Goldsmiths' Company for ten married couples and ten widows, the building being most effectively set off by two splendid cedars of Lebanon in the forecourt.

Beyond Acton High Street the main Uxbridge Road traverses a good-class residential district and leads in about half a mile to Ealing Common, a breezy open space on the south side, extending for another half a mile westwards to Ealing town. The Common is bordered on the northern side by a number of first-class residences. By Ealing Common is All Saints Church, which was erected under the bequest of Miss Frederica Elizabeth Perceval as a memorial to her father the Rt. Hon. Spencer Perceval, the Prime Minister who was assassinated in the House of Commons on May 11 1812. Built to the designs of W. A. Pite, F.R.I.B.A. the special features of the church, which was consecrated in 1905, include the great arch and recessed east window and the detached tower adjoining the north aisle. In the Lady Chapel are stained glass windows designed by Francis Skeat.

Though today the name embraces the suburbs of Acton and Southall and constitutes a new borough, Ealing was little more than a century ago a quiet village. It was six miles from the Marble Arch and stood near the road from London to Oxford. But with the coming of the railway its modern development began, and today it is covered with houses and shops extending from Acton to Hanwell, and from Brentford to Perivale on the north. It is quite the hand-somest of all the western suburbs of London, both in respect of its fine residences and of its attractive shops, the principal of which are situated in the Mall adjoining Common, the High Street, Bond Street, and in the New Broadway. The Town Hall, on the main Uxbridge Road, lies to the west of the Broadway, and resembles a church; it is, indeed, frequently mistaken for one. Not far away, and also on the north side of the main road, is the prominent Christ Church with a tall spire, built in 1852 after designs by Sir Gilbert Scott.

During the second World War Ealing suffered much damage from successive air raids and more especially from rocket-bombs in 1944. Houses and shops in the High Street were demolished and also a portion of the large department store of Messrs Sanders & Son on the south-east corner of Ealing Broadway. Many shops at West Ealing were also destroyed.

Although the present-day centre of Ealing is generally considered to be the Broadway in the Uxbridge Road, the real and original village of Ealing is some distance further south, and it is there that we find the Parish Church of St Mary, in the district now known as South Ealing. The original twelfth century church 'fell down' in 1729 and a new one was built ten years later; this was a severe rectangular building of plain brickwork with a square tower. Extensive alterations almost amounting to rebuilding were made by S. S. Teulon in 1866 and the Byzantine style of the restoration with its coloured brickwork led the Bishop of London of the period to describe it as 'the conversion of a Georgian monstrosity into a Constantinopolitan basilica'. There are several memorials to the Perceval and Walpole families. The latest acquisition is the Church Lounge, furnished and equipped in modern style for parish meetings and social gatherings.

Some handsome terraces of shops have been erected in the New Broadway and here the Uxbridge Road widens out for a short distance into a thoroughfare extending towards West Ealing. Some fine new blocks of flats have been erected on the north side of Haven Green near Ealing Broadway Station. On a private estate which lies between Hanger Lane and Haven Green near the Western Region Railway is a large new self-contained colony of flats called Ealing Village. It is enclosed by hedges and low walls and the main buildings which front Madeley Road are four storeys high and faced with brickwork distempered a pale green. Its special amenities include a swimming-pool, tennis courts, a bowling green, a common room and a special ladies' room. On the west side of Hanger Lane which now forms part of the North Circular Road is Hanger Hill Park. This is Ealing's beauty spot and from the summit of the hill a fine view is obtained of Harrow and London's north-western countryside. At the busy five-road junction by Hanger Lane Station an underpass road for southbound traffic and two new slip roads have been constructed to reduce traffic congestion. There are some fine new blocks of flats on the adjoining estate of Greystone Park and at the new suburb of Brentham near the Western Avenue. In this vicinity at Park Royal are various new factories including the gigantic new building of Messrs Guinness Limited, who have transferred a portion of their works here from Dublin.

Ealing was the birthplace of T. H. Huxley, who was born here on 4 May 1825. To the west of the High Street is Walpole Park, purchased by the Council in 1899 from Sir Spencer Walpole for £40,000 and opened in 1901. The residence, formerly Pittshanger Manor, is now the Ealing Central Library. It was built in 1770 by George Dance the younger and purchased in 1801 by his pupil John Soane, who made considerable alterations in his own individual style of architecture. The house is chiefly of interest as a foretaste of Sir John Soane's next home, that remarkable building in Lincoln's Inn Fields, now the Soane Museum. Castlebar Hill on the north side of the main Uxbridge Road is a district of large houses in spacious gardens, extending towards Perivale two miles distant near the new Western Avenue. Until about 1924 Perivale was a purely agricultural district consisting principally of dairy farms. It was not even a village, but possessed no more than seven houses with a population of thirty-four. The tiny church of Perivale is reputed to be eight hundred years old and consists merely of a nave and chancel, with a massively constructed timber belfry at the west end. The extension of the Piccadilly Line from Hammersmith to Uxbridge and the construction of the Western Avenue has led to further building developments at Greenford which has become a thriving new suburb.

Near Perivale on the north side of Western Avenue is the factory of Messrs Hoover, manufacturers of vacuum cleaners. This is a handsome building of concrete standing back from the roadway in a pleasant lawn.

About half a mile beyond Ealing Broadway we come to West Ealing, which is less opulent than the other districts in the borough. The main Uxbridge Road is lined with shops on both sides extending most of the way to Hanwell Broadway. In this part of the Uxbridge Road there appears to have been some jealous rivalry among the shopping areas to claim the proud title of 'Broadway', for within a short distance of each other (between intervals of plain 'Uxbridge Road') Ealing, West Ealing, Hanwell and Southall each have their 'Broadway' – and Ealing scores with an additional *New* Broadway. It may be added that they are not all as impressive as they sound. Hanwell is situated in an undulating locality adjoining the River Brent, which flows under the Uxbridge Road at the western end of the town close to St Bernard's Hospital. Here is a recreation ground and the church of St Mary, rebuilt in 1841 but occupying the site of an earlier building erected in 1782.

St Bernard's Hospital is situated on the south side of the Uxbridge Road close to the River Brent and the Grand Union Canal. It is a plain and spacious brick structure erected in 1829-30 in the Italian style, with a wing on either side, and was opened on 16 May 1831. The contract for the building was placed with Mr William Cubitt for £63,000. It was designed to provide accommodation for three hundred patients, but this number was soon found to be far too small, and the hospital was enlarged from time to time and now provides accommodation for over 2,500 persons, three-fifths of whom are females. The grounds of the hospital cover an area of seventy-eight acres and are pleasantly laid out. The chapel, which is in the Early English style, was built in 1880.

Nothing is perhaps more typical of the progress which society has made since the dawn of the nineteenth century than the changed attitude displayed towards the insane. Before that time little discrimination was shown between the treatment of the criminal and the victim of insanity. What advantage there was rested with the criminal, for whereas he was punished for a crime and paid the penalty of the law, the insane were visited with an indefinite sentence, punishment for no crime, and were placed at the tender mercy of those whose brutal will was perhaps their only law. No adequate protection was afforded by the law to those who through the loss of their reason were unable to protect themselves.

In 1792 a noble-hearted Frenchman called Pinel introduced kindness and consideration within the walls of a lunatic asylum, and it was largely due to his courage and efforts that many beneficial changes were brought about in this country in the treatment of the insane. Before the nineteenth century there were no public institutions (other than workhouses) where the mentally afflicted could go and patients were sent to 'private madhouses' where their treatment was often of the worst kind. The first Medical Superintendent – or Governor, as he was then called – at Hanwell was Dr (later Sir William) Ellis.

He was a great believer in work for patients, and within a short time had over sixty per cent of them working, a high figure for the period. He also believed in humane treatment and introduced a 'modified restraint' system. He was not so kind to his staff, however, and enforced strict rules which included a system of fines ranging from 1s. to 5s. for various minor offences. Another famous physician was Dr John Conolly, who introduced the 'non-restraint' method, and maintained it, often against adverse criticism. The one-time Hanwell Lunatic Asylum is now St Bernard's, a psychiatric hospital.

The main Uxbridge Road, between the River Brent and Southall High Street, having been found too narrow for its traffic, and formerly monopolized by the tramlines, a new road was constructed alongside the old road. Between the bridge over the Brent and the point where British Railways (Western Region) crosses the Uxbridge Road, it runs on the north side, and thence to Southall High Street it follows the south side of the old road, skirting Southall Park on the left. It now forms a double road with grass verges down the centre.

Southall, now a large industrial and residential suburb of London, derives its modern name from Southolt, meaning the South Wood, in distinction to Northolt, signifying North Wood, which is a village and new suburb one and a half miles north of Greenford. Much building has taken place here of late years towards the west, and the modern Broadway, lined with good shops on both sides, now extends for a distance of over half a mile along the main Uxbridge Road to the Grand Union Canal. The industrial quarter lies to the south, and here are the A.E.C. works, employing 5,000 people in the construction of buses, coaches and other commercial vehicles, several important engineering firms and the factory of the well-known Quaker Oats. A large market granted by charter of William III in 1698 is held weekly for horses—it is the only *weekly* horse market in the country—and pigs, Wednesday being the market-day. The oldest and most picturesque building in Southall is the sixteenth century Manor House, on The Green, which is now occupied by the borough Public Health Department. In the Southall Public Library an upper room is devoted to an exhibition of Martinware, a celebrated salt-glazed stoneware pottery that used to be manufactured by four brothers, Robert, Walter, Edwin and Charles Martin. Established at Fulham in 1873, they moved (by barge—and were nearly sunk at Brentford) to Havelock Road, Southall in 1878, where they continued to produce this very attractive pottery until 1923.

The western end of the town comes to an abrupt finish near the bridge which crosses the Grand Union Canal which has been rebuilt and widened. From here to Wood End, about a mile farther west, the Uxbridge Road has also been widened and now has a dual carriageway with cycle-tracks on both sides. To the south of Wood End, via Coldharbour Lane, is the busy industrial district of Hayes.

The old village of Hayes is situated about half a mile south of the Uxbridge Road, and until recent years was one of the most rural and picturesque villages in Middlesex. Early in the nineteenth century the surrounding country was an uncultivated waste, infested by the highwayman and the footpad, but it is now covered with orchards, market gardens, and scattered houses. The parish church of St Mary, restored in 1873-74, is one of the oldest in the rural villages near London, having a thirteenth-century square tower of grey flint and stone and a sixteenth century lych gate that revolves on the axis of its central post. The old village survives in a few cottages near the church and in Freeman's Lane, but the village pond has been filled in and becomes, *ipso facto,* a village green—albeit a very small one.

The new industrial quarter lies one mile farther to the south, and is centred near Hayes and Harlington Station on the Western Region Railway. Here are manufacturers of gramophones, aeroplanes, condensed milk, butterscotch and also engineering and cable works. Adjacent to the railway are the extensive works of the E.M.I. Group — Electric and Musical Industries — covering 150 acres and employing 12,000 people. Of the Group turnover, about a half is represented by gramophone records, the remainder comprising electronics, radio and television, domestic electric appliances etc. Of late years the industries of Great Britain have been moving southwards, and this is particularly noticeable in the various new industries which have established themselves in the western side of the metropolis in such places as Acton, Wembley, Hayes, and Slough.

Hayes End, on the main Uxbridge Road, three miles from Uxbridge town, is an offshoot of Hayes Village, which is rapidly assuming a suburban appearance with its long stretches of private houses and shops. Both here and at Wood End important new shopping centres have been developed. Beyond Hayes End is the new suburb of East Hillingdon which also has a handsome shopping centre extending for some distance along the Uxbridge Road. Adjoining Uxbridge on the east side is the old-world village of Hillingdon, which stands at the western end of what was once Hillingdon Heath. It still suggests a seventeenth-century retreat and contains the Red Lion Inn, where Charles I halted on 27 April 1646 during his flight from the besieged city of Oxford to the Scottish army at Nottingham. The old parish church of St John is built in the Decorated style of Gothic architecture and is surmounted by a tall and massive tower. It was restored in 1848 by Sir Gilbert Scott, and has a fine interior containing many memorials. The village street being very narrow, a new double roadway was formed by widening the north side of the Uxbridge Road starting from the parish church. Here a row of shops has been erected. On this side of Uxbridge is a depot of the Royal Air Force. In Field Heath Road by Colham Green is the modern addition to Hillingdon Hospital, which is a 9-storey wing comprising 210 beds and all the supporting services for a hospital of 800 beds. Hillingdon Hospital provides a full district service for a population of 208,000 from the Borough of Hillingdon and part of Ealing, and is also the accident hospital for London Airport.

The ancient market-town of Uxbridge is situated fifteen miles from Marble Arch. It still retains its old-fashioned appearance, but since the coming of the electric tramways, replaced first by trolley and now by diesel oil buses, which have their terminus at the western end of the High Street, and the opening of the branch line of the London Underground Railway, it has grown rapidly and with the suburbs of Ickenham and Hillingdon now has an estimated population of 60,100. The railway station, which is on the north side of the High Street, has been rebuilt on a sumptuous scale and includes a handsome colonnade of shops. The new houses on the eastern side of the town now extend to Hillingdon. Uxbridge was granted a weekly market and an annual fair in 1294, and the market-house, erected in 1789, is supported on columns. The town once contained a spacious Corn Exchange, there being several large corn mills situated on the banks of the River Colne and the Grand Union Canal, at the western end of the town. From here a great quantity of flour was dispatched by water to the London market. The Colne, which forms the boundary between London and Buckinghamshire, is crossed here by a seven-arched brick bridge, and broadens out with wooded islands, forming a very agreeable landscape. Here also are sawing, planing, and moulding mills and wharves located on the River Colne, which provide the local district with its principal supply of timber, slates, and coal. Other industries include two small breweries, iron foundries, brick-works, and engineering works.

The parish church of St Margaret's is hidden behind the market-house and was built as a chapel-of-ease to Hillingdon in 1448. It is in the Perpendicular style and was restored in 1872. It has a low embattled tower with a clock and six bells. Now that Uxbridge is part of the London Borough of Hillingdon, local government has been transferred to Hayes Park, but the old Town Hall is situated on the south side of the High Street, and comprises a large hall with a gallery and various committee rooms. The modern church of St Andrew, situated at the eastern end of the town, with a lofty spire, was designed by Sir Gilbert Scott. The western end of Uxbridge town is intimately associated with the armed struggle between King Charles I and his Parliament. Here a conference was held in January 1645 between the King's Commissioners and the Parliamentary delegates in a futile endeavour to come to terms. The house where the parties met was a fine mansion built in 1575 and surrounded by beautiful gardens. The present Crown Inn at the western end of the town forms a fragment of the old mansion and is known as the Old Treaty House. From here the Oxford Road leads in about a mile and a half to Denham, where it is joined by the Western Avenue. This leads from Greenford via South Ruislip, Northolt Airport, East Hillingdon and Uxbridge, beyond which it crosses the River Colne by a long viaduct. The final section between Uxbridge and Denham was opened in 1943.

By turning north along Harefield Road, at the western end of the High Street, we first cross Western Avenue and then leave the suburban area behind us, and from here it was a peaceful country walk to Ickenham, now unfortunately very much built up. Situated at the junction of several roads, the small village of Ickenham lies scattered round its village green, horsepond and pump. Its ancient and picturesque church, like many others in Middlesex, has no tower, but only a wooden bell-turret. The body of the church is built of flint. The surrounding country is beautifully wooded, and in this immediate vicinity is the red-brick Jacobean mansion of the Swakeleys, rising in stately fashion in its own large park. This fine house was built in 1638 by Sir Edmund Wright, who became Lord Mayor of London in 1641. The mansion is now used by the London Postal Region Sports Club as their headquarters. Until about 1930 there was very little land for sale near Ickenham, but many new houses have since been erected in this locality.

One mile north of Ickenham is the old-world village of Ruislip, which of late years has become the nucleus of a garden suburb. This has been largely due to the construction about 1910 of a branch line of the Metropolitan Railway from Harrow to Uxbridge, before which time Ruislip was about four miles from the nearest railway station. The former village consisted of a small cluster of houses, some of them ancient and timbered and still in existence, a few shops, two or three small inns and a group of 17th century almshouses, now no longer used as such. Nearby there used to stand an alehouse, the Bell Inn, which later became a curio shop frequented on more than one occasion by Her late Majesty Queen Mary. It is now a restaurant. Behind this group of buildings stands the ancient church of St Martin, partly restored in 1870 and again in 1956-57, with its grey battlemented tower forming the centre of this picturesque village. Ruislip has long ceased to be rural in respect of its government, having been associated with the neighbouring residential locality under the Ruislip-Northwood Urban District Council since 1904, but now absorbed in the new borough of Hillingdon. The new residential quarter and shopping centre of Ruislip, with two cinemas, lies mainly to the south and east of the old village. Near Ruislip Common, to the north, is the Ruislip Reservoir, covering an area of forty-six acres and originally formed to supply the Grand Union Canal which runs to the south-west; but now this and the surrounding land form part of a popular open-air venue known as Ruislip Lido, where may be enjoyed boating, bathing and woodland walks in a delightful setting. The Lido is surrounded by many hundreds of acres of Green Belt woodlands. It is much frequented by anglers and upon rare occasions, when thoroughly frozen over, affords ideal skating. South Ruislip is a new residential suburb which has sprung up of late years near Northolt Aerodrome. In 1948 the Central London Railway was extended to West Ruislip via Greenford and South Ruislip.

Ruislip village stands at the meeting-place of several roads, and from here we follow that leading north-east through the new suburb of Eastcote to Pinner, about two miles distant. Pinner derives its name from a small stream called the Pinn, which is one of the tributaries of the River Colne. The old village, situated on rising ground, forming the north-western side of Harrow Vale, consists principally of one broad main street sloping down to the Pinn. It contains a mixture of old-fashioned shops and dwellings and well-built modern houses, and its attractiveness is enhaced by its fine old parish church of St John-the-Baptist, with its Perpendicular tower, which stands at its eastern or upper end. The oldest portions of the church date from the thirteenth century, but the building was restored in 1879-80. A wall monument to Sir Christopher Clitherow who died in 1685, records that 'He lived a very honest man in a corrupt, seditious and wicked age'. The Queen's Head Inn dates from 1705, and close to the London Midland Region Railway Station, about a mile and a half distant, is the Royal Pinner School, formerly the Commercial Traveller's School, opened in 1855. Founded as a boarding school for the orphans of commercial travellers, it is likely to close in the near future, the number of pupils having steadily decreased in recent years. Several large country houses are situated in this locality, but various residential estates are being rapidly developed, particularly in the direction of Harrow-on-the-Hill, two and three-quarter miles distant, which is now joined to Pinner by a continuous line of houses and shops along the main London and Rickmansworth Road. Every year on the Wednesday after Whitsun, the ancient Pinner Fair still occupies the whole of the High Street and Bridge Street.

Harrow-on-the-Hill, as its name implies, tops the slope of the broad vale which extends north-eastwards towards Stanmore and Edgware. The crest of the hill, which is the highest in the County of Middlesex, is crowned by the beautiful parish church of St Mary, the tall spire of which is visible for many miles around. It stands some 400 feet above sea level, and was originally built by Archbishop Lanfranc in the time of the Conqueror, and some parts of the original church are still standing. The church was largely rebuilt in the fifteenth century and was restored by Sir Gilbert Scott in 1847. The church has thirteen old brasses, one of which portrays John Lyon and his wife. In the churchyard is the famous Peachey tomb where Lord Byron used to sit for hours when a boy at Harrow School. The views from the summit of the hill embrace several counties, those towards the west and south-west being very extensive, but the views on the north side are intercepted by the high ground near Stanmore and Harrow Weald.

The famous Harrow School was founded by John Lyon, a yeoman of Preston, in 1571. It was originally intended for the sons of natives, but a clause in the statutes permitted the master to receive foreigners and provision was made for alterations in the rules whenever occasion should arise. Thus, in spite of its slender endowment, Harrow has risen to the foremost rank among the public schools of England. The original school building, with the Fourth Form Room, is a small plain red-brick structure in Jacobean style, and the inner walls are covered with oak panelling, on which are carved the names of Byron, Sir Robert Peel, Lord Palmerston (Henry Temple), Sir William Jones, and other illustrious pupils, one of whom was Sir Winston Churchill. In most of the later buildings the style of the old schoolroom has been preserved. The boys were formerly housed in the school buildings, but they now live in the headmaster's residence, adjoining the Library, and in the houses of the undermasters in the town. That great Victorian philanthropist the seventh Earl of Shaftsbury is commemorated by the famous Eros fountain in Piccadilly Circus, but the *fons et origo* of his good works is recorded by a bronze plaque on an outside wall of the school near the spot from which 'while yet a boy in Harrow School, he saw with shame and indignation the pauper's funeral which helped to awaken his life-long devotion to the service of the poor and oppressed'.

Harrow High Street, which straggles down the hill on either side, still retains much of its old-fashioned character, and contains an inn, called the King's Head, dating from 1553. The intermingling of shops and houses old and new, among which the school buildings form a prominent feature, coupled with the varying levels and the shape of the ground, give the town a very charming aspect. Largely because of its accessibility from town by the Metropolitan and British Railways (Midland Region), Harrow has become a favourite suburb of London, and including the adjoining districts of Wealdstone, Harrow Weald, Pinner, Kenton, Stanmore and Hatch End, has the unique distinction among all the 32 new London Boroughs, of retaining its original borough boundaries, unaffected by the London Government Act of 1963. The principal shopping centres of the Borough of Harrow are Station Road and High Street, Wealdstone. Wealdstone affords all the advantages of a large self-contained town and here many handsome terraces of shops have been erected of late years.

A journey of two miles from Harrow along the main London Road brings us to Sudbury, which forms part of the new borough of Brent. Since the extension of the Bakerloo and the Metropolitan Railways to this locality, it has grown from one of the most rural districts near London into a large suburb with a population estimated in 1956 at 128,000. Until 1803 the land between Sudbury and the foot of Harrow Hill was known as Sudbury Common. The old village of Wembley, seven miles from the Marble Arch, stood round the parish church of St John-the-Evangelist, but all traces of it have vanished in the rapid development of this flourishing suburb. The churchyard which fronts the north side of Harrow Road is called God's Acre. In Harrow Road or Wembley High Road, which is the central shopping area, are many attractive new terraces of shops extending towards Sudbury Hill. In 1938 the new Wembley Town Hall was erected on the north side of Forty Lane near Wembley Park. This is a building of glazed brick with a severely plain façade without any claim to ornamentation. It is said to have cost the Wembley ratepayers a lot of money, but whatverer its internal appoint-ments, it more closely resembles a factory or a large packing case than a Town Hall or public building when viewed from outside. Carmel Court, next to the Town Hall, is a new colony of flats for ladies only. Some of the finest homes in Wembley are located in Park Lane, Wembley Park Drive and on the high ground above Forty Lane.

Wembley Park, the scene of the British Empire Exhibition of 1924 and 1925, is situated to the north of Harrow Road between the Midland Region and the Metropolitan Railway lines, and covers an area about equal to that of Hyde Park. It was purchased by a company in 1890 with the object of converting it into a popular pleasure resort and of erecting the so-called Watkin Tower, which was designed to rival the Eiffel Tower in Paris and to reach a height of 1,200 feet. The building was commenced, but languished for want of funds and never got beyond the first storey, which was 200 feet high, and some years later was taken down again.

In 1922 work was begun at Wembley Park on the great Stadium, and on laying out the grounds for the British Empire Exhibition, which was formally opened on 23 April 1924 by the late King George V and Queen Mary. Although it was the largest and most magnificent exhibition ever held in any great city it lack-ed the glamour of the White City and the earlier International Exhibitions, and failed to prove a financial success, thus necessitating a call upon the guarantors. Handicapped to a certain extent by the wet weather which marked the summer of 1924, it was visited by only about 9,000,000 people, and on many days the attendance failed to exceed 50,000. The largest attendance on any single day was that of Whit Monday in 1924, when some 300,000 people visited the Exhibition, and many people fainted in the great crush that occurred. In 1925 the total number of visitors was little more than 5,000,000, and the support given to the Exhibition by the people of London proved very disappointing. This was doubtless because Wembley was too remote from the centre of London to suit the convenience of those people living on the south and east sides of the metropolis. The site chosen was the best and most convenient that could have been obtained for such a vast exhibition within a similar distance from the centre of London, there being very little vacant land nearer town available for the purpose.

The great Wembley Stadium, the largest in the country, was completed in time for the Football Association Cup Final on 23 April 1923, the year before the Exhibition opened. It has a capacity of 100,000 people, so it was confidently proclaimed that there would be 'room for everybody'; and everybody came! Some 300,000 people descended upon Wembley Park, and it was with difficulty that sufficient space could be cleared to allow the game to commence. To this day nobody knows exactly how many people swarmed past the crash barriers on to the ground, but the gates were closed with an official attendance of 126,047. Here also the Military Tattoos, the Rodeo, and various firework displays took place during the Exhibition. The undulating scenery combined with an artificial lake rendered it an admirable site for the laying out of a great exhibition. The main entrance was at Wembley Park Station, in front of which was the King's Way, leading up to the high ground in front of the Stadium. Near the main entrance were situated the Palace of Industry and the Palace of Engineering, each covering an area about six times as large as that of Trafalgar Square. Centred round the lake, which was at right angles to the King's Way, were the Australian, Canadian, Indian, and New Zealand Buildings, the combined effect being most impressive. Other interesting features of the British Empire Exhibition were the South African Pavilion, the Burmese Pavilion, the West African village, the Lucullus Garden Club, the amusement park, and the circular railway round the Exhibition grounds. Of late years Wembley has become an industrial centre and some of the exhibition buildings have been converted into factories.

A part of the grounds are now occupied by the Empire Pool and Sports Arena which is close to the Stadium. Raglan Gardens on the west side of Wembley Park, now renamed Empire Way, is lined with new blocks of flats. Half a mile north of Wembley Park Station is Barn Hill Recreation Ground. This is Wembley's beauty spot and covers the top of a steep hill 282 feet above sea level from which fine views are obtained of Harrow-on-the-Hill and the surrounding countryside. Another similar public Recreation Ground is Horsenden Wood Park about half a mile south of Sudbury Station. This too is on the summit of a steep hill which involves a strenuous climb, but the view from the highest point is worth the effort of getting there. Most of the adjoining open land belongs to the Sudbury Golf Club. Kingsbury, formerly a rural parish on the west side of the Edgware Road, has of late years become a large industrial suburb which was added to Wembley in 1934. The rapid growth of Kingsbury and the adjoining suburb of Queensbury has been furthered by the extension in 1933 of the Metropolitan Railway from Wembley Park to Stanmore via Whitchurch Lane and Canon's Park. Queensberry has an attractive shopping centre which is built round a turfed square and there is a larger one at Queensbury Circus in Honeypot Lane. Near Kingsbury is Woodfield Park which fronts the north side of the Welsh Harp Lake.

The neighbouring industrial suburb of Neasden, like Wembley, is mainly a development of the period between the two World Wars. It has a fine shopping centre which is located at the junction of Neasden Lane and the North Circular Road, where there is a large roundabout. Near Stonebridge Park Station, at the junction of Harrow Road and the North Circular Road, a new office building of unusual triangular shape was completed in 1965; this has a 21-storey tower block, 245 feet high. A little further south the North Circular Road is crossed by the Grand Union Canal which is here carried over the roadway by a viaduct bridge. In 1939 rebels of the Irish Republican Army tried to destroy the canal bridge, but the bomb which they hurled at it failed to cause any serious damage.

In the opposite direction the North Circular Road leads from Neasden past the south bank of the Welsh Harp Lake to Edgware Road. Here several large factories have been erected of late years, notably those of Messrs Kemp, the biscuit manufacturers, and Messrs Staples, the firm of mattress and bedstead makers, both of which are situated close to the junction of the North Circular and the Edgware Roads. From here we proceed through West Hendon to the Hyde and Colindale, a new district which has sprung up on the east side of the Edgware Road since the establishment of the London Aerodrome in this immediate vicinity. Hendon aerodrome was the venue of the annual pageant of the Royal Air Force, but this no longer takes place. The main Edgware Road at Colindale has unfortunately been marred in places by the erection of several very unsightly factories with frontages of corrugated iron, but there is also a fine shopping centre. Beyond Colindale a large new suburb was developed by the London County Council at Burnt Oak, about a mile to the south of Edgware. It has a station on the Northern Line Tube, and like St Helier, the town built at the other end of that railway, it has direct access to the West End of London. Its busy shopping centre extends for half a mile along the main Edgware Road and includes a handsome store erected by the London Co-operative Society. Thus the Edgware Road from West Hendon to Edgware has been changed between the two World Wars from a quiet country road into one of the busiest suburban districts near London. So rapid has been the growth of the outer area of North-West London that Harrow, Wembley, Hendon and Finchley are now all contiguous. Whereas their combined population forty years ago numbered little more than 100,000, to-day it is over half-a-million.

Edgware, distant eight miles from the Marble Arch, was little more than forty years ago a quaint rural village of 1,516 inhabitants, consisting principally of one long street on the ancient Watling Street; but since the extension of the Hamp-

stead Tube Railway from Golder's Green, opened in 1923, it has been transformed into a large suburb and dormitory of London. Facing Edgware Road was
the Chandos Arms, with a projecting signboard representing the old heraldic
coat of the Brydges family, Dukes of Chandos. Edgware was formerly called
Eggesware and Edeworthg, and in former times was the first village of importance
on Watling Street. The parish church of St Margaret is at the corner of the High
Street and Station Road, and was rebuilt in 1705 and 1845. It has a square tower
and is said to have once been part of a monastery. Near it was a refreshment-
house for the monks of St Albans as they travelled to and from London. At
a court held at Edgware in 1551, two men were fined for playing at cards; in the
next year the inhabitants were prosecuted for not having a tumbril and ducking
stool; and in 1558 a man was fined for selling ale at the exorbitant price of a pint
and a half for a penny.

The new Edgware has been designed somewhat on the lines of Golder's Green,
with the best shops in Station Road and on the east side of Edgware Road.
Standing back from the main road, facing the parish church, is a distinctive-
looking parade of shops called the Forum. A new omnibus terminus has been
erected next to the Underground Railway Station. The west side of the Edgware
Road is in the new Borough of Harrow, and so also is the new residential district
of Canon's Park about half a mile north of Edgware. Here the roads fork, that
on the right leading to Elstree and St Albans, and that on the left to Stanmore,
Bushey Heath, and Watford. The village of Stanmore, ten miles from the Marble
Arch, is picturesquely situated on the slope of a hill 480 feet above the level of the
sea, leading up to Bushey Heath. The parish church of St John-the-Evangelist
is a handsome modern structure consecrated in 1850 and stands near the ruins
of an earlier church erected in 1632. The situation of the old church is marked
by a flat tombstone planted round with firs. Behind the church are some
picturesque old almshouses. Stanmore is rapidly developing into a high-class
residential district, many fine new houses and shops having been erected both
here and at Canon's Park since the opening of the branch line of the Bakerloo
Railway from Wembley Park to Stanmore. This was constructed at a cost of
£170,000. Stanmore is now the terminus of the eastern branch of the Bakerloo
Line. Stanmore Common, covered with birch and bracken, flanks the main
Watford Road, leading in about a mile to Bushey Heath, situated on high ground
rising to over five hundred feet above the sea level.

Little Stanmore, or Whitchurch, as it is more usually called, lies about a mile
to the west of Edgware. The church of St Lawrence, with a 16th century tower,
was rebuilt in 1715 at the expense of John Brydges, Duke of Chandos, as the
chapel of his magnificent mansion 'Canons' — demolished in 1747 after little
more than 30 years existence. The interior walls and ceilings of the church are
covered with paintings of biblical subjects, of which Pope wrote 'Here sprawl
the saints of Verrio and Laguerre'. At the west end is the Duke's private gallery,
while on the north side of the church some steps lead to the mausoleum containing memorial statues of his Grace with two of his wives and also other members

of the family (reminding the visitor of the tombs of the Russels at Chenies).

East of the Edgware Road is the Borough of Barnet which, with East and Friern Barnet, Finchley and Hendon, totals 22,123 acres, with a population of 318,000. The ancient town of Chipping or High Barnet, situated eleven miles from London, is built upon a hill rising to four hundred feet above the sea level, on the main road from London to York. Its picturesque High Street extends for a considerable distance along the hillside and debouches upon Hadley Green, where stands the stately church of St Mary, Hadley. The keyhole of the church door is said to be on a level with the cross on the top of the dome of St Paul's Cathedral. The church of St John the Baptist, erected about 1420, is situated in the High Street, at the southern end of the town. It is built in the Perpendicular style, with a square stone tower and has a clock with chimes and a peal of eight bells. It was restored and enlarged in 1875. In Wood Street, near the church, is Tudor Hall, a well-preserved turretted building of red brick, dated 'E.R. 1573', that was formerly the Queen Elizabeth Grammar School. The school moved to new premises in 1932 and the hall is now used for social purposes.

Barnet was the scene of the decisive battle fought between the houses of York and Lancaster on Easter morning, 1471. When the fight began the bells were ringing for morning service, and, before the evening closed, the fate of a dynasty was sealed and the power of the Barons broken for ever. Although named after Barnet, where Edward of York spent the night before the battle, and from which he marched out to meet the great Earl of Warwick, who was advancing from St Albans, the actual fight took place at Hadley Green, half a mile north of the town. Here an obelisk was erected in 1740 by Sir Jeremy Sambrooke, Bart., to commemorate this great event, and two trees close by are supposed to occupy the spot where Warwick fell. About ten thousand men, all feudal retainers, were engaged on either side. Near Hadley Green on the east side is Hadley Common, a richly-wooded public open space which extends to Cockfosters and is a favourite pleasure resort of Londoners.

Barnet was an important posting place in coaching days and still holds its horse-fair in September, which is one of the largest in England. High Barnet is now practically joined to North Finchley and the metropolis by the straggling suburb of Whetstone, which contains picturesque old houses, shops, and inns, and many fine suburban residences fronting the Great North Road for a considerable distance. The Woodside Home for Incurables, of the female sex only, was removed here from London in 1888. This building was demolished in 1964 and the inmates removed to a new and much improved Home built for them on another part of the extensive grounds, further back from the noisy main road. On the site of the old Woodside Home now stands the new 12-storey 'Ever-Ready' building. About a mile and a half to the west is the peaceful village of Totteridge, and to drive along pretty Totteridge Lane, though not the quiet country lane it once was, is still a delightful experience on a fine summer's day. Totteridge seems to have made an appeal to the High Court, for among the legal notabilities buried in the little churchyard of St Andrew are Lord Chancellor

Cottenham (a descendant of John Pepys of Cottenham in Cambridgeshire, great-uncle to the diarist), Lord Chief Justice Hewart of Bury and Mr Justice Bailhache. T. E. Colcutt, architect of the Imperial Institute in Kensington, now—except for its conspicuous 280 foot tower—demolished, lies here; also Harry Vardon, professional golfer. Among the oldest yew trees in country churchyards, St Andrew's makes a claim for 700-1000 years with one whose girth is 27 feet at three feet from the ground.

About midway between Totteridge and Edgware is the residential suburb of Mill Hill, with a population of 12,000. The straggling picturesque old village is situated on the top of the hill at a height of over four hundred feet, but the new town which lies to the west now extends towards the Hale and Edgware. It has grown with amazing rapidity of late years and is now a select suburb of London with beautiful homes standing in spacious gardens and some good shops in the Broadway. Here a very large roundabout called 'Apex Corner', has been constructed at the cross-roads of the main Watford by-pass road. Mill Hill Park is a large open space which extends for some distance along both sides of Watford Way towards Hendon. The healthiness of Mill Hill is attested by the presence of three large institutions, namely, the Linen and Woollen Drapers' Cottage Homes, on the slope of the hill, the Roman Catholic Missionary College of St Joseph, an imposing building, and the celebrated Nonconformist public school known for generations past as Mill Hill School. It is a fine range of buildings, standing in seventy acres of ground, and has accommodation for three hundred boys. The parish church of St Paul, which has no claim to distinction, was erected in 1829-30.

Returning to the Great North Road, we next come, after passing Whetstone, to North Finchley, distant about seven and a half miles from London. Here is a shopping centre at the junction of the main roads from Golder's Green and Highgate which is known as Tally Ho Corner, and from here the wide High Street extends for some distance along the Great North Road. With the rapid growth of London's outer suburban area, the old village of Finchley has lost its former rural appearance. The parish of Finchley is a large one, having a length of about five miles and an area of 3,478 acres. It extends from Hampstead to Whetstone from south to north, and from Hendon to Highgate from west to east, and is now part of the borough of Barnet. It is a veritable network of suburban streets, terraces, and detached villa residences, and includes North Finchley, East Finchley, and Church End. The last-mentioned district contains the Perpendicular parish church of St Mary, restored in 1872, and Christ's College, founded in 1857. There are also many fine houses, terraces of shops and blocks of flats in Falloden Way, Lyttelton Road and Aylmer Road which form part of the Barnet by-pass road.

Finchley once consisted for the most part of common land, extending for more than 1,500 acres. It was the scene of frequent robberies, until the common was enclosed and placed under cultivation early in the nineteenth century. Jack Sheppard was captured on Finchley Common in 1724. Ninety acres of the original common, parts of which still remain, are occupied by the Islington and St Pancras cemeteries, and that of Marylebone is situated between East Finchley and Church End. General Monck marshalled his forces in Finchley Common in 1660 when approaching the metropolis to effect the restoration of Charles II, and here also the Guards were mustered in 1745 upon the invasion of England by the Young Pretender.

Between North Finchley and New Southgate, which lies to the east, is Friern Barnet, a small area that was formerly an Urban District with Council Offices at the junction of Friern Barnet Lane and Road. This is a crescent-shaped building of multi-red brick, with a pitched roof and a bell-turret. In Friern Barnet Road is the Friern Hospital of the London County Council. It was erected between 1849 and 1851 and has accommodation for two thousand patients. The grounds, consisting of 119 acres, are situated on the west side of New Southgate Station, with a gradual slope towards the south-west. The building was designed by Mr Dawkes, and in 1903 was the scene of a fire involving the death of fifty-one persons.

The adjoining district of Southgate was so named as being the gate of Enfield Chase. It is a beautiful suburb of wide tree-lined roads and includes Old Southgate, Palmers Green and Winchmore Hill within its area. Here much building has taken place of late years in the direction of Palmers Green and towards Muswell Hill. A part of this parish was united in 1873 with Colney Hatch to form New Southgate, after which the Gothic church of St Paul was erected. Leigh Hunt was born at Southgate, and the rural lanes between Colney Hatch and Southgate were favourite haunts of Charles Lamb. The principal shopping centre is at Palmers Green on the main road from Wood Green to Enfield.

In Alderman's Hill which branches off towards Old Southgate is the beautiful Broomfield Park covering sixty acres. It was purchased in 1903 by the Urban District Council. Broomfield House, with a fine oak staircase of the period of Charles II, has wall and ceiling paintings of mythological subjects which, in a sale catalogue of 1903, were described as the work of Sir James Thornhill. The house is now a museum of an essentially local character, relating to Southgate, and therefore of particular interest. The present building, which was certainly built over 200 years ago, was, before it became public property, the residence for some 28 years of Sir Ralph Littler, Q.C., a magistrate who was noted for the severity of his sentences.

In Cannon Hill, a fine wide thoroughfare leading up from here to the Green and Old Southgate High Street is Northmet House, formerly Arnos Grove, a splendid mansion of red brick with stone dressings, now the headquarters of the Eastern Electricity Board, Northmet Division. It stands back from the road in spacious grounds and was formerly the residence of the Walker family of brewers who became active supporters of the Southgate Cricket Club which has its playing-field close to the Green. Adjoining the Green, which retains much of its rural atmosphere, in Waterfall Road is Christ Church, a building of stone which has a tower and spire and was built in 1862 by Sir Gilbert Scott. Farther down Waterfall Road is Arnos Park through which flows the Pymmes Brook. Round Southgate Underground Station, a fine new shopping centre has been developed of late years. Between here and Winchmore Hill is Grovelands Park which covers ninety-two acres and contains a beautiful boating-lake of seven acres adjoining dense woods and bracken. Farther north of the west side of Cockfosters Road on steep sloping ground is Oakhill Park which covers more than a hundred acres and extends westwards to Church Hill Road, East Barnet. This concludes our tour of the north-west suburbs.

Index